No.	Date	Title	Auditing Section
25	Nov. 1979	The Relationship of Generally Accepted Auditing Standards to Quality Control Standards	161
26	Nov. 1979	Association With Financial Statements	504
27	Dec. 1979	Supplementary Information Required by the Financial Accounting Standards Board	553
28	June 1980	Supplementary Information on the Effects of Changing Prices	554
29	July 1980	Reporting on Information Accompanying the Basic Financial Statements in Auditor-Submitted Documents	551
30	July 1980	Reporting on Internal Accounting Control	642
31	Aug. 1980	Evidential Matter	326
32	Oct. 1980	Adequacy of Disclosure in Financial Statements	431
33	Oct. 1980	(Superseded by SAS 45.)	
34	Mar. 1981	The Auditor's Considerations When a Question Arises About an Entity's Continued Existence	340
35	April 1981	Special Reports—Applying Agreed-upon Procedures to Specified Elements, Accounts, or Items of a Financial Statement	622
36	April 1981	Review of Interim Financial Information	722
37	April 1981	Filings Under Federal Securities Statutes	711
38	April 1981	(Superseded by SAS 49.)	
39	June 1981	Audit Sampling	350
40	Feb. 1982	Supplementary Mineral Reserve Information	556
41	April 1982	Working Papers	339
42	Sept. 1982	Reporting on Condensed Financial Statements and Selected Financial Data	552
43	Aug. 1982	Omnibus Statement on Auditing Standards	1010
44	Dec. 1982	Special-Purpose Reports on Internal Accounting Control at Service Organizations	324
45	Aug. 1983	Omnibus Statement on Auditing Standards—1983	1020
46	Sept. 1983	Consideration of Omitted Procedures After the Report Date	390
47	Dec. 1983	Audit Risk and Materiality in Conducting an Audit	312
48	July 1984	The Effects of Computer Processing on the Examination of Financial Statements	1030
49	Sept. 1984	Letters for Underwriters	634

MODERN AUDITING

Accounting Textbooks from John Wiley & Sons

Arpan and Radebaugh: **International Accounting and Multinational Enterprises, 2nd**

Burch and Grudnitski: **Information Systems: Theory and Practice, 4th**

DeCoster and Schafer: **Management Accounting: A Decision Emphasis, 3rd**

Defliese, Jaenicke, Sullivan, Gnospelius: **Montgomery's Auditing, College Version**

Delaney and Gleim: **CPA Examination Review—Auditing**

Delaney and Gleim: **CPA Examination Review—Business Law**

Delaney and Gleim: **CPA Examination Review—Theory and Practice**

Gaffney, Skadden, Wheeler, Laverty, Outslay and Skadden: **Wiley Federal Income Taxation**

Gleim and Delaney: **CPA Examination Review** Volume I **Outlines and Study Guide**

Gleim and Delaney: **CPA Examination Review** Volume II **Problems and Solutions**

Guy: **Introduction to Statistical Sampling in Auditing, 2nd**

Haried, Imdieke, and Smith: **Advanced Accounting, 3rd**

Helmkamp, Imdieke, and Smith: **Principles of Accounting, 2nd**

Kam: **Accounting Theory**

Kell, Boynton and Ziegler: **Modern Auditing, 3rd**

Kieso and Weygandt: **Intermediate Accounting, 5th**

Laughlin: **Financial Accounting**

McCullers and Schroeder: **Accounting Theory, 2nd**

Moscove and Simkin: **Accounting Information Systems, 2nd**

Ramanathan: **Management Control in Nonprofit Organizations, Text and Cases**

Ramanathan and Hegstad: **Readings in Management Control in Nonprofit Organizations**

Romney, Cherrington, and Hansen: **Casebook in Accounting Information Systems**

Sardinas, Burch, and Asebrook: **EDP Auditing: A Primer**

Taylor and Glezen: **Auditing: Integrated Concepts and Procedures, 3rd**

Taylor, Glezen, and Ehrenreich: **Case Study in Auditing, 3rd**

Tricker: **Management Information and Control Systems**

Wilkinson: **Accounting and Information Systems, 2nd**

THIRD EDITION

MODERN AUDITING

WALTER G. KELL

WILLIAM C. BOYNTON

RICHARD E. ZIEGLER

JOHN WILEY & SONS

NEW YORK / CHICHESTER / BRISBANE / TORONTO / SINGAPORE

TO THE STUDENT: A Study Guide for the textbook is available through your college bookstore under the title Study Guide to accompany MODERN AUDITING by *Walter G. Kell, William C. Boynton,* and *Richard E. Ziegler.* The Study Guide can help you with course material by acting as a tutorial, review and study aid. If the Study Guide is not in stock, ask the bookstore manager to order a copy for you.

Cover design by Rafael Hernandez

Material from the Certificate in Management Accounting Examinations, Copyright © 1972, 1973, 1974, 1975, 1976, 1977, 1978, 1979, 1980, 1981, 1982, 1983, 1984 by the Institute of Management Accounting, is reprinted or adapted with permission.

Material from the Uniform CPA Examinations and Unofficial Answers, Copyright © 1961, 1962, 1963, 1964, 1965, 1966, 1967, 1968, 1969, 1970, 1971, 1972, 1973, 1974, 1975, 1976, 1977, 1978, 1979, 1980, 1981, 1982, 1983, 1984, 1985 by the American Institute of Certified Public Accountants, Inc. is reprinted or adapted with permission.

Material from the Certified Internal Auditor Examination, Copyright © 1976, 1977, 1979, 1980, 1983, 1984 by the Institute of Internal Auditors, Inc. is reprinted or adapted with permission.

Library of Congress Cataloging in Publication Data:

Kell, Walter Gerry, 1921–
   Modern auditing.

   Includes index.
   1. Auditing.   I. Boynton, William C.   II. Ziegler,
Richard E.   III. Title.
HF5667.K39 1986   657'.45   85-29496
ISBN 0-471-81919-0

Printed in the United States of America

10 9 8 7 6 5 4 3

ABOUT THE AUTHORS

WALTER G. KELL (Ph.D., University of Illinois at Urbana—Champaign) is Professor of Accounting at the University of Michigan, where he has served as Chairman of the Department of Accounting. A certified public accountant, he has had professional experience with several accounting firms, including Arthur Andersen & Co., Touche Ross & Co., and Arthur Young & Company. He has been an active member of the American Institute of Certified Public Accountants and has served on its Committee on Auditing Procedure (predecessor to the Auditing Standards Board) and Auditing Standards Advisory Council. He is a past president of the American Accounting Association and has been a consulting editor to the *Accountants' Handbook.* He is a member of the Michigan Association of Certified Public Accountants and has served on its Committee on Accounting and Auditing Procedures and Board of Directors.

WILLIAM C. BOYNTON (Ph.D., Michigan State University) is Professor of Accounting and Accounting Department Head at the California Polytechnic State University—San Luis Obispo. A certified public accountant, he has served on the audit staffs of Deloitte Haskins & Sells and Ernst & Whinney. He is the author of several articles on accounting and auditing and has served as a codirector of the American Institute of Certified Public Accountants' National Banking School. A past chairman of the Accounting and Auditing Procedures Committee of the Virginia Society of Certified Public Accountants, he has also served on several committees of the American Accounting Association and the Federation of Schools of Accountancy.

RICHARD E. ZIEGLER (Ph.D., University of North Carolina at Chapel Hill) is Associate Professor and Associate Head of the Department of Accountancy at the University of Illinois in Urbana—Champaign, where he is the Alexander Grant & Co. Faculty Fellow. A certified public accountant, he worked for five years with an international accounting firm. More recently, he completed a professional internship on the audit staff of Arthur Young & Company. In addition to authoring several articles on accounting, he has served on committees of the American Accounting Association and served as Chair of its Auditing Standards Committee.

PREFACE

MODERN AUDITING continues to offer a unique blend of the contemporary and traditional approaches to the study of auditing. It recognizes the importance of transaction cycles in the study and evaluation of internal control while retaining the time-honored balance sheet approach in the verification of transaction cycle balances.

This textbook is designed primarily for the first course in auditing either at the undergraduate or graduate level. Throughout the book, every effort has been made to integrate auditing concepts with auditing methodology and auditing theory with auditing practice. In addition, emphasis is given to the professional responsibilities of the independent auditor.

ORGANIZATION

As in the previous editions, the book is divided into four parts:

Part	Subject	Chapters
I	Fundamental Relationships	1–4
II	Study and Evaluation of Internal Control	5–11
III	Verification of Account Balances	12–16
IV	Reporting and Other Responsibilities	17–21

This arrangement reflects both sound pedagogy and current auditing practices within the public accounting profession. Part I establishes basic auditing concepts and relationships, Part II describes interim field work, Part III explains year-end work, and Part IV emphasizes the auditor's reporting and professional responsibilities.

The first three chapters in Part I are essentially new chapters. Chapter 1 describes the professional practice of auditing. It includes expanded coverage of internal, operational, and governmental auditing; identifies three sets of prescribed auditing standards; explains the public accounting profession; and discusses the regulation of the profession. Chapter 2 focuses exclusively on financial statement audits. This chapter describes the need, importance, and limitations of this type of audit; the auditor's standard report; and the auditor's responsibilities in financial statement audits. Chapter 3 covers the first two phases of an audit engagement: accepting the engagement and planning the audit. The chapter includes extensive discussion of the role of analytical review and materiality and audit risk in audit planning. Chapter 4 was chapter 3 in previous editions. It combines a conceptual explanation of audit evidence and auditing procedures with a practical discussion of the nature and importance of working papers.

Part II deals with internal control systems and the auditor's study and evaluation of internal control. Internal control principles and review concepts are explained in Chapter 5. These basic relationships are then applied to electronic data processing systems in Chapter 6. Chapter 7 explains the role of audit sampling in the study and evaluation of internal control, and a case study is used to demonstrate a statistical sampling application. Chapters 8 to 11 discuss internal control principles and the auditor's methodology for reviewing and testing internal controls for significant classes of transactions within three transaction cycles: revenue, expenditure and production. These chapters also contain case studies of statistical sampling and electronic data processing applications.

There are five chapters in Part III. Chapter 12 explains the role of audit sampling in the verification of account balances and contains case study applications of both probability-proportional-to-size and classical variables sampling. Chapters 13 and 14 contain audit programs for verifying the principal account balances resulting from the transaction cycles described in Part II. Chapter 15 discusses the auditing of investing and financing cycles. The concluding chapter (Chapter 16) considers the verification of income statement balances and the steps in completing the audit.

Part IV deals with the independent auditor's reporting and professional responsibilities. Chapter 17 explains the four reporting standards, and actual audit reports are used to illustrate departures from the standard report. Chapter 18 describes and illustrates additional reports that may be issued in an audit engagement and the reporting standards in review and accounting service engagements. Chapter 19 focuses primarily on the AICPA Code of Professional Ethics, but also considers the Institute of Internal Auditor's Code of Ethics. Chapter 20 describes the auditor's potential legal liability under both common and statutory law. Ethics and legal liability are presented in Chapters 19 and 20 because we believe that students can obtain a much greater understanding of the CPA's responsibilities in these two areas at the end of the course rather than at the beginning. These are freestanding chapters, however, and may be assigned earlier by the instructor. The concluding chapter of this textbook (Chapter 21) provides in-depth coverage of the independent accountant's responsibilities relating to the filing of reports with the Securities and Exchange Commission.

SPECIAL FEATURES

The third edition continues the following features of earlier editions:

- Study objectives for each chapter.
- Identification of functions, common documents, accounting records, and data files for transaction cycles.
- Extensive coverage of the prevention and detection of errors and irregularities.

- Manual and electronic data processing flowcharts for significant classes of transactions within transaction cycles.
- Statistical sampling case studies for tests of transactions and tests of balances.
- Electronic data processing case studies for transaction cycles and computer-assisted techniques in the verification of account balances.
- Integration of authoritative auditing and professional literature throughout the text.
- Case studies drawn from actual practice.
- Full chapter coverage of SEC accounting and reporting requirements.

NEW TOPICS

This edition contains the following new topics.

- Database Management Systems (Chapter 6).
- Small Computer Systems (minis and micros) (Chapter 6).
- Audit Planning in an EDP Environment (Chapter 6).
- Substantive Tests Prior to the Balance Sheet Date (Chapter 13).
- Analytical Review Procedures in Verifying Income Statement Balances (Chapter 16).
- Final Assessment of Materiality and Audit Risk (Chapter 16).
- Omitted Procedures Discovered After the Report Date (Chapter 16).
- Special Purpose Reports on Internal Accounting Control at Service Organizations (Chapter 18).
- The Single Audit Act (Chapter 18).

END-OF-CHAPTER MATERIALS

As in previous editions, there is an abundance of end-of-chapter materials that are carefully integrated with the chapter content. Each chapter contains 20 review questions; 6–10 multiple-choice questions from professional examinations, 10–15 comprehensive questions, and a case study. The comprehensive questions and case studies include numerous professional examination questions and materials from staff training programs of three public accounting firms—Arthur Young & Company, Ernst & Whinney, and Peat, Marwick, Mitchell & Co. These materials are identified by an asterisk (*) in the text. In total, there are more than 850 questions and cases that have been carefully edited and adapted to the text.

SUPPLEMENTARY MATERIALS

The supplements to this edition consist of (1) a software package, (2) an Instructor's Manual, and (3) a Student Study Guide.

The software package consists of a disk and a workbook that is usable with

Lotus 1-2-3 or an IBM-PC microcomputer. The package requires the student to solve a variety of attribute and variables sampling problems.

The Instructor's Manual again contains (1) solutions to end-of-chapter materials, (2) selected exhibits and teaching aids for use as transparencies, and (3) a test bank of examination questions. The test bank consists of multiple-choice questions, correct/incorrect statements, matching questions, and essay and analysis questions. There are over 300 questions in the test bank.

The format of the Study Guide remains the same as in previous editions. The study guide for this edition contains 30 chapter highlights per chapter, 25 true or false statements, 15 completion statements, and 20 multiple-choice questions from professional examinations. Solutions to the statements and questions are included at the end of the Study Guide.

ACKNOWLEDGMENTS

We take this opportunity to thank the individuals who have made significant contributions to this edition.

David B. Pearson of Arthur Young & Company made many helpful suggestions on all substantive changes in this edition, and we are especially grateful for his insights and perceptive comments.

We are very fortunate to have received comprehensive reviews of the manuscript of this edition from the following professors: Roderick S. Barclay, Cleveland State University; Robert C. Fess, San Francisco State University; James C. Lampe, University of Missouri; Paul Miranti, Rutgers University; and Ben S. Trotter, Texas Tech University. In addition, we benefited greatly from critiques of the second edition by professors Alan P. Johnson, California State University, Hayward and Curtis C. Verschoor, DePaul University.

The following individuals made helpful suggestions on selected chapters: Richard W. Andrews, George D. Cameron, III, and George J. Siedel, III, all of The University of Michigan; Mary Finan, Arthur Young & Company and Robert W. Scharff, Peat, Marwick, Mitchell & Co.

Special thanks are extended to the many adopters of the previous editions for their comments and suggestions.

We appreciate the cooperation of the American Institute of Certified Public Accountants to quote from their professional pronouncements. We also acknowledge the permission obtained from the American Institute of Certified Public Accountants, the Institute of Certified Management Accounting, and the Institute of Internal Auditors to adapt and use material from the Uniform CPA Examinations, the CMA Examinations, and the CIA Examination.

We also wish to express our appreciation to our editor, Lucille Sutton, supervising copy editor, John F. Patton, and production supervisor, Debra Fratello, of John Wiley & Sons.

December 1985

Walter G. Kell
William C. Boynton
Richard E. Ziegler

CONTENTS

PART III / VERIFICATION OF ACCOUNT BALANCES   **407**

Chapter 18 / Other Reports and Services 657

Chapter 19 / Professional Ethics 693

Chapter 20 / Accountant's Legal Liability 733

Chapter 21 / The Independent Accountant and the Securities and Exchange Commission 772

Appendix X

Content Specification Outline for the Auditing Section of the Uniform Certified Public Accountant Examination (Effective May 1986)

Index

PART I

FUNDAMENTAL RELATIONSHIPS

In auditing, as in other fields of knowledge, there are fundamental relationships that are essential to a comprehensive understanding of the subject. The basic relationships of auditing are discussed in the chapters that comprise Part 1 of this text.

Chapter 1 describes the function of auditing in society, professional auditing standards, the public accounting profession, and regulation of the profession.

In Chapter 2, consideration is given to the reasons for a financial statement audit, the auditor's standard report, and the four phases of a financial statement audit.

Chapter 3 explains the primary considerations and professional standards that relate to accepting and planning a financial statement audit.

In Chapter 4, attention is focused on obtaining and evaluating audit evidence and the importance of documenting the auditor's work and findings in working papers.

Chapter 1

The Professional Practice of Auditing

Study Objectives

After studying this chapter, you should be able to

- Explain the essential parts of the term *auditing*.
- Distinguish among the different types of audits and auditors.
- Describe the professional standards for the practice of auditing.
- Identify the entities associated with the public accounting profession.
- Explain the three levels of regulation that exist within the profession.
- Enumerate the quality control standards for CPA firms.
- Indicate the types of services a CPA firm may render.

Auditing plays a vital role in business, government, and our economy. Evidence of the importance of auditing is provided by the following:

- The financial statements of over 10,000 public companies are audited annually, including all companies whose securities are traded on the New York Stock Exchange.
- Each state and local government unit receiving $100,000 or more per year in financial assistance from the federal government must have an annual audit under the Single Audit Act.
- In 1984, the Internal Revenue Service audited 1.2 million individual tax returns.

As a vocation, auditing offers the opportunity for challenging and rewarding careers in public accounting, industry, and government.

AUDITING DEFINED

Auditing may be defined as

> a systematic process of objectively obtaining and evaluating evidence regarding assertions about economic actions and events to ascertain the degree of correspondence between those assertions and established criteria and communicating the results to interested users.[1]

Several parts of this definition merit special comment:

- A *systematic process* connotes a logical, structured, and organized series of steps or procedures.
- *Objectively obtaining and evaluating evidence* means examining the bases for the assertions (representations) and judiciously evaluating the results without bias or prejudice either for or against the individual (or entity) making the representations.
- *Assertions about economic actions and events* are the representations made by the individual or entity. They comprise the subject matter of auditing. Assertions include information contained in financial statements, internal operating reports, and tax returns.
- *Degree of correspondence* refers to the closeness with which the assertions can be identified with established criteria. The expression of correspondence may be quantified, such as the amount of a shortage in a petty cash fund, or it may be qualitative, such as the fairness (or reasonableness) of financial statements.
- *Established criteria* are the standards against which the assertions or representations are judged. Criteria may be specific rules prescribed by a legislative body, budgets and other measures of performance set by management, or generally accepted accounting principles (GAAP) established by the Financial Accounting Standards Board (FASB) and other authoritative bodies.
- *Communicating the results* is often referred to as attestation. By attesting to the degree of correspondence with established criteria, the investigator enhances (or weakens) the credibility of the representations or claims that have been made by another party. The communication of findings is achieved through a written report.
- *Interested users* are all individuals who use (rely on) the auditor's findings. In a business environment, this includes stockholders, management, creditors, governmental agencies, and the public.

---

[1]Auditing Concepts Committee, "Report of the Committee on Basic Auditing Concepts," *The Accounting Review*, Vol. 47, Supp. (Sarasota, Fla.: American Accounting Association, 1972), p. 18.

TYPES OF AUDITS

Audits are generally classified into three categories: financial statement, compliance, or operational. The basic nature of each is briefly described below.

FINANCIAL STATEMENT AUDIT

A financial statement audit involves an examination of an entity's statements for the purpose of expressing an opinion on whether they are presented fairly in conformity with established criteria—usually GAAP. This type of an audit is made by *external auditors* appointed by the company whose statements are being examined. The results of financial statement audits are distributed to a wide spectrum of users such as stockholders, creditors, regulatory agencies, and the general public. Financial statement audits for major corporations are indispensable to the functioning of our national securities markets. Extensive consideration will be given to financial statement audits in later chapters of this text.

COMPLIANCE AUDIT

A compliance audit involves a review of certain financial or operating activities of an entity for the purpose of determining whether they conform to specified conditions, rules, or regulations. The established criteria in this type of audit may come from a variety of sources. Management, for example, may prescribe internal control procedures such as depositing all cash receipts intact daily and requiring two signatures on company checks. In addition, management may have policies (or rules) pertaining to overtime work, participation in a pension plan, and conflicts of interest. Compliance audits based on criteria established by management may be made frequently during the year. In some cases, they are made on a regular schedule such as weekly or monthly, or they may be conducted intermittently or on a surprise basis. This type of audit is usually made by company employees who perform an *internal audit function*.

Compliance audits may also be based on criteria established by creditors. For instance, a bond contract may require the maintenance of a specified current ratio and periodic payments into bond sinking funds during the term of the bond issue. These criteria are frequently related to a company's financial statements. In many cases, therefore, this type of compliance audit is made in conjunction with, or as a by-product of, a financial statement audit.

Possibly the widest application of compliance audits relates to criteria based on governmental regulations. Business enterprises, not-for-profit organizations, governmental units, and individuals are required to prove compliance with myriad regulations. A corporation, for example, must comply with various labor-related laws such as the Equal Employment Opportunity Act and the Fair Labor Standards Act, and defense contractors must comply with the terms and conditions of the government contract. In addition, they are required to satisfy extensive income and other tax regulations. Individuals, of course, are required to meet the income tax provisions of the Internal Revenue Code in filing their annual tax returns. Compliance audits based on governmental regulations are made by auditors employed by the governmental agency responsible for administering the regulation or external auditors. The findings in compliance audits are generally reported to the authority that established the criteria.

OPERATIONAL AUDIT

An operational audit involves a systematic review of an organization's operating activities in relation to specified objectives. This type of an audit is sometimes referred to as a *performance audit* or a *management audit*. In an operational audit, the auditor is expected to make an objective observation and comprehensive analysis of specific operations. The scope of the audit may be the entire organization or a stipulated subset thereof. For a business enterprise, the audit may relate to a segment such as a division, department, or branch, or a function such as production, marketing, or data processing. In contrast, an operational audit for the federal government may relate to a segment such as an agency or unit, or a function such as urban development, maintenance of national parks, and distribution of food stamps.

Operational audits are usually made to satisfy a combination of the following three purposes:

- *Assess Performance.* The reviewed organization's performance is compared with policies, standards, and goals established by management or other appropriate measurement criteria.
- *Identify Opportunities for Improvement.* From the assessment of performance, the auditor generally recognizes opportunities for either increased economy, efficiency, or effectiveness.
- *Develop Recommendations for Improvement or Further Action.* Recommendations will vary depending on the nature of the problem and the opportunities for improvement. In some cases, the auditor can make specific recommendations. In other instances, it may be necessary to recommend further study.[2]

Operational audits may be requested by management or a third party. The results of an operational audit are reported to the party who requested the audit. Further insight into this type of audit can be obtained from the summaries of operational audit engagements in Appendix 1A to this chapter.

A comparative analysis of significant differences among financial statement audits and specific examples of compliance and operational audits are shown

[2]Special Committee on Operational and Management Auditing, *Operational Audit Engagements* (New York: American Institute of Certified Public Accountants, 1982), p. 3.

Type of Audit	Nature of Assertion	Established Criteria	Degree of Correspondence	Primary Users of Audit Report
Financial statement	Entity's financial statement data	GAAP	Fairness	Stockholders, creditors, regulatory agencies, and general public
Compliance	Entity's income tax return information	Internal revenue code and regulations	Correctness	IRS
Operational	Performance statistics on delivery of city services	Performance goals established by city council	Closeness	City council

Figure 1-1. EXAMPLES OF DIFFERENT TYPES OF AUDITS.

in Fig. 1-1. It should be recognized that the assertions for the last two types of audits are only examples of the assertions that may be made.

TYPES OF AUDITORS

Individuals who are engaged to audit economic actions and events for individuals and legal entities are generally classified into three groups: (1) independent auditors, (2) internal auditors, and (3) government auditors. A brief description of each group and the type of auditing done by each are explained below.

INDEPENDENT AUDITORS

Independent auditors are either sole practitioners or members of public accounting firms who render professional auditing services to clients. By virtue of their education, training, and experience, independent auditors are qualified to perform each of the types of audits described above. The clients of independent auditors may include profit-making business enterprises, not-for-profit organizations, governmental agencies, and individuals.

Like members of the medical and legal professions, independent auditors work on a fee basis. There are similarities between the role of an independent auditor in a public accounting firm and an attorney who is a member of a law firm. However, there is also a major difference: The auditor is expected to be *independent* of the client in making an audit and in reporting the results, whereas the attorney is expected to be an *advocate* for the client in rendering legal services.

Audit independence involves both conceptual and technical considerations. It is enough to say at this point that to be independent, an auditor should be without bias with respect to the client under audit and should appear to be objective to those relying on the results of the audit. More attention will be given to independence in later chapters.

Most independent auditors are licensed to practice as certified public accountants (CPAs). In general, licensing involves passing a uniform CPA examination and obtaining practical experience in auditing. The national association of CPAs that prepares the CPA examination and establishes standards of practice for its members is the American Institute of Certified Public Accountants (AICPA).[3] The standards for financial statement audits, known as *generally accepted auditing standards* (GAAS), are shown in Figure 1-2.

As shown, there are ten standards grouped into three categories: general, field work, and reporting. GAAS must be approved by the membership of the AICPA. They are enforced through the AICPA's Code of Professional Ethics. GAAS establish the quality of performance and the overall objectives to be achieved by the auditor in a financial statement audit. Accordingly, they are used by peers, courts, and regulatory agencies in evaluating the auditor's performance. GAAS are applicable regardless of the size of the client, the form of business organization, the type of industry, or whether the entity is for profit or nonprofit. They apply equally to an examination of the financial statements of an unincorporated corner grocery store, a school district, and a large corporation such as Exxon or International Business Machines Corporation. Guidelines for meeting GAAS are provided by the AICPA. The most authoritative source is *Statements on Auditing Standards* (*SASs*) that are discussed later in the chapter. Further consideration is given to each of the ten GAAS in subsequent chapters.

INTERNAL AUDITORS

Internal auditors are employees of the companies they audit. This type of auditor is involved in an independent appraisal activity, called *internal auditing*, within an organization as a service to the organization. The objective of internal auditing is to assist the management of the organization in the effective discharge of its responsibilities.

The attainment of this overall objective involves such activities as:

- Reviewing and appraising the soundness, adequacy, and application of accounting, financial, and other operating controls, and promoting effective control at reasonable cost.
- Ascertaining the extent of compliance with established policies, plans, and procedures.
- Ascertaining the extent to which company assets are accounted for and safeguarded from losses of all kinds.
- Ascertaining the reliability of management data developed within the organization.

[3]The specifications for the auditing section of the CPA examination are reproduced in an appendix on page 808.

GENERALLY ACCEPTED AUDITING STANDARDS

General Standards

- The examination is to be performed by a person or persons having adequate technical training and proficiency as an auditor.
- In all matters relating to the assignment, an independence in mental attitude is to be maintained by the auditor or auditors.
- Due professional care is to be exercised in the performance of the examination and the preparation of the report.

Standards of Field Work

- The work is to be adequately planned and assistants, if any, are to be properly supervised.
- There is to be a proper study and evaluation of the existing internal control as a basis for reliance thereon and for the determination of the resultant extent of the tests to which auditing procedures are to be restricted.
- Sufficient competent evidential matter is to be obtained through inspection, observation, inquiries, and confirmations to afford a reasonable basis for an opinion regarding the financial statements under examination.

Standards of Reporting

- The report shall state whether the financial statements are presented in accordance with generally accepted accounting principles.
- The report shall state whether such principles have been consistently observed in the current period in relation to the preceding period.
- Informative disclosures in the financial statements are to be regarded as reasonably adequate unless otherwise stated in the report.
- The report shall contain either an expression of opinion regarding the financial statements, taken as a whole, or an assertion to the effect that an opinion cannot be expressed. When an overall opinion cannot be expressed, the reasons therefor should be stated. In all cases where an auditor's name is associated with financial statements, the report should contain a clear-cut indication of the character of the auditor's examination, if any, and the degree of responsibility he is taking.

Figure 1-2. AICPA STANDARDS FOR FINANCIAL STATEMENT AUDITS. (SOURCE: Auditing Standards Board, *Codification of Statements on Auditing Standards* (New York: American Institute of Certified Public Accountants, 1985), Auditing Section 150.02.)

- Appraising the quality of performance in completing assigned responsibilities.
- Recommending operating improvements.[4]

The scope of the internal audit function extends to all phases of an organization's activities. Internal auditors are primarily involved with compliance

[4]*Statement of Responsibilities of Internal Auditors* (Altamonte Springs, Fla.: Institute of Internal Auditors, 1978), pp. 3–4.

and operational audits. However, as is explained later, the work of internal auditors may supplement the work of independent auditors in financial statement audits.

Many internal auditors are certified (CIAs) and some are also CPAs. The international association of internal auditors is the Institute of Internal Auditors (IIA), which prescribes certification criteria and administers the certified internal auditor examination. In addition, the IIA has established practice standards for internal auditing as illustrated in Figure 1–3 and a code of ethics. It also has started to issue *Statements on Internal Auditing Standards* (*SIASs*) to assist its members in meeting the practice standards.

As indicated in the practice standards, internal auditors are expected to be independent of the activities they audit and objective in performing their audits. Independence depends on whether internal auditors are independent of the individuals responsible for the activities being audited. Internal auditors are not independent if they perform record-keeping functions or make management decisions. The objectivity of internal auditors depends to a large extent on the organizational level to which they report. When they report, or have direct access, to the board of directors, their objectivity ordinarily is greatly enhanced. The role and stature of internal auditors have increased significantly in the past decade.

A comparison of the IIA standards with the AICPA standards shows significant similarities between (1) the IIA standards for independence and professional proficiency and the AICPA's general standards and (2) the IIA standards for scope of work and performance of work (through standard 420)

SUMMARY OF GENERAL AND SPECIFIC STANDARDS FOR THE PROFESSIONAL PRACTICE OF INTERNAL AUDITING

100 **INDEPENDENCE.** Internal auditors should be independent of the activities they audit.

    110 *Organizational Status.* The organizational status of the internal auditing department should be sufficient to permit the accomplishment of its audit responsibilities.

    120 *Objectivity.* Internal auditors should be objective in performing audits.

200 **PROFESSIONAL PROFICIENCY.** Internal audits should be performed with proficiency and due professional care.

The Internal Auditing Department

    210 *Staffing.* The internal auditing department should provide assurance that the technical proficiency and educational background of internal auditors are appropriate for the audits to be performed.

    220 *Knowledge, Skills, and Disciplines.* The internal auditing department should possess or should obtain the knowledge, skills, and disciplines needed to carry out its audit responsibilities.

    230 *Supervision.* The internal auditing department should provide assurance that internal audits are properly supervised.

Figure 1-3. IIA PRACTICE STANDARDS. [SOURCE: *Standards for the Professional Practice of Internal Auditing* (Altamonte Springs, Fla.: Institute of Internal Auditors, 1980), pp. 3–4. (NOTE: There are also five standards for managing an internal auditing department.)]

The Internal Auditor

240 *Compliance with Standards of Conduct.* Internal auditors should comply with professional standards of conduct.

250 *Knowledge, Skills, and Disciplines.* Internal auditors should possess the knowledge, skills, and disciplines essential to the performance of internal audits.

260 *Human Relations and Communications.* Internal auditors should be skilled in dealing with people and in communicating effectively.

270 *Continuing Education.* Internal auditors should maintain their technical competence through continuing education.

280 *Due Professional Care.* Internal auditors should exercise due professional care in performing internal audits.

300 **SCOPE OF WORK.** The scope of the internal audit should encompass the examination and evaluation of the adequacy and effectiveness of the organization's system of internal control and the quality of performance in carrying out assigned responsibilities.

310 *Reliability and Integrity of Information.* Internal auditors should review the reliability and integrity of financial and operating information and the means used to identify, measure, classify, and report such information.

320 *Compliance with Policies, Plans, Procedures, Laws, and Regulations.* Internal auditors should review the systems established to ensure compliance with those policies, plans, procedures, laws, and regulations which could have a significant impact on operations and reports and should determine whether the organization is in compliance.

330 *Safeguarding of Assets.* Internal auditors should review the means of safeguarding assets and, as appropriate, verify the existence of such assets.

340 *Economical and Efficient Use of Resources.* Internal auditors should appraise the economy and efficiency with which resources are employed.

350 *Accomplishment of Established Objectives and Goals for Operations or Programs.* Internal auditors should review operations or programs to ascertain whether results are consistent with established objectives and goals and whether the operations or programs are being carried out as planned.

400 **PERFORMANCE OF AUDIT WORK.** Audit work should include planning the audit, examining and evaluating information, communicating results, and following up.

410 *Planning the Audit.* Internal auditors should plan each audit.

420 *Examining and Evaluating Information.* Internal auditors should collect, analyze, interpret, and document information to support audit results.

430 *Communicating Results.* Internal auditors should report the results of their audit work.

440 *Following Up.* Internal auditors should follow up to ascertain that appropriate action is taken on reported audit findings.

Figure 1-3. (*Continued*)

and the AICPA field work standards. The IIA's reporting standard (430) is not as extensive as the AICPA's reporting standards.

GOVERNMENT AUDITORS

Government auditors are employed by various local, state, and federal governmental agencies. At the federal level, the three primary agencies are the

U.S. General Accounting Office (GAO), the Internal Revenue Service (IRS), and the Defense Contract Audit Agency (DCAA).

The GAO is a nonpartisan federal agency responsible for conducting the audit function for Congress. The term *audit* is used by the GAO to describe work done in examining (1) financial reports, (2) compliance with applicable laws and regulations, (3) efficiency and economy of operations, and (4) effectiveness in achieving program results.[5] This definition includes financial statement, compliance, and operational audits.

The GAO has established practice standards classified as General, Examination and Evaluation, and Reporting. The general standards applicable to all

---

SUMMARY OF STANDARDS FOR AUDIT OF GOVERNMENTAL ORGANIZATIONS, PROGRAMS, ACTIVITIES, AND FUNCTIONS

General Standards

1. Qualifications: The auditors assigned to perform the audit must collectively possess adequate professional proficiency for the tasks required.
2. Independence: In all matters relating to the audit work, the audit organization and the individual auditors, whether government or public, must be free from personal or external impairments to independence, must be organizationally independent, and shall maintain an independent attitude and appearance.
3. Due professional care: Due professional care is to be used in conducting the audit and preparing related reports.
4. Scope impairments: When factors external to the audit organization and the auditor restrict the audit or interfere with the auditor's ability to form objective opinions and conclusions, the auditor should attempt to remove the limitation or, failing that, report the limitation.

Figure 1-4. GAO GENERAL AUDIT STANDARDS. (SOURCE: Comptroller General of the United States, *op. cit.*, p. 6.)

---

governmental audits are shown in Figure 1-4. Note that the first three standards are similar to those prescribed for independent and internal auditors.

Separate field work and reporting standards are prescribed for (1) financial and compliance audits and (2) economy, efficiency, and program results audits. The first standard of field work and reporting for financial and compliance audits adopts and incorporates the AICPA standards for field work and reporting. The specific standards are presented in Appendix 1B to this chapter.

The IRS is an agency of the Treasury Department that is responsible for administering the federal tax laws. IRS auditors (or agents) audit the returns of taxpayers for compliance with applicable tax laws. Their findings are generally restricted to the agency and the taxpayer. The Defense Contract Audit Agency, as its name suggests, conducts audits of defense contractors and their operations, and reports to the Department of Defense.

[5]Comptroller General of the United States, *Standards for Audit of Governmental Organizations, Programs, Activities and Functions* (Washington, D.C.: U.S. General Accounting Office, 1981), p. 4.

The national association for government accountants is the Association of Government Accountants (AGA). The AGA has not yet developed a certification program for government accountants. However, some government auditors hold CPA and/or CIA certificates.

THE PUBLIC ACCOUNTING PROFESSION

CPAs and other professionals employed by firms of certified public accountants are considered to be part of the public accounting profession. This profession is widely recognized as one of the leading growth professions in the world, and its stature is comparable to the professions of law and medicine. The profession of public accounting consists of (1) entities that function within the profession itself and (2) entities that have a direct influence on the profession through their regulatory and standard-setting activities as shown in Figure 1-5.

An explanation of each entity is given below.

AMERICAN INSTITUTE OF CERTIFIED PUBLIC ACCOUNTANTS

The public accounting profession's national professional organization is the AICPA. Membership in the AICPA is voluntary. Currently, there are approximately 260,000 CPAs in the United States, of whom 230,000 are members of the AICPA. One of the AICPA's major objectives is to promote and maintain high professional standards within the profession.

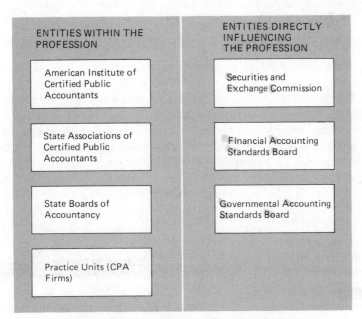

Figure 1-5. ENTITIES ASSOCIATED WITH THE PUBLIC ACCOUNTING PROFESSION.

The AICPA operates through a number of divisions. Those that pertain most directly to the audit function are (1) Auditing Standards, (2) Division for CPA Firms, and (3) Professional Ethics. The Auditing Standards Division is briefly explained below; the other divisions are described later.

The *Auditing Standards Division* is headed by a vice-president of auditing. It consists of the Auditing Standards Board (ASB), subcommittees, task forces, a director of auditing research, and a small staff. The ASB currently consists of 15 CPAs. It is the senior technical body designated to issue pronouncements on auditing matters. The board makes its pronouncements through *Statements on Auditing Standards* (*SASs*). Before issuance, each statement is widely circulated for public comment. SASs are

- Recognized as interpretations of generally accepted auditing standards (GAAS) under the AICPA's Code of Professional Ethics.
- Mandatory for AICPA members who must be prepared to justify departures from such statements.

The SASs that have been issued to date and the section reference to the AICPA's codification of SASs are identified in the inside front cover of this text.

Other AICPA publications of interest to auditors are (1) auditing interpretations, (2) audit guides, and (3) audit and accounting guides. These publications are not as authoritative as SASs.

In addition to prescribing standards for financial statement audits, the AICPA has established standards for quality control and for other areas of service rendered by CPA firms. The AICPA has also adopted a comprehensive code of professional ethics for its members.

STATE ASSOCIATIONS (SOCIETIES) OF CERTIFIED PUBLIC ACCOUNTANTS

CPAs within each state have formed a state society or association of CPAs. Like the national organization, membership in a state society is voluntary. Many CPAs are members of both the AICPA and a state society. State societies function through small full-time staffs and committees composed of their members. State associations have their own codes of professional ethics that closely parallel the AICPA Code of Ethics. Although they are autonomous, state societies usually cooperate with both each other and the AICPA in areas of mutual interest, such as continuing professional education and ethics.

STATE BOARDS OF ACCOUNTANCY

There are 54 boards of accountancy: one in each state, one in the District of Columbia, and one in each U.S. territory. State boards usually consist of five to seven CPAs and at least one public member who are generally appointed by the governor. A full-time executive secretary and a small (three- to five-member) administrative staff are common. Each board administers its state accountancy laws which set forth the conditions for licensing of CPAs, codes of professional ethics, and in some cases mandatory continuing professional education requirements. State boards are also becoming more active in positive enforcement programs aimed at maintaining the quality of audit practice. The primary functions of the boards are issuing licenses to practice as a CPA, renewing licenses, and suspending or revoking licenses to practice. State boards work independently of the AICPA and state societies.

PRACTICE UNITS

A CPA may practice as a sole practitioner or as a member of a firm. A CPA firm may be organized as a proprietorship, a partnership, or a professional corporation. There are approximately 30,000 practice units (CPA firms) in the United States. These firms are generally classified into four groups: (1) international, (2) national, (3) regional, and (4) local.

International firms have offices in the principal cities of the United States and major cities throughout the world. The eight largest firms in this group are referred to as the "Big Eight."[6] Over 90 percent of the "Fortune 500" companies and thousands of smaller clients are served by the Big Eight. The combined annual revenues of this group of firms in 1984 exceeded $8.3 billion worldwide and $5 billion in the United States. One of the Big Eight firms has 100 offices in the United States and 375 offices in 90 countries worldwide. This firm has approximately 1,300 partners and a professional staff approaching 25,000.

National firms have offices in the major cities in the United States. These firms serve some SEC clients and thousands of medium and small clients. National firms compete with international firms for domestic clients.

Regional firms have offices in a limited geographical area such as the East or Midwest. These firms usually serve smaller clients than international and national firms.

Local firms may have one office or several offices within a state or county. The local firm is by far the most common form of practice unit. Local firms serve small entities and individual clients.

SECURITIES AND EXCHANGE COMMISSION

The Securities and Exchange Commission (SEC) is a federal government agency that was created under the 1934 Securities Exchange Act to regulate the distribution and trading of securities offered for public sale and subsequent trading of securities on stock exchanges and over-the-counter markets. Under the provisions of this Act, the SEC has the authority to establish GAAP for companies under its jurisdiction. Throughout its history, the SEC has, with few exceptions, delegated this authority to the private sector, and it currently recognizes the pronouncements of the FASB as constituting GAAP in the

---

[6]The Big Eight are Arthur Andersen & Co.; Coopers & Lybrand; Deloitte Haskins & Sells; Ernst & Whinney; Peat, Marwick, Mitchell & Co.; Price Waterhouse; Touche Ross & Co.; and Arthur Young & Company.

filing of financial statements with the agency. In some instances, however, the SEC's disclosure requirements exceed GAAP.

The SEC also exerts considerable influence over auditing and the public accounting profession. Its regulations contain qualifications for determining the independence of the accountant, as well as standards of reporting. These requirements are basically the same as the standards prescribed by the AICPA. The SEC has the authority to take punitive action against independent accountants who do not comply with their regulations. Over the years, the SEC has not been reluctant to use this authority.

FINANCIAL ACCOUNTING STANDARDS BOARD

The FASB is an independent private body whose primary function is the development of GAAP. Statements and intepretations issued by this board have been officially recognized by the AICPA as constituting GAAP. The board consists of seven full-time members who are assisted by a large research staff and an advisory council. Before *Statements of Financial Accounting Standards* (SFASs) are issued, the statements are exposed to the public for comment, and public hearings are often held.

GOVERNMENTAL ACCOUNTING STANDARDS BOARD

Formed in 1984, the Governmental Accounting Standards Board (GASB) is the standard-setting body for the government sector of our economy. The GASB consists of five members who have the authority to promulgate accounting principles for state and local governmental entities. The process of issuing *Statements of Governmental Accounting Standards* (SGASs) is similar to the process followed by the FASB in issuing SFASs.

REGULATION OF THE PROFESSION

In 1977, the public accounting profession initiated a major program of self-regulation to increase the basis for reliance on financial statement audits by the general public. The program of regulation for the accounting profession includes provisions for the following:

- Admission of qualified people to professional practice.
- Establishment of generally accepted accounting principles and professional standards for accounting and auditing services and quality control.
- Continuing education for practicing accountants in accounting principles and professional standards.
- Periodic and regular determination of compliance with professional standards.
- Investigation of alleged deficiencies in complying with professional standards.

- Punishment of those found guilty of unacceptable practices.
- Maintenance of adequate competition.[7]

Regulation of the public accounting profession occurs at three levels: private, peer, and public. The levels are interrelated and each level aspires to the same goal, which is to improve the quality of practice. However, as explained below, each level uses different means to achieve the desired objective.

PRIVATE REGULATION

Private regulation occurs within the public accounting firm. In its audit practice, the firm has the responsibility to meet generally accepted auditing standards. To meet this responsibility and remain viable and competitive within the profession, most firms have a *system of quality control*. The system is designed to provide reasonable assurance of compliance with professional standards. Guidance in the establishment of necessary quality control policies and procedures is provided by the AICPA in the form of nine elements (or standards) of quality control.[8] The nature and purpose of each element and examples of specific policies and procedures are provided in Figure 1-6.

The elements of quality control are interrelated. For example, a firm's recruiting policies affect the quality of personnel assigned to engagements and the competency of personnel affects the firm's practices pertaining to consultation and supervision. The quality control policies and procedures adopted by a firm may vary because of its size, organizational structure, and operating philosophy.

The quality of auditing services rendered by a firm is therefore dependent on two sets of standards: GAAS for each engagement and quality control standards for the firm's auditing practice as a whole. These relationships are graphically depicted in Figure 1-7.

Private regulation involves the continuous monitoring of the day-to-day actions of the firm's professional staff by the firm's management. This aspect of regulation is usually direct and immediate. While seldom publicized, private regulation is generally very effective. Personnel who meet the standards receive pay raises and promotions. In contrast, individuals who perform substandard work do not receive such rewards and if improvement is not forthcoming, their employment may be terminated. Private regulation is primarily concerned with improving the competency of its professional staff. To assist its staff in meeting professional standards, firms provide on-the-job training and require their professionals to participate in continuing professional education courses.

For a CPA firm, there are numerous incentives to do good work. These include pride, professionalism, and a desire to be competitive with other firms.

---

[7]*Audit Quality: The Profession's Program,* Public Oversight Board, SEC Practice Section, Division for CPA Firms, AICPA, 1984, p. 8.

[8]Quality Control Standards Committee, *Statement on Quality Control Standards No. 1* (New York: American Institute of Certified Public Accountants, November 1979), p. 3.

Element	Purpose	Policies and Procedures
Independence	All professionals should be independent of clients.	Communicate rules on independence to professional staff. Monitor compliance with independence rules.
Assigning personnel to engagements	Personnel should have the technical training and proficiency required by the engagement.	Designate an appropriate person to assign personnel to engagements. Permit partner in charge of engagement to approve assignments.
Consultation	Personnel should seek assistance, when necessary, from persons having appropriate expertise, judgment, and authority.	Designate individuals as experts or specialists. Identify areas and specialized situations for which consultation is required.
Supervision	Work at all levels should be supervised to assure that it meets the firm's standards of quality.	Establish procedures for reviewing work papers and reports. Provide for on-going supervision of work.
Hiring	Only individuals who possess the qualities of integrity, competency, and motivation should be hired.	Maintain a recruiting program to obtain new hires at the entry level. Establish qualifications for evaluating potential hirees at each professional level.
Professional development	Personnel should have the knowledge required to fulfill assigned responsibilities.	Provide programs to develop expertise in specialized areas and industries. Make available to personnel information about new professional pronouncements.
Advancement	Personnel should have the qualifications to fulfill responsibilities they may be called on to assume in the future.	Establish qualifications necessary for each level of responsibility in the firm. Make periodic evaluations of personnel.
Acceptance and continuance of clients	The firm should not be associated with clients whose management lacks integrity.	Establish criteria for evaluating new clients. Establish review procedures for continuing a client.
Inspection	Determine that procedures relating to the other elements are being effectively applied.	Define scope and content of inspection program. Provide for reporting inspection results to appropriate management levels in the firm.

Figure 1-6. QUALITY CONTROL ELEMENTS.

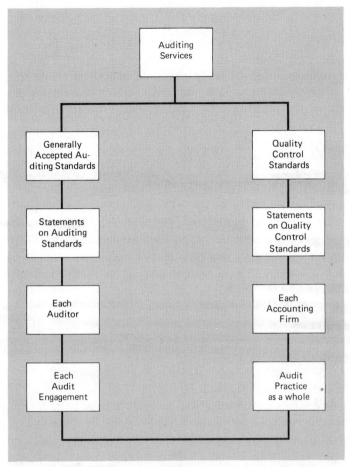

Figure 1-7. RELATIONSHIP BETWEEN GAAS AND QUALITY CONTROL STANDARDS IN AUDITING.

Additional motivation results from the desire to avoid the expense and damage to the firm's reputation that accompanies litigation and other actions brought against the firm for alleged noncompliance with professional standards.

PEER REGULATION

Peer regulation relates to the activities and requirements of professional organizations that are designed to enhance the quality of performance by individuals and CPA firms. This level of regulation extends to all professional standards.

One of the important parts of peer regulation is the AICPA Division for CPA Firms. The division consists of two sections: the SEC Practice Section and the Private Companies Practice Section. Membership in either or both sections is voluntary. Virtually all entities subject to SEC regulations are audited by firms who are members of the SEC Practice Section. Each section has its own objectives, membership and peer review requirements, and governing body (executive committee). In general, the objectives and requirements of the SEC Section are more extensive than those of the Private Section. In addition, the effectiveness of the SEC Section's regulatory system is monitored and evaluated by an independent public oversight board consisting of five members drawn from prominent individuals of high integrity and reputation. The objectives and membership requirements common to both sections are as follows:

Objectives

- Improve the quality of service (or practice) by CPA firms through the establishment of practice requirements for member firms.
- Establish and maintain an effective system of self-regulation of member firms by means of mandatory peer reviews, required maintenance of appropriate quality controls, and the imposition of sanctions for failure to meet membership requirements.

Membership Requirements

- Adhere to quality control standards established by the AICPA.
- Submit to peer reviews of the firm's accounting and audit practice every three years or at such additional times as designated by the executive committee, the reviews to be conducted in accordance with review standards established by the section's peer review committee.
- Ensure that all professionals in the firm resident in the United States, including CPAs and non-CPAs, participate in at least 20 hours of continuing professional education every year and in at least 120 hours every three years.

The quality control standards for peer reviews are based on the nine elements of quality control discussed earlier in this chapter. Peer reviews are conducted by review teams (1) appointed by the peer review committee of the section, (2) formed by a member firm engaged by the firm under review (currently, for example, every Big Eight firm is reviewed by another Big Eight firm), or (3) formed by an authorized entity engaged by the firm under review such as a state CPA society or an association of CPA firms. Each review team is required to report its findings to the Section, and these reports are included in the public files of the section.

The primary goal of the peer review process is to improve future practice. However, when a firm fails to take the corrective action considered necessary by the Section, the Section may impose such sanctions as: (1) additional continuing professional education requirements; (2) accelerated or special peer reviews; (3) admonishments, censures, or reprimands; (4) monetary fines; (5) suspension from membership; or (6) expulsion from membership in the section.

In addition, members of the SECPS must report to the Section's Special Investigation Committee (SIC) all litigation and regulatory proceedings involving the firm that alleges deficiencies in the conduct of an audit (technically referred to as an *audit failure*). The committee reviews each case and determines whether the charges indicate the need for (1) corrective action by the firm or (2) reconsideration of professional standards. The activities of the SIC supplement the peer review process.

Peer regulation extends to the AICPA Professional Ethics Division and state societies of CPAs that promulgate and enforce rules of ethical conduct for CPAs. Further consideration will be given to this aspect of peer regulation in Chapter 19.

The FASB, the GASB, and the AICPA Auditing Standards Division also contribute to peer regulation through the issuance of technical pronouncements on accounting and auditing matters. These pronouncements enable the independent auditor to follow professional standards in an audit engagement.

PUBLIC REGULATION

Public regulation is imposed by governmental agencies. It is basically punitive in nature. This level of regulation involves both state and federal agencies and occurs in several forms. State boards of accountancy, for example, establish the qualifications needed to be able to take the uniform CPA examination. Moreover, they handle licensing and continuing education requirements, and establish and enforce the state's code of professional ethics for CPAs. Boards of accountancy have considerable authority as they can suspend or revoke the license to practice of a CPA who does not meet professional standards.

Federal regulation is done primarily by the SEC. The primary objective of federal regulation is protecting the investing public from substandard audits. SEC sanctions for noncompliance with professional standards may include public censure, injunction, temporary or permanent suspension from practicing before the SEC, and legal action. Further consideration is given to the SEC's role in public regulation in Chapter 21.

Public regulation also occurs in state and federal courts where a CPA may be tried and punished for failing to meet the profession's standards of practice. More will be said about the CPA's legal liability in Chapter 20.

A summary of the three levels of regulation of CPAs and CPA firms is presented in Figure 1-8.

CONGRESSIONAL INVESTIGATION OF THE PROFESSION

The public accounting profession has been subjected to three congressional investigations in the past two decades. Each investigation focused on whether more government regulation of the profession is needed to prevent substandard audits. Two of the investigations occurred in the 1970s. They resulted in significant increases in the self-regulation process, including the development of the AICPA's quality control standards and the formation of the Division for CPA Firms.

Level of Regulation	Regulatory Organization	Primary Activities
Private	CPA firms	Establish and maintain a system of quality control.
		Supervise and review work done on each audit.
		Provide and encourage continuing education for individual CPAs.
Peer	AICPA Division for Firms	Administer peer review programs.
	AICPA and state societies of CPAs	Establish and enforce rules of ethical conduct.
	FASB and GASB	Promulgate generally accepted accounting principles.
	AICPA	Establish generally accepted auditing standards and quality control standards
Public	State Boards of Accountancy	Establish qualifications for taking the CPA examination and issue licenses to practice public accounting.
		Establish and enforce code of ethics.
	Securities and Exchange Commission	Establish qualifications for accountants to practice before the SEC and punish violators of securities acts.
	State and federal courts	Try alleged offenders and punish violators of the law.

Figure 1-8. REGULATION OF PUBLIC ACCOUNTING PROFESSION.

The most recent investigation, chaired by Congressman Dingell (Democrat of Michigan), began in February 1985. Its purpose is to examine

- The effectiveness of independent accountants who audit publicly owned corporations.
- The performance of the Securities and Exchange Commission in meeting its regulatory reponsibility in accounting and auditing matters.

This investigation is also probing the independence of CPA firms and whether the profession's regulatory system is adequate to protect the public.

OTHER TYPES OF SERVICES BY CPA FIRMS

Through their professional staffs, CPA firms are qualified to render a variety of services in addition to auditing. The principal types of nonauditing services are tax, management advisory, and accounting and review services.

TAX SERVICES

Individuals and business enterprises are required to file and pay a variety of taxes. CPAs who specialize in taxation are thoroughly knowledgeable about the intricacies of the tax laws.

Most CPA firms have tax specialists and many have separate tax departments. Tax services include assistance in filing tax returns, tax planning, estate planning, and representation of clients before governmental agencies in tax matters. Tax services constitute a very significant part of the practice of individual practitioners and small (local) CPA firms.

The AICPA, through its Division of Federal Taxation, issues *Statements on Responsibilities in Tax Practice*. These statements will be considered in Chapter 19.

MANAGEMENT ADVISORY SERVICES

Management advisory services (MAS) are defined as "the management consulting function of providing advice and technical assistance where the primary purpose is to help the client improve the use of its capabilities and resources to achieve its objectives."[9] The AICPA, through its MAS Executive Committee, issues *Statements on Standards for Management Advisory Services*. These standards will be considered in Chapter 19.

When rendering management advisory services, the CPA is acting as an outside, expert business consultant. In this capacity, the CPA should not make management decisions. Many of the larger firms have separate management services departments. Today, MAS represents a significant and rapidly growing proportion of the total billings of many CPA firms.

ACCOUNTING AND REVIEW SERVICES

A CPA firm may be engaged by a client to perform a variety of accounting services. These services include doing manual or automated bookkeeping, journalizing and posting adjusting entries, and preparing (or compiling) financial statements. In performing an accounting service, the firm serves as a substitute for or a supplement to the accounting personnel of the client. Accounting services are a major activity for some individual practitioners and local firms.

A review service consists primarily of inquiries of management and comparative analyses of financial information. The purpose of a review is to give limited assurance that no material modifications are necessary for the financial statements to be in conformity with GAAP. The scope of a review is significantly less than the scope of an audit. Reviews are rendered by all types of CPA firms in accordance with standards established by the AICPA. Further consideration is given to accounting and review services in Chapter 18.

[9]Management Advisory Services Executive Committee, *Statements on Standards for Management Advisory Services No. 1*, Definitions and Standards for MAS Practice (New York: American Institute of Certified Public Accountants, December 1981), p. 2.

CONCLUDING COMMENTS

The professional practice of auditing is an important activity in our society. There are three types of auditors—independent, internal, and government—each with its own practice standards. The public accounting profession, which includes the American Institute of Certified Public Accountants and CPA firms, has an extensive program of regulation designed to increase the basis for reliance on financial statement audits by the general public. This program includes quality control standards, the Division for CPA Firms, and peer reviews.

Appendix 1A

Illustrative Operational Audits

ILLUSTRATIVE OPERATIONAL AUDIT ENGAGEMENT SUMMARY NO. 1[10]

Organization audited	Data processing department.
Type of organization	Financial institution.
Background of operational audit	The senior management of the organization was concerned that the data process department was not operating effectively.
Principal recipients of operational audit report	President, executive vice president, and vice president of data processing.
Purpose(s)	To assess performance, identify opportunities for improvement, and outline recommendations for improvement.
Objective	To assess the adequacy of data processing operations in meeting the needs of the organization.
Scope	The review included administration, organization, user evaluation, planning and operations, hardware utilization, data communication, and information resource management.

[10]Report of the Special Committee on Operational and Management Auditing, *op. cit.*, p. 19.

General procedures/ approach to conducting engagement	Key users in the organization were interviewed. Major documents were reviewed, including plans, budgets, employee training records. Actual operations were observed over a period on a random basis. Hardware records on use were analyzed.
Measurement criteria	The areas contained in the AICPA publication, *Operational Reviews of the Electronic Data Processing Function.*
Specific findings and recommendations	Findings and recommendations were presented in six major categories: Administration, Organization, Planning, Hardware, Utilization, and Information Resources.
Special comments and limitations	None.

ILLUSTRATIVE OPERATIONAL AUDIT ENGAGEMENT SUMMARY NO. 2[11]

Organization audited	Public utility.
Type of organization	Investor owned utility.
Background of operational audit	The Public Service Commission requested an evaluation of the efficiency and effectiveness with which the company was being managed.
Principal recipients of operational audit report	Public service commission members.
Purpose(s)	To assess performance, identify opportunities for improvement and develop recommendations for improvement.
Objective	To evaluate current operational efficiency and effectiveness and present ways in which it might be improved.
Scope	The review included all organizational and functional areas.
General procedures/ approach to conducting engagement	Management efforts to minimize revenue requirements were evaluated. A financial and statistical profile (seven-year period) was developed. Current practices, procedures, and results were documented. Areas of good practice were documented and candidate areas for improvement were identified. An in-depth study of candidate areas for improvement was conducted.

[11]Report of the Special Committee on Operational and Management Auditing, *op. cit.,* p. 23.

Measurement criteria	Internal comparisons—unit price levels and resource units per workload unit experienced by the utility for each year of the review period by cell matrix (function/resource matrix), and among like organizational units of the utility. External comparisons—comparison of price levels with market indices and similar utilities: comparison of resource units per workload unit with similar utilities.
Specific findings and recommendations	The report provided a summary of overall impressions, significant conclusions for each functional area, recommendations, and possible plan for implementation.

Appendix 1B

Additional GAO Standards[12]

EXAMINATION AND EVALUATION (FIELD WORK) AND REPORTING STANDARDS FOR FINANCIAL AND COMPLIANCE AUDITS

1. AICPA Statements on Auditing Standards for field work and reporting are adopted and incorporated in this statement for government financial and compliance audits. Future statements should be adopted and incorporated, unless GAO excludes them by formal announcement.

2. Additional standards and requirements for government financial and compliance audits.
   a. Standards on examination and evaluation:
      (1) Planning shall include consideration of the requirements of all levels of government.
      (2) A review is to be made of compliance with applicable laws and regulations.
      (3) A written record of the auditors' work shall be retained in the form of working papers.
      (4) Auditors shall be alert to situations or transactions that could be indicative of fraud, abuse, and illegal expenditures and acts and if such evidence exists, extend audit steps and procedures to identify the effect on the entity's financial statements.
   b. Standards on reporting:
      (1) Written audit reports are to be submitted to the appropriate officials of the organization audited and the appropriate officials of the organizations requiring or arranging for the audits unless legal restrictions

[12]Comptroller General of the United States, *op. cit.*, pp. 7–11.

or ethical considerations prevent it. Copies of the reports should also be sent to other officials who may be responsible for taking action and to others authorized to receive such reports. Unless restricted by law or regulation, copies should be made available for public inspection.

(2) A statement in the auditors' report that the examination was made in accordance with generally accepted government auditing standards for financial and compliance audits will be acceptable language to indicate that the audit was made in accordance with these standards.

(3) Either the auditors' report on the entity's financial statements or a separate report shall contain a statement of positive assurance on those terms of compliance tested and negative assurance on those items not tested. It shall also include material instances of noncompliance and instances or indications of fraud, abuse, or illegal acts found during or in connection with the audit.

(4) The auditors shall report on their study and evaluation of internal accounting controls made as part of the financial and compliance audit. They shall identify as a minimum: (a) the entity's significant internal accounting controls, (b) the controls identified that were evaluated, (c) the controls identified that were not evaluated (the auditor may satisfy this requirement by identifying any significant classes of transactions and related assets not included in the study and evaluation), and (d) the material weaknesses identified as a result of the evaluation.

(5) Either the auditors' report on the entity's financial statements or a separate report shall contain any other material deficiency findings identified during the audit not covered in (3) above.

(6) If certain information is prohibited from general disclosure, the report shall state the nature of the information omitted and the requirement that makes the omission necessary.

EXAMINATION AND EVALUATION STANDARDS FOR ECONOMY AND EFFICIENCY AUDITS AND PROGRAM RESULTS AUDITS

1. Work is to be adequately planned.

2. Assistants are to be properly supervised.

3. A review is to be made of compliance with applicable laws and regulations.

4. During the audit a study and evaluation shall be made of the internal control system (administrative controls) applicable to the organization, program, activity, or function under audit.

5. When audits involve computer-based systems, the auditors shall:
   a. Review general controls in data processing systems to determine whether
      (1) the controls have been designed according to management direction

and known legal requirements and (2) the controls are operating effectively to provide reliability of, and security over, the data being processed.

b. Review application controls of installed data processing applications upon which the auditor is relying to assess their reliability in processing data in a timely, accurate, and complete manner.

6. Sufficient, competent, and relevant evidence is to be obtained to afford a reasonable basis for the auditors' judgments and conclusions regarding the organization, program, activity, or function under audit. A written record of the auditors' work shall be retained in the form of working papers.

7. The auditors shall:
   a. Be alert to situations or transactions that could be indicative of fraud, abuse, and illegal acts.
   b. If such evidence exists, extend audit steps and procedures to identify the effect on the entity's operations and programs.

REPORTING STANDARDS FOR ECONOMY AND EFFICIENCY AUDITS AND PROGRAM RESULTS AUDITS

1. Written audit reports are to be prepared giving the results of each governmental audit.

2. Written audit reports are to be submitted to the appropriate officials of the organization audited and to the appropriate officials of the organizations requiring or arranging for the audits unless legal restrictions or ethical considerations prevent it. Copies of the reports should also be sent to other officials who may be responsible for taking action on audit findings and recommendations and to others authorized to receive such reports. Unless restricted by law or regulation, copies should be made available for public inspection.

3. Reports are to be issued on or before the dates specified by law, regulation, or other special arrangement. Reports are to be issued promptly so as to make the information available for timely use by management and by legislative officials.

4. The report shall include:
   a. A description of the scope and objectives of the audit.
   b. A statement that the audit (economy and efficiency or program results) was made in accordance with generally accepted government auditing standards.
   c. A description of material weaknesses found in the internal control system (administrative controls).
   d. A statement of positive assurance on those items of compliance tested and negative assurance on those items not tested. This should include significant instances of noncompliance and instances of or indications

of fraud, abuse, or illegal acts found during or in connection with the audit. However, fraud, abuse, or illegal acts normally should be covered in a separate report, thus permitting the overall report to be released to the public.

e. Recommendations for actions to improve problem areas noted in the audit and to improve operations. The underlying causes of problems reported should be included to assist in implementing corrective actions.

f. Pertinent views of responsible officials of the organization, program, activity, or function audited concerning the auditors' findings, conclusions, and recommendations. When possible their views should be obtained in writing.

g. A description of noteworthy accomplishments, particularly when management improvements in one area may be applicable elsewhere.

h. A listing of any issues and questions needing further study and consideration.

i. A statement as to whether any pertinent information has been omitted because it is deemed privileged or confidential. The nature of such information should be described, and the law or other basis under which it is withheld should be stated. If a separate report was issued containing this information it should be indicated in the report.

5. The report shall:
a. Present factual data accurately and fairly. Include only information, findings, and conclusions that are adequately supported by sufficient evidence in the auditors' working papers to demonstrate or prove the bases for the matters reported and their correctness and reasonableness.

b. Present findings and conclusions in a convincing manner.

c. Be objective.

d. Be written in language as clear and simple as the subject matter permits.

e. Be concise but, at the same time, clear enough to be understood by users.

f. Present factual data completely to fully inform the users.

g. Place primary emphasis on improvement rather than on criticism of the past; critical comments should be presented in a balanced perspective considering any unusual difficulties or circumstances faced by the operating officials concerned.

REVIEW QUESTIONS

1-1 Identify the essential parts of the definition of auditing.

1-2 Describe the principal types of audits and indicate the primary purpose(s) of each.

1-3 Distinguish between the three types of auditors and indicate the types of audits each may perform.

1-4 a. Describe the nature and importance of generally accepted auditing standards (GAAS).
b. Identify the three categories of GAAS.

1-5   a. Identify the categories of standards for the practice of internal auditing.
      b. Indicate the principal similarities between GAAS and the internal auditing standards.

1-6   a. How is the term audit used by the Government Accounting Office (GAO)?
      b. Identify the categories of GAO practice standards for governmental audits.

1-7   a. What entities are included in the public accounting profession?
      b. What entities directly influence the profession?

1-8   a. Indicate the principal AICPA divisions that directly affect auditing.
      b. Describe the composition of the AICPA's Auditing Standards Division.

1-9   Explain the nature and primary purpose of the Auditing Standards Board.

1-10 a. What are Statements on Auditing Standards (SASs)?
      b. What are the effects and authority of SASs?

1-11 a. Contrast the authority of state associations of CPAs and state boards of accountancy.
      b. Identify the categories of practice units within the public accounting profession.

1-12 What factors are relevant in the regulation of the public accounting profession?

1-13 Identify the three levels of regulation and their common objective.

1-14 Identify the nine elements of quality control that have been established by the AICPA.

1-15 Explain the relationship between GAAS and quality control standards.

1-16 a. Identify the two sections within the Division for CPA Firms.
      b. Indicate the objectives that are common to both sections.

1-17 What membership requirements are common to both sections of the Division for CPA Firms?

1-18 What sanctions may be imposed under peer review?

1-19 a. What organizations are involved in public regulation of the profession?
      b. For each organization in (a) above, indicate the sanctions each regulatory agency may impose.

1-20 What types of services other than auditing are CPA firms qualified to render?

OBJECTIVE QUESTIONS FROM PROFESSIONAL EXAMINATIONS

Indicate the *best* answer for each of the following multiple choice questions.

1-21 These questions pertain to types of audits.

   1. Independent auditing can best be described as
      a. A branch of accounting.
      b. A discipline that attests to the results of accounting and other functional operations and data.
      c. A professional activity that measures and communicates financial and business data.
      d. A regulatory function that prevents the issuance of improper financial information.

   2. Governmental auditing often extends beyond examinations leading to the expression of opinion on the fairness of financial presentation and includes audits of efficiency, economy, effectiveness, and also
      a. Accuracy.   c. Compliance.
      b. Evaluation.   d. Internal control.

3. Operational audits generally have been conducted by internal auditors and governmental audit agencies, but may be performed by certified public accountants. A primary purpose of an operational audit is to provide
   a. A means of assurance that internal accounting controls are functioning as planned.
   b. Aid to the independent auditor, who is conducting the examination of the financial statements.
   c. The results of internal examinations of financial and accounting matters to a company's top-level management.
   d. A measure of management performance in meeting organizational goals.

1-22 These questions involve generally accepted auditing standards (GAAS) and Statements on Auditing Standards (SASs).

1. The "generally accepted auditing standards" are standards that
   a. Are sufficiently established so that independent auditors generally agree on their existence.
   b. Are generally accepted based on a pronouncement of the Financial Accounting Standards Board.
   c. Are generally accepted as a consequence of approval of the AICPA membership.
   d. Are generally accepted in response to the changing needs of the business community.

2. Which of the following statements best describes the phrase "generally accepted auditing standards?"
   a. They identify the policies and procedures for the conduct of the audit.
   b. They define the nature and extent of the auditor's responsibilities.
   c. They provide guidance to the auditor with respect to planning the audit and writing the audit report.
   d. They set forth a measure of the quality of the performance of audit procedures.

3. Statements on Auditing Standards issued by the ACIPA's Auditing Standards Board are
   a. Part of the generally accepted auditing standards under the AICPA Code of Professional Ethics.
   b. Interpretations of generally accepted auditing standards under the AICPA Code of Professional Ethics, and departures from such statements must be justified.
   c. Interpretations of generally accepted auditing standards under the AICPA Code of Professional Ethics, and such statements must be followed in every engagement.
   d. Generally accepted auditing procedures that are not covered by the AICPA Code of Professional Ethics.

1-23 These questions relate to quality control standards.

1. A basic objective of a CPA firm is to provide professional services to conform with professional standards. Reasonable assurance of achieving this basic objective is provided through
   a. Continuing professional education.
   b. A system of quality control.
   c. Compliance with generally accepted reporting standards.
   d. A system of peer review.

2. A CPA firm's personnel partner periodically studies the CPA firm's personnel advancement experience to ascertain whether individuals meeting stated criteria are

assigned increased degrees of responsibility. This is evidence of the CPA firm's adherence to prescribed standards of
a. Quality control.
b. Due professional care.
c. Supervision and review.
d. Field work.

3. Within the context of quality control, the primary purpose of continuing professional education and training activities is to enable a CPA firm to provide personnel within the firm with
a. Technical training that assures proficiency as an auditor.
b. Professional education that is required in order to perform with due professional care.
c. Knowledge required to fulfill assigned responsibilities and progress within the firm.
d. Knowledge required in order to perform a peer review.

COMPREHENSIVE QUESTIONS

1-24 After performing an audit, the auditor determines that

1. The financial statements of a corporation are presented fairly.
2. A company's receiving department is inefficient.
3. A company's tax return does not conform with IRS regulations.
4. A government supply depot is not meeting planned program objectives.
5. The financial statements of a physician are properly prepared on a cash basis.
6. A foreman is not carrying out his assigned responsibilities.
7. The IRS is in violation of an established government employment practice.
8. A company is meeting the terms of a government contract.
9. A municipality's financial statements correctly show actual cash receipts and disbursements.
10. The postal service in midtown is inefficient.
11. A company is meeting the terms of a bond contract.
12. A department is not meeting the company's prescribed policies concerning overtime work.

Required

a. Indicate the type of audit that is involved: (1) financial, (2) compliance, or (3) operational.
b. Identify the type of auditor that is involved: (1) independent, (2) internal, (3) government–GAO, or (4) government–IRS.
c. Identify the primary recipient(s) of the audit report: stockholders, management, Congress, and so on. Use the following format for your answers:

Type of Audit	Type of Auditor(s)	Primary Recipient(s)

1-25 J. Cowan, an engineer, is the president of Arco Engineering. At a meeting of the board of directors, Cowan was asked to explain why the company has audits made by (1) internal auditing, (2) external auditing, and (3) governmental auditing. One board member suggested that the company's total audit expense might be less if all auditing was consolidated under internal auditing. J. Cowan was unable to distinguish between the three types of audits or to satisfactorily respond to the board member's suggestion.

Required

a. Explain the different purposes served by each type of audit.

b. Identify the categories of auditing standards applicable to each type of audit.

c. Comment on the board members suggestion to consolidate all auditing under internal auditing.

1-26 There are ten GAAS. Listed below are statements that relate to these standards:

1. The auditor is careful in doing the audit and writing the audit report.

2. A more experienced auditor supervises the work of an inexperienced auditor.

3. The auditor investigates and reaches conclusions about the client's internal controls.

4. A predesigned schedule is followed during the examination.

5. The auditor is an accounting graduate with several years of experience in auditing.

6. In the auditor's judgment, the financial statements conform to all FASB statements.

7. The auditor is objective and unbiased in performing the examination.

8. The client used the same accounting principles this year as last year.

9. The examination produced all the evidence needed to reach a conclusion about the client's financial statements.

10. The client's notes to the financial statement contain all essential data.

11. The auditor expresses an opinion on the financial statements.

Required

a. Identify by category and number within each category the GAAS to which each statement relates (i.e., general standard no. 1, field work standard no. 2, etc.).

b. For each answer in (a) above, provide the full statement of the standard. Use the following format for your answers:

Identification of Standard	Statement of Standard

1-27 Lajod Company has an Internal Audit Department consisting of a manager and three staff auditors. The Manager of Internal Audits, in turn, reports to the Corporate Controller. Copies of audit reports are routinely sent to the Board of Directors as well as the Corporate Controller and individual responsible for the area or activity being audited.

The Manager of Internal Audits is aware that the external auditors have relied on the internal audit function to a substantial degree in the past. However, in recent months, the external auditors have suggested there may be a problem related to the objectivity of the internal audit function. This objectivity problem may result in more extensive testing and analysis by the external auditors.

The external auditors are concerned about the amount of nonaudit work performed by the Internal Audit Department. The percentage of nonaudit work performed by the internal auditors in recent years has increased to about 25% of their total hours worked. A sample of five recent nonaudit activities is as follows.

1. One of the internal auditors assisted in the preparation of policy statements on internal control. These statements included such items as policies regarding sensitive payments and standards of control for systems.

2. The bank statements of the corporation are reconciled each month as a regular assignment for one of the internal auditors. The Corporate Controller believes this strengthens the internal control function because the internal auditor is not involved in the receipt and disbursement of cash.

3. The internal auditors are asked to review the budget data in every area each year for relevance and reasonableness before the budget is approved. In addition, an internal auditor examines the variances each month, along with the associated explanations. These variance analyses are prepared by the Corporate Controller's staff after consultation with the individuals involved.

4. One of the internal auditors has recently been involved in the design, installation, and initial operation of a new computer system. The auditor was primarily concerned with the design and implementation of internal accounting controls and the computer application controls for the new system. The auditor also conducted the testing of the controls during the test runs.

5. The internal auditors are frequently asked to make accounting entries for complex transactions before the transactions are recorded. The employees in the accounting department are not adequately trained to handle such transactions. In addition, this serves as a means of maintaining internal control over complex transactions.

The Manager of Internal Audits has always made an effort to remain independent of the Corporate Controller's office and believes the internal auditors are objective and independent in their audit and nonaudit activities.

Required

a. Define objectivity as it relates to the internal audit function.

b. For each of the five situations outlined above, explain whether the objectivity of Lajod Company's Internal Audit Department has been materially impaired. Consider each situation independently.

c. The Manager of Audits reports to the Corporate Controller.
1. Does this reporting relationship result in a problem of objectivity? Explain your answer.
2. Would your answer to any of the five situations in Requirement b above have changed if the Manager of Internal Audits reported to the Board of Directors? Explain your answer.

CMA(adapted)

1-28 Standards for the professional practice of internal auditing have been established by the Institute of Internal Auditors. Listed below are specific policies and procedures adopted by the Marco Corporation for its internal auditors:

1. Internal auditors must comply with the Institute of Internal Auditor Code of Ethics.
2. Internal auditors should periodically inspect the safeguards over inventories and cash.
3. Internal auditors should have valid evidence for audit findings.
4. Inexperienced internal auditors must be supervised by certified internal auditors.
5. Internal auditors should attend professional seminars on EDP.
6. Internal auditors should be unbiased in performing audits.
7. Internal auditors should make a study of the efficiency of personnel in the receiving department.
8. Internal auditors should make post-audit reviews of actions taken by a department following an audit.
9. Internal auditors should periodically review the company's compliance with federal government regulations.
10. Internal auditors' reports of audit findings should be communicated to appropriate levels of management.
11. Internal auditors should exercise due care in doing each audit.
12. All new internal auditors must be college graduates.

Required

a. Identify and state the specific IIA standard that pertains to each policy.
b. For each specific standard identified in (a), identify the related general standard (independence, professional proficiency, scope of work, and performance of audit work.) Use the following format for your answers:

Policy/Procedure No.	Specific Standard	General Standard

1-29 Jones and Todd, a local CPA firm, received an invitation to bid for the audit of a local, federally assisted program. The audit is to be conducted in accordance with the audit standards published by the General Accounting Office (GAO), a federal auditing agency. Jones and Todd has become familiar with the GAO standards and recognizes that the GAO standards are not inconsistent with generally accepted auditing standards (GAAS). The GAO standards, unlike GAAS, are concerned with more than the financial aspects of an entity's operations. The GAO standards broaden the definition of auditing by establishing that the full scope of an audit should encompass the following elements:

1. An examination of *financial* transactions, accounts, and reports, including an evaluation of *compliance* with applicable laws and regulations.
2. A review of *efficiency* and *economy* in the use of resources, such as personnel and equipment.
3. A review to determine whether desired results are effectively achieved (*program results*).

Jones and Todd has been engaged to perform the audit of the program and the audit is to encompass all three elements.

Required

a. Jones and Todd should perform sufficient audit work to satisfy the *financial* and *compliance* element of the GAO standards. What should such audit work determine?

b. After making appropriate review and inquiries, what uneconomical practices or inefficiencies should Jones and Todd be alert to in satisfying the *efficiency* and *economy* element encompassed by the GAO standards?

c. After making appropriate review and inquiries, what should Jones and Todd consider to satisfy the *program results* element encompassed by the GAO standards?

AICPA

1-30 The following organizations are directly associated with the public accounting profession: (1) the AICPA, (2) state associations of CPAs, (3) state boards of accountancy, (4) the SEC, (5) the FASB, and (6) the GASB. Listed below are activities pertaining to these organizations:

1. License individuals to practice as CPAs.
2. Promulgate GAAP.
3. Issue Statements on Auditing Standards.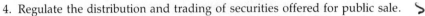
4. Regulate the distribution and trading of securities offered for public sale.
5. Establish its own code of professional ethics.
6. Issue Statements of Financial Accounting Standards.
7. Impose mandatory continuing education as a requirement for renewal of license to practice as a CPA.
8. Issue disclosure requirements for companies under its jurisdiction that may exceed GAAP.
9. Issue auditing interpretations.
10. Cooperate with the AICPA in areas of mutual interest such as continuing professional education and ethics enforcement.
11. Take punitive action against an independent auditor.
12. Establish accounting principles for state and local governmental entities.
13. Establish GAAS.
14. Suspend or revoke a CPA's license to practice.
15. Establish quality control standards.

Required

List the number of each activity and indicate the organization(s) associated with each activity.

1-31 The AICPA has established nine elements of quality control. Listed below are specific policies and procedures adopted by the CPA firm of Baily, Brown & Co.:

1. Periodic evaluations are made of personnel.
2. On-going supervision is given to less experienced personnel.
3. An experienced CPA is designated as a public utility industry expert.
4. Rules on independence are communicated to the professional staff.
5. The scope and content of the firm's inspection program are defined.
6. All new hires must be college graduates.

7. Copies of Statements on Auditing Standards are provided for all professional staff.
8. A partner assigns personnel to engagements.
9. All new clients must be solvent at the time the engagement is accepted.

Required

a. Identify the quality control element that applies to each of the foregoing items.
b. For each element of quality control identified in (a), state the purpose of the element.
c. Indicate another policy or procedure that applies to the element. Use the following format for your answer.

Policy/ Procedure No.	Element (a)	Purpose (b)	Additional Procedure (c)

1-32 The AICPA Division for CPA Firms provides for an SEC Practice Section and a Private Companies Practice Section.

Required

a. Identify the similarities in objectives between the two sections.
b. Enumerate the requirements of membership that are common to both sections.
c. Indicate the responsibilities and functions of the peer review teams that are common to both sections.
d. Identify the similarity in peer review objectives between the two sections.
e. Enumerate the types of sanctions that are applicable to both sections.

1-33 Regulation is an important part of the public accounting profession.   P 16

Required

a. Identify the provisions that contribute to a program of regulation for the public accounting profession.
b. Identify the three levels of regulation and state the objective that is common to each level.
c. For each level of regulation, (1) indicate the applicable regulatory organization(s) and (2) identify one primary activity for each organization.

CASE STUDY

1-34 Ray, the owner of a small company, asked Holmes, CPA, to conduct an audit of the company's records. Ray told Holmes that an audit is to be completed in time to submit audited financial statements to a bank as part of a loan application. Holmes immediately accepted the engagement and agreed to provide an auditor's report within three weeks. Ray agreed to pay Holmes a fixed fee plus a bonus if the loan was granted.

Holmes hired two accounting students to conduct the audit and spent several hours telling them exactly what to do. Holmes told the students not to spend time reviewing the controls, but instead to concentrate on proving the mathematical accuracy of the ledger accounts and summarizing the data in the accounting records that support Ray's financial statements. The students followed Holmes' instructions and after two weeks gave Holmes the financial statements that did not include footnotes. Holmes reviewed the statements and prepared an unqualified auditor's report. The report, however, did not refer to generally accepted accounting principles nor to the year-to-year application of such principles.

Required

Briefly describe each of the generally accepted auditing standards and indicate how the action(s) of Holmes resulted in a failure to comply with *each* standard.

Organize your answer as follows:

Brief Description of Generally Accepted Auditing Standards	Holmes' Actions Resulting in Failure to Comply with Generally Accepted Auditing Standards

AICPA

Chapter 2

Financial Statement Audits

Study Objectives

After you have completed your study of this chapter, you should be able to

- State the reasons for financial statement audits.

- Distinguish between the responsibilities of the independent auditor and management for audited financial statements.

- Prepare the auditor's standard report and explain the key words in the report.

- Enumerate the different types of opinions an auditor may express.

- Explain the auditor's responsibilities for the discovery of errors and irregularities.

- Enumerate the limitations of financial statement audits.

- Give an overview of an audit engagement.

Financial statement audits are by far the most common type of audit made by independent auditors. Such audits are made for a wide variety of entities including all large publicly held companies, privately owned enterprises, governmental agencies, universities, and charitable and research organizations. In terms of third party reliance, the financial statement audit clearly ranks as the most important audit made by independent auditors.

In this chapter, we will discuss the importance of financial statement audits, explain and illustrate the auditor's standard report, consider the limitations of financial statement audits, and give an overview of an audit engagement.

NEED FOR FINANCIAL STATEMENT AUDITS

The Financial Accounting Standards Board (FASB) has stated that *relevance* and *reliability* are the two primary qualities that make accounting information useful for decision making.[1] Users of financial statements look to the independent auditor's report for assurance that these two qualities have been met. The need for independent audits of financial statements is attributed to four conditions: (1) conflict of interest, (2) consequence, (3) complexity, and (4) remoteness.[2] To users, these conditions collectively contribute to *information risk*, which is the risk that the financial statements may be incorrect, incomplete, or biased.

CONFLICT OF INTEREST

Users of financial statements may have diverse interests in the reporting entity, and their interests may not coincide with the interests of those who have prepared the data. Many users are particularly concerned about an actual or potential conflict of interest between themselves and the management of the entity. This apprehension extends to the fear that the financial statements and accompanying data that management is providing may be intentionally or unintentionally biased by the provider. Thus, users seek assurance from outside independent experts that the data are free from the perceived conflict of interest.

A conflict of interest may also exist among the users of financial statements. For example, a stockholder may prefer a liberal dividend policy, whereas a creditor may prefer no dividends. For the statements to be reliable for each prospective user, the data must be *neutral*. That is, they should not favor one set of interested parties over another. The independent auditor is expected to give equal consideration to the needs of each user group in issuing an opinion on the fairness of the client's financial statements.

CONSEQUENCE

Published financial statements represent an important and, in many cases, the only source of information for decision making by users. In making significant investment, lending, and other decisions, users want the financial statements to contain as much relevant data as possible. This need is recognized by the extensive disclosure requirements imposed by the SEC on companies under its jurisdiction. Statement users look to the independent auditor for assurance that the financial statements are prepared in conformity with

[1] "Qualitative Characteristics of Accounting Information," *Statement of Financial Accounting Concepts No. 2*, (Stamford, Conn.: Financial Accounting Standards Board, May 1980), par. 15.

[2] Auditing Concepts Committee, "Report of the Committee on Basic Auditing Concepts," *The Accounting Review*, Vol. 47, Supp. (Sarasota, Fla., American Accounting Association 1972), p. 25.

GAAP and that the statements contain disclosures necessary for a reasonably knowledgeable user.

COMPLEXITY

Both the subject matter of accounting and the process of preparing financial statements are becoming more and more complicated. The accounting and reporting of earnings per share, leases, and pensions are but a few of many examples of this fact.

As the subject matter becomes more complicated, there is a greater risk of misinterpretation and a greater possibility of unintentional error. Users therefore are finding it more difficult or even impossible to evaluate the quality of the statements. Accordingly, they look to the report on the statements by the independent auditor for assurance about the quality of the information being received.

REMOTENESS

Few users have direct access to the accounting records from which financial statements are prepared. Furthermore, in instances when records are available for scrutiny, time and cost constraints normally prevent users from making a meaningful examination. Remoteness prevents users from directly assessing the quality of the statements. Under such circumstances, users have two alternatives: (1) accept the quality of the financial data on faith or (2) rely on the attestation of a third party. In terms of financial statements included in published annual reports, users clearly prefer the second alternative.

ECONOMIC BENEFITS OF AN AUDIT

Financial statement audits provide many economic benefits. Large companies like General Electric and IBM are willing to incur the $3–$5 million annual audit fee in order to maintain access to capital markets and meet statutory requirements under federal securities acts. In contrast, small companies often have financial statement audits to obtain bank loans or more favorable borrowing terms. Because of reduced information risk resulting from audited financial statements, potential creditors may offer lower interest rates and potential investors may be willing to accept a lower rate of return on their investment. In short, audited financial statements improve an entity's credibility.

Financial statement audits frequently have a favorable affect on employee efficiency and honesty. Knowledge that an independent audit is to be made results in fewer errors in the accounting process and reduces the likelihood of misappropriation of assets by employees. Similarly, the auditor's involvement in an entity's financial reporting process is a restraining influence on management. The fact that its financial statement assertions are to be verified increases the probability that management will be more truthful and forthright in its representations.

An audit frequently is of direct benefit to the management of the client. Based on the examination, the independent auditor can make suggestions to improve controls and achieve greater operating efficiencies within the client's organization. This economic benefit is especially valuable to small and medium size companies.

Audited financial statements generally have little or no effect on the market price of a company's securities. The audited statements are essentially historical in nature and therefore rarely contain information that is new to investors. However, such statements help to assure the efficiency of the market by limiting the life of inaccurate information or deterring its dissemination.[3]

RESPONSIBILITIES OF MANAGEMENT AND THE INDEPENDENT AUDITOR

Fundamental to a financial statement audit is the division of responsibility between management and the independent auditor. The critical distinction is:

- Management is responsible for preparing the financial statements and the contents of the statements are the assertions of management.
- The independent auditor is responsible for examining management's financial statements and expressing an opinion on their fairness.

This division of responsibility is well established as indicated in the following quotations:

> . . . [The] fairness of the representations made through the financial statements is an implicit and integral part of management's responsibility.[4]
>
> Management has a responsibility to furnish shareholders and potential investors with reliable information on a timely basis.[5]
>
> The financial statements are the responsibility of the client and all decisions with respect to them must ultimately be assumed by the client.[6]
>
> The fundamental and primary responsibility for the accuracy of information filed with the Commission [SEC] . . . rests upon management. Management does not discharge its obligations in this respect by employment of independent public accountants, however reputable . . . .[7]

In discharging its responsibility, management is expected to (1) devise a system of internal control that will safeguard assets and help assure the pro-

---

[3]The Commission on Auditors' Responsibilities, *Report, Conclusions and Recommendations* (New York: American Institute of Certified Public Accountants, 1978), p. 7.

[4]Auditing Standards Board, *Codification of Statements on Auditing Standards* (New York: American Institute of Certified Public Accountants, 1985), Auditing Section 110.02 (hereinafter referred to and cited as AU §).

[5]Exchange Act Release No. 13185, "Promotion of the Reliability of Financial Information . . . ," January 19, 1977.

[6]SEC Accounting Series Release No. 126, "Independence of Accountants," July 5, 1972.

[7]*In re* Interstate Hosiery Mills, Inc., 4 S.E.C. 706, 721 (1930).

Management	Independent Auditor
PRIMARY RESPONSIBILITY	
Prepare the financial statements.	Examine the financial statements.
END PRODUCT	
Financial statements that contain management's representations.	Audit report that contains an expression of opinion on the fairness of the financial statements.
CRITERIA IN DISCHARGING RESPONSIBILITY	
GAAP	GAAS

Figure 2-1 FINANCIAL STATEMENT RESPONSIBILITIES.

duction of reliable financial statements, (2) maintain an adequate and effective system of accounts, and (3) adopt appropriate accounting policies. The criteria followed by management in preparing financial statements ordinarily are generally accepted accounting principles (GAAP). The criteria followed by the independent auditor in his examination are generally accepted auditing standards (GAAS). Figure 2-1 summarizes the principal differences in responsibilities.

In order to highlight the division of responsibilities between management and the independent auditor, many companies include a *report on management's responsibility* in their annual reports to stockholders. A sample report in Dow Chemical is shown in Figure 2-2. Note that the report also includes comments pertaining to internal control, internal auditing, and independent auditor access to the board of directors. The auditor's report on Dow Chemical is shown on page 48.

The auditor may assist in the preparation of financial statements. For example, he may counsel management as to the applicability of a new accounting principle, and, during the course of the audit, he may propose adjustments to the client's statements. However, acceptance of this advice and the inclusion of the suggested adjustments in the financial statements do not alter the basic separation of responsibility. Ultimately, management is responsible for all decisions concerning the form and content of the statements.

INDEPENDENT AUDITOR RELATIONSHIPS

The auditor is an intermediary in the communication of accounting data. In the discharge of his responsibilites, the auditor must be independent of both the preparers and the users of the financial statements that represent summaries of such data. In an audit engagement, the auditor maintains professional relationships with four important groups: (1) management, (2) the board of directors, (3) internal auditors, and (4) stockholders.

RESPONSIBILITY FOR FINANCIAL STATEMENTS

The following consolidated financial statements and related notes of The Dow Chemical Company and its subsidiaries were prepared by management in accordance with generally accepted accounting principles. The Board of Directors, through its Audit Committee, assumes an oversight role with respect to the preparation of the financial statements.

The Company is responsible for the integrity and objectivity of the consolidated financial statements, which are presented in a consistent manner on the accrual basis of accounting. Established accounting procedures are designed to provide accurate books, records and accounts, which fairly reflect the transactions of the Company.

The training of qualified personnel and the assignment of duties are intended to provide internal controls at a cost appropriate to management's evaluation of the risks involved. Such controls are monitored by an internal audit staff, providing reasonable assurances that transactions are executed in accordance with management's authorization and that adequate accountability for the Company's assets is maintained.

Deloitte Haskins & Sells, independent public accountants, with direct access to the Board of Directors through its Audit Committee, have examined the consolidated financial statements prepared by the company, and their report follows.

Figure 2-2. MANAGEMENT RESPONSIBILITY REPORT.

MANAGEMENT

The term *management* refers collectively to individuals who actively plan, coordinate, and control the operations and transactions of the client. In an auditing context, management refers to the company officers, controller, and key supervisory personnel.

During the course of an audit, there is extensive interaction between the auditor and management. To obtain the evidence needed in an audit, the auditor often requires confidential data about the entity. It is imperative, therefore, to have a relationship based on mutual trust and respect. An adversary relationship will not work.

The auditor should have an interest in the well-being and future of his client. However, this concern should be tempered by a posture of professional skepticism about management's assertions. Moreover, the auditor must be prepared to evaluate critically the fairness of management's financial statement representations.

BOARD OF DIRECTORS

The board of directors of a corporation is responsible for seeing that the corporation is operated in the best interests of the stockholders. The auditor's relationship with the directors depends largely on the composition of the board. When the board consists primarily of company officers, the auditor's relationship with the board may be the same as with management.

However, when the board has a number of outside members, a different relationship is possible. Outside members are not officers or employees of the company. In such case, the board, or a designated audit committee composed primarily of outside members of the board, can serve as an intermediary between the auditor and management.

In the past decade, there has been a marked increase in the use of audit committees as a means of strengthening the independence of auditors. For example, the General Motors' audit committee is chaired by the former chairman of the board of American Telephone and Telegraph, and General Electric's committee is chaired by a former managing partner of a large public accounting firm that does not perform the company's audit. The functions of an audit committee that directly affect the independent auditor are:

- Nominating the public accounting firm to conduct the annual audit.
- Discussing the scope of the examination with the auditor.
- Inviting direct auditor communication on major problems encountered during the course of the audit.
- Reviewing the financial statements and the auditor's report with the auditor on completion of the engagement.

Audit committees have been endorsed by the AICPA, the American Stock Exchange, and the SEC, and they are required by the New York Stock Exchange.

INTERNAL AUDITORS

An independent auditor ordinarily has a close working relationship with the client's internal auditors. Management, for example, may ask the independent auditor to review the internal auditors' planned activities for the year and report on the quality of their work. The independent auditor also has a direct interest in the work of internal auditors that pertains to the client's system of internal control.

The *internal auditor's* work cannot be used as a *substitute* for the independent auditor's work. However, it can be an important *complement*. In determining the effect of such work on his own examination, the independent auditor should (1) consider the competence and objectivity of the internal auditor and (2) evaluate the quality of the internal auditor's work.

The competence of an internal auditor can be ascertained by inquiring into his technical training, experience, and proficiency. The objectivity of an internal auditor can be evaluated by considering the organizational level to which he reports and reviewing the substance of his reports. When he reports to the audit committee, he may have considerable independence. In evaluating the quality of the internal auditor's work, the independent auditor should examine, on a test basis, the audit programs and working papers of the work performed. In addition, he should personally test a portion of the internal auditor's work.

It is permissible under GAAS for the internal auditor to provide *direct assistance* to the independent auditor in performing a financial statement audit. When this occurs, the independent auditor should supervise the internal auditor to the extent considered necessary. In addition, all judgments required in the examination must be made by the independent auditor.

STOCKHOLDERS

Stockholders rely on audited financial statements for assurance that management has properly discharged its stewardship responsibility. The auditor therefore has an important responsibility to stockholders as the primary users of his report. During the course of an engagement, the auditor is not likely to have direct personal contact with stockholders who are not officers or key employees of the client.

VERIFIABILITY OF FINANCIAL STATEMENT DATA

Auditing is based on the assumption that financial data are verifiable. Data are verifiable when two or more qualified individuals, working independently of one another, reach essentially similar conclusions from an examination of the data. *Verifiability* is primarily concerned with the availability of evidence attesting to the validity of the data being considered.[8]

In some disciplines, data are considered verifiable only if the examiners can prove beyond all doubt that the data are either true or false, or right or wrong, but this is not the case in accounting and auditing. The auditor seeks a reasonable basis for the expression of an opinion on the financial statements, and his opinion is an assertion on the *fairness* of the statements. In making his examination, he obtains evidence in order to ascertain the validity and propriety of the accounting treatment of transactions and balances. In this context, *validity* means *sound* or *well-grounded*, and *propriety* means *conforming to established accounting rules and customs*.

Financial statements contain many specific assertions about individual items. With respect to inventories, for example, management asserts that inventory is in existence, owned, and properly stated at cost (or market). In examining the statements, the auditor believes the individual assertions are verifiable (or auditable) and that it is possible to reach a conclusion about the fairness of the statements taken as a whole by verifying the accounts that comprise the statements. The use and importance of audited financial statements provide proof that the assumption of verifiability is well founded.

RELATIONSHIP BETWEEN ACCOUNTING AND AUDITING

There are significant differences in both methodology and objectives between the accounting process by which the financial statements are prepared and the audit of the statements.

[8]Committee to Prepare a Statement of Basic Accounting Theory, *A Statement of Basic Accounting Theory* (Sarasota, Fla.: American Accounting Association, 1966), p. 1.

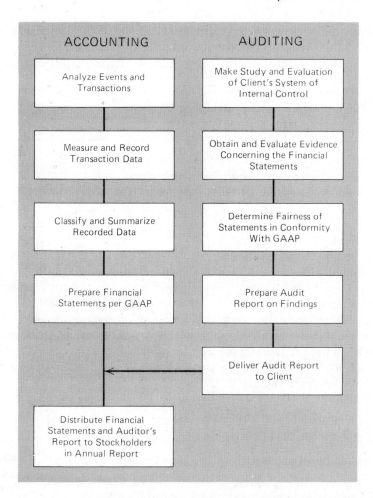

Figure 2-3. RELATIONSHIP BETWEEN ACCOUNTING AND AUDITING.

Accounting methodology involves identifying the events and transactions that affect the entity. Once identified, these items are measured, recorded, classified, and summarized in the accounting records. The result of this process is the preparation and distribution of financial statements and other types of accounting reports. The ultimate objective of accounting is the communication of relevant and reliable financial data that will be useful for decision making. Thus, accounting is clearly a creative process. The individuals directly involved in the company's accounting are generally employees of the company.

The audit of financial statements includes studying and evaluating internal control and obtaining and evaluating evidence concerning management's financial statements, as required by the second and third standards of field work. Auditing culminates in the issuance of an audit report that contains the auditor's opinion on the client's financial statements. Rather than creating new accounting information, auditing adds credibility to the financial statements. The relationship between accounting and auditing in the preparation and audit of financial statements is graphically depicted in Figure 2–3.

AUDITOR'S STANDARD REPORT

The audit report is the auditor's formal means of communicating his findings to interested parties. In issuing an audit report, the auditor must meet the four generally accepted auditing standards of reporting. A standard (unqualified) report is the most common report issued.[9] Because of its importance in a financial statement audit, a basic understanding of the form and content of the standard report is essential.

The standard report consists of two paragraphs and standardized language as illustrated in Figure 2-4. The two paragraphs are referred to as the *scope* and *opinion* paragraphs respectively. Any substantive change in wording in either paragraph is considered to be a departure from the standard report.

In published annual reports, the three most common designations for the auditor's report are the independent accountants' report, auditors' report, and accountants' report. The report may be addressed to the company being audited, its board of directors, or stockholders. It is signed in the name of the firm that completed the audit.

OPINION OF INDEPENDENT PUBLIC ACCOUNTANTS

To the Stockholders and Board of Directors of The Dow Chemical Company

We have examined the consolidated balance sheets of The Dow Chemical Company and its subsidiaries as of December 31, 1984 and 1983 and the related consolidated statements of income, stockholders' equity, and changes in financial position for each of the three years in the period ended December 31, 1984. Our examinations were made in accordance with generally accepted auditing standards and, accordingly, included such tests of the accounting records and such other auditing procedures as we considered necessary in the circumstances.

In our opinion, such financial statements present fairly the financial position of The Dow Chemical Company and its subsidiaries at December 31, 1984 and 1983 and the results of their operations and the changes in their financial position for each of the three years in the period ended December 31, 1984, in conformity with generally accepted accounting principles applied on a consistent basis.

Deloitte Haskins & Sells   *Midland, Michigan*
                                              February 15, 1985

Figure 2-4. AUDITOR'S STANDARD REPORT.

[9] *Accounting Trends & Techniques* (New York: American Institute of Certified Public Accountants, 1984), p. 399.

The standard report contains three assertions by the auditor:

- An examination was made of specified financial statements.
- The examination was made in accordance with *generally accepted auditing standards (GAAS).*
- The financial statements (in the auditor's opinion) *present fairly* the financial position, results of operations, and changes in financial position in conformity with *GAAP* applied on a consistent basis.

SCOPE PARAGRAPH

This paragraph describes the nature and scope of the auditor's examination. It satisfies the portion of the fourth reporting standard that requires the auditor to give a clear-cut indication of the character of the examination and the degree of responsibility that he is taking.

We have examined the . . . balance sheets . . . for the years then ended.   The scope paragraph begins with a representation that the auditor has made an examination of certain specified statements of a designated company. This sentence implies, but does not explicitly state, that the financial statements examined by the auditor were prepared by management and that the statements are management's responsibility. Each of the financial statements examined by the auditor is identified in the first sentence, together with the dates appropriate to each statement.

Our examinations were made in accordance with generally accepted auditing standards.   These words refer to the ten generally accepted auditing standards and assert that the auditor's examination has met these standards. Neither the source of the standards (the AICPA) nor the specific standards are identified.

. . . such tests of the accounting records and such other auditing procedures as we considered necessary in the circumstances.   This clause further explains the nature of the auditor's examination. The word *tests* is used to indicate that less than a 100% examination was made of the data included in the accounting records. The reference to *such other auditing procedures* denotes that not all procedures were done on a test basis and that some procedures involve other than the accounting records. For example, the auditor ordinarily reads all the minutes of board of directors' meetings.

In contrast to GAAS that establish the quality of performance and the overall objectives to be obtained in an audit, *auditing procedures* are the methods used and the acts performed by the auditor during his examinations. Auditing procedures include such steps as counting petty cash, reviewing a client-prepared bank reconciliation, observing an inventory count, and examining legal title to a motor vehicle purchased by a company. The specific procedures used by the auditor are not disclosed in the auditor's report. In contrast to auditing standards that are applicable in every financial statement audit, auditing procedures may vary from client to client. Thus, an auditor will usually perform more auditing procedures or apply the same procedure more extensively for clients with poor internal control than those with good internal control.

The concluding phrase, *as we considered necessary in the circumstances,* indicates that the auditor used professional judgment in deciding what tests to make and auditing procedures to apply. It further implies that decisions pertaining to this aspect of the examination were made independently of management. Stated conversely, this phrase says that the auditor's examination was not circumscribed by any management-imposed limitations on the scope of the work.

OPINION PARAGRAPH

This paragraph satisfies the first three reporting standards and the portion of the fourth standard that requires an expression of an opinion. The specific wording of the opinion paragraph is explained below.

In our opinion, such financial statements. . . .   In interpreting the meaning and significance of this clause, it is proper to conclude that the opinion is being expressed by a *professional, experienced,* and *expert* person or persons. Alternatively, the word *judgment* could be substituted for *opinion.* It is incorrect, however, to conclude that this phrase says, *We certify, We guarantee,* or *We are certain (or positive).* The second part of this clause makes reference to the financial statements identified in the scope paragraph; the titles of the individual statements are not repeated.

The opinion expressed in the auditor's standard report is an *unqualified opinion.* Such an opinion is justified when (1) the examination has been made in accordance with GAAS, (2) the financial statements satisfy the first three reporting standards, and (3) the statements are not affected by a major uncertainty (such as a lawsuit) whose outcome depends on a future event. When these conditions are not present, other types of opinions should be expressed, as described later in the chapter. An unqualified opinion also means that any differences between management and the auditor on accounting matters have been resolved to the auditor's satisfaction.

. . . present fairly the . . . financial position . . . results of operations and . . . changes in financial position . . .   The intended connotation of present fairly is *reasonably* or, in a slightly more technical sense, *in all material (or important) respects.* It also means that the statements are free of material misstatements and/or omissions, and are not misleading. Such terms as *accurately, truly, factually, correctly,* or *exactly* are not used because of the existence of estimates in the financial statements and the nature of the examination.

The auditor's opinion on fairness pertains to each financial statement taken as a whole. It does not apply to the accuracy or correctness of individual accounts or components of each financial statement. An unqualified opinion expresses the auditor's belief that the financial statements accomplish their stated purpose by presenting fairly financial position (balance sheet), the results of operations (income and retained earnings statements), and changes in financial position (statement of changes in financial position).

. . . in conformity with generally accepted accounting principles. . . . This clause satisfies (1) the first standard of reporting that states the report shall indicate whether the financial statements are prepared in accordance with GAAP and (2) the third standard of reporting that provides that the disclosures in the statements are adequate unless otherwise stated in the auditor's report. The term *generally accepted accounting principles* provides the criteria for the auditor's judgment as to the fairness of the financial statements. Statements of the FASB, for example, are recognized as GAAP, which includes adequate disclosure.[10]

. . . applied on a consistent basis. The concluding words of the opinion paragraph satisfy the second standard of reporting that says the report should state whether the principles have been consistently observed (applied). These words assure interested parties that comparisons between the statements being reported on have not been affected by changes in accounting principles. This acknowledgment is not a guarantee that the statements are comparable. Other changes that may affect comparability, such as the purchase of a business, discontinuance of a product line, or adoption of a pension plan, are not included in the auditor's opinion on consistency. However, if the effects of such changes are material, they may require disclosure in the financial statements.

OTHER TYPES OF OPINIONS

Circumstances may arise in an audit that make it inappropriate for the auditor to issue an unqualified opinion. In such cases, the auditor can express a qualified opinion, an adverse opinion, or a disclaimer of opinion.

QUALIFIED OPINION

A qualified opinion states that "except for" or "subject to" the effects of a matter, the financial statements as a whole are presented fairly. This type of opinion is expressed when the following conditions exist:

- The auditor is unable to obtain sufficient evidence concerning one or more important items in the statements.
- The financial statements contain a material departure from GAAP.

[10]Auditing Standards Board, *op. cit.,* AU § 411.04.

- There has been a material change in the application of accounting principles from one or more preceding periods.
- There are significant uncertainties affecting one or more important financial statement items.

The most frequent cause of a qualified opinion is the inconsistent application of accounting principles, such as a change in inventory costing methods or a change in depreciation methods. For an inconsistency, the only change in the auditor's report is the addition of "except for" language at the end of the opinion paragraph as follows:

> . . . In conformity with generally accepted accounting principles applied on a consistent basis *except for the change, with which we concur, in the method of computing depreciation as described in Note X to the financial statements.*

When any of the other conditions result in a qualified opinion, the form of the report changes. In these instances, an explanatory third paragraph is added between the scope and opinion paragraphs to explain the circumstances pertaining to the qualification. In addition, the qualifying language is inserted immediately after the words "In our opinion." An example of a report qualified for nonconformity with generally accepted accounting principles is as follows:

> (Separate Explanatory Paragraph)
> The Company has excluded from property and debt in the accompanying balance sheet certain lease obligations, which, in our opinion, should be capitalized in order to conform with generally accepted accounting principles. If these lease obligations were capitalized, property would be increased by $. . . . . ., long-term debt by $. . . . . ., and retained earnings by $. . . . . . as of December 31, 19XX, and net income and earnings per share would be increased (decreased) by $. . . . . and $. . . . . respectively for the year then ended.
> (Opinion Paragraph)
> In our opinion, except for the effects of not capitalizing lease obligations, as discussed in the preceding paragraph, the financial statements present fairly. . . . .[11]

When a qualified opinion is issued because of an uncertainty, the words "subject to" are used instead of "except for." This type of a qualification is illustrated later in the chapter.

ADVERSE OPINION

An adverse opinion states that the financial statements are not presented fairly in conformity with GAAP. This type of opinion is expressed when departures

[11]Auditing Standards Board, *op. cit.,* AU § 509.36.

from GAAP are so significant that, in the auditor's judgment, a qualified opinion is not appropriate. An adverse opinion would ordinarily be appropriate if a manufacturing company reported all of its property, plant, and equipment at appraised values. When an adverse opinion is expressed, a three-paragraph audit report is required and the following wording should be used in the opinion paragraph.

(Opinion Paragraph)

In our opinion, because of the effects of the matters discussed in the preceding paragraph, the financial statements referred to above do not present fairly, in conformity with generally accepted accounting principles, the financial position of X Company as of December 31, 19XX, or the results of its operations and changes in its financial position for the year then ended.[12]

DISCLAIMER OF OPINION

A disclaimer of opinion states that the auditor is unable to express an opinion on the fairness of the financial statements taken as a whole. This type of opinion is appropriate when (1) the auditor is unable to obtain sufficient evidence concerning the statements as a whole (often called a scope limitation) or (2) there are significant uncertainties affecting the financial statements as a whole and in the auditor's judgment the expression of a qualified opinion is not appropriate. A three-paragraph auditor's report is required with a disclaimer of opinion as illustrated below.

(Scope Paragraph)

. . . Except as set forth in the following paragraph, our examination was made in accordance with generally accepted auditing standards and accordingly included such tests of the accounting records and such other auditing procedures as we considered necessary in the circumstances.

(Separate Explanatory Paragraph)

The Company did not take a physical inventory of merchandise, stated at $. . . . . . in the accompanying financial statements as of December 31, 19XX, and at $. . . . . . as of December 31, 19X1. Further, evidence supporting the cost of property and equipment acquired prior to December 31, 19XX is no longer available. The Company's records do not permit the application of adequate alternative procedures regarding the inventories or the cost of property and equipment.

---

[12]Auditing Standards Board, *op. cit.*, AU § 509.43.

(Disclaimer Paragraph)

Since the Company did not take physical inventories and we were unable to apply adequate alternative procedures regarding inventories and the cost of property and equipment, as noted in the preceding paragraph, the scope of our work was not sufficient to enable us to express, and we do not express, an opinion on the financial statements referred to above.[13]

Figure 2-5 summarizes the circumstances that require the auditor to issue other than an unqualified opinion.

The importance (materiality) of the circumstance is the primary factor when alternative opinions may be expressed. The more material the circumstance, the more likely will be the choice of a disclaimer of an opinion and an adverse opinion rather than a qualified opinion.

OTHER RESPONSIBILITIES OF THE AUDITOR

Users of audited financial statements sometimes place too much reliance on the auditor's examination. Three of the more common misconceptions are that the examination will (1) detect all material errors and irregularities in the financial statements, (2) discover all illegal acts committed by the client, and (3) insure the financial health of the entity. The auditor's responsibilities for these items are explained below.

ERRORS AND IRREGULARITIES

These terms are defined as follows:

- The term *errors* refers to unintentional mistakes, including (1) mathematical or clerical mistakes in underlying accounting data from which financial statements are prepared, (2) mistakes in the application of accounting principles, and (3) oversight or misinterpretation of facts in preparing financial statements.

Circumstance	Type of Opinion
Lack of sufficient evidence concerning the financial statements	Qualified or disclaimer
Material departure from generally accepted accounting principles	Qualified or adverse
Material change in application of GAAP	Qualified
Significant uncertainties in the financial statements	Qualified or disclaimer

Figure 2-5. CIRCUMSTANCES REQUIRING OTHER THAN UNQUALIFIED OPINIONS.

[13]Auditing Standards Board, *op. cit.*, AU § 509.47.

- The term *irregularities* refers to intentional distortions of financial statements resulting from deliberate misrepresentations (fraud) by management, or misappropriations (defalcations) of assets. Irregularities may result from such acts as the falsification or omission of transactions and/or the related accounting records, intentional misapplication of accounting principles, and improper diversion of assets.[14]

The two terms differ significantly in relation to underlying motive and effect. An error is accidental and the individual responsible for the error neither expects nor realizes any personal gain. In contrast, an irregularity is premeditated and the perpetrator usually hopes to achieve personal gain or some other specific objective.

The auditor is required to plan his examination *to search* for errors and irregularities that would have a *significant or material effect* on the financial statements and to exercise due care in the conduct of his audit. When the auditor believes that material errors or irregularities may exist, he should discuss the matter with an appropriate level of management, and if practicable, he should extend the scope of his examination. The expression of an unqualified opinion by the auditor implicitly states that the financial statements are not materially misstated because of errors or irregularities.

If the auditor either knows or is uncertain about the existence of material errors or irregularities in the financial statements, he should either appropriately modify his opinion or disclaim an opinion. An examination made in accordance with GAAS, however, cannot guarantee the detection of all material errors or irregularities. An audit involves selective testing of transactions and balances. Thus, the items examined may not contain any material errors or irregularities. Moreover, detection may be prevented by forgeries, unrecorded transactions or collusion between client personnel and outside parties or among management or employees of the client.

ILLEGAL CLIENT ACTS

An *illegal act* refers to such acts as the payment of bribes, the making of illegal political contributions, and the violation of other specific laws and regulations. All U.S. companies are subject to the illegal payments provisions of the Foreign Corrupt Practices Act, which prohibits payments to foreign government officials for the purpose of obtaining or retaining business in a foreign country. An examination made in accordance with GAAS may result in the detection of illegal client acts. However, it cannot be relied on to do so for the following reasons:

- The determination of whether an act is illegal involves matters of law that usually are beyond the auditor's professional competence.
- Illegal acts may pertain to aspects of the company's operations, such as the Occupational Safety and Health Act, that are not ordinarily specifically reflected in the financial statements.[15]

[14]Auditing Standards Board, *op. cit.*, AU § 327.02–.03.
[15]Auditing Standards Board, *op. cit.*, AU § 328.03.

The auditor does not have a responsibility to search for illegal acts. However, in making an examination in accordance with GAAS, the auditor should be aware that illegal acts may have a material effect on the financial statements. Procedures performed for the purpose of expressing an opinion on the client's financial statements may provide evidence of possible illegal acts. When the auditor believes illegal acts may have occurred, he should (1) inquire of management, (2) consult with the client's legal counsel, and (3) consider performing additional procedures to obtain an understanding of the acts and their possible effects on the financial statements.

When the auditor determines that an illegal act has occurred, the findings should be reported to a level of authority high enough for appropriate action. In some cases, this may be the board of directors. If an illegal act has a material effect on the financial statements, the auditor should appropriately modify his audit report. The auditor has no obligation to notify authorities or other outside parties concerning illegal acts. Such notification is the responsibility of management.

FINANCIAL HEALTH

Statement users are often dismayed when a company files for bankruptcy shortly after the auditor has concluded that its financial statements have been fairly presented. This occurred recently when the United American Bank (UAB) of Knoxville was declared insolvent by bank regulators three weeks after its independent auditors had issued an unqualified opinion on the bank's financial statements. The regulators' action set off a chain of bank failures that collectively was the largest commercial bank collapse in U.S. history.[16] If the independent auditor followed GAAS in issuing his report, he fulfilled his responsibilities in this case. However, if he did not perform his examination in accordance with GAAS, statement users have reason to be dismayed over the auditor's performance.

Under GAAS, the auditor is required to state whether the financial statements are presented fairly in conformity with GAAP. Fair presentation is not a guarantee of financial health. For example, financial statements showing a poor financial position, such as a current ratio of less than one, may be just as fairly presented as statements showing an excellent current ratio of 5 to 1. The appraisal of a company's financial health is the responsibility of the users of audited financial statements. If users make incorrect appraisals on the basis of fairly presented data, they alone are responsible. Of course, if the auditor expresses an unqualified opinion on financial statements that he knows or should have known are not presented fairly, the auditor has not followed GAAS.

Under GAAS, the auditor also has a responsibility to disclose in his report the existence of any *significant uncertainties* that prevent him from expressing an unqualified opinion on the fairness of the financial statements. One un-

---

[16]"Auditing the Auditors: Why Congress May Tighten Up," *Business Week*, December 12, 1983, p. 130. (*Note:* The head of UAB subsequently admitted to numerous counts of fraud and was sentenced to prison by a federal court.)

certainty that clearly relates to the financial health of a company is its ability to continue in business as a going concern. When the auditor is in doubt about this matter, he is required to modify his opinion. During Chrysler Corporation's financial crisis in the early 1980s, the auditor issued a qualified opinion stating:

> In our opinion, *subject to the effects of such adjustments, if any, which might have been required had the outcome of the uncertainties regarding the Corporation's going concern status . . . been known,* the financial statements present fairly the financial position of Chrysler Corporation. . . .

When significant uncertainty exists, the auditor's report should also contain explanatory information concerning the extenuating circumstances. It is important to recognize that the resolution of the uncertainties depends on the outcome of future events that are not known when the auditor's report is issued. Thus, the auditor cannot be expected to predict the eventual outcome. The auditor fulfills his responsibilities by modifying his opinion and making appropriate reference to the extenuating circumstances disclosed in the financial statements.

LIMITATIONS OF AN AUDIT

A financial statement audit made in accordance with GAAS is subject to a number of inherent limitations. One constraint is that the auditor works within fairly restrictive economic limits. To be useful, the audit must be made at a reasonable cost and within a reasonable length of time. The limitation on cost results in selective testing, or sampling, of the accounting records and supporting data. Thus, as explained in the preceding section, there is a risk that the examination will not detect all material errors or irregularities that may exist in the financial statements. Even without cost constraints, however, the auditor cannot be expected to discover management fraud that is associated with collusion and supported by documents that appear to be authentic.

The auditor's report on the financial statements is usually issued within three months of the balance sheet date. This time constraint may affect the amount of evidence that can be obtained concerning events and transactions after the balance sheet date that may have an effect on the financial statements. Moreover, there is a relatively short time period available for the resolution of uncertainties existing at the statement date.

Another significant limitation is the established accounting framework for the preparation of financial statements. Alternative principles are often permitted under GAAP, estimates are an inherent part of the accounting process, and no one, including auditors, can foresee the outcome of uncertainties. An audit cannot add exactness and certainty to the financial statements when they do not exist.

Despite these limitations, a financial statement audit adds credibility to the financial statements. As a result, this type of audit has become an indispensable part of our society.

OVERVIEW OF AN AUDIT ENGAGEMENT

The audit of a small company may involve only one or a few auditors, less than 100 hours of work, and an audit fee of less than $5,000. In contrast, for a Fortune 500 corporation, an audit engagement may require scores of auditors, many thousands of hours of work, and an audit fee of several million dollars.

Four separate and distinct phases (steps) can be identified in an audit engagement. The phases and their relationships to generally accepted auditing standards and quality control standards are indicated in Figure 2–6. Note that two sets of standards, the general category of GAAS and the quality control standards, apply to each phase of an audit engagement.

Accepting the engagement extends both to new clients and the continuation of existing audit clients. As shown in Figure 2–6, only the general standards of GAAS apply to this phase of an audit engagement. Further consideration of this phase and an illustration of an engagement letter are given in the next chapter.

Audit planning involves the development of a game plan for doing the audit. From the exhibit, it can be seen that both the general and field work standards apply to this phase of an audit engagement. Audit planning includes such tasks as scheduling the examination, assigning personnel to the audit,

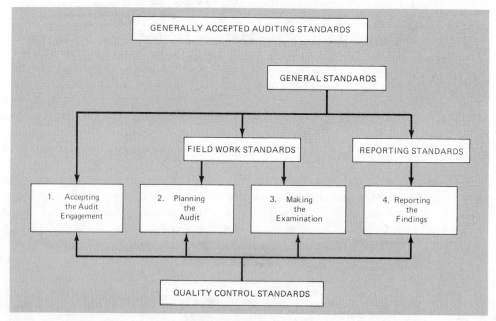

Figure 2-6. OVERVIEW OF AN AUDIT ENGAGEMENT

and designing audit programs. These and other aspects of audit planning are considered in Chapter 3.

The third phase of the audit, making the examination, consists of (1) making a study and evaluation of the client's system of internal control and (2) obtaining and evaluating evidence about the fairness of the financial statements. As illustrated, both the general and field work standards are applicable in making the examination. The major portion of the auditor's examination occurs during this phase of the audit as explained in Chapters 4–16.

The fourth and final phase of the audit is reporting the findings. Both the general standards and reporting standards must be met in issuing an audit report. Further consideration is given to audit reports in Chapters 17 and 18.

CONCLUDING COMMENTS

Financial statement audits are the most common type of audit performed by independent auditors. These audits fill the need of financial statement users for relevant and reliable financial information. In issuing a standard audit report, the auditor explicitly states that the financial statements are presented fairly in conformity with GAAP. In addition, the auditor implicitly indicates that the statements are not materially misstated because of errors or irregularities. Financial statement audits add credibility to the financial statements and they play an important role in our free enterprise system.

REVIEW QUESTIONS

2-1 Why do financial statements need to be audited?

2-2 What are the economic benefits of an audit?

2-3 What are the auditor's responsibilities and functions in a financial statement audit?

2-4 Some people claim there is no basic difference between the responsibility of management and the responsibility of the auditor for financial statements. Do you agree? Why or why not?

2-5 a. What is the primary purpose of a report on management's responsibility?
b. Identify four accounting and auditing matters that are included in this report.

2-6 a. How does the auditor's relationship with management differ, if at all, from his relationship with the board of directors and stockholders?
b. What relationships may exist between the independent auditor and an internal auditor?

2-7 a. What are audit committees?
b. What benefit can an independent auditor derive from an audit committee?
c. Enumerate the functions of the audit committee that pertain to a financial statement audit.

2-8 What is meant by the words *verifiability of data?*

2-9 Contrast accounting and auditing as to (a) methodology and (b) purpose.

2-10 a. Identify the two paragraphs of the auditor's standard report and indicate the purpose(s) of each.

b. Explain the applicability of the four reporting standards to the standard report.

2-11 a. What assertions are made by the auditor in the auditor's standard report?

b. What circumstances justify the issuance of an unqualified opinion?

2-12 Explain the meaning of the following phrases in the scope paragraph of the auditor's report: (a) tests of the accounting records and (b) auditing procedures we considered necessary in the circumstances.

2-13 Explain both the meaning and misconceptions of "present fairly" as used in the auditor's report.

2-14 The consistency standard guarantees that financial statements will be comparable in all respects. Comment on the accuracy of this statement.

2-15 Identify the three types of opinions that may appear in a nonstandard audit report and indicate the circumstances when each opinion is appropriate.

2-16 a. Distinguish between errors and irregularities.

b. What is the auditor's basic responsibility for detecting errors or irregularities?

2-17 a. What responsibility does the auditor have when he believes material errors or irregularities may exist?

b. What are the possible effects of the foregoing on the auditor's standard report.

2-18 a. Define illegal acts.

b. What is the auditor's basic responsibility for detecting illegal acts?

c. Can an examination made in accordance with generally accepted auditing standards be relied on to detect illegal acts? Why or why not?

2-19 a. What responsibility does the auditor have to report on the financial health of a company?

b. How may an auditor inform investors of potential insolvency?

2-20 a. Identify the four phases of an audit engagement.

b. Indicate the applicability of each of the categories of GAAS to the phases of an audit engagement.

OBJECTIVE QUESTIONS FROM PROFESSIONAL EXAMINATIONS

Indicate the *best* answer for each of the following multiple-choice questions.

2-21 These questions pertain to basic considerations in financial statement audits.

1. One of the following is not a proper condition that supports the need for an independent audit of financial statements.
   a. Conflict of interest between management and the CPA.
   b. Complexity of the financial statements.
   c. Remoteness of users from the accounting records.
   d. Consequence of the financial statements in the user's decision process.
2. An independent audit aids in the communication of economic data because the audit
   a. Confirms the accuracy of management's financial representations.
   b. Lends credibility to the financial statements.
   c. Guarantees that financial data are fairly presented.
   d. Assures the readers of financial statements that any fraudulent activity has been corrected.

3. The responsibility for the proper preparation of a company's financial statements rests with its
   a. Management.
   b. Audit committee.
   c. Internal auditors.
   d. External auditors.
   e. Board of Directors.

2-22 These questions relate to the auditor's report.

1. The auditor's standard report is generally considered to have a scope paragraph and an opinion paragraph. In the report, the auditor refers to both generally accepted accounting principles (GAAP) and generally accepted auditing standards (GAAS). In which of the paragraphs are these terms used?
   a. GAAP in the scope paragraph and GAAS in the opinion paragraph.
   b. GAAS in the scope paragraph and GAAP in the opinion paragraph.
   c. GAAS in both paragraphs and GAAP in the scope paragraph.
   d. GAAP in both paragraphs and GAAS in the opinion paragraph.
2. When financial statements are presented that are *not* in conformity with generally accepted accounting principles, an auditor may issue a(an)

	Except for *Opinion*	*Disclaimer* *of an Opinion*
a.	Yes	No
b.	Yes	Yes
c.	No	Yes
d.	No	No

3. If a company's external auditor issues an unqualified opinion as a result of the audit of the company's financial statements, readers of the audit report can assume that
   a. The external auditor found no irregularities.
   b. The company is financially sound.
   c. The financial statements are accurate.
   d. Internal accounting control is strong.
   e. All disagreements between the company and the external auditor were resolved to the satisfaction of the external auditor.

2-23 These questions involve the auditor's responsibilities for errors, irregularities, and illegal acts.

1. In an audit made in accordance with generally accepted auditing standards, an auditor
   a. Has a responsibility to discover all material errors or irregularities.
   b. Has a responsibility to search for material errors or irregularities.
   c. Has responsibility to detect errors but not irregularities.
   d. Guarantees the discovery of all material errors or irregularities.
2. When an audit examination provides evidence that material errors or irregularities may exist, the auditor should
   a. Withdraw from the engagement and present such evidence to appropriate regulatory authorities.
   b. Immediately extend his audit procedures to determine if material errors or irregularities do, in fact, exist.

      c. Refer the matter to the board of directors with the recommendation that it be pursued to a conclusion.

      d. Discuss the matter and the extent of any further investigation with an appropriate level of management, after which, if his suspicions have not been eliminated, he should communicate with the board of directors and, if practicable, extend his audit procedures.

3. An auditor's examination performed in accordance with generally accepted auditing standards generally should

      a. Be expected to provide assurance that illegal acts will be detected when internal control is effective.

      b. Be relied on to disclose violations of truth in lending laws.

      c. Encompass a plan to actively search for illegalities that relate to operating aspects.

      d. *Not* be relied on to provide assurance that illegal acts will be detected.

COMPREHENSIVE QUESTIONS

2-24 Feiler, the sole owner of a small hardware business, has been told that the business should have financial statements reported on by an independent CPA. Feiler, having some bookkeeping experience, has personally prepared the company's financial statements and does not understand why such statements should be examined by a CPA. Feiler discussed the matter with Farber, a CPA, and asked Farber to explain why an audit is considered important.

Required

a. Describe the objectives of an independent audit.

b. Identify 10 ways in which an independent audit may be beneficial to Feiler.

AICPA

2-25 The following two statements are representative of attitudes and opinions sometimes encountered by CPAs in their professional practices:

1. Today's audit consists of test checking. This is dangerous because test checking depends on the auditor's judgment, which may be defective. An audit can be relied on only if every transaction is verified.

2. An audit by a CPA is essentially negative and contributes to neither the gross national product nor the general well-being of society. The auditor does not create; he merely checks what someone else has done.

Required

Evaluate each of the above statements and indicate

a. Areas of agreement with the statement, if any.

b. Areas of misconception, incompleteness or fallacious reasoning included in the statement, if any.

Complete your discussion of each statement (both parts a and b) before going on to the next statement.

AICPA (adapted)

2-26 Footnotes are important in determining whether the financial statements are presented fairly in accordance with generally accepted accounting principles. Following are two sets of statements concerning footnotes.

1. Student A says that the primary responsibility for the adequacy of disclosure in the financial statements and footnotes rests with the auditor in charge of the audit field work. Student B says that the partner in charge of the engagement has the primary responsibility. Student C says that the staff person who drafts the statements and footnotes has the primary responsibility. Student D contends that it is the client's responsibility.

Required

Which student is correct?

2. It is important to read the footnotes to financial statements, even though they often are presented in technical language and are incomprehensible. The auditor may reduce his exposure to third-party liability by stating something in the footnotes that contradicts completely what he has presented in the balance sheet or income statement.

Required

Evaluate the above statements and indicate:

a. Areas of agreement with the statements, if any.

b. Areas of misconception, incompleteness, or fallacious reasoning included in the statements, if any.

AICPA (adapted)

2-27 For many years, the financial and accounting community has recognized the importance of the use of audit committees and has endorsed their formation. At this time, the use of audit committees has become widespread. Independent auditors have become increasingly involved with audit committees and consequently have become familiar with their nature and function.

Required

a. Describe what an audit committee is.

b. Identify the reasons why audit committees have been formed and are currently in operation.

c. What are the functions of an audit committee?

AICPA

2-28 Listed below in alphabetical order are the steps that are included in preparing, auditing, and distributing financial statements.

1. Analyze events and transactions.

2. Classify and summarize recorded data.

3. Deliver audit report to client.

4. Determine fairness of statements in conformity with GAAP.

5. Distribute financial statements and auditor's report to stockholders in annual report.

6. Make study and evaluation of client's system of internal control.
7. Measure and record transaction data.
8. Obtain and evaluate evidence concerning the financial statements.
9. Prepare audit report on findings.
10. Prepare financial statements per GAAP.

Required

a. Prepare a diagram of the relationship between accounting and auditing in the preparation and audit of financial statements. Show each of the steps in the proper sequence.
b. Management and the independent auditor share the responsibility for the assertions contained in financial statements. Evaluate and discuss the accuracy of this statement.

2-29 The auditor's standard report contains the terms *generally accepted auditing standards, auditing procedures,* and *generally accepted accounting principles.*

Required

a. Indicate the paragraph(s) of the standard report in which each term appears.
b. Distinguish between the three terms.
c. Why is it important that the auditor state that the audited financial statements are in conformity with GAAP?
d. What is the relationship, if any, between Statements on Auditing Standards and GAAS?

2-30 The auditor's standard report contains standardized wording. Listed below are a number of incorrect sentences, clauses, and phrases pertaining to the standard report. Assume that the report pertains to the balance sheets at December 31, 19X1 and 19X0, and the related statements of income, retained earnings, and changes in financial position of the X Company for each of the three years ended December 31, 19X1.

1. In our opinion, the aforementioned statements present accurately. . . .
2. Our examinations were made in accordance with auditing standards promulgated by the AICPA. . . .
3. We have examined the balance sheets at December 31, 19X1 and 19X0 and the accompanying statements for the years then ended.
4. Our examinations . . . accordingly included such tests of the financial statements. . . .
5. . . . on a basis consistent with last year.
6. . . . in conformity with promulgated accounting principles. . . .
7. . . . present fairly the balance sheet of X Company at December 31, 19X1 and 19X0. . . .
8. Our examinations . . . and such other auditing principles as we considered necessary. . . .
9. . . . present fairly the financial position and results of its operations for each of the three years then ended. . . .

10. We have reviewed . . . and the related statements of income, retained earnings, and changes in working capital for each of the three years. . . .

Required

a. Rewrite the portions of the above items that are incorrect using standard report language. You may assume that the portions of sentences identified as . . . are correct.

b. Following each revision, indicate whether the item will appear in (1) the scope paragraph or (2) the opinion paragraph of the auditor's standard report.

2-31 An inexperienced auditor for the CPA firm of Wagner and Witus prepared the following standard audit report on the conventional basic financial statements (balance sheet, income statement, retained earnings statement and statement of changes in financial position) of the Wilson Corporation.

(0) I have audited the balance sheets of the Wilson Corporation as of December 31, 19X3 and December 31, 19X2, and (1) the related statements of income and retained earnings for each of the three years in the period ended December 31, 19X3. (2) Our examination was made in accordance with (3) Statements on Auditing Standards, and accordingly included such tests of (4) the financial statements and (5) such other tests as we considered necessary in the circumstances.

In our opinion, the financial statements referred to above (6) present reasonably the (7) financial position of the Wilson Corporation at December 31, 19X2 and (8) the results of its operations and changes in working capital for each of the three years ended December 31, 19X3, in (9) accordance with generally accepted accounting principles applied on (10) a basis consistent with the preceding period.

Required

Comment on each of the numbered items in the audit report. If the numbered item is correct, so state. If the numbered item is incorrect, indicate the correct wording. Number 0 is given as an example.

0. "I have audited" should be "We have examined."

2-32 On completion of all field work on September 23, 19X1, the following report was rendered by Timothy Ross to the directors of The Rancho Corporation:

To the Directors of The Rancho Corporation:

We have examined the balance sheet, the related statement of income and retained earnings of The Rancho Corporation and the statement of changes in financial position as of July 31, 19X1 and 19X0. Our examinations were made in accordance with the standards of the profession and included all tests of the statements that you considered appropriate in the circumstances.

In our opinion, with the exception of some minor errors that are considered immaterial, the aforementioned financial statements present fairly the financial position of The Rancho Corporation at July 31, 19X1 and 19X0, and the results of its operations for the years then ended, in conformity with pronouncements of the Financial Accounting Standards Board applied consistently throughout the period.

Timothy Ross, CPA
September 23, 19X1

Required

a. List and explain deficiencies and omissions in the auditor's report.

b. Organize your answer sheet by paragraph (scope and opinion) of the auditor's report.

AICPA (adapted)

2-33 The following audit report was issued at the turn of this century:†

To the Stockholders of the United States Steel Corporation:

We have examined the books of the U.S. Steel Corporation and its Subsidiary Companies for the year ending December 31, 1902, and certify that the Balance Sheet at that date and the Relative Income Account are correctly prepared therefrom.

We have satisfied ourselves that during the year only actual additions and extensions have been charged to Property Account; that ample provision has been made for Depreciation and Extinguishment, and that the item of "Deferred Charges" represents expenditures reasonably and properly carried forward to operations of subsequent years.

We are satisfied that the valuations of the inventories of stocks on hand as certified by the responsible officials have been carefully and accurately made at approximate cost; also that the cost of material and labor on contracts in progress has been carefully ascertained, and that the profit taken on these contracts is fair and reasonable.

Full provision has been made for bad and doubtful accounts receivable and for all ascertainable liabilities.

We have verified the cash and securities by actual inspection or by certificates from the Depositories, and are of opinion that the Stocks and Bonds are fully worth the value at which they are stated in the Balance Sheet.

And we certify that in our opinion the Balance Sheet is properly drawn up so as to show the true financial position of the Corporation and its Subsidiary Companies, and that the Relative Income Account is a fair and correct statement of the net earnings for the fiscal year ending at that date.

Price, Waterhouse & Co.
New York
March 12, 1903

Required

a. Contrast the scope of the examination in this report with the scope of the examination in the auditor's standard report.

b. Contrast the manner in which the nature of the examination is indicated in this report with the manner of explaining the nature of the examination in the standard report.

c. Compare the last paragraph of the above report with the opinion paragraph of the auditor's standard report.

2-34 An auditor may issue four types of opinions: (1) unqualified, (2) qualified, (3) adverse, and (4) disclaimer (no opinion). Listed below are unrelated circumstances pertaining to different types of opinions. Assume in each case that the auditor would issue an unqualified opinion except for the identified circumstance.

†The Commission on Auditors' Responsibilities, *op. cit.*, p. 2.

1. The financial statements are not in conformity with GAAP.
2. A major uncertainty exists at the balance sheet date that will not be resolved until next year.
3. The auditor is unable to perform all auditing procedures deemed to be necessary in the circumstances.
4. Accounting principles are not applied on a consistent basis.
5. There is inadequate disclosure of essential supplemental information in the financial statements.

Required

a. Identify the conditions that must exist to justify the issuance of an unqualified opinion.
b. Indicate the opinion(s) that an auditor may render for each of the above circumstances.
c. Give the modifying language in the opinion paragraphs for (1) a qualified opinion because of inconsistency in applying GAAP, (2) an adverse opinion for nonconformity with GAAP, (3) a qualified opinion due to an uncertainty, and (4) a disclaimer of opinion because of a scope limitation.

2-35 Frequently, questions have been raised ". . . regarding the responsibility of the independent auditor for the discovery of fraud (including defalcations and other similar irregularities), and concerning the proper course of conduct of the independent auditor when his examination discloses specific circumstances which arouse his suspicion as to the existence of fraud."

Required

a. What are (1) the function and (2) the responsibilities of the independent auditor in the examination of financial statements? Discuss fully, but in this part do not include fraud in the discussion.
b. What are the responsibilities of the independent auditor for the detection of fraud? Discuss fully.
c. What is the independent auditor's proper course of conduct when his examination discloses specific circumstances that arouse his suspicion as to the existence of fraud?

AICPA (adapted)

CASE STUDY

2-36 Several years ago, Dale Holden organized Holden Family Restaurants. Holden started with one restaurant that catered to the family trade. Holden's first restaurant became very popular because the quality of the food and service was excellent, the restaurant was attractive yet modest, and the prices were reasonable.

The success with his first restaurant encouraged Dale Holden to expand by opening additional Holden Family Restaurants in other metropolitan locations throughout the state. Holden has opened at least one new restaurant each year for the last five years, and there are now a total of eight restaurants. All of the restaurants are successful because Holden has been able to maintain the same high standards that were achieved with the original restaurant.

With the rapid expansion of the business, Holden has hired a controller and supporting staff. The financial operations of the restaurants are managed by the controller and his department. This allows Holden to focus his attention on the restaurant operations and plan for future locations.

Holden has applied to the bank for additional financing to open another restaurant this year. For the first time ever, the bank asked him to provide financial statements audited by a CPA. The bank assured Holden that the certified statements were not being required because it doubted his integrity or thought him to be a poor credit risk. The loan officer explained that bank policy required all businesses over a certain size to supply audited statements with loan applications, and Holden's business had reached that size.

Holden was not surprised by the bank's requirement. He had ruled out an audit previously because he has great respect for his controller's ability, and he wanted to avoid the fee associated with the first audit as long as possible. However, the growth of his business and the increased number of restaurant locations make an audit a sound business requirement. He also believes that an additional benefit of the independent audit will be the probable detection of any fraud which may be occurring at his restaurants.

To fulfill the bank request for audited statements, Dale Holden has hired Hill & Associates, CPAs.

Required

a. Hill & Associates has been hired to perform an audit leading to the expression of an opinion on Holden Family Restaurants' financial statements. Discuss Hill & Associates' responsibilities for the review of internal control and the detection of fraud in a general-purpose audit.

b. What effect, if any, would the detection of fraud during the audit of Holden Family Restaurants by Hill & Associates have on their expression of an opinion on the financial statements? Give the reasons for your answer.

CMA

Chapter 3

Accepting and Planning the Audit

Study Objectives

When you have completed a careful study of this chapter, you should be able to

- Indicate the steps involved in accepting an audit engagement.

- State the applicability of generally accepted auditing standards (GAAS) to accepting an engagement.

- Enumerate the components of audit planning.

- Identify the sources that may enable the auditor to obtain information about the client's business and industry.

- Explain the importance of materiality and audit risk in audit planning.

- Describe the relationship between audit objectives and audit programs.

- List the factors that pertain to scheduling the work and assigning personnel to the engagement.

Within the public accounting profession, there is considerable competition among firms for clients. In a recent year, for example, there were slightly over 500 auditor changes by publicly held clients, of which approximately 200 occurred within the group of Big 8 firms.[1] Within the past several years, such large companies as Bendix, Pennzoil, Hertz, and Bank of New York have changed auditors. Auditor changes result from a variety of factors including

[1]*Public Accounting Report* (Atlanta, GA.: Professional Publications, Inc., January 1985), p. 4.

(1) mergers between corporations with different independent auditors, (2) the need for expanded professional services, (3) dissatisfaction with a firm, and (4) a desire to reduce the audit fee.

In this chapter, we will first explain the factors to be considered in accepting an audit engagement. Then, we will describe and illustrate the components of audit planning.

ACCEPTING THE ENGAGEMENT

In undertaking an examination of financial statements, an auditor accepts professional responsibilities to the public, his client, and the members of his own profession. He must sustain the public's confidence in the profession by maintaining his independence, integrity, and objectivity. He must serve his client with competence and professional concern for their best interests. And to the members of his profession, he has a responsibility to enhance the stature of the profession and its ability to serve the public. Thus, a decision to accept a new audit client or continue a relationship with an existing client should not be taken lightly.

An auditor is not obligated to perform a financial statement audit for any entity that requests it. Accepting an engagement involves three steps: (1) evaluating the integrity of management, (2) assessing the auditor's ability to conduct the examination in accordance with GAAS, and (3) preparing an engagement letter. Each step is considered in some detail below.

EVALUATE INTEGRITY OF MANAGEMENT

The primary purpose of a financial statement audit is to express an opinion on management's financial statements. Accordingly, it is important that an auditor only accept an audit engagement when reasonable assurance exists that the client's management can be trusted. When management lacks integrity, there is a greater likelihood that material errors and irregularities may occur in the accounting process from which the financial statements are developed. This, in turn, increases the risk that an unqualified opinion will be expressed when the financial statements are materially misstated. As explained in Chapter 1, evaluating the integrity of management is required by the AICPA quality control element pertaining to the acceptance and continuance of clients. The auditor may obtain information about the integrity of management by making inquiries of third parties and reviewing his previous experience with the client.

Make Inquiries of Third Parties

For a new client, information about the client's management may be obtained by (1) inquiring of knowledgeable persons in the community and (2) communicating with the prior auditor if the client has been audited previously.

Knowledgeable persons include attorneys, bankers, and others in the financial and business community who have had business relationships with the prospective client. In some cases, making an inquiry of the local chamber of commerce, the better business bureau, and the credit bureau may also be helpful. These sources are especially useful when the client has not been audited previously.

For a client who has been audited, the knowledge of the client's management acquired by the prior (predecessor) auditor is considered to be essential information for a new (successor) auditor. Before accepting the engagement, the successor auditor should take the initiative to communicate, either orally or in writing, with the predecessor auditor. The communication should be made with the client's permission, and the client should be requested to authorize the predecessor to respond fully to the successor's inquiries. Authorization is required because the profession's code of ethics prohibits an auditor from disclosing confidential information obtained in an audit without the client's permission.

In the communication, the successor auditor should make specific and reasonable inquiries regarding matters that may affect his decision to accept the engagement, such as

- The integrity of management.
- Disagreements with management about accounting principles and auditing procedures.
- The predecessor's understanding of the reasons for a change in auditors.

The predecessor auditor is expected to respond promptly and fully, assuming the client gives consent. If the client's consent is not given or the predecessor auditor does not respond fully, the successor auditor should consider the implications in deciding whether to accept the engagement.[2]

Review Previous Experience With Existing Clients

Before making a decision to continue an engagement with an audit client, the auditor should carefully consider his prior experiences with the client's management. For example, the auditor should consider any material errors or irregularities and illegal acts discovered in prior audits. During an examination, the auditor makes inquiries of management about such matters as the existence of contingencies, the completeness of all minutes of board of director meetings, and compliance with regulatory requirements. The truthfulness of management's responses to such inquiries in prior audits should be carefully considered in evaluating the integrity of management.

---

[2]For prospective SEC clients who have been audited previously, additional information may be obtained by the successor auditor from reading a report filed with the SEC concerning a change in the company's auditors. This report is explained in Chapter 21.

ASSESS ABILITY TO MEET GAAS

In deciding to accept an engagement with a new client or to continue with a client, the auditor should consider whether the engagement can be completed in accordance with GAAS. The three general standards are of particular importance in making this decision because they also apply to the standards of field work and reporting. The general standards relate to the personal qualifications of the auditor and the quality of his work, as explained below.

Technical Training and Proficiency

In every profession, there is a premium on technical competence. Consider, for instance, the training and proficiency required to be a physician, attorney, or dentist. Similar demands for competence are made on members of the public accounting profession as indicated by the first general standard that states

> The examination is to be performed by a person or persons having adequate technical training and proficiency as an auditor.

The competency of the auditor is determined not only by education and practical experience, but also by his skill and efficiency in carrying out his work. Accordingly, this standard refers to (1) education for entry into the profession, (2) practical training and experience in auditing, and (3) continuing professional education. In most states, a CPA is required to complete 120 hours of professional education over a three-year period. This requirement must also be met by all professionals in firms that are members of the AICPA Division for CPA Firms.

Before accepting an audit engagement, the auditor should determine whether he has the *professional competence* to complete the engagement in accordance with GAAS. If the auditor concludes that he does not have the necessary expertise, he should decline the engagement.

Independence

Competency and technical training alone are not sufficient for an auditor. An auditor must also be free of client influence in performing his work. Thus, the second general standard stipulates

> In all matters relating to the assignment, an independence in mental attitude is to be maintained by the auditor or auditors.

This standard likens the auditor's role in an audit engagement to the role of an umpire in a baseball game, an arbitrator in a labor dispute, or a one-person grand jury in a criminal indictment.

To comply with this standard, the auditor must be independent both in fact and appearance. Independence in fact relates to the auditor's ability to act with integrity and objectivity. Integrity pertains to an individual's honesty; objectivity refers to his impartiality. Neither quality is precisely measurable because they relate to an individual's character and state of mind. Nonetheless, these qualities are recognized as imperative in meeting the independence standard.

To be independent in appearance, the auditor should avoid relationships with a client that may cause a reasonable person to conclude that the auditor will be unable to act with integrity and objectivity. These relationships fall into two broad categories: (1) financial and (2) business. For example, the auditor may not have a direct financial (ownership) interest in the client. Similarly, the auditor may not be a member of management or the board of directors.

Before accepting an audit engagement, the auditor should determine whether he and his firm can be independent of the client throughout the engagement. The requirements for independence extend beyond GAAS. In making this determination, the auditor must also meet the rules on independence contained in the AICPA's Code of Ethics, described in Chapter 19. In addition, if the prospective client is required to file audited financial statements with the SEC, the auditor must also comply with the agency's requirements pertaining to independence, as discussed in Chapter 21. If the auditor concludes that he is not independent, he should decline the engagement or inform the potential client that he is precluded from expressing an opinion on the financial statements.

Due Professional Care

Just as the patient expects the physician to follow professional standards of care in performing a physical examination and rendering a diagnosis, so the client and the general public expect the auditor to exercise due care in making an audit. The third general standard states

> Due professional care is to be exercised in the performance of the examination and the preparation of the report.

Criteria for judging the care exercised by a professional are based primarily on custom, convention, and judgment in light of the attendant circumstances, rather than a list of universally accepted steps or procedures.

The standard of due care requires the critical review of both the work done and the judgment exercised by those assisting in the examination. This standard has been associated with the image of a prudent, reasonably competent practitioner whose degree of skill is taken as the standard of measurement whenever the quality of performance of a fellow practitioner is questioned.[3]

[3]Robert K. Mautz and Hussein A. Sharaf, *The Philosophy of Auditing* (Sarasota, Fla.: American Accounting Association, 1961), p. 132.

The auditor should decline an engagement if he believes that he will not be able to exercise due professional care throughout the audit.

PREPARE ENGAGEMENT LETTER

It is good professional practice to confirm the terms of each engagement in an engagement letter, such as the letter shown in Figure 3-1. Of paramount importance in an engagement letter is a clear statement of the nature of the auditor's examination and the responsibilities assumed by the auditor. In Figure 3-1, this is done in paragraphs 2 through 4. In addition, the letter should indicate the basis for determining the audit fee, as shown in paragraph 6. If there are any limitations on the scope of the audit, they should be identified. Paragraph 5 of the sample letter states that the auditor will review the client's income tax returns and that he will be available for consultation on the tax effects of transactions. These are services that are not required in an audit engagement.

As illustrated, an engagement letter should contain space for the client's acceptance. It should be sent to the client in duplicate, with one copy to be signed and returned to the auditor. An engagement letter constitutes a legal contract between the auditor and the client and should be renewed each year.

TIMING OF THE ACCEPTANCE

An auditor may accept an engagement both before and after the close of the client's fiscal year. Early appointment by the client and acceptance by the auditor facilitate audit planning. For example, acceptance of the engagement in the first month of the client's fiscal year gives the auditor much greater flexibility in scheduling his field work. In contrast, acceptance of the audit near or after the close of the fiscal year may impose severe constraints on planning the examination and performing the field work. Before accepting an engagement at these late dates, the auditor should ascertain whether the circumstances will permit an examination in accordance with GAAS. When the auditor is uncertain on this vital issue, he should discuss with the client the possibility that he may be unable to express an unqualified opinion on the financial statements because of the limitations on the timing and scope of his examination.

AUDIT PLANNING

A vital phase of every audit engagement is planning. Planning serves much the same purpose in auditing that it does in personal planning for college or a ski trip to Aspen and in business planning for the development of a new product like the GM Saturn. In each instance, planning results in an orderly

REDDY & ABEL CERTIFIED PUBLIC ACCOUNTANTS

March 15, 19X1

Mr. Thomas Thorp, President
Melville Co., Inc.
Route 32
Midtown, New York 11746

Dear Mr. Thorp:

This will confirm our understanding of the arrangements for our examination of the financial statements of Melville Co., Inc., for the year ending December 31, 19X1.

We will examine the Company's balance sheet at December 31, 19X1, and the related statements of income, retained earnings, and changes in financial position for the year then ended, for the purpose of expressing an opinion on them. Our examination will be in accordance with generally accepted auditing standards and will include such auditing procedures as we consider necessary to accomplish this purpose.

These procedures will include tests (by statistical sampling, if feasible) of documentary evidence supporting the transactions recorded in the accounts, tests of the physical existence of inventories, and direct confirmation of receivables and certain other assets and liabilities by correspondence with selected customers, creditors, legal counsel, and banks.

Although defalcations and similar irregularities may occasionally be disclosed by this type of examination, it is not designed for this purpose and should not be relied on to disclose fraud, should any exist. We will, of course, report to you anything that appears to us during our examination to be unusual or abnormal.

We will review the Company's Federal and State [identify states] income tax returns for the year ended December 31, 19X1. These returns, we understand, will be prepared by you. Further, we will be available during the year to consult with you on the tax effects of transactions or contemplated changes in business policies.

Our fee for this examination will be at our regular per diem rates, plus travel and other costs. Invoices will be rendered every two weeks and are payable on presentation.

We are pleased to have this opportunity to serve you. If this letter correctly expresses your understanding, please sign the enclosed copy and return it to us.

Very truly yours,

REDDY & ABEL

Ivan M. Reddy

Partner

APPROVED:

By: _____
Date: _____

Figure 3-1. ENGAGEMENT LETTER.

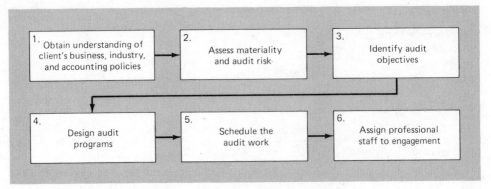

Figure 3-2. COMPONENTS OF AUDIT PLANNING.

arrangement of the parts or steps to achieve the desired objective. The first standard of field work states

> The work is to be adequately planned and assistants, if any, are to be properly supervised.

Audit planning involves the development of an overall strategy or game plan for the expected conduct and scope of the examination. The amount of planning required in an engagement will vary with the size and complexity of the client, and the auditor's knowledge and experience with the client. As to be expected, considerably more effort is needed to adequately plan an initial audit than a continuing audit. The components of audit planning and the sequence in which they are performed are shown in Figure 3-2. Each component is explained below.

OBTAIN UNDERSTANDING OF CLIENT

In order to adequately plan an audit, the auditor should obtain sufficient knowledge of the client's business to enable him to understand events, transactions, and practices that may have a significant effect on the financial statements. The auditor needs knowledge about the

- Entity's business, its organization, and its operating characteristics.
- Industry in which the entity operates.
- Government regulations that affect the client.
- Entity's accounting policies and procedures.
- Entity's data processing methods and controls.
- Reports expected to be rendered, such as data to be filed with the SEC.

A variety of techniques may be used to acquire this knowledge. Those with the widest application are discussed below.

Communicate With Audit Committee

The audit committee of the board of directors may provide the auditor with special insights into the client's business and industry. For example, the committee may have information about strengths or weaknesses in the company's internal controls in a specific division, a recently acquired subsidiary, or a newly implemented EDP systems application. The committee may also be able to inform the auditor of significant changes in the company's management and organizational structure. In addition, the audit committee should be knowledgeable about new industry and governmental regulations that affect the company.

As previously explained, one of the primary functions of an audit committee is to discuss the scope of the examination with the auditor. In some cases, the audit committee may request additions or modifications to the auditor's planned examination.

Review Prior Years' Working Papers

In a recurring audit engagement, the auditor can review his own working papers for knowledge about the client. In addition, the working papers may indicate problem areas that have occurred in prior audits that may be expected to continue in the future. For instance, the client may have on-going inventory control weaknesses and complicated pension and profit-sharing bonus plans.

For a new client, the predecessor auditor's working papers may be helpful. The client must consent to the successor's review of the working papers and the predecessor auditor is then expected to cooperate. The review of the working papers is normally limited to matters of continuing audit significance, such as analyses of balance sheet accounts and contingencies. During the review, the predecessor auditor should be available for consultation. At such time, the successor auditor can make inquiries concerning matters that may affect the examination.

Review Industry and Business Data

For a new client, information about the industry in which the client operates may be obtained from reading industry data accumulated by the auditing firm and industry publications. The auditor may also obtain useful information from the many industry audit and accounting guides published by the AICPA.

To obtain knowledge about the client's business, the auditor may

- Review the articles of incorporation and bylaws.
- Read the minutes of directors' and stockholders' meetings.
- Analyze recent financial statements, tax returns, and reports to regulatory agencies.
- Become familiar with applicable government regulations.
- Read important continuing contracts.

- Read trade and industry publications concerning current business and industry developments.

The information obtained should be documented by the auditor and retained in a permanent file for use in subsequent examinations.

Tour Client Operations

A tour of the operating facilities and offices is a significant help to an auditor in obtaining knowledge about a new client's operating characteristics. From a tour of the plant, an auditor should become familiar with the layout of the plant, the operating (manufacturing) process, storage facilities, and potential trouble spots, such as unlocked storerooms, obsolete materials, and excessive scrap.

During a tour of the office, an auditor should become knowledgeable about the types and locations of the accounting records and EDP facilities, and the work habits of personnel. An important by-product of both tours is the opportunity to meet personnel who occupy key positions with the client's organization. The auditor should document the information obtained from the plant and office tours.

In a recurring engagement, the tour of client operations is often limited to major changes that have occurred since the completion of last year's audit. For a multidivisional company, tours may be done on a rotating basis.

Review Accounting Manuals

A company's accounting policies and procedures are often summarized in accounting manuals. From a study of the manuals, the auditor can obtain an understanding of a new client's accounting system, methods of data processing, and system of internal control. In addition, the auditor may be able to identify accounting policies that are unique to the company or the industry in which the client operates. During this review, the auditor should also consider the applicable effects of new accounting and auditing pronouncements on the client's financial statements.

In a recurring engagement, the review of manuals is limited to changes in policies and procedures.

Make Inquiries of Management

For both new and recurring clients, discussions with management may reveal current business developments affecting the entity that may have audit significance. Moreover, areas of particular interest to management may be discussed.

Inquiries may also be made of management as to whether client personnel will be able to prepare schedules and analyses for the auditor. In addition, the auditor can inquire about the existence and extent of an internal audit function and matters pertaining to corporate accountability such as codes of conduct, potential conflicts of interest, and possible illegal payments.

Perform Analytical Review

Analytical review procedures involve the study and comparison of relationships among data. The comparisons may be made in dollars, ratios, percentages, or physical quantities. Analytical review is used in audit planning to enable the auditor to (1) obtain a better understanding of the client's business and industry and (2) identify unusual relationships and unexpected fluctuations in the data that may require investigation during the examination. By using analytical review, the auditor should be able to plan a more effective and efficient audit.

The subject matter for analytical review is the principal financial and operating data used by the client to evaluate its financial position and results of operations. In most companies, the data are accumulated monthly and should be available to the auditor on request. From the study of the data, which often will include prior year and budget data for the company and relevant industry data, the auditor should be able to obtain considerable insight into the company's current business activities and relative position in the industry.

Analytical review procedures include

- Comparison of the financial information with information for comparable prior period(s).
- Comparison of the financial information with anticipated results (for example, budgets and forecasts).
- Study of the relationships of elements of financial information that would be expected to conform to a predictable pattern based on the entity's experience.
- Comparison of the financial information with similar information regarding the industry in which the entity operates.
- Study of relationships of the financial information with relevant nonfinancial information.[4]

A basic premise underlying the application of analytical review procedures is that relationships among data may be expected to continue in the absence of known conditions to the contrary. When the procedures identify unusual relationships, fluctuations that are unexpected, or the absence of expected fluctuations that may have a significant effect on the financial statements, the auditor should plan to investigate them during his examination.

The first three analytical review procedures above relate to internal company data. Comparisons of such data over time may reveal significant trends such as an increasing current ratio or a decreasing rate of return on sales. When

[4]Auditing Standards Board, *Codification of Statements on Auditing Standards* (New York: American Institute of Certified Public Accountants, 1985), Auditing Section 318.06 (hereinafter referred to and cited as AU §).

the current year's results are expected to follow the projected trend, less audit work on the related accounts may be planned. Conversely, when conformity with a predictable pattern is not anticipated, additional audit work should be planned.

Figure 3-3 presents selected financial relationships for the Boxkraft Container Corporation for five years. The auditor examines the data for indications of significant trends. In this case, the auditor may conclude that there is an unfavorable trend for the current and quick ratios but the relationships appear to be normal. In contrast, the auditor may conclude that the change in the length of the collection period in 19X5 is an unusual fluctuation. If this fluctuation had been identified in planning the 19X5 audit, the auditor may have scheduled more audit work on accounts receivable and the allowance for bad debts.

The fourth analytical review procedure involves external comparisons as it relates client data to relevant industry data. Industry data represent a composite of all companies within an industry. There are many sources of industry data, including Dun & Bradstreet which publishes 14 key ratios for 125 lines of business. Figure 3-4 illustrates data for eight of the ratios showing upper, median, and lower quartiles for ten lines of manufacturing companies. The usefulness of external comparisons depends on the similarity of the client's business and significant accounting policies with other companies in the industry.

In external comparisons, the auditor wants to identify significant differences between client data and industry data. For example, if industry sales are projected to be down, but client sales are expected to be up, the auditor may plan to do more audit work in sales in his examination. If we assume Boxkraft Container Corporation is in the paperboard container and box line of business,

	Boxkraft Container Corporation Financial Ratios 12/31/X5				
Ratio	12/31/X5	12/31/X4	12/31/X3	12/31/X2	12/31/X1
1. Quick ratio	1.17	1.23	1.31	1.70	1.86
2. Current ratio	2.04	2.04	2.25	2.41	2.52
3. Total liabilities to net worth	88%	91%	93%	98%	84%
4. Collection period (days)	47.40	41.40	40.80	40.90	41.50
5. Net sales to inventory (times)	8.77	8.84	9.82	9.85	9.20
6. Return on net sales	2.02%	1.76%	6.28%	6.52%	6.57%
7. Return on total assets	1.92%	1.58%	6.40%	6.67%	7.01%
8. Return on net worth	3.60%	3.21%	12.36%	13.20%	12.91%

Figure 3-3. FINANCIAL RATIOS.

Manufacturing

Line of Business (and number of concerns reporting)	Quick Ratio	Current Ratio	Total Liabilities to Net Worth	Collection Period	Net Sales to Inventory	Return on Net Sales	Return on Total Assets	Return on Net Worth
	Times	Times	Percent	Days	Times	Percent	Percent	Percent
2011–2017	2.1	4.2	33.3	12.7	44.2	2.9	11.6	25.7
MEAT	1.3	2.2	71.8	17.8	29.0	1.5	6.5	13.9
PRODUCTS (113)	0.8	1.6	177.2	24.8	16.3	0.6	2.4	4.8
2021–2026	1.2	2.0	64.3	18.9	55.0	2.8	9.5	23.1
DAIRY	1.0	1.4	114.7	26.4	26.9	1.2	5.2	11.1
PRODUCTS (125)	0.7	1.2	205.0	32.8	13.9	0.5	1.1	3.1
2051–2052	2.0	3.3	24.1	17.0	41.5	5.5	12.7	21.8
BAKERY	1.1	1.9	49.1	24.4	29.8	2.4	6.9	13.8
PRODUCTS (113)	0.8	1.3	112.0	31.7	17.4	1.2	2.7	6.7
2082–2087	1.5	3.3	34.0	16.7	20.1	7.3	14.6	27.3
BEVERAGES	0.9	2.0	68.2	24.9	13.2	4.1	8.3	15.6
(140)	0.5	1.3	136.7	37.2	5.1	1.8	3.6	8.5
2321–2329	1.6	3.5	43.4	23.3	10.8	5.5	10.2	23.3
MEN'S AND	1.0	2.4	97.2	43.8	6.3	3.0	5.1	11.4
BOY'S APPAREL (114)	0.6	1.7	180.9	66.0	4.2	1.6	2.4	6.2
2331–2339 WOMEN'S, MISSES, AND	1.5	2.7	59.7	23.7	16.4	3.2	10.4	31.4
JUNIORS	1.0	1.7	131.6	43.0	10.7	2.0	6.2	16.3
OUTERWEAR (107)	0.7	1.4	235.9	62.6	7.3	0.5	1.2	3.8
2511–2519	2.0	3.9	31.3	18.2	13.2	6.1	13.5	25.9
HOUSEHOLD	1.1	2.6	71.3	34.1	9.4	3.0	7.0	13.3
FURNITURE (116)	0.7	1.8	148.4	47.4	5.2	0.9	2.6	4.2
2651–2655 PAPERBOARD	2.1	3.3	39.5	30.2	21.9	5.0	9.7	18.7
CONTAINERS	1.3	2.1	99.6	41.5	13.1	3.4	7.0	12.5
AND BOXES (115)	0.9	1.5	197.4	46.3	7.6	0.9	2.6	4.6
2731–2732	1.9	4.2	30.0	32.1	14.1	12.6	14.8	20.7
BOOKS	1.2	2.7	69.4	48.5	7.3	6.7	9.3	13.5
(101)	0.7	1.8	150.5	81.3	3.6	2.8	5.4	7.6
2851	2.2	4.1	34.7	18.4	10.0	5.8	12.4	23.3
PAINT,	1.4	2.8	63.2	34.1	8.0	3.4	8.7	12.4
VARNISHES, AND ALLIED PRODUCTS (109)	1.0	2.0	121.5	65.4	5.8	2.0	5.4	7.9

Figure 3-4. INDUSTRY DATA: EIGHT KEY RATIOS FOR TEN LINES OF BUSINESS. [SOURCE: *Selected Key Business Ratios in 125 Lines of Business* (New York: Dun & Bradstreet, Inc. 1981), p. 6 (adapted).]

the auditor may ask the client to explain why the company is in the median quartile in some ratios and the lowest quartile in others. If a satisfactory explanation is not obtained, additional audit work may be planned.

Since planning is generally done well before current year-end account balances are available, analytical review data for planning purposes may be based on actual year-to-date data and/or projected year-end data derived from company budgets and forecasting models. The compilation of client data is facilitated by the use of computer software packages. These packages may also include the ability to access on-line data retrieval services to obtain comparative industry data, thereby eliminating the need to consult hard-copy services.

ASSESS MATERIALITY AND AUDIT RISK

Materiality and audit risk underlie the application of generally accepted auditing standards. Materiality and audit risk thus have a pervasive effect in a financial statement audit. The auditor should consider materiality and audit risk both in (a) planning the audit and (b) evaluating whether the financial statements taken as a whole are presented fairly in conformity with generally accepted accounting principles.[5] The meaning of these concepts and their relevance to audit planning are explained below.

The Concept of Materiality

The Financial Accounting Standards Board defines materiality as

> The magnitude of an omission or misstatement of accounting information that, in the light of surrounding circumstances, makes it probable that the judgment of a reasonable person relying on the information would have been changed or influenced by the omission or misstatement.[6]

This definition requires the auditor to consider both the circumstances pertaining to the entity and the information needs of those who will rely on the audited financial statements. Accordingly, the auditor may conclude that the materiality levels for working capital accounts should be lower for a company on the brink of bankruptcy than for a company with a 4:1 current ratio. The auditor's assessment of materiality is a matter of professional judgment, which may or may not be explicitly quantified.

The auditor makes a *preliminary judgment* about materiality levels in planning the audit. This assessment, often referred to as *planning materiality,* may ultimately differ from the materiality levels used in evaluating the audit findings because (1) the surrounding circumstances may change and (2) additional

[5] Auditing Standards Board, *op. cit.,* AU § 312.08.
[6] "Qualitative Characteristics of Accounting," *Statement of Financial Accounting Concepts No. 2.* (Stamford, Conn.: Financial Accounting Standards Board, 1980), p. xv.

information about the client will have been obtained during the course of the examination. For example, the client may have obtained the financing needed to continue as a going concern, and the auditor's examination may affirm that the company's short-term solvency has significantly improved.

Materiality involves both quantitative and qualitative considerations. In assessing the quantitative importance of a misstatement, it is necessary to relate the dollar amount of the error to the financial statements under examination. A 25% understatement of merchandise inventory would be material to Sears Roebuck, whereas a similar misstatement of prepaid insurance would likely be immaterial. Likewise, a $50,000 misstatement in inventory would be material to a small corner grocery store, but it would be immaterial to the consolidated financial statements of a supermarket chain such as Safeway or Kroger. In planning the examination, the auditor generally is concerned only with misstatements that are quantitatively material.

Qualitative considerations relate to the causes of the misstatement. An error that is quantitatively immaterial may be qualitatively material. This may occur, for instance, when the misstatement is attributable to an irregularity or an illegal act by the client.

In an audit engagement, it is necessary for the auditor to assess materiality at two levels

- The *financial statement level* because his opinion on fairness extends to the financial statements taken as a whole.
- The *account balance level* because he verifies account balances in reaching an overall conclusion on the fairness of the financial statements.[7]

Factors that should be considered in making preliminary judgments of materiality at each level are explained below.

Financial Statement Materiality

Financial statements are materially misstated when they contain errors or irregularities whose effect, individually or in the aggregate, is important enough to prevent the statements from being presented fairly in conformity with GAAP.[8] In this context, errors or irregularities may result from misapplication of GAAP, departures from fact, or omissions of necessary information. For convenience, the designation *error* will be used in the following discussion to include all of the foregoing factors.

In audit planning, the auditor should recognize that there may be more than one level of materiality relating to the financial statements. Each statement, in fact, could have several levels. For the income statement, materiality could be related to total revenues, operating income, income before taxes, or net income. For the balance sheet, materiality could be based on total assets, current assets, working capital, or shareholders' equity.

---

[7]This level also may be identified with *classes of transactions,* such as sales, purchases, and so on.
[8]Auditing Standards Board, *op. cit.,* AU § 312.04.

The auditor's preliminary judgment of materiality is often made six to nine months before the balance sheet date. Thus, the assessment may be based on annualized interim financial statement data. Alternatively, it may be premised on one or more prior years' financial results adjusted for current changes, such as the general condition of the economy and industry trends.

In making a preliminary judgment about materiality, the auditor initially determines the aggregate (overall) level of materiality for each statement. For example, he may estimate that errors totaling $100,000 for the income statement and $200,000 for the balance sheet would be material. It would be inappropriate in this case for the auditor to use balance sheet materiality in planning the audit because if balance sheet errors also affect the income statement, the income statement would be materially misstated. For planning purposes, the auditor should use the *smallest aggregate level of errors considered to be material to any one of the financial statements.* This decision rule is appropriate because (1) the financial statements are interrelated and (2) many auditing procedures pertain to more than one statement. For instance, the audit procedure to determine whether year-end credit sales are recorded in the proper period provides evidence about both accounts receivable and sales.

Account Balance Materiality

The materiality level for an account balance is the maximum error that can exist in the account before it is considered to be materially misstated.[9] It is generally recognized that there is an inverse relationship between the materiality level for an account and the amount of audit evidence needed to verify the account balance. Accordingly, more evidence will be required for an inventory balance of $1 million when materiality is $100,000 than when it is $200,000.

In making judgments about materiality levels for account balances, the auditor should consider the relationship between account balance materiality and financial statement materiality. This consideration should lead the auditor to plan his examination to detect errors that may be immaterial in relation to individual accounts, but when aggregated, may be material to the financial statements taken as a whole. The amount of error that can exist in an account without causing aggregate errors to exceed financial statement materiality may or may not be explicitly quantified in audit planning.

The Concept of Audit Risk

Audit risk is the risk that the auditor may unknowingly fail to appropriately modify his opinion on financial statements that are materially misstated.[10] The more certain the auditor wants to be that he is expressing the correct opinion, the lower will be the audit risk he is willing to accept. If 99% certainty is

---

[9]Maximum error is often referred to as *tolerable error.* This term is more fully explained in Chapter 12.

[10]Auditing Standards Board, *op. cit.,* AU § 312.02.

desired, audit risk is 1%, whereas if 95% certainty is considered satisfactory, audit risk is 5%.

The auditor formulates his opinion on the financial statements taken as a whole primarily on the basis of evidence obtained through the verification of individual account balances. Thus, to be useful in audit planning, audit risk must be related to account balances. The objective is to restrict audit risk at the individual account balance level so that at the conclusion of the examination, the audit risk in expressing an opinion on the financial statements will be at an appropriately low level.

There are three components of audit risk:

- *Inherent Risk.* The susceptibility of an account balance to material error assuming the client does not have any related internal controls.
- *Control Risk.* The risk that a material error in an account will not be prevented or detected on a timely basis by the client's system of internal control.
- *Detection Risk.* The risk that the auditor's examination will not detect a material error in an account balance.[11]

Inherent risk is greater for some accounts than for others. For example, complex calculations for leases and pensions are more likely to contain errors than simple computations of straight-line depreciation. Accounts may also differ in their susceptibility to loss, theft, and fraud. Cash is more likely to be stolen than plant assets, and inventories are more vulnerable to declines in value than other tangible resources. In addition to factors pertaining to individual accounts, inherent risk extends to factors that may affect all accounts. These include potential conflicts of interest, critical shortages of working capital, and impending bankruptcy.

Control risk is a function of the effectiveness of the client's system of internal control. Effective internal controls over an account reduce control risk, whereas ineffective internal controls increase control risk. Control risk can never be zero because internal control systems cannot provide complete assurance that all material errors will be prevented or detected. For instance, controls may be ineffective on occasion because of human failures due to carelessness or fatigue.

Detection risk is a function of the effectiveness of the auditor's verification of account balances. This risk is influenced by the nature, timing, and extent of the auditor's procedures. More evidence, obviously, is obtained in a 100% examination of a balance than a 50% testing. In estimating detection risk, the auditor should also consider the likelihood that he will make an error, such as misapplying an auditing procedure or misinterpreting the evidence obtained.

There is an inverse relationship between the inherent and control risks for an account and the level of detection risk that the auditor can accept for that account. Thus, at a given level of audit risk, a decrease in inherent and control

---

[11]Auditing Standards Board, *op. cit.*, AU § 312.20 (adapted).

risks can be offset by a corresponding increase in detection risk. Inherent and control risks relate to the client's circumstances, whereas detection risk is controllable by the auditor. Accordingly, the auditor controls his audit risk by adjusting his detection risk according to the perceived levels of inherent and control risks. It should be recognized, however, that it is not appropriate under GAAS for the auditor to conclude that inherent and control risks are so low that it is not necessary to verify account balances. The auditor must always perform some verification procedures on material account balances.

The components of audit risk may be expressed in quantitative terms such as percentages, or in nonquantitative terms such as low, moderate, or high. A model for quantitatively expressing the components of audit risk is explained in Appendix A on page 92. Additional consideration is given to both materiality and audit risk in later chapters.

IDENTIFY AUDIT OBJECTIVES

The identification of audit objectives is an essential part of audit planning. As indicated previously, the objective of a financial statement audit is to express an opinion on whether the financial statements are presented fairly in accordance with GAAP. To meet this overall objective, it is customary to identify specific objectives for each account reported in the financial statements. These objectives are derived from the assertions made by management that are contained in the components of the financial statements. Some of management's assertions are explicit; some are implicit. Explicit assertions include the identification of the component (cash, inventories, and so forth), its dollar amount, and its classification (such as current assets). Implicit assertions for an asset account include (1) the asset exists, (2) the company has ownership rights to the asset, and (3) unless disclosed, there are no restrictions on the company's use of the asset.

The development of audit objectives from management assertions is illustrated below using inventories as an example. The objectives will include, but are not limited to, a determination that the inventories reported on the balance sheet

- Physically exist.
- Show the effects of all merchandising transactions that have occurred to the balance sheet date.
- Are owned by the company.
- Are properly valued at the lower of cost or market.
- Are properly classified on the balance sheet, and the basis of valuation is adequately disclosed.

For accounts payable, the objectives include whether (1) the payables exist, (2) the amount owed includes all obligations to suppliers at the statement date, (3) the amounts owed are actual obligations of the client, (4) the amounts are properly reported at the amount owed, and (5) the payables are properly classified on the balance sheet. Additional consideration is given to audit objectives in later chapters.

DESIGN AUDIT PROGRAMS

Audit programs are lists of the audit procedures to be performed during the field work phase of the audit. The procedures in an audit program should be sufficiently comprehensive to ensure that the audit objectives are met. Audit programs provide

- An outline of the work to be done and instructions on how it is to be accomplished.
- A basis for coordinating, supervising, and controlling the audit.
- A record of the work done.

Figure 3-5 illustrates a partial audit program for verifying inventory balances. Each procedure provides audit evidence for the corresponding audit objective shown on page 86. Audit programs for verifying account balances pertain to the auditor's detection risk. Generally, there is an inverse relationship between the comprehensiveness of an audit program and the risk that the auditor's examination will fail to detect a material error in an account.

In practice, more than one procedure may be necessary to achieve an audit objective. Moreover, a given procedure may be applicable to more than one objective. In the case of cash on hand, the procedure of counting cash provides evidence as to the existence and ownership of cash and the amount to be reported on the balance sheet.

ABC Company
Verification of Inventory Balances

Work Paper Reference	Audit Procedures	Done by	
		Auditor	Date
	1. Observe client's physical inventory taking.		
	2. Test purchases and sales cut-off procedures at year end.		
	3. Examine paid invoices and consignment agreements (if any).		
	4. Compare unit costs used in costing the inventory to vendors' invoices and verify cost computations.		
	5. Review client's proposed balance sheet presentation of inventory.		

Figure 3-5 PARTIAL AUDIT PROGRAM.

The basic design of audit programs occurs during audit planning. However, as the field work proceeds, it may be necessary to modify the planned program. Audit programs for the auditor's study and evaluation of internal controls and more complete audit programs for verifying account balances are illustrated in later chapters.

Audit Programs in Initial Engagements

The design of audit programs for new clients is complicated by uncertainties. In an initial engagement, it may not be possible for the auditor to obtain a good understanding of the strengths and weaknesses of the company's internal controls (control risk), the actual complexity of the client's transactions (inherent risk), or the number of problem areas before he is well into his field work. The design of the audit programs in such cases may be done in stages, beginning with the procedures to be followed to study and evaluate the client's internal control system. When this phase of the examination is completed, the programs for verifying account balances can be designed.

In initial engagements, two additional audit concerns must be recognized in designing programs: (1) determining the propriety of the account balances at the beginning of the period being examined and (2) ascertaining the accounting principles used in the preceding period as a basis for determining the consistency of application of such principles in the current year.

Audit Programs in Recurring Engagements

In a repeat engagement, the auditor has access to audit programs used in the preceding year(s) and the working papers pertaining to those programs. From a review of such data and his experience and knowledge of the client, the auditor should be aware of troublesome areas and unusual items in the past, and be able to anticipate the likelihood of similar problems recurring in the current year. Thus, he should be able to design on a preliminary basis all of the audit programs for the current year prior to performing any field work.

When audit programs for verifying account balances are designed prior to field work, assumptions are made about inherent and control risks for each account. If the auditor's evaluation of internal control confirms the assumptions, the audit programs can remain unchanged. However, if the assumptions prove to be incorrect, the programs must be modified in order to keep audit risk at the desired level.

SCHEDULE THE WORK

Scheduling the work relates to when the audit programs are executed on the client's premises. Field work may be performed at almost any time during, or shortly after the end, of the client's fiscal year. It is customary to classify the timing of field work into two categories:

- *Interim work* that typically extends from six months prior to the balance sheet date to the balance sheet date.
- *Year-end work* that normally extends from the balance sheet date to two or more months thereafter.

Interim work is primarily concerned with the auditor's study and evaluation of internal control, and year-end work pertains primarily to the verification of account balances. However, in some cases, as explained in later chapters, it is permissible for the auditor to do some verification work at interim dates. A substantial part of the auditor's examination may be completed at interim dates. The performance of field work at interim dates permits the auditing firm to spread its workload more evenly throughout the year and helps to compensate for the fact that December 31 is the end of the fiscal year for most companies.

The time dimensions of an audit engagement are graphically portrayed in Figure 3-6. The time frames are intended to suggest that the related activity would be done during that time period, rather than the length of time that should be allocated to the given activity.

The February 15 date in this example is of considerable importance. It marks the end of the auditor's basic responsibilities under GAAS. The time period from this date to the issuance of the report relates to the preparation and processing of the audit report.

The timing of audit work also involves other considerations. In some instances, there is a need for the simultaneous examination of related items.

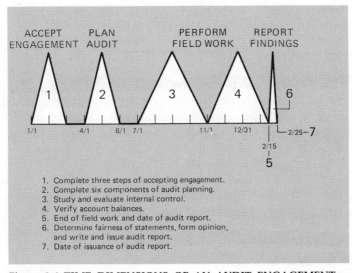

Figure 3-6 TIME DIMENSIONS OF AN AUDIT ENGAGEMENT

For example, in a count of cash, both cash and negotiable instruments must be controlled by the auditor until all items have been counted. In other cases, an unannounced performance of an auditing procedure may be appropriate. Thus, the audit program may call for a surprise count of cash on hand. Alternatively, the timeliness of the procedure may be important. A count of securities on hand 10 days after the balance sheet date does not establish the securities on hand at the statement date unless measures are taken to control changes in the intervening period.

ASSIGN PROFESSIONAL STAFF TO THE ENGAGEMENT

The final component of audit planning is the assigning of professional staff to the engagement. Assigning personnel to the engagement is also one of the elements of quality control. From a knowledge of the client's business and the planned audit program, the auditor is in a position to determine the professional staff needs for the engagement. In making staff assignments, consideration should be given to the composition of the audit team in terms of overall experience, responsibility, supervision, and technical expertise. Staff assignments should also be coordinated with the nature and timing of the audit tests to be performed. A typical audit team consists of

- A partner who has both overall and final responsibility for the engagement.
- One or more managers who coordinate and supervise the execution of the audit program.
- One or more seniors who may have responsibility for parts of the audit program and who supervise and review the work of staff assistants.
- Staff assistants who perform most of the required procedures.

The audit team ordinarily has backup resource staff in the accounting firm, as needed, such as an EDP expert, a tax specialist, and an industry expert.

In order to make individual staff assignments and control overall audit costs, it is customary to prepare a time budget for the engagement. The more detailed the budget, the easier it is to compare actual time worked with the time expected. In some cases, a time budget may be prepared for each financial statement account. The establishment of time budgets should be approved by the partner in charge of the engagement on the basis of his knowledge of the client and the field work involved.

The assignment of professional staff should be influenced by the auditor's expected use of the client's internal auditors and accounting personnel in the engagement. Accounting personnel may

- Prepare a trial balance of the general ledger.
- Reconcile control and subsidiary accounts.
- Age accounts receivable (i.e., current, 30-days past due, etc.).

- Prepare schedules of insurance policies in force, notes receivable, and plant assets.

Material prepared by the client must be so identified (usually by the letters PBC to signify "prepared by client") and must be reviewed and tested for accuracy and completeness by the auditor.

AUDIT SUPERVISION

In addition to audit planning, the first standard of field work states that assistants, if any, are to be properly supervised. Planning and supervision are closely related. They both continue throughout the engagement, and they frequently overlap. Supervision involves directing the work of less experienced auditors while the audit engagement is in progress. It includes (1) instructing assistants as to the objectives of the procedures they are to perform, (2) keeping informed of significant problems encountered in performing the procedures, (3) reviewing the work done, and (4) dealing with differences of opinion among members of the audit staff.[12] This requirement applies to every level of supervision. Audit supervision is also an element of a firm's quality control system.

The supervision standard is not satisfied by just reviewing the working papers and holding "after the fact" discussions and evaluations of the work done by assistants. Supervision requires the supervisor to watch, analyze, and question the work of assistants as it is being done. Such factors as the complexity of the engagement and the technical training and experience of the assistants will influence the nature and extent of the supervision appropriate in a given instance.

CONCLUDING COMMENTS

The auditor must meet both quality control and generally accepted auditing standards in accepting an audit engagement. These standards require the auditor to evaluate the integrity of the client's management and meet the GAAS standards of technical training and proficiency, independence, and due care. The terms of each engagement should be formalized by issuing an engagement letter.

Audit planning is an important part of an audit engagement. In planning, the auditor should become knowledgeable about the client's business, industry, and accounting policies. Based on this information, the auditor proceeds to assess materiality and audit risk, identify audit objectives, design the audit programs, schedule the work, and assign staff. Adequate planning is essential if the auditor's examination is to be both efficient and effective.

---

[12]Auditing Standards Board, *op. cit.,* AU § 311.11.

Appendix 3A

Audit Risk Model

The components of audit risk may be expressed in an audit risk model as follows:

$$AR = IR \times CR \times DR$$

The symbols represent audit, inherent, control, and detection risk, respectively. While auditors disagree about the wisdom or practicality of quantifying the risk components, a study of the model is helpful in understanding the interaction among the components. Assume, for example, that the auditor has made the following risk assessments in examining inventories:

Desired audit risk	5%
Inherent risk	50%
Control risk	50%

Use of the model indicates that detection risk should be 20% as shown below

$$
\begin{aligned}
DR &= AR \div (IR \times CR) \\
&= .05 \div (.5 \times .5) \\
&= 20\%
\end{aligned}
$$

If the auditor decides that inherent risk cannot be quantified, or that the effort to do so will exceed the potential reduction in the auditing procedures expected to be derived from such an evaluation, he can take the conservative approach by assessing inherent risk at the maximum (100%). In this case, the model yields a detection risk of 10% ($.05/(1.00 \times .5) = .10$). Similarly, if control weaknesses related to the account balance being tested suggest no basis for relying on internal controls, the auditor can set control risk at 100%. In this case, if we assume the desired audit risk remains at 5%, the model shows that detection risk should also be 5% ($.05/(1.00 \times 1.00) = .05$).

REVIEW QUESTIONS

3-1 What is the applicability of quality control standards and generally accepted auditing standards (GAAS) in accepting an audit engagement?

3-2 Identify the steps that are involved in accepting an audit engagement.

3-3 Contrast the manner in which the auditor can determine the integrity of management between a new and a recurring audit engagement.

3-4 The general standards are sometimes considered to be pervasive in auditing. Do you agree? Why or why not?

3-5 State the first general standard and identify the three ways the auditor can meet this standard.

3-6 a. Independence is not as important as competence in auditing. Do you agree? Explain.
     b. What factors should be considered by the auditor in determining whether he is independent with respect to a client?

3-7 a. The standard of due professional care only applies to accepting an audit engagement. Do you agree? If not, explain.
     b. What standards may be used for due care?

3-8 a. State the first standard of field work.
     b. Identify the components of audit planning in the sequence in which they are performed.

3-9 a. What information about a client is essential in audit planning?
     b. What techniques may be used by the auditor to acquire the information?

3-10 a. What purposes are served by analytical review procedures in audit planning?
     b. What types of comparisons and studies may be made in an analytical review?

3-11 a. Define materiality.
     b. Contrast the importance of materiality and planning materiality in an audit.

3-12 a. When is an item considered to be material at the financial statement level?
     b. In audit planning, what is the decision rule concerning materiality when all of the basic financial statements are considered?

3-13 a. Define materiality at the account level.
     b. What factors should be considered in making the materiality judgment at this level?

3-14 a. What is audit risk?
     b. Identify and explain the three components of audit risk.

3-15 a. Indicate the relationships among the components of audit risk?
     b. How does the auditor control audit risk?

3-16 a. How are audit objectives derived?
     b. Identify the audit objectives that may be used for inventories.

3-17 a. What is the nature and scope of an audit program?
     b. What are the advantages of using audit programs?

3-18 a. Identify the time frames for the four parts of an audit engagement for a client who prepares financial statements on a calendar year basis.
     b. Contrast the time periods for (1) interim work and (2) year-end work, and indicate the primary activity in each time frame.

3-19 a. What is the composition of a typical audit team?
     b. What types of assistance may client personnel provide in an audit?

3-20 a. What procedures are expected from an auditor in meeting the standard of proper supervision?
     b. Supervision involves more than post audit review of an assistant's work. Discuss.

OBJECTIVE QUESTIONS FROM PROFESSIONAL EXAMINATIONS

Indicate the *best* answer for each of the following multiple choice questions.

3-21 These questions involve accepting an audit engagement.

1. A CPA is most likely to refer to one or more of the three general auditing standards in determining
   a. The nature of the CPA's report qualification.
   b. The scope of the CPA's auditing procedures.
   c. Requirements for the review of internal control.
   d. Whether the CPA should undertake an audit engagement.
2. Early appointment of the independent auditor will enable
   a. A more thorough examination to be performed.
   b. A proper study and evaluation of internal control to be performed.
   c. Sufficient competent evidential matter to be obtained.
   d. A more efficient examination to be planned.
3. Engagement letters are widely used in practice for professional engagements of all types. The primary purpose of the engagement letter is to
   a. Remind management that the primary responsibility for the financial statements rests with management.
   b. Satisfy the requirements of the CPA's liability insurance policy.
   c. Provide a starting point for the auditor's preparation of the preliminary audit program.
   d. Provide a written record of the agreement with the client as to the services to be provided.
4. Which of the following should an auditor obtain from the predecessor auditor prior to accepting an audit engagement?
   a. Analysis of balance sheet accounts.
   b. Analysis of income statement accounts.
   c. All matters of continuing accounting significance.
   d. Facts that might bear on the integrity of management.

3-22 These questions relate to planning the engagement.

1. Those procedures specifically outlined in an audit program are primarily designed to
   a. Gather evidence.
   b. Detect errors or irregularities.
   c. Test internal systems.
   d. Protect the auditor in the event of litigation.
2. Which of the following would be *least* likely to be comparable between similar corporations in the same industry line of business?
   a. Earnings per share.
   b. Return on total assets before interest and taxes.
   c. Accounts receivable turnover.
   d. Operating cycle.
3. Which of the following situations would *most* likely require special audit planning by the auditor?

a. Some items of factory and office equipment do *not* bear identification numbers.
b. Depreciation methods used on the client's tax return differ from those used on the books.
c. Assets costing less than $500 are expensed even though the expected life exceeds one year.
d. Inventory is comprised of precious stones.

4. Audit programs are modified to suit the circumstances on particular engagements. A complete audit program for an engagement generally should be developed
a. Prior to beginning the actual audit work.
b. After the auditor has completed an evaluation of the existing internal accounting control.
c. After reviewing the client's accounting records and procedures.
d. When the audit engagement letter is prepared.

COMPREHENSIVE QUESTIONS

3-23 The audit committee of the Board of Directors of Unicorn Corp. asked Tish & Field, CPAs, to audit Unicorn's financial statements for the year ended December 31, 19X3. Tish & Field explained the need to make an inquiry of the predecessor auditor and requested permission to do so. Unicorn's management agreed and authorized the predecessor auditor to respond fully to Tish & Field's inquiries.

After a satisfactory communication with the predecessor auditor, Tish & Field drafted an engagement letter that was mailed to the audit committee of the Board of Directors of Unicorn Corp. The engagement letter clearly set forth arrangements concerning the involvement of the predecessor auditor and other matters.

Required
a. What information should Tish & Field have obtained during their inquiry of the predecessor auditor prior to acceptance of the engagement?
b. Describe what other matters Tish & Field would generally have included in the engagement letter.

AICPA

3-24 A CPA has been asked to audit the financial statements of a company for the first time. All preliminary verbal discussions and inquiries have been completed between the CPA, the company, the predecessor auditor, and all other necessary parties. The CPA is now preparing an engagement letter.

Required
a. List the items that should be included in the typical engagement letter.
b. Describe the benefits derived from preparing an engagement letter.
c. Who should prepare and sign the engagement letter?
d. Why should the engagement letter be sent?
e. Why should the engagement letter be renewed periodically?

AICPA (adapted)

3-25 The CPA firm of Test & Check has been appointed auditors for the XYZ Corporation by the company's audit committee. The engagement is limited to making an audit of the company's financial statements. The audit fee is to be at the firm's regular per diem rates plus travel costs. To confirm the arrangements, Test & Check sends the following engagement letter.

March 10, 19X1

Mr. D. R. Brink, Controller
XYZ Corporation
Maintown, ME. 03491

Dear Mr. Brink:

This will confirm our understanding of the arrangements for our review of the financial statements of XYZ Corporation Inc., for the year ending December 31, 19X1.

We will examine the Company's balance sheet at December 31, 19X1, and the related statements of income, retained earnings, and changes in financial position for the year then ended, for the purpose of auditing them. Our examination will be in accordance with generally accepted auditing standards and will include such auditing procedures as we consider necessary to express an unqualified opinion.

These standards will include tests (by statistical sampling, if feasible) of documentary evidence supporting the transactions recorded in the statements, tests of the physical existence of inventories, and direct confirmation of receivables and certain other assets and liabilities by correspondence with selected customers, creditors, legal counsel, and banks.

Although defalcations and similar irregularities should be uncovered by this type of examination, it is not designed for this purpose and we therefore cannot guarantee this result. We will, of course, report to you anything that looks suspicious to us during our examination.

Our fee for this examination will be on a cost plus basis, including travel costs. Invoices will be rendered every two weeks and are payable on presentation.

We are pleased to have this opportunity to serve you. If this letter correctly expresses your understanding, please sign the enclosed copy and return it to us.

Very truly yours,
Test & Check, CPAs

Approved:
By: _____
Date: _____

M. E. Test
Partner

Required

List the deficiencies in the engagement letter. For each deficiency, indicate the proper wording. Use the following format for your answer—do not write a proper engagement letter:

Deficiency	Proper Wording

3-26 You are meeting with executives of Cooper Cosmetics Corporation to arrange your firm's engagement to examine the Corporation's financial statements for the year ending December 31, 19X3. One executive suggests that the audit work be divided among three audit staff members, with one man examining asset accounts, a second examining liability accounts, and the third examining income and expense accounts in order to minimize audit time, avoid duplication of staff effort, and curtail interference with company operations.

Required

a. To what extent should a CPA follow the client's suggestions for the conduct of an audit? Discuss.

b. List and discuss the reasons why audit work should not be assigned solely according to asset, liability, and income and expense categories.

AICPA (adapted)

3-27 Johnson, Inc., a closely held company, wishes to engage Norr, CPA, to examine its annual financial statements. Johnson was generally pleased with the services provided by its prior CPA, Diggs, but thought the audit work performed was too detailed and interfered excessively with Johnson's normal office routines. Norr asked Johnson to inform Diggs of the decision to change auditors but Johnson did not wish to do so.

Required

a. List and discuss the steps Norr should follow before accepting the engagement.

b. What additional procedures should Norr perform on this first-time engagement over and beyond those Norr would perform on the Johnson engagement of the following year?

AICPA

3-28 The first standard of field work includes adequate planning of the work.

Required

a. What is the objective of audit planning?

b. What information about the client is essential in planning?

c. Identify the principal techniques used by the auditor to obtain the essential information?

d. Explain two specific types of information that can be obtained from each of the techniques identified in (c) above.

AICPA (adapted)

3-29 In late spring of 19X4, you are advised of a new assignment as in-charge accountant of your CPA firm's recurring annual audit of a major client, the Lancer Company. You are given the engagement letter for the audit covering the calendar year December 31, 19X4, and a list of personnel assigned to this engagement. It is your responsibility to plan and supervise the field work for the engagement.

Required

Discuss the necessary preparation and planning for the Lancer Company annual audit prior to beginning field work at the client's office. In your discussion, include the sources you should consult, the type of information you should seek, the preliminary plans and preparation you should make for the field work, and any actions you should take relative to the staff assigned to the engagement. Do not write an audit program.

AICPA

3-30 You are engaged in your second annual examination of the financial statements of the Claren Corporation, a medium-sized manufacturing company with 25 stockholders that manufactures optical instruments. During the audit, the following matters come to your attention.

A new controller was employed six months ago. He also serves as office manager but apparently exercises little disciplinary control over his 15 subordinates, who include a cashier, two bookkeepers, a supply room attendant, and two technicians who show the company products in a factory salesroom attached to the office. The office staff seems to be continually talking about social matters, visiting, making personal telephone calls, or engaged in other private matters that are generally indicative of inefficiency. You know that the office has fallen about three weeks behind in its accounting work for the year. On numerous occasions, you have been unable to obtain answers to questions that arose during the audit because the person who could supply the information was out of the office.

Required

a. Discuss what you would do when you found that you were frequently unable to obtain answers to questions because the person who could supply the information was out of the office.

b. Discuss your responsibility for drawing attention to the apparent general inefficiency of the office operations.

c. What steps would you take if you found numerous errors in the books?

d. What effect, if any, would the errors have upon your audit opinion?

3-31 Pro–Tex Company is a wholesale distributor of professional equipment and supplies. The company's sales have averaged about $900,000 annually for the three-year period 19X3–19X5. The firm's total assets at the end of 19X5 amounted to $850,000. Pro–Tex is a new audit client. At your request, the controller and his staff accumulate the following ratios for the three-year period ending December 31, 19X5.

	19X3	19X4	19X5
Current ratio	1.80	1.92	1.96
Acid–test (quick) ratio	1.08	0.99	0.87
Accounts receivable turnover	8.75	7.71	6.42
Inventory turnover	4.73	4.32	3.42
Percent of total debt to total assets	48.0	45.0	42.0
Percent of long-term debt to total assets	28.0	24.0	21.0
Sales to fixed assets (fixed asset turnover)	1.58	1.69	1.79
Sales as a percent of 19X1 sales	1.00	1.03	1.05
Gross margin percentage	36.0	34.7	34.6
Net income to sales	7.0%	7.0%	7.2%
Return on total assets	7.7%	7.7%	7.8%
Return on stockholders' equity	13.6%	13.1%	12.7%

Required

a. Identify any unusual relationships in individual ratios that you believe may have audit significance for your 19X6 audit.

b. From the data, identify significant trends in the company's financial position and operating results.

c. Identify any unusual fluctuations in the trend results that you believe may have audit significance for your 19X6 audit.

3-32 In Figure 3-6, the phases or steps of an audit are identified in a time matrix.

Required

a. Indicate in tabular form the time dimensions of each step, assuming a company has a fiscal year that ends on (1) February 28 and (2) September 30.

b. Is it permissible under GAAS to accept an engagement after the fiscal year has ended? Explain.

c. What advantages are derived from early appointment of the auditor?

d. How much of the audit can be performed at interim dates?

CASE STUDY

3-33* Sunny Energy Applications Co. sells solar-powered swimming pool heaters. Sunny contracts 100% of the work to other companies. As Sunny is a new company, its balance sheet has total assets of $78,000, including $24,000 of "stock subscriptions receivable." The largest asset is $42,000 worth of "unrecovered development costs." The equity side of the balance sheet is made up of $78,000 of "Common Stock Subscribed."

The company is contemplating a public offering to raise $1 million. The shares to be sold to the public for the $1 million will represent 40% of the then issued and outstanding stock. There are two officers-employees of the company, Mike Whale and Willie Float. Whale and Float are former officers of Canadian Brass Co. Float is being sued by the SEC for misusing funds raised by Canadian Brass in a public offering. The funds were used as compensatory balances for loans to a Physics Inc. Physics Inc. was controlled by Float and is the predecessor of Sunny Energy Applications.

Canadian Brass is being sued by the SEC for reporting improper (exaggerated) income. Float was chief executive at the time. There are many organizations engaged in researching the feasibility of using solar energy. Most of the organizations are considerably larger and financially stronger than Sunny Energy. The company has not been granted any patents that would serve to protect it from competitors.

Required

a. What potential risks may be present in this engagement?

b. What specific auditing and accounting problems appear to exist?

c. What additional information do you feel you need to know about the company?

d. Do you believe the engagement should be accepted or rejected? Why?

Chapter 4

Evidential Matter/ Working Papers

Study Objectives

When you have completed the study of this chapter, you should be able to

- Distinguish between the two categories of evidential matter.

- Recognize the factors that affect the sufficiency and competency of evidential matter.

- State the presumptions pertaining to the reliability of evidential matter.

- Identify the types of corroborating information available to the auditor.

- Enumerate and describe the types of auditing procedures that may be used to gather evidential matter.

- Define substantive tests.

- Indicate the possible effects of evidential matter on the auditor's report.

- Explain the nature and purpose of working papers.

As indicated in Chapter 1, the purpose of the ordinary examination is the expression of an opinion on the fairness of the client's financial statements. To have a basis for an opinion, the auditor must gather and evaluate evidence.

This chapter focuses on the third standard of field work, which requires the auditor to obtain sufficient competent evidential matter. The chapter is divided into three sections: (1) audit evidence, (2) obtaining and evaluating audit evidence, and (3) working papers.

Throughout this chapter, emphasis is given to the role of evidence in verifying balances. The accumulation of evidence in making a study and evaluation of internal control, as required by the second standard of field work, is explained in Chapter 5.

AUDIT EVIDENCE

NATURE OF EVIDENTIAL MATTER

In auditing, evidential matter consists of underlying accounting data (e.g., the underlying accounting or financial records) and all corroborating information available to the auditor.[1] The types of evidence in each category and the relationship of the categories to the third standard of field work are shown in Figure 4-1. In an electronic data processing (EDP) system, the underlying accounting data may consist of machine-readable media such as magnetic tapes and disks. The impact of the computer on audit evidence is explained in Chapter 6.

Both categories of evidential matter are required in making an examination in accordance with generally accepted auditing standards (GAAS). It should

Nature of Evidential Matter	Third Standard of Field Work
UNDERLYING ACCOUNTING DATA • Books of original entry. • General and subsidiary ledgers. • Related accounting manuals. • Informal and memorandum records, such as work sheets, computations, and reconciliations. CORROBORATING INFORMATION • Documents such as checks, invoices, contracts, etc. • Confirmations and other written representations. • Information from inquiry, observation, inspection, and physical examination. • Other information obtained or developed by the auditor.	SUFFICIENT COMPETENT EVIDENTIAL MATTER

Figure 4-1. CATEGORIES AND TYPES OF EVIDENTIAL MATTER.

[1]Auditing Standards Board, *Codification of Statements on Auditing Standards* (New York: American Institute of Certified Public Accountants, 1985), Auditing Section 326.14 (hereinafter referred to and cited as AU §).

be obvious that underlying accounting data are indispensable, for they provide the basis for the client's financial statements. However, these records may not be reliable. Thus, it is imperative that the auditor obtain supportive evidence of the reliability of the financial records. Much of this evidence is available within the client organization, but recourse to knowledgeable persons outside the company is also necessary.

EVIDENTIAL MATTER AND AUDIT OBJECTIVES

As indicated in Chapter 3, auditing involves identifying audit objectives related to management's representations or assertions in the financial statements. While the opinion ultimately rendered is on the fairness of the financial statements taken as a whole, most of the auditor's work in forming that opinion consists of obtaining and evaluating evidential matter concerning the assertions in the financial statements.

The process of identifying specific sources of evidence to meet specific audit objectives is covered extensively in Part III of this book. This chapter establishes a general framework for identifying the types of evidence and understanding their usefulness in auditing.

STATEMENT AND PURPOSE OF THE THIRD STANDARD OF FIELD WORK

The third standard of field work states

Sufficient competent evidential matter is to be obtained through inspection, observation, inquiries, and confirmations to afford a reasonable basis for an opinion regarding the financial statements under examination.

Four possible courses of action that an auditor may use in obtaining evidential matter are identified in the third standard. These are examples of *auditing procedures*. At this point, it should be recognized that there are more than four auditing procedures available to the auditor. These and other procedures are explained later in the chapter. The standard also specifies that *sufficient* (i.e., enough) *competent* (i.e., reliable) evidential matter should be obtained to provide a reasonable (i.e., rational) basis for an opinion. Each of these key elements of the standard requires subjective judgment by the auditor in the specific audit engagement. Considerations that may influence the auditor's judgment are discussed below.

Sufficiency of Corroborating Information

This element of the third standard of field work pertains to the quantity of evidential matter. Considerations that may affect the auditor's judgment as to sufficiency include

- Materiality and audit risk.
- Economic factors.
- Size and characteristics of the population.

Materiality and Audit Risk.   The importance of materiality and audit risk in audit planning was explained in Chapter 3. It will be recalled that the auditor is expected to make a preliminary judgment concerning materiality at both the financial statement and account balance levels. In verifying an account balance, there is an inverse relationship between its materiality level and the quantity of corroborating information required by the auditor. When the materiality level is low, more evidence is needed than when the level is high. It follows that when financial statement materiality is low, more corroborating information will be required to obtain a reasonable basis for an opinion than when the materiality level is high.

Audit risk affects the sufficiency of audit evidence through the component of detection risk. As explained in Chapter 3, the auditor controls audit risk by adjusting detection risk according to his perceived level of inherent and control risks. There is also an inverse relationship between the level of detection risk and the quantity of corroborating information to be obtained. The auditor needs more evidence when detection risk is low than when it is high.

Economic Factors.   An auditor works within economic limits that dictate that sufficient evidence must be obtained within a reasonable time and at reasonable cost. He is frequently faced with a decision as to whether the additional time and cost will produce commensurate benefits in terms of both the quantity and the quality of the evidence obtained. However, time and/or cost constraints alone are invalid reasons for not obtaining required evidence. In accepting audit engagements, an auditor should reject unreasonable client-imposed time and cost limitations. Such constraints are not conducive to making an examination in accordance with GAAS.

Population Size and Characteristics.   Sampling is a practical necessity in the accumulation of evidential matter for many statement items. The size of a population refers to the number of items that comprise the total, as, for example, the number of credit sales transactions, the number of customer accounts in the accounts receivable ledger or the number of dollars in an account balance. Generally, the larger the population, the larger the quantity of evidence required. However, as explained in later chapters, for certain sampling techniques, increases in population size beyond 5,000 units have a negligible effect on the quantity of evidence required.

The characteristics of a population refer to the homogeneity or variability of the individual items that comprise the population. In the case of the customer accounts, one such factor is the range of the dollar amount of individual balances. The auditor may require a larger sample and more evidential matter for diverse populations than for uniform populations.

Competency of Evidential Matter

The competency (or reliability) of both underlying accounting data and corroborating information are involved in this aspect of the third standard of field work. The reliability of the accounting records is directly related to the effectiveness of the client's system of internal accounting control. Strong internal controls enhance the accuracy and reliability of the accounting records, whereas weak internal controls often do not prevent or detect errors and irregularities in the accounting process, as is explained in Chapter 5.

The competency of corroborating information depends on many factors. The considerations that have the widest applicability in auditing are

- Relevance.
- Source.
- Timeliness.
- Objectivity.

Relevance. This criterion means that the evidence must be pertinent to the auditor's decision. Accordingly, if the objective is the quantity of goods on hand, the auditor can obtain relevant evidence by test counting the inventory. However, such evidence would not be relevant in determining whether the goods are owned by the client or their cost.

In executing an audit program, the auditor should be aware of the importance of this criterion. Unnecessary cost and time result when the auditor obtains irrelevant evidence. Moreover, such evidence may also lead to erroneous conclusions in forming an opinion on the client's financial statements.

Source. The circumstances in which evidence is obtained affect the reliability of the evidence. The importance of this criterion can be illustrated by some examples. Suppose that as an auditor, you seek evidence concerning the amount of cash on hand and the amount owed by customer X. For cash, you conclude that it should be counted. But by whom—you or the client? If you count it, you have direct personal knowledge of the amount on hand; if the client makes the count and gives you a report, you have indirect knowledge. Clearly, the former provides better evidence.

For the customer's balance, you can examine evidence within the client's organization, such as the shipping order and the duplicate sales invoice, or the customer could be asked to communicate directly to you the balance he owes. In this case, the latter evidence is considered more reliable because the respondent is a third party who is independent of the client. Moreover, the client is not able to alter the response.

For a third example, assume you are reviewing the bank reconciliation prepared by two different clients. For client A, the reconciliation is prepared by an internal auditor who is independent of the cashier and the accountant; for client B, it is prepared by the cashier who also serves as the company accountant. Greater credence would undoubtedly be given to the client A

reconciliation because it was generated under a better system of internal control.

From these examples, it is possible to recognize the following presumptions about the effects of the source of the information on the reliability (competency) of evidential matter:

- When evidential matter can be obtained from independent sources outside an enterprise, it provides greater assurance of reliability for the purposes of an independent audit than that secured solely within the enterprise.
- When accounting data and financial statements are developed under satisfactory conditions of internal control, there is more assurance as to their reliability than when they are developed under unsatisfactory conditions of internal control.
- Direct personal knowledge of the independent auditor obtained through physical examination, observation, computation, and inspection is more persuasive than information obtained indirectly.[2]

Timeliness. This criterion relates to the date to which the evidence is applicable. The timeliness of the evidence is especially important in verifying current asset, current liability, and related income statement balances. For these accounts, the auditor seeks evidence that the client has made a proper cutoff of cash, sales, and purchase transactions at the statement date. This task is facilitated when appropriate auditing procedures are applied at or near that date. Similarly, evidence obtained from physical counts at the balance sheet date provides better evidence of quantities on hand at that date than counts made at other times.

Objectivity. Evidence that is objective in nature is generally considered to be more reliable than evidence that is subjective. For example, evidence of the existence of tangible resources can be ascertained with a substantial degree of conclusiveness through physical inspection. Furthermore, evidence obtained from outside independent sources is considered more objective than evidence provided solely by the client.

In contrast, evidence in support of management's estimates of inventory obsolescence and product warranties may be largely subjective. In such case, the auditor should (1) consider the qualifications and integrity of the individual making the estimate and (2) assess the appropriateness of the decision-making processes followed by the client in making the judgments.

Figure 4-2 summarizes the effects of these considerations on the competency of evidential matter.

Reasonable Basis

The auditor is not expected, or required, by the third standard of field work to have an absolute, certain, or guaranteed basis for an opinion. The require-

[2]Auditing Standards Board, *op. cit.,* AU § 326.19.

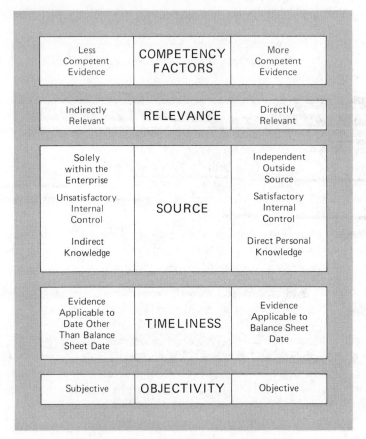

Figure 4-2. COMPETENCY OF EVIDENTIAL MATTER.

ment of a reasonable basis pertains to the overall level of assurance the auditor needs at the conclusion of the audit to express an opinion on the financial statements.

In executing an audit program, the auditor may quantify statistically the levels of assurance for the individual items in the statements, as is explained in Chapter 12. It is not possible, however, to combine statistically the individual levels of assurance into an objective evaluation of the overall reasonableness of the financial statements taken as a whole. The auditor's judgments concerning reasonableness are influenced by the following factors:

Professional Considerations.   Professional considerations contribute to a fairly uniform application of the quality and amount of evidence that is required. Statements on Auditing Standards (SASs) contain specific objectives to be attained during the course of an examination and provide guidance about specific ways to achieve them. Auditors are required to justify any departure from these statements.

In the practice of public accounting, there are also two counterbalancing forces. On the one hand, competition among firms tends to make the individual firm cost- and fee-conscious. Accordingly, the firm is restrained from obtaining an inordinately high degree of assurance in a specific engagement since other firms may be able to perform the audit at less cost. On the other hand, the auditing firm is well aware that an inadequate basis for an opinion may result in lawsuits by those harmed by reliance on the auditor's report and sanctions by peer review committees.

Integrity of Management. Management is responsible for the financial statement assertions, and it is also in a position to control much of the corroborating evidence and underlying accounting data supporting the statements. Accordingly, an auditor will clearly require more competent evidence when there is doubt about the integrity of management.

Related Party Transactions. Related party transactions are transactions for which one of the participants is in a position to significantly influence the other participant to the extent that "arm's length" bargaining of terms and conditions is not possible. Such transactions include those between a parent company and its subsidiaries, and between a company and its management or principal stockholders. Related party transactions may be motivated by a desire to obscure financial or other business problems that would otherwise manifest themselves in the financial statements. Hence, the auditor will ordinarily require more competent evidence for related party transactions than for transactions between unrelated parties. Further consideration is given to related party transactions in Chapter 16.

Public Versus Private Ownership. Auditors generally believe that a higher overall level of assurance is needed for publicly held companies than for closely held companies. Not only are there more users of the auditor's report in large corporations, but these users may rely primarily on audited statements in making investment decisions.

Financial Condition. The threat of bankruptcy tends to raise the auditor's subjective evaluation of reasonable basis. In bankruptcy proceedings, creditors often seek financial relief by suing the auditors on the premise that the audited statements did not adequately forewarn them of their impending disaster. In such case, the auditor must be in a position to defend his opinion and the quality of his work.

TYPES OF CORROBORATING INFORMATION

The principal types of corroborating information are

- Physical evidence.
- Confirmations.

- Documentary evidence.
- Written representations.
- Mathematical evidence.
- Visual evidence.
- Oral evidence.
- Analytical evidence.

Each type of evidence is discussed separately below, together with the circumstances in which each is most relevant. As will be seen, the types of evidence are not mutually exclusive.

Physical Evidence

This form of evidence is widely used by the auditor in the verification of tangible asset balances. Physical evidence is obtained from physical examination of the resources. This type of evidence provides the auditor with direct personal knowledge of the existence of an item. Such evidence, however, does not establish the ownership, cost, or market value of the asset. Physical evidence will be helpful in determining quality (or condition) if the auditor is capable of making that determination. The representation of an outside expert on precious gems in a jewelry store audit would ordinarily be considered more reliable in evaluating quality than the auditor's direct personal knowledge.

Confirmations

Confirmations are a distinctive type of documentary evidence. They generally represent direct written responses by knowledgeable third parties to specific requests for financial information. When confirmations are obtained directly by the auditor, from third parties, they are generally considered to have a very high degree of reliability. Confirmations are especially useful in verifying the existence and accuracy of an account balance. It is common practice in an audit engagement to make extensive use of this form of evidence. The following are illustrative of the items that are frequently confirmed:

Item	Knowledgeable Respondent
Cash in bank	Bank
Accounts receivable	Individual customers
Inventory stored in public warehouse	Warehouse custodian
Bonds payable	Bond trustee
Lease terms	Lessor
Shares of common stock outstanding	Registrar

Documentary Evidence

This type of corroborating information includes checks, invoices, contracts, and minutes of meetings. Ordinarily, such documentation is contained in the client's files and is available to the auditor on request. The reliability of a document depends on the manner in which the document is created, how it is obtained by the auditor, and the nature of the document itself. Generalizations concerning the first two factors have already been indicated in the discussion of the competency of evidential matter.

Documentary evidence may be created outside the client organization or within it. Externally created documents may be sent directly to the auditor by the third party, or such documentation may be held by the client. The former are generally given a higher degree of reliability since the client does not have an opportunity to alter the documents.

Examples of third-party documentation that may be obtained directly by an auditor include bank statements and statements of escrow account balances held by banks. These documents will not become directly available to the auditor as a matter of course. They will be sent to the client, unless by prearrangement, the client requests the preparer to send the document directly to the auditor. Third-party documents held by the client include customer purchase orders, suppliers' invoices, and tax bills.

The reliability of internally created documents depends on several factors. First is the distribution or circulation of the documents. Documents originated by the client that circulate outside the client organization are considered more reliable than documents that remain entirely within the company. The former include canceled checks and receipted bank deposit slips. The latter include time tickets, material requisition slips, and copies of sales invoices. Second is the quality of the system of internal control from which the documents are generated. The effects of circulation of documents on the reliability of documentary evidence are graphically illustrated in Figure 4–3.

The nature of the document is also important in appraising the probable existence of error or irregularity in the evidence. The amount on a manually prepared check, for example, is more easily altered than an amount that has been indelibly imprinted by a check-writing machine. Similarly, there is greater opportunity for a dishonest employee to create fictitious checks when blank check forms are used than when prenumbered company checks are required.

Documentary evidence is extensively used in auditing. The auditor relies on documentation to establish the occurrence, terms, and propriety of exchange transactions, the ownership of assets, the claims of creditors, and the accuracy and completeness of the accounting records. Documentary evidence also plays a vital role in the auditor's study and evaluation of internal control, as is explained in Chapter 5.

Written Representations

A written representation is a signed statement by responsible and knowledgeable individuals about a particular account, circumstance, or event. Written representations are a form of documentary evidence. Such evidential matter may originate from within the client's organization or external sources.

The auditor is required by GAAS to obtain certain written representations

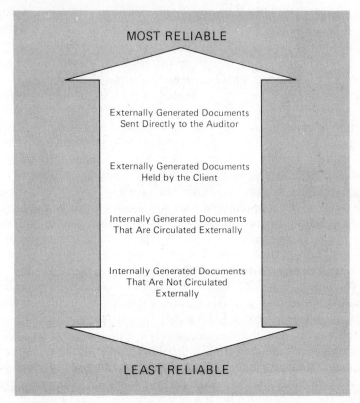

MOST RELIABLE

Externally Generated Documents
Sent Directly to the Auditor

Externally Generated Documents
Held by the Client

Internally Generated Documents
That Are Circulated Externally

Internally Generated Documents
That Are Not Circulated
Externally

LEAST RELIABLE

Figure 4-3. EFFECTS OF CIRCULATION ON RELIABILITY OF DOCUMENTARY EVIDENCE.

from management in meeting the third standard of field work.[3] Such representations are designed to document management's replies to inquiries made by the auditor during the audit engagement. Management representations, commonly presented in the form of a *rep letter,* may reveal information not shown in the accounting records such as the existence of contingencies that may require further investigation.

The reliability of a rep letter depends on the auditor's ability to corroborate the representations by other evidence. A rep letter is usually obtained near the end of the examination. An example of a rep letter is presented in Chapter 16 under the discussion of "Completing the Audit."

During the course of an audit, the auditor may also request written representations from outside experts. The independent auditor is not expected to possess the expertise of a lawyer in evaluating litigation pending against the client, a geologist in estimating the quantity of ore in a mine, or an appraiser in valuing a fine arts collection. When such evidence is needed, the auditor may use the work of a specialist to obtain competent evidential matter.[4] The

[3]Auditing Standards Board, *op. cit.,* AU § 333.01.
[4]Auditing Standards Board, *op. cit.,* AU § 336.04.

response may be received in the form of a letter, report, or other written communication. A relatively high degree of reliance may be placed on this type of documentation, especially when the response validates preliminary conclusions already formed by the auditor.

Mathematical Evidence

This type of evidence results from the auditor's computations or recomputations. Computations usually provide reliable evidence as to the accuracy of an amount determined by the client. This type of mathematical evidence may result from such routine tasks as checking the footings (totals) of journals and ledgers or from complicated calculations pertaining to pension plans and earnings-per-share data. Mathematical evidence provides the auditor with direct personal knowledge of the arithmetical accuracy of an amount.

Visual Evidence

During the course of an examination, the auditor makes many observations. For example, he witnesses the performance of assigned responsibility and observes the security in a storeroom. This type of evidence enables the auditor to acquire direct personal knowledge concerning the matter at issue. The reliability of this evidence is limited only by the auditor's perception of what he observes.

Oral Evidence

During an examination, an auditor will make frequent oral inquiries of officers and employees of the client. Oral evidence is rarely reliable by itself. Its primary value to the auditor lies in corroborating other evidential matter and disclosing matters that may merit further investigation and documentation. Oral evidence may cover a broad range of topics such as an interpretation of a board of directors' resolution, an explanation of the accounting treatment of a merger, and an evaluation of the collectibility of a customer's account. When an auditor uses oral evidence, it should be noted in the audit working papers. The auditor may ask management to confirm some oral data in its rep letter.

Analytical Evidence

This type of evidence involves the use of ratios and comparisons of client data with industry trends, general economic conditions, and prior and/or expected company results. Analytical evidence provides a basis for supporting an inference on the fairness of a specific financial statement item or relationship. The reliability of analytical evidence is largely dependent on the relevance of the comparable data. When industry trends and similar data provide a valid basis for comparison, the reliability of this type of evidence is enhanced.

OBTAINING AND EVALUATING AUDIT EVIDENCE

SUBSTANTIVE TESTS

The evidential matter required by the third standard of field work is obtained through two general classes of auditing procedures: (1) tests of details of transactions and balances and (2) analytical review procedures applied to financial information.[5] Collectively, these procedures are called *substantive tests.* The nature and purpose of these tests are explained below.

Tests of Details of Transactions and Balances

These procedures are designed to obtain evidence on the validity and propriety of the accounting treatment of transactions and balances. Conversely, their purpose is to determine the existence of any monetary errors or irregularities therein. A substantive test of the details of a transaction occurs when a sales invoice is traced by the auditor to the accounting records to determine whether any monetary errors have occurred in journalizing and posting. Substantive tests of transactions may be performed during the year under audit or at or near the balance sheet date.

A substantive test of the details of an account balance occurs when the auditor counts cash on hand to determine whether the amount of cash agrees with the recorded balance. Substantive tests of balances are generally performed at or near the balance sheet date.

Analytical Review Procedures

Analytical review procedures involve a study and comparison of relationships among data. These procedures may be used in (1) audit planning as explained in Chapter 3, (2) during the examination to obtain corroborating information about an account, and (3) at or near the end of the examination as an overall review.

Analytical evidence is provided by these procedures. When the comparative data confirm the reasonableness of the relationships, the auditor has obtained additional corroborating information about an account balance. When the reverse is true, the auditor ordinarily will require additional evidential matter in meeting the third standard of field work.

PROCEDURES FOR TESTS OF DETAILS OF TRANSACTIONS AND BALANCES

In making an examination in accordance with GAAS, the auditor is required to use the auditing procedures necessary in the circumstances. Auditing procedures are the acts performed by the auditor to obtain corroborating infor-

---

[5]Auditing Standards Board, *op. cit.,* AU § 320.79.

mation. The procedures themselves are not evidence. The most widely used procedures in performing tests of transactions and balances are

- Inspecting.
- Observing.
- Confirming.
- Inquiring.
- Retracing.
- Recalculating.
- Vouching.
- Counting.
- Scanning.

Each procedure is discussed below. In the discussion, consideration will also be given to the types of circumstances to which each procedure is applicable.

Inspecting

Inspecting involves careful scrutiny or detailed examination of documents and physical resources. This procedure is used extensively in auditing. The inspecting of documents enables the auditor to assess the authenticity of the evidential matter or, conversely, the existence of alterations or questionable items. Examination of documents also permits a determination of the precise terms of invoices, contracts and agreements. Through the inspection of physical resources, the auditor obtains direct personal knowledge of their existence and physical condition.

In using this procedure, the auditor seeks reasonable assurance that the document or tangible resource supports management's representations. However, the auditor is not expected to be an expert in determining the authenticity of endorsements on checks or a specialist in determining the quality of highly technical inventory components.

Inspecting documents provides a means for evaluating documentary evidence, whereas the inspection of tangible assets provides a means for evaluating physical evidence. Audit program instructions such as reviewing, reading, and examining are synonymous with inspecting.

Observing

This auditing procedure pertains to watching or witnessing the performance of some activity. The activity may be the manner in which cash is safeguarded, vouchers are prepared and approved, and the care taken by the client in counting inventory. The subject matter of observation is personnel, procedures, and processes. From this observation, the auditor obtains direct personal knowledge of the activity in the form of visual evidence.

Confirming

Confirming is a form of inquiry that enables the auditor to obtain information directly from an independent source outside the client organization. In the usual case, the client makes the request of the outside party in writing, but the auditor controls the mailing of the inquiry. The request should include instructions requiring the recipient to send the response directly to the auditor. This auditing procedure produces confirmation evidence. It is extensively used in performing tests of account balances, and it may also be used in tests of transactions.

Inquiring

This auditing procedure involves either oral or written inquiry by the auditor. Such inquiries may be made internally to management, as in the case of questions pertaining to the obsolescence of inventory items and the collectibility of receivables, or externally to lawyers concerning the probable outcome of litigation, and other specialists. Inquiry produces either oral evidence or evidence in the form of written representations.

Retracing

In retracing, the auditor begins with the document(s) created when the transaction is executed and follows the evidence through the accounting process. Thus, the auditor can trace a sales transaction from the receipt of the customer's order through filling and shipping the order, billing the customer, journalizing and posting the sale, and summarizing and presenting the transaction in the financial statements. This auditing procedure is extensively used in performing tests of transactions, and it is also applicable to tests of account balances. Retracing is a useful procedure for detecting understatement since it provides a basis for determining the completeness of the accounting records. The effectiveness of this procedure is enhanced when serially prenumbered documents are used by the client. Retracing pertains primarily to documentary evidence.

Recalculating

This procedure involves a reperformance of calculations and reconciliations made by the client. Recalculations may be made of amounts computed for depreciation, accrued interest, and unit price extensions on inventory summary sheets. In addition, the auditor will ordinarily verify the accuracy of totals on supporting schedules and reconciliations. Mathematical evidence is produced by this procedure.

Vouching

This procedure involves (1) inspecting documents in support of transactions or financial data to determine their propriety and validity and (2) comparing the documents with the accounting records. In vouching, the auditor works from the accounting records back to the documentation that served as the basis for the entry. Notice that the direction of testing is opposite to that used in retracing. Vouching is a primary means of detecting overstatements in account balances.

Counting

The two most common applications of this procedure are (1) the physical counting of tangible resources such as the amount of cash on hand and (2) accounting for all prenumbered documents. The first provides physical evidence of the quantity on hand and is used in tests of balances. The second may be used by the auditor to obtain evidence on the completeness of the accounting records.

Scanning

The auditing procedure of scanning involves a less detailed level of scrutiny than inspection. Scanning may be described as the rapid review or *eye-balling* of documents, records, and schedules for the purpose of detecting unusual items or events that may require further investigation. For instance, an audit program may require the auditor to scan (1) the June voucher register for unusual account classifications and (2) additions to repairs expense for large expenditures.

RELATIONSHIP OF AUDIT EVIDENCE AND AUDITING PROCEDURES

During the course of an audit, the auditor will likely use each of the auditing procedures described above to obtain sufficient competent evidential matter. The relationship between the types of evidential matter and auditing procedures is summarized in Figure 4-4. Further consideration is given to these relationships in Part III of this text.

EVALUATION OF EVIDENTIAL MATTER

The auditor should be objective, careful, and thorough in his evaluation of evidential matter. Proper evaluation of the evidence is essential to the preparation of a correct audit report. All relevant evidential matter should be considered by the auditor, regardless of whether it substantiates or negates management's financial statement assertions.

In evaluating evidence, the auditor considers whether specific audit objectives have been achieved. Some audit objectives relate to matters of fact, such as the determination of the amount of cash in a bank account and the face value of bonds payable outstanding at the balance sheet date. However, many audit objectives pertain to matters of judgment such as the determination of the adequacy of the allowance for bad debts and the proper statement presentation of a contingency.

Type of Evidence	Auditing Procedure	Illustrative Application of Auditing Procedure
Physical	Inspecting Counting	Inspect new warehouse. Count cash on hand.
Confirmations	Confirming	Confirm bank balance with bank.
Documentary	Inspecting Retracing Vouching	Inspect (examine) bank statement. Trace sales invoices to customers' ledger. Vouch entries in check register to paid checks.
Written representations	Inquiring	Ask management for representation letter.
Mathematical	Recalculating	Recompute accrued interest payable.
Visual	Observing Scanning	Observe storeroom security. Scan repairs expense for large expenditures.
Oral	Inquiring	Ask storeroom supervisor about obsolete inventory items.
Analytical	Analytical review	Compare sales with sales budget.

Figure 4-4. AUDIT EVIDENCE AND AUDITING PROCEDURES.

The auditor should exercise care in interpreting the evidence that has been obtained. One concern is making an unwarranted conclusion. For example, it is not correct to conclude from a physical inspection of a plant asset that it is owned by the client. Similarly, it is incorrect to infer that a delivery truck exists from an examination of a purchase invoice for the vehicle. The auditor must also be prudent in interpreting analytical evidence. Changed company circumstances and unforeseen industry developments may negate relationships that previously were assumed to be reasonable.

The auditor should also recognize that relatively little evidential matter is absolutely conclusive. Because of economic constraints pertaining to the cost of obtaining evidence and the nature of financial statement assertions, it is usually unrealistic for the auditor to seek proof beyond all doubt. On the other hand, an auditor should not be satisfied with inconclusive or contradictory evidence. To have a reasonable basis for expressing an opinion, the auditor needs a preponderance (i.e., a consensus or majority) of persuasive evidence about each financial statement assertion that is material.

EFFECTS ON AUDITOR'S REPORT

When the auditor has obtained sufficient competent evidential matter as required by the third standard of field work, he must express the opinion appropriate to the circumstances. However, when the auditor is unable to obtain a reasonable basis for an opinion on a material financial statement assertion, an opinion should be deferred until the necessary evidence is acquired, or a qualified opinion or disclaimer of opinion should be expressed on the financial statements. The process of meeting the third standard of field

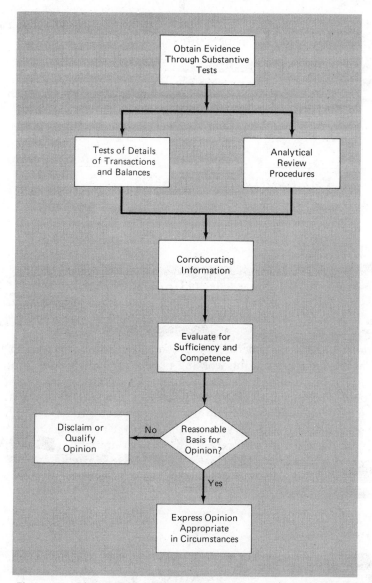

Figure 4-5. OBTAINING AND EVALUATING EVIDENTIAL MATTER.

work and determining the effects on the auditor's report is summarized in Figure 4-5.

WORKING PAPERS

NATURE AND PURPOSE OF WORKING PAPERS

The auditor should prepare and maintain working papers. Working papers are the records kept by the auditor of the procedures applied, the tests performed, the information obtained, and the pertinent conclusions reached in the engagement.[6] Working papers provide

- The principal support for the auditor's report.
- Evidence that the examination was made in accordance with GAAS.
- A means for coordinating and supervising the examination.

Working papers should be tailored to meet the needs of the specific engagement.

WORKING PAPERS AND AUDITING STANDARDS

Working papers have direct application to GAAS, as explained below.

General Standards

Working papers provide evidence of the auditor's technical training and proficiency by showing his knowledge of GAAP and his ability to apply auditing procedures applicable in the circumstances. Similarly, the conclusions reached by the auditor, as set forth in the working papers, help demonstrate the objectivity or independence of the auditor in his examination.

Working papers are especially important in meeting the standard of due care. The completeness of the working papers provides evidence of the care exercised by the auditor during his examination, and the content of the working papers reveals the scope of the work. On completion of the audit, the working papers should not contain any unresolved questions (other than those whose resolution depends on some future event). Unresolved questions could suggest the absence of due care during the examination. Working papers should provide evidence that each step of the audit program has been performed or an explanation of why a specified procedure was omitted and alternative methods employed.

Field Work Standards

A major use of working papers during the audit is in the coordination and control of the work by the manager and/or partner in charge of the engagement. Working papers also facilitate the review, at every level of supervision, of the work done. Accordingly, working papers are important in meeting the first standard of field work.

Working papers are indispensable in meeting the second and third standards of field work. As is explained in Chapter 5, the auditor's study and evaluation of internal control should be clearly documented in the working papers. As suggested in this chapter, working papers provide the means for documenting the evidential matter obtained during the examination.

---

[6]Auditing Standards Board, *op. cit.*, AU § 339.03.

Reporting Standards

Working papers not only facilitate the preparation of the auditor's report, but represent the primary support for the auditor's opinion. The working papers should contain evidence pertaining to the conformity of the financial statements with GAAP consistently applied.

TYPES OF WORKING PAPERS

There are many varieties and types of working papers an auditor accumulates during an examination. In most situations, working papers are classified into the following groupings: (1) audit plans and audit programs, (2) working trial balance, (3) schedules and analyses, (4) audit memoranda and documentation of corroborating information, and (5) adjusting and reclassifying entries. The nature of the items to be included in the first category is explained in Chapter 3. The other groupings are explained below.

Working Trial Balance

A partial working trial balance is illustrated in Figure 4-6. It will be noted that columns are provided for several types of balances including the client's ledger balance and final balances at both the end of the prior year and the current year. There also are columns for adjustments and reclassifications. The accounts listed in the working trial balance represent either individual accounts such as Marketable Securities and Inventories or groups of accounts such as Cash and Receivables.

The working trial balance may be prepared by the client or the auditor. When the former occurs, the auditor verifies the trial balance by footing the columns and tracing the account balances to the general ledger. A working trial balance is of paramount importance during the conduct of the audit. It provides a basis for controlling all of the individual working papers and summarizing the data obtained during the course of the engagement. In addition, it is the connecting link between the general ledger and the financial statements.

Schedules and Analyses

In many audits, the terms *schedules* and *analyses* are used interchangeably. However, for purposes of illustration and explanation, it is possible to distinguish between the two types of working papers.

A schedule shows the composition of individual accounts and groups of accounts at a given point in time. A schedule of the marketable securities shows the specific types of securities that comprise the account balance at the statement date. In contrast, group schedules, also identified as *lead* or *summary schedules*, summarize the working paper data pertaining to a given type of statement item such as cash, receivables, and so on. A lead schedule for cash

OMNI, INC.
WORKING TRIAL BALANCE - BALANCE SHEET
DECEMBER 31, 19X1

PREPARED BY: *QBC* DATE 2/10/X2
REVIEWED BY: *ACE* DATE 2/15/X2

W/P REF	ACCT. NO.	DESCRIPTION	FINAL BALANCE 12/31/X0	LEDGER BALANCE 12/31/X1	ADJUSTMENTS AJE REF	DEBIT (CREDIT)	ADJUSTED BALANCE 12/31/X1	RECLASSIFICATIONS RJE REF	DEBIT (CREDIT)	FINAL BALANCE 12/31/X1
		ASSETS								
		CURRENT								
A		CASH	392,000	427,000	(1)	50,000	477,000			477,000
B	150	MARKETABLE SECURITIES	52,200	62,200			62,200			62,200
C		RECEIVABLES (NET)	1,601,400	1,715,000	(1)	(50,000)	1,665,000	(A)	10,000	1,675,000
D	170	INVENTORIES	2,542,500	2,810,200	(2)	133,000	2,943,200			2,943,200
E		PREPAID EXPENSES	24,900	19,500			19,500			19,500
		TOTAL CURRENT	4,613,000	5,033,900		133,000	5,166,900		10,000	5,176,900
F	240	LONG-TERM INVESTMENTS		190,000			190,000			190,000
G		PROPERTY, PLANT & EQUIPMENT (NET)	3,146,500	3,310,900			3,310,900			3,310,900
		TOTAL	7,759,500	8,534,800		133,000	8,667,800		10,000	8,677,800
		LIABILITIES AND STOCKHOLDERS' EQUITY								
		CURRENT LIABILITIES								
M	400	NOTES PAYABLE	750,000	825,000			825,000			825,000
N	410	ACCOUNTS PAYABLE	2,150,400	2,340,300	(2)	(133,000)	2,473,300	(A)	(10,000)	2,483,300
O	420	ACCRUED PAYABLES	210,600	189,000			189,000			189,000
P	430	INCOME TAXES PAYABLE	150,000	170,000			170,000			170,000
		TOTAL CURRENT	3,261,000	3,524,300		(133,000)	3,657,300		(10,000)	3,667,300
R	500	BONDS PAYABLE	1,000,000	1,200,000			1,200,000			1,200,000
S	600	COMMON STOCK	2,400,000	2,400,000			2,400,000			2,400,000
T	700	RETAINED EARNINGS	1,098,500	1,410,500			1,410,500			1,410,500
		TOTAL	7,759,500	8,534,800		(133,000)	8,667,800		(10,000)	8,677,800

Figure 4-6. PARTIAL WORKING TRIAL BALANCE WORKING PAPER.

is illustrated in Figure 4-7. Such schedules are common in audits of large companies. Group schedules serve as an intermediate summary before the data are transferred to the working trial balance.

An analysis of a ledger account shows all the changes in the account during the period covered by the financial statements. Account analyses may be made for any balance sheet or income statement account. In many instances, a single analysis may pertain to more than one account. For example, the analysis of

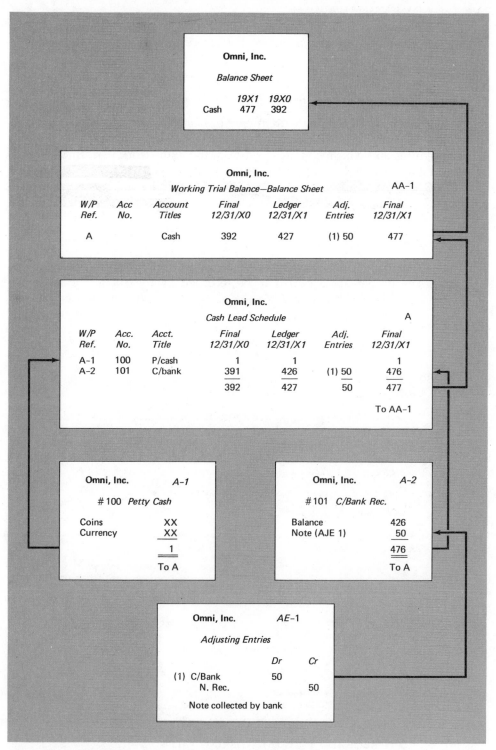

Figure 4-7. INTEGRATED WORKING PAPERS FOR CASH.

notes receivable may also include interest receivable and interest earned, as illustrated in Figure 4-8.

Audit Memoranda and Corroborating Information

Audit memoranda refer to written data prepared by the auditor in narrative form. Memoranda may include comments on the performance of auditing procedures and conclusions reached from the audit work performed. Documentation of corroborating information includes (1) extracts of minutes of board of director meetings, (2) confirmation responses, (3) written representations from management and outsiders, and (4) copies of important contracts.

Adjusting and Reclassifying Entries

It is important to distinguish between adjusting entries and reclassifying entries. The former are expected to be recorded by the client; the latter are intended solely for the auditor's working papers. Adjusting entries are corrections of client errors of omission or commission or corrections resulting

OMNI, INC.
NOTES RECEIVABLE AND INTEREST
DECEMBER 31, 19X1

W/P REF: *C-4*
PREPARED BY: *Q.C.E.* DATE *1/20/X2*
REVIEWED BY: *P.A.R* DATE *2/4/X2*

ACCTS. 160, 161, 450

MAKER	DATE MADE	DUE	INTEREST RATE	FACE AMOUNT	NOTES RECEIVABLE BALANCE 12/31/X0	DEBITS	CREDITS	BALANCE 12/31/X1	INTEREST ACCRUED 12/31/X0	EARNED 19X1	COLLECTED 19X1	ACCRUED 12/31/X1
COFFMAN, INC.	7/1/X0	6/30/X1	10%	25,000	25,000 x		25,000 c	–	1,250 x	1,250 φ	2,500 C	–
MORRISON BROS.	11/1/X0	10/31/X1	10%	30,000	30,000 x		30,000 c	–	500 x	2,500 φ	3,000 C	–
SHIRLEY AND SON	4/1/X1	3/31/X2	12%	40,000 v	–	40,000		40,000 n	–	3,600 φ	–	3,600
WARNER CORPORATION	10/1/X1	9/30/X2	12%	20,000 v	–	20,000		20,000 n	–	600 φ	–	600
					55,000 x	60,000	55,000	60,000 ∧	1,750 x	7,950	5,500	4,200 ∧
					F	F	F	FF To C	F	F	F	FF To C

x Agreed to 12/31/X0 working papers
n Confirmed with maker - no exceptions
v Examined note during cash count
F Footed
FF Footed and Crossfooted
∧ Traced to ledger balance
C Traced collections to cash receipts and deposit slips
φ Verified computations

Figure 4-8. NOTES RECEIVABLE AND INTEREST WORKING PAPER

from misunderstandings or misinterpretations of GAAP. In contrast, reclassifying entries pertain to the proper financial statement presentation of a correct account balance.

To determine the reclassifying entry that is required, the auditor must ascertain the composition of the account balance. Accordingly, if the balance of Bonds Payable includes some bonds due next year, those bonds should be reported as a current liability. The reclassification entry is (Dr) Bonds Payable and (Cr) Current Maturities of Bonds Payable. For another illustration, assume that the balance in Accounts Receivable includes some credit balances pertaining to customer advances. The reclassifying entry is (Dr) Accounts Receivable and (Cr) Customers' Advances, a liability account.

Adjusting and reclassifying entries, with accompanying explanations, should be summarized on separate lists in the working papers. The list of adjusting entries is usually labeled "proposed adjusting entries," since there frequently is a considerable amount of discussion and negotiation between the client and the auditor regarding proposed adjustments. The auditor should explain the entries to the client, when necessary, but not make the entries. To do so would technically make the auditor a company accountant rather than an independent auditor.

Both adjusting and reclassifying entries should pertain only to items that individually or collectively are material to the financial statements. In the working papers, each entry should be shown on (1) the schedule or analysis of the account, (2) the working trial balance, (3) the summary of adjusting or reclassifying entries, and (4) the lead schedules, if any, as summarized in Figure 4-7. To facilitate identification, adjusting entries may be numbered and reclassifying entries may be lettered.

PREPARING WORKING PAPERS

There are a number of basic techniques that are widely used in preparing a working paper. These pertain to the mechanics of working paper preparation and include the following essential points:

Heading.   Each working paper contains the name of the client, a descriptive title identifying the content of the working paper, such as *Bank Reconciliation— City National Bank,* and the balance sheet date or the period covered by the audit.

Index Numbers.   Each working paper is given an index number, such as A–1, B–2, and so forth, for identification purposes. In addition, there is *cross- referencing* of data both to and from other working papers to facilitate the flow of information.

Tick Marks.   Tick marks are symbols used by an auditor that provide a reference to a narrative explanation elsewhere in the working paper. The symbols are, in essence, the auditor's shorthand. Each tick mark or symbol must be accompanied by an explanation of the nature and extent of the work done.

Signature and Dates. Both the preparer and reviewer should initial and date the working paper. The signatures establish responsibility for the work and the review.

Each of the basic techniques is illustrated in Figure 4-8.

AUTOMATED WORKING PAPERS

Many public accounting firms are beginning to use software developed for microcomputers to produce automated working papers. These packages provide for the automatic generation of integrated working papers while sharply limiting data entry requirements. Data entered on related working papers generally need be entered only once. Thus, data entered on a lead schedule can automatically be carried forward to the working trial balance, and data entered on adjusting and reclassifying journal entry working papers can automatically be posted to the relevant lead schedules and working trial balance. In addition, all line and column totals are calculated by the software, saving the auditor considerable time that would otherwise be spent footing and crossfooting. Further, once the working trial balance and related schedules have been created for a client, final balances can be automatically rolled forward for the next year's engagement.

The working trial balance in Figure 4-6 is an example of a microcomputer-generated automated working paper. Other illustrations will be provided in subsequent chapters. Automated working paper software also offers efficiencies in the preparation of consolidated financial statements and in reclassifying amounts for tax returns.

REVIEWING WORKING PAPERS

There are several levels in the review of working papers within a CPA firm. The first-level review is made by the preparer's supervisor, such as a senior or manager. This review occurs when the work on a specific segment of the audit has been completed. The reviewer is primarily interested in the work done, the evidence obtained, the judgment exercised, and the conclusions reached by the preparer of the working paper.

Other reviews are made of the working papers when all of the field work has been completed. These reviews are explained in Chapter 16 under "Completing the Audit."

WORKING PAPER FILES

Working papers are generally filed under two categories: (1) a permanent file and (2) a current file. The *permanent file* contains data that are expected to be useful to the auditor on many future engagements with the client. In contrast, the *current file* contains corroborating information pertaining to the execution of the current year's audit program.

Items typically found in the permanent file are

- Copies of the articles of incorporation and bylaws.
- Chart of accounts and procedure manuals.
- Organization charts.
- Plant layout, manufacturing processes, and principal products.
- Terms of capital stock and bond issues.
- Copies of long-term contracts, such as leases, pension plans, and profit-sharing and bonus agreements.
- Summary of accounting principles used by the client.

OWNERSHIP AND CUSTODY OF WORKING PAPERS

Working papers belong to the auditor. The auditor's ownership rights, however, are subject to constraints imposed by the auditor's own profession. The AICPA's Code of Professional Ethics stipulates that a CPA shall not disclose any confidential information obtained during the course of a professional engagement, except with the consent of the client.

Custody of the working papers rests with the auditor, and he is responsibile for their safekeeping. Working papers included in the permanent file are retained indefinitely. Current working papers should be retained for as long as they are useful to the auditor in servicing his client or are needed to satisfy legal requirements for record retention. The statute of limitations rarely extends beyond six years.

CONCLUDING COMMENTS

Sufficient competent evidential matter cannot be measured in terms of audit hours worked or the number of working papers accumulated during the engagement. This determination requires the exercise of audit judgment. Every auditor, new or experienced, must make this evaluation for each segment of the audit to which he has been assigned. This responsibility begins on the first assignment of the first audit and continues in every engagement. The beginning auditor is well advised to work diligently and continuously on this important responsibility. The judgment exercised by an auditor must be documented. Working papers may prove to be a friend or foe of the auditor. Good working papers contribute to advancement within the firm and strengthen an auditor's defense in a lawsuit. Poor working papers produce contrary results.

REVIEW QUESTIONS

4-1 Identify the two categories of evidential matter and indicate their relative importance to the third standard of field work.

4-2 What is the relationship of audit evidence to audit objectives and to the expression of an opinion on the financial statements?

4-3 State the purpose of the third standard of field work.

4-4 What factors are relevant in determining the sufficiency of corroborating information?

4-5 What factors affect the competency of corroborating information?

4-6 Identify the sources of evidential matter and rank them as to competency.

4-7 Identify the three presumptions concerning the competency of evidential matter.

4-8 a. An auditor is expected to have an absolute basis for the expression of an opinion. Do you agree? Why or why not?
b. What types of considerations are relevant concerning the basis for the auditor's opinion?

4-9 Identify the types of corroborating information that can be obtained by the auditor during an examination.

4-10 a. What are the objectives of a management representation letter?
b. Indicate the relationship of this form of evidence to generally accepted auditing standards.

4-11 What factors affect the reliability of documentary evidence?

4-12 Identify the two general classes of auditing procedures that are applicable to the third standard of field work and indicate the primary purpose(s) of each.

4-13 a. When may analytical review procedures be used?
b. What effects may analytical evidence have on the auditors examination?

4-14 Identify the types of procedures that may be performed in making tests of details of transactions and balances.

4-15 a. What approach should the auditor take in evaluating evidence?
b. What constraints should be exercised in the evaluating process?

4-16 What effects will the failure to meet the third standard of field work have on the auditor and the auditor's standard report.

4-17 a. Define the term *working papers* and indicate their principal functions in auditing.
b. Enumerate the principal types of working papers.

4-18 Distinguish between (a) schedules and analyses and (b) adjusting and reclassifying entries.

4-19 Indicate the nature of the permanent working paper file and identify four types of data that would ordinarily be included in such a file.

4-20 Who owns and who should maintain custody of working papers?

OBJECTIVE QUESTIONS FROM PROFESSIONAL EXAMINATIONS

Indicate the *best* answer choice for each of the following multiple choice questions.

4-21 These questions relate to evidential matter.

1. The most reliable type of documentary audit evidence that an auditor can obtain is
   a. Physical examination by the auditor.
   b. Documentary evidence calculated by the auditor from company records.
   c. Confirmations received directly from third parties.
   d. Internal documents.
2. Which of the following statements relating to the competence of evidential matter is always true?
   a. Evidential matter gathered by an auditor from outside an enterprise is reliable.
   b. Accounting data developed under satisfactory conditions of internal control are more relevant than data developed under unsatisfactory internal control conditions.
   c. Oral representations made by management are not valid evidence.
   d. Evidence gathered by auditors must be both valid and relevant to be considered competent.
3. Audit evidence can come in different forms with different degrees of persuasiveness. Which of the following is the least persuasive type of evidence?
   a. Documents mailed by outsiders to the auditor.
   b. Correspondence between auditor and vendors.
   c. Sales invoices inspected by the auditor.
   d. Computations made by the auditor.

4-22 These questions pertain to audit procedures.

1. In the context of an audit of financial statements, substantive tests are audit procedures that
   a. May be eliminated under certain conditions.
   b. Are designed to discover significant subsequent events.
   c. May be either tests of transactions, direct tests of financial balances, or analytical tests.
   d. Will increase proportionately with the auditor's reliance on internal control.
2. Analytical review procedures are
   a. Substantive tests designed to evaluate a system of internal control.
   b. Compliance tests designed to evaluate the validity of management's representation letter.
   c. Substantive tests designed to evaluate the reasonableness of financial information.
   d. Compliance tests designed to evaluate the reasonableness of financial information.
3. Which of the following ultimately determines the specific audit procedures necessary to provide an independent auditor with a reasonable basis for the expression of an opinion?
   a. The audit program.
   b. The auditor's judgment.
   c. Generally accepted auditing standards.
   d. The auditor's working papers.

4-23 These questions apply to working papers.

1. Which of the following is *not* a primary purpose of working papers?
   a. To coordinate the examination.
   b. To assist in preparation of the audit report.

      c. To support the financial statements.

      d. To provide evidence of the audit work performed.

2. Which of the following is *not* a factor that affects the independent auditor's judgment as to the quantity, type, and content of working papers?

      a. The timing and the number of personnel to be assigned to the engagement.

      b. The nature of the financial statements, schedules, or other information on which the auditor is reporting.

      c. The need for supervision of the engagement.

      d. The nature of the auditor's report.

3. Which of the following eliminates voluminous details from the auditor's working trial balance by classifying and summarizing similar or related items?

      a. Account analyses.

      b. Supporting schedules.

      c. Control accounts.

      d. Lead schedules.

COMPREHENSIVE QUESTIONS

4-24 The third GAAS of field work requires that the auditor obtain sufficient competent evidential matter to afford a reasonable basis for an opinion regarding the financial statements under examination. In considering what constitutes sufficient competent evidential matter, a distinction should be made between underlying accounting data and all corroborating information available to the auditor.

Required

a. Discuss the nature of evidential matter to be considered by the auditor in terms of the underlying accounting data, all corroborating information available to the auditor, and the methods by which the auditor tests or gathers competent evidential matter.

b. State the presumptions that can be made about the validity of the evidential matter with respect to (1) corroborating information and (2) underlying accounting data.

AICPA (adapted)

4-25 In this examination of financial statements, the CPA is concerned with the examination and accumulation of audit evidence.

Required

a. What is the objective of the CPA's examination and accumulation of audit evidence during the course of his audit?

b. The source of the audit evidence is of primary importance in the CPA's evaluation of its quality. Audit evidence may be classified according to source. For example, one class originates within the client's organization, passes through the hands of third parties, and returns to the client, where it may be examined by the auditor. List the classifications of audit evidence according to source, briefly discussing the effect of the source on the reliability of the evidence.

c. In evaluating the quality of the audit evidence, the CPA also considers factors other than the sources of the evidence. Briefly discuss these other factors.

AICPA (adapted)

4-26 In his examination of financial statements, an auditor must judge the validity of the audit evidence he obtains.

Required

a. In the course of his examination, the auditor asks many questions of client officers and employees.
   1. Describe the factors that the auditor should consider in evaluating oral evidence provided by client officers and employees.
   2. Discuss the validity and limitations of oral evidence.

b. An auditor's examination may include computation of various balance-sheet and operating ratios for comparison to prior years and industry averages. Discuss the validity and limitations of ratio analysis.

c. In connection with his examination of the financial statements of a manufacturing company, an auditor is observing the physical inventory of finished goods, which consists of expensive, highly complex electronic equipment. Discuss the validity and limitations of the audit evidence provided by the procedure.

AICPA

4-27 During the course of an examination, the auditor examines a wide variety of documentation. Listed below are some forms of documentary evidence and the source from which they are obtained.

1. Bank statement sent directly to the auditor by the bank.
2. Creditor monthly statement obtained from client's files.
3. Vouchers in client's unpaid voucher file.
4. Duplicate sales invoices in filled order file.
5. Time tickets filed in payroll department.
6. Credit memo in customer's file.
7. Material requisitions filed in storeroom.
8. Bank statement in client's files.
9. Invoices from suppliers attached to unpaid vouchers.
10. Paid checks returned with bank statement in (1) above.
11. Letter in customer file from collection agency on collectibility of balance.
12. Memo in customer file from treasurer authorizing the write-off of the account.

Required

a. Classify the evidence by source into one of four categories: (1) directly from outsiders, (2) indirectly from outsiders, (3) internal but validated externally, and (4) entirely internal.

b. Comment on the reliability of the four sources of documentary evidence.

4-28 A variety of specific audit procedures for obtaining audit evidence are listed below:

1. Inspect and count securities on hand.
2. Confirm inventories stored in public warehouses.
3. Obtain written report from a chemical engineer on grades of gasoline held as inventory by an oil company.
4. Recompute depreciation charges.

5. Learn about possible lawsuit during conversation with client's legal counsel during luncheon.
6. Compute and compare gross profit rates for the current and preceding years.
7. Examine certificates of title to delivery trucks purchased during the year.
8. Obtain letter from management on matters of audit interest.
9. Vouch sales journal entries to sales invoices.
10. Observe the client's count of cash on hand.
11. Review minute book for dividend authorizations.
12. Trace "paid" checks to check register entries.
13. Scan voucher register for unusual account classifications.

Required

a. Indicate the type of evidence obtained by each procedure.
b. List by number the types of evidence that are (1) obtained directly from independent sources outside the enterprise and (2) obtained by the auditor's direct personal knowledge.

4-29 In meeting the third standard of field work, the auditor may perform (a) substantive tests of transactions, (b) substantive tests of balances, and (c) analytical review procedures. Below are listed specific audit procedures that fall within one of these categories:

1. Compare actual results with budget expectations.
2. Vouch entries in check register to "paid" checks.
3. Recalculate accrued interest payable.
4. Confirm customer balances.
5. Calculate inventory turnover ratios and compare with industry data.
6. Reconcile bank accounts at year-end.
7. Vouch sales journal entries to sales invoices.
8. Count office supplies on hand at year-end.
9. Examine deeds of ownership for land purchased during year.
10. Obtain representation letter from management.
11. Scan postings to repair expense for evidence of charges that should be capitalized.
12. Ask storeroom supervisor about obsolete items.

Required

List the numbers of the foregoing procedures. For each procedure, indicate the type of substantive test and the type of evidence obtained. Use the following format for your answer:

Procedure No.	Type of Substantive Test	Type of Corroborating Information

4-30 Auditors frequently refer to the terms "standards" and "procedures." Standards deal with measures of the quality of the auditor's performance. Standards specifically refer to the ten GAAS. Procedures relate to those acts that are performed by the auditor while trying to gather evidence. Procedures specifically refer to the methods or techniques used by the auditor in the conduct of the examination.

Required

List the different types of procedures that an auditor would use during an examination of financial statements. For example, a type of procedure that an auditor would frequently use is the observation of activities and conditions. Do not discuss specific accounts.

AICPA (adapted)

4-31 An important part of every examination of financial statements is the preparation of working papers.

Required

a. Discuss the relationship of working papers to the standards of field work.
b. You are instructing an inexperienced staffman on his first auditing assignment. He is to examine an account. An analysis of the account has been prepared by the client for inclusion in the working papers. Prepare a list of the comments and notations that the staffman should make or have made on the account analysis to provide an adequate working paper as evidence of his examination. (Do not include a description of auditing procedures applicable to the account.)

AICPA (adapted)

4-32 The preparation of working papers is an integral part of a CPA's examination of financial statements. On a recurring engagement, a CPA reviews his audit programs and working papers from his prior examination while planning his current examination to determine their usefulness for the current engagement.

Required

a. 1. What are the purposes or functions of working papers?
   2. What records may be included in working papers?
b. What factors affect the CPA's judgment of the type and content of the working papers for a particular engagement?
c. To comply with GAAS, a CPA includes certain evidence in his working papers— for example, "evidence that the engagement was planned and work of assistants was supervised and reviewed." What other evidence would a CPA include in audit working papers to comply with generally accepted auditing standards?

AICPA (adapted)

4-33 The accountant for the Brian Co. is preparing financial statements for the year ended December 31. Your review of the accounting records discloses the need for the following adjusting and reclassifying entries.

1. Office Supplies has a balance of $2,400. An inventory at December 31 shows $1,700 of supplies on hand.

2. There are two insurance accounts in the trial balance, Prepaid Insurance—$9,200 and Insurance Expense—$2,800. Unexpired insurance at the statement date is $3,000.

3. All rent receipts ($25,000) were credited to rent income. At the end of the year, $5,000 of rentals are unearned.

4. The allowance for uncollectibles has a credit balance of $6,000. An aging schedule shows estimated uncollectibles of $14,000.

5. The balance in accounts payable is $122,400. Included in this amount is $10,400 of advance deposits made by Brian Co. on future purchases.

6. The ledger shows interest receivable of $3,200 at the beginning of the year. All interest collections have been credited to interest revenue. At December 31 of the current year, accrued interest receivable totals $3,800.

7. A capital expenditure of $6,000 was debited to repairs expense on October 1. The annual rate of depreciation on the machinery is 10%.

8. Freight-in of $5,000 was debited to Freight-out.

9. Accounts receivable has a balance of $118,400. This balance is net of customers with credit balances of $15,000.

10. Bonds payable has a balance of $550,000. Bonds maturing within the next year total $50,000.

Required

Journalize the adjusting and reclassifying entries. Identify the adjustments by number and the reclassifications by letter.

4-34 Smith is the partner in charge of the audit of Blue Distributing Corporation, a wholesaler that owns one warehouse containing 80% of its inventory. Smith is reviewing the working papers that were prepared to support the firm's opinion on Blue's financial statements and Smith wants to be certain essential audit records are well-documented.

Required

What evidence should Smith find in the working papers to support the fact that the audit was adequately planned and the assistants were properly supervised.

AICPA (adapted)

4-35* As a staff assistant on the Portage Developers Corp. audit, you have been asked by your supervisor, Mary Reed, to prepare a cash summary or lead schedule for the working papers for the December 31, 19X0 cash balances. Portage Developers Corp. maintains a petty cash account and four checking accounts at local banks. At December 31, 19X0, the five accounts had a total balance of $3,645,486.28 consisting of

Account Title	Account Number	December 31, 19X0 Balance
Petty cash	101	$ 27,000.00
Payroll account, Eaton National Bank	102	1,322,750.00
General account, Eaton National Bank	103	1,631,342.20

Special account, Tanglewood Bank of Commerce	104	928,487.18
General account, Commercial Bank Corp.	105	(264,093.10)

Working paper documentation of the work done on these accounts have been indexed on working papers A1–A5, respectively.

During her review of the working papers. Mary Reed concludes that (1) the overdraft in the Commercial Bank Corp. account should be reclassified as a current liability and (2) that an adjusting entry should be made for a $20,000 payment by a customer on account that was properly included in deposits in transit to the Eaton National Bank general account, but not recorded on the books prior to December 31, 19X0.

Required

a. Prepare only the cash summary working paper. Use the following column headings: *Account Number, Account Title, Working Paper Reference 12/31/X0 Balance per Books. Adjusting and Reclassifying Entries Dr. and Cr., and 12/31/X0 Final Balance.*

b. Below the summary totals, journalize the adjusting and reclassifying entries. Your firm uses numbers to identify adjusting entries and letters to identify reclassification entries.

CASE STUDY

4-36* The following schedule was prepared by staff accountant C. B. Sure on completing the verification of a December 31 client-prepared reconciliation of the City Bank General Account in the audit of Bold, Inc.

Bold, Inc.	A–1
	Prepared by: Client
#102 City Bank—Reconciliation	**Reviewed by: C. B. Sure**

Per Bank	$62,765.18 ✔
Deposit in transit	1,452.20 ✔
Outstanding checks:	
87.10✔ 619.75✔	
232.90✔ 1,100.00✔	
17.20✔ 472.19✔	(2,529.14)
Other (see AJE's 12 and 13 on cash lead Schedule A)	510.55
Reconciled balance	$62,198.79
✔ Verified	✔

As a senior on the job, you discuss the work done with Sure and determine

1. The balance per bank agreed with the amount shown on the bank confirmation received directly from the bank.

2. The deposit in transit was traced to the January bank statement.

3. All outstanding checks were traced to the December check register.

4. Adjusting entry 12 was for the collection of a $515 noninterest bearing note by the bank; entry 13 was for December bank charges of $4.45.

5. The recorded balance per books at December 31, is $61,267.69.

6. In comparing "paid" checks with the check register, an error was discovered. Check number 2640 for $980 to a creditor was recorded by Bold, Inc. as $890. The bank paid the correct amount.

7. The final step, done on January 7, was to check the mathematical accuracy of the schedule.

Required

a. Prepare the bank reconciliation working paper in good form, showing adjusted balances per bank and per books.

b. Prepare the adjusting entries that presumably were made.

c. Prepare a cash lead schedule assuming (1) account number 101, Petty Cash $5,000 (working paper A–2, no adjustments) and (2) account number 103, City Bank— Payroll $20,000 (working paper A–3, no adjustment).

d. Show how cash will appear in the working trial balance.

PART II

STUDY AND EVALUATION OF INTERNAL CONTROL

The study and evaluation of internal control are essential parts of an audit. Seven chapters are included in Part II.

In Chapter 5, attention is given to the basic features of internal control systems and the nature and scope of the auditing standard that requires the auditor to make a study and evaluation of a client's system of internal control.

The following two chapters expand on this requirement by considering the impact of electronic data processing (Chapter 6) and the applicability of statistical sampling (Chapter 7).

The remaining chapters provide comprehensive coverage of internal control principles and the methodology for making a study and evaluation of internal control of specific classes of transactions within three transaction cycles—revenue, expenditure, and production.

Chapter 5

Internal Control Principles and Review Concepts

Study Objectives

When you have finished your study of this chapter, you should be able to

- Explain the meaning and purpose of internal accounting control.

- Enumerate the environmental factors and basic principles that pertain to internal control.

- State the scope and objective of the second standard of field work.

- Identify and describe the steps required in making a review of a client's system of internal accounting control.

- Point out the nature, purpose, and extent of compliance tests.

- Explain the factors that should be considered in making a final evaluation of a client's system of internal accounting control.

- Indicate the effects the auditor's evaluation of internal control may have on substantive tests.

As indicated in earlier chapters, the client's system of internal control is an important factor in an audit engagement. It may be recalled, for example, that the effectiveness of the system affects control risk, which is a major component of audit risk. Moreover, the auditor's study and evaluation of internal control usually represent a significant part of field work. This chapter is divided into two segments: (1) basic considerations about internal control systems and (2) the auditor's methodology for meeting the second standard of field work.

BASIC CONSIDERATIONS

IMPORTANCE OF INTERNAL CONTROL

The importance of internal control to management and independent auditors has been recognized in the professional literature for many years. A 1947 American Institute of Certified Public Accountants (AICPA) publication cited the following factors as contributing to the constantly expanding recognition of the significance of internal control:

- The scope and size of the business entity has become so complex and widespread that management must rely on numerous reports and analyses to effectively control operations.
- The check and review inherent in a good system of internal control afford protection against human weaknesses and reduce the possibility that errors or irregularities will occur.
- It is impracticable for auditors to make audits of most companies within economic fee limitations without relying on the client's system of internal control.[1]

During the three decades following this publication, even greater importance has been placed on internal control by management and independent auditors. In 1977, a new dimension was imposed with the passage of the Foreign Corrupt Practices Act. Under this Act, management and directors of companies subject to the reporting requirements of the Securities Exchange Act of 1934, whether or not they operate outside the United States, are required to comply with antibribery and accounting standards provisions. The latter requires the maintenance of a satisfactory system of internal control. The act is administered by the Securities and Exchange Commission (SEC), and management and directors who do not comply with the provisions are subject to fines, penalties, and/or imprisonment.

ADMINISTRATIVE AND ACCOUNTING CONTROL

Two subdivisions of internal control are recognized in auditing: (1) administrative control and (2) accounting control:

Administrative control includes, but is not limited to, the plan of organization and the procedures and records that are concerned with the decision processes leading

---

[1]Committee on Auditing Procedure, *Internal Control* (New York: American Institute of Certified Public Accountants, 1947), p. 5.

to management's authorization of transactions . . . and is the starting point for establishing accounting control over transactions.[2]

Accounting control comprises the plan of organization and procedures and records that are concerned with the safeguarding of assets and the reliability of financial records and consequently are designed to provide reasonable assurance that:

a. Transactions are executed in accordance with management's general or specific authorization.
b. Transactions are recorded as necessary (1) to permit preparation of financial statements in conformity with generally accepted accounting principles or any other criteria applicable to such statements and (2) to maintain accountability for assets.
c. Access to assets is permitted only in accordance with management's authorization.
d. The recorded accountability for assets is compared with the existing assets at reasonable intervals and appropriate action is taken with respect to any differences.[3]

The definition of *administrative control* indicates that these controls may extend beyond the process leading to the authorization of transactions. Such controls include statistical analyses, time and motion studies, performance reports, and quality controls. These types of controls have little or no impact on a company's financial records. However, the definition also recognizes that the two subdivisions of internal control are not mutually exclusive because some administrative controls lead to the authorization of transactions, which is the starting point for accounting control.

The definition of accounting control focuses on two *broad objectives:* (1) the safeguarding of assets and (2) the reliability of financial records, and four *operative objectives* (items a–d). Any administrative control that directly affects any of these aspects is considered to be an accounting control.

CLARIFYING ACCOUNTING CONTROL

The auditor should have a thorough understanding of accounting control. Further clarification about the meaning of accounting control is given below.

Safeguarding of Assets

In a broad sense, the safeguarding of assets includes any precautionary measure taken by management to prevent something undesirable from happening to the company's resources. Such measures might apply to all losses, whether they result from "acts of God" or bad business decisions. This interpretation extends considerably beyond the accounting process.

---

[2]Auditing Standards Board, *Codification of Statements on Auditing Standards* (New York: American Institute of Certified Public Accountants, 1985), Auditing Section 320.27 (hereinafter referred to and cited as AU §).

[3]Auditing Standards Board, *op. cit.,* AU § 320.28.

A more meaningful interpretation is to limit this element to the measures taken by management to protect the company from losses resulting from executing and recording transactions and from custody of the related assets. Losses, in such cases, may be due to either errors or irregularities. Errors consist of unintentional mistakes such as understatement of sales invoices by unknowingly applying incorrect unit prices and overpayment of employees by inadvertently using incorrect wage rates. In contrast, irregularities are intentional distortions that may involve deliberate misrepresentations by management or misappropriations of assets (defalcations).

Reliability of Financial Records

Financial records provide the basis for reporting (1) internally to management and (2) externally to stockholders and other interested parties. While both uses are important, it should be recognized that the auditor reports his findings to stockholders. Thus, for auditing purposes, the reliability of the financial records applies primarily to external reporting.

In this context, external reporting is broader than just financial statements. It includes all financial data in the annual report (financial highlights, comparative summaries, etc.) and other forms of financial reporting (interim reports and earnings releases). The term *financial records* is synonymous with the term *accounting records* in the scope paragraph of the auditor's standard report, *accounting data* in the time-honored definition of internal control, and *underlying accounting data* in the classification of evidential matter.

Reasonable Assurance

The establishment and maintenance of a system of internal accounting control is the responsibility of management. Management normally seeks reasonable, rather than absolute, assurance that the objectives of the system will be achieved. Two significant factors underlie this conclusion.

First is the recognition that the cost of the system should not exceed the benefits expected to be attained. The cost-benefit criterion is critical in the management decision-making process. This is complicated by the fact that the cost-benefit relationship involves estimates and judgments, rather than precise measurements. In airports, the cost of personal security surveillance for passengers was deemed to be worth the benefit of protection from hijackers and bombs. In contrast, managements of retail establishments, to date, have decided that a similar personal surveillance system is not worth the benefit of eliminating shoplifting losses. Many stores, however, have installed strategically located closed-circuit television cameras and electronic sensing devices in an effort to cope with this problem.

Second is the realization that the control procedure should not have a significant adverse effect on efficiency or profitability. For example, a company could eliminate losses from bad checks by accepting only certified or cashiers' checks from customers. However, because of the possible adverse effect on sales, most companies believe that requiring identification from the check writer offers reasonable assurance against this type of loss.

Transactions

Transactions include exchanges of assets and services between a business enterprise and outside parties, as well as the transfer or use of assets and services within a company. Transactions constitute the basic components of business operations and they are directly or indirectly related to the four operative objectives of internal accounting control. Accordingly, they are the primary subject matter of internal accounting control.

The flow of transactions through a system of internal accounting control involves the authorization, execution, and recording of transactions and accountability for the resulting assets. Ideally, a company's system of internal accounting control should provide a complete *transaction* (or audit) *trail* for each major class of transactions. A transaction trail is a chain of evidence provided by coding, cross references, and documentation connecting account balances and other summary results with original transactions and calculations.[4]

Different types of controls may be required for different types of transactions. Thus, the establishment of controls and the auditor's interest in them are centered on specific types or classes of transactions such as sales, purchases, and so on. Moreover, the auditor is concerned about specific control procedures pertaining to each function (or step) involved in the flow of transactions for each class. For example, in executing credit sales in a manufacturing company, there should be controls in approving credit, filling and shipping the order, and billing the customer.

Limitations

All systems of internal accounting control are subject to inherent limitations. One limitation is the human factor that exists in most control procedures. The effectiveness of a specific control can be nullified by misunderstanding of instructions, carelessness, fatigue, and absenteeism. It is also possible for the effectiveness of a procedure to be minimized through deliberate circumvention by one employee or jointly by several employees. The latter situation is usually referred to as *collusion*.

A second limitation is that internal control procedures may not encompass all transactions. Internal control may not apply to (1) nonroutine transactions such as officers' bonuses and extraordinary events or (2) management's judgments involving accounting estimates that are required in the preparation of financial statements.

In addition, it should be recognized that internal accounting control exists in a dynamic rather than a static business environment. Changed conditions,

---

[4]Auditing Standards Board, *op. cit.,* AU § 320.33.

such as the resignation or retirement of a key employee, or the installation of self-service by customers or "on-line, realtime" consoles in a computer system, may necessitate major modifications in existing controls. Consequently, special care should be taken in making projections about the future effectiveness of a system solely on the basis of its current effectiveness.

INTERNAL ACCOUNTING CONTROL ENVIRONMENT

Every system of internal accounting control operates within a set of conditions or circumstances that collectively is referred to as the internal control environment. A good internal control environment complements prescribed control procedures, whereas a poor environment adversely affects such controls. A company's internal control environment includes the following factors:

- Management leadership.
- Organizational structure.
- Budgets and internal reports.
- Internal auditing.
- Personnel.
- Sound practices.
- Company circumstances.

These factors apply regardless of whether the method of data processing is manual, mechanical, or electronic.

Management Leadership

Management is responsible for establishing a favorable control environment within the organization. The board of directors, particularly its audit committee, and top management should provide leadership in establishing an appropriate level of control consciousness. The communication of control policies, the frequency and extent of management's surveillance of the system, and management's disposition of exceptions to prescribed controls affect the potential effectiveness of a system.

The control environment is adversely affected when management fails to adhere to established control procedures or is unwilling to prescribe appropriate control procedures. Lack of adherence occurs, for example, when management directs subordinates to ignore prescribed controls and when top management elects to override existing controls.

Organizational Structure

An organizational structure contributes to a good internal control environment by providing an overall framework for planning, coordinating, and controlling operations. The organizational structure of a company involves (1) establishing the organizational independence of functional areas, divisions, and/or departments and (2) providing for the assignment of responsibility and delegation of authority within each organizational unit. The organizational structure of a company usually is depicted graphically in an organization chart. An organizational structure should also provide job descriptions for key positions within each unit.

To enable individuals to effectively discharge their assigned responsibilities, they should be knowledgeable about policies, procedures, and activities that directly and indirectly affect their duties. Appropriate communication of these factors is essential to developing an attitude of control consciousness throughout the organization.

Budgets and Internal Reports

Budgets make several contributions to a company's internal accounting control environment. They provide the means of formulating and communicating company objectives throughout the organization, and they furnish a basis for measuring performance against planned goals. The budgeting process should follow the divisions of responsibility set forth in the organizational structure of the company. Budgets should be updated periodically to reflect management's revised expectations resulting from changed operating conditions and other factors.

An effective system of internal reporting to all levels of management is essential to a sound control environment. When properly prepared and analyzed, internal reports provide a basis for evaluating performance and the manner in which delegated responsibility is being discharged. Internal reporting should be on both a regular and timely basis.

Internal Auditing

As explained in Chapter 1, internal auditing is an appraisal function. Internal auditing contributes to a good control environment through the monitoring of the functioning of prescribed control procedures. An effective internal audit function can assist management in exercising continuous supervision over the system. In addition, it can offer constructive suggestions for improving the system. A company's control environment is enhanced when internal auditors are independent of the units they audit and they report or have direct access to the board of directors.

Personnel

Basic to a proper control environment are the competence and integrity of the personnel who must carry out the prescribed control procedures. Dishonest and/or incompetent personnel can make most control procedures inoperative or ineffective. People in positions of responsibility, such as officers, department heads, managers, and cashiers, should be individuals who have both the training and the experience to discharge their assigned responsibilities efficiently and economically. On the one hand, it would be inefficient and injudicious to place an inexperienced accountant as the controller of a company; on the other hand, it would be uneconomical to use an experienced certified public accountant (CPA) as a bookkeeper. In addition to competency, personnel should have high personal and ethical standards. The competence and integrity of personnel are largely dependent on a company's policies and procedures pertaining to hiring, training, compensation, performance evaluation, and promotions.

Sound Practices

Sound practices relate to miscellaneous measures taken by a company in creating a good control environment. The following are representative of practices that are widely used:

- Carrying fidelity insurance on personnel in positions of trust (this practice is commonly referred to as *bonding of employees*).
- Having a written *code of officer and employee conduct* pertaining to moral standards of behavior and prohibition against illegal acts.
- Having a clear-cut *conflict of interest policy* relating to actions that are incompatible with company objectives.
- Establishing a *mandatory vacation policy* for personnel in positions of trust.

Company Circumstances

This aspect of a company's environment pertains to such factors as: (1) the geographical dispersion of its operations, (2) the existence of wholly or partially owned subsidiaries, and (3) the recent acquisition of entities whose controls may not be comparable to the company's. These conditions suggest that there may be a lack of uniformity of controls throughout a company. This factor may be especially important in multinational companies with subsidiaries in foreign countries.

INTERNAL ACCOUNTING CONTROL PRINCIPLES

To achieve the objectives of internal accounting control, a system should have certain essential features. The following six principles are basic to an effective system of accounting control:

- Authorization procedures.
- Segregation of functions.
- Documentation procedures.
- Accounting records and procedures.
- Physical controls.
- Independent internal verification.

Authorization Procedures

The purpose of this basic principle is to assure that transactions are authorized by management personnel acting within the scope of their authority. Authorizations may be general or specific. The former relates to the general conditions under which transactions are authorized, such as standard price lists for products and credit policies for charge sales. The latter relates to the granting of the authorization on a case-by-case basis. This may occur, for example, in nonroutine transactions, such as major capital expenditures and the issuing of capital stock. Specific authorization may also apply to routine transactions that exceed the limits prescribed in the general authorization such as granting credit to a customer who does not meet specified credit conditions.

There is a difference between management's authorization of a transaction and employee approval. Acting within the scope of authorized credit policies, for instance, credit department personnel can approve credit to individual customers.

Authorization procedures are also important in limiting access to assets. For instance, only authorized personnel should have access to storage areas for inventories, cash, and marketable securities. Similarly, there should be restricted access to storage areas for unused documents, such as blank checks and vouchers, that may be used for the improper disposition of assets. In addition, direct access to the accounting records should be restricted to authorized accounting personnel.

Segregation of Functions

This basic principle applies to each of the four operative objectives of internal accounting control and therefore is all-pervasive. It involves the assignment of responsibility for a transaction in a manner such that the duties of one employee automatically provide a cross-check on the work of one or more other employees. The primary purpose of segregation of functions is the prevention and prompt detection of errors or irregularities in the performance of assigned responsibilities. Functions are considered to be incompatible from a control standpoint when it is possible for an individual to commit errors or irregularities in the normal course of his duties and to prevent their detection by the system.

The primary application of this principle is that the responsibility for executing a transaction, recording the transaction, and custody of the assets resulting from the transaction should be assigned to different departments and individuals. In the case of purchase transactions, purchasing department personnel should make the purchase, accounting department personnel should record the goods received, and storeroom personnel should assume custody of goods received. Before recording the purchase, accounting personnel should ascertain that the purchase was authorized and that the goods ordered were received. The accounting entry, in turn, provides a basis of accountability for the goods in the storeroom.

The principle of segregation of duties also applies to the various steps involved in the execution of a transaction. Thus, in executing a sales transaction in a manufacturing company, different departments or individuals should be responsible for authorizing the sale, filling the order, shipping the goods, and billing the customer. Similarly, within the accounting department, different personnel should maintain the general ledger and the customers' subsidiary ledger.

Adherence to this principle is more difficult in a small company than a large one because of the smaller number of employees. However, in such companies, it is common for the owner to be an active participant in the business. Thus, he may assume specific duties that may result in an appropriate segregation of functions. For example, in executing a sales transaction, the owner may approve credit and bill customers while employees fill and ship (or deliver) the order. Alternatively, owners may exercise closer supervision and review of employees' work to compensate for the inadequate segregation of duties.

Documentation Procedures

Proper documentation is important to effective internal accounting control. Documents provide evidence of the occurrence of transactions and the price, nature, and terms of the transactions. Invoices, checks, contracts, and time tickets are illustrative of common types of documents. When duly signed or stamped, documents also provide a basis for establishing responsibility for the executing and recording of transactions. Prenumbered documents are useful in maintaining control and accountability. Prenumbering helps to assure that (1) all transactions are recorded and (2) that no transactions are recorded more than once. When prenumbering exists, all voided documents should be retained.

Documentation procedures should provide for the timely preparation of the document by operating personnel when transactions are executed. The recording of transactions is facilitated when documents are promptly forwarded to accounting. Documents should subsequently be filed in an orderly manner.

Accounting Records and Procedures

This basic principle focuses on the recording of transactions within the accounting department. The objectives of this control are (1) prompt preparation of accurate accounting records and (2) timely reporting of accounting data to users. Both a chart of accounts and an accounting procedures manual are important. A *chart of accounts* provides the basis for the classification of transactions and greatly facilitates the preparation of financial statements. In many companies, an accounting supervisor periodically reviews journal entries to evaluate the reasonableness of the account classifications.

Accounting procedures relate to the timely processing of documents within the accounting department. They include accounting for all serially pre-numbered documents in journalizing and controls to assure that transactions occurring near the end of an accounting period are recorded in the proper time period.

Physical Controls

Physical controls pertain primarily to security devices and measures for the safekeeping of assets, accounting records, and unused preprinted forms. Security devices include onsite safeguards such as fireproof safes and locked storerooms, and offsite safeguards such as bank deposit vaults and certified public warehouses. Security measures involve limiting access to storage areas to authorized personnel.

Physical controls also involve the use of mechanical and electronic equipment in executing transactions. For example, cash registers help to assure that all cash receipts transactions are rung up, and they provide locked-in summaries of daily receipts.

Independent Internal Verification

This basic principle of internal accounting control relates to reviewing the accuracy and propriety of an employee's work by another employee. For this principle to be effective, three conditions should exist:

- The review should be performed by an employee who is unrelated to, and independent of, the personnel who originally prepared the data or had custody of the related assets.
- The review should be made frequently either in total or on a sampling basis.
- Errors and exceptions should be promptly communicated to the employees involved for corrective action. Recurring and material inaccuracies and all improprieties should, of course, be reported to management.

Independent internal verification may involve comparing recorded accountability with existing assets (as in the case of a cash or inventory count) by an individual who does not have custody of the assets, or agreeing control accounts with their subsidiary records, and recalculating employee earnings by an individual who did not prepare the original data.

METHODOLOGY FOR MEETING THE SECOND STANDARD OF FIELD WORK

Now that the essential underlying information about internal accounting control has been explained, consideration can be given to the second generally accepted auditing standard of field work, which states:

> There is to be a proper study and evaluation of the existing internal control as a basis for reliance thereon and for the determination of the resultant extent of the tests to which auditing procedures are to be restricted.

Internal control systems are unique to each client since they are developed by different individuals with different skills for different managements and for different size companies utilizing different personnel, records, and data processing methods. Thus, the study of internal control systems cannot be standardized but must be tailored to the system used by the specific client.

SCOPE AND OBJECTIVE OF THE STANDARD

The second standard of field work extends to internal accounting control, as defined earlier in the chapter, but not to internal administrative control. Internal control systems can change significantly from year to year as new controls are introduced and personnel changes occur in key positions. Thus, this standard must be met in each audit engagement.

The stated (and primary) objective of the standard is to ascertain the amount of reliance the auditor can place on the system in determining the extent to which other auditing procedures will be necessary in completing the engagement. The phrase *basis for reliance thereon* refers to specific aspects of the system and not to the system in its entirety. For example, the auditor wants to know the amount of reliance that can be placed on control procedures pertaining to the granting of credit in sales transactions. The phrase *for the determination of the resultant extent to which auditing procedures are to be restricted* implies that there is a relationship between the amount of reliance and the amount of additional work that will be needed. The auditing procedures referred to are the substantive tests of transactions and balances and analytical review procedures explained in Chapter 4.

In addition to the stated objective, the auditor's study and evaluation provide a basis for informing management about weaknesses in the system and making recommendations for improvement.

OVERVIEW OF METHODOLOGY

The study of the system of internal accounting control, which provides the basis for evaluating the system, consists of two closely related parts:

- A *review of the system* to obtain knowledge and understanding of the client's prescribed system.
- *Tests of compliance* to determine whether prescribed control procedures are in use and are operating as planned.

The review, in turn, is divided into phases. In the first or *preliminary phase*, the auditor seeks general knowledge about the client's internal control environment and accounting system. At the conclusion of the preliminary phase of the review, the auditor decides whether further study is likely to justify any restriction of substantive tests. If a negative answer results, the auditor proceeds directly to the design and execution of expanded substantive tests. If an affirmative answer results, the auditor continues to the second or *completion phase* of the review. In this part of the review, the auditor obtains specific knowledge of the design of the client's system of internal accounting control. At the conclusion of the completion phase of the review, the auditor makes a *preliminary evaluation* of prescribed controls.

The primary purpose of the preliminary evaluation is to identify specific control procedures that can be relied on in performing substantive tests, assuming satisfactory compliance with the prescribed procedures. If there are no controls on which reliance is planned, the auditor goes directly to the design and execution of expanded substantive tests. However, when reliance is planned on a control procedure, the auditor performs tests of compliance to determine whether the controls are in use and operating as planned. On completing the tests of compliance, the auditor makes a *final evaluation*. This evaluation identifies the control procedures that can be relied on in performing restricted substantive tests. The courses of action and the decision points for the auditor in meeting the second standard of field work are shown in Figure 5-1. Observe that the auditor can discontinue the study and evaluation after either phase of the review. Note also that three decision paths will result in expanded substantive tests.

To satisfy GAAS with respect to the second standard of field work, the auditor is only required to perform the preliminary phase of the review. Further study of the system depends entirely on the auditor's judgment about whether such effort will be cost-beneficial in completing the audit. Each of the parts of the study and evaluation is explained more fully below.

PRELIMINARY PHASE OF REVIEW

This phase of the review is the minimum study contemplated by the second standard of field work. In the preliminary phase of the review, the auditor seeks information about (1) the internal control environment and (2) the flow of transactions through the accounting system. For the former, the auditor is interested in each of the environmental factors discussed earlier in this chapter. For the latter, he is interested in how transactions in each of the major classes are authorized, executed, and recorded, including the methods of data processing. In this phase of the review, the auditor needs only general knowledge. The auditor's preliminary understanding is usually obtained by inquiry, but it may also be acquired by review of documentation, observation, previous experience with the client, and reference to prior-year working papers.

At the conclusion of the preliminary phase of the review, the auditor must decide, for each of the major classes of transactions, whether to continue or

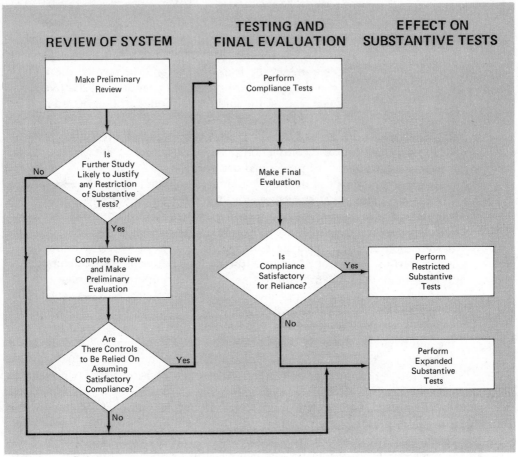

Figure 5-1. OVERVIEW OF METHODOLOGY FOR THE STUDY AND EVALUATION OF INTERNAL ACCOUNTING CONTROL.

terminate his review. A decision to continue results when the auditor believes that

- Further study will likely justify some restriction of substantive tests.
- The audit effort required to complete the review and perform tests of compliance will not exceed the reduction in substantive tests that could be achieved by relying on internal accounting control.

When both conditions do not exist, the auditor ends his review and proceeds to the design of expanded substantive tests that do not contemplate reliance on any control procedures. This course of action is fully in accord with GAAS and is often followed in audits of small clients.

The auditor's decision, which requires professional judgment, should be documented by explaining the reasons for terminating the review in the working papers. When the auditor plans no reliance on internal accounting control, he does not need to document his understanding of the client's system.

COMPLETION PHASE OF REVIEW

In this phase of the review, the auditor obtains specific knowledge and understanding of the client's prescribed control procedures as they pertain to particular classes of transactions or balances. In making the review, the auditor should consider the potential effectiveness of the prescribed controls, either individually or collectively, in preventing or detecting specific types of errors or irregularities. The completion phase of the review involves the following steps: (1) gathering the information, (2) verifying the understanding, and (3) making a preliminary evaluation.

Gathering the Information

The information required for this phase of the review is ordinarily obtained from inquiries of appropriate client personnel, review of written documentation such as internal accounting control manuals and flowcharts, and observation of the processing of transactions and the handling of related assets.[5] Auditors differ in their approaches to gathering the information. Generally, the information is organized according to one of the following approaches:

- *Transaction Cycles,* such as the revenue cycle that includes sales, cash receipts, and sales adjustments transactions. This grouping transcends organizational differences among companies and functional lines within a company.
- *Financial Statement Classifications,* such as the cash account that includes cash receipts and cash disbursement transactions. This approach facilitates the design of substantive tests of related account balances.
- *Business Functions,* such as financial management, sales, and production. This grouping follows established organizational lines within a company and is helpful in determining whether assigned responsibility has been properly discharged.[6]

In this text, we will use a *transaction cycle* grouping because this approach currently predominates in practice.

The information obtained in the review should be documented in the working papers. This is often done through answers to questionnaires, flowcharts, and narrative memoranda.

---

[5]Auditing Standards Board, *op. cit.,* AU § 320.56.

[6]AICPA *Audit and Accounting Manual* (New York: American Institute of Certified Public Accountants, 1984), Section 4200.14 (adapted).

Questionnaires. A questionnaire consists of a series of questions relating to control procedures normally required to prevent or detect errors and irregularities that may occur for each type of transaction. The questions are usually phrased in a manner that results in either a "yes" or "no" answer, with the former indicating that the necessary control procedure is prescribed by the client. Some firms have standardized questionnaires that are adaptable to many clients. A questionnaire minimizes the possibility of overlooking important aspects of the system. A further advantage is the ease with which a questionnaire can be completed. A completed questionnaire for the Campus Theater is shown in Figure 5-2.

Flowcharts. A flowchart is a schematic diagram using symbols, interconnecting lines, and annotations that portrays the steps involved in the processing of a transaction and the custody of related assets. Separate flowcharts

Prepared by: _CAB_ Date: _9/8/X1_
Reviewed by: _WAS_ Date: _9/13/X1_

Campus Theater
Internal Accounting Control Questionnaire
December 31, 19X1

CYCLE: Revenue		CLASS OF TRANSACTIONS: Cash Receipts	
Control Procedure	Yes	No	Remarks
1. Are prenumbered tickets used and subsequently accounted for?	√		
2. Is there restricted access to rolls of unused tickets?	√		
3. Is a ticket machine used in issuing tickets?	√		
4. Are tickets voided upon admission of patrons?	√		
5. Is there segregation of duties between the issuance of tickets and admission of patrons?	√		
6. Is there an independent daily cash count and reconciliation with tickets issued?	√		
7. Are cash receipts deposited in total daily?		√	*cash is deposited weekly*

Figure 5-2. INTERNAL ACCOUNTING CONTROL QUESTIONNAIRE.

are prepared for each major class of transactions. The fundamental techniques and principles of flowcharting are explained and illustrated in Appendix 5A at the end of this chapter.

A flowchart enables the auditor to see the relationships that exist between controls and facilitates the identification of key controls. In addition, it is believed that the knowledge needed to prepare a flowchart requires the auditor to obtain a clear understanding of the system.

Narrative Memoranda. Narrative memoranda consist of written comments by the auditor about the system under review. The memoranda may indicate the source(s) of the information, provide a specific description of the controls reviewed, and identify aspects of the system that have audit significance. This method of documentation offers flexibility in its design. As in the case of flowcharts, narrative memoranda require the auditor to make a comprehensive review.

Verifying the Understanding

To reinforce his understanding of the information gathered from the various sources, the auditor may perform a *transaction walk-through review.* This review is an *optional* step in the study of the client's system. To perform the review, one or a few transactions within each of the major classes of transactions are traced through the transaction trail and the related accounting control procedures are observed. The primary purpose of a walk-through review is to verify (or clarify) the auditor's understanding of the flow of transactions through the client's system. In addition, some auditors consider the walk-through to be part of the tests of compliance.

As a practical matter, a transaction walk-through review may start with any step in the execution and recording of a transaction so long as the complete sequence of steps performed and the persons performing them are identified. The transaction walk-through should be documented in the working papers.

Making a Preliminary Evaluation

An explanation of this step in the completion phase of the review requires a consideration of both the nature and purpose of this evaluation.

Nature. In making a preliminary evaluation, the auditor should

- Consider the errors and irregularities that could occur for each significant class of transactions and related assets.
- Identify the control procedures that should prevent or detect such occurrences.
- Determine whether the necessary procedures are prescribed in the client's system.

In the first two parts, the auditor often uses generalized materials available within his firm. For example, the firm may have checklists that contain specific types of errors and irregularities, along with the control procedures that should prevent or detect them. The auditor then adapts the checklists, as necessary, to the particular client. The third part in the evaluation is accomplished through reviewing the client's system as described above.

Purpose. The primary purpose of this evaluation is to determine whether, assuming satisfactory compliance, specific procedures can be relied on by the auditor in performing substantive tests. A control is considered to be reliable when there is reasonable assurance that it will prevent or detect errors or irregularities pertaining to the particular class of transactions or balances. Professional judgment is indispensable in making this evaluation.

The auditor may decide not to rely on a prescribed control procedure because

- The control procedure is unsatisfactory or unreliable for its intended purpose.
- There are other compensating controls that appear to be more reliable.
- The time and effort to test the control procedure are expected to be greater than the reduction in subsequent testing expected to be realized from such reliance.

When there is no planned reliance on a control procedure, the auditor foregoes any testing of the control and proceeds to the design of expanded substantive tests.

A secondary purpose of this evaluation is to identify any weaknesses in prescribed controls that should be communicated to management. A weakness in internal accounting control is a condition in which the specific control procedures, or the degree of compliance with them, are not sufficient to achieve a specific control objective—that is, errors or irregularities may occur and not be detected within a timely period by employees in the normal course of performing their assigned functions.[7] A weakness may be immaterial or material. A material weakness exists when there is more than a relatively low risk that errors or irregularities, either individually or collectively, would have a material effect on the financial statements.

In evaluating an individual weakness, the auditor should recognize that

- The amounts of errors or irregularities that may occur and remain undetected range from zero to the gross amount of assets or transactions exposed to the weakness.
- The risk or probability of errors or irregularities is likely to be different for the different possible amounts within that range. For example, the risk of errors or irregularities in amounts equal to the gross exposure

---

[7]Auditing Standards Board, *op. cit.*, AU § 642.30.

may be very low, but the risk of smaller amounts may be progressively greater.[8]

A similar approach should be taken in evaluating the combined effect of individually immaterial errors.

The working paper in Figure 5-3 illustrates the documentation of the auditor's preliminary evaluation. Each error or irregularity in this example is numbered to correspond with the questions shown in Figure 5-2. In Campus Theater, the auditor concludes that if compliance is satisfactory, all control procedures can be relied on in performing substantive tests, except for the control over the depositing of cash.

TESTS OF COMPLIANCE

Tests of compliance are performed to obtain reasonable assurance that controls expected to be relied on are in use and operating as planned. This phase of the study of internal control does not extend to any control that will not be relied on in making substantive tests.

Nature

Compliance tests focus on the performance of prescribed procedures. They are generally performed during interim work and are concerned with three questions:

- Were the prescribed control procedures performed?
- How were the prescribed control procedures performed?
- By whom were the prescribed control procedures performed?[9]

The failure to perform a required procedure or the failure to perform it properly is referred to as an *exception*, an *occurrence*, or a *deviation*. Such terminology is superior to the use of the term *error*, for the lack of compliance only indicates that there may be an error in the accounting records. For instance, the failure of a second person to verify the accuracy of a voucher is an exception, but the accounting record could still be correct if the first clerk correctly prepared the document.

Three auditing procedures are commonly used in performing compliance tests:

- *Inquiring* of personnel concerning the performance of their duties.
- *Observing* personnel in the performance of their duties.
- *Inspecting* documentation for evidence of performance of control procedures.

---

[8]*Ibid,* AU § 642.31.

[9]Auditing Standards Board, *op. cit.,* AU § 320.64.

Campus Theater
Preliminary Evaluation: Cash Receipts Transactions
12/31/X1

Errors and Irregularities	Necessary Control Procedure	Prescribed Control Procedure	Planned Reliance Yes	No
1. Tickets may be issued without accounting for the cash	Prenumbering of tickets	All tickets are prenumbered; theater manager accounts for tickets issued	✓	
2. Unused tickets may be stolen and sold for cash	Physical control and restricted access to storage area	Unused tickets are stored in a safe; manager has only access	✓	
3. Tickets may be issued out of sequence and cash may not be accounted for	Mechanical equipment for issuing tickets	Ticket machines are used in issuing tickets	✓	
4. Doorperson could resell tickets or combine with cashier to resell tickets and keep the cash	Mutilation of tickets upon admission of patron	Doorperson tears tickets in half when admitting patrons	✓	
5. The cashier may collect cash and admit patron without issuing a ticket	Separation of functions in admissions	Cashier issues tickets; doorperson admits patrons with tickets	✓	
6. Cash may be over or short due to mistakes in making change	Independent daily cash count and reconciliation with tickets issued	Theater manager makes daily count and reconciliation	✓	
7. All cash receipts may not be deposited	Depositing total cash receipts daily	Cash receipts are deposited weekly		✓

Figure 5-3. PRELIMINARY EVALUATION WORKING PAPER.

156

Inquiring is designed to determine (1) the employee's understanding of his job, (2) the employee's performance in his job, and (3) the frequency, causes, and disposition of exceptions. The inability of the employee to answer inquiries may indicate that the employee is not performing or is improperly performing the prescribed control procedure. Observing the employee's work serves similar purposes. Ideally, this procedure should be performed without the employee's direct knowledge or on a surprise basis. Inquiring and observing are the only procedures that can be used in performing compliance tests of control procedures that involve segregation of functions and leave no transaction trail of performance.

Inspecting (reviewing or examining) documentation is applicable when there is a transaction trail of performance in the form of documents that contain signatures and validation stamps that indicate whether and by whom the controls were performed. When inspection of documents is used, any document that fails to have evidence of performance of the control procedure is an exception, regardless of whether the document itself is in error.

Compliance Tests by Reperformance

In practice, some auditors test compliance with prescribed controls by reperforming the control procedure that was presumably done by the employee. These same auditors maintain that this form of testing provides the best evidence of how well the control procedure is performed.

To illustrate *reperformance*, assume a control procedure requires a second clerk in the billing department to independently verify the correctness of unit selling prices on invoices by comparing them to an authorized price list. On doing so, the clerk initials a copy of the invoice to indicate performance. In testing compliance by reperformance, the auditor compares selling prices on invoices initialed by the clerk to the authorized price lists, and each instance of the use of incorrect prices is regarded as an exception. Thus, in this example, there would be two types of exceptions to prescribed control procedures: (1) invoices that do not have the employee's initials and (2) initialed invoices for which unit selling prices do not agree with the authorized price list. From the foregoing, it can be seen that reperformance is a more costly procedure than inspecting documentation for evidence of performance.

Extent and Timing

Tests of compliance should be applied to control procedures used in executing transactions throughout the accounting period being audited because the financial statements cover the entire year. These tests, however, are often made during interim work and may occur several months before the end of the accounting period. Such testing is acceptable under GAAS, if the auditor also determines that the control procedures are still functioning properly throughout the remainder of the period under audit. The nature and extent of additional compliance tests, if any, depend on such factors as the

- Effectiveness of the controls based on the interim tests.
- Length of the remaining period.
- Responses to inquiries concerning changes in controls and operating conditions during the remaining period.
- Results of tests made by internal auditors in the remaining period.
- Discovery of monetary errors in the accounts in the remaining period through substantive testing.[10]

The extent of compliance testing and the interpretation of results may be based entirely on the auditor's subjective judgment. Alternatively, the auditor's judgment may be based, in part, on statistical sampling as explained in Chapter 7. For control procedures that depend primarily on segregation of functions and leave no transaction trail, inquiries should cover the entire year. However, observation may be limited to periods when the auditor is conducting field work on the client's premises.

Compliance and Substantive Tests of Transactions

Two types of tests are concerned with the details of transactions: (1) substantive tests, which are explained in Chapter 4, and (2) compliance tests. The primary purpose of each type of test and the field work standard to which each relates are as follows:

Type of Transaction Test	Primary Purpose	Field Work Standard
Compliance	Determine extent of compliance with prescribed accounting controls, or conversely, exceptions therefrom.	Second
Substantive	Determine the validity and propriety of the accounting treatment of transactions, or conversely, monetary errors or irregularities therein.	Third

In most audits, compliance tests are performed primarily during interim work and substantive tests are performed primarily during year-end work. However, it is permissible under GAAS to perform substantive tests of transactions during interim work. When this occurs, the auditor may perform compliance tests concurrently on the same transactions. That is, the auditor will simultaneously examine the transactions for exceptions to prescribed control procedures and monetary errors in the accounting records. The simul-

---

[10]Auditing Standards Board, *op. cit.*, AU § 320.70.

taneous execution of these two tests, often referred to as *dual purpose testing*, is widely used in practice where there is documentary evidence of performance with prescribed controls because it is cost-efficient. More will be said about substantive tests of transactions at an interim date in Chapter 13.

Audit Program

As in the case of the verification of account balances, an audit program should be prepared for compliance tests. The program should be sufficiently comprehensive to obtain evidence of whether each control procedure to be relied on is operating as planned. Accordingly, if the control is *documents should be prenumbered*, the audit program should state:

> Examine documents for prenumbering.

In performing the procedure, the auditor will select a representative sample of documents from the client's files and examine them for prenumbering. Figure 5-4 illustrates a partial audit program for testing controls over cash receipts transactions in the revenue cycle of the Campus Theater.

	Campus Theater Partial Audit Program December 31, 19X1		
TYPE OF TEST: Compliance CYCLE: Revenue	PURPOSE: Functioning of Controls CLASS OF TRANSACTIONS: Cash Receipts		
Working Paper Ref.	Audit Procedure	Done by	
		Auditor	Date
	1. Examine tickets for prenumbering.		
	2. Observe storage of unused tickets and inquire about authorized access to safe.		
	3. Observe use of ticket machines in issuing tickets.		
	4. Observe doorperson in admitting patrons and examine ticket receptacle for complete tickets.		
	5. Observe segregation of duties between cashier and doorperson.		
	6. Examine documentary evidence of daily cash counts and reconciliations with tickets issued.		

Figure 5-4. PARTIAL AUDIT PROGRAM.

The alignment of the audit procedures in the audit program parallels the arrangement of prescribed control procedures on which reliance is planned (Figure 5-3). The prescribed control procedure over depositing cash is not tested because no reliance is planned on this control. The results of compliance testing should be documented in the working papers.

Using the Work of Internal Auditors

Large companies with many divisions, such as IBM and Hewlett–Packard, or many branches, such as Chase Manhattan and Montgomery Ward, usually employ internal auditors. As part of their regular duties, these auditors periodically review the internal control systems of each division and branch. Thus, it is possible for the external (independent) auditor to use the reports of the internal auditors on their findings in his study and evaluation of internal control. As indicated in Chapter 2, the independent auditor may use the work of internal auditors as a supplement to, but not as a substitute for, his own work. In addition, all judgments about the effectiveness of the internal accounting controls must be made by the independent auditor.[11]

FINAL EVALUATION OF THE CONTROLS

On completing the compliance tests, the auditor makes a final evaluation of the controls in the system. The nature and purpose of this evaluation are explained below.

Nature

This evaluation is similar to the preliminary evaluation. However, in this case, the evaluation is based on both the review of the system and the results of compliance testing. In making the final evaluation, it should be recognized that strengths and weaknesses affecting different classes of transactions are not offsetting in their effects. For example, weaknesses in billing procedures for sales transactions are not mitigated by strong controls over cash collections.

The final evaluation involves both a quantitative and a qualitative appraisal. The number of exceptions found in a compliance test of a given control may be of such magnitude that there is reason to doubt that the control procedure can be relied on. This might be true, for instance, if many sales were made without credit approval. However, in order to judge the significance of exceptions, it usually is necessary to search for the underlying causes. Thus, the auditor may attach different importance to exceptions traceable to (1) a new employee, (2) a vacation replacement, and (3) an experienced regular employee. It is also essential to attempt to ascertain whether the failure to follow the prescribed control is attributable to errors or irregularities. One

---

[11] Auditing Standards Board, *op. cit.*, AU § 322.11.

instance of an exception or a pattern of exceptions that suggest the possibility of irregularities ordinarily will be more important in the auditor's evaluation than the frequency of the exceptions.

Purpose

The purpose of this evaluation is to determine the extent to which the client's actual control procedures can be relied on in performing substantive tests. The auditor's judgment of reliance may be expressed in terms of the risk that errors or irregularities will not be detected by the client's controls. Three levels of risk may be identified:

- *Low.* The auditor expects few, if any, errors and no irregularities.
- *Moderate.* The auditor expects some immaterial errors and no irregularities.
- *High.* The auditor expects material errors or irregularities.

This evaluation is directed at the specific control procedures tested for each major class of transactions. The evaluation should be documented in the working papers. A useful format is to identify (1) strengths (effective controls), (2) weaknesses (ineffective or missing controls), if any, (3) effects on substantive tests, and (4) matters to be communicated to management, if any. These conclusions are vital in every audit engagement in which reliance is to be placed on internal accounting control. Figure 5-5 shows the evaluation of the control procedures in the Campus Theater.

DETERMINING EFFECTS ON OTHER AUDITING PROCEDURES

The second standard of field work does not permit the auditor to place complete reliance on internal control to the exclusion of other auditing procedures with respect to material amounts in the financial statements. This standard clearly is not an end in itself. It suggests a correlation of reliance on accounting controls with substantive tests, rather than the elimination of other work by the auditor. The ultimate purpose of the second standard of field work is to assist the auditor in obtaining a reasonable basis for an opinion on the client's financial statements as required by the third standard of field work.

In considering the interrelationship of these standards, it is useful to recognize that they relate to two aspects of audit risk discussed in Chapter 3:

- *Control Risk.* The risk that material errors could occur in the accounting process by which the financial statements are developed and not be prevented or detected on a timely basis by the system of internal control.
- *Detection Risk.* The risk that any material errors that occur will not be detected in the auditor's examination.

Campus Theater
Evaluation of Internal Control Over Execution of Cash
Receipts Transaction   12/31/x1

Strengths

All of the controls on which reliance is planned were tested for compliance. These controls were found to be functioning as planned. In my judgment, the control risk associated with these controls is low.

Weaknesses

Cash is deposited in the bank only once each week. This procedure is not satisfactory for good internal control.

Effects on Substantive Tests

For controls in which control risk is low, the planned audit program should be implemented. For the control over depositing cash intact, they should be extended.

Management Communication

Indicate that the failure to deposit cash intact daily also makes cash vulnerable to theft. Suggest that the manager make daily deposits using the bank's night depository vault.

Figure 5-5. FINAL EVALUATION OF INTERNAL CONTROL OVER EXECUTION OF CASH RECEIPTS TRANSACTIONS.

The auditor relies on internal accounting control to reduce control risk and substantive tests to reduce detection risk. The relative weight to be given each factor is a matter for the auditor's professional judgment in light of the circumstances. Thus, reliance on substantive tests may properly vary inversely with the reliance on internal accounting control.[12] The auditor's reliance on internal accounting control may affect the nature, timing, or extent of substantive testing.

Nature

The nature of the test refers to the kind of auditing procedures to be performed. For example, in verifying the cash in bank account, it is customary to include the bank reconciliation in the audit evidence. When the auditor believes there is a low risk of errors in processing cash transactions, he may be satisfied to review the bank reconciliation prepared by the client. However, when the risk of errors is high, the auditor may deem it necessary to (1) obtain the bank

[12]Auditing Standards Board, *op. cit.*, AU § 320.82.

statement directly from the bank and (2) prepare the bank reconciliation himself.

Timing

The extent of the auditor's reliance on internal control may affect the time when the testing is done. For instance, when there is low risk of errors in processing sales transactions, a major portion of the examination of accounts receivable may be done several months prior to the end of the year. In contrast, when the risk of errors is high, most, if not all, of the examination is likely to be performed at or near the balance sheet date.

Extent

The auditor's reliance on internal control may also affect the degree or amount of substantive testing to be performed. Thus, fewer customer accounts (a smaller sample) will be examined when the risk of errors in processing sales transactions is low than when the risk of errors is high.

REQUIRED COMMUNICATION OF MATERIAL WEAKNESSES

During a financial statement audit, the auditor is required by GAAS to communicate any material weaknesses in internal accounting control that come to his attention to senior management and the board of directors or its audit committee.[13] The communication should be made at the earliest practicable date. The auditor may communicate orally or in writing. Further consideration is given to this requirement, including the form and content of a written report on material weaknesses, in Chapter 16 under the section "Completing the Audit."

ENGAGEMENT TO REPORT ON INTERNAL ACCOUNTING CONTROL

A CPA may be engaged to report on an entity's system of internal accounting control. The circumstances and types of reports are explained and illustrated in Chapter 18.

CONCLUDING COMMENTS

The study and evaluation of internal accounting control are vital parts of field work in a financial statement audit. The basic principles of internal accounting control and the methodology described in this chapter to meet this standard provide the framework for considering additional aspects of internal accounting control in future chapters. This consideration begins in the next chapter, where we explain the internal control implications of electronic data processing (EDP) systems.

---

[13] Auditing Standards Board, *op. cit.*, AU § 323.01.

Appendix 5A

Flowcharting

Auditors frequently use an internal control questionnaire or a narrative memorandum, or both, to document their understanding of relevant aspects of an internal control system. This documentation serves as the basis for the auditor's evaluation of the internal control system. Increasingly, auditors are supplementing the information derived from questionnaires or memoranda with flowcharts of their clients' systems. This is due, in part, to the pervasive use of flowcharts by clients with EDP systems.

A flowchart is a schematic representation of the flow of data through a sequence of operations performed in a control system. Flowcharting is a particularly effective method of showing relationships among the various functions performed. For auditing purposes, flowcharts often are prepared for the major classes of transactions such as sales, cash receipts, purchases, cash disbursements, payroll, and manufacturing. In practice, flowcharts range from very abbreviated to very detailed portrayals, and employ a variety of symbols and techniques. The more commonly used symbols are shown in Figure 5A-1.

To be of maximum usefulness in the evaluation process, a flowchart should reveal the source, flow, and disposition of all important documents, including the locations of major files and records used in processing. Additionally, each operation or should be depicted and identified with some function or department (e.g., purchasing, billing, or general accounting) or an individual performing the task (e.g., purchasing agent, billing clerk, or general ledger clerk). Segregation of functions may be indicated either by partitioning the flowchart into areas labeled by function, department, or individual, or by striping, a technique in which the function, department, or individual performing the task is shown in a stripe across the top of an operation or process symbol.

The use of these and other flowcharting techniques is demonstrated in many illustrative flowcharts in subsequent chapters of this book. For example, Figures 8-2 and 8-3 on pages 267 and 269, respectively, contain sample flowcharts for the execution and recording of sales transactions in a manual system. Figure 8-7 on page 277 presents a more abbreviated form of flowchart for the computerized processing of sales transactions.

Study of these flowcharts reveals a number of additional flowcharting techniques. Generally, the direction of flow is from top to bottom and from left to right. Figures 8-2 and 8-3 illustrate the use of connectors to enhance clarity by avoiding the need for long flow lines crossing through one or more partitions. On the other hand, in the more abbreviated flowchart in Figure 8-7,

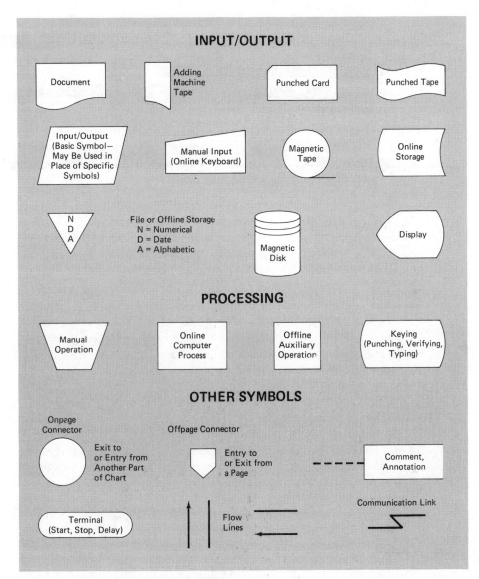

Figure 5A-1. FLOWCHARTING SYMBOLS.

flow lines running between partitions have been used, omitting the need for connector symbols.

Flowcharting is a creative task making it unlikely that any two people would draw flowcharts exactly alike for a given system. However, the following guidelines should prove helpful:

- Identify the classes of transactions to be flowcharted.
- Collect the necessary information through interviews, observations, and review of documents.

- Visualize an organizational format for the flowchart (e.g., whether to use partitions or striping to indicate segregation of functions) and prepare a rough sketch.
- Prepare the flowchart in good form.
- Test the completeness and accuracy of the flowchart by tracing a hypothetical transaction through the flowchart.

It should be emphasized that flowcharting is a means to an end, not an end in itself. From flowcharts and information obtained from questionnaires and other sources, the auditor should have ample knowledge to make an evaluation of the client's prescribed controls.

REVIEW QUESTIONS

5-1 What are the basic similarities and differences between administrative control and accounting control?

5-2 What are the four operative objectives of internal accounting control?

5-3 Explain the meaning of the terms (a) safeguarding of assets, (b) reliability of financial records, and (c) transactions, as these terms relate to accounting control.

5-4 Enumerate the factors that pertain to the internal control environment.

5-5 Identify the six basic principles of internal accounting control.

5-6 a. When is the assignment of duties among personnel deemed to be compatible? Incompatible?
b. What conditions are important in independent internal verification?

5-7 a. State the second standard of field work.
b. Indicate the scope and objectives of this standard.

5-8 a. Identify the parts and phases of the study of a system of internal accounting control.
b. How much of the study must be completed in each audit engagement?

5-9 Distinguish between the two phases of the review of the system as to (a) nature, (b) method, and (c) purpose.

5-10 Contrast the advantages and disadvantages of using (a) questionnaires and (b) flowcharts in the completion phase of the review.

5-11 Describe the nature and purpose of a transaction walk-through review.

5-12 Indicate (a) the steps required in making a preliminary evaluation and (b) the method used by the auditor in performing each step.

5-13 What is the difference between a weakness and a material weakness?

5-14 Indicate (a) the three questions that are of concern in performing compliance tests and (b) the auditing procedures used in these tests.

5-15 Distinguish between compliance and substantive tests as to (a) primary purpose and (b) applicable standards of field work.

5-16 "Compliance tests are normally performed during both interim and year-end work." Evaluate the accuracy of this statement.

5-17 What is meant by dual purpose testing?

5-18 a. To what extent can the independent auditor use the work of internal auditors in his study and evaluation of internal accounting control?

b. What responsibility does the independent auditor have in regard to all judgments about the system of internal control?

5-19 Explain (a) the nature and purpose of the final evaluation of the system and (b) the levels of risk that may be identified.

5-20 a. What are the two aspects of audit risk that pertain to the standards of field work?

b. How does the auditor attempt to minimize these risks?

OBJECTIVE QUESTIONS FROM PROFESSIONAL EXAMINATIONS

Indicate the *best* answer for each of the following multiple choice questions.

5-21 These questions relate to basic considerations about internal control.

1. Of the following statements about an internal control system, which one is *not* valid?
   a. No one person should be responsible for the custodial responsibility and the recording responsibility for an asset.
   b. Transactions must be properly authorized before such transactions are processed.
   c. Because of the cost/benefit relationship, a client may apply control procedures on a test basis.
   d. Control procedures reasonably insure that collusion among employees cannot occur.
2. Proper segregation of functional responsibilities calls for separation of the
   a. Authorization, approval, and execution functions.
   b. Authorization, execution, and payment functions.
   c. Receiving, shipping, and custodial functions.
   d. Authorization, recording, and custodial functions.
3. In a properly designed internal accounting control system, the same employee should *not* be permitted to
   a. Sign checks and cancel supporting documents.
   b. Receive merchandise and prepare a receiving report.
   c. Prepare disbursement vouchers and sign checks.
   d. Initiate a request to order merchandise and approve merchandise received.
4. In general, a material internal control weakness may be defined as a condition in which material errors or irregularities would ordinarily *not* be detected within a timely period by
   a. An auditor during the normal study and evaluation of the system of internal control.
   b. A controller when reconciling accounts in the general ledger.
   c. Employees in the normal course of performing their assigned functions.
   d. The chief financial officer when reviewing interim financial statements.
5. Which of the following would be *least* likely to be considered an objective of a system of internal control?
   a. Checking the accuracy and reliability of accounting data.
   b. Detecting management fraud.
   c. Encouraging adherence to managerial policies.
   d. Safeguarding assets.

5-22 These questions pertain to the study and evaluation of internal control.

1. An auditor evaluates the existing system of internal control in order to
   a. Determine the extent of compliance tests that must be performed.
   b. Determine the extent of substantive tests that must be performed.
   c. Ascertain whether irregularities are probable.
   d. Ascertain whether any employees have incompatible functions.

2. A secondary objective of the auditor's study and evaluation of internal control is that the study and evaluation provide
   a. A basis for constructive suggestions concerning improvements in internal control.
   b. A basis for reliance on the system of internal accounting control.
   c. An assurance that the records and documents have been maintained in accordance with existing company policies and procedures.
   d. A basis for the determination of the resultant extent of the tests to which auditing procedures are to be restricted.

3. After finishing the review phase of the study and evaluation of internal control in an audit engagement, the auditor should perform compliance tests on
   a. Those controls that the auditor plans to rely on.
   b. Those controls in which material weaknesses were identified.
   c. Those controls that have a material effect on the financial statement balances.
   d. A random sample of the controls that were reviewed.

4. Which of the following is the correct order of performing the auditing procedures A through C below?
   A = Compliance tests.
   B = Preparation of a flowchart depicting the client's system of internal control.
   C = Substantive tests.
   a. ABC.
   b. ACB.
   c. BAC.
   d. BCA.

5. When reviewing the system of internal control, the auditor would ordinarily prepare and obtain answers to an internal control questionnaire based upon a tentative flowchart of the system. The next step should ordinarily be to
   a. Determine the extent of audit work necessary to form an opinion.
   b. Arrive at a decision regarding the effectiveness of the internal control system.
   c. Gather enough evidence to determine if the internal control system is functioning as described.
   d. Make a preliminary evaluation of the internal control system assuming satisfactory compliance.

COMPREHENSIVE QUESTIONS

5-23 An important procedure in the CPA's audit programs is his review of the client's system of internal control.

Required

a. Distinguish between accounting controls and administrative controls in a properly coordinated system of internal control.

b. What bearing do these controls have on the work of the independent auditor?

c. List the basic principles of a sound system of accounting control.

AICPA (adapted)

5-24 Jones, CPA, who has been engaged to examine the financial statements of Ajax Inc., is about to commence a study and evaluation of Ajax's system of internal control and is aware of the inherent limitations that should be considered.

Required

a. What are the objectives of a system of internal accounting control?

b. What are the reasonable assurances that are intended to be provided by the system of internal accounting control?

c. When considering the potential effectiveness of any system of internal accounting control, what are the inherent limitations that should be recognized?

AICPA

5-25 Six principles of internal accounting control are identified in the chapter. Listed below are specific control procedures:

1. Cash registers are used for over-the-counter cash receipts.
2. Different individuals approve the payroll, write the payroll checks, and distribute the checks.
3. Checks are prenumbered.
4. Bank statements are independently reconciled each month.
5. Credit is approved by the credit department prior to sale.
6. A chart of accounts is maintained.
7. Inventory is stored in locked warehouses.
8. A voucher system is used.
9. Material requisitions are required to withdraw raw materials from the storeroom.
10. Control accounts and subsidiary ledgers are periodically agreed.

Required

a. Identify the internal control principle to which each procedure relates.

b. Identify two other procedures that apply to each internal control principle.

5-26 The Richmond Company, a client of your firm, has come to you with the following problem. It has three clerical employees who must perform the following functions:

1. Maintain general ledger.
2. Maintain accounts payable ledger.
3. Maintain accounts receivable ledger.
4. Prepare checks for signature.
5. Maintain disbursements journal.
6. Issue credits on returns and allowances.
7. Reconcile the bank account.
8. Handle and deposit cash receipts.

Required

Assuming there is no problem as to the ability of any of the employees, the company requests your advice on assigning the above functions to the three employees in such a manner as to achieve the highest degree of internal control. It may be assumed that these employees will perform no other accounting functions than the ones listed.

a. State how you would recommend distributing the above functions among the three employees. Assume that, with the exception of the nominal jobs of the bank reconciliation and the issuance of credits on returns and allowances, all functions require an equal amount of time. (*Hint:* Give each employee a job title.)

b. List four possible unsatisfactory combinations of the above listed functions.

AICPA (adapted)

5-27 As an audit manager, you find it necessary to provide an inexperienced assistant with an overview and an explanation of the auditor's study and evaluation of a client's system of internal accounting control.

Required

a. Present a flowchart of the auditor's study and evaluation of internal accounting control.

b. Explain the decision paths that may be followed with respect to substantive tests and indicate the effect of each path on the amount of substantive testing.

c. Explain the two conditions that normally justify a decision to complete the review.

d. Indicate the factors that might cause the auditor to forego compliance testing of prescribed controls.

e. Give the assistant an explanation of the manner in which the final evaluation of the system may be expressed.

5-28 ToysGalore Inc., a privately owned retail chain of toy stores operating in the Midwest, is having its financial statements audited for the first time by an external auditor. Management believes that the audited financial statements will help it to obtain the financing that will be needed for an expansion of operations.

The partner in charge of the audit engagement has suggested that the review and testing of the ToysGalore's internal accounting control system be performed at an interim date. Tom Kodd, President of ToysGalore, has replied by asking, "What is the purpose of reviewing and testing internal accounting controls? Won't that take a lot of time and add significantly to the cost of the audit? What criteria would you use for evaluating our internal accounting control system, and what kind of evidence would you require?"

Required

a. Explain the purpose of the external auditor's study and evaluation of internal accounting control in connection with an audit of financial statements.

b. Identify the four criteria that would be used by the external auditor to determine if an audit client's internal accounting controls are adequate.

c. There are two parts in the internal accounting control study conducted by an external auditor that lead to a final evaluation of the system.

1. Identify the two parts of the internal accounting control study.

2. Explain what the external auditor would review to gather evidence during each of these two phases of the internal accounting control study.

CMA (adapted)

5-29 Adherence to GAAS requires, among other things, a proper study and evaluation of the existing internal control. The most common approaches to reviewing the system of internal control include the use of a questionnaire, preparation of a written description, preparation of a flowchart, and combinations of these methods.

Required

a. What is a CPA's objective in reviewing internal control for an opinion audit?
b. Discuss the advantages to a CPA of reviewing internal control by using
   1. An internal control questionnaire.
   2. The written description approach.
   3. A flowchart.
c. If after completing his description of internal control for an opinion audit, the CPA is satisfied that no material weaknesses in the client's internal control system exist, is it necessary to perform compliance tests? Explain.

AICPA (adapted)

5-30 For each of the following questions appearing on an internal accounting control questionnaire, assume that a "No" answer is given:

1. Is there separation of duties between the journalizing of transactions and posting of subsidiary ledgers?
2. Are cash registers used to register cash receipts?
3. Is voucher preparation and check signing done by different individuals?
4. Are independent counts made of raw materials in storeroom?
5. Are all sales transactions authorized?
6. Are all bad debt write-offs authorized in writing prior to recording?
7. Is access to storeroom restricted to storeroom personnel?
8. Are prenumbered checks journalized in sequence?
9. Are prenumbered vouchers used in approving purchases for payment?
10. Are bank statements independently reconciled?
11. Is storeroom enclosed and locked?
12. Is a chart of accounts used in journalizing?

Required

a. Indicate the error or irregularity that could occur for each weakness.
b. Identify the internal control principle(s) involved in each situation.
c. Indicate by name (execution, recording, access, or comparison) the operative objective of internal accounting control to which the condition relates.

5-31 In your capacity as a staff assistant, you have worked on a number of audits during the year. Listed below are a list of possible internal control weaknesses that you have noted in your working papers:

1. A supermarket deposits cash intact every fourth day.

2. The cashier makes bank deposits, records cash transactions, and reconciles the bank statements.

3. The board of directors of a multinational company delegates the authorization of capital budgeting expenditures of less than $100,000 to the vice-president of manufacturing.

4. The reconciliation of the bank statement is made by a subsidiary ledger accounting clerk who does not have access to cash.

5. Office supplies in a large manufacturing company are stored in an unlocked closet in the office.

6. The write-off of bad debts is authorized by the accounts receivable clerk whenever a balance is two months past due.

7. Prenumbered receiving reports are not used in the receiving department.

8. The shipping department orally notifies the billing department of goods shipped.

9. Storeroom personnel and all foreman have access to the raw materials storeroom.

10. Monthly statements are not sent to customers.

Required

a. Classify the foregoing as (1) no weakness, (2) immaterial weakness, and (3) material weakness. Give the reasons for your answer.

b. For immaterial and material weaknesses, indicate the internal control principle that has been violated.

c. Indicate your suggestions for eliminating any immaterial or material weaknesses.

5-32 The system of internal accounting control of the Trusty Company includes the following control procedures:

1. An approved voucher is required for each check issued.

2. Two signatures are required on every check.

3. A supervisor makes daily cash register counts.

4. Overtime work must be approved by a supervisor.

5. Prenumbered sales invoices are used in billing.

6. A second clerk is required to verify the accuracy of each voucher.

7. Employee payroll records are kept in a locked file cabinet.

8. An accounting supervisor reviews journal entries periodically for reasonableness of account classifications.

9. Accounts receivable accounting personnel only make postings to the customers' ledger.

10. All vouchers must be stamped *paid* on payment.

11. Only EDP equipment operators are allowed in the computer room.

12. A supervisor reconciles accounts receivable control with the customer ledger monthly.

Required

a. Indicate the internal control principle(s) applicable to each procedure.

b. Indicate an error or irregularity that could be prevented by each procedure.

c. Identify a compliance test that may be performed for each procedure.

5-33 The following is a list of prescribed accounting control procedures:

1. After the treasurer of the Ardent Company signs disbursement checks, the supporting data are returned to the accounting department, and the checks are given to his secretary for mailing.
2. The ticket-taker of a theater is required to tear each ticket presented for admission in half and present the stub to the patron.
3. The clerks of a department store are instructed to give the customer his cash register receipt along with the proper change.
4. The waitresses of the Elite Restaurant prepare the customer's check, which the customer then pays to the cashier. The waitresses are instructed not to make corrections on the check, but if an error is made to void the check and issue a new check. All voided checks are to be given to the manager at the end of the day.
5. The Larson Manufacturing Company prepares six copies of each purchase order. The third copy is sent to the receiving department to be used as a receiving memo, but the form is so designed that the quantity ordered does not print on this copy.
6. Hourly workers are required to punch clock cards.
7. A manager reconciles cash on hand with cash register readings daily.
8. An internal auditor reconciles the bank statements each month.
9. The credit department approves all credit sales.
10. Unused checks are stored in a safe under the custody of the treasurer.

Required

For each procedure, indicate

a. The applicable internal control principle(s).
b. Identify the operative objective of accounting control to which the procedure relates.
c. Give an example of an error or irregularity that may be prevented.

5-34 At the Main Street Theater, the cashier, located in a box office at the entrance, receives cash from customers and operates a machine that ejects serially numbered tickets. To gain admission to the theater, a customer hands the ticket to a doorperson stationed some 50 feet from the box office at the entrance to the theater lobby. The doorperson tears the ticket in half, opens the door for the customer, and returns the stub to him. The other half of the ticket is dropped by the doorperson into a locked box.

Required

a. What internal controls are present in this phase of handling cash receipts?
b. What steps should be taken regularly by the manager or other supervisor to give maximum effectiveness to these controls?
c. Assume that the cashier and doorperson decided to collaborate in an effort to abstract cash receipts. What action might they take?
d. Continuing the assumption made in (c) above of collusion between the cashier and doorperson, what features of the control procedures would be likely to disclose the embezzlement?

AICPA

5-35 A description of some of the operating procedures of the Greystone Manufacturing Corporation is given in the succeeding paragraphs:

1. When materials are ordered, a duplicate of the purchase order is sent to the receiving department. When the materials are received, the receiving clerk records the receipt on the copy of the order, which is then sent to the accounting department to support the entry to Accounts Payable and Purchases. The materials are then taken to stores where the quantity is entered on bin records.

2. Timecards of employees are sent to a data processing department that prepares punched cards for use in the preparation of payrolls, payroll checks, and labor cost distribution records. The payroll checks are compared with the payrolls and signed by an official of the company who returns them to the supervisor of the data processing department for distribution to employees.

3. A sales branch of the company has an office force consisting of the manager and two assistants. The branch has a local bank account in which it deposits cash receipts. Checks drawn on this account require the manager's signature or the signature of the treasurer of the company. Bank statements and paid checks are returned by the bank to the manager, who retains them in his files after making the reconciliation. Reports of disbursements are prepared by the manager and submitted to the home office on scheduled dates.

Required

For each of the activities described, you are to point out

a. The deficiencies, if any, in internal control, including an explanation of the errors or irregularities that might occur.

b. Recommendations for changes in procedures that would correct the existing weaknesses.

AICPA (adapted)

CASE STUDY

5-36* Harlan, Inc., is a large, highly diversified organization engaged in feed and flour milling, the manufacture of plastic products, the manufacture of highly specialized machinery, and the operation of poultry hatcheries, farms, and processing plants. The company's facilities are located throughout the United States.

During the past several years, the company has been expanding the business through acquisitions, mergers, and natural growth of the original operations.

The company finances poultry growing operations of feed customers until the flocks are marketed. Poultry prices have been depressed for the past several years, and as a result, large bad debt losses have been sustained. Many accounts are secured by collateral other than poultry and are not considered current assets.

Your review of the current internal controls and accounting procedures disclosed the following changes from prior years:

1. The company organized an internal audit staff during the year.

2. The internal audit staff is reconciling all bank accounts.

3. The company has instituted a procedure whereby divisions send the Home Office an "invoice apron" that lists the information required for payment of the invoices and the due date. The other invoices and other supporting data (e.g., receiving reports, purchase orders) remain at the receiving location.

4. Excess funds are now invested in short-term securities. The treasurer has sole authority for purchase and sale of the investments. Securities purchases are credited to a company account at a local brokerage house. The securities are held in the treasurer's name. All correspondence related to the investments is sent directly to the treasurer. He, in turn, forwards brokerage advices to the controller's office for recording in the accounts.

5. A physical inventory of office furniture and fixtures has been taken at the home office.

Discussions with company personnel and compliance testing disclosed the following information:

1. The company plans to discontinue extending credit to certain customers whose poultry raising operations have deteriorated to the point that their ability to repay the company is doubtful. It is anticipated that a large provision for doubtful accounts may be necessary to reduce these accounts to estimated realizable value on a forced realization basis (the company has second mortgages as collateral on many of the farms).

2. The tool crib inventory consists of a conglomeration of miscellaneous items, most of which are small quantities with very minor unit prices. This inventory totals $42,395.89 which is an insignificant portion of the total inventories.

3. The purchased parts stockroom at another plant is segregated from the production areas by a wire fence. While visiting this plant, you noted that the gate was left open all day and access to the stockroom (which contains many valuable and easily concealed items) was available to any employee. The stockroom's perpetual inventory records were formerly checked by an employee who made periodic test counts. This employee has retired and not been replaced. As a result, such counting has ceased. You expanded your tests in view of these situations and are satisified that the perpetual records reasonably reflect the quantities on hand.

Required

a. Identify the environmental factors that impact on the company's internal accounting controls.

b. List identified strengths and weaknesses in Harlan's procedures.

c. From your list of weaknesses, identify those you consider material and indicate your suggestions for improvement in your required communication to management.

d. Indicate the areas in which you would likely extend your substantive tests.

Chapter 6

Auditing Electronic Data Processing Systems

Study Objectives

When you have finished your study of this chapter, you should be able to

- Describe the basic components of an EDP system.
- Identify the types of accounting controls in an EDP system.
- Explain the similarities and differences in making a study and evaluation of internal control between a manual and an EDP system.
- Prepare and execute an audit program for testing general controls.
- Describe the computer-assisted techniques for testing application controls.
- Indicate the nature and uses of generalized audit software.
- Explain the auditor's responsibilities in auditing small computer systems and service center-produced data.

Electronic Data Processing (EDP) has been one of the most important technological developments in the latter half of the twentieth century. Computer installations now range in size from microcomputers to minicomputers to large mainframe computers linked together in complex international financial communication networks. A company may elect to lease or own its computer system or to use outside, independent computer service centers to process accounting data. Thus, even a very small audit client may have some data processed electronically. Coupled with the greater use of computers in business has been a corresponding increase in computer-related frauds.

In this chapter, consideration is given initially to the basic components and types of accounting controls in a computerized system. Then attention is given to the auditor's study and evaluation of internal controls in EDP systems, and to the audit effects of small computer systems and computer service organizations.

EDP SYSTEM COMPONENTS

The auditor should be familiar with the following components of an EDP system:

- Hardware.
- Software.
- Data organization and processing methods.

COMPUTER HARDWARE

Hardware is the physical equipment associated with the system. The basic hardware configuration consists of the central processing unit (CPU) and peripheral input and output devices. The principal hardware component is the CPU. It is composed of a control unit, an internal storage unit, and an arithmetic-logic unit. The control unit directs and coordinates the entire system, including the entry and removal of information from storage, and the routing of the data between storage and the arithmetic-logic unit. The internal storage unit, or computer "memory," stores the program instructions and the data to be processed. The arithmetic logic-unit is so named because it is capable of performing mathematical computations and certain logical operations. Peripheral to the CPU are input devices, output devices, and auxiliary storage devices. Figure 6-1 illustrates common types of computer hardware.

Terminals are directly connected to the CPU. Generally, they are located in remote locations. Keyboard printer terminals have keyboards similar to a typewriter that provide hard copy of the data being entered. Visual display terminals also have keyboards and show the data on a screen. Character recognition devices consist of optical character recognition (OCR) and magnetic ink character recognition (MICR) devices. These devices read documents containing typed or coded characters and enter the data directly into the CPU or onto machine-readable media.

The printer is a widely used output device. It produces hard copy in the form of documents, reports, and so on. Peripheral equipment in direct communication with the CPU is considered to be on-line.

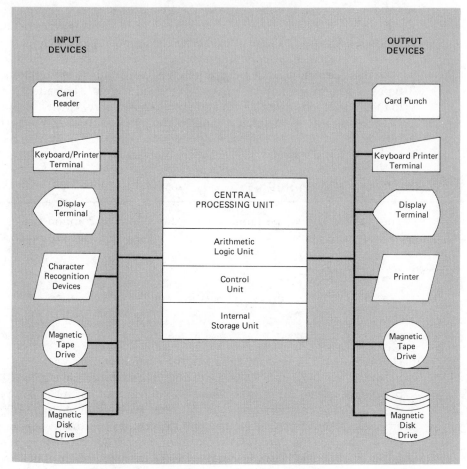

Figure 6-1. COMPUTER HARDWARE.

COMPUTER SOFTWARE

This component consists of the programs and routines that facilitate the programming and operation of a computer. There are several kinds of computer software. Of particular interest to auditors are: (1) systems programs and (2) application programs.

Systems Programs

These programs, sometimes called *supervisory programs,* perform general functions required for the operation of the computer as it executes specific tasks. Systems programs include the following:

- *Operating systems* direct the operation of the computer, including input and output devices, main storage, execution of programs, and management of files.

- *Utility programs* perform common data processing tasks, such as copying, reorganizing data in a file, sorting, merging, and printing. Other kinds of utility programs may be used to gather information about the use of the hardware and software, aid in the detection of unauthorized use or changes to programs and data, provide documentation of program logic, and facilitate testing of new systems.

- *Compilers and assemblers* translate specific programming languages into instructions in a language that can be understood by the computer. Each computer has a specific machine language determined by the engineers who designed it.

- *Database management systems* are utilized by companies employing a computerized database; these programs control the data records and files independently of the application programs that allow changes in or use of the data.

Systems programs generally are purchased from hardware suppliers and software companies. They are then adapted, as necessary, by each user to suit individual needs.

Application Programs

Application programs contain instructions that enable the user to perform data processing tasks appropriate for specific applications—such as payroll, inventory, and so on. These programs are generally written by the user of the equipment, but they may also be purchased from software vendors.

The instructions can be classified into four types: (1) input-output, (2) data movement, (3) arithmetic, and (4) logic. The input instruction enables the computer to read data from an appropriate input medium and store it in the computer memory. To get the data out of storage and onto an output medium, the output instruction must be provided. The data movement instruction allows a computer to move data from one storage location to another. Arithmetic instructions are used to specify the arithmetic operations and the data fields to be operated on. The basic concept of the logic instruction is the comparison of two sets of data in storage and the branching of the program to a particular step when a certain condition (equal, greater than, or less than) is found after the comparison of the data.

DATA ORGANIZATION AND PROCESSING METHODS

The accounting function often involves recording, updating, retrieving, and reporting on large volumes of transaction data and related information. In an EDP environment, data organization refers to the method(s) used to organize data within files. In contrast, data processing methods refer to (1) entering the data into the computer and (2) processing of the data by the computer. Collectively, these activities are referred to as *data management*. The two principal methods of data organization and the three most widely used processing methods are explained below.

Traditional File Method

The traditional file method of data organization predominates in accounting applications. Under this method, two types of files are maintained: (1) *master files* that contain up-to-date information about a given class of data such as the current balances of customers' accounts or the current quantities of inventory items and (2) *transaction files* that contain the details of individual transactions of the same class such as a day's credit sales or a day's cash disbursements.

These files may be organized for *sequential* or *direct access* processing. In sequential files, information is maintained in a particular sequence or order. When a master file is organized sequentially, related transaction file data must be sorted into the same order before it can be used to update the master file. For example, if an accounts receivable master file is organized by customer number, the daily credit sales transaction file must be sorted into the same sequence before updating occurs. Also, each time a sequential master file is updated, the entire file must be read by the computer even though only a few accounts or records on the file may be affected by the day's transaction file. Sequential files are usually kept on magnetic tape.

In direct access files, neither the master nor related transaction file data are maintained in any particular order. The transaction file need not be sorted prior to processing. Furthermore, the computer is able to skip over those accounts on the master file not being updated, reading only those accounts for which the transaction file contains updating data. Thus, direct access files may be processed more efficiently. These files are usually kept on magnetic disks. Differences in the processing of sequential and direct access files are illustrated in Figure 6-2.

Under the traditional file method, separate master and transaction files are maintained for each application such as accounts receivable, inventory, payroll, and sales. Typically, the data in these files are accessible only by the single application program for which the files were created. Because of this, redundancy of data across files is common. For instance, a payroll file generally includes the following data elements among others: employee name, social security number, address, and pay rate. All of these same data elements are likely to be repeated in a separate personnel file. The creation and maintenance of the same data elements in several files is costly. The single program access and redundancy drawbacks of the traditional file method are overcome in the database method as explained below.

Database Method

The database method of data organization is the principal alternative to the traditional file method. This method is based on the creation and maintenance

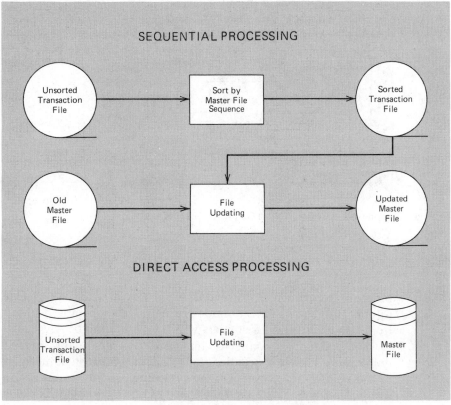

Figure 6-2. SEQUENTIAL AND DIRECT ACCESS PROCESSING.

of a single common file for all applications using common data. Thus, each data element is stored only once but is accessible by all authorized application programs. In the case of the payroll and personnel applications mentioned above, the employee name, social security number, address, and pay rate data would be included in the file just once, but would be useable in both application programs. Sophisticated *database management system software* is designed to provide control over which users and applications can access and change specific data elements.

File organization under this method is based on logical, rather than physical, relationships among data. One technique used to logically relate the data elements is the *chain (or list) and pointer system.* In this system, related records need not be physically adjacent to each other. Rather, logically related records are linked by pointers. A pointer is a data field within a record that contains the storage address of the next logical record in the chain. Figure 6-3 illustrates the use of dual pointers, one to give the address of the previous logically related record in the file and one to give the address of the next logically related record. The logical relationship identified through the pointers is "em-

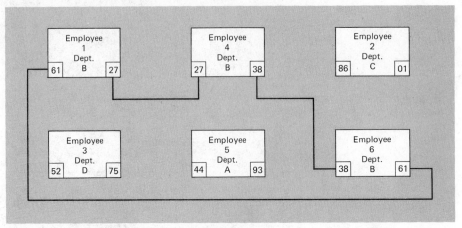

Figure 6-3. CHAIN AND POINTER METHOD.

ployee in Department B." Most data elements will be logically related to several records and chains. Other examples of logical relationships include "purchases from Vendor B" and "customers with a credit rating of AA."

Though data redundancy is eliminated, this file organization generally requires more storage space than traditional files because of the space occupied by the pointers. However, efficiencies in the procedures for entering, updating, and retrieving data, and the speed of processing usually more than compensate for the additional storage space. Direct access devices such as magnetic disks are used as the storage medium. Once used only in very large systems, the database method is gaining popularity in medium and smaller systems as well.

Batch Entry/Batch Processing

In this type of EDP processing, data are accumulated by classes of transactions, such as sales or cash disbursements, and are both entered and processed in batches. Data entry may involve conversion of the data from source documents to machine-readable form by keying the data onto punch cards or magnetic tape or disk. Usually, a second data entry clerk verifies the accuracy of the conversion by rekeying the same data. Alternatively, the data may already be machine-readable in the form of *turnaround documents* such as the punched cards or documents with optical or magnetic ink characters required to be returned with payments on utility and credit card billings. Once in machine-readable form, the file may or may not have to be sorted depending on whether sequential or direct access files are used.

Batch entry/batch processing is generally efficient because similar transactions are processed together. Other advantages include the ability to generate batch or control totals prior to processing and the use of batch numbers as transaction trail or processing references. One disadvantage of this type of processing is that the master file cannot be updated until the batch data are accumulated. In addition, there are usually delays in correcting processing errors identified by edit routines because errors in source documents or in converting data into machine-readable form must be completely recycled. An illustration of batch entry/batch processing is provided in Figure 6-4.

On-Line Entry/Batch Processing

Under this method of processing, individual transactions are entered directly into the computer via a terminal as they occur. A machine-readable validated transaction file is accumulated as the transactions are entered. This file is subsequently processed to update the master file. An advantage of this method is that the data are subjected to certain edit or validation checks by the computer program at the time of entry and error messages are communicated immediately to the terminal operator. For example, the programmed edit routine may detect missing, incomplete, or invalid data such as a nonexistent customer number. This permits immediate detection and correction of most data entry errors. The method also retains the control advantages of batch entry/batch processing—namely, batch control totals and batch reference numbers.

On-line entry/batch processing may be used either with reference access to the related master file or with no access. In reference access, the file may be read but not updated from the terminal. Reference access is necessary in

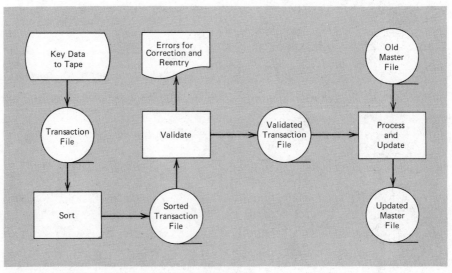

Figure 6-4. BATCH ENTRY/BATCH PROCESSING.

cash receipts processing in which payments received from customers must be matched with open invoices in the customer's file. In contrast with no access, the related master file cannot be read when the transaction data are entered. The reading of the master file usually is not required prior to batch processing sales and payroll transactions. Figure 6-5 illustrates on-line entry/batch processing both with and without access.

On-Line Entry/On-Line Processing

Also called on-line/realtime processing (OLRT), this type of processing permits immediate validation of data entry, as described above. It differs from on-line entry/batch processing in two respects: (1) master files are updated concurrently with data entry and (2) a transaction log is produced that consists of a chronological record of all transactions. The log is not sorted by class of transactions. To provide a transaction trail, each transaction is assigned a unique identifying number by the computer program.

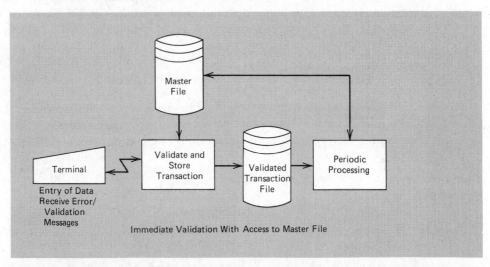

Immediate Validation With Access to Master File

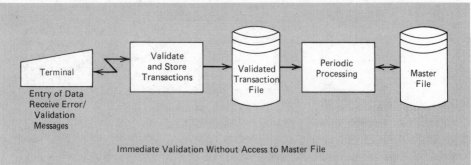

Immediate Validation Without Access to Master File

Figure 6-5. ON-LINE ENTRY/BATCH PROCESSING. (SOURCE: Gordon B. Davis, Donald L. Adams, and Carol A. Schaller, *Auditing and EDP*, Second Edition (New York: American Institute of Certified Public Accountants, 1983), p. 147–148.) (adapted)

On-line entry/on-line processing is used in airline and hotel reservations systems. A common accounting application is found in many retail stores where electronic cash registers immediately update inventory records when the sale is rung up.

The major disadvantages of this type of processing are the risk of errors in the master file from concurrent updating and the possible loss of part or all of the master files in case of hardware failure. To minimize these risks, some companies use memo updating of the master file at the time of data entry. This involves the use of a copy of the master file. The transaction log is then used to update the actual master file periodically. Figure 6-6 illustrates both immediate processing and memo updating of the master file under on-line entry/on-line processing.

INTERNAL CONTROL IN AN EDP SYSTEM

Most EDP systems involve a combination of manual and computer processing activities. In the usual case, separate control procedures are developed for each phase of the processing. As in a completely manual system, management has the responsibility for providing the control environment and for establishing and maintaining the system of internal control when EDP is used. The broad objectives of internal control also remain the same: to safeguard assets and produce reliable financial records.

INTERNAL CONTROL ENVIRONMENT

The method of data processing may significantly affect the organizational structure and the control procedures necessary to meet the broad objectives of internal accounting control. Typically, EDP has a significant impact on internal control. In determining its effect on the control environment, the auditor should consider the following differences between manual and EDP activities:

- There is often less documentary evidence of the performance of control procedures in computer systems than in manual systems.
- Information in manual systems is visible. In contrast, files and records in EDP systems are usually in machine-sensible form and cannot be read without a computer.
- The decrease of human involvement in EDP processing can obscure errors that might be observed in manual systems.
- Information in EDP systems may be more vulnerable to physical disaster, unauthorized manipulation, and mechanical malfunction than information in manual systems.
- Various functions may be concentrated in EDP systems, with a corresponding reduction in the traditional segregation of duties followed in manual systems.

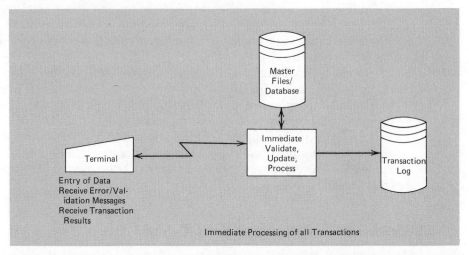

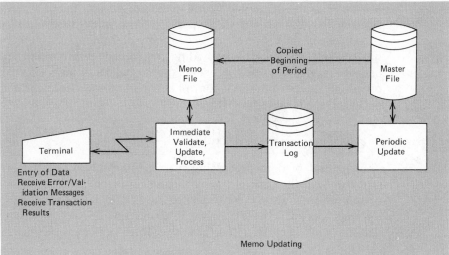

Figure 6-6. ON-LINE ENTRY/ON-LINE PROCESSING. (SOURCE: *Auditing and EDP*, op. cit., p. 145.) (adapted)

- Changes in the system are often more difficult to implement and control in EDP systems than in manual systems.
- EDP systems can provide greater consistency in processing than manual systems because they uniformly subject all transactions to the same controls.

The concentration of functions within EDP systems tends to combine duties that would be incompatible in a manual system. For example, in the processing of payroll transactions, the computer may be programmed to compute gross and net earnings, record the payroll, update employee earning records, and prepare the payroll checks. If one individual performed these duties in a manual system, that person would be in a position to both perpetrate and conceal errors. The safeguard in an electronic system rests in the computer program. Once the program has been tested (debugged) and approved, that program will process transactions uniformly. The risk, from a control standpoint, is in the possibility of unauthorized changes in the program rather than the possibility of processing errors. It is for this reason that programming and machine operation should be separated.

Similarly, an individual should not be able to make unapproved changes in EDP data files. In the preceding payroll application, an individual should not be able to add fictitious employees or false pay rates to the file data, thereby causing the payroll program to process incorrect payroll checks. An individual who can make unapproved changes in systems programs or file data also performs incompatible functions. When incompatible duties exist, other compensating controls should be provided.

A good control environment pertaining to EDP activities complements prescribed EDP control procedures whereas a poor environment may impede the effectiveness of such procedures. The auditor's evaluation of the control environment ordinarily will influence his study and evaluation of prescribed EDP controls.

ACCOUNTING CONTROLS

There are two categories of accounting controls in a computerized system: general and application.

General controls pertain to the EDP environment and all EDP activities. These controls tend to be pervasive in their effect. Included within this category are the following:

- Organization and operation controls.
- Systems development and documentation controls.
- Hardware and systems software controls.
- Access controls.
- Data and procedural controls.[1]

Application controls relate to specific tasks to be performed by the computer. These controls are designed to provide reasonable assurance that the recording, processing, and reporting of data by EDP are properly performed. Included within this category of EDP controls are

- Input controls.
- Processing controls.
- Output controls.

Each of the specific types of controls is explained below.

[1]Computer Services Executive Committee, Audit and Accounting Guide, *The Auditor's Study and Evaluation of Internal Control in EDP Systems* (New York: American Institute of Certified Public Accountants, 1977), p. 25.

ORGANIZATION AND OPERATION CONTROLS

Organization and operation controls pertain to segregation of functions within the EDP department and between EDP and user departments. Weaknesses in these controls usually affect all EDP applications. The organization structure shown in Figure 6-7 illustrates an arrangement that provides for clear-cut lines of authority and responsibility within the EDP department. The primary responsibilities for each position are as follows:

Position	Primary Responsibilities
EDP manager	Exercises overall control, develops short- and long-range plans, and approves systems.
Systems analyst	Evaluates existing systems, designs new systems, outlines the systems, and prepares specifications for programmers.
Programmer	Flowcharts logic of computer programs, develops and documents programs, and debugs programs.
Computer operator	Operates the computer hardware and executes the program according to operating instructions.
Data entry operator	Prepares data for processing by recording it on machine-readable media, e.g., by keying data onto magnetic tape.
Librarian	Maintains custody of systems documentation, programs, and files.
Data control group	Acts as liaison with user departments and monitors input, processing, and output.
Database administrator	Designs content and organization of the database and controls access to and use of the database.

In small installations, the systems analysis and programming functions may be combined. However, the combining of these two functions with computer operations generally results in incompatible functions. When these three func-

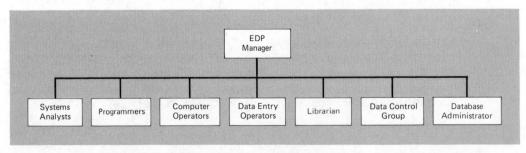

Figure 6-7. ORGANIZATION CHART OF AN EDP DEPARTMENT IN A LARGE COMPANY.

tions are performed by one individual, that person is in a position to both commit and conceal errors. A number of computer frauds have resulted when these duties were combined.

The EDP department should be organizationally independent of user departments. Thus, the EDP manager should report to an executive, such as the chief financial officer, who is not regularly involved in authorizing transactions for computer processing. In addition, EDP personnel should not correct errors unless they originate within EDP. For example, EDP can correct keypunching errors, but it should return a sales order with an invalid code number to sales for correction. Furthermore, EDP personnel should not authorize or initiate transactions or have custody of resulting assets. When the organizational plan does not provide for appropriate segregation of functions, the auditor may have serious doubts about the reliability of the results produced by the system.

SYSTEMS DEVELOPMENT AND DOCUMENTATION CONTROLS

Systems development controls relate to (1) review, testing, and approval of new systems; (2) control of program changes; and (3) documentation procedures. The following procedures are helpful in providing the necessary controls:

- Systems design should include representatives of user departments and, as appropriate, the accounting department and internal auditors.
- Each system should have written specifications that are reviewed and approved by management and the user department.
- Systems testing should be a cooperative effort of users and EDP personnel.
- The EDP manager, the database administrator, user personnel, and the appropriate level of management should give final approval to a new system before it is placed in normal operation.
- Program changes should be approved before implementation to determine whether they have been authorized, tested, and documented.[2]

Documentation controls pertain to the documents and records maintained by a company to describe computer processing activites. Adequate documentation is important to both management and the auditor. For management, documentation provides a basis for (1) reviewing the system, (2) training new personnel, and (3) maintaining and revising existing systems and programs. For the auditor, documentation provides the primary source of information about the flow of transactions through the system and the related accounting controls. Documentation includes

- Descriptions and flowcharts of the systems and programs.
- Operating instructions for computer operators.

---

[2]Computer Services Executive Committee, *op. cit.*, pp. 30–34.

- Control procedures to be followed by operators and users.
- Descriptions and samples of required inputs and outputs.

In database management systems, an important documentation control is the *data dictionary/directory*. The directory is software which keeps track of the definitions and locations of data elements in the database.

HARDWARE AND SYSTEMS SOFTWARE CONTROLS

Modern computer technology has achieved a high degree of reliability in computer equipment. Contributing factors are the existence of built-in hardware control features and systems software controls that are designed to detect any malfunctioning of the equipment. This category of controls includes the following.

Dual Read. Input data are read twice and the two readings are compared.

Parity Check. Data are processed by the computer in arrays of bits (binary digits of 0 or 1). In addition to bits necessary to represent the numeric or alphabetic characters, a parity bit is added, when necessary, to make the sum of all the "1" bits always odd or even. As data are entered and ultimately transferred within the computer, the parity check is applied by the computer to assure that bits are not lost during the process.

Echo Check. The echo check involves transmitting data received by an output device back to the source unit for comparison with the original data.

Read After Write. The computer reads back the data after they have been recorded, either in storage or on the output device, and verifies the data by comparison with their original source.

To achieve maximum benefit from these controls, (1) there should be a program of preventive maintenance on all hardware and (2) controls over changes in systems software should parallel the systems development and documentation controls described above.

ACCESS CONTROLS

Access controls should prevent unauthorized use of EDP equipment, data files, and computer programs. The specific controls include both physical and procedural safeguards.

Access to computer hardware should be limited to authorized individuals, such as computer operators. Physical safeguards include the housing of the equipment in an area that is separate from user departments. Access to the area should be restricted by security guards, door locks, or special keys. Procedural safeguards involve management review of computer utilization reports.

Access to data files and programs should be designed to prevent unauthorized use of such data. Physical controls exist in the form of a library and a librarian. Access to program documentation and data files should be limited to individuals authorized to process, maintain, or modify particular systems. Ordinarily, the librarian keeps a log of the use of files and programs. Alternatively, under the database method of filing, the data dictionary software provides an automated log of access to programs and data elements.

In systems with on-line entry of data, many users have direct access to the CPU through remote input devices. Access often extends beyond company employees to outside agents and even to customers who have special keys, such as magnetic cards issued by banks, that activate the computer. To provide the necessary control, each user of a remote input device is given a key, code, or card that identifies the holder as an authorized user. Other access controls are (1) computer call-back procedures when the telephone is used to dial the computer and (2) passwords that are checked by the computer before a person can enter a transaction.

OTHER DATA AND PROCEDURAL CONTROLS

This category of general controls provides a framework for controlling daily computer operations, minimizing the likelihood of processing errors, and assuring the continuity of operations in the event of a physical disaster or computer failure.

The first two objectives are achieved through a control function performed by individuals or departments that are organizationally independent of computer operations. This responsibility is often assumed by the data control group within EDP. The control function involves

- Receiving and screening all data to be processed.
- Accounting for all input data.
- Following up on processing errors.
- Verifying the proper distribution of output.

The ability to maintain the continuity of computer operations involves (1) the use of off-premises storage for important files, programs, and documentation; (2) physical protection against environmental hazards; (3) formal record retention and recovery plans for data; and (4) arrangements for use of backup facilities at another location in the event of a disaster.

The ability to reconstruct data files is equally important. When sequential processing is used, a common method of records reconstruction is the grandfather-father-son concept illustrated in Figure 6-8. Under this concept, the new updated master file is the son. The master file utilized in the updating run that produced the son is the father, and the previous master file is the grandfather. To update these earlier master files, records of transactions for the current and prior periods also must be retained. In the event that the current computer master file is destroyed, the system then has the capability to replace it. Ideally, the three generations of master files and the transaction

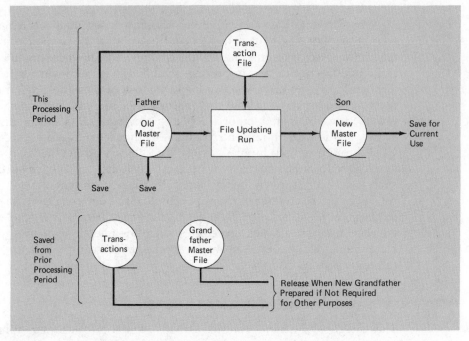

Figure 6-8. GRANDFATHER-FATHER-SON IN MAGNETIC TAPE FILES. (SOURCE: Gordon B. Davis, Donald L. Adams, and Carol A. Schaller, *Auditing and EDP*, Second Edition (New York: American Institute of Certified Public Accountants, 1983), p. 128.)

files should be stored in separate locations to minimize the risk of losing all the files at one time. When direct access processing is used, the master file and transaction logs should be dumped, or copied, periodically to tape. In the event the on-line files are destroyed or damaged, these tapes may be used with a special recovery program to reconstruct the master file.

INPUT CONTROLS

Input controls are one type of application controls. They are of vital importance in an EDP system because most of the errors occur at this point. Input controls are designed to provide reasonable assurance that data received for processing have been (1) properly authorized, (2) converted into machine-sensible form, and (3) subsequently accounted for. These controls also include the rejection, correction, and resubmission of data that were initially incorrect.

Authorization

Each transaction entry should be properly authorized and approved in accordance with management's general or specific authorization. When documents are individually processed, authorization is usually provided in the form of a signature or stamp on the source document; in contrast, when input data are assembled in batches, there ordinarily is user department approval of each batch of documents. In some cases, the computer performs the authorization function. For instance, a purchase requisition is automatically initiated when inventory quantities are reduced to a specified reorder level. Control here occurs after the fact by review of the output by the data control group or the user department.

Conversion of Input Data

Controls over the conversion of data into machine-sensible form are intended to assure that (1) the data are correctly entered, and (2) the converted data are valid. Control techniques include the following.

Verification Controls.   These include (1) rekeying of all or a selected portion of the input data from the source document by a second person, with a comparison of the results, or (2) the use of turn-around documents. The use of these techniques was explained earlier in the section on batch entry/batch processing.

Computer Editing.   These are computer routines that are intended to detect incomplete, incorrect, or unreasonable data. They include

- *Missing data check* to assure that all required data fields have been completed and no blanks are present.
- *Valid character check* to verify that only alphabetical, numerical, or other special characters appear as required in data fields.
- *Limit (reasonableness) check* to determine that only data falling within predetermined limits are entered (e.g., time cards exceeding a designated number of hours per week may be rejected).
- *Valid sign check* to determine that the sign of the data, if applicable, is correct.
- *Valid code check* to match a classification (i.e., expense account number) or transaction code (i.e., cash receipts entry) against a master list of codes permitted for the type of transaction to be processed.
- *Check digit* to determine that an account, employee, or other identification number has been correctly entered by applying a specific arithmetic operation to the identification number and comparing the result with the check digit.

Batch Controls.   Common forms of batch controls include

- *Document or record counts* which are totals of the number of documents or records to be processed.
- *Financial totals* which are computed from source documents containing financial information.

- *Hash totals* which are computed by adding values that would not usually be added together (e.g., employee or product numbers, which sums have no meaning other than as a control device).

Subsequent Accountability

Controls are needed to ascertain that input data have not been lost, added, duplicated, or otherwise changed during movement between processing steps or between departments. Transmittal controls, routing slips, and control totals are techniques that are frequently used for this purpose.

Error Correction

The correction and resubmission of incorrect data are vital to the accuracy of the accounting records. For example, if processing of a valid sales invoice is stopped because of an error, accounts receivable and sales will both be understated until the error is eliminated and the processing completed. Errors should be corrected by those responsible for the mistake. Thus, errors in source documents should be corrected by user departments, whereas errors in conversion or movement of input data should be corrected by the EDP department. For control purposes, errors should be logged and their disposition should be periodically reviewed by the data control group.

PROCESSING CONTROLS

This class of application controls is designed to provide reasonable assurance that the computer processing has been performed as intended for the particular application—that is, all transactions are processed as authorized, no authorized transactions are omitted, and no unauthorized transactions are added.

Processing controls take many forms, but the most common are programmed controls incorporated into the individual applications software. Widely used techniques include the following:

Control Totals. Provision for accumulating control totals is written into the computer program to facilitate the balancing of input totals with processing totals for each run. Similarly, run-to-run totals are accumulated to verify processing performed in stages.

File Identification Labels. External labels are physically attached to magnetic tape or disks to permit visual identification of a file. Internal file labels are in machine-readable form and are matched electronically with specified operator instructions (or commands) incorporated into the computer program before processing can begin or be successfully completed.

Limit and Reasonableness Checks. This technique is the same as described earlier under computing editing.

Before-and-After Report. This report shows a summary of the contents of a master file before and after each update.

Sequence Tests. If transactions are given identification numbers (as in some direct-entry systems) or if records should be processed in a specific order, the transaction file can be tested for sequence, as well as for duplicate or missing items.

Process Tracing Data. This technique involves a printout of specific data for visual inspection to determine if the processing is correct. For evaluating changes in critical data items, tracing data may include the contents before and after the processing.

OUTPUT CONTROLS

Output controls are designed to assure that the processing result is correct and that only authorized personnel receive the output. The accuracy of the processing result includes both updated machine-sensible files and printed output. This objective is met by the following.

Reconciliation of Totals. Output totals that are generated by the computer programs are reconciled to input and processing totals by the data control group and user departments.

Comparison to Source Documents. Output data are subject to detailed comparison with source documents.

Visual Scanning. The output is reviewed for completeness and apparent reasonableness. Actual results may be compared with estimated results.

Control over the distribution of output is usually maintained by the data control group. Special care should be exercised by this group over the distribution of confidential output. To facilitate control over the disposition of output, systems documentation should include a report distribution sheet.

METHODOLOGY FOR THE STUDY AND EVALUATION OF EDP CONTROLS

There are both similarities and differences in making a study and evaluation of internal control between a manual and an EDP system.

APPLICABILITY OF GENERALLY ACCEPTED AUDITING STANDARDS

All of the generally accepted auditing standards (GAAS) apply to an examination of financial statements prepared in accordance with generally accepted accounting principles (GAAP). This is true regardless of the method of data processing used by the client. The impact of a computerized data system on three of the standards merits special comment.

- *The First General Standard.* This standard states that the examination is to made by individuals with adequate technical training and proficiency as an auditor. This means that the auditor must have sufficient expertise to understand and evaluate the system's essential accounting control features. The extent of the knowledge depends on the complexity of the EDP system and the responsibilities the individual is assuming. The individual may be a (a) general audit staff member, (2) computer audit specialist, or (3) management advisory services EDP professional.
- *The First Standard of Field Work.* This standard states that the work is to be adequately planned and assistants, if any, are to be adequately supervised. In planning the examination for clients who use computer processing, the auditor should consider matters such as
  ○ The extent to which the computer is used in each significant accounting application,
  ○ The complexity of the client's computer operations, including the use of an outside service center;
  ○ The organizational structure of the computer processing activities;
  ○ The availability of data in hard copy and computer-readable forms; and
  ○ The use of computer-assisted audit techniques to increase the efficiency of performing audit procedures.[3]
- *The Second Standard of Field Work.* This standard states that there is to be a proper study and evaluation of the existing internal control. The applicability of this standard is not affected by whether the EDP facilities used are those of the client or an outside third party.

OVERVIEW OF METHODOLOGY

The methodology for making a study and evaluation of internal controls in an EDP system is conceptually the same as in a manual system. For example, the steps and decision paths in Figure 5-1 for a manual system are identical with those applicable to a computer system. The methodology for an EDP system is as follows:

Steps	Decision Paths
• Make preliminary review of accounting system and general and application controls to decide whether further study is justifiable.	• Continue review or go to expanded substantive tests.

[3]Auditing Standards Board, *Codification of Statements on Auditing Standards* (New York: American Institute of Certified Public Accountants, 1985), Auditing Section 311.09 (adapted) (hereinafter referred to and cited as AU §).

Steps	Decision Paths
• Complete review of general and application controls and make preliminary evaluation of prescribed controls.	• Identify controls to be relied on, assuming satisfactory compliance, and proceed to compliance testing; or go to expanded substantive tests.
• Perform compliance tests on controls to be relied on.	
• Make final evaluation of control procedures.	• For controls for which compliance is satisfactory, go to restricted substantive tests; when compliance is not satisfactory, go to expanded substantive tests.

Each of the steps and decision paths is explained below.

REVIEW OF THE SYSTEM

An auditor's review of a client's system of accounting control should encompass all significant and relevant manual, mechanical, and EDP activities and the interrelationship between EDP and user departments. As in the case of a manual data processing system, the review consists of two phases: (1) preliminary and (2) completion.

Preliminary Phase of Review

In the preliminary phase of the review of EDP controls, the auditor obtains information about three matters: (1) the flow of transactions through the system, (2) the extent to which EDP is used in each significant accounting application, and (3) the basic structure of accounting control within the client organization. Significant accounting applications relate to classes of transactions, such as sales and payroll in a manufacturing company, that will materially affect the client's financial statements. The basic structure of accounting controls includes a consideration of the relationships between manual and EDP-based controls and the extent and availability of the transaction trail.

In performing the preliminary phase of the review, the auditor relies primarily on inquiry, but knowledge also may be obtained by observation of the performance of control procedures and by reviewing organization charts, procedures manuals, and other documentation.

At the conclusion of the preliminary review, the auditor must decide whether further study is likely to justify any restriction of substantive tests. Basically, this is a "go" or "no go" decision. A "go" decision results in moving to the completion phase of the review. A "no go" decision terminates the review phase, and the auditor proceeds directly to substantive testing.

A decision to terminate the review may occur when

- EDP is not used in any significant accounting applications.
- EDP is used in significant accounting applications, but other auditing

procedures (i.e., substantive tests) are more cost-efficient than performing compliance tests on the EDP controls.

- EDP controls in significant accounting applications are redundant because of other accounting controls, such as user department controls over input and output.

- EDP controls in significant accounting applications are too weak to rely on.

Completion Phase of Review

In the completion phase of the review, the auditor is expected to expand on the knowledge about accounting controls obtained during the preliminary review through additional inquiry, observation, review of documentation, and transaction walk-through reviews. As in a manual system, the findings should be documented in the form of completed questionnaires, flowcharts, or narrative memoranda.

This phase of the review process begins with a review of general EDP controls pertaining to all significant accounting applications. In making this review, the auditor should obtain answers to such questions as the following:

- How does the organization of the data processing department provide adequate supervision and segregation of functions within EDP and between EDP and users?

- What procedures provide for control over systems development and access to systems documentation?

- What procedures provide for control over program and systems maintenance?

- What procedures provide control over computer operations, including access to data files and programs?

- What procedures, during the period under review, assure that file reconstruction and processing recoveries were complete?

- To what extent do internal auditors perform a review and evaluation of EDP activities?[4]

If material weaknesses are discovered in general controls, the auditor may terminate the review because general controls often have pervasive effects on application controls. However, when there are no material weaknesses in general controls, the auditor proceeds to make his review of application controls pertaining to each significant accounting application. Thus, answers should be obtained to questions relating to the adequacy of prescribed EDP accounting controls over input, processing, and output. With respect to input data that were initially incorrect, the auditor will ascertain whether

[4]Computer Services Executive Committee, *op. cit.*, p. 16.

- User department errors are corrected in the initiating department.
- Such data are subsequently resubmitted.
- Error logs are kept of such data.

Preliminary Evaluation.   The nature and purpose of this evaluation of accounting controls in an EDP system is the same as in a manual system. Accordingly, the auditor should (1) consider the types of errors and irregularities that could occur, (2) determine the control procedures that should prevent or detect such occurrences, and (3) determine whether the necessary control procedures are prescribed. Possible errors and irregularities and necessary control procedures relating to application controls are shown in Figure 6-9.

After completing this analysis, the auditor uses professional judgment to identify the control procedures to be relied on, assuming satisfactory com-

Errors and Irregularities	Necessary Control Procedures
INPUT	
Valid data are incorrectly converted to machine-sensible form.	Verification controls Computer editing Batch controls Data control group monitoring
Properly converted input is lost, duplicated, or distorted during handling.	Transmittal controls Control totals
Detected erroneous data are not corrected and resubmitted for processing.	Error logs Data control group monitoring
PROCESSING	
The wrong files are processed and updated.	External file labels Internal file labels
Processing errors are made on valid input data.	Control totals
Illogical or unreasonable input is processed.	Limit and reasonableness tests
OUTPUT	
Output may be incorrect because of processing errors.	Output control totals
Output may be incorrect because file revisions are unauthorized or approved changes are not made.	Periodic comparisons of file data with source documents
Output is distributed to unauthorized users.	Data control group monitoring Report distribution control sheet

Figure 6-9. PRELIMINARY EVALUATION CONSIDERATIONS: APPLICATION CONTROLS.

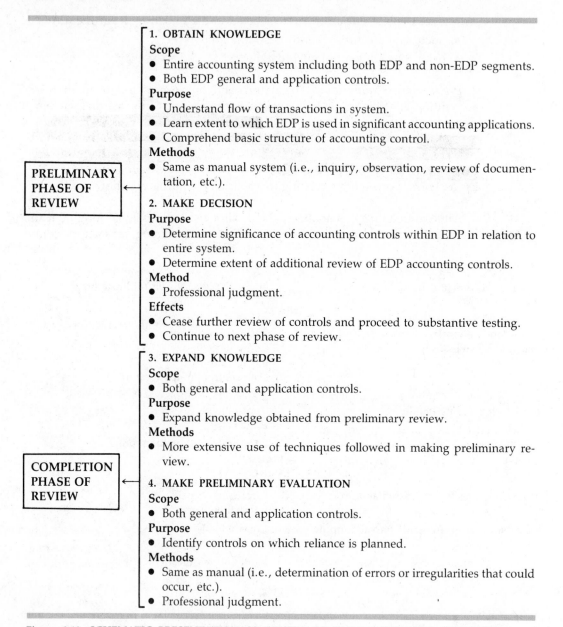

1. OBTAIN KNOWLEDGE

Scope
- Entire accounting system including both EDP and non-EDP segments.
- Both EDP general and application controls.

Purpose
- Understand flow of transactions in system.
- Learn extent to which EDP is used in significant accounting applications.
- Comprehend basic structure of accounting control.

Methods
- Same as manual system (i.e., inquiry, observation, review of documentation, etc.).

PRELIMINARY PHASE OF REVIEW

2. MAKE DECISION

Purpose
- Determine significance of accounting controls within EDP in relation to entire system.
- Determine extent of additional review of EDP accounting controls.

Method
- Professional judgment.

Effects
- Cease further review of controls and proceed to substantive testing.
- Continue to next phase of review.

3. EXPAND KNOWLEDGE

Scope
- Both general and application controls.

Purpose
- Expand knowledge obtained from preliminary review.

Methods
- More extensive use of techniques followed in making preliminary review.

COMPLETION PHASE OF REVIEW

4. MAKE PRELIMINARY EVALUATION

Scope
- Both general and application controls.

Purpose
- Identify controls on which reliance is planned.

Methods
- Same as manual (i.e., determination of errors or irregularities that could occur, etc.).
- Professional judgment.

Figure 6-10. SCHEMATIC PRESENTATION OF REVIEW OF EDP ACCOUNTING CONTROLS.

pliance. A schematic presentation of the review of EDP accounting controls is provided in Figure 6-10.

TESTS OF COMPLIANCE

Tests of compliance are performed for the purpose of providing assurance that the internal control procedures that exist within the client's system are in use and are functioning as planned. For EDP control procedures that leave visible evidence of performance, the auditor inspects the document or record containing the evidence. An example is a file that documents the program changes for an EDP application and approval of the changes. Performance of some control procedures within the EDP activity leaves no visible evidence. These include input validation routines or processing controls designed to detect erroneous or invalid data. To test for the effectiveness of such controls, the auditor may examine transactions submitted for processing to determine that no transactions tested have unacceptable conditions or that the unacceptable conditions present were reported and appropriately resolved. Effective performance of other control procedures is dependent largely on an adequate segregation of functions. The performance of these procedures is largely self-evident from the operation of the system or the existence of its records. Consequently, tests of compliance with such procedures are primarily to determine whether the procedures were performed by persons having no incompatible functions.[5]

In an EDP system, the auditor's procedures for performing tests of compliance are determined by the adequacy of the transaction trail. When an adequate trail exists, the auditor may be able to follow ordinary manual audit procedures. In other cases, the auditor may need to use the computer to carry out the procedures.

Tests of General Controls

Because general controls are pervasive in their effect, an evaluation of these controls must precede any testing of applications controls. Thus, the auditor may review controls over access to and changing of computer programs prior to reviewing a specific programmed control procedure in an application program. An illustrative audit program for testing general controls is presented in Figure 6-11.

Tests of Application Controls Without the Computer

If the processing application being tested is well documented and sufficient printed output exists, or can be generated by the client, the auditor may decide to use audit procedures traditionally applied in a manual accounting system to test the existence and effectiveness of internal controls. This is done by using conventional source documents and printed output.

Auditing by testing input and output instead of the computer itself does not enable the auditor to detect program errors that do not show up in the output samples. Error listings generated by the processing function give evidence that a control does exist to detect such an error, but missing controls are not revealed. Instead, the auditor must rely on existing procedural and output controls to detect such omissions.

Auditing without the computer offers the following advantages:

- The auditor can use familiar manual system techniques.
- Recourse to the complexities of computer programs is unnecessary.

[5]Auditing Standards Board, *op. cit.*, AU § 320.67 (adapted).

AUDIT PROGRAM

TYPE OF TESTING: Compliance   **PURPOSE:** Effectiveness of EDP General Controls

A. ORGANIZATION AND OPERATION CONTROLS ARE PROPERLY FUNCTIONING.

1. Observe and make inquiries concerning segregation of functions between EDP and user departments and within EDP.
2. Selectively test preprocessing, postprocessing, and programmed controls to determine if they provide for processing in accordance with management's authorization.

B. SYSTEMS DEVELOPMENT AND DOCUMENTATION CONTROLS ARE PROPERLY FUNCTIONING.

1. Examine evidence for approval of new systems and programs and changes therein.
2. Trace selected program changes to supporting documentation.
3. Review results of tests to verify correctness of system and program changes.

C. HARDWARE AND SYSTEMS SOFTWARE CONTROLS ARE PROPERLY FUNCTIONING.

1. Review and evaluate the hardware controls included in the operating system.
2. Review documentation in support of systems software changes to ascertain whether prescribed procedures are being followed.
3. Examine results of selected pretesting of software programs.

D. ACCESS CONTROLS ARE PROPERLY FUNCTIONING.

1. Inquire of librarian as to compliance with procedures for controlling unauthorized access to programs and data files.
2. Examine data files and program access records to test the library function as it applies to significant accounting applications.
3. Observe procedures for limiting access to computer hardware.

E. DATA AND PROCEDURAL CONTROLS ARE PROPERLY FUNCTIONING.

1. Review on a test basis reconciliations of control totals by the data control group.
2. Selectively review computer operator manuals and observe whether prescribed procedures are being followed.
3. Determine the extent, nature, and quality of internal auditing review of EDP activities.
4. Observe distribution of computer output to ascertain that only authorized users receive copies.

Figure 6-11. AUDIT PROGRAM: COMPLIANCE TESTS OF GENERAL CONTROLS. (SOURCE: Computer Services Executive Committee, *op. cit.*, pp. 25–40 [adapted]).

The principal disadvantages of auditing without the computer are that the auditor may fail to utilize the capabilities of the computer in gathering audit evidence, and cost savings in audit time and effort may not be realized.

Tests of Application Controls with the Computer

If the auditor decides that auditing around the computer is not an effective approach to test the functioning of programmed application controls, another approach must be used. The auditor may elect to use either computer-assisted audit techniques or, alternatively, to place reliance on controls over the maintenance and processing of specific application programs. In either case, the auditor needs to obtain reasonable assurance of the consistency of the operation of the controls throughout the period under examination. The auditor may find it advantageous to test programmed controls with the aid of the computer when

- A significant part of the internal control is embodied in a computer program.
- There are significant gaps in the visible transaction trail.
- There are large volumes of records to be tested.

There are three common computer-assisted audit techniques used to test the operation of specific programmed application controls: *parallel simulation, test data,* and *integrated test facility.*

Parallel Simulation. In this approach (sometimes called *controlled reprocessing* or *modeling*), actual company data are reprocessed using an auditor-controlled software program. This method is so named because the software is designed to reproduce or simulate the client's processing of real data. A graphic portrayal of this approach is shown in Figure 6–12.

Parallel simulation may be performed at different times during the year under audit, and it may also be applied to the reprocessing of historical data. This approach does not contaminate client files, and it may be conducted at an independent computer facility.

This approach has the following advantages:

- Since real data are used, the auditor can verify the transactions by tracing them back to source documents and approvals.
- The size of the sample can be greatly expanded at relatively little additional cost.
- The auditor can independently run the test.

If the auditor decides to use parallel simulation, care must be taken to determine that the data selected for simulation are representative of actual client transactions. It is also possible that the client's system may perform operations that are beyond the capacity of the software program.

Test Data. Under the test data approach (sometimes referred to as *test decks*), dummy transactions are prepared by the auditor and processed under auditor control by the client's computer program. The test data consist of one transaction for each valid or invalid condition the auditor wishes to test. For example, a payroll test deck may include both a valid and an invalid overtime pay condition. The output from processing the test data is then compared by the auditor with planned results to determine whether prescribed controls are operating as planned. This approach to testing is relatively simple, quick, and inexpensive. However, the method has the following major audit deficiencies:

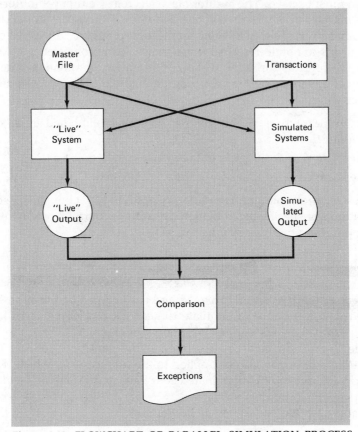

Figure 6-12. FLOWCHART OF PARALLEL SIMULATION PROCESS.

- The client's program is tested only at a specific point in time rather than throughout the audit period.
- The method is only a test of the presence and functioning of controls in the program tested.
- There is no examination of documentation actually processed by the system.
- Computer operators know that test data are being run, which could reduce the validity of the output.
- The scope of the test is limited by the auditor's imagination and knowledge of the controls within the system.

Integrated Test Facility. This method of testing programmed controls requires the creation of a small subsystem (a minicompany) within the regular EDP system. This may be accomplished by creating dummy master files or appending dummy master records to existing client files. Test data, specially coded to correspond to the dummy master files, are introduced into the system together with actual transactions. The test data should include all kinds of transaction errors and exceptions that may be encountered. In this manner, the test data are subjected to the same programmed controls as the actual data. For the subsystem, or dummy files, a separate set of outputs is produced. The results can be compared with those expected by the auditor.

The ITF method has as a disadvantage the risk of potentially creating errors in client data. In addition, modifications may be necessary to client's programs in order to accommodate the dummy data.

Comparison of Approaches. The primary differences between the parallel simulation and test data approaches are shown in Figure 6–13. The comparison of the output under each approach is done manually by the auditor. The integrated test facility technique combines features of each of these methods as both test data and actual transactions are processed simultaneously.

Irrespective of the choice among these three methods of testing the effectiveness of programmed controls, the procedures performed are analogous to the manual procedure of tracing transactions through all or selected components of the client's control system to determine the existence and effectiveness of selected accounting controls. Unlike the manual case, however, the procedures are performed by the computer and leave no visible trail. Only in the case of a transaction that does not satisfy a specific control incorporated into the program will an error message be generated. Audit programs for testing

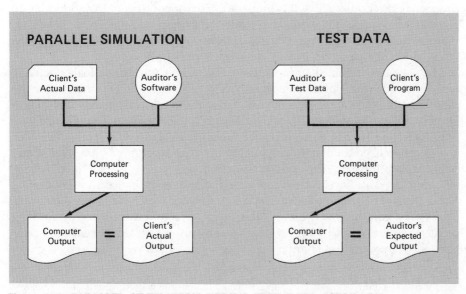

Figure 6-13. PARALLEL SIMULATION VERSUS TEST DATA APPROACH.

application controls for specific classes of transactions will be illustrated in Chapters 8–11.

FINAL EVALUATION OF CONTROLS

After performing compliance tests, the auditor's evaluation of EDP accounting controls is conceptually the same as the corresponding evaluation of manual controls. As in a completely manual system, the evaluation will affect the nature, timing, and extent of the auditor's substantive tests.

OTHER CONSIDERATIONS

In an EDP environment, an auditor has an opportunity to use generalized audit software. It may also be necessary for the auditor to consider the audit effects of small computer systems and computer service centers. These matters are discussed below.

GENERALIZED AUDIT SOFTWARE

When a client uses EDP for significant accounting applications, the auditor should consider using computer audit software to assist him in carrying out a variety of auditing procedures. The most common type of audit software in use today is known as *generalized audit software.* This software is adaptable for use with client EDP files produced under a variety of data organization and processing methods.[6] Thus, it is transportable from one client to another. Until recently these packages were very costly to develop and maintain. However, they are now available at moderate cost from software vendors and CPA firms who market their own internally developed packages.

The use of generalized audit software enables the auditor to deal effectively with large quantities of data. This may permit the accumulation of either the same quantity of evidence at less cost compared to performing an examination without the computer, or more evidence at an economical cost. Its use also permits the auditor to place less reliance on the client's EDP personnel. The use of generalized audit software in auditing is limited only by the availability of client data files and the auditor's ingenuity.

Generalized audit software can be used in both compliance and substantive tests. Examples of compliance testing applications include a comparison of prices on a computerized file of sales invoices to a master file of authorized prices to determine the frequency of use of unauthorized prices, or a comparison of the detail of charges to customer accounts with authorized credit

---

[6]Special considerations are usually required when audit software is used with database management systems.

file data to determine the frequency with which credit was granted in excess of authorized limits. In both cases, the software would be used to produce exception reports. Examples of substantive testing applications include the following.

Selecting and Printing Audit Samples

The computer can be programmed to select audit samples according to whatever criteria are specified by the auditor. These samples can be used for a variety of purposes. Individual customer accounts receivable accounts may be selected for confirmation, or the auditor may be interested in obtaining a listing of all items over a certain dollar amount. In examining supporting documentation for charges to a "repairs and maintenance expense" account, the auditor may wish to specify a lower limit of $500. The samples selected may be based on multiple criteria. In the case of confirmation requests, the computer may also be used to print the confirmation letter as well as the envelope.

Testing Calculations and Making Computations

Another common use of the computer is to test the accuracy of computations in machine-readable data files. Tests of extensions, footings, or other computations may be performed. Inventory quantities may be extended by a unit cost and the amount of the inventory recalculated; individual customer accounts receivable records may be individually footed and a total of all accounts prepared. If client files contain sufficient information, the recalculation of certain year-end adjusting entries also may be possible. Because of the speed with which computer processing is performed, recomputations can be performed on a more extensive basis than is practicable in a manual system.

Summarizing Data and Performing Analyses

The auditor frequently desires to have the client data reorganized in a manner that will suit a special purpose. For instance, the auditor may want to determine slow-moving inventory items, debit balances in accounts payable, or the age of accounts receivable. Similarly, in performing analytical review procedures, the auditor may utilize the computer to compute desired ratios and other comparative data.

Comparing Audit Data with Company Records

Audited data resulting from work performed by the auditor may be compared with the information in a company's records. The audited data must, of course, first be converted into machine-readable form. Test counts made by the auditor of inventory quantities on hand may be keypunched and compared with the quantity shown on the perpetual inventory record or the quantity determined by the company as the result of a physical inventory count.

SMALL COMPUTER SYSTEMS

The decade of the 1980s has seen widespread proliferation of small computer systems. These systems may be used as stand alone computers, or they may be linked in networks. The distinction once made between two classes of these computers, minicomputers and microcomputers, is no longer precise. Some of today's "supermicros" with high-speed processing chips, large hard disk storage capacity, and data communications abilities rival minicomputers in their serviceability.

Minicomputers may be used to process a particular accounting application such as inventories or several applications comprising an integrated general ledger package in large- and medium-sized businesses. In these businesses, however, microcomputers are more often used as personal productivity tools to prepare special analyses rather than to process routine accounting applications. Accounting applications, or even an integrated general ledger package, however, may be maintained on a microcomputer in a small business. In any case, the audit considerations when mini and microcomputers are used to process accounting data are similar.

Control Considerations

Both of the two categories of EDP accounting controls discussed earlier in the chapter are relevant to small computer systems. However, the characteristics of these systems may limit the applicability of specific controls.

General controls may be weak because of

- *Lack of Segregation of Functions Between the EDP Department and Users.* In many cases, the user can initiate and authorize transactions and control both the processing and distribution of the output.
- *Location of the Computer.* In many systems, the computer is located in the user department. As a result, there may be weaknesses in access controls that may result in improper use or manipulation of data files and unauthorized modifications of computer programs.
- *Lack of Segregation of Functions Within the EDP Department.* Because of the limited number of personnel in the EDP department, the functions of programming and operations may not be separated.
- *Limited Knowledge of EDP.* Personnel in the EDP department may have limited experience and knowledge of computers. Thus, systems may not meet management's objectives and the review and approval of new programs by such individuals may be ineffective.[7]

The application controls described earlier for large systems are equally important in small systems. Areas that may require special consideration in small computer systems are as follows:

---

[7]Computer Services Guidelines, *Audit and Control Considerations in a Minicomputer or Small Business Computer Environment* (New York: American Institute of Certified Public Accountants, 1981), pp. 3–5 (adapted).

- *Data Entry.* Since data are entered directly into the system through terminals, more importance is attached to controls over original source data and the detection of errors at the time of entry.
- *Data Processing.* Controls to prevent the processing of wrong files may not exist. To compensate for this weakness, greater reliance must be placed on external file labels.
- *Absence of Limit and Reasonableness Tests.* Most systems use purchased software packages that may not contain these tests, or the tests provided may not be useful to the user. More reliance on controls over original source documents may help to compensate for this weakness.[8]

Study and Evaluation of Internal Control

The auditor's responsibility for meeting the second standard of field work is not affected by the size of the computer system. When EDP is used in significant accounting applications, the auditor must make a study of internal controls. As explained above, general controls are often weak in a small computer environment. Thus, the auditor may find it more cost-effective to concentrate on application controls in his review of the system. With due recognition of weaknesses in general controls, the auditor should be able to anticipate errors and irregularities that could occur in specific EDP applications. In some cases, application controls and manual controls may be sufficient to provide a basis for reliance on the system. When this does not occur, the auditor will be required to perform expanded substantive tests.

The compliance testing of controls involves the same techniques described earlier for large computer systems. Special considerations, however, may be required in planning the tests due to the number of data records that can be retained on magnetic media in small systems, and the limited time period the transaction trail can be retained.

COMPUTER SERVICE ORGANIZATIONS

A computer service organization is an entity that provides EDP services for another entity. The service organization may be a *computer service center* that records transactions and processes related data for small companies. These services may involve the processing of a company's payrolls, sales orders, billings, collections, and maintaining a company's general ledger. Alternatively, the service organization may be a *trust department* of a bank or a similar entity that invests and holds assets for a company's employee benefit or pension plan.[9] Under either type of arrangement, transactions affecting the company's financial statements flow through an accounting system that is, at least in part, physically and operationally separate from the company.

---

[8]Davis, Adams, and Schaller, *Auditing and EDP, op. cit.,* p. 299 (adapted).
[9]Auditing Standards Board, *op. cit.,* AU § 324.03.

In such circumstances, the accounting controls of the service organization should be included in the auditor's study and evaluation of the company's system of internal control. At a minimum, the service organization's controls should be included in the preliminary phase of the review in order to determine the extent of the service organization's processing of transactions and the basic structure of accounting controls. Following the preliminary review, the auditor has the same decision options that are available for a company's own system of internal control. If the auditor intends to rely on the service organization's controls in performing substantive tests of transactions processed by the organization, it is necessary to establish a basis for reliance. This may be done by either

- Completing the review of the service organization's controls and performing compliance tests on the controls expected to be relied on, or
- Relying on an internal control report prepared by the service organization's independent auditors for customers of the service organization.

Using the independent auditor's report is often the most cost-efficient approach. This report is discussed and illustrated in Chapter 18.

CONCLUDING COMMENTS

The methodology of making a study and evaluation of internal accounting control in an EDP system is under continuing scrutiny within the accounting profession. Auditing methodology must keep pace with the increased sophistication of the computer.

This chapter has provided an introduction to the current "state of the art." Through practical experience and continuing professional education, the auditor of today must also be equipped to be the auditor of tomorrow. One conclusion appears indisputable: There will be more EDP systems in the future than there are today.

REVIEW QUESTIONS

6-1 a. What is the principal hardware component in an EDP system?
b. What hardware components are peripheral to the principal hardware component?

6-2 a. Explain the nature and functions of computer software.
b. Distinguish between systems programs and application programs.

6-3 a. Distinguish between the traditional file and database method of organizing data.
b. Distinguish between sequential and direct access processing.

6-4 For each of the three methods of data processing, indicate (a) their essential characteristics and (b) an advantage and a disadvantage.

6-5 Indicate four differences between EDP and manual systems that may affect the control environment.

6-6 Distinguish between general and application controls and indicate the category of controls that is pervasive in its effect.

6-7 a. Identify the customary positions in an EDP department.

b. Explain the primary applications of segregation of functions in an EDP department.

6-8 a. What areas are related to systems development and documentation controls?

b. Why is documentation important to (1) management and (2) the auditor?

6-9 a. Indicate the purpose of hardware and systems software controls.

b. Identify four kinds of hardware and systems software controls.

6-10 a. Explain the purpose(s) and nature of access controls.

b. Enumerate the access controls that may be used in an on-line entry system.

6-11 a. Indicate the scope of data and procedural controls.

b. Describe the activities involved in the control function and identify the group that would perform this function.

6-12 a. Indicate the internal accounting control objectives for each of the three types of application controls.

b. Identify the categories of controls pertaining to the conversion of input data.

6-13 a. Indicate the applicability of the first GAAS to EDP.

b. What information about the EDP system is needed in meeting the first standard of field work?

6-14 a. In the preliminary phase of the review, indicate (1) its scope, (2) the information desired, and (3) the procedures used.

b. Why may the auditor decide to terminate the review at the end of the preliminary phase?

6-15 What questions about the general controls are of interest to the auditor in the completion phase of the review?

6-16 What are the advantages and disadvantages of auditing without the computer?

6-17 Contrast compliance testing by (a) parallel simulation, (b) test data, and (c) integrated test facility.

6-18 a. What is generalized audit software?

b. Explain how generalized audit software may be used in (1) compliance tests and (2) substantive tests.

6-19 a. Identify three weaknesses in general controls in small computer systems.

b. Indicate three types of application controls that should receive special consideration by the auditor.

c. What approach may be followed in the study and evaluation of internal control in small computer systems.

6-20 a. Describe the types of computer service organizations that may be used by a company.

b. Indicate the effects of service organizations on the auditor's study and evaluation of internal control.

OBJECTIVE QUESTIONS FROM PROFESSIONAL EXAMINATIONS

Indicate the *best* answer for each of the following multiple-choice questions.

6-21 These questions pertain to internal control in an EDP system.

1. Which of the following constitutes a weakness in the internal control of an EDP system?

a. One generation of backup files is stored in an off-premises location.

b. Machine operators distribute error messages to the control group.

c. Machine operators do *not* have access to the complete systems manual.

d. Machine operators are supervised by the programmer.

2. One of the major problems in an EDP system is that incompatible functions may be performed by the same individual. One compensating control for this is the use of

a. Echo checks.

b. A self-checking digit system.

c. Computer-generated hash totals.

d. A computer log.

3. When erroneous data are detected by computer program controls, such data may be excluded from processing and printed on an error report. This error report should be reviewed and followed up by the

a. Computer operator.

b. Systems analyst.

c. EDP control group.

d. Computer programmer.

4. An EDP input control is designed to ensure that

a. Machine processing is accurate.

b. Only authorized personnel have access to the computer area.

c. Data received for processing are properly authorized and converted to machine-readable form.

d. Electronic data processing has been performed as intended for the particular application.

6-22 These questions apply to the auditor's study and evaluation of internal control in an EDP system.

1. When testing a computerized accounting system, which of the following is *not* true of the test data approach?

a. Test data are processed by the client's computer programs under the auditor's control.

b. The test data must consist of all possible valid and invalid conditions.

c. The test data need consist of only those valid and invalid conditions in which the auditor is interested.

d. Only one transaction of each type need be tested.

2. Auditing by testing the input and output of an EDP system instead of the computer program itself will

a. Not detect program errors that do *not* show up in the output sampled.

b. Detect all program errors, regardless of the nature of the output.

c. Provide the auditor with the same type of evidence.

d. Not provide the auditor with confidence in the results of the auditing procedures.

3. Which of the following methods of testing application controls utilizes a generalized audit software package prepared by the auditors?

a. Parallel simulation.

b. Integrated testing facility approach.

c. Test data approach.

d. Exception report tests.

4. Which of the following is likely to be of *least* importance to an auditor in reviewing the internal control in a company with automated data processing?

a. The segregation of duties within the EDP center.

b. The control over source documents.

c. The documentation maintained for accounting applications.

d. The cost/benefit ratio of data processing operations.

COMPREHENSIVE QUESTIONS

6-23 Two categories and eight types of EDP accounting control procedures are identified in the chapter. Listed below are a number of specific control procedures:

1. EDP manager reports to chief financial officer.
2. Backup files.
3. Written approval of all program changes.
4. Physical controls for data files and programs.
5. Batch controls.
6. Reconciliation of output totals.
7. File identification labels.
8. Echo checks.
9. Limit and reasonableness checks.
10. Record counts

Required

a. Indicate the category and type of control to which each procedure pertains.

b. Identify and explain one other control procedure for each of the eight types.

6-24 The plan of organization is an important aspect of an EDP activity.

Required

a. Diagram an appropriate structure for an EDP department.

b. Briefly describe the primary responsibilities of each individual or group identified in the diagram.

c. Indicate the conditions in an EDP structure that would result in incompatible functions.

6-25 When auditing an EDP accounting system, the independent auditor should have a general familiarity with the effects of the use of EDP on the various characteristics of accounting control and on the auditor's study and evaluation of such control. The independent auditor must be aware of those control procedures that are commonly referred to as "general" controls and those that are commonly referred to as "application" controls. General controls relate to all EDP activities and application controls relate to specific accounting tasks.

Required

a. What are the general controls that should exist in EDP-based accounting systems?

b. What are the purposes of each of the following categories of application controls?
    1. Input controls.
    2. Processing controls.
    3. Output controls.

AICPA

6-26 Johnson, CPA, was engaged to examine the financial statements of Horizon Incorporated, which has its own computer installation. During the preliminary review, Johnson found that Horizon lacked proper segregation of the programming and operating functions. As a result, Johnson intensified the study and evaluation of the system of internal control surrounding the computer and concluded that the existing compensating general controls provided reasonable assurance that the objectives of the system of internal control were being met.

Required

a. In a properly functioning EDP environment, how is the separation of the programming and operating functions achieved?

b. What are the compensating general controls that Johnson most likely found? *Do not discuss hardware and application controls.*

AICPA

6-27 A well-designed management information system using EDP equipment will include methods of assuring that the data are appropriate to the situation and are accurate.

Required

a. Describe procedures that should exist in order to assure that the input data are accurate and appropriate.

b. Describe procedures that would assure that all data were processed and processed properly.

c. Describe procedures that would assure that the output data are accurate and appropriate.

CMA

6-28 Talbert Corporation hired an independent computer programmer to develop a simplified payroll application for its newly purchased computer. The programmer developed an on-line, datebased microcomputer system that minimized the level of knowledge required by the operator. It was based on typing answers to input cues that appeared on the terminal's viewing screen, examples of which follow:

a. Access routine:
   1. Operator access number to payroll file?
   2. Are there new employees?

b. New employees routine:
   1. Employee name?
   2. Employee number?
   3. Social security number?
   4. Rate per hour?
   5. Single or married?
   6. Number of dependents?
   7. Account distribution?

c. Current payroll routine:
   1. Employee number?
   2. Regular hours worked?
   3. Overtime hours worked?
   4. Total employees this payroll period?

The independent auditor is attempting to verify that certain input validation (edit) checks exist to ensure that errors resulting from omissions, invalid entries, or other inaccuracies will be detected during the typing of answers to the input cues.

Required

Identify the various types of input validation (edit) checks the independent auditor would expect to find in the EDP system. Describe the assurances provided by each identified validation check. Do not discuss the review and evaluation of these controls.

AICPA

6-29 The requirement to make a study and evaluation of internal control applies regardless of the method of data processing used by a company. However, the methodology of complying with this standard may be affected by the form of the data processing system.

Required

a. Describe the nature, purpose, and methods of the preliminary phase of the review.

b. Explain the purpose and methods of the completion phase of the review.

c. Identify the major differences and similarities between manual and EDP systems in making a study and evaluation of internal control.

6-30 You are performing an audit of the EDP function of a chemical company with about $150 million in annual sales. Your preliminary review discloses the following points:

1. The EDP manager reports to the director of accounting, who, in turn, reports to the controller. The controller reports to the treasurer, who is one of several vice presidents in the company. The EDP manager has made several unsuccessful requests to the director of accounting for another printer.

2. There is no written charter for the EDP function, but the EDP manager tells you that the primary objective is to get the accounting reports out on time.

3. Transaction tapes are used daily to update the master file and are then retired to the scratch tape area.

4. A third generation computer with large disk capacity was installed three years ago. The EDP acitivity previously used a second generation computer, and many of the programs written for that computer are used on the present equipment by means of an emulator.

5. You observe that the output from the computer runs is written on tape for printing at a later time. Some output tapes from several days' runs are waiting to be printed.

6. The EDP manager states that the CPU could handle at least twice the work currently being processed.

Required

a. Identify the defect inherent in each of the six conditions shown above.

b. Briefly describe the probable effect if the condition continues.

Note: On your answer sheet, show the defect, followed immediately by the probable effect, for each condition.

IIA

6-31 To test the effectiveness of general controls in an EDP system, the auditor may perform the following procedures:

1. Trace selected program changes to supporting documentation.
2. Review and evaluate the hardware controls included in the operating system.
3. Observe and make inquiries concerning segregation of functions between EDP and user departments and within EDP.
4. Selectively review computer operator manuals and observe whether prescribed procedures are being followed.
5. Inquire of librarian as to compliance with procedures for controlling unauthorized access to programs and data files.
6. Examine results of selected pretesting of software programs.
7. Examine evidence for approval of new systems and programs and changes therein.
8. Selectively test preprocessing, postprocessing, and programmed controls.
9. Review on a test basis reconciliations of control totals by the data control group.
10. Examine data files and program access records to test the library function as it applies to significant accounting applications.

Required

a. Indicate the type of general control to which each procedure relates.
b. Identify an error or irregularity that could occur if the procedure is lacking or is improperly functioning.

6-32 Listed below are a number of errors or irregularities pertaining to application controls in an EDP system:

1. An incorrect file is updated.
2. Output is distributed to unauthorized users.
3. Input data are duplicated during handling.
4. Processing errors are made on valid input data.
5. Valid data are improperly converted into machine-readable form.
6. Illogical or unreasonable input is processed.
7. Erroneous data are not corrected and resubmitted for processing.
8. Unauthorized data are converted into machine-sensible form.
9. Output control totals do not agree with input or processing controls.
10. Output data do not agree with original source documents.

Required

For each error or irregularity, identify (a) the control procedures that should prevent or detect such occurrences and (b) the type of application controls (input, processing, and output) that is involved.

6-33 CPAs may audit "around" or "through" computers in examining financial statements of clients who use computers to process accounting data.

Required

a. Describe the auditing approach referred to as auditing "around" the computer.
b. Under what conditions does the CPA decide to audit "through" the computer instead of "around" the computer?

c. In auditing "through" the computer, the CPA may use a test deck.
   1. What is a test deck?
   2. Why does the CPA use a test deck?
d. How can the CPA satisfy himself that the computer program tapes presented to him are actually being used by the client to process its accounting data?

AICPA

6-34 You have been engaged by Central Savings and Loan Association to examine its financial statements for the year ended December 31, 19X1. The CPA who examined the financial statements at December 31, 19X0 rendered an unqualified opinion.

In January 19X1, the Association installed an on-line realtime computer system. Each teller in the association's main office and seven branch offices has an on-line input-output terminal. Customers' mortgage payments and savings account deposits and withdrawals are recorded in the accounts by the computer from data input by the teller at the time of the transaction. The teller keys the proper account by account number and enters the information in the terminal keyboard to record the transaction. The accounting department at the main office has both punched card and typewriter input-output devices. The computer is housed at the main office.

In addition to servicing its own mortgage loans, the association acts as a mortgage servicing agency for three life insurance companies. In this latter activity, the association maintains mortgage records and serves as the collection and escrow agent for the mortgages (the insurance companies), who pay a fee to the Association for these services.

Required

You would expect the association to have certain internal controls in effect because an on-line realtime computer system is employed. List the internal controls that should be in effect solely because this system is employed, classifying them as

1. Those controls pertaining to input of information.
2. All other types of computer controls.

AICPA (adapted)

6-35 The independent auditor must evaluate a client's system of internal control to determine the extent to which various auditing procedures must be employed. A client who uses a computer should provide the CPA with a flowchart of the information processing system so the CPA can evaluate the control features in the system. Shown below is a simplified flowchart, such as a client might provide. Unfortunately, the client had only partially completed the flowchart when it was requested by you.

Required

a. Complete the flowchart shown on page 218.
b. Describe what each item in the flowchart indicates. When complete, your description should provide an explanation of the processing of the data involved. Your description should be in the following order:
   1. "Orders From Salesmen" to "Run 5."
   2. "From Mailroom" to "Run 5."
   3. "Run 5" through the remainder of the chart.

AICPA (adapted)

FLOWCHART

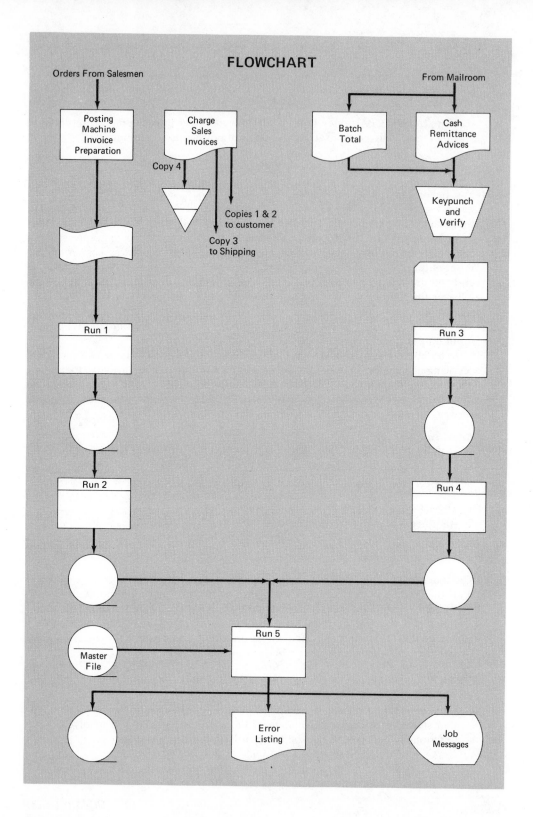

Orders From Salesmen

From Mailroom

Posting Machine Invoice Preparation

Charge Sales Invoices

Batch Total

Cash Remittance Advices

Copy 4

Copies 1 & 2 to customer

Copy 3 to Shipping

Keypunch and Verify

Run 1

Run 3

Run 2

Run 4

Master File

Run 5

Error Listing

Job Messages

6-36 George Beemster, CPA, is examining the financial statements of the Louisville Sales Corporation, which recently installed an off-line electronic computer. The following comments have been extracted from Mr. Beemster's notes on computer operations and the processing and control of shipping notices and customer invoices:

1. To minimize inconvenience, Louisville converted without change its existing data processing system, which utilized tabulating equipment. The computer company supervised the conversion and has provided training to all computer department employees (except keypunch operators) in systems design, operations, and programming.

2. Each computer run is assigned to a specific employee, who is responsible for making program changes, running the program, and answering questions. This procedure has the advantage of eliminating the need for records of computer operations because each employee is responsible for his own computer runs.

3. At least one computer department employee remains in the computer room during office hours, and only computer department employees have keys to the computer room.

4. System documentation consists of those materials furnished by the computer company—a set of record formats and program listings. These and the tape library are kept in a corner of the computer department.

5. The corporation considered the desirability of programmed controls but decided to retain the manual controls from its existing system.

6. Corporation products are shipped directly from public warehouses, which forward shipping notices to general accounting. There, a billing clerk enters the price of the item and accounts for the numerical sequence of shipping notices from each warehouse. The billing clerk also prepares daily adding machine tapes ("control tapes") of the units shipped and the unit prices.

7. Shipping notices and control tapes are forwarded to the computer department for keypunching and processing. Extensions are made on the computer. Output consists of invoices (in six copies) and a daily sales register. The daily sales register shows the aggregate totals of units shipped and unit prices, which the computer operator compares to the control tapes.

8. All copies of the invoice are returned to the billing clerk. The clerk mails three copies to the customer, forwards one copy to the warehouse, maintains one copy in a numerical file, and retains one copy in an open invoice file that serves as a detail accounts receivable record.

Required

a. Describe weaknesses in internal control over information and data flows and the procedures for processing shipping notices and customer invoices, and recommend improvements in these controls and processing procedures. Organize your answer sheets as follows:

Weakness	Recommended Improvement

b. Indicate which of the eight EDP controls is applicable to each weakness.

AICPA (adapted)

6-37 "The EDP function ran in a mode that courted disaster but left the EDP staff apparently isolated from knowledge of the fraud. An open shop functioned where a central staff developed and ran the primary programs for the business, but programmers in other departments could also write and run their own programs and they had unrestricted access to the live data base of insurance policies. The special processing required to carry out the fraud could have been done, and, it is claimed, was done by the programmers outside of the central EDP staff.

"It is also claimed that EDP management had proposed on numerous occasions the establishment of an internal audit group for the EDP environment, but it was always rejected by top management.

"The EDP staff also observed the external auditors from a revealing point of view. The auditors were apparently handed EDP listings of policy records printed from the master files and accepted them as documents of record since they had no capability or skills to directly access the master files in the system themselves. When the auditors happened to select a fake policy for confirmation, they were told that policy folder was in use by somebody in the company and would be available the next day.

"The way it worked was that Equity's head, Stanley Goldblum, set standards for growth in income, assets, and earnings. The desired quarterly and annual profits were relayed to Alan Green through Lewis and another executive. . . . Green would then go on the computer and crank out the necessary fictitious policies."[10]

Required

a. What controls were violated in this case?

b. As auditor of Equity Funding, how would you have reacted to the above?

CASE STUDY

6-38* You have been assigned to the annual audit of Explosives, Inc. You contact the senior, Bob Good, as instructed and arrange a date to discuss the client and the current year's audit.

At your meeting with Good, the company and the current year's audit were discussed. During the discussion, Good emphasized that he wanted to take a good look at the data processing (DP) department. He had attended the firm's one-week course on computer auditing and felt strongly about the need for such review.

On the eighth day of the job, Bob received word that his immediate attention was needed on another job. He had performed most of the review in the DP department and wants you to complete it. Good left the following workpapers to help you complete the review of the DP department.

General Background

The DP department has evolved from a tab operation and currently uses IBM 360 equipment. The department is under the supervision of Gus Sampson, who has worked in it since its inception. He reports to the controller.

---

[10]Donn B. Parker, "Futher Comment on the Equity Funding Insurance Fraud Case," *EDPACS*, January 1975, p. 16.

The department is located on the third floor of the east office wing. It shares office space with the research department and the general accounting department. The machines, however, are physically separated from the other departments by glass doors. The chemical mixing department is located just below on the second floor. The first floor houses the plant personnel department, various conference rooms, and other administrative offices.

The DP department services corporate accounting, the local plant, and three other plant locations elsewhere in the country. The department has an IBM 360/30 computer. Card input is used on most applications. There are two IBM card sorters that are used extensively to sort the card input. Cards are retained for at least one year.

Within the DP department, there are three groups, each with specific duties:

1. Keypunch.
2. Systems analysis.
3. Programming and operations.

Each group has its own supervisor who reports to the DP manager.

Computer Room Operations

All of the machine operators know the jobs they run quite well and have the knowledge to make changes in the operating procedures and programs when they encounter difficulties. This has greatly increased efficiency as less time is lost due to machine halts caused by program interruptions. Gus stated that because of the operators' familiarity with the various jobs, he does not have to devote much time to supervising them.

When asked about operating manuals for the operators, Gus replied it would be a waste of time to prepare them since the operators are so familiar with the programs and jobs. If a problem develops, an operator can simply look at a source program listing and make the necessary correction. Gus said he seldom reviewed any console sheets because of the confidence he had in his operators. He complained, however, about the accounting people always giving him bad data and then complaining about the output, "GIGO is the rule," he said.

During my tour of the computer room with Gus, I noticed that reels of tape, some with labels and some without, were in file racks, on tables, on top of equipment, and in the corner of the floor. In another corner, I noticed open boxes of various forms and payroll checks. I had expected to see only two or three operators in the computer room, but there were five or six people in it. When I asked Gus about these conditions, he said he had read all the books and publications on controlling the computer room and felt most of the alleged dangers were exaggerated. He trusted his employees and felt his shop was one of the best in the area. As for the additional people, he felt that too many people are mystified by the computer. Consequently, he maintains an open door policy so people can come in and see "what the monster is all about."

Programming Group

Information about this group was obtained from Betty James, the head programmer, who reports to Gus Sampson. The members of this group mainly write new programs and maintain current programs, about 75% of which were written years ago using a second generation (1401) programming language. These programs are currently being rewritten in a more modern and efficient language.

Documentation for the old programs and some of the new ones consists of source listings. The old programs were written by Gus, Betty, and a fellow who has left the company. Since Gus and Betty are still around, there has not been any need to prepare additional documentation. Betty said, however, that Gus has been thinking about developing documentation standards for all programs.

Betty mentioned numerous problems have arisen lately due to an operator or programmer making an undocumented "patch" in a program so the job can be run. Sometimes, the change causes other errors to occur. Gus has attempted to stop the operators from making changes, but with the program cards being accessible to everyone, it has been impossible to enforce.

Required

a. Draw an organization chart of the EDP department.
b. For each of the eight EDP controls mentioned in the chapter, discuss the weaknesses in the system and your recommendations for improvement.

Chapter 7

Audit Sampling in Compliance Testing

Study Objectives

After studying this chapter, you should be able to

- State the relationship of generally accepted auditing standards (GAAS) to audit sampling.

- Recognize and define the risks associated with audit sampling.

- Explain the essential steps in the design, execution, and evaluation of an attribute sampling plan for compliance tests.

- Prepare working papers for statistical sampling plans.

- Identify circumstances when discovery sampling is appropriate and explain how this technique is used.

- Describe the differences between nonstatistical and statistical sampling in compliance testing.

In contemporary auditing, sampling is well established. The importance of audit sampling in current practice is underscored by the issuance of a Statement on Auditing Standards (SAS) on audit sampling. In addition, the AICPA has published a comprehensive audit and accounting guide entitled *Audit Sampling* to assist auditors in implementing the SAS.

This chapter explains the basic concepts of audit sampling and emphasizes the application of statistical sampling in compliance testing. The chapter is divided into four sections: (1) basic concepts (2) attribute sampling in compliance testing, (3) discovery sampling, and (4) nonstatistical sampling in compliance testing.

BASIC AUDIT SAMPLING CONCEPTS

NATURE AND PURPOSE OF AUDIT SAMPLING

Audit sampling is the application of an audit procedure to less than 100% of the items within an account balance or class of transactions for the purpose of evaluating some characteristic of the balance or class.[1]

Audit sampling is applicable to both compliance and substantive testing. However, it is not equally applicable to all of the auditing procedures that may be used in performing these tests. For example, audit sampling is widely used in vouching, confirming, and retracing, but it is ordinarily not used in inquiry, observing, and analytical review procedures.

UNCERTAINTY AND AUDIT SAMPLING

Both the second and third standards of field work contain an element of uncertainty. For example, the auditor's reliance on internal control affects the *extent of tests* to which other auditing procedures are to be restricted. In meeting the evidential matter standard, the auditor is required only to have a *reasonable basis* for an opinion.

The auditor is justified in accepting some uncertainty when the cost and time required to make a 100% examination of the data are, in his judgment, greater than the adverse consequences of possibly expressing an erroneous opinion from examining only a sample of the data. Since this is normally the case, sampling is widely used in auditing.

The uncertainties inherent in auditing are collectively referred to as audit risk. Audit sampling applies to two components of audit risk: (1) control risk and (2) detection risk. As explained in earlier chapters, control risk is the risk that the system of internal control will not detect or prevent material errors in the financial statements, and detection risk is the risk that the material errors in the financial statements will not be discovered by the auditor's examination. Audit sampling in compliance testing provides information that is directly related to the auditor's assessment of control risk, and audit sampling in substantive testing assists the auditor in quantifying and controlling detection risk.

When sampling is used in meeting the second and third standards of field work, it should be recognized that uncertainties may result from factors (1) associated directly with the use of sampling (sampling risk) and (2) unrelated to sampling (nonsampling risk).

Sampling Risk

This risk relates to the possibility that a properly drawn sample may not be representative of the population. Thus, the auditor's conclusion about internal

---

[1]Auditing Standards Board, *Codification of Statements on Auditing Standards* (New York: American Institute of Certified Public Accountants, 1985), Auditing Section 350.01 (hereinafter referred to and cited as AU §).

control procedures or the details of transactions and balances based on the sample may be different from the conclusion that would result from the examination of the entire population. In performing compliance and substantive tests, the following types of sampling risk may occur.[2]

Compliance Testing

The risk of overreliance on internal accounting control is the risk that the sample supports the auditor's planned degree of reliance on the control when the true compliance rate does not justify such reliance.[3]

The risk of underreliance on internal accounting control is the risk that the sample does not support the auditor's planned degree of reliance on the control when the true compliance rate supports such reliance.[4]

Substantive Testing

The risk of incorrect acceptance is the risk that the sample supports the conclusion that the recorded account balance is not materially misstated when it is materially misstated.[3]

The risk of incorrect rejection is the risk that the sample supports the conclusion that the recorded account balance is materially misstated when it is not materially misstated.[4]

These risks have a significant impact on both the effectiveness and efficiency of the audit. The risk of overreliance and the risk of incorrect acceptance relate to audit effectiveness. When the auditor reaches either of these erroneous conclusions, his examination may not be sufficient to detect material errors and irregularities, and he may not have a reasonable basis for an opinion. In contrast, the risks of underreliance and incorrect rejection relate to the efficiency of the audit. When either of these erroneous conclusions are reached, the auditor will increase substantive tests unnecessarily. However, such effort will ordinarily lead ultimately to a correct conclusion, and the audit will nevertheless be effective.

Nonsampling Risk

This risk refers to the portion of audit risk that is not due to examining only a portion of the data. This risk results from (1) human mistakes, such as failing to recognize errors in documents in a sample, (2) applying auditing procedures inappropriate to the audit objective, and (3) misinterpreting the results of a sample. Nonsampling risk can never be mathematically measured. However,

---

[2]Auditing Standards Board, *op. cit.*, AU § 350.12.

[3]This risk is sometimes identified as the *beta* risk.

[4]This risk is sometimes identified as the *alpha* risk.

by proper planning and supervision and adherence to the quality control standards described earlier, nonsampling risk can be held to a negligible level.

NONSTATISTICAL AND STATISTICAL SAMPLING

In performing audit tests in accordance with GAAS, the auditor may use either nonstatistical or statistical sampling or both. Both types of sampling require the exercise of judgment in planning and executing the sampling plan and evaluating the results. Moreover, both types of sampling can provide sufficient evidential matter as required by the third standard of field work. Both types of audit sampling are also subject to some sampling and nonsampling risk. The critical difference between the two types of sampling is that the laws of probability are used to control sampling risk in statistical sampling.

The choice between the two types of sampling is based primarily on cost/benefit considerations. Nonstatistical sampling may be less costly than statistical sampling, but the benefits from statistical sampling may be significantly greater than nonstatistical sampling.

In nonstatistical sampling, the auditor determines sample size and evaluates sample results entirely on the basis of subjective criteria and his own experience. Thus, he may unknowingly use too large a sample in one area and too small a sample in another. To the extent that the sufficiency of audit evidence is based on a sample, the auditor may, in turn, obtain more (or less) evidence than is actually needed to have a reasonable basis for expressing an opinion. However, a properly designed nonstatistical sample may be just as effective as a statistical sample.

In statistical sampling, substantial costs may be required to train auditors in the use of statistics and the design and implementation of the sampling plan. However, statistical sampling should benefit the auditor in (1) designing an efficient sample, (2) measuring the sufficiency of the evidence obtained, and (3) evaluating sample results.[5] Most important, statistical sampling enables the auditor to quantify and control sampling risk.

The choice of nonstatistical or statistical sampling does not affect the selection of auditing procedures to be applied to a sample. Moreover, it does not affect the competence of evidence obtained about individual sample items or the appropriate response by the auditor to errors found in sample items. These matters require the exercise of professional judgment. The relationship between nonstatistical and statistical sampling is graphically shown in Figure 7-1.

AUDIT SAMPLING TECHNIQUES

An auditor may use sampling to obtain information about many different characteristics of a population. However, most audit samples lead either to

[5]Statistical Sampling Subcommittee, Audit and Accounting Guide, *Audit Sampling* (New York: American Institute of Certified Public Accountants, 1983), p. 13 (hereinafter referred to as *Audit Sampling Guide*).

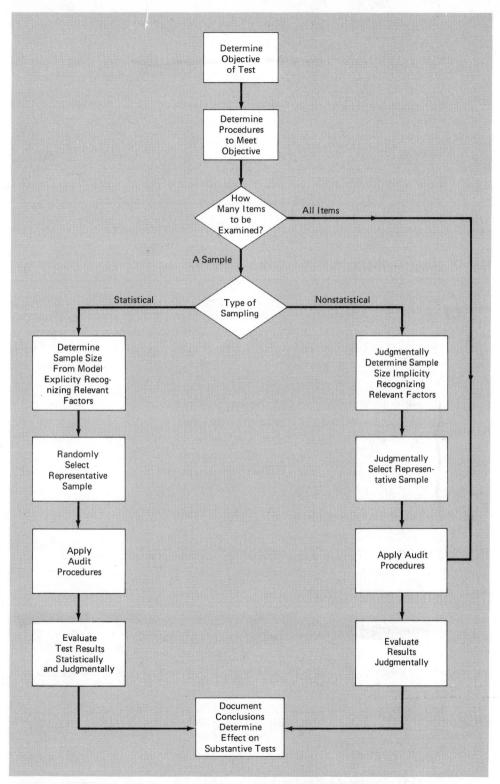

Figure 7-1. AUDIT SAMPLING: STATISTICAL AND NONSTATISTICAL.

an estimate of (1) a deviation rate or (2) a dollar amount. When statistical sampling is used, these sampling techniques are identified as *attribute sampling* and *variables sampling,* respectively. The essential differences between these techniques are summarized in Figure 7-2.

There are several variations within each of these techniques, including a method of estimating the monetary amount of transactions involving compliance deviations. In the remaining pages of this chapter, consideration is given to the following aspects of attribute sampling: (1) statistical sampling in compliance testing, (2) discovery sampling, and (3) nonstatistical sampling in compliance testing. Variables sampling techniques are explained in Chapter 12.

STATISTICAL SAMPLING

Attribute sampling for compliance tests generally is used only if there is a trail of documentary evidence of the performance of control procedures. This type of sampling is ordinarily not applicable to controls that depend primarily on segregation of functions or controls that produce no documentary evidence of performance. The steps in a statistical sampling plan for compliance tests are as follows:

1. Determine the audit objectives.
2. Define the population and sampling unit.
3. Specify the attributes of interest.
4. Determine the sample size.
5. Determine the sample selection method.
6. Execute the sampling plan.
7. Evaluate the sample results.

Steps 1–5 involve audit planning. The remaining steps are performed during field work. Each of the steps should be documented in the working papers.

DETERMINE THE AUDIT OBJECTIVES

The overall purpose of compliance testing is to determine whether prescribed control procedures are in use and operating as planned. It is necessary, there-

Sampling Technique	Type of Testing	Purpose
Attribute sampling	Compliance	Estimate the rate of deviations from prescribed control procedures in a population.
Variables sampling	Substantive	Estimate the total dollar amount of a population or the dollar amount of error in a population.

Figure 7.2. ATTRIBUTE AND VARIABLES SAMPLING TECHNIQUES.

fore, to identify the controls that are of interest to the auditor in terms of specific internal control objectives. For instance, when the auditor tests controls over the execution of sales transactions, the specific objectives may relate to the control procedures over granting credit, filling and shipping the order, and billing the customer.

DEFINE THE POPULATION AND SAMPLING UNIT

In compliance testing, the population is the class of transactions being tested. The auditor should determine that the population is appropriate for the objectives of the plan. For example, if the objective is whether all approved vouchers have been recorded, the population should be all approved vouchers, not all entries in the voucher register. If the voucher register were used as the population, unrecorded vouchers could not be included in the sample.

The identification of the population also includes a consideration of the population's homogeneity with respect to the control procedures to be tested. Accordingly, cash disbursements may be stratified as to amount when there are significant differences in prescribed controls for disbursements over a specified dollar amount.

When there are multiple client locations, such as branches and divisions, the auditor may elect to regard each segment as a separate population. This choice would clearly be warranted when there are significantly different control procedures at each location. However, when the controls are similar throughout the organization and consolidated statements are prepared, one population for all locations may suffice.

The auditor is faced with a similar choice when the client has made a change in a control procedure during the year. If the auditor wishes to rely on both controls, the population should include transactions processed both before and after the change. In contrast, if reliance is to be placed only on the new control, the population may be defined solely for transactions processed after the change.

It is not necessary in attribute sampling to know the exact size of the population, although a reasonable approximation of population size may be needed when the population is relatively small (e.g. 5,000 or less). As will be shown later, population size has little or no effect on sample size.

The sampling unit is an individual element in the population. A sampling unit may be a document, a line item of a document, or a line item of a journal or register. It is imperative that the sampling unit be compatible with the objective of the test. For the voucher example above, the sampling unit should be the voucher. In contrast, if the objective is to determine the existence of improperly recorded transactions in the voucher register, the sampling unit should be the line item in the register.

The sampling unit may impact significantly on audit efficiency. Assume, for instance, that sales invoices average four line items per invoice. If, in testing a control over pricing, the sampling unit is defined as the invoice, and sample size is 150, the auditor would have to test 600 items. In contrast, if the line item is the sampling unit, only 150 items would be tested for compliance.

SPECIFY THE ATTRIBUTES OF INTEREST

On the basis of his knowledge of the internal control system, the auditor should be able to identify attributes that indicate compliance with the control procedure expected to be relied on in substantive testing. Attributes should be identified for each control procedure necessary to achieve the related specific internal control objective for the particular class of transactions. If the control procedure requires credit department approval of credit prior to shipment, the attribute may be defined as "sales order with credit approval." When the control procedure requires action by a specified individual, the attribute of interest is "approval of voucher by Jones."[6] Care should be exercised in specifying the attributes since they provide the basis for the subsequent determination of the number of deviations from prescribed procedures.

Figure 7-3 illustrates the attributes that may be specified in an attribute sampling plan to test controls over the execution of credit sales transactions. It is assumed in this illustration that the company prepares a sales order on receipt of the customer order.

Each attribute should relate to a control procedure on which the auditor intends to rely. However, each attribute may not be of equal importance. In a given case, the auditor may consider credit approval to be more important than the verification of mathematical accuracy. The relative importance of each attribute should be considered in setting desired statistical objectives. Ordinarily, more stringent statistical parameters are set for the more critical controls.

The attributes in Figure 7-3 relate to documentary evidence of performance of a control procedure. In each case, the employee is expected to initial, sign,

Attribute	Description of Attribute
1	Authorization of sale by appropriate sales order department personnel
2	Sales order department verification of agreement of sales order with customer order as to quantities, descriptions, and prices
3	Credit approval by authorized credit department personnel
4	Shipping department verification of agreement of goods shipped with sales order
5	Billing department verification of agreement of sales invoice with shipping document
6	Billing department verification of agreement of sales invoice with sales order
7	Billing department verification of agreement of unit prices on sales invoice with specific price authorization and/or catalog or list prices
8	Billing department verification of mathematical accuracy of sales invoice

Figure 7-3. ATTRIBUTES OF INTEREST FOR COMPLIANCE TESTS OF SALES TRANSACTIONS.

[6]Some auditors define attributes of interest as *deviation conditions* rather than control procedures. The deviation conditions for the two attributes here would be "sales order lacking credit approval" and "voucher not approved by Jones."

or stamp the document upon completing the control procedure. The auditor then obtains evidence of compliance with the control by reviewing (or inspecting) the documents for the initials, and so on.

DETERMINE THE SAMPLE SIZE

The objective in determining sample size is to obtain a sample that will meet desired statistical objectives for each control procedure being tested. The factors that affect the determination of sample size are (1) acceptable level of risk of overreliance, (2) tolerable deviation rate, (3) expected population deviation rate, and (4) population size.

Acceptable Level of Risk of Overreliance

As explained earlier, two types of sampling risk are associated with internal control: (1) the risk of underreliance, which relates to the efficiency of the audit, and (2) the risk of overreliance, which relates to the effectiveness of the audit. Due to the potentially serious consequences associated with an ineffective audit, and because compliance testing may be the only source of evidence regarding deviations, the auditor desires to keep the risk of overreliance at a low level.

In statistical sampling, the risk of overreliance must be stated explicitly. The level of acceptable risk has an inverse affect on sample size; at a 5% risk, sample size will be larger than at a 10% risk. Determining the appropriate sample size for varying levels of risk of overreliance and other factors may be accomplished by the use of tables like those illustrated later in Figure 7-4. The effects of varying levels of risk of overreliance on sample size can be seen by holding the other sample size factors constant. If we assume a tolerable deviation rate of 5%, an expected population deviation rate of 1%, and a large population, the following sample sizes result when the risk of overreliance is changed:

Risk of Overreliance	Sample Size
10%	77
5	93
1	165

Most auditors either specify one level of risk of overreliance for all compliance tests or select 5 or 10% depending on the importance of the control.[7]

Tolerable Deviation Rate

The tolerable deviation rate is the maximum rate of deviations from a prescribed control procedure that an auditor is willing to accept and still rely on

---

[7]The factor *reliability* or *confidence level* is sometimes used in attribute sampling. This factor is the complement of the risk of overreliance. Thus, a 5% risk of overreliance is the equivalent of specifying 95% reliability.

the control. In deciding on the tolerable rate, the auditor should consider the relationship of each deviation to

- The accounting records being tested.
- Any related internal accounting control procedures.
- The purpose of the auditor's evaluation.[8]

The auditor should recognize that deviations from prescribed control procedures increase the *risk*, but not necessarily the number, of errors in the financial records. For example, the lack of approval on a voucher is a deviation, but the voucher may nevertheless pertain to a valid transaction that is properly recorded.

Related control procedures exist when there are compensating or auxiliary controls to a specified procedure. The significance of a deviation from the specified procedure, such as the approval of a voucher, is affected by the potential effectiveness of related controls, such as the review of supporting documentation by one or more authorized signers of company checks.

The purpose of the auditor's evaluation of internal control is to provide a basis for determining the extent to which other auditing procedures are to be restricted. As explained in earlier chapters, the auditor cannot entirely eliminate substantive testing. Thus, the auditor should recognize that other auditing procedures may detect errors or irregularities resulting from a deviation from prescribed control procedures.

Tolerable deviation rates vary with the auditor's planned reliance on the control procedure—the greater the reliance, the lower the tolerable rate and vice versa. The following guidelines have been suggested in quantifying an acceptable range[9]:

Planned Reliance	Tolerable Rate Range
Substantial	2–7%
Moderate	6–12
Little	11–20
No reliance	Omit test

Tolerable rate has an inverse affect on sample size. The effect of tolerable rate on sample sizes assuming a risk of overreliance of 5%, a zero expected population deviation rate, and a large population is illustrated by the following:

Tolerable Deviation Rate	Sample Size	Tolerable Deviation Rate	Sample Size
2%	149	6%	49
4	74	8	36

Expected Population Deviation Rate

The auditor uses one or more of the following to estimate the expected population rate for each control procedure.

[8]Auditing Standards Board, *op. cit.*, AU § 350.33.
[9]*Audit Sampling Guide, op. cit.*, p. 32.

- Last year's sample deviation rate, adjusted judgmentally for current year changes in the control procedure.
- The current year's preliminary evaluation of internal control.
- The rate found in a preliminary sample of approximately 50 items.

If the expected deviation rate is equal to or greater than the tolerable rate, the auditor cannot reasonably expect to rely on the control. Thus, he should omit compliance testing and design substantive tests without any reliance on that control procedure.

The expected population rate has a significant and direct effect on sample size. When the risk of overreliance and tolerable rate are held constant, increases and decreases from a given expected population deviation rate will result in larger and smaller sample sizes repectively. The effect of this factor on sample size is as follows, assuming a 5% risk of overreliance, a 5% tolerable deviation rate, and a large population:

Expected Population Deviation Rate	Sample Size	Expected Population Deviation Rate	Sample Size
0.0%	59	1.5%	124
1.0	93	2.0	181

These effects recognize that as the expected population deviation rate approaches the tolerable rate, more precise information is needed and a larger sample size results.

Population Size

As previously explained, population size has little of no effect on sample size. If we assume a 5% risk of overreliance, a 5% tolerable rate, and a 1% expected population deviation rate, the effects of changes in population size on sample size are as follows[10]:

Population Size	Sample Size	Population Size	Sample Size
100	64	2,000	92
500	87	5,000	93
1,000	90	100,000	93

When the population is over 5,000 sampling units, it is appropriate in statistical sampling to consider the population as infinite. A large population will be assumed in all remaining examples and end-of-chapter problems.

Sample Size Tables

When each of the factors affecting sample size has been quantified, sample size is determined objectively through the use of sample size tables like those shown in Figure 7-4. The tables are based on an upper deviation limit (or one-tailed) approach because the auditor is concerned only that the actual pop-

---

[10]*Audit Sampling Guide, op. cit.*, p. 35.

Statistical Sample Sizes for Compliance Testing (for large populations)

Table 1.   5% Risk of Overreliance

Expected Population Deviation Rate	Tolerable Deviation Rate								
	2%	3%	4%	5%	6%	7%	8%	9%	10%
0.00%	149	99	74	59	49	42	36	32	29
0.50	*	157	117	93	78	66	58	51	46
1.00	*	*	156	93	78	66	58	51	46
1.50	*	*	192	124	103	66	58	51	46
2.00	*	*	*	181	127	88	77	68	46
2.50	*	*	*	*	150	109	77	68	61
3.00	*	*	*	*	195	129	95	84	61
4.00	*	*	*	*	*	*	146	100	89
5.00	*	*	*	*	*	*	*	158	116
6.00	*	*	*	*	*	*	*	*	179

Table 2.   10% Risk of Overreliance

Expected Population Deviation Rate	Tolerable Deviation Rate								
	2%	3%	4%	5%	6%	7%	8%	9%	10%
0.00%	114	76	57	45	38	32	28	25	22
0.50	194	129	96	77	64	55	48	42	38
1.00	*	176	96	77	64	55	48	42	38
1.50	*	*	132	105	64	55	48	42	38
2.00	*	*	198	132	88	75	48	42	38
2.50	*	*	*	158	110	75	65	58	38
3.00	*	*	*	*	132	94	65	58	52
4.00	*	*	*	*	*	149	98	73	65
5.00	*	*	*	*	*	*	160	115	78
6.00	*	*	*	*	*	*	*	182	116

*Sample size is too large to be cost/effective for most audit applications.

Figure 7-4. SAMPLE SIZE TABLES. [SOURCE: *Audit Sampling Guide, op. cit.*, pp. 106–107 (adapted).]

ulation deviation rate does not *exceed* the tolerable deviation rate. To use the tables, it is necessary to

- Select the table that corresponds to the acceptable risk of overreliance.
- Locate the column that pertains to the specified tolerable deviation rate.
- Locate the row that contains the expected population deviation rate.

• Read the sample size from the intersection of the column and row determined in steps two and three.

Illustrative sample sizes are:

Risk of Overreliance	Tolerable Deviation Rate	Expected Population Deviation Rate	Sample Size
5%	4%	1.0%	156
5	6	2.0	127
10	5	1.0	77
10	6	2.0	88

DETERMINE THE SAMPLE SELECTION METHOD

Once sample size has been determined, a method of selecting sampling units from the population must be chosen. Sample items should be selected in a manner that results in a sample that is representative of the population. Thus, all items in the population should have a chance of being selected. To accomplish this, statistical sampling plans require the use of *random* selection methods. The principal random selection methods used in attribute sampling are random number sampling and systematic sampling.

Random Number Sampling

To use random number sampling (sometimes called *simple random sampling*), the auditor must have a basis for relating a unique number to each item in the population. Then, either by reference to a table of random numbers or a computer program that generates random numbers, a selection of numbers can be made to choose the individual items that will make up the sample.

The use of random number tables is facilitated when the items in a population are consecutively numbered. In using tables, the auditor must (1) pick a starting point in the tables by making a "blind stab" or arbitrarily choosing a starting point, and (2) determine the direction or route (top to bottom, left to right, etc.) to be used in reading the tables. The route must be followed consistently.

A random number table is shown in Figure 7-5. To illustrate its use, assume that a sample is desired from a population of sales invoices numbered 0001 to 4000. Assume further that the auditor elects to use the first set of four digits, start with row 6 of column 1, and read from top to bottom. In such case, the first four invoices in the sample would be numbers 0050, 3486, 2580, and 3942. Numbers 9287 and 7748 would be discarded because these digits do not correspond to the numbers in the population.

In using a random number table, it is possible that the same number may be drawn more than once. When the duplicate number is ignored (i.e., skipped), the auditor is said to be *sampling without replacement*. Statistical tables used by auditors to determine sample size, like those illustrated earlier in this chapter,

	Columns				
Row	(1)	(2)	(3)	(4)	(5)
1	04734	39426	91035	54839	76873
2	10417	19688	83404	42038	48226
3	07514	48374	35658	38971	53779
4	52305	86925	16223	25946	90222
5	96357	11486	30102	82679	57983
6	92870	05921	65698	27993	86406
7	00500	75924	38803	05386	10072
8	34862	93784	52709	15370	96727
9	25809	21860	36790	76883	20435
10	77487	38419	20631	48694	12638

Figure 7-5. PARTIAL RANDOM NUMBER TABLE.

are often based on sampling with replacement. As a practical matter, however, the auditor usually samples without replacement since no new information would be obtained from examining the same item twice. The use of tables based on sampling with replacement results in larger sample sizes and is therefore considered by auditors to be a conservative approach.

Many computer software packages offer a standard program that includes a random number generator. Such a program can provide a list of random numbers to fit any size sample. In addition, the software can be instructed to produce numbers that correspond solely to numbers appearing in the population. Random number generators greatly expedite the process of obtaining the list of sample items.

Systematic Sampling

This method of selection consists of selecting every nth item in the population from one or more random starts. The interval between items is usually referred to as the *skip interval*. When a single random start is used, the interval can be computed by dividing the population size by the sample size. Therefore, when a sample of 400 is to be obtained from a population of 2,000, the skip interval is 5 (2,000/400). The starting point in this method of selection should be a number from a random number table that falls within the interval from 1 to 5.

A major advantage of systematic selection is that it may take less time than other selection methods. Once the interval and starting point are determined, selection of the sample can be started immediately. In addition, it is unnecessary to number the items in the population to use this method. The auditor (or the computer) simply counts every nth item. Thus, the method can be used when the data are in the form of punched cards, magnetic tapes, or ledger cards.

Whenever the auditor considers using systematic selection, he must be alert to the possibility of any cyclical pattern within the population coinciding with the skip interval. In that event, systematic selection could produce a nonrandom sample, and another selection method should be considered. Alternatively, he can minimize the chance of bias by picking multiple starting points for the selection process. When multiple random starting points are used, the skip interval, as determined earlier in this section, is multiplied by the number of random starts, thus keeping total sample size the same.

EXECUTING THE SAMPLING PLAN

After the sampling plan has been designed, sample items are selected and examined to determine the nature and frequency of deviations from prescribed control procedures.

When the sampling unit is a document, the auditor may select a quantity that is slightly larger than the required amount. The "extras" are used as replacements when voided, unused, or nonapplicable items are selected in the required sample. A nonapplicable item occurs when a control procedure or attribute does not pertain to the item selected. For instance, if the attribute being examined is "existence of receiving report to support voucher," a voucher for the payment of a monthly bill from a public utility would not be applicable because receiving reports are not prepared for such services. Thus, this voucher would be replaced by an extra in executing the sample plan.

An unused item refers to the selection of an item from a portion of the population that has not yet been used. This may occur when the auditor defines the population to include the entire year and the sampling plan is executed during interim work. In such cases, any numbers selected that exceed those for which documents are available are replaced by an extra. When a sample item cannot be located, the item should be counted as a deviation. The auditor may discontinue the sampling plan whenever the number of deviations found in the sample will not support the planned reliance on the control procedure.

EVALUATE THE SAMPLE RESULTS

Deviations found in the sample must be tabulated, summarized, and evaluated. Professional judgment is required in the evaluation of the following factors leading to an overall conclusion.

Calculate the Sample Deviation Rate

A sample deviation rate for each control tested is calculated by dividing the number of deviations found by the sample size examined. This rate is the auditor's best estimate of the true deviation rate in the population.

Determine the Upper Deviation Limit

This limit indicates the maximum deviation rate in the population based on the *number* of deviations discovered in the sample. The upper limit is expressed as a percentage, which is sometimes alternately referred to as the *achieved upper precision limit* or *maximum population deviation rate.*

The upper deviation limit is determined from evaluation tables like those shown in Figure 7-6. To use the tables, it is necessary to

- Select the table that corresponds to the acceptable risk of overreliance.
- Locate the column that contains the actual *number* of deviations (not the deviation rate) found in the sample.
- Locate the row that contains the sample size used.
- Read the upper deviation limit from the intersection of the column and row determined in steps two and three.

Illustrative upper deviation limits are as follows:

Risk of Overreliance	Number of Deviations	Sample Size	Upper Deviation Limit
5%	1	100	4.7%
5	2	150	4.1
10	3	120	5.5
10	4	200	4.0

When the sample size used does not appear in the evaluation tables, the auditor may (1) use the largest sample size in the table not exceeding the actual sample size used, (2) interpolate, (3) obtain more extensive tables, or (4) use a computer program that will produce an upper limit for any sample size. The upper deviation limit determined from tables implicitly includes an allowance for sampling risk. Thus, the upper deviation limit can be used to determine whether a sample supports reliance on the control tested. If the upper deviation limit is less than or equal to the tolerable rate specified in designing the sample, the results support relying on the control; otherwise, the results do not support reliance.

Allowance for Sampling Risk

It will be recalled that sampling risk relates to the possibility that a properly drawn sample may nonetheless not be representative of the population. As indicated above, the evaluation of a sample can be made without explicitly calculating the allowance for sampling risk. However, knowing how the allowance can be determined and its effects is helpful in the evaluation process. The allowance for sampling risk is added to the sample deviation rate to produce an upper deviation limit that will exceed the true population deviation rate a known proportion of the time. When evaluation tables are used, the allowance for sampling risk is determined by subtracting the sample deviation rate from the upper deviation limit. Therefore, in the first case above, the

Statistical Sample Results Evaluation Table for Compliance Tests
Upper Deviation Limit
(for large populations)

Table 3.   5% Risk of Overreliance

Sample Size	Actual Number of Deviations Found								
	0	1	2	3	4	5	6	7	8
25	11.3	17.6	*	*	*	*	*	*	*
30	9.5	14.9	19.5	*	*	*	*	*	*
35	8.2	12.9	16.9	*	*	*	*	*	*
40	7.2	11.3	14.9	18.3	*	*	*	*	*
45	6.4	10.1	13.3	16.3	19.2	*	*	*	*
50	5.8	9.1	12.1	14.8	17.4	19.9	*	*	*
55	5.3	8.3	11.0	13.5	15.9	18.1	*	*	*
60	4.9	7.7	10.1	12.4	14.6	16.7	18.8	*	*
65	4.5	7.1	9.4	11.5	13.5	15.5	17.4	19.3	*
70	4.2	6.6	8.7	10.7	12.6	14.4	16.2	18.0	19.7
75	3.9	6.2	8.2	10.0	11.8	13.5	15.2	16.9	18.4
80	3.7	5.8	7.7	9.4	11.1	12.7	14.3	15.8	17.3
90	3.3	5.2	6.8	8.4	9.9	11.3	12.7	14.1	15.5
100	3.0	4.7	6.2	7.6	8.9	10.2	11.5	12.7	14.0
125	2.4	3.7	4.9	6.1	7.2	8.2	9.3	10.3	11.3
150	2.0	3.1	4.1	5.1	6.0	6.9	7.7	8.6	9.4
200	1.5	2.3	3.1	3.8	4.5	5.2	5.8	6.5	7.1

Table 4.   10% Risk of Overreliance

Sample Size	Actual Number of Deviations Found								
	0	1	2	3	4	5	6	7	8
20	10.9	18.1	*	*	*	*	*	*	*
25	8.8	14.7	19.9	*	*	*	*	*	*
30	7.4	12.4	16.8	*	*	*	*	*	*
35	6.4	10.7	14.5	18.1	*	*	*	*	*
40	5.6	9.4	12.8	15.9	19.0	*	*	*	*
45	5.0	8.4	11.4	14.2	17.0	19.6	*	*	*
50	4.5	7.6	10.3	12.9	15.4	17.8	*	*	*
55	4.1	6.9	9.4	11.7	14.0	16.2	18.4	*	*
60	3.8	6.3	8.6	10.8	12.9	14.9	16.9	18.8	*
70	3.2	5.4	7.4	9.3	11.1	12.8	14.6	16.2	17.9
80	2.8	4.8	6.5	8.3	9.7	11.3	12.8	14.3	15.7
90	2.5	4.3	5.8	7.3	8.7	10.1	11.4	12.7	14.0
100	2.3	3.8	5.2	6.6	7.8	9.1	10.3	11.5	12.7
120	1.9	3.2	4.4	5.5	6.6	7.6	8.6	9.6	10.6
160	1.4	2.4	3.3	4.1	4.9	5.7	6.5	7.2	8.0
200	1.1	1.9	2.6	3.3	4.0	4.6	5.2	5.8	6.4

*Over 20%.

Figure 7-6. STATISTICAL SAMPLE EVALUATION TABLES. [SOURCE: *Audit Sampling Guide, op. cit.,* pp. 108–109 (adapted).

sample deviation rate is 1% (1/100) and the allowance is 3.7% (4.7% − 1.0%).[11] If three deviations had been found in the sample of 100, the upper deviation limit is 7.6%, the sample deviation rate is 3% (3/100), and the allowance for sampling risk is 4.6% (7.6% − 3.0%).

The allowance for sampling risk is directly related to the number of deviations found in the sample as illustrated by the increase from 3.7 to 4.6% in this example. It follows, in statistical sampling, that when the sample deviation rate exceeds the expected population deviation rate, the allowance for sampling risk will be large enough to cause the upper deviation limit to exceed the tolerable deviation rate specified in designing the sample. Thus, the following generalizations can be stated:

- Whenever the sample deviation rate exceeds the expected population deviation rate used to determine sample size, the upper deviation limit will exceed the tolerable deviation rate at the specified risk of overreliance and the sample results will not support reliance on the control.
- Conversely, whenever the sample deviation rate is less than or equal to the expected population deviation rate, the upper deviation limit will be less than or equal to the tolerable deviation rate at the specified risk of overreliance and the sample results will support reliance on the control.

From the above, it can be seen that it is not always necessary to compare the upper deviation limit with the tolerable deviation rate in evaluating sample results. The basis for the auditor's evaluation should be documented in the working papers. The working paper in Figure 7-7 permits an evaluation using either the upper deviation limit or the sample deviation rate.

Consider the Qualitative Aspects of Deviations

It would be a mistake to conclude that the auditor is interested only in the frequency of the deviations. Each deviation from a prescribed control procedure should be analyzed to determine its nature and cause. Deviations may result from such factors as a new employee, an inexperienced replacement, an employee on vacation or sick leave, misunderstanding of instructions by new employees, incompetence, carelessness, and deliberate violation.

The auditor should also consider whether the deviation may have a direct effect on the financial statements. For instance, the failure of unit prices on a sales invoice to agree with authorized prices has an impact on the statements. In contrast, the absence of verification of the mathematical accuracy of an invoice that is mathematically correct does not indicate an error in the financial statements. A further consideration is whether the deviation constitutes an irregularity. Nonsystematic deviations are generally accidental and unintentional. However, a systematic pattern of deviations may be indicative of a serious breakdown in a control leading to numerous unintentional errors or deliberate efforts to misrepresent facts or conceal misappropriations. Ob-

---

[11]The allowance for sampling risk can also be computed directly using binomial probability distribution theory.

viously, deviations that directly affect the financial statements or appear to be irregularities have greater audit significance.

Reach an Overall Conclusion

The auditor uses the results of the sample and professional judgment to reach a conclusion about the reliance to be placed on each of the control procedures that have been tested. As explained in Chapter 5, the auditor may express his conclusion in terms of whether control risk is low, medium or high. When, in the auditor's judgment, the sample results do not support the planned reliance, the auditor ordinarily will have to modify the nature, timing, or extent of substantive tests, or if applicable, test other compensating controls for compliance.

ILLUSTRATIVE CASE STUDY

In the audit of the Dexter Company, the auditor decides to use attribute sampling in compliance testing of sales transactions. The plan and the auditor's working papers are explained and illustrated below. This case study is divided into three parts: (1) the design of the sampling plan, (2) executing the plan, and (3) evaluating the results.

The *design of the sampling plan* involves the first five steps of the sampling plan. These are presented in the sample design section of the working paper in Figure 7-7. The objective of the plan, the sampling unit and population, and the sample selection method are identified at the top of the working paper. Then, the attributes of interest are listed in column 1, and the factors used to determine sample size are specified in columns 2–4. In this plan, attributes 2 and 4 are considered less critical than the others; hence, the statistical parameters for these conditions are less stringent than for the more critical conditions. Sample sizes are next determined from the tables shown in Figure 7-4 and are entered in column 5. In the Dexter Company, the auditor decides to round up sample sizes to provide extra units. These amounts are entered in column 6. For purposes of this illustration, assume that these are actual numbers of items examined for each attribute.

In *executing the plan*, the sample items are randomly selected and the invoices are examined for each attribute. As deviations are found, they are recorded and summarized on a worksheet as shown in Figure 7-8.

In *evaluating the results*, the number of deviations from each attribute is entered in column 7 of Figure 7-7. Then, the deviation rates are computed and entered in column 8 and may be compared with the corresponding expected population deviation rates in column 4. In this case study, the sample rate for attribute 3 exceeds the expected rate. Thus, it can be foreseen that the upper deviation limit will exceed the tolerable rate for this attribute. Next, the auditor uses the evaluation tables in Figure 7-6 to determine the upper deviation limit for each attribute. These results are entered in column 9. The upper deviation limit is then compared with the tolerable rate for each attribute. When the upper deviation limit exceeds the tolerable rate, the sample

DEXTER COMPANY
ATTRIBUTE SAMPLE -- SALES TRANSACTIONS
12/31/X1

PREPARED BY: CJR DATE 10/6/X1
REVIEWED BY: RCR DATE 10/10/X1
W/P REF: H-2

SAMPLE DESIGN   SAMPLE RESULTS

OBJECTIVE: TO DETERMINE WHETHER CONTROLS OVER THE EXECUTION OF SALES TRANSACTIONS ARE APPLIED AS PRESCRIBED

SAMPLING UNIT AND POPULATION: SALES INVOICE; POPULATION = 5000 INVOICES NUMBERED A76500 - A81499

SELECTION METHOD: SIMPLE RANDOM; COMPUTER GENERATED LIST

(1) ATTRIBUTES NO. DESCRIPTION	(2) RISK OF OVERRE-LIANCE	(3) TOLER-ABLE DEVIA-TION RATE	(4) EXPTD. POP. DEVIA-TION RATE	(5) SAMPLE SIZE PER TABLE	(6) SAMPLE SIZE USED	(7) NUMBER OF DEVIA-TIONS	(8) SAMPLE DEVIA-TION RATE	(9) UPPER DEVIA-TION LIMIT	(10) ALLOW-ANCE FOR SAMPLING RISK	(11) TEST UDL <= TDR
1 AUTHORIZATION OF SALES BY APPROPRIATE SALES ORDER DEPT. PERSONNEL	5	3	0.5	0	160	0	0.0	2.0	2.0	YES
2 ORDER DEPT. VERIF. OF AGREEMENT OF SALES ORDER WITH CUSTOMER ORDER	10	6	2	0	90	1	1.1	4.3	3.2	YES
3 APPROVAL OF CREDIT BY AUTHORIZED CREDIT DEPT. PERSONNEL	5	3	0.5	0	160	5	3.1	6.9	3.8	NO
4 SHIPPING DEPT. VERIF. OF GOODS SHIPPED WITH SALES ORDER	10	5	1.5	0	105	0	0.0	2.3	2.3	YES
5 BILLING DEPT. VERIF. OF AGREEMENT OF SALES INVOICE WITH SHIPPING DOCUMENT	5	3	0.5	0	160	0	0.0	2.0	2.0	YES
6 BILLING DEPT. VERIF. OF AGREEMENT OF SALES INVOICE WITH SALES ORDER	5	4	1	0	160	1	0.6	3.1	2.5	YES
7 BILLING DEPT. VERIF. OF AGREEMENT OF SALES INVOICE WITH AUTHORIZED PRICES	5	4	1	0	160	1	0.6	3.1	2.5	YES
8 BILLING DEPT. VERIF. OF MATH ACCURACY OF SALES INVOICE	5	4	1	0	160	0	0.0	2.0	2.0	YES

CONCLUSION: All controls can be relied on except approval of credit (Attribute #3). This is a material weakness. Confirmation procedures and procedures to evaluate allowance account to be extended.

MANAGEMENT COMMUNICATION: Inform management of material weakness regarding deviations from credit approval process.

Figure 7-7. STATISTICAL SAMPLING PLAN WORKING PAPER: SAMPLE DESIGN AND SAMPLE RESULTS

Prepared by: *C.J.A.*   Date: *10/6/X1*
Reviewed by: *R.C.P.*   Date: *10/9/X1*

Dexter Company

Sampling for Attributes – Execution of Sales Transactions

Deviation Listings

12/31/X1

Invoice Number			Attribute						
		1	2	3	4	5	6	7	8
A76504			✓						
A76550				✓					
A76720				✓					
A76745							✓		
A77001				✓					
A77022								✓	
A79268				✓					
A80743				✓					
Total No. of Deviations		0	1	5	0	0	1	1	0
Sample Size		160	90	160	105	160	160	160	160
Sample Deviation Rate		0	1.1	3.1	0	0	.6	.6	0

Figure 7-8. DEVIATIONS LISTING WORKING PAPER

results do not support the auditor's planned reliance on the prescribed control. In the Dexter Company, as foreseen, attribute 3 again is the only deviation. Finally, for illustrative purposes, the allowance for sampling risk (column 9– column 8) is entered in column 10.

In order to form an overall conclusion about each control procedure, the auditor makes a qualitative assessment of the deviations to determine their nature, cause, and significance. This analysis is documented in the working papers as shown in Figure 7-9. Observe that this working paper also indicates the effects of the deviations on substantive testing and whether any weaknesses should be reported to management.

In this case, the auditor concludes both the statistical evaluation and the qualitative assessment support planned reliance on all of the tested controls except the one related to attribute 3, which should be discussed with man-

		Prepared by:	Date: 10/6/X1
		Reviewed by:	Date: 10/9/X1

Dexter Company
Sampling of Attributes – Execution of Sales Transactions
Analysis of Sample Deviations
12/31/X1

Attribute	Number of Deviations	Explanation of Deviations	Effects on Substantive Tests	Management Communication
2	1	Verification of agreement of sales order and customer order not indicated but they did in fact agree.	None	No
3	5	Authorized credit approval not evident on five invoices. No explanation offered by credit dept. personnel.	Expand procedures for confirmation of account balances and review of adequacy of allowances for doubtful accounts.	Yes
6	1	Verification not indicated on one invoice involving a backorder. Processing of backorders otherwise appropriate.	None	No
7	1	Evidence of verification not indicated on one invoice; however invoice price agreed with authorized price list.	None	No

Figure 7-9. ANALYSIS OF SAMPLE DEVIATIONS WORKING PAPER

agement. These conclusions are documented on the bottom of the working paper in Figure 7-7.

DISCOVERY SAMPLING

NATURE AND PURPOSE

Discovery sampling is a form of attribute sampling that is designed to locate at least one exception if the rate of deviation in the population is at or above a specified rate. This method of sampling is used to search for critical deviations that may indicate the existence of an irregularity. Discovery sampling is appropriate when the expected deviation rate is quite low and the auditor wants a sample that will provide a specified chance to observe one occurrence.

Discovery sampling is useful when the auditor

- Is examining a large population composed of items that contain a very high proportion of control risk.
- Suspects that irregularities have occurred.
- Seeks additional evidence in a given case to determine whether a known irregularity is an isolated occurrence or part of a recurring pattern.

Discovery sampling generally is not used to find a "needle in the haystack" or a "once in a lifetime occurrence."

DESIGN AND EVALUATION

In using discovery sampling, it is necessary to specify two statistical parameters: (1) the critical rate of deviations and (2) the probability. The former refers to that rate of deviations in the population that must be present (or exceeded) to provide the auditor with the desired probability of producing one deviation. Additionally, population size must be estimated to permit selection of an appropriate table for determining sample size. A discovery sampling table for use with populations over 10,000 is illustrated in Figure 7-10. Other tables are available for smaller population sizes.

To illustrate, assume a population of 14,000 in which you conclude that 70 or more deviations would indicate a serious problem. Assume also that you wish to have a 90% probability of finding at least one deviation if there are 70 or more. The critical rate of deviations is 0.5% (70/14,000) and the sample size shown in the table is 460, as indicated by the row corresponding to a 90% probability in the 0.5% column. It may be observed from Figure 7-10 that discovery sampling produces inordinate sample sizes when the critical rate of deviations is less than 0.5 percent and probability is greater than 90%.

In the above example, if one deviation is discovered in examining the randomly selected sample items, the auditor is 90% certain that a serious problem exists. Thus, the auditor would proceed to expand his examination of the population. In contrast, if no deviations are found, the auditor can

Probability in Percent of Including at Least One Deviation in a Sample (for populations over 10,000)

Sample Size	Upper Limit on Critical Rate of Deviations							
	0.01%	0.05%	0.1%	0.2%	0.3%	0.5%	1%	2%
50		2%	5%	9%	14%	22%	39%	64%
60	1%	3	6	11	16	26	45	70
70	1	3	7	13	19	30	51	76
80	1	4	8	15	21	33	55	80
90	1	4	9	16	24	36	60	84
100	1	5	10	18	26	39	63	87
120	1	6	11	21	30	45	70	91
140	1	7	13	24	34	50	76	94
160	2	8	15	27	38	55	80	96
200	2	10	18	33	45	63	87	98
240	2	11	21	38	51	70	91	99
300	3	14	26	45	59	78	95	99+
340	3	16	29	49	64	82	97	99+
400	4	18	33	55	70	87	98	99+
460	5	21	37	60	75	90	99	99+
500	5	22	39	63	78	92	99	99+
600	6	26	45	70	84	95	99+	99+
700	7	30	50	75	88	97	99+	99+
800	8	33	55	80	91	98	99+	99+
900	9	36	59	83	93	99	99+	99+
1,000	10	39	63	86	95	99	99+	99+
1,500	14	53	78	95	99	99+	99+	99+
2,000	18	63	86	98	99+	99+	99+	99+
2,500	22	71	92	99	99+	99+	99+	99+
3,000	26	78	95	99+	99+	99+	99+	99+

Figure 7-10. DISCOVERY SAMPLING TABLE.

reach a conclusion about the probability of the existence of a specified number of deviations in the population. For example, the probability of fewer than 42 deviations (a rate of less than 0.3%) is 75%, as indicated by the percentage shown at the intersection of the sample size row (460) and the 0.3% column.

NONSTATISTICAL SAMPLING

As explained earlier, the auditor may use nonstatistical sampling in compliance testing. The steps involved in the design and execution of the sampling plan are similar regardless of the type of sampling. Moreover, the factors to be considered in determining sample size and evaluating sample results are identical, although they may not be quantified and explicitly stated in nonstatistical applications. The major differences between nonstatistical and statistical sampling in performing the steps are summarized below.

DETERMINE THE SAMPLE SIZE

As in statistical sampling applications, the major determinants of sample size in nonstatistical sampling are: (1) the acceptable risk of overreliance, (2) the tolerable deviation rate, and (3) the expected population deviation rate for each attribute. In nonstatistical sampling, it is not necessary for the auditor to quantify these factors explicitly in determining sample size. However, he must subjectively recognize the following effects on sample size of a change in one factor when other factors are held constant.

Factor	Effect on Sample Size
Risk of overreliance	Inverse
Tolerable deviation rate	Inverse
Expected population deviation rate	Direct

The auditor may, but is not required to, use the information from statistical tables as a guide in determining sample size in a nonstatistical sample.

DETERMINE THE SAMPLE SELECTION METHOD

In addition to random number and systematic sampling described earlier, the auditor may use block or haphazard sampling in selecting items in nonstatistical sampling.

Block Sampling

At one time, block sampling was the most common selection method. The method consists of selecting similar transactions occurring within a specified time period. For example, the sample may consist of all vouchers processed during a two-week period. If enough blocks are selected, this method of selection may be suitable in nonstatistical sampling. However, selection of a single block from a whole year's transactions is no longer considered appropriate in most circumstances.

Haphazard Sampling

This method involves selecting items at will, without regard to document number, amount, or other feature. Thus, the auditor may haphazardly select a sample of 50 invoices from a file. If bias is avoided in making the selection, the sample may be representative of the population.

EVALUATE THE SAMPLE RESULTS

In nonstatistical samples, it is not possible to determine (1) an upper deviation limit or (2) a statistically derived allowance for sampling risk associated with a sample result and a specified risk of overreliance. However, the auditor should relate the deviation rate found in a sample to the corresponding tolerable rate specified in determining sample size. The difference may be viewed as an allowance for sampling risk.[12]

To illustrate, if a sample deviation rate of one percent is found for an attribute for which the tolerable rate was 7%, the auditor may view the difference of 6% as an adequate allowance for sampling risk and conclude the sample provides an acceptably low level of risk of overreliance. In doing so, he is relying on his experience and professional judgment that the sample deviation rate is sufficiently small relative to the tolerable rate (the allowance for sampling risk is sufficiently large) to ensure that the true population deviation rate does not exceed the tolerable rate. On the other hand, if a sample deviation rate of 5% is found for an attribute for which a tolerable rate of 6% was specified, the difference of 1% may be viewed as an inadequate allowance for sampling risk, resulting in an unacceptably high risk of overreliance. That is, the auditor is concerned that even though the sample deviation rate is less than the specified tolerable rate, the actual population deviation rate may nonetheless exceed the tolerable rate.

In evaluating the results of nonstatistical samples, as is the case in evaluating statistical samples, the auditor should consider the qualitative aspects of deviations found in a sample, as well as the frequency of the deviations.

CONCLUDING COMMENTS

Audit sampling is well established in contemporary auditing. Both statistical and nonstatistical sampling may be used in performing compliance tests. The critical difference between the two types of sampling is that the laws of probability are used to control sampling risk in statistical sampling. Under either type of sampling, the auditor is primarily concerned about the risk of overreliance on internal accounting control. Further consideration is given to attribute sampling applications in Chapters 8–11.

REVIEW QUESTIONS

7-1 a. Why may the second and third standards of field work be described as containing an element of uncertainty?

[12]It should be recognized that this determination of sampling risk differs significantly from the allowance for sampling risk in statistical sampling.

b. How do uncertainty, audit risk, and audit sampling relate to one another?

7-2 a. Distinguish between sampling risk and nonsampling risk.

b. Identify the types of sampling risk that may occur in auditing and identify the type of testing to which each risk pertains.

7-3 Indicate the impacts of the sampling risks on (a) audit effectiveness and (b) audit efficiency.

7-4 Explain the basic similarities and differences between nonstatistical and statistical sampling in audit testing.

7-5 Contrast nonstatistical and statistical sampling in regard to cost/benefit considerations.

7-6 How should audit objectives be defined for an attribute sampling plan?

7-7 a. Define an "attribute."

b. What evidence of performance should exist for attributes?

7-8 Identify four factors that may affect the auditor's identification of the population.

7-9 a. Define the sampling unit.

b. Identify the different kinds of sampling units that may be selected.

7-10 What factors affect the determination of sample size?

7-11 a. Does the auditor normally set the risk of overreliance high or low? Why?

b. What effect does this risk have on sample size?

7-12 a. Define the term "tolerable deviation rate" and indicate the factors that should be considered in deciding on the tolerable rate.

b. What effect does this rate have on the sample size?

7-13 a. Indicate the information that may be used by the auditor to estimate the expected population deviation rate.

b. What effect does this factor have on sample size?

7-14 Enumerate the steps that must be followed in determining sample size from sample size tables.

7-15 a. Identify and briefly explain the sample selection methods that may be used in statistical sampling.

b. Using Figure 7-5, select the first five vouchers from a population of 8,000 vouchers prenumbered consecutively from number 2001 under each of the following assumptions:

Case	Start Row	Start Column	Digits to Be Used in Table	Selection Path
(1)	3	2	First 4	Top/bottom: left to right
(2)	9	3	Last 4	Bottom/top: right to left

7-16 a. Identify the three steps involved in quantitatively evaluating sample results.

b. Indicate the steps involved in using the evaluation tables.

7-17 a. What factors should be considered in qualitatively evaluating sample results?

b. What alternative courses of action should be considered when sample results do not support the auditor's planned reliance on a control procedure?

7-18 a. Describe the circumstances in which discovery sampling may be useful in auditing.

b. What factors are necessary to determine sample size in discovery sampling?

7-19 Contrast the method of (a) determining sample size and (b) evaluating sample results between a nonstatistical and a statistical sampling plan.

7-20 Distinguish between block and haphazard sampling selection and identify the circumstances under which each method may produce a representative sample.

OBJECTIVE QUESTIONS FROM PROFESSIONAL EXAMINATIONS

Indicate the *best* answer for each of the following multiple choice questions.

7-21 These questions pertain to the use of statistical sampling in auditing.

1. The application of statistical sampling techniques is *least* related to which of the following generally accepted auditing standards?
   a. The work is to be adequately planned and assistants, if any, are to be properly supervised.
   b. In all matters relating to the assignment, an independence in mental attitude is to be maintained by the auditor or auditors.
   c. There is to be a proper study and evaluation of the existing internal control as a basis for reliance thereon and for the determination of the resultant extent of the tests to which auditing procedures are to be restricted.
   d. Sufficient competent evidential matter is to be obtained through inspection, observation, inquiries, and confirmations to afford a reasonable basis for an opinion regarding the financial statements under examination.

2. Statistical sampling provides a technique for
   a. Exactly defining materiality.
   b. Greatly reducing the amount of substantive testing.
   c. Eliminating judgment in testing.
   d. Measuring the sufficiency of evidential matter.

3. The tolerable rate of deviations for a compliance test is generally
   a. Lower than the expected rate of errors in the related accounting records.
   b. Higher than the expected rate of errors in the related accounting records.
   c. Identical to the expected rate of errors in the related accounting records.
   d. Unrelated to the expected rate of errors in the related accounting records.

7-22 These questions pertain to sampling risk.

1. At times, a sample may indicate that the auditor's planned degree of reliance on a given control is reasonable when, in fact, the true compliance rate does not justify such reliance. This situation illustrates the risk of
   a. Overreliance.
   b. Underreliance.
   c. Incorrect acceptance.
   d. Incorrect rejection.

2. Which of the following best illustrates the concept of sampling risk?
   a. A randomly chosen sample may *not* be representative of the population as a whole on the characteristic of interest.
   b. An auditor may select audit procedures that are *not* appropriate to achieve the specific objective.
   c. An auditor may fail to recognize errors in the documents examined for the chosen sample.
   d. The documents related to the chosen sample may *not* be available for inspection.

3. In assessing sampling risk, the risk of incorrect rejection and the risk of underreliance on internal accounting control relate to the
   a. Efficiency of the audit.
   b. Effectiveness of the audit.
   c. Selection of the sample.
   d. Audit quality controls.

7-23 These questions pertain to the selection of items for a statistical sample.

1. An underlying feature of random-based selection of items is that each
   a. Stratum of the accounting population be given equal representation in the sample.
   b. Item in the accounting population be randomly ordered.
   c. Item in the accounting population should have an opportunity to be selected.
   d. Item must be systematically selected using replacement.
2. When performing a compliance test with respect to control over cash disbursements, a CPA may use a systematic sampling technique with a start at any randomly selected item. The biggest disadvantage of this type of sampling is that the items in the population
   a. Must be recorded in a systematic pattern before the sample can be drawn.
   b. May occur in a systematic pattern, thus destroying the sample randomness.
   c. May systematically occur more than once in the sample.
   d. Must be systematically replaced in the population after sampling.
3. An auditor plans to examine a sample of 20 checks for countersignatures as prescribed by the client's internal control procedures. One of the checks in the chosen sample of 20 cannot be found. The auditor should consider the reasons for this limitation and
   a. Evaluate the results as if the sample size had been 19.
   b. Treat the missing check as a deviation for the purpose of evaluating the sample.
   c. Treat the missing check in the same manner as the majority of the other 19 checks, that is, countersigned or not.
   d. Choose another check to replace the missing check in the sample.

COMPREHENSIVE QUESTIONS

7-24 One of the generally accepted auditing standards states that sufficient competent evidential matter is to be obtained through inspection, observation, inquiries, and confirmation to afford a reasonable basis for an opinion regarding the financial statements under examination. Some degree of uncertainty is implicit in the concept of "a reasonable basis for an opinion," because the concept of sampling is well established in auditing practice.

Required

a. Explain the auditor's justification for accepting the uncertainties that are inherent in the sampling process.
b. Discuss the uncertainties that collectively embody the concept of audit risk.
c. Discuss the nature of sampling risk and nonsampling risk. Include the effect of sampling risk on compliance tests of internal accounting control.

AICPA (adapted)

7-25 Jiblum, CPA, is planning to use attribute sampling in order to determine the degree of reliance to be placed on an audit client's system of internal accounting control over sales. Jiblum has begun to develop an outline of the main steps in the sampling plan as follows:

1. State the objective(s) of the audit test (e.g., to test the reliability of internal accounting controls over sales).
2. Define the population (define the period covered by the test, define the sampling unit, define the completeness of the population).
3. Define the sampling unit (e.g. client copies of sales invoices).

Required

a. What are the remaining steps in the above outline that Jiblum should include in the statistical test of sales invoices? *Do not present a detailed analysis of tasks that must be performed to carry out the objectives of each step. Parenthetical examples need not be provided.*

b. How does statistical methodology help the auditor to develop a satisfactory sampling plan?

AICPA

7-26 This problem focuses on the determination of sample sizes.

Required

a. Given the constraints of an 8% tolerable deviation rate and an expected population deviation rate of from 1 to 5%, indicate the specific combinations of these factors at both 5 and 10% levels of risk of overreliance that will result in sample sizes that will not be less than 125 or more than 200.

b. At a 5% risk of overreliance, a 5% tolerable deviation rate, and a 2% expected population deviation rate, sample size is 181. Compute the new sample size for each of the following changes, assuming other factors are held constant:
1. Increase tolerable deviation rate to 7%.
2. Decrease tolerable deviation rate to 4%.
3. Decrease expected population deviation rate to 1%.
4. Increase expected population deviation rate to 3%.
5. Increase risk of overreliance to 10%.

7-27 The use of statistical sampling techniques in an examination of financial statements does not eliminate judgmental decisions.

Required

a. Identify and explain four areas in which judgment may be exercised by a CPA in planning a statistical sampling test.

b. Assume that a CPA's sample shows an unacceptable deviation rate. Describe the various actions that he may take based on this finding.

c. A nonstratified sample of 80 accounts payable vouchers is to be selected from a population of 3,200. The vouchers are numbered consecutively from 1 to 3,200 and are listed, 40 to a page, in the voucher register. Describe two different techniques for selecting a sample of vouchers for review.

AICPA (adapted)

7-28 An audit of inventory records disclosed that the population comprises 20,000 items of inventory. Units within the items vary from 30 to 750. The values of the units vary from 20¢ to $1,500. The auditor had estimated the error rate at not over 5%, and since a risk of overreliance of 5% and a tolerable rate of 8% was desired, the tables used showed a sample of 200 items. The selection was made from the north end of the storeroom, picking items having 100 or more units.

In the test, 40 instances were found in which the number of units in stock varied by one or more units from the number shown on the inventory records.

The report to management states that the auditor is 95% confident (5% risk of overreliance) that the number of records in the population which are in error is somewhere between 970 and 1,030.

Required

Describe five errors in the auditor's techniques.

IIA

7-29 In the audit of the Joan Company, the auditor specifies 10 attributes of interest. The statistical parameters for each condition and the number of deviations found in the sample are as follows:

Attribute	Tolerable Deviation Rate	Risk of Overreliance	Expected Population Deviation Rate	Number of Sample Deviations
1	4%	5%	1.5%	1
2	3	5	0.5	0
3	6	5	2.0	4
4	6	5	2.5	5
5	8	5	3.0	2
6	3	10	1.0	0
7	4	10	1.5	2
8	5	10	2.0	4
9	6	10	2.0	1
10	7	10	3.0	4

Required

a. Assuming a large population, determine the sample size for each attribute.

b. Rounding sample size down to the nearest sample size in the tables in Figure 7-6, determine the upper deviation limit for each attribute.

c. Assess the allowance for sampling risk for each attribute.

d. Identify the controls that can be relied on.

e. Identify the controls that cannot be relied on.

f. Indicate the range of tolerable rates for each of the three levels of auditor reliance on a control procedure.

7-30 In the development of an audit program, it is determined that to achieve acceptable levels of the allowance for sampling risk and the risk of overreliance, a sample of 186 items from a population of 10,000 is adequate on a statistical basis.

Required

a. Briefly define each of the following terms used in the above statement:
   1. Population.
   2. Sample.
   3. Allowance for sampling risk.
   4. Risk of overreliance.
b. If the population is 100,000 and the specifications for allowance for sampling risk and risk of overreliance are unchanged from the situation above for a population of 10,000, which of the following sample sizes could be expected to be statistically correct for the larger population: 186; 504; 3,000; 4,360? Justify your answer. (Your answer should be based on judgment and reasoning, rather than actual calculation.)
c. Statistical sampling techniques are being used in auditing. A sample is taken and analyzed to draw an inference or reach a conclusion about a population, but there is always a risk that the inference or conclusion may be incorrect. What value, then, is there in using statistical sampling techniques?

7-31 Mavis Stores had two billing clerks during the year. Snow worked three months and White worked nine months. As the auditor for Mavis Stores, Jones, CPA, uses attribute sampling to test clerical accuracy for the entire year, but due to the lack of internal verification, the system depends heavily on the competence of the billing clerks. The quantity of bills per month is constant.

Required

a. Jones decided to treat the billing by Snow and White as two separate populations. Discuss the advisability of this approach, considering the circumstances.
b. Jones decided to use the same risk of overreliance, deviation rate, and tolerable deviation rate for each population. If we assume he decided to select a sample of 200 to test Snow's work, approximately how large a sample is necessary to test White's?

AICPA (adapted)

7-32 In the Leo Company, 36,000 checks were issued during a designated period of time. Concern exists within management that some of these checks may be forgeries. As part of your regular audit engagement, you agree to use discovery sampling to test for such deviations.

Required

a. Assuming you desire 95% probability of detecting at least one deviation, determine sample size when the critical number of deviations is (1) 72, (2) 180, and (3) 360.
b. Assuming no deviations are found in the above samples, what is the probability that the number of deviations is less than 36 in (1), less than 72 in (2), and less than 108 in (3)?
c. Repeat part (a) assuming a 70% probability is desired.
d. Repeat part (b) for the samples determined in part (c).

7-33 As the auditor for the Harns Company, you elect to use statistical sampling in performing tests of sales transactions. You decide to use shipping documents for the purpose of testing whether all shipments have been billed. The shipping document is selected as the sampling unit. There are 5,000 shipping documents in the population and you elect to use random sampling in drawing your sample. Pertinent data concerning attributes of interest are as follows:

Attribute	Tolerable Deviation Rate (%)	Risk of Over-reliance (%)	Expected Population Deviation Rate (%)
1. Prenumbered sales order for each shipping document	7	5	1.0
2. Prenumbered sales invoice for each shipping document	7	5	1.0
3. Agreement of details of shipping document with details of sales order	7	10	1.0
4. Agreement of details of shipping document with details of sales invoice	6	5	1.0
5. Signature of shipping clerk on shipping document	7	10	2.0
6. Receipt from carrier attached to shipping document	8	10	0.5

Assume that the results of the sample reveal the following number of deviations for each attribute: (1) 2, (2) 0, (3) 2, (4) 2, (5) 1, (6) 0.

Required

a. Prepare a sampling plan worksheet using Figure 7-7 as an example (round sample size per table up to next number ending in zero for sample size used; e.g., 78 to 80).

b. Statistically interpret the results of the sample.

c. Explain the alternative courses of action that are available to the auditor when the sample deviation rate plus the allowance for sampling risk exceeds the tolerable deviation rate.

7-34 The Tomlin Company's principal activity is buying milk from dairy farmers, processing the milk, and delivering the milk to retail customers. You are engaged in auditing the sales transactions of the company and determine the following:

1. The company has 50 retail routes; each route consists of 100 to 200 accounts, the number that can be serviced by a driver in a day.

2. The driver enters cash collections from the day's deliveries to each customer directly on a statement form in record books maintained for each route. Mail remittances are posted in the route record books by office personnel. At the end of the month, the statements are priced, extended, and footed. Xeroxes of the statements are prepared and left in the customers' milk boxes with the next milk delivery.

3. The statements are reviewed by the office manager, who prepares a monthly list for each route of accounts with 90-day balances or older. The list is used for intensive collection action.

4. The audit program used in prior audits for the selection of sales transactions for compliance tests stated: "Select two accounts from each route, one to be chosen by

opening the route book at random and the other as the third account on each list of 90-day or older accounts. For each account selected, choose the latest transaction for testing.''

Your review of sales transactions leads you to conclude that statistical sampling techniques may be applied to their examination.

Required

a. Since statistical sampling techniques do not relieve the CPA of his responsibilities in the exercise of his professional judgment, of what benefit are they to the CPA? Discuss.

b. Give the reasons why the audit procedure previously used for selection of sales transactions (as given in 4 above) would not produce a valid statistical sample.

c. Suggest two ways to select a valid statistical sample.

d. Assume that the company has 10,000 sales transactions and that your statistical sampling disclosed 6 errors in a sample of 200 transactions. Is it reasonable to assume that 300 transactions in the entire population are in error? Explain.

7-35 In an attribute sampling plan for the Mid-East Sales Co., you examine 200 sales invoices. In your working papers, you make the following listing of possible deviations to prescribed control procedures in the execution of the transactions:

Invoice Number	Prescribed Procedure	Findings
248	Written authorizations of sales by sales order department	Verbal notation authorization by phone by sales order department.
333	Sales order verification of quantities and prices	No evidence of verification but quantities and prices are correct.
377	Sales order verification of quantities and prices	No evidence of verification; quantities and prices are incorrect.
472	Credit department authorization of credit	Evidence of credit department approval on invoice, but amount of invoice exceeds maximum credit limits of company.
545	Shipping department verification of agreement of goods shipped with sales order	No shipping department verification but invoice agrees with sales order.
617	Billing department verification of unit prices	Price verification indicated on invoice; by reperformance, you ascertain that the prices do not agree with price list in effect at time of sale.
701	Billing department verification of mathematical accuracy of invoice	No verification of accuracy on invoice; by recalculation, you determine mathematical accuracy of invoice.
719	Credit department authorization of credit	Credit department signature not on signature list; investigation discloses a new hire in credit whose name was not added to authorized list of signers.

Invoice Number	Prescribed Procedure	Findings
762	Billing department verification of invoice with sales order	No evidence of verification on invoice; investigation reveals that verification was done but employee forgot to initial invoice.

Required

a. List the numbers of the foregoing items and indicate whether there is or is not a deviation from a prescribed procedure.

b. Briefly explain the reason for each answer.

7-36 You are now conducting your third annual audit of the financial statements of Elite Corporation for the year ended December 31, 19X1. You decide to employ unrestricted random number statistical sampling techniques in testing the effectiveness of the company's internal control procedures relating to sales invoices, which are all serially numbered. In prior years, after selecting one representative two-week period during the year, you tested all invoices issued during that period and resolved all of the errors that were found to your satisfaction.

Required

a. Explain the statistical procedure you would use to determine the size of the sample of sales invoices to be examined.

b. Once the sample size has been determined, how would you select the individual invoices to be included in the sample? Explain.

c. Would the use of statistical sampling procedures improve the examination of sales invoices as compared with the selection procedure used in prior years? Discuss.

7-37 You have made a review and preliminary evaluation of the Morgan Company's system of internal control, and based on this, you have designed a tentative audit program. Your next step is to perform compliance tests in order to confirm or challenge your evaluation.

A major area of compliance testing is cash disbursements. Monthly, the company processes an average of 360 vouchers, paying 600 invoices. Each voucher contains a copy of the check along with supporting documentation, such as vendor's invoices, purchase orders, and receiving reports.

You intend to examine a sample of vouchers using attribute sampling to evaluate compliance with several control procedures in which you are interested. The attributes for testing the controls are set forth in your audit program as

1. Approval of account distribution.
2. Invoice and purchase order agreement.
3. Purchase order approval.
4. Purchase order and requisition agreement.
5. Invoice and receiving report agreement.
6. Discounts taken.
7. Invoice canceled after approval.
8. Approval of check request.

From experience, you expect a noncompliance rate of about 2% for attributes 1, 2, 5, and 6, and a noncompliance rate of 1% for all others.

After consideration of a number of related audit steps, you decide on a tolerable deviation rate for noncompliance of 7% for controls 1 through 6 and 5% for attributes 7 and 8. A low risk of overreliance, 5%, is elected because compliance tests, as part of your review and evaluation of internal control, serve as the foundation for the greater part of the audit yet to come.

Required

a. What is the sampling unit and the population size?

b. Determine the appropriate sample size for each attribute.

c. Assume that on examining each sample item, given the sample sizes determined in b, you find that there were seven occurrences of inappropriate account distributions, two occurrences of invoices being paid after the discount date, and three cases of invoices not being canceled after approval for payment.
   1. Determine the upper deviation limit for each attribute. (Round sample size down to next largest value in evaluation tables.)
   2. State what impact these findings would have on the execution of the remainder of your audit program.

CASE STUDY

7-38*   The audit team has reviewed the internal accounting controls of Yates Company and has determined that it is cost-beneficial to perform a compliance test on the *disbursement cycle*. The test will be restricted to inventory purchases. The results of this test will affect the nature, timing, and extent of the substantive test work related to inventory price tests.

The audit team has determined that they are willing to accept a 10% risk of overreliance.

The audit team has had many favorable results in performing this test in prior years, but the client has experienced a significant number of personnel changes this past year.

The audit team has asked you to provide them with a number of alternative sampling plans from which they could make a selection.

Required

a. Assuming that the number of deviations expected is 2%, what is (1) the minimum sample size based on substantial planned reliance on internal control and (2) the maximum sample size based on moderate planned reliance.

b. Based on the assumptions stated in a(1) above, what conclusions can the auditor make if the sample results show (1) one deviation, and (2) three deviations?

c. One of the attributes tested is "evidence of management approval of vendor's invoice." In your testing, you discover the following:
   1. The manager's initials are not present, although you observed the manager reviewing the documentation. There were no errors in information contained on the documents or in the invoice extensions.
   2. Management reviewed and approved the invoice and initialed the documents. However, the supporting documentation shows a difference in quantities received compared to the invoice, and no correction has been made.
   3. The invoice was reviewed and approved by management prior to payment. The manager's initials are present, and the auditor reviewed the steps performed and found no exceptions.
   Which of the foregoing, if any, represent a deviation from the control procedure?

Chapter 8

Compliance Tests of Revenue Cycle: Sales Transactions

Study Objectives

After you have completed the study of this chapter, you should be able to

- Identify the activities and types of transactions that occur in a company's revenue cycle.

- Relate the internal accounting control objectives to sales transactions.

- Explain the essential features of internal control over sales transactions.

- Describe the auditor's methodology for making a study and evaluation of internal control over sales transactions.

- State the applicability of statistical sampling to compliance tests of sales transactions.

- Prepare an audit program for testing EDP controls over sales transactions.

This is the first of four consecutive chapters pertaining to systems of internal accounting control for specific classes of transactions. Each chapter contains a discussion of internal accounting control objectives and principles that are applicable to each class of transactions. Then, attention is given to the auditor's study and evaluation of internal control, including case study applications of statistical sampling and electronic data processing (EDP).

TRANSACTION CYCLE APPROACH

In these chapters, we will use the transaction cycle approach. The transaction cycle approach requires the identification of

- The major areas of activity.
- The major classes of transactions within the activity.
- The steps or functions associated with each class of transactions.

The identification of major areas of business activity may be broad or narrow. For example, one company may elect to use a revenue cycle and include both sales and cash receipts within that grouping. In contrast, another company may decide to identify sales and cash receipts as separate cycles. While the identification of cycles may differ among entities, the cycles selected should include all repetitive transactions in which the entity normally engages. For purposes of discussion and illustration in this book, the following cycles and specific classes of transactions will be used:

Cycle	Principal Classes of Transactions	Chapter Coverage
Revenue	Sales (and cost of sales)	8
	Cash receipts and sales adjustments	9
Expenditure	Purchases and cash disbursements	10
	Payroll	11
Production	Manufacturing	11
Investing	Temporary and long-term investments	15
Financing	Long-term debt and capital stock	15

INTERNAL ACCOUNTING CONTROL OBJECTIVES

As explained in Chapter 5, there are four operative objectives of internal accounting control. To facilitate subsequent discussion, we will condense these into three objectives with the following text identifications and applicable internal control principles.

Internal Accounting Control Objectives	Text Classification and Identification	Primary Internal Control Principles
Transactions are executed in accordance with management's general or specific authorization.	Transactions are properly executed.	Segregation of functions Authorization procedures Documentation procedures Physical controls Independent internal verification

Internal Accounting Control Objectives	Text Classification and Identification	Primary Internal Control Principles
Transactions are recorded as necessary (1) to permit preparation of financial statements in conformity with generally accepted accounting principles or any other criteria applicable to such statements and (2) to maintain accountability for assets.	Transactions are properly recorded.	Segregation of functions Accounting records and procedures Independent internal verification
Access to assets is permitted only in accordance with management's authorization.		
The recorded accountability for assets is compared with the existing assets at reasonable intervals and appropriate action is taken with respect to any differences.	Custody of assets is properly maintained.	Segregation of functions Authorization procedures Physical controls Independent internal verification

These three objectives will provide the framework for discussing (1) the basic features of accounting control over specific classes of transactions within a cycle and (2) the auditor's study and evaluation of internal controls for each of the classes.

NATURE OF THE REVENUE CYCLE

An entity's revenue cycle consists of the activities relating to the exchange of goods and services with customers and to the collection of the revenue in cash. Different entities may have different sources of revenue. For example, merchandising and manufacturing companies have sales; doctors, attorneys, and CPAs have fees; theaters, sports arenas, and amusement parks have admissions; banks and financial institutions have interest and dividends; and mass transit companies and airlines have fares. The discussions and illustrations in this chapter are based on a merchandising company. However, much of the commentary can easily be adapted to other types of entities.

For a merchandising company, the classes of transactions in the revenue cycle include (1) sales, (2) sales adjustments (discounts, returns and allowances, and uncollectible accounts [provisions and write-offs]), and (3) cash receipts (collections on account and cash sales). Sales transactions are discussed in this chapter; the other classes of transactions are considered in Chapter 9.

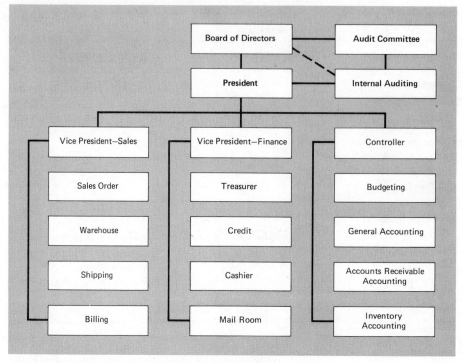

Figure 8-1. ORGANIZATION CHART FOR REVENUE CYCLE.

INTERNAL CONTROL ENVIRONMENT

An organization plan that provides clear lines of authority and responsibility is an important aspect in the internal control environment over transactions in the revenue cycle. An organizational structure for a wholesale or mail order company is illustrated in Figure 8–1. In this example, billing is the responsibility of the vice president of sales. In some companies, billing is part of the controller's responsibility. A good control environment also requires

- Competent and trustworthy personnel.
- Monitoring of prescribed controls by internal auditing.
- Sales and cash budgets, with periodic comparisons of actual results with planned objectives.

MATERIALITY AND AUDIT RISK

Sales are the principal source of operating revenue for many business enterprises and they are a major component in determining net income. It is also common in merchandising and manufacturing companies for cost of sales to be the largest cost in the income measurement process. Similarly, cash receipts transactions usually have a material affect on a company's financial statements. Thus, the auditor seeks to keep audit risk that the financial statements as a whole are materially misstated because of revenue cycle transactions at a relatively low level.

The volume of transactions in the revenue cycle is usually high and cash is very vulnerable to theft and misappropriation. As a result, there are numerous opportunities for errors and irregularities to occur. In order to assess the probability that material errors or irregularities may exist in the financial statements, it is necessary for the auditor to determine the effectiveness of the client's system of internal control over revenue cycle transactions. The auditor's assessment of control risk, which is the risk that internal control will not prevent or detect material errors or irregularities, will then influence the auditor's judgment of the amount of detection risk he can accept in performing substantive tests of revenue cycle balances.

INTERNAL CONTROL OVER SALES TRANSACTIONS

BASIC CONSIDERATIONS

Sales may be made on a credit or cash basis. In a corner grocery store, all sales may be for cash in over-the-counter transactions. By contrast, national retailers such as Lord & Taylor, Montgomery Ward, and Sears Roebuck have both cash and credit over-the-counter sales as well as mail order sales. The time period involved in executing the sales transaction may range from a matter of minutes in an over-the-counter sale in a retail store to days, weeks, and months in wholesaling and manufacturing companies. Attention in this chapter is directed primarily at credit sales transactions. Cash sales are considered in Chapter 9. Because the filling of a sales order requires the release of inventory, the costing of goods sold is considered to be a recording function associated with sales transactions. However, the internal controls associated with the acquisition and custody of inventory are discussed under the expenditure cycle.

The following matters are basic to an understanding of sales transactions in the revenue cycle:

Functions

Executing

- Accepting the customer's order.
- Approving credit.
- Filling the sales order.
- Shipping the sales order.
- Billing the customer.

Recording
- Journalizing and posting sales transactions.
- Updating the customers' ledger.
- Updating inventory records.

Custody
- Protecting the customers' ledger.
- Maintaining correctness of customer balances.

Common Documents

- *Customer Order.* A request for merchandise by a customer that may be received directly from customers or through salespersons.
- *Sales Order.* A form showing the description, quantity, and other data pertaining to a customer order. It serves as the basis for internal processing of the customer order by the seller.
- *Shipping Document.* A form used to show the details and date of each shipment. It may be in the form of a *bill of lading,* which is a formal acknowledgment of the receipt of goods for delivery by a freight carrier.
- *Sales Invoice.* A form stating the particulars of a sale, including the amount owed, terms, and date of sale. It is used to bill customers and provides the basis for recording the sale.
- *Daily Sales Summary.* A report showing total sales invoices issued during the day. It is used as a control device to assure that all invoices are recorded.
- *Customer Monthly Statement.* A report sent to each customer showing the beginning balance, transactions during the month, and the ending balance.

Accounting records

- *Book of Original Entry.* Sales journal (or register) with columns for both sales and cost of sales. It may also have columns for classifying sales by departments, product lines, and geographical location.
- *General Ledger Accounts.* Cash, accounts receivable, notes receivable, inventory, sales, and cost of sales.
- *Subsidiary Ledgers.* Customers' ledger and perpetual inventory.

File Data

- *Approved Customer File.* Contains a list of customers from whom orders may be accepted.
- *Customer Credit File.* Shows the credit and collection history for each customer.
- *Customer Order File.* Contains unfilled sales orders.
- *Customer Account File.* Contains supporting documentation of postings to each customer's account.
- *Sales Invoice File.* Holds copies of invoices sent to customers.

SALES TRANSACTIONS ARE PROPERLY EXECUTED

Sales transactions are properly executed when they (1) are authorized by personnel acting within the scope of their authority and (2) conform with the terms of the authorizations. The execution of sales transactions involves a sequence of functions or steps. It is desirable therefore to recognize specific accounting control objectives for each function as follows:

Function	Specific Accounting Control Objective
1. Accepting customer orders	Orders for sales or for services are accepted in accordance with management's authorized criteria.
2. Approving credit	Credit is granted on basis of management's established credit policies and limits.
3. Filling sales orders	Orders are filled or services rendered in accordance with approved sales orders.
4. Shipping sales orders	Shipments are made on basis of approved sales orders.
5. Billing customers	All shipments are billed at authorized prices and terms.

The internal control principles applicable to the execution of sales transactions are explained below.

Authorization Procedures

The vice president of sales has the responsibility for general authorizations of selling prices, terms, and conditions of sales. Specific authorizations are necessary at four points: (1) granting credit, (2) setting prices and terms, (3) filling and shipping the order, and (4) billing the customer. Authorization procedures should provide for the (1) assignment of responsibility for authorizations and approvals to departments and/or individuals and (2) documentation of the action taken.

For over-the-counter credit sales, the credit department may issue company credit cards to customers that sales clerks are authorized to accept. In other cases, clerks may be permitted to accept national credit cards such as American Express, Visa, and MasterCard.

Segregation of Functions

Each of the functions involved in executing sales transactions should be assigned to different departments and/or individuals. Personnel participating in these functions should not record the transactions or have custody of the resulting receivables. Based on the organization chart in Figure 8-1, the assignment of responsibility for each function is as follows:

Function	Department	Related Activities
1. Accepting customer orders	Sales Order	Receive orders, trace customers to approved customer file, investigate acceptability of new customers, issue sales orders, and maintain customer order file.
2. Approving credit	Credit	Trace customers to credit files, indicate approval on sales orders, and maintain customer credit files.
3. Filling sales orders	Warehouse	Maintain custody over inventory, fill orders per specifications, and initial filled sales orders.
4. Shipping sales orders	Shipping	Agree goods for shipment with sales orders, pack and ship goods, prepare shipping documents, and obtain receipts from carriers.
5. Billing customers	Billing	Match shipping documents with sales orders, bill customers at authorized prices and terms, prepare and mail sales invoices, and prepare batch or daily sales summaries of billings.

It should also be recognized that the functions are completed in sequence. Thus, the order cannot be filled before credit is approved, and the customer is not billed before the goods are shipped. A flowchart of a manual system for executing sales transactions is shown in Figure 8-2.

Documentation Procedures

The essential source documents in executing sales transactions are the (1) *sales order*, (2) *shipping document (bill of lading)*, (3) *sales invoice*, and (4) *daily sales summary*. To achieve maximum accountability, the first three types of documents should be prenumbered and subsequently accounted for. The sales order and sales invoice should indicate the proper account classification and coding for each transaction.

Documentation procedures should provide for the prompt billing of customers. To achieve this objective, some companies require a billing department supervisor to determine periodically that the billing date on invoices is not more than one business day later than the shipping date.

Physical Controls

Physical controls in the form of mechanical equipment are useful in executing sales transactions. The primary example is the use of a cash register to indicate the amount of over-the-counter sales. Another device is the autographic register to control the issuance of sales slips. This equipment contains prenumbered sales slips that are manually cranked through the machine as they are used. The original copy is given to the customer, and the duplicate is locked inside the register as evidence of the sale.

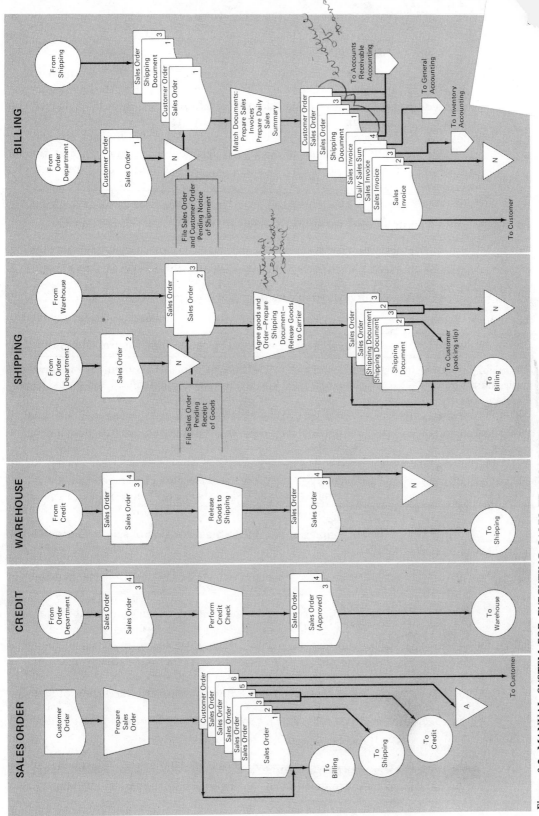

Figure 8-2. MANUAL SYSTEM FOR EXECUTING SALES TRANSACTIONS.

Independent Internal Verification

There are numerous opportunities for independent internal verification in executing sales transactions. For example, the shipping department is generally required to compare the goods received from the warehouse with the sales order before shipping the merchandise. In the billing department, the sales orders are matched with shipping documents before invoices are prepared. In addition, in a manual system, a second billing clerk verifies the correctness of each invoice before it is mailed, and accounts for all prenumbered sales invoices.

SALES TRANSACTIONS ARE PROPERLY RECORDED

To meet this operative internal control objective, the functions or steps in the recording of sales transactions must be properly performed. It is desirable therefore to recognize specific accounting control objectives and the assignment of responsibility for each function as follows:

Function	Department	Specific Accounting Control Objective
1. Journalizing and posting sales transactions	General Accounting	Only actual sales are recorded, and all actual sales are correctly journalized and posted as to amount, classification, and accounting period.
2. Updating customers' ledger	Accounts Receivable Accounting	Sales are promptly and correctly posted to customer accounts.
3. Updating inventory records	Inventory Accounting	Goods sold are promptly and correctly posted to inventory records.

The internal control principles applicable to the recording of sales transactions are explained below.

Segregation of Functions

An appropriate segregation of functions is shown in the above tabulation. General Accounting Department personnel should not participate in the execution of sales transactions or have custody of the resulting assets. If the same employee bills the customer, records the sale, and maintains the accounts receivable ledger, that person could misstate the amount of the sale and conceal the error. Figure 8-3 illustrates a flowchart for the recording of sales transactions.

Accounting Records and Procedures

The source document for recording sales transactions is the sales invoice. Invoices should be journalized in the sales journal in numerical sequence. In

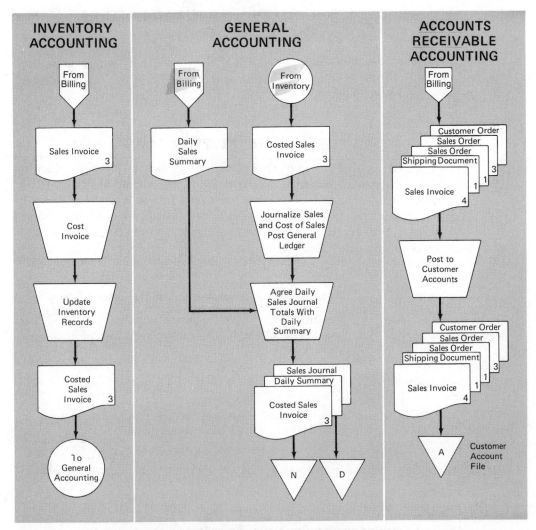

Figure 8-3. MANUAL SYSTEM FOR RECORDING SALES TRANSACTIONS.

journalizing, all sales invoices in a series should be accounted for. In addition, care should be exercised to assure that sales transactions occurring near the end of the year are journalized in the proper time period. Postings to customer accounts and inventory records should be made directly from the invoices. Following posting to the customers' ledger, the invoice and supporting documentation are filed alphabetically in the customer account file. This file is often used extensively by the auditor in testing controls over sales transactions.

Independent Internal Verification

The completeness of daily sales journal entries can be internally verified by having a second accounting clerk (1) account for the numerical sequence of entries in the sales journal, and (2) establish the agreement of the daily sales summary with corresponding sales journal totals. In some companies, a supervisor reviews the journal entries periodically to verify the reasonableness of the account classifications. In addition, there should be independent reconciliations of the agreement of accounts receivable control with the total of the customers' ledger.

CUSTODY OF ACCOUNTS RECEIVABLE IS PROPERLY MAINTAINED

As explained earlier, this operative objective pertains to limiting access to assets and comparing recorded accountability with existing assets. Both accounts receivable and cash may result from sales transactions. The former is considered here; the latter is discussed with cash receipts in the next chapter. For custody over accounts receivable, the functions and specific accounting control objectives are as follows:

Function	Department	Specific Accounting Control Objective
1. Protecting the customers' ledger	Accounts Receivable Accounting	Access to the customers' ledger is limited to authorized accounting personnel.
2. Maintaining correctness of customer balances	Accounts Receivable Accounting	Recorded customer balances are independently verified with customers at reasonable intervals.
	General Accounting	Customers' ledger is periodically agreed with accounts receivable control.

The internal control principles applicable to these functions are explained below.

Physical Controls and Authorization Procedures

The customers' ledger should be kept in locked and fireproof files, and access should be restricted to authorized accounting personnel. Similarly, customer files should be locked to prevent unauthorized access to documentation that could be used to make unauthorized entries in customer accounts.

Segregation of Functions and Independent Internal Verification

Segregation of functions exists when individuals who have physical custody over the customers' ledger do not execute or record sales transactions. Independent internal verification occurs when an accounting department supervisor controls the mailing of monthly statements to customers and the investigation of differences reported by customers.

STUDY AND EVALUATION OF INTERNAL CONTROL

The auditor's methodology for meeting the second standard of field work for sales transactions consists of the steps and decision paths explained in Chapter 5.

REVIEW OF THE SALES SYSTEM

It will be recalled that the review consists of two phases: (1) preliminary and (2) completion. In the preliminary review of sales transactions, the auditor makes inquiries and reviews documentation to obtain a general understanding of the internal control environment and the flow of sales transactions through the accounting system. In the completion phase, the auditor is expected to obtain specific knowledge of the client's prescribed control procedures in the sales system. The principal steps in the completion phase of the review of the controls over sales are described below.

Gathering Information

Information concerning specific controls over sales transactions is obtained through inquiry, observation, and review of documentation. A questionnaire for sales transactions is shown in Figure 8-4. The questions relate to control procedures that the auditor considers to be necessary for effective control over sales. Each question is referenced to a specific function. For example, (E1) is the first function under executing (i.e., accepting customer orders); (R1) and (C1) refer to the first functions under recording and custody respectively. A *YES* answer to a question indicates that the client has the control; a *NO* response suggests a possible weakness in internal control over sales. In addition to answers to questionnaires, the information gathered by the auditor may be documented in flowcharts and narrative memoranda.

Making a Preliminary Evaluation

The primary purpose of this evaluation of sales transactions is to identify control procedures that can be relied on in performing substantive tests of sales transaction balances, assuming satisfactory compliance with the control procedures. The preliminary evaluation is made by (1) considering the errors and irregularities that could occur in performing each function, (2) identifying the controls necessary to prevent or detect the occurrences, and (3) determining whether the necessary controls are prescribed by the client. A representative listing of possible errors and irregularities and necessary control procedures is shown in Figure 8-5.[1] Columns 2 and 3 of the form are based on generalized knowledge, adapted as needed by the auditor to the specific

[1]Figure 5–3 shows two additional columns in the preliminary evaluation: Prescribed Controls and Reliance (Yes/No). These columns have been omitted here in the interest of simplification.

CYCLE: Revenue	CLASS OF TRANSACTIONS: Sales	

EXECUTING	Yes	No
1. Are customer orders compared to an approved customer list? (E1)		
2. Is a prenumbered sales order issued for each accepted customer order? (E1)		
3. Is there internal verification of the agreement of sales order with customer order? (E1)		
4. Are all credit sales approved prior to the sale? (E2)		
5. Is a sales order required before an order is filled? (E3)		
6. Is there internal verification of the goods in filling a sales order? (E3)		
7. Are the goods compared with the sales order in shipping? (E4)		
8. Is each shipment supported by a prenumbered shipping document? (E4)		
9. Are shipping documents and sales orders compared in billing? (E5)		
10. Are prenumbered sales invoices used in billing? (E5)		
11. Is there internal verification of prices and mathematical accuracy of sales invoices? (E5)		
12. Are daily sales summaries prepared and agreed to the invoices issued? (E5)		

RECORDING

1. Are daily sales journal entries agreed to daily sales summaries? (R1)
2. Are invoices journalized in numerical sequence? (R1)
3. Is there periodic independent reconciliation of accounts receivable control and the customers' ledger? (R2)
4. Are postings to the subsidiary ledgers made independent of journalizing and posting the general ledger (R2, R3)

CUSTODY

1. Are there adequate physical controls over accounts receivable records? (C1)
2. Is there independent mailing of monthly statements to customers? (C2)

Figure 8-4 INTERNAL CONTROL QUESTIONNAIRE: SALES TRANSACTIONS.

client. Information about prescribed controls over sales is obtained from step 1 of the completion phase of the review.

From a comparison of the necessary controls and the prescribed controls, the auditor makes a preliminary evaluation of the controls. If a necessary control is not prescribed or a prescribed control will not prevent the possible error or irregularity, the auditor looks for compensating controls or concludes that there is a weakness in the client's sales system. The auditor's evaluation should be fully documented in the working papers.

COMPLIANCE TESTS OF CONTROLS TO BE RELIED ON

Based on his preliminary evaluation and the possible compliance tests shown in Figure 8-5, the auditor prepares the audit program for performing compli-

Function	Possible Errors and Irregularities	Necessary Control Procedures	Possible Compliance Tests
EXECUTING			
1. Accepting customer orders	The sales order may be incorrect as to quantities and types of goods.	Internal verification of agreement of sales order with customer order.	Examine evidence of verification.
2. Approving credit	Sales may be made to customers who are poor credit risks.	Approval of credit by credit department.	Examine evidence of credit approval.
3. Filling sales orders	Order specifications may not be met as to type and quantity.	Internal verification of goods by warehouse and shipping.	Examine evidence of verifications.
4. Shipping sales orders	Goods may be shipped to unauthorized customers.	Approved sales order for each shipment.	Determine existence of approved sales order for each shipping document.
5. Billing the customer	Some shipments may not be billed.	Accounting for all pre-numbered shipping documents and determining that each has a sales invoice.	Examine evidence of internal verification and existence of a sales invoice for each shipping document.
	Sales invoices may be incorrect in terms of prices and mathematical accuracy.	Internal verification of accuracy of invoice.	Examine evidence of internal verification.
RECORDING			
1. Journalizing and posting of sales transactions	Invoices may not be journalized.	Internal verification of agreement of sales journal entries with daily sales summaries.	Review evidence of internal verification.
2. Updating customers' ledger	Invoices may not be posted to customer accounts.	Independent reconciliation of accounts receivable control and customers' ledger.	Examine evidence of reconciliation.
3. Updating inventory records	Inventory sold may not be posted to inventory records.	Segregation of functions between general accounting and inventory accounting.	Observe segregation of functions.
CUSTODY			
1. Protecting the customers' ledger	Customer accounts may be stolen.	Customers' ledger is locked in safe and access is limited to authorized personnel.	Observe storage; inquire about access.
2. Maintaining correctness of customer balances	Mathematical errors may be made in computing a customer's balance.	Independent mailing of monthly statements to customers.	Observe mailing of monthly statements.

Figure 8-5. PRELIMINARY EVALUATION CONSIDERATIONS—SALES TRANSACTIONS.

ance tests on the controls to be relied on. As shown in the audit program in Figure 8-6, the objective of the testing is to determine whether the controls are operating as planned. The steps in the programs are classified under the related operative objective.

Note that the audit program includes each of the auditing procedures that are applicable to compliance tests: (1) review of documentation showing evidence of performance of control procedures, (2) observation of controls that do not leave an audit trail of documentation, (3) inquiry, and (4) reperformance of some controls.

Compliance tests of sales transactions should include invoices for each of the company's principal operating segments. The tests should also extend to transactions for the entire year. Such tests, however, are usually made during

---

TYPE OF TESTING: Compliance	**PURPOSE: Study and Evaluation of Internal Control**
CYCLE: Revenue	**CLASS OF TRANSACTIONS: Sales**

A. CONTROLS IN EXECUTING SALES TRANSACTIONS ARE OPERATING AS PLANNED.

  1. Examine sample of sales invoices for

- Accompanying sales order. (E1)
- Evidence of agreement of sales order with customer order. (E1)
- Evidence of credit approval. (E2)
- Shipping department verification of agreement of goods to be shipped with sales order. (E4)
- Accompanying shipping document and receipt from freight carrier. (E4)
- Evidence of verification of prices and mathematical accuracy. (E5)

  2. Observe segregation of functions in performing control procedures.
  3. Inquire of personnel about performing control procedures.
  4. Reperform control procedures in step 1 on selected invoices.

B. CONTROLS IN RECORDING SALES TRANSACTIONS ARE OPERATING AS PLANNED.

  1. Examine evidence of verification of daily sales summaries with sales journal totals. (R1)
  2. Examine evidence that all invoices are accounted for in journalizing. (R1)
  3. Examine evidence of independent reconciliations of accounts receivable control and the customers' ledger. (R2)
  4. Observe segregation of duties between general ledger and subsidiary ledger accounting personnel. (R2, R3)

C. CONTROLS OVER THE CUSTODY OF ACCOUNTS RECEIVABLE ARE OPERATING AS PLANNED.

  1. Observe security over accounts receivable records. (C1)
  2. Observe mailing of monthly statements to customers. (C2)

Figure 8-6. AUDIT PROGRAM: COMPLIANCE TESTS OF SALES TRANSACTIONS.

interim work. This is permissible if the auditor also obtains evidence about the functioning of the controls during the remainder of the year. The additional evidence may be acquired through inquiry, observation, and, if necessary, by additional testing.

In the program, the sampling unit is the sales invoice. By using this unit, the auditor can reach a conclusion about whether controls to assure that all billings have been shipped are operating effectively. Alternatively, the auditor could use the shipping document as the sampling unit to determine whether controls to assure that all shipments have been billed are functioning properly.

Dual Purpose Testing

As explained in Chapter 5, the auditor may also perform substantive tests of details of transactions in conjunction with compliance tests. Substantive tests are designed to determine the validity and propriety of the accounting treatment of transactions and balances or, conversely, the existence of any monetary errors. Thus, while the sample of sales invoices is available for use, the auditor may perform the following substantive tests:

- Compare the amount, date, customer name, and account classification on the invoice with the corresponding sales journal entry for accuracy.
- Compare the same data with the corresponding postings to individual accounts in the customers' ledger for accuracy.

In addition, in reperforming the control procedures (step A4 of the audit program), the auditor may accumulate the dollar amount of any monetary errors that are discovered. From these tests, the auditor can estimate the number, nature, and magnitude of monetary errors in the processing of sales transactions.

FINAL EVALUATION OF THE CONTROLS

This evaluation is based on the preliminary evaluation and an analysis of the results of compliance testing. In making the analysis, the auditor considers both the number of deviations from prescribed control procedures and the causes of the deviations. The results of any substantive tests of transactions should also be considered in evaluating the controls. The existence of monetary errors in the accounting treatment of the transactions indicates that the system of internal control did not prevent or detect their occurrence.

The auditor then determines the effects of his evaluations of specific control procedures over sales transactions on the nature, timing, and extent of substantive tests of revenue cycle balances. For example, if there is moderate risk of errors in approving sales for credit, the auditor will apply more extensive substantive tests in determining the adequacy of the client's allowance for uncollectible accounts than when the risk of such errors is low. Substantive tests of revenue cycle balances are explained in Chapter 13.

STATISTICAL SAMPLING IN COMPLIANCE TESTING

As explained in Chapter 7, statistical sampling may be used in compliance testing. In that chapter, a comprehensive case study is presented in which statistical sampling is used in performing compliance tests of controls over sales transactions. The reader is encouraged to review that illustration at this time.

ELECTRONIC DATA PROCESSING

Many companies use electronic data processing in executing and recording sales transactions. To illustrate some of the effects of EDP on internal control and the auditor's study and evaluation of EDP controls, the following case study is presented.

DESCRIPTION OF THE SALES SYSTEM

For its sales transactions, the Joiner Company uses the batch entry–batch processing method to prepare the sales invoices, prepare the sales journal, and update customer account balances. Magnetic tape input is utilized and file data are maintained on magnetic tape and magnetic disk. A flowchart of the sales system is shown in Figure 8-7.

In the manual portion of the sales system, the key control procedures are (1) preparing batch totals in the billing department, (2) verifying and logging the totals in data control, and (3) keying and verifying the data in data entry.

As shown in Figure 8-7, there are two computer runs:

Run 1. In this run, the sales transaction tape is sorted by customer number and is then validated by the application of an *edit check* routine consisting of tests for completeness, validity, and reasonableness. The outputs of this run are the valid sales transaction tape and a report showing control totals and a listing of rejected transactions. The report is sent to data control, where the control totals are compared with the logged totals. In addition, data control assumes the responsibility for seeing that (1) the rejected transactions are corrected by the department making the error and (2) the corrected data are resubmitted for computer processing.

Run 2. This run involves the processing of the valid transaction tape. As shown, both accounts receivable and sales price master files are used in the run. The price master file is on magnetic disk to facilitate access to the individual prices as the various products are encountered on the sales transaction tape. The outputs consist of an updated accounts receivable master file on magnetic tape and printouts of sales invoices, the sales journal, and a control and exception report. Each printout is forwarded to data control, where the

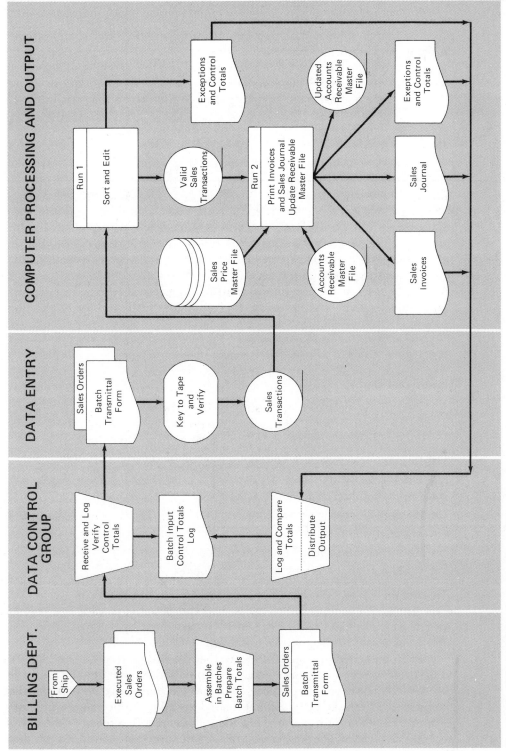

Figure 8-7. EDP SYSTEM FOR SALES TRANSACTIONS.

277

totals are compared and the other outputs are distributed to the appropriate departments within the company.

A third run, the costing of the sales invoices and the updating of inventory records, is not included in the flowchart in the interest of simplification. Figure 8-7 shows only one aspect of updating the accounts receivable master file.

STUDY AND EVALUATION OF EDP CONTROLS

As explained in Chapter 6, the auditor must make a preliminary review of EDP controls. Thus, through observation and review of documentation, the auditor obtains information about (1) the flow of sales transactions through the accounting system, (2) the extent to which EDP is used in processing sales transactions, and (3) the basic structure of accounting control. The auditor may terminate his review at this point and design substantive tests that do not contemplate any reliance on EDP accounting controls. However, in the Joiner Company, the auditor decides to complete the review and perform compliance tests of the accounting controls expected to be relied on in substantive testing. The audit program for compliance testing of the application controls is shown in Figure 8-8. The program provides for the use of both test data and generalized audit software.

Use of Test Data

Test data are applicable to the testing of the program controls in run 1 and the program logic in run 2. For testing the proper functioning of the controls incorporated into the edit routine (program) of run 1, the auditor prepares both valid and invalid sales transaction test data. The latter include

- Missing or invalid customer number.
- Invalid product code.
- Incomplete customer name and address.
- Missing quantities.
- Abnormal (unrealistic) sales quantities.
- Alphabetical characters in numerical fields.

The data are keyed onto magnetic tape and run on the client's program. The error listing of invalid transactions is then compared with expected results. Any discrepancies in the comparison are investigated by the auditor for possible weaknesses in the controls of the edit routine.

For run 2, the auditor seeks evidence that the program controls pertaining to the decision steps and mathematical computations in the program are properly functioning. For this purpose, separate test data may be prepared or, alternatively, the valid test data that cleared the edit routine test of run 1 may be used. Test data for run 2 may include transactions that result in the use of recently changed unit sales prices and credit terms, discontinued product lines, and invalid pricing codes. As in the preceding test, the auditor compares

TYPE OF TESTING: Compliance   **PURPOSE: EDP Application Controls**
CYCLE: Revenue   **CLASS OF TRANSACTIONS: Sales**

A. INPUT CONTROLS ARE PROPERLY FUNCTIONING.

1. Randomly select sample of executed sales orders and trace to sales invoices.
2. Review, on test basis, the reconciliation of batched sales input totals with control totals in run 1.
3. Selectively review exception listings of run 1 and investigate items that have remained uncleared for an unreasonably long time.
4. Design and use test data to test program controls of edit routine in run 1.

B. PROCESSING CONTROLS ARE PROPERLY FUNCTIONING.

1. Observe the procedures for reconciling control totals in run 2 and selectively trace control totals to related input controls.
2. Review exception lists for unusual items and determine the disposition of rejected data.
3. Use test data to test the program logic in the preparation of sales invoices, the sales journal, and updating the accounts receivable master file.
4. Use generalized audit software to test master file data controls.

C. OUTPUT CONTROLS ARE PROPERLY FUNCTIONING.

1. Review reconciliation of output controls with other control totals.
2. Obtain printout of the two accounts receivable master files of run 2 and selectively reconcile changes in customer balances with sales invoices.

Figure 8-8. AUDIT PROGRAM: COMPLIANCE TESTS OF EDP APPLICATION CONTROLS FOR SALES TRANSACTIONS.

the output of the test run with expected results and investigates any differences.

To be a valid test of a program, the auditor must make sure the program tested is actually used by the client. Thus, the auditor requests on a surprise basis, the client's program for sales from the librarian. The identification numbers on the program tapes are traced to program documentation in the library to assure that the client's regular programs are being obtained. The test data are then processed against a copy of the client's master file data under the auditor's supervision.

Use of Generalized Audit Software

Generalized audit software is used in this example to test the reliability of the client's master file. The extent of this form of testing depends on the effectiveness of the general controls pertaining to file security and program changes. When such controls are strong and the foregoing compliance tests produce no exceptions, some auditors may not use this form of testing.

In the Joiner Company, the auditor decides to use the generalized audit software to test the accounts receivable master file. To do so, the auditor first obtains a copy of the file at the beginning of the day and updates it by processing the actual sales transactions for the day. The audit software is then used to compare the detail of the client's updated file with the updated file produced by the generalized audit software. Any differences are identified and printed out by the computer. Generalized audit software may also be used to select and print a sample of sales prices from the sales price master file. These prices can then be compared manually with the authorized prices established by the company and any differences noted. Differences found from the use of generalized audit software indicate that applicable control procedures are not operating as planned.

On completing the compliance tests of EDP general and application controls, the auditor evaluates the system and then determines the extent to which substantive tests of revenue cycle balances are to be restricted.

CONCLUDING COMMENTS

An entity's revenue cycle includes the activities in processing customer orders for goods and services and in achieving settlement of the selling price from the customer. The scope of the chapter has been limited to the sales transactions phase of the revenue cycle. Each of the operative objectives of internal accounting control and the six principles of internal control are applicable to sales transactions. In performing compliance tests of sales transactions, the auditor works extensively with the sales invoices. Either statistical or nonstatistical sampling may be used in performing compliance tests of sales transactions.

EDP methods may affect the nature of the control procedures and the audit trail of sales transactions. In a system that utilizes magnetic tape for both input and file data, the auditor may use test data in testing program controls and generalized audit software to test controls over updating master file data.

REVIEW QUESTIONS

8-1 Describe the nature of the revenue cycle and identify the classes of transactions that are part of this cycle.

8-2 State the framework of internal control objectives for revenue cycle transactions.

8-3 Indicate the functions that pertain to the executing and recording of sales transactions and custody of assets.

8-4 How important are sales transactions in terms of materiality and audit risk?

8-5 What are the specific accounting control objectives for each of the functions involved in executing sales transactions?

8-6 Indicate an appropriate segregation of duties among the departments involved in executing sales transactions.

8-7 a. When are authorizations required in executing sales transactions?
b. What forms of authorization exist in over-the-counter credit sales?

8-8 a. Identify the specific internal accounting control objectives for each function associated with the recording of sales transactions.

b. Indicate an appropriate segregation of duties for these functions.

8-9 Indicate the flow of sales orders and sales invoices in the manual execution of sales transactions.

8-10 Indicate applications of the principle of independent internal verification to the recording of sales transactions.

8-11 a. What internal accounting control principles are applicable to the custody of assets in the revenue cycle?

b. Indicate one application of each principle.

8-12 What is the purpose of making a preliminary evaluation of accounting controls over sales transactions?

8-13 Explain the relationship between the internal control questionnaire and the auditor's preliminary evaluation of sales transactions.

8-14 Identify the four types of audit procedures that may be used in performing compliance tests of sales transactions.

8-15 Contrast the purposes served by using (a) the sales invoice and (b) the shipping document in compliance testing.

8-16 Contrast the verifications made by (a) data control and (b) data entry in the case study.

8-17 Identify the control totals that are available to data control in the case study.

8-18 a. What objectives are served by the edit check routine in an EDP system?

b. Identify three types of test data that may be used in an edit routine.

8-19 What precautions should the auditor take to make a valid test of a computer program?

8-20 How may test data and generalized audit software be used in compliance testing of EDP application controls over sales transactions?

OBJECTIVE QUESTIONS FROM PROFESSIONAL EXAMINATIONS

Indicate the *best* answer for each of the following multiple choice questions.

8-21 These questions relate to the study and evaluation of internal control over sales transactions.

1. Tracing copies of sales invoices to shipping documents will provide evidence that all

    a. Shipments to customers were recorded as receivables.

    b. Billed sales were shipped.

    c. Debits to the subsidiary accounts receivable ledger are for sales shipped.

    d. Shipments to customers were billed.

2. To determine whether the system of internal accounting control operated effectively to minimize errors of failure to invoice a shipment, the auditor would select a sample of transactions from the population represented by the

    a. Customer order file.

    b. Bill of lading file.

    c. Subsidiary customer accounts ledger.

    d. Sales invoice file.

3. After the auditor has prepared a flowchart of the internal accounting controls surrounding sales and evaluated the design of the system, the auditor would perform compliance tests on all internal accounting control procedures
   a. Documented in the flowchart.
   b. Considered to be weaknesses that might allow errors to enter the accounting system.
   c. Considered to be strengths that the auditor plans to rely on.
   d. That would aid in preventing irregularities.

4. Smith Corporation has numerous customers. A customer file is kept on disk storage. Each customer file contains name, address, credit limit, and account balance. The auditor wishes to test this file to determine whether credit limits are being exceeded. The best procedure for the auditor to follow would be to
   a. Develop test data that would cause some account balances to exceed the credit limit and determine if the system properly detects such situations.
   b. Develop a program to compare credit limits with account balances and print out the details of any account with a balance exceeding its credit limit.
   c. Request a printout of all account balances so they can be manually checked against the credit limits.
   d. Request a printout of a sample of account balances so they can be individually checked against the credit limits.

COMPREHENSIVE QUESTIONS

8-22 The internal control questionnaire in Figure 8-4 includes the following questions:

1. Are all credit sales approved prior to sale?
2. Are customer orders compared to an approved customer list?
3. Is there internal verification of the goods in filling a sales order?
4. Are the goods compared with sales order in shipping?
5. Are prenumbered sales invoices used in billing?
6. Is there internal verification of prices and mathematical accuracy of sales invoices?
7. Are postings to the subsidiary ledgers made independent of journalizing and posting to the general ledger?
8. Are daily sales journal entries agreed to daily sales summaries?
9. Is there periodic independent reconciliation of accounts receivable control and the customers' ledger?
10. Are shipping documents and sales orders compared in billing?

Required

a. Identify the operative internal accounting control objective to which each question relates (i.e., executing, recording, or custody).
b. Identify the function and specific internal accounting control objective to which each question pertains.
c. Indicate the internal accounting control principle that is involved.
d. Identify an error or irregularity that may result from a No answer to each question. (Present your answers in tabular form, using separate columns for each of the four parts.)

8-23 The following control procedures over sales transactions are prescribed by the Harlan Company:

1. Credit department approval of credit sales.
2. Sales invoice for each shipping document.
3. Internal verification of prices, terms, and accuracy of sales invoice.
4. Prenumbered sales invoices.
5. Agreement of daily sales summaries with recorded entries.
6. Authorization of prices and terms.
7. Monthly statements independently mailed to customers.
8. Reconciliation of control accounts and subsidiary ledgers.
9. Sales orders agreed with customers orders.

Required

For each control procedure,

a. Indicate the function and the specific internal accounting control objective of each procedure.
b. Identify an error or irregularity that may be prevented or detected.
c. Indicate a compliance test that may be performed to determine whether each control is operating as prescribed. (Present your answers in tabular form using separate columns for each part.)

8-24 Assume the following exceptions to prescribed control procedures over sales transactions occurred in the Lane Company:

1. A shipment to a bona fide customer was not billed.
2. A sales invoice was correctly journalized but was not posted to the customer's account in the subsidiary ledger.
3. Sales are billed at unauthorized prices.
4. A sales invoice was incorrectly totaled.
5. A sales order was incorrectly filled and shipped.
6. Sales were made to customers who were poor credit risks.
7. A sales invoice was not journalized.
8. A customer's records were stolen.
9. Sales entries were incorrectly classified.
10. A sales order shows incorrect quantities.

Required

a. Indicate the function and specific internal accounting control objective associated with each occurrence.
b. Indicate the control procedure(s) that could prevent or detect the occurrences.
c. Indicate a compliance test for each procedure in (b). (Present your answers in tabular form using separate columns for each part.)

8-25 A flowchart of credit sales activities in the Top Manufacturing Company is shown on page 284.

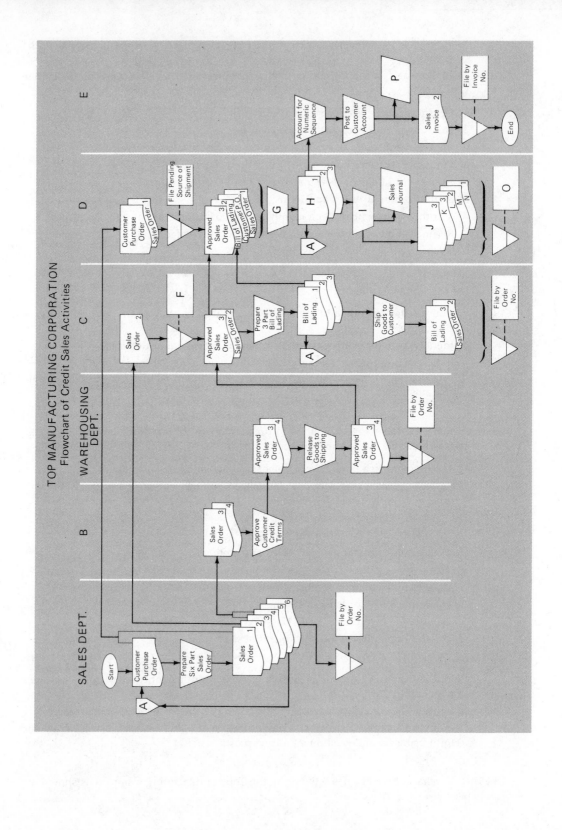

TOP MANUFACTURING CORPORATION
Flowchart of Credit Sales Activities

Required

Indicate what each of the code letters "B" through "P" represents. Do *not* discuss adequacies or inadequacies in the system of internal control.

AICPA

8-26 A partially completed charge sales systems flowchart is shown below. The flowchart depicts the charge sales activities of the Bottom Manufacturing Corporation.

A customer's purchase order is received and a six-part sales order is prepared therefrom. The six copies are initially distributed as follows:

Copy 1: Billing copy—to billing department.
Copy 2: Shipping copy—to shipping department.
Copy 3: Credit copy—to credit department.
Copy 4: Stock request copy—to credit department.
Copy 5: Customer copy—to customer.
Copy 6: Sales order copy—file in sales order department.

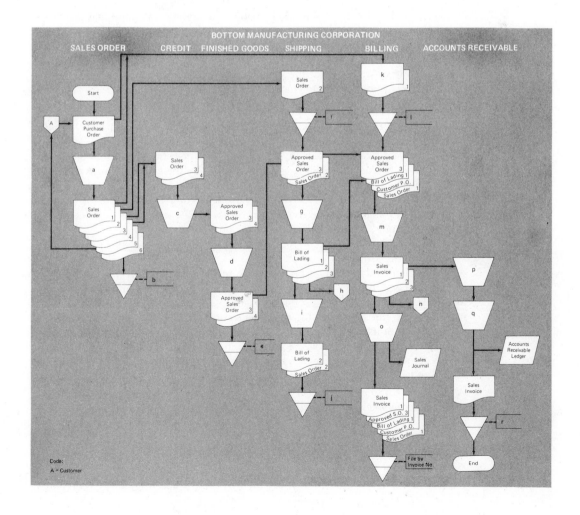

When each copy of the sales order reaches the applicable department or destination, it calls for specific internal control procedures and related documents. Some of the procedures and related documents are indicated on the flowchart. Other procedures and documents are labeled letters a to r.

Required

List the procedures or the internal documents that are labeled letters c to r in the flowchart of Bottom Manufacturing Corporation's charge sales system. Organize your answers as follows (note that an explanation of the letters a and b that appear in the flowchart are entered as examples):

Flowchart Symbol Letter	Procedures or Internal Document
a	Prepare six-part sales order
b	File by order number

AICPA

8-27 The customer billing function of the Robinson Company, a small paint manufacturer, is attended to by a receptionist, an accounts receivable clerk, and a cashier who also serves as a secretary. The company's paint products are sold to wholesalers and retail stores.

The following describes *all* of the procedures performed by the employees of the Robinson Company pertaining to customer billings.

1. The mail is opened by the receptionist who gives the customers' purchase orders to the accounts receivable clerk. Fifteen to 20 orders are received each day. Under instructions to expedite the shipment of orders, the accounts receivable clerk at once prepares a five-copy sales invoice form that is distributed as follows:
   a. Copy 1 is the customer billing copy and is held by the accounts receivable clerk until notice of shipment is received.
   b. Copy 2 is the accounts receivable department copy and is held for ultimate posting of the accounts receivable records.
   c. Copies 3 and 4 are sent to the shipping department.
   d. Copy 5 is sent to the storeroom as authority for release of the goods to the shipping department.
2. After the paint ordered has been moved from the storeroom to the shipping department, the shipping department prepares the bills of lading and labels the cartons. Sales invoice copy 4 is inserted in a carton as a packing slip. After the trucker has picked up the shipment, the customer's copy of the bill of lading and copy 3, on which are noted any undershipments, are returned to the accounts receivable clerk. The company does not "back order" in the event of undershipments; customers are expected to reorder the merchandise. The Robinson Company's copy of the bill of lading is filed by the shipping department.
3. When copy 3 and the customer's copy of the bill of lading are received by the accounts receivable clerk, copies 1 and 2 are completed by numbering them and inserting quantities shipped, unit prices, extensions, discounts, and totals. The accounts receivable clerk then mails copy 1 and the copy of the bill of lading to the customer. Copies 2 and 3 are stapled together.
4. The individual accounts receivable ledger cards are posted by the accounts receivable clerk by a bookkeeping machine procedure, whereby the sales register is prepared

as a carbon copy of the postings. Postings are made from copy 2, which is then filed, along with staple-attached copy 3, in numerical order. Monthly, the general ledger clerk summarizes the sales register for posting to the general ledger accounts.

Required

a. Identify (1) errors and irregularities and (2) necessary control procedures. Organize your answer around the primary functions for sales transactions.

b. Which weaknesses, if any, do you consider material? Discuss.

AICPA (adapted)

8-28 Your examination of the financial statements of General Department Store, Inc. disclosed the following:

1. The store has 30,000 retail accounts that are billed monthly on a cycle basis. There are 20 billing cycle divisions of the subsidiary accounts receivable ledger, and accounts are apportioned alphabetically to the divisions.

2. All charge sales tickets, which are prenumbered, are microfilmed in batches for each day's sales. These sales tickets are then sorted into their respective cycle divisions, and adding machine tapes are prepared to arrive at the total daily sales for each division. The daily totals for the divisions are then combined for comparison with the grand daily total charge sales determined from cash register readings. After the totals are balanced, the daily sales tickets are filed behind the related customer account cards in the respective cycle divisions.

3. Cycle control accounts for each division are maintained by postings of the tapes of daily sales.

4. At the cycle billing date, the customers' transactions (sales, remittances, returns, and other adjustments) are posted to the accounts in the individual cycle. The billing machine used automatically accumulates six separate totals: previous balances, purchases, payments, returns, new balances, and overdue balances. After posting, the documents and the customers' statements are microfilmed and then mailed to the customer.

5. Within each division, a trial balance of the accounts in the cycle, obtained as a by-product of the posting operation, is compared with the cycle control account.

6. Credit terms for regular accounts require payment within 10 days of receipt of the statement. A credit limit of $300 is set for all accounts.

7. Before the statements are mailed, they are reviewed to determine which are past due. Accounts are considered past due if the full balance of the prior month has not been paid. Past due accounts are noted for subsequent collection effort by the credit department.

8. Receipts on account and customer account adjustments are accumulated and posted in a similar manner.

Required

List the audit procedures that you would apply to testing transactions of one billing cycle division. Confine your audit procedures to the sales tickets and charges to the accounts. Do not discuss the audit of cash receipts or customer account adjustments.

AICPA (adapted)

8-29 The Meyers Pharmaceutical Company, a drug manufacturer, has the following system for billing and recording accounts receivable:

1. An incoming customer's purchase order is received in the order department by a clerk who prepares a prenumbered company sales order form in which is inserted the pertinent information, such as the customer's name and address, customer's account number, quantity, and items ordered. After the sales order form has been prepared, the customer's purchase order is stapled to it.

2. The sales order form is then passed to the credit department for credit approval. Rough approximations of the billing values of the orders are made in the credit department for those accounts on which credit limitations are imposed. After investigation, approval of credit is noted on the form.

3. Next, the sales order form is passed to the billing department, where a clerk types the customer's invoice on a billing machine that cross-multiplies the number of items and the unit price, then adds the automatically extended amounts for the total amounts of the invoice. The billing clerk determines the unit prices for the items from a list of billing prices.

   The billing machine has registers that automatically accumulate daily totals of customer account numbers and invoice amounts to provide "hash" totals and control amounts. These totals, which are inserted in a daily record book, serve as predetermined batch totals for verification of computer inputs.

   The billing is done on prenumbered, continuous, carbon-interleaved forms having the following designations:
   a. "Customer's copy."
   b. "Sales department copy," for information purposes.
   c. "File copy."
   d. "Shipping department copy," which serves as a shipping order. Bills of lading are also prepared as carbon copy by-products of the invoicing procedure.

4. The shipping department copy of the invoice and the bills of lading are then sent to the shipping department. After the order has been shipped, copies of the bill of lading are returned to the billing department. The shipping department copy of the invoice is filed in the shipping department.

5. In the billing department, one copy of the bill of lading is attached to the customer's copy of the invoice and both are mailed to the customer. The other copy of the bill of lading, together with the sales order form, is then stapled to the invoice file copy and filed in invoice numerical order.

6. A keypunch machine is connected to the billing machine so that punched cards are created during the preparation of the invoices. The punched cards then become the means by which the sales data are transmitted to a computer.

   The punched cards are fed to the computer in batches. One day's accumulation of cards comprises a batch. After the punched cards have been processed by the computer, they are placed in files and held for about two years.

Required

List the procedures that a CPA would employ in his examination of his selected audit samples of the company's (1) typed invoices, including the source documents, and (2) punched cards.

(The listed procedures should be limited to the verification of the sales data being fed into the computer. Do not carry the procedures beyond the point at which the cards are ready to be fed to the computer.)

AICPA

8-30 In an audit of the credit authorization function of Dawson Manufacturing Company, the auditor is concerned with detecting unauthorized credit sales. Different control procedures are applicable to the three categories of sales transactions described below. After performing a preliminary review of the different levels of control in the credit function, the auditor decides to treat each sales category as a separate population and develops the following estimates:

Dollar Amount Per Sales Transaction	Number of Sales Transactions Per Year	Maximum Percent of Unauthorized Credit Sales That Can Be Tolerated	Estimated Percent of Credit Sales Lacking Proper Authorization
A. Less than $1,000	10,000	5	2
B. Between $1,000 and $5,000	6,000	4	1
C. Over $5,000	5,000	3	0.5

Required

a. The auditor chooses to use a 5% risk of overreliance. How many items should be selected from each sales category given the auditor's preliminary estimates?

b. Without regard to your answer to a above, assume the following findings:

Dollar Amount Per Sales Transaction	Sample Size Selected	Number of Credit Sales Lacking Proper Authorization
A. Less than $1,000	200	8
B. Between $1,000 and $5,000	150	3
C. Over $5,000	150	0

Estimate, at the 5% level of risk of overreliance, the maximum number of credit sales in each category that have not been properly authorized.

c. Interpret the sample results obtained in b above in light of the criteria established by the auditor in preliminary planning. Be sure to indicate (1) whether or not the sampling results meet the auditor's criteria, and (2) the recommended alternative courses of action to be taken by the auditor if the criteria are not met for one or more of the sales categories.

IIA (adapted)

8-31 Huron Company manufactures and sells eight major product lines with 15 to 25 items in each product line. All sales are on credit, and orders are received by mail or telephone. Huron has a computer-based system that employs magnetic tape as a file medium.

All sales orders received during regular working hours are typed on Huron's own sales order form immediately. This typed form is the source document for the keypunching of a shipment or back-order card for each item ordered. These cards are employed in the after-hours processing at night to complete all necessary recordkeeping for the current day and to facilitate the shipment of goods the following day. In summary, an order received one day is to be processed that day and night and shipped the next day.

The daily processing that has to be accomplished at night includes the following activities:

1. Preparing the invoice to be sent to the customer at the time of shipment.
2. Updating accounts receivable file.
3. Updating finished goods inventory
4. Listing of all items back-ordered and short.

Each month, the sales department would like to have a sales summary and analysis. At the end of each month, the monthly statements should be prepared and mailed to customers. Management also wants an aging of accounts receivable each month.

Required

a. Identify the master files that Huron should maintain in this system to provide for the daily processing. Indicate the data content which should be included in each file and the order in which each file should be maintained.

b. Prepare a systems flowchart of the daily processing required to update the finished goods inventory records and produce the necessary inventory reports (assume that the necessary magnetic tape devices are available). Use the annotation symbol to describe or explain any facts that cannot be detailed in the individual symbols.

c. Describe (1) the items that should appear in the monthly sales analysis report(s) the sales department should have and (2) the input data and master files that would have to be maintained to prepare these reports.

CMA (adapted)

8-32* John Carr, controller for the General Corporation, provides you with the following information relative to the company's sales system:

The sales department prepares a six-part sales invoice form from the customer's order and files the order alphabetically by customer. Part 2 is sent to the credit department for approval; the remaining parts are held until credit is approved. After credit approval, the credit slip is returned to sales and filed with the customer's order. If credit is not approved, the customer is notified and the order is not processed. If approved, parts 1 (customer invoice) and 3 (accounting) are then sent to billing and held in a temporary customer file; part 4 is sent to shipping as a package slip; part 5 is sent to the warehouse as a stock request; and part 6 is sent to the customer to acknowledge the order.

The warehouse releases the goods and sends the stock request with the goods to shipping. In shipping, the goods are compared with the description on the stock request and units shipped are noted on this request and on the packing slip. Shipping then sends the packing slip with the goods to the customer. The stock request is sent to billing. For back-ordered items, a back-order report is prepared in billing after part 5 is returned from shipping. The report is sent to the sales department for preparation of a new sales invoice.

Billing enters the items shipped from the stock request on the customer invoice and accounting copy. Billing also makes extensions and checks them, compares prices to price list, and runs a tape of amounts on the accounting copies. The stock requests are filed numerically and numerical sequence is accounted for at this time. The customer invoice is sent to the customer.

The accounting copy is sent to accounting, where it is posted to the customer ledger card and placed in the invoice file according to shipping date. A tape of invoices is also sent to accounting, where the total is posted to the general ledger sales and accounts receivable control accounts. The total daily posting to customer ledger cards is balanced to the general ledger sales entry. The tape of invoices is discarded after balancing.

Required

Prepare a flowchart of the sales system.

8-33* The Joppa Corporation's sales department receives each sales order (mail or phone), prepares the sales order form, and forwards a copy to the credit manager for credit approval. On indicating approval, the sales order copy is returned to the sales department, where the shipping order copy is sent to the shipping department for assembling the order. After the order is prepared for shipping, a prenumbered bill of lading is prepared for the shipment.

On shipment of the order, the shipping order copy is returned with a copy of the bill of lading to the sales department, where it is matched with the copy in the open sales order file. All the documents are forwarded to the accounting department.

From the information supplied by the sales department, the prenumbered sales invoices are prepared in the accounting department. Two copies are mailed to the customer and the invoice information entered in detail in the sales journal. Invoice amounts are posted to the customers' accounts receivable cards at the same time they are entered in the sales journal. Totals from the sales journal are posted to the general ledger at month-end.

Required

a. List the procedures you would perform to compliance test the recorded sales.

b. Since this company maintains a file of unfilled sales orders in the sales department, list the recommendations you would give to the client for review of the file and pursuit of old unfilled sales orders.

c. Comment on the internal control system.

CASE STUDY

8-34* The Alpha Company is a medium-sized company that assembles robots from parts and subassemblies ordered to specification. All work done by outside processors is completed prior to the time the Alpha Company receives the component parts and/ or subassemblies. These robots are sold to steel mills, automobile companies, and other manufacturing companies. Sales prices of the robots range from $8,000 to $25,000 depending on their capacity, complexity, and variation from the standard model formats specified by the customer.

The company has been in operation approximately five years and has enjoyed increased gross revenue and earnings during each year. This year, sales are expected to be about $10 million and net income about $500,000.

In the past, we have always considered internal controls over sales and accounts receivable to be very reliable. This year you find that, for the first time, a significant portion (about 20%) of sales is composed of replacement parts for robots. Instead of employing the same sales and accounts receivable system as for sales of new robots, which system appears very reliable again this year, the following procedures are employed for sales of replacement parts:

> (The new procedures have been authorized by J. B. Brown, the vice-president of sales, to facilitate filling the replacement parts orders as expeditiously as possible so customers can minimize the "down time" of the Alpha robots in their plants. Brown believes very strongly that customers' satisfaction with Alpha robots depends, to a large extent, on the time required to repair the robots they have.)

Customers may telephone their replacement orders (which average about $150) to the sales order department, which orally transmits them to the shipping department, where the replacement parts inventory is stocked. The replacement parts inventory is not commingled with parts used in the assembly of new robots. The shipping department fills the order and prepares a scratch paper listing of the parts shipped, which is forwarded to the billing department. The billing department prepares a special three-part prenumbered sales invoice. It enters quantities from the memo received from the shipping department and prices from a current price list, makes extensions and footings, and mails the original after someone else in the department has completely checked it. The first copy is sent to the accounts receivable clerk for entry in the sales journal and on the accounts receivable ledger card and for filing in numerical order. The accounts receivable clerk frequently checks for missing invoice numbers and requests any missing invoices from the billing department. The second copy is sent to the sales order department for filing by customer.

Perpetual inventory records are not maintained for the replacement parts. However, a physical inventory of the replacement parts inventory is taken at the end of each month by a member of the controller's department, assisted by someone from the shipping department.

Required

a. Identify the errors and irregularities that may occur in Alpha's system.

b. Opposite each items listed in a, indicate the necessary control procedures that may prevent or detect such occurrences.

c. Enumerate the compliance tests you would apply in testing sales of replacement parts transactions.

Chapter 9

Compliance Tests of Revenue Cycle: Cash Receipts and Sales Adjustments Transactions

Study Objectives

When you have completed your study of this chapter, you should be able to

- Describe the applicability of the principles of internal accounting control to cash receipts and sales adjustments transactions.

- Comprehend and evaluate flowcharts of cash receipts transactions.

- Prepare an internal control questionnaire for cash receipts transactions.

- Identify errors and irregularities that may occur in cash receipts transactions.

- Design audit programs for compliance tests of cash receipts and sales adjustments transactions.

- Indicate the applicability of statistical sampling in compliance tests of cash receipts and sales adjustments transactions.

- Explain the essential steps of an audit program for testing EDP controls over cash receipts transactions.

This chapter completes the coverage of the revenue cycle. In the chapter, cash receipts transactions associated with the earning of revenues and sales adjustments transactions are considered. The format of the chapter parallels the approach used in the preceding chapter. Accordingly, consideration will be given first to the internal control environment, basic principles of internal control, and specific accounting control objectives. Then, attention is given to the study and evaluation of internal accounting control over cash receipts and sales adjustments, including applications of statistical sampling and electronic data processing (EDP).

INTERNAL CONTROL OVER CASH RECEIPTS AND SALES ADJUSTMENTS TRANSACTIONS

BASIC CONSIDERATIONS

Cash receipts may result from a variety of sources. For example, cash receipts may result from revenue transactions, short- and long-term borrowing, issuance of capital stock, and the sale of marketable securities, long-term investments, and other assets. The scope of this chapter is limited to cash receipts from sales transactions. Such receipts include cash sales and collections from trade customers on credit sales. Other sources of cash receipts are discussed in the investing and financing cycles in Chapter 15. Sales adjustments transactions include sales discounts, sales returns and allowances, and uncollectible accounts.

The following are basic to an understanding of cash receipts and sales adjustments transactions in the revenue cycle:

Functions

Executing

- Receiving mail receipts.
- Receiving over-the-counter receipts.
- Aggregating total receipts.
- Depositing cash in bank.
- Granting cash discounts.
- Granting sales returns and allowances.
- Determining uncollectible accounts.

Recording

- Journalizing and posting cash receipts transactions.
- Journalizing and posting sales adjustments transactions.
- Updating the customers' ledger.

Custody

- Protecting cash.
- Maintaining correctness of cash balances.

Common Documents

- *Remittance Advice.* A memo attached to or separate from a check indicating the item(s) paid by a check. If not sent by the customer, it usually is prepared by the recipient.
- *Check.* An order directing a bank to pay a specified sum of money to a payee on demand. On receipt, a check should be restrictively endorsed by stamp or signature *for deposit only*.
- *Cash Register Tape.* A chronological listing of cash receipts produced internally by the register of amounts registered by a cashier. The customer's copy is in the form of a *cash register receipt slip*.
- *Prelisting of Cash Receipts.* A detailed compilation of each cash remittance received through the mail.
- *Cash Register Reading.* A machine produced total of cash rung up on a register for a specified period of time such as a day. The reading is generally done by a cashier supervisor.
- *Cash Count Sheet.* A listing of cash and checks in a register and a reconciliation of the total with the cash register reading.
- *Daily Cash Summary.* A report showing total mail and over-the-counter receipts for the day.
- *Bank Deposit Slip.* A listing of the detail and total cash deposited in the bank prepared by the depositor.
- *Bank Statement.* A report sent to the depositor periodically (usually monthly) by the bank. It shows the beginning and ending balances and transactions posted to the depositor's account.
- *Credit Memo.* A notice to a customer issued by the seller granting credit for unsatisfactory merchandise.
- *Write-Off Authorization Memo.* A notice used internally for writing off an uncollectible customer account.

Accounting Records

- *Books of Original Entry.* Cash receipts journal and general journal.
- *General Ledger Accounts.* Cash, accounts receivable, notes receivable, sales, sales discounts, sales returns and allowances, allowance for uncollectible accounts, and uncollectible accounts expense.
- *Subsidiary Ledger.* Customers' ledger.

File Data

- *Customer Account File.* Contains documentation of postings to each customer's account.

ADDITIONAL INTERNAL CONTROL ENVIRONMENT CONSIDERATIONS

The internal control environment described in Chapter 8 applies to all transactions in the revenue cycle. Additional comment is warranted here concerning the control environment for cash receipts transactions.

In the organization structure illustrated in Figure 8-1, the position of vice president of finance is shown. In most companies, this individual has the overall responsibility for cash management.

Responsibility for executing cash receipts transactions and custody of cash funds is usually delegated to departments or offices, such as the treasurer's office and the cashier's office. Personnel in these departments should be competent in the handling of cash transactions and should be knowledgeable of banks and banking practices.

When there is an internal auditing function within an entity, there can be independent monitoring of the receiving and depositing of cash receipts. Cash budgets play an important role in effective cash management. Monthly reports that compare actual results with budget expectations contribute to the control of cash.

Many companies bond employees who handle cash. Bonding involves the purchase of a fidelity insurance policy against loss of cash from theft and similar defalcations perpetrated by a dishonest employee. Before the insurer issues a policy or adds an employee to an existing policy, it generally makes an investigation as to the individual's honesty and integrity in previous positions. Bonding contributes to the control environment over cash receipts in two ways: (1) it may prevent the hiring of dishonest individuals, and (2) it serves as a deterrent to dishonesty because employees know that the insurance company may vigorously investigate and prosecute any dishonest act.

Other sound controls over cash receipts include (1) having employees who handle cash take vacations and (2) rotating their assigned duties periodically. The thrust of these controls is to deter dishonesty by making employees aware that they may not be able to permanently conceal their transgressions. Some bank embezzlements, for example, have been traced to the apparently dedicated employee who had the same job and did not take a vacation in 25 years.

CASH RECEIPTS TRANSACTIONS ARE PROPERLY EXECUTED

The functions and specific accounting control objectives in executing cash receipts transactions are as follows:

Function	Specific Accounting Control Objective
1. Receiving mail receipts	Receipts are handled by authorized personnel and are promptly and accurately listed.
2. Receiving over-the-counter receipts	Receipts are handled by authorized personnel and are promptly and correctly registered.
3. Aggregating total receipts	Receipts are totaled, verified, and summarized by authorized personnel.
4. Depositing cash	Receipts are promptly deposited intact in an authorized depository.

The internal control principles applicable to the execution of these transactions are explained below.

Authorization Procedures

Authorization of cash receipts transactions embodies procedures for opening
and closing bank accounts. The treasurer and/or the chief financial officer
usually have this authority. It is also necessary to identify personnel who are
authorized to handle cash. These may include all employees in the cashier's
department, mailroom employees who sort mail, and salespersons in retail
companies who also have the authority to operate cash registers.

Segregation of Functions

The separation of duties in executing cash receipts transactions is indicated
below.

Function	Department	Related Activities
1. Receiving mail receipts	Mailroom	Prepare prelist of individual checks, prepare remittance advices if necessary, restrictively endorse checks.
2. Receiving over-the-counter receipts	Sales	Make cash sales, ring up sales on cash register, restrictively endorse checks.
	Cashier (Individual Cashiers)	Ring up collections from customers on cash registers, prepare remittance advices, restrictively endorse checks.
3. Aggregating total cash received	Cashier (Supervisor)	Make cash register readings, make daily cash counts of registers, reconcile checks with prelists and remittance advices, prepare daily cash summary.
4. Depositing cash in bank	Cashier (Supervisor)	Prepare bank deposit slip, make bank deposit.
	Treasurer	Compare prelists and cash count sheets with daily cash summary, compare summary with bank deposit.

In addition to a separation of functions between departments, this tabulation
shows a separation of duties within the cashier's department. Many national
retailers, for example, accept payments on account from customers only at
the cashier's office. A flowchart of a manual system for executing mail receipts
and over-the-counter cash sales is shown in Figure 9-1.

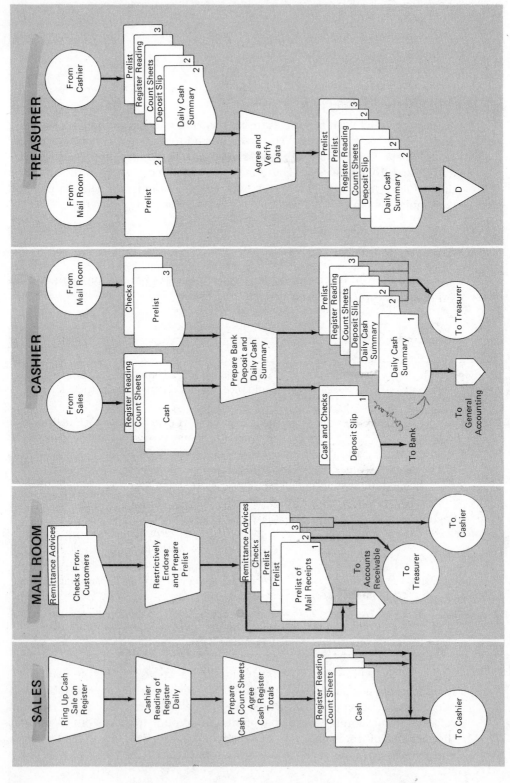

Figure 9-1. MANUAL SYSTEM FOR EXECUTING CASH RECEIPTS TRANSACTIONS.

Documentation Procedures

A major concern in executing cash receipts transactions is the possible diversion of cash before there is any documentation of the receipt. Hence, control procedures should provide reasonable assurance that documentation is produced at the moment cash is received. For mail receipts, documentation consists of remittance advices, checks, and daily listings (technically called pre-listings) of mail receipts. On receipt in the mail room, all checks should be restrictively endorsed for deposit only.

Documentation of over-the-counter receipts consists of *cash register tapes, checks,* and *remittance advices.* These documents are provided when the cash is received. Subsequently, the cashier's office will obtain cash register readings and prepare *cash count sheets, daily cash summaries,* and *bank deposit slips.* Responsibility for bank deposits is usually assigned to the cashier's office because all receipts are centralized at this location. Cash should be deposited in total (intact) daily for purposes of accountability, safekeeping, and good cash management. Consequently, the bank deposit should equal the total cash shown on the daily cash summary. Deposit slips are prepared in duplicate. One copy is retained by the bank and the other is validated by the bank and then sent by the depositor to the treasurer's office. The details of the deposit (e.g., the individual checks) should be indicated on the slip or shown in a separate listing. Figure 9-1 shows the origin, routing, and disposition of the documents.

Physical Controls

In retail establishments, the use of cash registers is a vital accounting control procedure in executing cash receipts transactions.

The control features of a cash register include:

- Immediate visual display for the customer of the amount of the receipt.
- A printed receipt which is available to the customer.
- Locked-in totals of the day's receipts.

Electronically operated registers, often referred to as electronic point-of-sale (POS) systems, provide even greater control over the execution of register receipts. Such registers have the capability of "reading" the sales price from the price tags and automatically adding the sales tax. In addition, the registers can be utilized to perform a variety of control functions, such as updating accounts receivable and perpetual inventory records, and accumulating sales data by salesperson, product line, and so on.

Companies with a large volume of mail receipts sometimes use a *lockbox system.* The lockbox is a post office box that is controlled by the company's bank. Under this type of security system, the bank picks up the mail daily, credits the company for the cash, and sends the remittance advices to the company. This system also expedites the depositing of checks, with the result that the company receives credit for them sooner.

Other examples of physical controls include coin machines in transit companies, automatic receptacles on interstate toll roads, ticket machines in theaters, and metered gas pumps in service stations.

Independent Internal Verification

For cash register receipts, each register is read (totaled) by a cashier department supervisor, and a reconciliation is made on cash count sheets of the total cash with the actual cash in the register. In the treasurer's office, there should be daily comparisons of (1) prelists and cash register totals with the daily cash summary and (2) the summary with the corresponding duplicate deposit slip.

CASH RECEIPTS TRANSACTIONS ARE PROPERLY RECORDED

The functions and accounting control objectives for recording cash receipts transactions are as follows:

Function	Department	Specific Accounting Control Objective
1. Journalizing and posting cash receipts transactions	General Accounting	Only valid cash receipts are recorded, and all valid receipts are correctly recorded as to amount, account classification, and accounting period.
2. Updating customers' ledger	Accounts Receivable Accounting	Collections from customers are promptly and correctly posted to customer accounts.

The internal control principles applicable to these functions are explained below.

Segregation of Functions

As in the case of sales transactions, there should be a separation of duties between journalizing and posting to the general ledger and updating the customers' ledger. In addition, accounting personnel should not participate in the execution of the transactions or have custody of the cash receipts.

Accounting Records and Procedures

The primary source documents for journalizing cash receipts transactions are the daily cash summaries and prelists. Postings to the customers' ledger are made directly from the prelists and accompanying remittance advices.

Independent Internal Verification

Applications of this principle include (1) agreeing remittance advices to prelists in accounts receivable accounting and (2) agreeing the prelist to the daily cash summary in general accounting as shown in the flowchart in Figure 9-2.

CUSTODY OF CASH IS PROPERLY MAINTAINED

The functions and specific accounting control objectives for proper custody of cash receipts are as follows:

Functions	Department	Specific Accounting Control Objective
1. Protecting cash	Treasurer	Cash is stored in secure areas and access thereto is limited to authorized personnel.
2. Maintaining correctness of cash balances	General Accounting	Recorded cash and bank balances are independently reconciled with cash on hand and in banks at reasonable intervals.

The internal control principles applicable to these functions are explained below.

Physical Controls and Authorization Procedures

Because cash offers a great temptation for misappropriation, every effort should be made by a company to store cash (and checks) in a safe place from the moment it is received to its ultimate disposition. Direct physical access to cash held on company premises can be effectively limited by the use of safes, vaults, and similar protective equipment. Access to such security devices should be restricted to authorized personnel only and be strictly enforced. Whenever possible, cash should be stored off premises where the greater security of a bank can be utilized. All cash, except possibly small change and petty cash funds, should be deposited in the bank daily through regular or night depository facilities.

Segregation of Functions and Independent Internal Verification

Personnel responsible for the custody of cash on hand and in banks should not otherwise be involved in executing and recording cash receipts transactions.

Independent verifications of cash balances are generally made monthly. Recorded cash on hand and petty cash balances are compared with cash counts, and recorded bank balances are reconciled to balances shown on bank statements. These verifications should be made by personnel who have no other duties pertaining to cash receipts.

SALES ADJUSTMENTS TRANSACTIONS ARE PROPERLY EXECUTED

The functions and specific accounting control objectives in executing sales adjustments transactions are as follows:

Function	Specific Accounting Control Objective
Granting cash discounts	Discounts are granted in accordance with authorized terms.
Granting sales returns and allowances	Returns and allowances are granted in accordance with management's policies.
Determining uncollectible accounts	Uncollectible accounts are determined on the basis of established criteria.

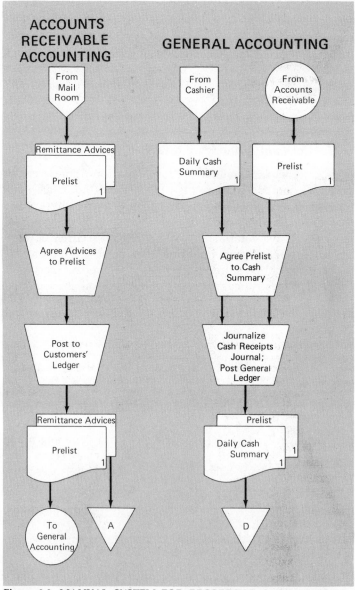

Figure 9-2. MANUAL SYSTEM FOR RECORDING CASH RECEIPTS TRANSACTIONS.

The internal control principles applicable to the execution of these transactions are as follows.

Authorization Procedures

Authorization procedures usually provide for personnel in (1) the accounts receivable department to approve discounts, (2) the sales order department to grant credit for sales returns and allowances, and (3) the treasurer's department to approve the write-off of bad debts. Before approving a discount, the customer's remittance must be traced to the sales invoice in the customer account file for compliance with discount terms. Before approving other adjustments, there should be evidence in the form of a receiving report for returned goods, written communication from the customer requesting an allowance, or a collection agency report on the delinquent customer. Unauthorized sales adjustments result in improper credits to customer accounts and an understatement of the balance due.

Segregation of Functions

The segregation of functions for sales adjustments are tabulated below.

Function	Department	Related Activities
Granting cash discounts	Accounts receivable accounting	Compare customer remittances with discount terms and indicate approval of discount.
Granting sales returns and allowances	Sales	Evaluate requests for adjustments, review evidence of returned goods, and authorize issuance of credit memos.
	Billing	Issue credit memos to customers.
Determining uncollectible accounts	Treasurer	Review credit and collection history of delinquent customers, examine collection agency data, and approve and issue write-off memos for bad accounts.

Individuals performing these functions have incompatible duties if they also handle cash collections from customers. In such case, they could make unauthorized credits to the accounts and divert the collections when received to personal use.

Documentation Procedures

The approval of cash discounts should be indicated by accounts receivable on the prelists from the mail room and on the remittance advices from over-the-counter collections. Returns and allowances should be supported by credit memos, and write-offs of uncollectible accounts should be based on write-off memos. These documents should be prenumbered and subsequently accounted for.

SALES ADJUSTMENTS TRANSACTIONS ARE PROPERLY RECORDED

The functions and internal control objectives in recording these transactions are as follows:

Function	Department	Specific Accounting Control Objective
Journalizing and posting sales adjustments transactions	General Accounting	Only valid sales adjustments are recorded, and all valid sales adjustments are correctly recorded as to amount, classification, and accounting period.
Updating the customers' ledger	Accounts Receivable Accounting	Sales adjustments are promptly and correctly posted to customer accounts.

The internal control principles of segregation of functions and accounting records and procedures are applicable to the recording of these transactions. As for other classes of transactions, all prenumbered documents should be accounted for in journalizing.

CUSTODY OF ASSETS IS PROPERLY MAINTAINED

The assets relating to sales adjustments transactions include cash, accounts receivable, and the goods returned for credit. The internal accounting control objectives and principles pertaining to the custody of cash and accounts receivable have already been explained. Custody of goods returned ordinarily is assumed by the warehouse where the goods were originally stored.

STUDY AND EVALUATION OF INTERNAL CONTROL

The auditor's methodology for meeting the second standard of field work for cash receipts and sales adjustments transactions is identical with the steps described for sales transactions in Chapter 8.

REVIEW OF THE CASH RECEIPTS SYSTEM

The auditor is required to make a preliminary review of the internal control environment and the flow of cash receipts transactions through the accounting system. A decision to complete the review is made when the auditor believes it will be cost-efficient to rely on the client's control procedures in performing substantive tests of resulting balances. The principal steps in the completion phase of review are explained below.

CYCLE: Revenue	CLASS OF TRANSACTIONS: Cash Receipts

EXECUTING	Yes	No
1. Are prelists prepared for mail receipts? (E1)		
2. Are checks restrictively endorsed on receipt? (E1, E2)		
3. Are persons who handle cash prohibited from recording cash and making postings to the customers' ledger? (E1, E2)		
4. Are cash registers used for over-the-counter receipts? (E2)		
5. Is there periodic surveillance of cash register procedures? (E2)		
6. Are prelists and checks independently reconciled with cash summaries? (E3)		
7. Are cash registers read daily and reconciled to cash on hand? (E3)		
8. Is cash deposited intact daily? (E4)		
9. Do only authorized personnel make deposits? (E4)		
10. Are deposits and daily cash summaries independently reconciled? (E4)		

RECORDING

1. Are accounting personnel prohibited from handling cash? (R1)
2. Is there internal verification of the agreement of daily cash summaries and cash receipts journal entries? (R1)
3. Is there separation of duties between the journalizing of cash receipts transactions and posting to the customers' ledger? (R2)

CUSTODY

1. Is cash stored in safes or vaults prior to deposit? (C1)
2. Are periodic independent counts made of cash on hand? (C2)

Figure 9-3. INTERNAL CONTROL QUESTIONNAIRE: CASH RECEIPTS TRANSACTIONS.

Gathering Information

In this step, the auditor seeks information about the specific internal controls prescribed by the client. A questionnaire for cash receipts transactions is illustrated in Figure 9-3. As in the preceding chapter, the questions relate to necessary control procedures and they are referenced to specific functions. In addition to inquiry, the auditor may also obtain information about prescribed controls through observation and review of documentation.

Making a Preliminary Evaluation

A representative listing of errors and irregularities for cash receipts transactions and the control procedures considered necessary to prevent or detect their occurrence is shown in Figure 9-4. Then, using the knowledge about the client's prescribed controls obtained in step 1 of this review, the auditor makes

Function	Possible Errors and Irregularities	Necessary Control Procedures	Possible Compliance Tests
EXECUTING			
1. Receiving mail receipts	Checks may be lost in the mailroom.	Restrictive endorsement of checks on receipt.	Examine checks for endorsement.
2. Receiving over-the-counter receipts	Cash sales may not be registered.	Periodic surveillance of cash register procedures.	Inquire of supervisors about findings.
	Errors may be made in making change.	Daily cash register readings and cash counts by supervisors.	Review cash count sheets.
	Collections from customers may be misappropriated (lapping).	Segregation of functions of cash handling and recording.	Observe segregation of functions.
3. Aggregating total cash received	Accompanying checks may not agree with prelist from mailroom.	Comparison of prelist with checks in cashier's department.	Review evidence of comparison.
4. Depositing cash in bank	Cash may not be deposited intact.	Verification of agreement of deposit slip with daily cash summary.	Review evidence of verification.
RECORDING			
1. Journalizing and posting cash receipts transactions	Some receipts may not be recorded.	Internal verification of agreement of cash receipts journal entries with daily cash summary.	Examine evidence of verification.
2. Updating customers' ledger	Recorded receipts may not be posted to customer accounts.	Segregation of functions between journalizing and updating.	Observe segregation of duties.
CUSTODY			
1. Protecting cash	Cash may be stolen before being deposited.	Storage of cash in vaults and safes.	Observe storage security.
2. Maintaining correctness of cash balances	Mathematical errors may be made in computing cash balances.	Periodic independent comparisons of cash balances with cash on hand.	Examine evidence of independent comparisons.

Figure 9-4. PRELIMINARY EVALUATION CONSIDERATIONS: CASH RECEIPTS TRANSACTIONS.

a preliminary evaluation of each control. The auditor's preliminary evaluation should be documented in the working papers.

Lapping of Cash Receipts

Lapping is an irregularity that results in the deliberate misappropriation of cash receipts. It may involve either a temporary or a permanent abstraction of cash receipts for the personal use of the individual perpetrating the unauthorized act. Lapping is usually associated with collections from customers, but it may also involve other types of cash receipts. Conditions conducive to lapping exist when an individual who handles cash receipts also maintains the customers' ledger. The auditor should assess the likelihood of lapping when making a preliminary evaluation of controls over cash receipts by carefully considering the segregation of functions that exists in the receiving and recording of collections from customers.

To illustrate lapping, assume on a given day that cash register tapes totaled $600 and mail receipts opened by the lapper consisted of one payment on account by check for $200 from customer A. The lapper would proceed to abstract $200 in cash and destroy all evidence pertaining to the mail receipt except for the customer's check. The cash receipts journal entry would agree with the register tape ($600) and the deposit slip would show cash $400 and A's check for $200. These facts can be tabulated as follows:

Actual Receipts		Documentation		Cash Receipts Journal Entry		Bank Deposit Slip	
Cash	$600	Cash tape	$600	Cash sales	$600	Cash	$400
A check	200		—		—	A check	200
	$800		$600		$600		$600

In an effort to conceal the shortage, the defrauder usually attempts to (1) keep bank and book amounts in daily agreement so that a bank reconciliation will not detect the irregularity and (2) correct the customer's account within three to four days of actual collection so that any discovered discrepancy in the customer's account can be explained as a delay in receiving the money or posting. To accomplish the latter, the abstraction is shifted to another customer's account several days later as follows:

Actual Receipts		Documentation		Cash Receipts Journal Entry		Bank Deposit Slip	
Cash	$500	Cash tape	$500	Cash sales	$500	Cash	$400
B check	300	A check	200	A check	200	B check	300
	$800		$700		$700		$700

The total shortage is now $300. Notice in both cases that the totals of the last two columns are in agreement. Thus, a comparison of totals will not detect lapping. However, a comparison of the details of the cash receipts journal entry with the details of the deposit slip will detect the shortage. If lapping exists at the balance sheet date, the confirmation of customer balances may also detect the irregularity.

COMPLIANCE TESTS OF CASH RECEIPTS CONTROLS

The auditor is required by GAAS to perform compliance tests of the controls expected to be relied on in substantive testing. In this case, the compliance tests are made to determine whether the prescribed controls over cash receipts transactions are operating as planned. An audit program is illustrated in Figure 9-5. This program includes most of the possible compliance tests shown in Figure 9-4.

In the program, daily cash summaries are used as the sampling unit in testing controls that leave a trail of documentary evidence in the execution and recording of cash receipts transactions. The comparison of daily cash summary *totals* with the total amount shown on the daily deposit slip and the bank statement focuses on whether all receipts have been deposited intact

---

TYPE OF TEST: Compliance   PURPOSE: Study and Evaluation of Internal Control
CYCLE: Revenue   CLASS OF TRANSACTIONS: Cash Receipts

A. CONTROLS IN EXECUTING CASH RECEIPTS TRANSACTIONS ARE OPERATING AS PLANNED.

1. Examine selected daily cash summaries for
   - Verification with prelists. (E1)
   - Verification with cash count sheets. (E2)
   - Verification with details and totals of daily deposit slips. (E4)
2. Observe mail clerks and cashiers in performance of required control procedures.
3. Inquire of supervisors about the results of their surveillance of cash register procedures.
4. Reperform verification procedures in step 1 for some cash summaries.

B. CONTROLS IN RECORDING CASH RECEIPTS TRANSACTIONS ARE OPERATING AS PLANNED.

1. Examine above sample of daily cash summaries for evidence of agreement with daily cash receipts entries. (R1)
2. Observe segregation of functions between journalizing of cash receipts and postings to customers' ledger. (R2)

C. CONTROLS OVER CUSTODY OF CASH ARE OPERATING AS PLANNED.

1. Observe storage of cash and means of limiting access to storage areas. (C1)
2. Review evidence of periodic comparisons of cash balances with cash on hand. (C2)

Figure 9-5. AUDIT PROGRAM—COMPLIANCE TESTS OF CASH RECEIPTS TRANSACTIONS.

daily. Any discrepancies in amount or time delays should be investigated. The comparison of the *details* of the deposit slip and the individual entries in the cash receipts journal is designed to detect lapping.

REVIEW AND COMPLIANCE TESTS OF SALES ADJUSTMENTS CONTROLS

The auditor may also use an internal control questionnaire to gather information about controls over sales adjustments transactions. Questions pertaining to the execution of these transactions will often include the following:

- Are all cash discounts approved?
- Are sales returns and allowances approved by sales personnel?
- Are prenumbered credit memos used for sales returns and allowances?
- Is there separation of duties between approval of sales returns and allowances and issuance of credit memos?
- Are all bad debt write-offs approved in writing?
- Is there separation of duties between the approval of bad debt write-offs and collections from customers?

A variety of errors may occur with sales adjustments transactions. For example, cash discounts may be incorrectly computed or discounts may be granted when the collection is received after the discount period has lapsed. Similarly, the amount of credit for a sales return or allowance may be incorrectly determined.

A number of irregularities are possible when there is inadequate segregation of duties in executing and recording sales adjustments transactions. This is especially true when an individual handles cash receipts and maintains the customers' ledger. In such case, an employee may credit a customer account for an unauthorized credit memo and subsequently misappropriate the customer's payment on account. Alternatively, an employee can write off a valid receivable as a bad debt and then divert the remittance to personal use.

In order to have a basis for reliance on internal controls over sales adjustments transactions, it is necessary to perform compliance tests on the controls. In the tests, the sampling unit may be (1) credit memos for sales returns and allowances and (2) bad debt authorizations for bad debt write-offs.

FINAL EVALUATION OF THE CONTROLS

Based on his preliminary evaluation and the results of compliance testing, the auditor determines the reliance that can be placed on specific control procedures in performing substantive tests. In analyzing the test results, the auditor considers both the qualitative and the quantitative aspects of deviations from prescribed control procedures. The auditor subsequently determines the effects of his evaluations on the nature, timing, and extent of substantive tests of account balances resulting from cash receipts and sales adjustments transactions.

STATISTICAL SAMPLING IN COMPLIANCE TESTING

Opportunities for the application of statistical sampling in compliance testing for cash receipts and sales adjustments transactions are more limited than for certain other classes of transactions. Note that several of the steps in the compliance testing program for cash receipts in Figure 9-5 involve inquiry about, or observations of, cash handling procedures. These procedures do not lend themselves to statistical sampling. Other steps in the program focus on the daily cash summaries as the sampling unit. Because this sampling unit relates to a small population (there would be a maximum of 365 summaries for the year in some companies), the attribute sampling tables in Chapter 7 (which are based on sampling from populations of 5000 or more items) would not apply. While other tables and formulas are available for attribute sampling from small populations, auditors frequently use nonstatistical audit sampling in these circumstances.

Alternatively, a different sampling unit might be chosen for a specific compliance test. For instance, step A1 in the audit program in Figure 9-7 (p. 313) specifies the customer remittance advice as the sampling unit. This would generally produce a population large enough to use the sampling theory and tables illustrated in Chapter 7. Such a sample could be selected by establishing correspondence between a random number table and prenumbered remittance advices, or by first randomly selecting daily prelists and then randomly selecting line items (remittances) on the prelists. Of course, appropriate selection of the sampling unit depends on the objective of the test.

In the compliance testing of sales adjustments transactions, a sample of remittance advices selected as described above could be examined for evidence of approval of any discounts taken. Also, statistical sampling of sales returns and allowances transactions could be performed when the volume of such transactions is large. This may occur for national mail order companies such as Spiegels and L. L. Bean. The sampling unit would be the credit memo, and the attributes to be examined could include evidence of (1) the request for credit (customer letter), (2) a receiving report for the goods returned for credit, (3) internal verification of the credit memo, and (4) approval of credit by a supervisor.

ELECTRONIC DATA PROCESSING

Cash receipts transactions may be processed in an electronic system by each of the data processing methods described in Chapter 6. The following case study illustrates the use of on-line entry/batch processing.

DESCRIPTION OF THE CASH RECEIPTS SYSTEM

The R. E. Birk Company uses the departments described earlier in this chapter for the manual processing of cash receipts. Customer checks are received in the mailroom where they are endorsed and listed on a prelist. As shown in the flowchart in Figure 9-6, accounts receivable receives the checks, remittance advices, and a copy of the prelist from the mailroom. Authorized accounts receivable clerks then enter the receipts directly into the computer using display-type terminals. The input data are edited by the computer, and the accounts receivable clerk receives an immediate response of any incorrect data on the display screen.

As shown in the flowchart, there are two computer runs. In run 1, the input data are edited and sorted. The outputs of this run consist of a printed exceptions and control report and a valid cash receipts transaction tape. In run 2, the valid cash receipts transaction tape is processed. The outputs of this run are an updated accounts receivable master file in machine-readable form, a printed report of individual customer payments, an exceptions and control report, and three printouts pertaining to the recording and depositing of cash receipts.

Daily, accounts receivable makes a detailed comparison of the report of customer activity with the remittance advices and prelist. In addition, the cashier's department makes the bank deposit after agreeing the checks received from accounts receivable with the daily cash summary and prelist. Evidence of the cash activity and bank deposit is then sent to the treasurer's office.

STUDY AND EVALUATION OF EDP CONTROLS

The audit program for testing application controls over cash receipts transactions in Figure 9-7 is similar to the program presented in Figure 8-8. Input and output controls that leave a visible transaction trail are tested by recourse to source documents and by reviewing reconciliations of batch and other control totals. The programmed controls in runs 1 and 2 do not leave a transaction trail. Accordingly, the testing of controls is done through the computer using test data. Valid and invalid test data are prepared to test the controls incorporated within the cash receipts edit routines in run 1 and the program logic in run 2.

Based on the tests of general controls and the tests of application controls, the auditor proceeds to evaluate EDP controls over cash receipts transactions and determines the extent to which substantive tests of balances are to be restricted.

CONCLUDING COMMENTS

Cash receipts and sales adjustments transactions are integral parts of an entity's revenue cycle. The explanation of internal control principles applicable to these classes of transactions and the study and evaluation of internal control of cash receipts transactions completes the coverage of interim work on the revenue cycle.

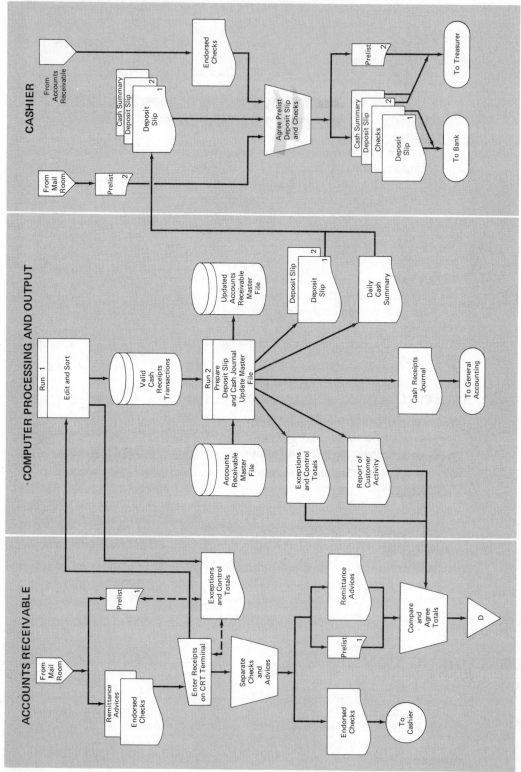

Figure 9-6. EDP SYSTEM FOR CASH RECEIPTS.

TYPE OF TEST: Compliance	PURPOSE: EDP Application Controls
CYCLE: Revenue	CLASS OF TRANSACTIONS: Cash Receipts

A. INPUT CONTROLS ARE PROPERLY FUNCTIONING.

1. Randomly select sample of customer remittance advices and trace to recorded customer remittances.
2. Review, on test basis, the reconciliation of batched remittance input totals with control totals in run 1.
3. Selectively review exception listings of run 1 and investigate items that have remained uncleared for an unreasonably long time.
4. Design and use test data to test program controls of edit routine in run 1.

B. PROCESSING CONTROLS ARE PROPERLY FUNCTIONING.

1. Observe the procedures for reconciling control totals in run 2 and selectively trace control totals to related input controls.
2. Selectively review exception lists of run 2 for unusual items and determine the disposition of rejected data.
3. Use test data to test program controls in run 2.

C. OUTPUT CONTROLS ARE PROPERLY FUNCTIONING.

1. Review reconciliation of output controls of run 2 with other controls.
2. Obtain printout of the two accounts receivable master files of run 2 and selectively reconcile changes in customer balances with remittance advices.

Figure 9-7. AUDIT PROGRAM: COMPLIANCE TESTS OF EDP APPLICATION CONTROLS FOR CASH RECEIPTS TRANSACTIONS.

In many engagements, the auditor places considerable emphasis on the review and compliance testing of control procedures over cash receipts transactions. The extent of reliance on these controls directly affects substantive testing of cash and accounts receivable balances. These tests are explained in Part III of this book.

REVIEW QUESTIONS

9-1 Indicate the scope of cash receipts and sales adjustments transactions in the revenue cycle.

9-2 What are the functions in executing and recording cash receipts transactions and in the custody of related assets?

9-3 Discuss the personnel and sound practices aspects of an internal control environment that relate to cash receipts transactions.

9-4 Indicate the materiality and audit risk of cash receipts transactions in the typical audit engagement.

9-5 Identify the specific internal accounting control objective and appropriate division of duties for each function involved in executing cash receipts transactions.

9-6 What authorizations are required in executing cash receipts transactions?

9-7 Describe the activities of each department that participates in the execution of cash receipts transactions.

9-8 Briefly discuss the use of cash registers, prelists, and daily cash summaries in controlling cash receipts.

9-9 Diagram the flow of data within the cashier's department when a company has both over-the-counter and mail receipts.

9-10 Identify the control procedures that offer reasonable assurance that cash receipts are deposited intact daily.

9-11 How does a lockbox system contribute to internal control over cash receipts?

9-12 What accounting control principles are applicable to the recording of cash receipts transactions?

9-13 Diagram the flow of data within general accounting in recording cash receipts transactions.

9-14 a. Indicate the specific accounting control objectives pertaining to the custody of cash receipts.
   b. Explain the applicability of physical controls and authorization procedures to the custody of cash.

9-15 a. Identify the functions and the related department(s) involved in the execution of sales adjustments transactions.
   b. What types of documentation should exist for sales adjustments?

9-16 a. What is *lapping*?
   b. What internal control principle should prevent this irregularity?
   c. Identify an audit test that is useful in detecting lapping.

9-17 a. List the steps in the audit program for compliance testing of cash receipts transactions that involve a review of documentary evidence.
   b. Indicate the steps in the audit program that involve observation of control procedures.

9-18 Indicate the circumstances in which statistical sampling may be used in compliance tests of (a) cash receipts and (b) sales adjustments transactions.

9-19 a. Identify the control(s) in the computer processing portion of Figure 9-6.
   b. Explain the controls in the cashier and accounts receivable departments.

9-20 a. List the steps in the audit program for determining whether input controls are properly functioning.
   b. How may test data be used in the compliance testing of processing controls?

OBJECTIVE QUESTIONS FROM PROFESSIONAL EXAMINATIONS

Indicate the *best* answer for each of the following multiple-choice questions.

9-21 These questions pertain to internal control over cash receipts transactions.

   1. Which one of the following would the auditor consider to be an incompatible operation if the cashier receives remittances from the mailroom?
      a. The cashier posts the receipts to the accounts receivable subsidiary ledger cards.

    b. The cashier makes the daily deposit at a local bank.

    c. The cashier prepares the daily deposit.

    d. The cashier endorses the checks.

2. The *least* crucial element of internal control over cash is

    a. Separation of cash record keeping from custody of cash.

    b. Preparation of the monthly bank reconciliation.

    c. Batch processing of checks.

    d. Separation of cash receipts from cash disbursements.

3. Which of the following is *not* a universal rule for achieving strong internal control over cash?

    a. Separate the cash handling and record-keeping functions.

    b. Decentralize the receiving of cash as much as possible.

    c. Deposit each day's cash receipts by the end of the day.

    d. Have bank reconciliations performed by employees independent with respect to handling cash.

4. In updating a computerized accounts receivable file, which one of the following would be used as a batch control to verify the accuracy of posting cash remittances?

    a. The sum of net sales.

    b. The sum of cash deposits less discounts taken by customers.

    c. The sum of cash deposits plus discounts taken by customers.

    d. The sum of net sales plus discounts taken by customers.

9-22 These questions relate to the study and evaluation of internal control over cash receipts transactions.

1. From prior experience, a CPA is aware of the fact that cash receipts contain a few unusually large receipts. In using statistical sampling, the CPA's best course of action is to

    a. Eliminate any unusually large receipts that appear in the sample.

    b. Continue to draw new samples until no unusually large receipts appear in the sample.

    c. Stratify the cash receipts population so that the unusually large receipts are reviewed separately.

    d. Increase the sample size to lessen the effect of the unusually large receipts.

2. The questions below appear on an Internal Control Questionnaire. Which question if answered NO would have disclosed that the cashier diverted cash received over the counter from a customer to his own use and wrote off the receivable as a bad debt?

    a. Are aging schedules of accounts receivable prepared periodically and reviewed by a responsible official?

    b. Are journal entries approved by a responsible official?

    c. Are receipts given directly to the cashier by the person who opens the mail?

    d. Are remittance advices, letters, or envelopes that accompany receipts separated and given directly to the accounting department?

3. In performing a review of his client's cash receipts, a CPA uses systematic sampling with a random start. The primary *disadvantage* of systematic sampling is that population items

    a. Must be reordered in a systematic pattern before the sample can be drawn.

    b. May occur in a systematic pattern, thus negating the randomness of the sample.

    c. May occur twice in the sample.

    d. Must be replaced in the population after sampling to permit valid statistical inference.

COMPREHENSIVE QUESTIONS

9-23 Jerome Paper Company engaged you to review its internal control system. Jerome does not prelist cash receipts before they are recorded and has other weaknesses in processing collections of trade receivables, the Company's largest asset. In discussing the matter with the controller, you find he is chiefly interested in economy when he assigns duties to the 15 office personnel. He feels the main considerations are that the work be done by people who are most familiar with it, capable of doing it, and available when it has to be done.

The controller says he has excellent control over trade receivables because receivables are pledged as security for a continually renewable bank loan and the bank sends out positive confirmation requests occasionally, based on a list of pledged receivables furnished by the Company each week. You learn that the bank's internal auditor is satisfied if he gets an acceptable response on 70% of his requests.

Required

a. Explain how prelisting of cash receipts strengthens internal control over cash.
b. Assume that an employee handles cash receipts from trade customers before they are recorded. List the duties which that employee should not do to withhold from him the opportunity to conceal embezzlement of cash receipts.

AICPA

9-24 The internal control questionnaire in Figure 9-3 includes the following questions:

1. Are prelists prepared for mail receipts?
2. Are cash registers used for over-the-counter receipts?
3. Are cash registers read daily and reconciled to cash on hand?
4. Are deposits and daily cash summaries independently reconciled?
5. Is cash deposited intact daily?
6. Is there internal verification of the agreement of daily cash summaries and cash receipts journal entries?
7. Is there separation of duties between the journalizing of cash receipts transactions and posting to the customers' ledger?
8. Is cash stored in safes or vaults prior to deposit?
9. Are periodic independent counts made of cash on hand?

Required

a. Identify the operative internal control objective to which each question relates (i.e., executing, recording, or custody).
b. Identify the function and specific internal accounting control objective to which the question pertains.
c. Indicate the internal accounting control principle that is involved.
d. Identify an error or irregularity that may result from a "no" answer to each question. (Present your answers in tabular form using a separate column for each part.)

9-25 The following control procedures over cash receipts transactions are prescribed by the David Company:

1. Restrictive endorsement of checks on receipt.
2. Daily cash register readings and cash counts by supervisors.

3. Daily cash deposits.
4. Internal verification of deposits and cash summaries by treasurer's office.
5. Internal verification of daily cash receipts journal entries with cash summaries.
6. Prelisting of remittances from customers in mailroom.
7. Segregation of functions between general accounting and accounts receivable accounting.
8. Storing cash in vaults and safes prior to deposit.
9. A supervisor's review of entries for reasonableness of account classifications.

Required

a. Indicate the function and the specific internal accounting control objective served by each procedure.
b. Identify an error or irregularity that may be prevented or detected by the control procedure.
c. Indicate a compliance test that may be performed to determine whether each control procedure is operating as prescribed. (Present your answers in tabular form using a separate column for each part.)

9-26 Assume the following exceptions to prescribed control procedures over cash receipts transactions occurred in the Janz Company:

1. A mail remittance was misappropriated after receipt.
2. A cash sale was not registered.
3. Cash on hand was $5 short of the cash register reading due to errors in making change.
4. Recorded receipts were diverted to personal use before deposit.
5. The cash account was incorrectly footed.
6. A prelist receipt was not journalized.
7. A journalized collection was not posted to the customer's account.
8. Cash was stolen from the cashier's desk.
9. The accompanying checks did not agree with the prelist.
10. An actual deposit did not agree with the deposit slip.

Required

a. Indicate the function associated with each occurrence.
b. Indicate the control procedure(s) that could prevent or detect each occurrence.
c. Identify a compliance test that would determine whether each control indicated in b above is operating as planned. (Present your answers in tabular form using a separate column for each part.)

9-27 Trapan Retailing Inc., has decided to diversify operations by selling through vending machines. Trapan's plans call for the purchase of 312 vending machines that will be situated at 78 different locations, within one city, and the rental of a warehouse to store merchandise. Trapan intends to sell only canned beverages at a standard price.

Management has hired an inventory control clerk to oversee the warehouse, and two truck drivers who will periodically fill the machines with merchandise, and deposit cash collected at a designated bank. Drivers will be required to report to the warehouse daily.

Required

What internal controls should the auditor expect to find in order to assure the integrity of the cash receipts function?

AICPA (adapted)

9-28 The town of Commuter Park operates a private parking lot near the railroad station for the benefit of town residents. The guard on duty issues annual prenumbered parking stickers to residents who submit an application form and show evidence of residency. The sticker is affixed to the auto and allows the resident to park anywhere in the lot for 12 hours if four quarters are placed in the parking meter. Applications are maintained in the guard office at the lot. The guard checks to see that only residents are using the lot and that no resident has parked without paying the required meter fee.

Once a week, the guard on duty, who has a master key for all meters, takes the coins from the meters and places them in a locked steel box. The guard delivers the box to the town storage building where it is opened, and the coins are manually counted by a storage department clerk who records the total cash counted on a "Weekly Cash Report." This report is sent to the town accounting department. The storage department clerk puts the cash in a safe and on the following day the cash is picked up by the town's treasurer who manually counts the cash again, prepares the bank deposit slip, and delivers the deposit to the bank. The deposit slip, authenticated by the bank teller, is sent to the accounting department where it is filed with the "Weekly Cash Report."

Required

Describe weaknesses in the existing system and recommend one or more improvements for each of the weaknesses to strengthen the internal control over the parking lot cash receipts. Organize your answer sheet as follows:

Weakness	Recommended Improvement(s)

AICPA

9-29 You have been asked by the board of trustees of a local church to review its accounting procedures. As a part of this review, you have prepared the following comments relating to the collections made at weekly services and recordkeeping for members' contributions:

1. The church's board of trustees has delegated responsibility for financial management and audit of the financial records to the finance committee. This group prepares the annual budget and approves major disbursements but is not involved in collections or recordkeeping. No audit has been considered necessary in recent years because the same trusted employee has kept church records and served as financial secretary for 15 years.

2. The collection at the weekly service is taken by a team of ushers. The head usher counts the collection in the church following each service. He then places the collection and a notation of the amount counted in the church safe. Next morning

the financial secretary opens the safe and counts the collection again. He withholds about $100 to meet cash expenditures during the coming week and deposits the remainder of the collection intact. In order to facilitate the deposit, members who contribute by check are asked to draw their checks to "cash."

Required

Describe the weaknesses and recommend improvements in procedures for collections made at weekly services. Organize your answer using the following format:

Weakness	Recommended Improvement(s)

AICPA (adapted)

9-30 The flowchart on page 320 depicts the activities relating to the shipping, billing, and collecting processes used by Smallco Lumber Company.

Required

Identify weaknesses in the system of internal accounting control relating to the activities of (a) warehouse clerk, (b) bookkeeper #1, (c) bookkeeper #2, and (d) collection clerk.

AICPA

9-31 In the Hamilton Company, a supplier of goods and services, several departments are involved in the processing of customer complaints and the issuance of any resulting credit memos. Following is a list of the departments:

a. Receiving.

b. Sales.

c. Production.

d. Customer service.

e. Accounts receivable.

Required

Explain briefly the control function each of the departments above performs when processing complaints and issuing credit memos.

IIA

9-32 The Art Appreciation Society operates a museum for the benefit and enjoyment of the community. During hours when the museum is open to the public, two clerks who are positioned at the entrance collect a five-dollar admission fee from each nonmember patron. Members of the Art Appreciation Society are permitted to enter free of charge on presentation of their membership cards.

At the end of the day, one of the clerks delivers the proceeds to the treasurer. The treasurer counts the cash in the presence of the clerk and places it in a safe. Each Friday afternoon, the treasurer and one of the clerks deliver all cash held in the safe to the bank and receive an authenticated deposit slip that provides the basis for the weekly entry in the cash receipts journal.

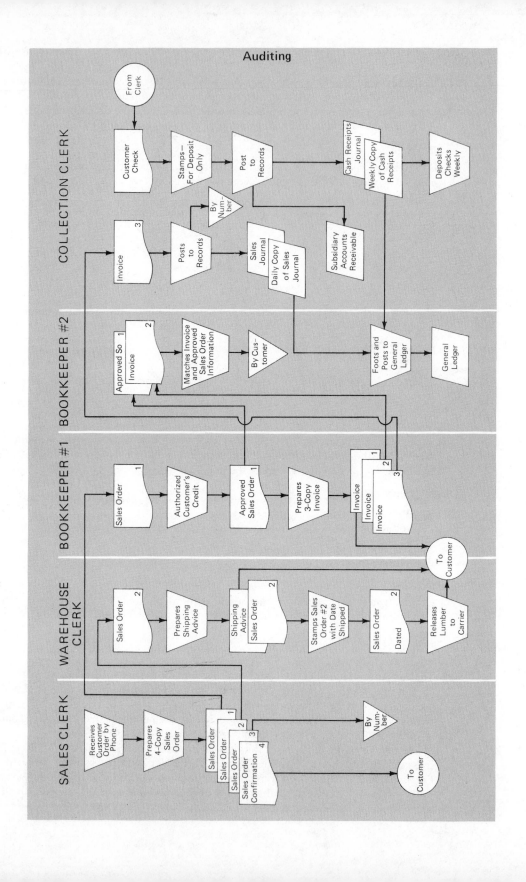

The board of directors of the Art Appreciation Society has identified a need to improve its system of internal control over cash admission fees. The board has determined that the cost of installing turnstiles or sales booths or otherwise altering the physical layout of the museum will greatly exceed any benefits that may be derived. However, the board has agreed that the sale of admission tickets must be an integral part of its improvement efforts.

Smith has been asked by the board of directors of the Art Appreciation Society to review the internal control over cash admission fees and provide suggestions for improvement.

Required

Indicate weaknesses in the existing system of internal control over cash admission fees that Smith should identify and recommend one improvement for each of the weaknesses identified.

Organize the answer as indicated in the following illustrative example:

Weakness	Recommendation
1. There is no basis for establishing the documentation of the number of paying patrons.	1. Prenumbered admission tickets should be issued on payment of the admission fee.

AICPA

9-33 Charting, Inc., a new audit client of yours, processes its sales and cash receipts documents in the following manner:

1. *Payment on Account.* The mail is opened each morning by a mail clerk in the sales department. The mail clerk prepares a remittance advice (showing customer and amount paid) if one is not received. The checks and remittance advices are then forwarded to the sales department supervisor, who reviews each check and forwards the checks and remittance advices to the accounting department supervisor.

The accounting department supervisor, who also functions as credit manager in approving new credit and all credit limits, reviews all checks for payments on past due accounts and then forwards the checks and remittance advices to the accounts receivable clerk, who arranges the advices in alphabetical order. The remittance advices are posted directly to the accounts receivable ledger cards. The checks are endorsed by stamp and totaled. The total is posted to the cash receipts journal. The remittance advices are filed chronologically.

After receiving the cash from the previous day's cash sales, the accounts receivable clerk prepares the daily deposit slip in triplicate. The third copy of the deposit slip is filed by date and the second copy and the original accompany the bank deposit.

2. *Sales.* Sales clerks prepare sales invoices in triplicate. The original and second copy are presented to the cashier. The third copy is retained by the sales clerk in the sales book. When the sale is for cash, the customer pays the sales clerk, who presents the money to the cashier with the invoice copies.

A credit sale is approved by the cashier from an approved credit list after the sales clerk prepares the three-part invoice. After receiving the cash or approving the invoice, the cashier validates the original copy of the sales invoice and gives it to the customer. At the end of each day, the cashier recaps the sales and cash received and forwards the cash and the second copy of all sales invoices to the accounts receivable clerk.

The accounts receivable clerk balances the cash received with cash sales invoices and prepares a daily sales summary. The credit sales invoices are posted to the accounts receivable ledger and then all invoices are sent to the inventory control clerk in the sales department for posting to the inventory control cards. After posting, the inventory control clerk files all invoices numerically. The accounts receivable clerk posts the daily sales summary to the cash receipts journal and sales journal and files the sales summaries by date.

The cash from cash sales is combined with the cash received on account to comprise the daily bank deposit.

3. *Bank Deposits.* The bank validates the deposit slip and returns the second copy to the accounting department, where it is filed by date by the accounts receivable clerk.

Monthly bank statements are reconciled promptly by the accounting department supervisor and filed by date.

Required

You recognize that there are weaknesses in the existing system and believe a chart of information and document flows would be beneficial in evaluating this client's internal control in preparing for your examination of the financial statements. Complete the flowchart for sales and cash receipts of Charting, Inc. by labeling the appropriate symbols and indicating information flows on page 323. The chart is complete as to symbols and document flows.

AICPA

9-34* PML Manufacturing, Inc., a privately held corporation, manufactures office equipment. The cash receipts portion of the revenue cycle is described below:

1. Mail is opened in the mailroom. Remittances (a check and a copy of the invoice) are separated.
2. A control list of checks is prepared and sent to the controller.
3. Checks are sent to the cashier and the remittance advices (copies of the invoices) to the accounts receivable department for posting.
4. Cashier 1 endorses the checks and prepares a duplicate deposit slip.
5. Cashier 2 compares the checks and deposit slips. He investigates any discrepancies and a messenger deposits the cash daily.
6. A messenger takes the deposit to the bank.
7. The messenger returns the validated duplicate deposit slip directly to the controller.
8. The controller reconciles the control list of checks and duplicate deposit slip and resolves any differences.
9. The controller files the reconciliation, duplicate deposit slip, and control list of checks received chronologically.

Required

Prepare a flowchart of the cash receipts procedures.

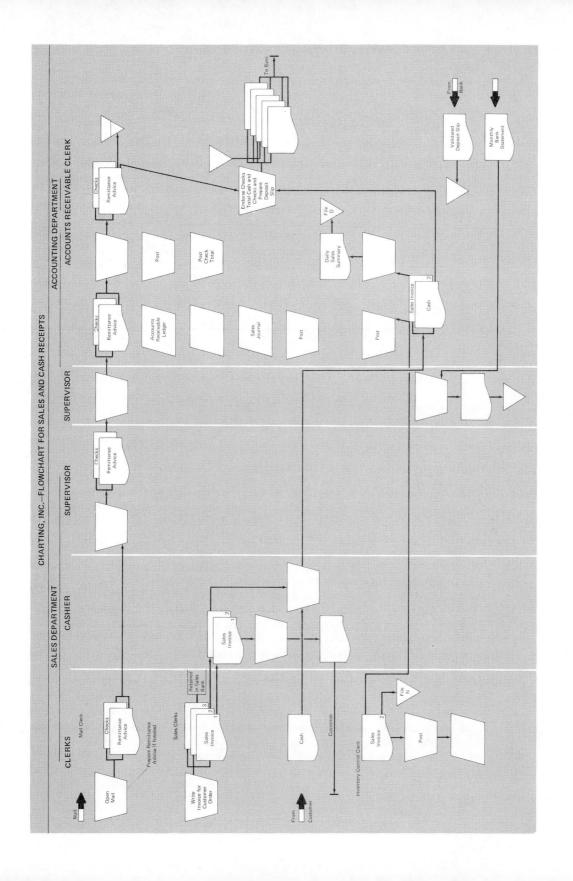

CHARTING, INC.—FLOWCHART FOR SALES AND CASH RECEIPTS

9-35 Your supervisor in the annual audit of the Milan Company asks you to design and execute an attribute sampling plan pertaining to the proper execution of sales returns and allowances. The population consists of 5,200 credit memos numbered consecutively beginning with number 830001.

Required

a. Using the additional information and instructions presented below, prepare a working paper similar to the one illustrated in Figure 7-7 to document the sampling plan.
   1. Identify four attributes to be examined in your sample.
   2. Determine an appropriate sample size for each attribute assuming the following:
      (a) You are willing to accept a 10% risk of overreliance for each attribute.
      (b) You are willing to accept the maximum tolerable rate for each attribute compatible with placing substantial reliance on the internal accounting controls.
      (c) You expect a deviation rate of 2% for the first two attributes listed in (1) above and a rate of 3% for attributes 3 and 4.
   3. Assume that the sample size used and the number of deviations found for each attribute were as follows:

Attribute	Sample Size Used	Number of Deviations
1	75	1
2	75	0
3	100	0
4	100	5

   For each attribute, determine the sample deviation rate, the upper deviation limit, and the allowance for sampling risk.

b. Comment on the results of your sample.

9-36 Until recently, Consolidated Electricity Company employed a batch processing system for recording the receipt of customer payments. The following narrative describes the procedures involved in this system.

The customer's payment and the remittance advice (a punch card) are received in the treasurer's office. An accounts receivable clerk in the treasurer's office keypunches the cash receipt into the remittance advice and forwards the card to the EDP department. The cash receipt is added to a control tape listing and then filed for deposit later in the day. When the deposit slips are received from EDP later in the day (approximately 2:30 PM each day), the cash receipts are removed from the file and deposited with the original deposit slip. The second copy of the deposit slip and the control tape are compared for accuracy before the deposit is made and then filed together.

In the EDP department, the remittance advices received from the treasurer's office are held until 2:00 PM daily. At that time, the customer payments are processed to update the records on magnetic tape and prepare a deposit slip in triplicate. During the update process, data are read, nondestructively, from the master accounts receivable tape, processed, and then recorded on a new master tape. The original and second copy of the deposit slip are forwarded to the treasurer's office. The old master tape (former accounts receivable file), the remittance advices (in customer number order), and the third copy of the deposit slip are stored and filed in a secure place. The updated accounts receivable master tape is maintained in the system for processing the next day.

Consolidated Electricity Company has revised and redesigned its computer system so that it has on-line capabilities. The new cash receipts procedures, described below, are designed to take advantage of the new system.

The customer's payment and remittance advice are received in the treasurer's office as before. A cathode ray tube terminal is located in the treasurer's office to enter the cash receipts. An operator keys in the customer's number and payment from the remittance advice and checks. The cash receipt is entered into the system once the operator has confirmed that the proper account and amount are displayed on the screen. The payment is then processed online against the accounts receivable file maintained on magnetic disk. The cash receipts are filed for deposit later in the day. The remittance advices are filed in the order they are processed; these cards will be kept until the next working day and then destroyed. The computer prints out a deposit slip in duplicate at 2:00 PM for all cash receipts since the last deposit. The deposit slips are forwarded to the treasurer's office. The cash receipts are removed from the file and deposited with the original deposit slip; the duplicate deposit slip is filed for further reference. At the close of business hours (5:00 PM) each day, the EDP department prepares a record of the current day's cash receipts activity on a magnetic tape. This tape is then stored in a secure place in the event of a systems malfunction; after 10 working days, the tape is released for further use.

Required

a. Prepare a systems flowchart for the company's new on-line cash receipts procedures.

b. Have the new cash receipts procedures as designed and implemented by Consolidated Electric Company created any internal and systems control problems for the company? Explain your answer.

CMA (adapted)

CASE STUDY

9-37* Empire Oil Company, an integrated oil company, operates throughout the United States.

Empire's treasury department is made up of two sections. One section handles cash receipts, and one section handles cash disbursements. The internal audit department approves all disbursements and reconciles all bank accounts.

Cash (includes currency, checks, and bank drafts) may be received in one of the following two ways:

1. In the home office directly from the customer.

2. In any one of 45 lockboxes maintained at various depository banks throughout the United States.

With regard to cash received in the home office, the mailroom forwards all mail addressed to the treasury department directly to the cash receipts section of that department unopened. Mail received with no department designation is opened by the mailroom personnel. Any of this mail that contains cash is then forwarded directly to the cash receipts section.

With respect to cash received at lockboxes, daily the respective banks credit Empire's account and forward directly to the cash receipts section of the treasury department all remittance advices and a detailed listing showing the amount and source of the cash.

On receipt of the cash from the mailroom and data from the depository banks, the cash receipts section prepares a four-part form showing the date cash was received, the party from whom received, and the amount. After running an adding machine tape of the amounts and numbering the forms consecutively by day, one copy is furnished to the internal auditors who use it in connection with their bank reconciliations and the original and two copies are sent to the appropriate accounting sections (production and pipeline accounting, refining accounting, marketing accounting, etc.). These sections insert the general ledger account to be credited and return one copy to the cash receipts section. The accounting sections then see that the proper accounts are credited in the subsidiary ledgers (e.g., retail accounts receivable).

The cash receipts section, on receipt of the copies from the accounting sections, combines the copies with the remittance advices to make up the daily cash receipts vouchers. The vouchers are then forwarded to the computer department where the data are keypunched and fed into the system generating the general ledger.

Required

Evaluate the company's internal control over cash receipts transactions and indicate your recommendations for improvement.

Chapter 10

Compliance Tests of Expenditure Cycle: Purchases and Cash Disbursements Transactions

Study Objectives

When you have completed a careful study of this chapter, you should be able to

- Identify the factors that relate to the internal control environment over expenditure cycle transactions.

- Relate the internal accounting control objectives to the expenditure cycle.

- Recognize the applicability of the principles of internal accounting control to purchases and cash disbursements transactions.

- Enumerate errors and irregularities, control procedures, and compliance tests for the two types of expenditure cycle transactions.

- Explain the essential features of audit programs for compliance tests of purchases and cash disbursements transactions.

- Describe the applicability of statistical sampling in testing controls over these two classes of transactions.

- Prepare an audit program for testing EDP controls over purchases and cash disbursements transactions.

This chapter begins with an explanation of the expenditure cycle and the internal control environment and objectives pertaining thereto. Then, consideration is given to internal controls over purchases and cash disbursements transactions and to the study and evaluation of controls over these two classes of transactions. The organization and content of this chapter are similar to the preceding chapters on the revenue cycle.

NATURE OF THE EXPENDITURE CYCLE

The expenditure cycle involves the activities associated with the acquisition of and payment for plant assets, goods and services, and labor. There are three major classes of transactions in this cycle: (1) purchasing, (2) cash disbursements, and (3) payroll. The first two classes of transactions are considered in this chapter; the third is discussed in Chapter 11.

This cycle does not include the acquisition of short- or long-term securities, the redemption of long-term debt, or the reacquisition of a company's capital stock. These transactions are considered to be part of the investing and financing cycles, respectively, and are explained in Chapter 15.

INTERNAL CONTROL ENVIRONMENT

The internal control environment in a company is influenced by the company's organizational structure, personnel, budgets and internal reports, internal auditing, and sound practices. An organization chart for the expenditure cycle is illustrated in Figure 10-1.

Both the competency and the integrity of personnel involved in purchases and cash disbursements transactions are important in creating a good internal accounting control environment. Purchasing agents, for example, may have direct personal interface with suppliers, and they may participate in extensive negotiations of price, quality specifications, and terms. Such personnel are frequently subjected to numerous pressures by solicitous vendors. In such cases, lack of integrity in a purchasing agent could lead to "kickbacks" from suppliers and the placing of purchase orders where the agent may have a vested interest. Similarly, dishonesty among receiving clerks and storeroom employees could lead to irregularities in the processing and safekeeping of goods received. Qualified and trustworthy personnel are equally important in the vouching and payment of purchases and the preparation and payment of the payroll.

Many companies prepare budgets for cash, capital expenditures, and repairs and maintenance expenses. Budget expectations should be compared with actual results periodically. Sound practices include the bonding of authorized check signers, custodians of petty cash funds, and storeroom employees.

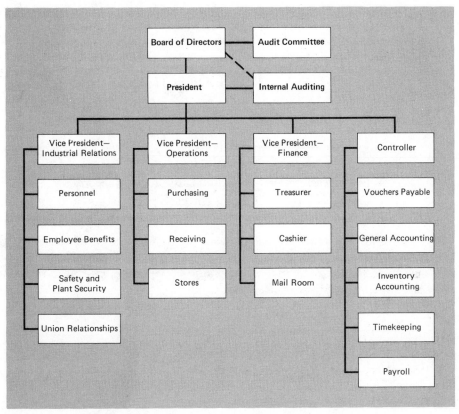

Figure 10-1. ORGANIZATION CHART FOR EXPENDITURE CYCLE.

MATERIALITY AND AUDIT RISK

Transactions in the expenditure cycle often affect more financial statement accounts than the other cycles combined. On the balance sheet, for example, the expenditure cycle impacts on all current assets, except marketable securities and receivables, all plant and intangible assets, and many current liabilities. The income statement effects are similarly pervasive as transactions in this cycle involve major expenses such as salaries and wages, taxes, utilities, advertising, and repairs. Thus, the auditor seeks to keep audit risk that the financial statements as a whole are materially misstated because of expenditure cycle transactions at a very low level.

The volume of transactions in the expenditure cycle is usually high and inventories are vulnerable to loss from obsolesence, deterioration, and theft. As a result, the likelihood of material errors or irregularities is high and the auditor looks to internal control to prevent and detect such occurrences. The auditor's study and evaluation of internal controls in the expenditure cycle provide the basis for assessing the control risk that errors or irregularities may exist in the financial statements from these transactions. This assessment, in turn, determines the amount of detection risk the auditor can accept in performing substantive tests of expenditure cycle balances.

INTERNAL ACCOUNTING CONTROL OBJECTIVES

For the expenditure cycle, the operative objectives of internal accounting control may be stated as follows:

- Expenditure cycle transactions (i.e., purchases, cash disbursements, and payroll) are properly executed.
- Expenditure cycle transactions are properly recorded.
- Custody of assets (i.e., inventories, plant assets, and prepayments) resulting from expenditure cycle transactions is properly maintained.

These three objective will provide the framework for discussing (1) the basic features of accounting control over specific classes of transactions within the expenditure cycle and (2) the study and evaluation of internal control over expenditure cycle transactions.

INTERNAL CONTROL OVER PURCHASES AND CASH DISBURSEMENTS TRANSACTIONS

BASIC CONSIDERATIONS

Purchasing (acquisition) and cash disbursements (payments) transactions involve the acquisition of goods and services from outsiders and the subsequent payment of the liabilities that have been incurred. The acquisition part of this cycle extends beyond the buying of merchandise for resale or raw materials for use in production. Purchasing also includes the methods and procedures that culminate in the acquisition of other assets (property, plant, equipment, intangibles, and prepayments) and myriad day-to-day operating expenses such as advertising, repairs, utilities, and insurance. Cash disbursement transactions, in turn, involve the process of preparing, signing, and mailing checks to vendors and providers of services for the benefits that have been received. Throughout the chapter, emphasis is given to the acquisition of and payment for goods in a company that utilizes a voucher system for cash disbursements.

The following matters are basic to an understanding of purchases and cash disbursements transactions in the expenditure cycle:

Functions

Executing

- Requisitioning goods, other assets, and services.
- Ordering the items requested.
- Receiving the items ordered.

- Storing goods received for inventory.
- Preparing the payment voucher.
- Paying the liability.

Recording

- Journalizing and posting purchases and cash disbursements.
- Updating unpaid voucher file.
- Updating inventory records.

Custody

- Protecting inventory.
- Maintaining correctness of inventory records and cash in bank.

Common Documents

- *Purchase Requisition.* A written request made by an employee to the purchasing department to buy goods and services.
- *Purchase Order.* A written offer by purchasing to another entity to purchase goods and services specified in the order.
- *Receiving Report.* A report prepared on the receipt of goods showing the kinds and quantities of goods received from vendors.
- *Vendor's Invoice.* A form stating the items shipped or services rendered, the amount due, and the payment terms.
- *Voucher.* A form indicating the vendor, amount due, and payment date of purchases received. It is used internally as the authorization for recording and paying the liability.
- *Check.* A formal order to a bank to pay the payee the amount indicated on demand.
- *Remittance Advice.* A memo stating the items being paid by a check.
- *Daily Voucher Summary.* A report of total vouchers processed during the day.
- *Daily Check Summary.* A report showing total checks issued during the day.

Accounting Records

- *Books of Original Entry.* Voucher register, with multiple columns for debit accounts, and check register.
- *General Ledger Accounts.* Cash, accounts payable, inventory, plant assets, manufacturing overhead control, and operating expenses.
- *Subsidiary Ledgers.* Creditors' ledger or unpaid voucher file, plant asset records, perpetual inventory records, and manufacturing overhead records.

File Data

- *Unfilled Purchase Requisition File.* Contains copies of requisitions forwarded to purchasing that are open (unfilled).
- *Unfilled Purchase Order File.* Holds open purchase orders.

- *Approved Vendor File.* Contains a list of vendors with whom orders may be placed.
- *Receiving Report File.* Contains copies of receiving reports issued.
- *Unpaid Voucher File.* Contains approved vouchers filed by date payment is due.
- *Paid Voucher File.* Holds vouchers that have been paid.

PURCHASES AND CASH DISBURSEMENTS TRANSACTIONS ARE PROPERLY EXECUTED

These transactions in the expenditure cycle are properly executed when they are authorized by management and executed in accordance with authorized terms. The execution of these two classes of transactions involves the following functions and specific accounting control objectives.

Function	Specific Accounting Control Objective
1. Requisitioning goods, other assets, and services	Requisitions are initiated and approved by authorized individuals.
2. Ordering items requested	Purchase orders are properly executed as to price, quantity, and quality.
3. Receiving items ordered	Goods received are counted, inspected, and agreed to purchase orders.
4. Storing goods received for inventory	Goods received are added to inventory and properly safeguarded and accounted for.
5. Preparing the payment voucher	Vouchers are for goods and services actually received and are correct as to amount, account classification, and payee.
6. Paying the liability	Checks are supported by approved vouchers, are correct as to amount and payee, and are signed by authorized signers.

The internal control principles applicable to these functions are explained below.

Authorization Procedures

Authorization is required at a number of control points: (1) initiating the request, (2) placing the order, (3) receiving the goods, and (4) paying the vendor. Most companies permit general authorizations for regular operating purposes. Such authorizations usually extend to purchases of inventory and raw materials when reorder points are reached, to normal repair and maintenance work, and to similar items. In contrast, company policy frequently requires specific authorization for capital expenditures and lease contracts. Operating within these policies, designated individuals are permitted to initiate purchase requests. Requisitions may be manually or electronically prepared. Each request should be signed by a supervisor who has budgetary responsibility for the category of expenditure.

The purchasing department has the authority to place (or issue) purchase orders for goods and services that have been requested. Before placing an order, purchasing should ascertain the best source of supply and for major items, it should obtain competitive bids. A valid purchase order represents the authorization to receive incoming goods and services.

Authorization for payment of the goods and services originates in the vouchers payable department through the preparation of a voucher and culminates in the signing of a check by authorized signers.

Segregation of Functions

The major functions involved in executing purchases and cash disbursements transactions should be assigned to different departments and individuals. Based on the organization chart in Figure 10-1, an appropriate segregation of functions is shown at the bottom of this page. Under this plan, the work of one employee provides a check on the accuracy of the work of another. For example, the storeroom receipt for goods received confirms the receiving department's representation that the goods were received.

Function	Department	Related Activities
1. Requisitioning goods, other assets, and services	Stores, Maintenance, Plant, etc.	Initiate and approve purchase requisitions.
2. Ordering the items requested	Purchasing	Prepare, approve, and issue purchase orders; perform follow-up on unfilled orders.
3. Receiving the items ordered	Receiving	Receive; count, and inspect goods and other assets received, deliver items received to initiating department; obtain signed receipt from initiator; prepare receiving reports.
4. Storing goods received for inventory	Stores	Maintain custody of goods received for stock, acknowledge receipt of goods ordered.
5. Preparing the payment voucher	Vouchers Payable	Prepare vouchers for payment; prepare daily voucher summary; maintain unpaid voucher file.
6. Paying the liability	Treasurer	Prepare, sign, and mail checks to vendors; prepare daily check summary; maintain paid voucher file.

Documentation Procedures

Documentation is necessary for each of the major steps in the purchasing and cash disbursements functions. The key documents in ordering goods and services are the purchase requisition and the purchase order.

The requisition should specify the item(s) desired and be approved by a supervisor in the originating department. Because requisitions may originate in any department, they are rarely prenumbered. Purchase orders are prepared in the purchasing department. The orders should contain a precise description of the goods and services desired, quantities, price, and vendor name and address. Purchase orders should be prenumbered and signed by an authorized purchasing agent. The purchase order is sent to the vendor, and copies are distributed internally to receiving, vouchers payable, and the department that made the request. On the receiving department copy, the quantity ordered is generally obliterated so that receiving clerks will make careful counts of the goods received.

Prenumbered receiving reports provide the documentation for goods and services received. In many companies, a purchase order must be on file before goods can be accepted. Receiving department personnel are expected to indicate the quantity and description of the goods and vendor name and address on the receiving report. On delivery of the goods to the initiating department, receiving clerks should obtain a signed receipt. In some cases, receipt may be indicated by initialing the receiving report. The key documents in recording and paying the liability are the voucher and the check.

Voucher. Vouchers are prepared in the vouchers payable department. The preparation of a voucher involves the following control procedures:

- Establish the agreement of the vendor's invoice with the receiving report and purchase order.
- Determine the mathematical accuracy of the vendor's invoice.
- Indicate on the documents (or voucher) that the preceding verification steps have been performed.
- Prepare the voucher in duplicate and attach supporting documents (purchase order, receiving report, and vendor's invoice).
- Verify the mathematical accuracy of each voucher.
- Approve the voucher for payment by having an authorized person sign the voucher.

Other kinds of supporting documentation may be required when the voucher relates to services and other assets. In no case, however, should a voucher be approved without appropriate documentation. One copy of the voucher with supporting documentation attached is filed in an unpaid voucher file, and a copy is sent to accounting for recording.

Check.   The issuance of checks is the responsibility of the treasurer's office. The control procedures for issuing checks include the following:

- The bank must be notified of the names of individuals authorized to sign checks, and samples of their signatures must be filed with the bank.
- Company imprinted and prenumbered checks should be used.
- Check-protection devices should be utilized in printing the amount of the check.
- Each check should be supported by an approved voucher and be accompanied by a remittance advice.
- Authorized check signers should review all supporting documentation before signing a check.
- Supporting documentation should be stamped, perforated, or otherwise mutilated after payment.
- The check signer, or last check signer when two signatures are required, should control the mailing of the check and remittance advice.
- No checks should be issued to "cash" or "bearer."

Daily summaries should be prepared of vouchers and checks for use in accounting. A flowchart for the execution of these two classes of transactions in the expenditure cycle is illustrated in Figure 10-2 on page 337.

Physical Controls and Independent Internal Verification

One application of physical controls is enclosed and locked storerooms. Other applications include scales for weighing bulk materials and protective check-writing equipment in issuing checks.

Independent internal verification occurs when a second voucher clerk validates the accuracy and completeness of the voucher before it is approved by a supervisor. A similar review is sometimes required in the treasurer's department before the voucher is sent to the check signers.

PURCHASES AND CASH DISBURSEMENTS TRANSACTIONS ARE PROPERLY RECORDED

The functions and the specific accounting control objectives pertaining to the recording of these transactions are as follows:

Function	Department	Specific Accounting Control Objective
1. Journalizing and posting purchases and cash disbursements transactions	General Accounting	Purchases and cash disbursements are correctly journalized as to amount, account classification, and accounting period.

Function	Department	Specific Accounting Control Objective
2. Updating unpaid voucher file	Vouchers Payable	Unpaid vouchers are properly filed in an unpaid voucher file.
3. Updating inventory records	Inventory Accounting	Purchases are promptly and correctly posted to perpetual inventory records.

The internal control principles applicable to these functions are explained below.

Segregation of Functions

Accounting personnel who record these transactions should not participate in the execution of the transactions. Moreover, within accounting, individuals who journalize vouchers should not maintain the unpaid voucher file.

Accounting Records and Procedures

The primary source documents for the accounting entries are the approved voucher and the disbursement check. In journalizing vouchers, accounting personnel should review the reasonableness of the account classifications and trace any unusual items to the chart of accounts. Accounting procedures include the posting of purchases to inventory records directly from the voucher and the filing of the vouchers in an unpaid (tickler) voucher file.

The check register entries should agree with the data on the check. Special care should be exercised in recording checks issued near the end of the accounting period to assure that the checks are entered in the proper period. Checks do not represent disbursements until they are either mailed or delivered to the payee. A flowchart for the recording of purchases and cash disbursements transactions is shown in Figure 10-3 on page 338.

Independent Internal Verification

Accounting receives daily summaries of vouchers and checks. As shown in Figure 10-3, these totals should be independently compared with the corresponding totals of the voucher and check registers, respectively. Accounting personnel are expected to also verify the numerical sequencing of the entries. In some companies, a supervisor reviews the account classifications in the voucher register for reasonableness. In addition, there should be independent reconciliations of accounts payable and inventory control accounts with their subsidiary records.

CUSTODY OF ASSETS IS PROPERLY MAINTAINED

Inventory, plant assets, and cash in bank are among the major types of assets associated with the expenditure cycle. Consideration here is focused on in-

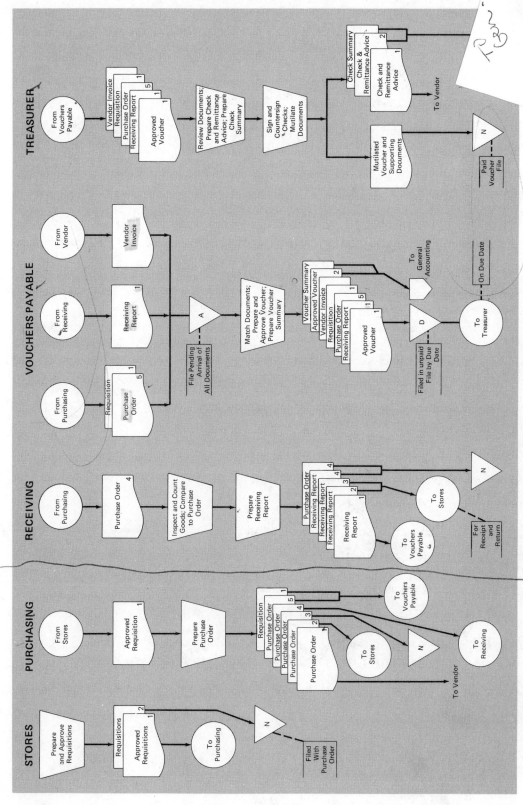

Figure 10-2. MANUAL SYSTEM FOR EXECUTING PURCHASES AND CASH DISBURSEMENTS TRANSACTIONS.

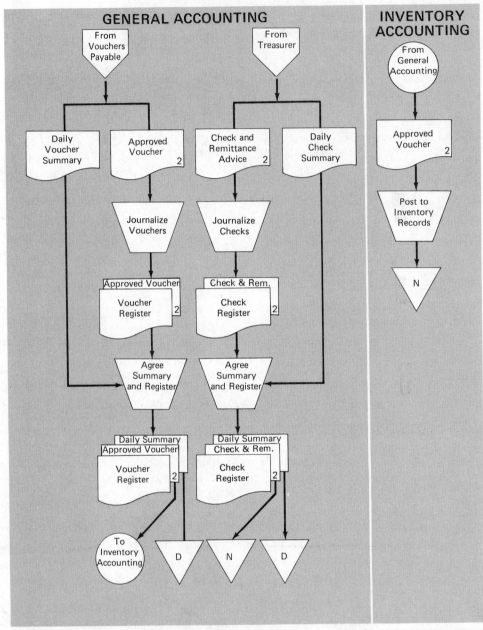

Figure 10-3. MANUAL SYSTEM FOR RECORDING PURCHASES AND CASH DISBURSEMENTS TRANSACTIONS.

ventories and cash in bank. The following functions and internal control objectives are applicable to the safeguarding of these assets.

Function	Department	Specific Accounting Control Objective
1. Protecting inventory	Stores	Access to inventory is restricted to authorized personnel.
2. Maintaining correctness of inventory records	Inventory Accounting	Recorded balances are independently compared with existing assets at reasonable intervals.
3. Maintaining correctness of cash in bank	General Accounting	Recorded balances are periodically independently reconciled with bank balances.

The internal control principles pertaining to these functions are explained below.

Physical Controls and Authorization Procedures

Physical controls over inventory include locked storerooms and warehouses. Access to storage areas should be restricted to authorized personnel.

Independent Internal Verification and Segregation of Functions

Periodically, there should be an independent comparison of recorded inventory balances with existing assets. This comparison is often made on a cycle basis where designated segments are counted or inventoried on a rotating basis. Similarly, monthly bank reconciliations should be made by personnel not otherwise involved with signing or recording of checks.

STUDY AND EVALUATION OF INTERNAL CONTROL

The auditor's methodology for making a study and evaluation of controls over purchases and cash disbursements transactions involves the same steps and decision paths followed for other major classes of transactions.

REVIEW OF PURCHASES AND CASH DISBURSEMENTS SYSTEMS

As previously explained, the review consists of two phases: (1) preliminary and (2) completion. In this case, the preliminary review pertains to the internal control environment for expenditure cycle transactions and the flow of purchases and cash disbursements transactions through the accounting system. The completion phase relates to the client's prescribed internal accounting controls over these two classes of transactions. The essential steps in the completion phase of the review are described below.

Gathering Information

In obtaining information about prescribed controls over purchases and cash disbursements transactions, the auditor uses inquiry, observation, and review of documentation. Questionnaires for these transactions are shown in Figures 10-4 and 10-5. It will be recalled that the questions relate to specific control procedures considered by the auditor to be necessary for effective control. As in the preceding two chapters, each question is referenced to a specific function. The auditor's understanding of prescribed controls should be docu-

---

CYCLE: Expenditure   **CLASS OF TRANSACTIONS: Purchases**

EXECUTING	Yes	No

1. Is an approved purchase requisition required for each purchase? (E1)
2. Is an authorized purchase order required for each purchase? (E2)
3. Are prenumbered purchase orders used and accounted for? (E2)
4. Is a purchase order required before receiving can accept a shipment? (E3)
5. Are goods counted, inspected, and compared with purchase order on receipt? (E3)
6. Are prenumbered receiving reports used, accounted for, and signed by a receiving clerk? (E3)
7. Is a signed receipt obtained from storeroom on delivery of goods by receiving? (E4)
8. Are purchase orders, receiving reports, and vendors' invoices matched in preparing vouchers? (E5)
9. Are vouchers internally verified for accuracy? (E5)
10. Are vouchers approved by authorized personnel? (E5)
11. Are daily voucher summaries prepared and agreed to vouchers issued? (E5)

RECORDING

1. Are all issued vouchers accounted for in journalizing? (R1)
2. Are voucher register entries reviewed for reasonableness? (R1)
3. Are unpaid voucher file and perpetual inventory records independently maintained? (R2, R3)
4. Are there periodic independent reconciliations of control accounts and subsidiary records? (R2, R3)

CUSTODY

1. Are goods stored in locked areas with restricted access? (C1)
2. Are there periodic independent comparisons of inventory records with goods on hand? (C2)

Figure 10-4. INTERNAL CONTROL QUESTIONNAIRE: PURCHASES TRANSACTIONS.

CYCLE: Expenditure	CLASS OF TRANSACTIONS: Cash Disbursements		
EXECUTING*		Yes	No

EXECUTING*

1. Are all disbursements (except for petty cash) made by check?
2. Are imprinted and prenumbered checks used?
3. Is a check-protection device used in printing the check amount?
4. Is each check supported by an approved voucher?
5. Is supporting documentation mutilated after payment?
6. Are two signatures required on each check?
7. Does last check signer mail the check and remittance advice?
8. Are there prohibitions against issuing checks to cash or bearer?
9. Is the signing of blank checks prohibited?
10. Is a daily summary of checks prepared and agreed to checks issued?

RECORDING

1. Are accounting personnel prohibited from signing checks? (R1)
2. Are daily summaries of checks compared with check register totals? (R1)
3. Are checks recorded in numerical sequence? (R1)

CUSTODY

1. Are there periodic independent reconciliations of bank accounts? (C3)

*All questions pertain to function E6, paying the liability.

Figure 10-5. INTERNAL CONTROL QUESTIONNAIRE: CASH DISBURSEMENTS TRANSACTI

mented in the working papers in the form of flowcharts, narrative memoranda, and answers to questionnaires.

Making the Preliminary Evaluations

The primary purpose of the preliminary evaluations of purchases and cash disbursements transactions is to identify control procedures that can be relied on in making substantive tests of related balances, assuming satisfactory compliance. The evaluations are made by (1) considering the errors and irregularities that could occur in performing each function, (2) identifying the controls necessary to prevent or detect the occurrences, and (3) determining whether the necessary controls are prescribed by the client. Representative listings of errors and irregularities and necessary control procedures for each of these classes of transactions are shown in Figures 10-6 (page 342) and 10-7 (page 343). Columns 2 and 3 of each form are based on generalized knowledge about these transactions, adapted as necessary by the auditor to the specific client. Information concerning the prescribed controls over purchases and cash disbursements is obtained from the information gathering step of the review.

Function	Possible Errors and Irregularities	Necessary Control Procedures	Possible Compliance Tests
EXECUTING			
Requisitioning	Excess quantities of goods may be ordered.	Review of requisitions for reasonableness by supervisor.	Examine evidence of supervisor approval.
Ordering	Purchases may be for unauthorized purposes.	Approved purchase requisition for each purchase order.	Examine purchase order for supporting requisition.
Receiving	Receiving reports may be prepared for goods that were not ordered.	Purchase order for each shipment.	Examine receiving report for accompanying purchase order.
	Goods received may be incorrectly counted.	Storeroom count and signed receipt for goods received.	Examine storeroom receipt for evidence of count and signature.
Storing	Goods received may not be as ordered.	Comparison of goods received with goods requisitioned.	Review evidence of storeroom verification.
Preparing the voucher	Vouchers may be prepared for goods that were unauthorized or not received.	Matching purchase order, receiving report, and vendor's invoice for each voucher.	Review voucher for evidence of supporting documents and agreement with voucher. Examine voucher for authorized signature.
	Vouchers may be incorrect as to payee and amount.	Internal verification of voucher accuracy.	Examine evidence of verification.
RECORDING			
Journalizing and posting purchases transactions	Vouchers may be incorrectly classified.	Supervisory review of entries for reasonableness.	Inquire of supervisor concerning findings.
	Vouchers may not be recorded.	Internal verification of entries with daily voucher summary.	Review evidence of internal verification.
Updating unpaid voucher file	A voucher may not be filed.	Periodic reconciliation of accounts payable with unpaid vouchers.	Review evidence of reconciliation.
Updating inventory records	A purchase may not be posted to inventory records.	Periodic reconciliation of control and subsidiary records.	Review evidence of reconciliation.
CUSTODY			
Protecting inventory	Inventory may be stolen.	Locked storerooms.	Observe storage security.
Maintaining correctness of inventory records	A purchase may be posted to the wrong inventory card.	Periodic independent comparisons of records with goods on hand.	Review evidence of reconciliation, observe count.

Figure 10-6. PRELIMINARY EVALUATION CONSIDERATIONS: PURCHASES TRANSACTIONS.

Function	Possible Errors and Irregularities	Necessary Control Procedures	Possible Compliance Tests
EXECUTING			
Paying the liability (review of documentation)	Voucher may be incomplete or lack supervisory approval.	Review voucher for completeness and approval.	Examine voucher for evidence of approval.
	A voucher may be paid twice.	Mutilation of voucher on payment.	Examine "paid" vouchers for cancellation.
Paying the liability (preparing and signing checks)	Checks may be incorrect as to payee and amount.	Internal verification of checks with supporting voucher.	Examine evidence of verification.
Paying the liability (distributing checks)	Checks may be diverted to unauthorized payees.	No checks payable to cash or bearer.	Review checks for names of payees.
RECORDING			
Journalizing and posting cash disbursements	A check may not be recorded.	Accounting for all prenumbered checks in journalizing.	Review evidence of verification.
CUSTODY			
Maintaining correctness of cash in bank	A mathematical error may be made in computing the bank balance.	Periodic independent bank reconciliations.	Review evidence of reconciliation.

Figure 10-7. PRELIMINARY EVALUATION CONSIDERATIONS: CASH DISBURSEMENTS TRANSACTIONS.

From a comparison of necessary and prescribed controls, the auditor makes a preliminary evaluation of the controls expected to be relied on. If a necessary control is not prescribed, or a prescribed control does not appear adequate to prevent or detect the error or irregularity, the auditor considers the effect of the weakness on the remainder of the audit. He may, for example, look for compensating controls or proceed directly to the design of expanded substantive tests. The auditor's preliminary evaluations of the prescribed control procedures for each of these two classes of transactions should be documented in the working papers.

COMPLIANCE TESTS OF CONTROLS TO BE RELIED ON

Using the possible compliance tests shown in Figures 10-6 and 10-7, the auditor prepares the audit programs for determining whether the controls to be relied on are operating as planned. Illustrative audit programs for purchases and cash disbursements transactions are shown in Figures 10-8 and 10-9 (pages 344 and 345). Note that for controls that leave a transaction trail of performance, the sampling unit for purchases is the voucher, and the sampling unit for cash disbursements is the "paid" check. Alternatively, the purchase order or the receiving report could be used as the sampling unit for purchases. Both programs also include observation, inquiry, and reperformance.

Dual Purpose Testing

As previously explained, the auditor may decide to perform *dual purpose tests* during interim work. Thus, while the samples of vouchers and checks are available for use, the auditor may perform substantive tests of the details of the accounting treatment of the transactions. It will be recalled that the purpose of substantive tests of details is to ascertain the correctness of the accounts or

---

TYPE OF TESTING: Compliance   **PURPOSE: Study and Evaluation of Internal Control**
CYCLE: Expenditure   **CLASS OF TRANSACTIONS: Purchases**

A. CONTROLS IN EXECUTING PURCHASES TRANSACTIONS ARE OPERATING AS PLANNED.

1. Examine sample of vouchers for the year to date for evidence of
   - Valid purchase requisition (E1), purchase order (E2), and receiving report (E3).
   - Storeroom verification of goods received (E3, E4).
   - Verification of agreement with supporting documentation (E5).
   - Verification of mathematical accuracy of the voucher (E5).
   - Authorized approval signature (E5).
2. Observe segregation of duties in performing control procedures.
3. Inquire of personnel about their performance of control procedures.
4. Reperform the verification procedures in (1) above on some vouchers.

B. CONTROLS IN RECORDING PURCHASES TRANSACTIONS ARE OPERATING AS PLANNED.

1. Examine a sample of daily voucher summaries for verification with daily voucher register entries (R1).
2. Observe segregation of functions between general ledger accounting and subsidiary ledger accounting (R2, R3).
3. Examine evidence of periodic agreement of control accounts with subsidiary records (R2, R3).

C. CONTROLS OVER THE CUSTODY OF INVENTORY ARE OPERATING AS PLANNED.

1. Observe storage of inventory and means for restricting access to storeroom (C1)
2. Review evidence of periodic inventory counts and reconciliations with inventory records. (C2)

Figure 10-8. AUDIT PROGRAM: COMPLIANCE TESTS OF PURCHASES TRANSACTIONS.

TYPE OF TESTING: Compliance   PURPOSE: Study and Evaluation of Internal Control
CYCLE: Expenditure   CLASS OF TRANSACTIONS: Cash Disbursements

A. CONTROLS IN EXECUTING CASH DISBURSEMENTS TRANSACTIONS ARE OPERATING AS PLANNED.*

1. Examine sample of "paid" checks for the year to date for evidence of
   - Supporting approved voucher.
   - Verification of agreement of check with voucher.
   - Cancellation of voucher on payment.
   - Signatures of authorized check signers.

2. Observe segregation of duties between voucher preparation and mailing of checks.
3. Inquire of personnel about their performance of control procedures.
4. Reperform the control procedures in (1) above on some checks.

B. CONTROLS IN RECORDING CASH DISBURSEMENTS TRANSACTIONS ARE OPERATING AS PLANNED.

1. Examine a sample of daily check summaries for evidence of verification with daily check register entries. (R1)
2. Observe segregation of functions between accounting and treasurer's department. (R1)
3. Inspect check register for numerical sequencing of checks. (R1)

C. CONTROLS OVER THE CUSTODY OF CASH IN BANK ARE OPERATING AS PLANNED.

1. Examine evidence of periodic bank reconciliations. (C1)

*All items pertain to function E6.

Figure 10-9. AUDIT PROGRAM: COMPLIANCE TESTS OF CASH DISBURSEMENTS TRANSACTIONS.

conversely the existence of any monetary errors in the accounts. The tests for purchases and cash disbursements transactions may consist of the following:

- Compare the amount, date, payee, and account classification on the voucher with the corresponding data in the related voucher register entry for accuracy
- Compare the detailed data on the check with the details of the related check register entry for accuracy.

In addition, the auditor notes the monetary errors found in reperforming control procedures in step A4 of each audit program.

From these tests, the auditor can estimate the magnitude of monetary errors in the processing of purchases and cash disbursements transactions.

FINAL EVALUATION OF THE CONTROLS

The final evaluation of the controls is based on the auditor's preliminary evaluation and the results from compliance testing of controls pertaining to these two classes of transactions. In analyzing the results, the auditor considers both the number of deviations from prescribed control procedures and the causes of the deviations. The auditor may express his reliance on the controls in terms of whether the risk of errors and irregularities in the processing of purchases and cash disbursements transactions is low, moderate, or high. The auditor then determines the effects of his evaluations of specific control procedures over these transactions on the nature, timing, and extent of substantive tests. For example, if there is moderate risk of errors in preparing vouchers, the auditor will perform more substantive tests on accounts payable balances than when the risk of such errors is low. Substantive tests of expenditure cycle balances are explained in Part III of this text.

STATISTICAL SAMPLING IN COMPLIANCE TESTING

Statistical sampling may be utilized in performing compliance tests of purchases and cash disbursements transactions. Each of the major steps in the design and implementation of an attribute sampling plan for purchase transactions for the Kemp Company is illustrated below.

DESIGN OF THE SAMPLING PLAN

In attribute sampling, the objectives of the test are usually expressed in terms of the proper execution or recording of transactions. In designing the sample, tests are made of the functions that relate to the overall objective of the plan. For this case study, the objective is execution of purchases transactions. The test includes the functions of ordering, receiving, and preparing the voucher. The sampling unit is the prenumbered voucher and the population consists of 18,000 vouchers. These elements of the sampling plan, together with the attributes corresponding to the controls the auditor wishes to test for reliance, are shown in the sample design section of the working paper in Figure 10-10.

EVALUATING THE RESULTS

In the concluding phase of the sampling plan, the auditor makes both a quantitative and qualitative assessment of the sample results. An upper deviation limit is determined for each attribute using the tables in Chapter 7 and entered in column 9. The allowance for sampling risk (column 9–column 8) may be calculated and entered in column 10.

Comparison of columns 9 and 3 reveals that the auditor's objective was met for each attribute. In each case, the upper deviation limit is less than the tolerable rate. Thus, the auditor can conclude that at the specified risk of overreliance, the true but unknown population deviation rate does not exceed the upper deviation limit.

KEMP COMPANY
ATTRIBUTE SAMPLE -- PURCHASES TRANSACTIONS
12/31/X1

W/P REF: X-2
PREPARED BY: CJH DATE 8/2/X1
REVIEWED BY: RCP DATE 8/4/X1

SAMPLE DESIGN   SAMPLE RESULTS

OBJECTIVE:	TO DETERMINE WHETHER CONTROLS OVER EXECUTION OF PURCHASE TRANSACTIONS ARE APPLIED AS PRESCRIBED

SAMPLING UNIT AND POPULATION: VOUCHERS; POPULATION = 18000 VOUCHERS NUMBERED 66245 - 84244

SELECTION METHOD: SIMPLE RANDOM USING RANDOM NUMBER TABLE

(1)		(2)	(3)	(4)	(5)		(6)	(7)	(8)	(9)	(10)	(11)
ATTRIBUTES		RISK OF OVERRE-LIANCE	TOLER-ABLE DEVIA-TION RATE	EXPTD. POP. DEVIA-TION RATE	SAMPLE SIZE PER TABLE		SAMPLE SIZE USED	NUMBER OF DEVIA-TIONS	SAMPLE DEVIA-TION RATE	UPPER DEVIA-TION LIMIT	ALLOW-ANCE FOR SAMPLING RISK	TEST UDL < TDR
NO.	DESCRIPTION											
1	APPROVED PURCHASE ORDER, RECEIVING REPORT, AND VENDOR'S INVOICE FOR EACH VOUCHER	5	5	1	93		100	1	1.0	4.7	3.7	YES
2	VERIFICATION OF AGREEMENT OF INVOICE WITH SUPPORTING DOCUMENTATION	5	7	2	88		90	1	1.1	5.2	4.1	YES
3	VERIFICATION OF MATHEMATICAL ACCURACY OF INVOICE	5	7	2	88		90	1	1.1	5.2	4.1	YES
4	SUPERVISORY APPROVAL OF VOUCHER	5	5	1	93		100	0	0.0	3.0	3.0	YES
5												
6												
7												
8												

CONCLUSION: MANAGEMENT COMMUNICATION: None.

All statistical objectives were met. All deviations were minor errors. Controls can be relied on.

Figure 10-10. STATISTICAL SAMPLING PLAN WORKING PAPER: COMPLIANCE TESTS OF PURCHASES TRANSACTIONS.

Further, qualitative assessment of the nature and causes of the deviations produced no evidence of any irregularities or other serious problems. Thus, the auditor feels justified in concluding that the controls that were tested may be relied on for the purpose of determining substantive tests of related account balances.

ELECTRONIC DATA PROCESSING

EDP may be utilized in executing and recording purchases and cash disbursements transactions. A case study is presented below together with an explanation of the methodology for making tests of controls in the system.

DESCRIPTION OF THE PURCHASES AND CASH DISBURSEMENTS SYSTEM

In Huran Inc., the batch entry/batch processing method is used to process approved vouchers, disbursement checks, and related output. Input to the system is in the form of magnetic tape, and file data also are maintained on this medium. A flowchart of the major features of the system is presented in Figure 10-11.

As shown in the flowchart, data control verifies and logs the control totals received from vouchers payable. It then sends the vouchers and transmittal form to data entry where the vouchers are keypunched onto tape and verified. Next, the purchases transaction tape is forwarded to computer processing where it is used in two computer runs.

Run 1. This run involves editing the data for reasonableness and completeness, and balancing the data. From this run, a valid tape of purchases transactions results and a printout is made of exceptions and control totals.

Run 2. As shown in Figure 10-11, this run involves the processing of the valid purchases transaction tape with the tapes of the accounts payable and inventory master files. The outputs from this run consist of updated master file tapes and printed reports of exceptions and control totals and the voucher register.

The processing of checks also involves two computer runs.

Run 3. In this run, the accounts payable master file is read to identify the vouchers due for payment and produce a vouchers payment tape.

Run 4. As shown in the flowchart, this run involves the processing of the vouchers payment tape to prepare the checks and check register and update the accounts payable master file.

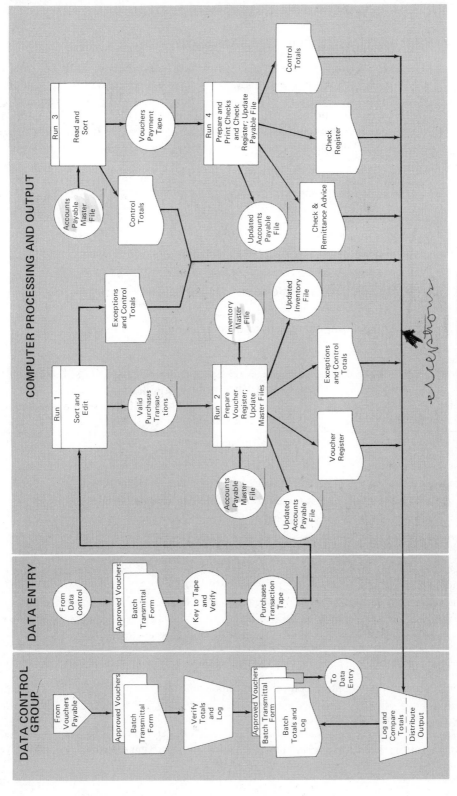

Figure 10-11. EDP SYSTEM FOR PURCHASES AND CASH DISBURSEMENTS TRANSACTIONS.

STUDY AND EVALUATION OF EDP CONTROLS

The methodology for making a study and evaluation of EDP controls over purchases transactions is similar to the procedures described in Chapters 8 and 9. Both general and application controls should be reviewed and compliance tests should be performed on all EDP controls on which reliance is to be placed in making substantive tests of resulting balances. An audit program for testing EDP application controls in this case study is shown in Figure 10-12.

The program provides for the use of test data in testing controls in the edit program of run 1 and the program logic in run 2. Invalid test data for run 1 may include:

1

- Missing or invalid vendor number.
- Missing or invalid purchases distribution code number.
- Missing dollar amount.
- Missing payment due date.
- Missing payment terms.
- Alphabetical characters in numerical field.

TYPE OF TESTING: Compliance
CYCLE: Expenditure

PURPOSE: EDP Application Controls
CLASS OF TRANSACTIONS: Purchases and Cash Disbursements

A. INPUT CONTROLS ARE PROPERLY FUNCTIONING.

1. Review, on test basis, reconciliation of batch totals in data control with control totals in run 1.
2. Selectively review exception listing of run 1 and investigate uncleared items.
3. Prepare and use test data to test program controls in edit routine of run 1.
4. Select sample of entries in voucher register and vouch entries to source documents.

B. PROCESSING CONTROLS ARE PROPERLY FUNCTIONING.

1. Observe reconciling procedures over control data in runs 2–4 and selectively trace control totals to input controls.
2. Review error listings of run 2 and investigate unusual items.
3. Use test deck data to test program of run 2.
4. Use generalized audit software to test accounts payable and inventory master files.

C. OUTPUT CONTROLS ARE PROPERLY FUNCTIONING.

1. Review reconciliation of output controls with input controls.
2. On a test basis, obtain printouts of master files used in runs 2 and 4 and use source documents to reconcile the two sets of file data.

Figure 10-12. AUDIT PROGRAM: COMPLIANCE TESTS OF EDP APPLICATION CONTROLS FOR PURCHASES AND CASH DISBURSEMENTS TRANSACTIONS.

Both valid and invalid data may be used in testing the controls in run 2. The latter may consist of a purchase for a negative amount, a purchase with invalid pricing data, and a purchase for a zero amount.

Generalized audit software applications to the master files parallel those described in Chapter 8 for the accounts receivable master file. Thus, software can be used to randomly select a sample of inventory or vendor accounts.

From evidence obtained in testing the system, the auditor proceeds to evaluate the EDP controls and determine the extent to which substantive tests of inventory and accounts payable balances are to be restricted.

CONCLUDING COMMENTS

An entity's expenditure cycle pertains to the acquisition and payment of plant assets, goods and services, and labor. The scope of this chapter has been limited to purchases and cash disbursements transactions. Each of the objectives and principles of internal control is applicable to these two classes of transactions. In performing compliance tests of transactions in a manual processing system, the auditor relies primarily on vouchers and paid checks. Compliance tests of the system may also involve statistical sampling and EDP.

Further attention is given to the expenditure cycle in the next chapter, where controls over payroll transactions are explained and illustrated.

REVIEW QUESTIONS

10-1 What classes of transactions are included in the expenditure cycle?

10-2 What departments report to (a) the vice president of operations and (b) the controller in the expenditure cycle?

10-3 Explain the materiality and audit risk associated with purchases and cash disbursements transactions?

10-4 The purchasing aspect of this cycle extends only to the acquisition of inventory items, and cash disbursements applies to all payments. Discuss the validity of these assertions.

10-5 Identify the functions pertaining to the executing and the recording of purchases and cash disbursements transactions and custody of related assets.

10-6 Indicate the specific internal accounting control objectives and a proper departmental assignment of duties for the first four functions involved in executing purchase transactions.

10-7 a. What authorizations are necessary in executing purchases transactions?
  b. What errors and irregularities may occur when these transactions are not authorized?

10-8 Describe the primary activities of (a) the receiving, (b) stores, and (c) vouchers payable departments in executing transactions.

10-9 Enumerate the steps in (a) preparing vouchers and (b) issuing checks.

10-10 What are the specific accounting control objectives for the three functions involved in recording purchases and cash disbursements?

10-11 Trace the flow of (a) purchase orders and (b) receiving reports in the flowchart in Figure 10-2.

10-12 Indicate the applicability of the internal control principle of independent internal verification to purchases and cash disbursements transactions.

10-13 How may physical controls be used for these two classes of transactions?

10-14 a. List the steps in the audit program for compliance tests of purchases that involve the use of a sample.

    b. What sampling unit(s) other than vouchers might be used in compliance tests of purchases?

10-15 Identify the steps in the audit program for compliance tests of cash disbursements that involve observation and inquiry.

10-16 Explain the applicability of dual purpose testing to purchases and cash disbursements transactions.

10-17 a. Enumerate the specific steps in designing a statistical sampling plan for purchases transactions?

    b. Identify the steps in determining the sample results section of Figure 10-10.

10-18 Explain the nature of the magnetic tape symbols show in Figure 10-11.

10-19 What aspects of the EDP system are subject to testing by the use of (a) test data and (b) generalized audit software?

10-20 Identify six types of invalid data that might be used in testing cash disbursements in an EDP system.

OBJECTIVE QUESTIONS FROM PROFESSIONAL EXAMINATIONS

Indicate the *best* answer for each of the following multiple choice questions.

10-21 These questions pertain to basic features of internal control over purchases and cash disbursements transactions.

1. A client erroneously recorded a large purchase twice. Which of the following internal accounting control measures would be most likely to detect this error in a timely and efficient manner?
    a. Footing the purchases journal.
    b. Reconciling vendors' monthly statements with subsidiary payable ledger accounts.
    c. Tracing totals from the purchases journal to the ledger accounts.
    d. Sending written quarterly confirmations to all vendors.

2. For effective internal control purposes, which of the following individuals should be responsible for mailing signed checks?
    a. Receptionist.
    b. Treasurer.
    c. Accounts payable clerk.
    d. Payroll clerk.

3. The accounts payable department receives the purchase order form to accomplish all of the following *except*
    a. Compare invoice price to purchase order price.
    b. Ensure the purchase had been properly authorized.

    c. Ensure the goods had been received by the party requesting the goods.
    d. Compare quantity ordered to quantity purchased.

10-22 These questions involve the study and evaluation of internal control over purchases and cash disbursements transactions.

1. In examining cash disbursements, an auditor plans to choose a sample using systematic selection with a random start. The primary advantage of such a systematic selection is that population items
   a. Which include irregularities will *not* be overlooked when the auditor exercises compatible reciprocal options.
   b. May occur in a systematic pattern, thus making the sample more representative.
   c. May occur more than once in a sample.
   d. Do *not* have to be prenumbered in order for the auditor to use the technique.
2. A client's materials-purchasing cycle begins with requisitions from user departments and ends with the receipt of materials and the recognition of a liability. An auditor's primary objective in reviewing this cycle is to
   a. Evaluate the reliability of information generated as a result of the purchasing process.
   b. Investigate the physical handling and recording of unusual acquisitions of materials.
   c. Consider the need to be on hand for the annual physical count if this system is *not* functioning properly.
   d. Ascertain that materials said to be ordered, received, and paid for are on hand.
3. An auditor employs sampling techniques to estimate the percentage of purchase orders that have been improperly prepared. Which of the following changes from one year to the next requires the greatest increase in the number of orders that the auditor examines?
   a. The auditor decided to decrease his risk of overreliance from 10 to 5%.
   b. The number of purchase orders in the population increased from 150,000 to 400,000
   c. The auditor's presampling estimate of the percentage of orders that had been improperly prepared decreased from 10 to 5%.
   d. The auditor decided to decrease the tolerable deviation rate from 8 to 4%.
   e. The average dollar value of each purchase order increased from $25 to $50.

COMPREHENSIVE QUESTIONS

10-23 The following questions appear in Figures 10-4 and 10-5:

1. Are imprinted and prenumbered checks used?
2. Is each check supported by an approved voucher?
3. Is supporting documentation mutilated after payment?
4. Are two signatures required on each check?
5. Does last check signer mail the check and remittance advice?
6. Are there prohibitions against issuing checks to cash or bearer?
7. Are all vouchers accounted for in journalizing?
8. Are daily summaries of checks compared with check register totals?

9. Is an authorized purchase order required for each purchase?

10. Is a signed receipt obtained from storeroom or other recipient on delivery of goods by receiving?

11. Are purchase orders, receiving reports, and vendors' invoices matched in preparing vouchers?

12. Are vouchers internally verified for accuracy?

13. Are goods stored in locked areas with restricted access?

Required

a. Identify the internal accounting control objective to which each question relates (i.e., executing, recording, or custody).

b. Identify the function and specific internal control objective to which the question pertains.

c. Indicate the internal control principle that is involved.

d. Identify an error or irregularity that may result from a "no" answer to each question. (Present your answers in tabular form using separate columns for each part.)

10-24 The following control procedures over purchases and cash disbursements transactions are prescribed by the Merlin Company:

1. Approved purchase order for each purchase.
2. Prenumbered receiving report for goods received.
3. Signed receipt from storeroom on acceptance of goods.
4. Matching of voucher with vendor's invoice.
5. Approved voucher for each check.
6. Cancellation of voucher on payment.
7. Review of voucher and supporting documentation by check signers.
8. Internal verification of voucher accuracy.
9. Locked storerooms for inventory.
10. Periodic reconciliation of inventory control and perpetual inventory records.
11. Accounting for all prenumbered checks in journalizing.
12. Periodic independent bank reconciliations.
13. No checks payable to cash or bearer.
14. Approved purchase requisition for each purchase order.
15. Review of purchase requisitions for reasonableness.

Required

a. Indicate the function served by each procedure.

b. Identify an error or irregularity that may be prevented or detected by the control procedure.

c. Indicate a compliance test that may be performed to determine whether the control procedure above is operating as prescribed. (Present your answers in tabular form using separate columns for each part.)

10-25 Properly designed and utilized forms facilitate adherence to prescribed internal accounting control policies and procedures. One such form might be a multicopy purchase order with one copy intended to be mailed to the vendor. The remaining copies would ordinarily be distributed to the stores, purchasing, receiving and accounting departments.

The following purchase order is currently being used by National Industrial Corporation:

PURCHASE ORDER

SEND INVOICE ONLY TO:
297 Hardingten Dr., Bronx, NY 10461

TO _____   SHIP TO _____

_____   _____

_____   _____

DATE TO BE SHIPPED	SHIP VIA	DISC. TERMS	FREIGHT TERMS	ADV. ALLOWANCE	SPECIAL ALLOWANCE

QUANTITY	DESCRIPTION

PURCHASE CONDITIONS

1. Supplier will be responsible for extra freight cost on partial shipment, unless prior permission is obtained.

2. Please acknowledge this order.

3. Please notify us immediately if you are unable to complete order.

4. All items must be individually packed.

Required

a. In addition to the name of the company, what other necessary information would an auditor recommend be included in the illustrative purchase order?

b. What primary internal control functions are served by the purchase order copies that are distributed to the stores, purchasing, receiving, and accounting departments?

AICPA

10-26 Dunbar Camera Manufacturing, Inc., is a manufacturer of high-priced precision motion picture cameras in which the specifications of component parts are vital to the manufacturing process. Dunbar buys valuable camera lenses and large quantities of sheetmetal and screws. Screws and lenses are ordered by Dunbar and are billed by the vendors on a unit basis. Sheetmetal is ordered by Dunbar and is billed by the vendors on the basis of weight. The receiving clerk is responsible for documenting the quality and quantity of merchandise received.

A preliminary review of the system of internal control indicates that the following procedures are being followed:

1. *Receiving Report.* Properly approved purchase orders, which are prenumbered, are filed numerically. The copy sent to the receiving clerk is an exact duplicate of the

copy sent to the vendor. Receipts of merchandise are recorded on the duplicate copy by the receiving clerk.

2. *Sheetmetal.* The company receives sheetmetal by railroad. The railroad independently weighs the sheetmetal and reports the weight and date of receipt on a bill of lading (waybill), which accompanies all deliveries. The receiving clerk only checks the weight on the waybill to the purchase order.

3. *Screws.* The receiving clerk opens cartons containing screws, then inspects and weighs the contents. The weight is converted to number of units by means of conversion charts. The receiving clerk then checks the computed quantity to the purchase order.

4. *Camera Lenses.* Each camera lens is delivered in a separate corrugated carton. Cartons are counted as they are received by the receiving clerk and the number of cartons are checked to purchase orders.

Required

a. Explain why the internal control procedures as they apply individually to receiving reports and the receipt of sheetmetal, screws, and camera lenses are adequate or inadequate. Do not discuss recommendations for improvements.

b. What financial statement distortions may arise because of the inadequacies in Dunbar's system of internal control and how may they occur?

AICPA

10-27 Taylor, a CPA, has been engaged to audit the financial statements of University Books, Incorporated. University Books maintains a large revolving cash fund exclusively for the purpose of buying used books from students for cash. The cash fund is active all year because the nearby univeristy offers a large variety of courses with varying starting and completion dates throughout the year.

Receipts are prepared for each purchase and reimbursement vouchers are periodically submitted.

Required

Construct an internal control questionnaire to be used in the evaluation of the system of internal control of University Books' revolving cash fund. The internal control questionnaire should elicit a yes or no response. *Do not discuss the internal controls over books that are purchased.*

AICPA

10-28 You are involved in an attribute sampling plan for testing the proper execution of vouchers in the Hickox Company. You elect to use the attributes shown in Figure 10-10 for testing and decide on the following sample design specifications:

1. The risk of overreliance for each attribute test is 10%.

2. The tolerable deviation rate is 6% for attributes 1 and 2 and 8% for attributes 3 and 4.

3. The expected deviation rate is 1% for attributes 1 and 2 and 2% for attributes 3 and 4.

Your examination reveals the following number of deviations, respectively, for attributes 1, 2, 3, and 4; 0, 1, 1, 3.

Required

a. Prepare a schedule showing details of the sample design and sample results.

b. Comment on your findings.

10-29 You have completed an audit of activities within the purchasing department of Zale Company. The department employs 30 buyers, seven supervisors, a manager, and clerical personnel. Purchases total about $500 million a year. Your audit disclosed the following conditions:

1. The company has no formal rules on conflicts of interest. Your analysis produced evidence that one of the 30 buyers in the department owns a substantial interest in a major supplier and that he procures supplies averaging $50,000 a year from that supplier. The prices charged by the supplier are competitive.

2. Buyers select proposed sources without submitting the lists of bidders for review. Your tests disclosed no evidence that higher costs were incurred as a result of that practice.

3. Buyers who originate written requests for quotations from suppliers receive the suppliers' bids directly from the mailroom. In your test of 100 purchases based on competitive bids, you found that in 75 cases the low bidders were awarded the purchase orders.

4. Requests to purchase (requisitions) received in the purchasing department from other departments in the company must be signed by persons authorized to do so. Your examination of 200 such requests disclosed that three, all for small amounts, were not properly signed. The buyer who had issued all three orders honored the requests because he misunderstood the applicable procedure. The clerical personnel charged with reviewing such requests had given them to the buyer in error.

Required

For each of the four conditions, state

a. The risk, if any, which is incurred if each condition described above is permitted to continue.

b. The control, if any, you would recommend to prevent continuation of the condition described.

IIA

10-30 Long, CPA, has been engaged to examine and report on the financial statements of Maylou Corporation. During the review phase of the study of Maylou's system of internal accounting control over purchases, Long was given the document flowchart on page 358 for purchases.

Required

a. Identify the procedures, relating to purchase requisitions and purchase orders, that Long would expect to find if Maylou's system of internal accounting control over purchases is effective. For example, purchase orders are prepared only after giving proper consideration to the time to order and quantity to order. Do not comment on the effectiveness of the flow of documents as presented in the flowchart or on separation of duties.

b. What are the factors to consider in determining
1. The time to order?
2. The quantity to order?

10-31 A manual system flowchart for executing purchases and cash disbursements transactions is shown on page 359.

Required

Indicate what each of the letters (A) through (L) represent. Do not discuss adequacies or inadequacies in the system of internal control.

AICPA

10-32 Anthony, CPA, prepared the flowchart on page 360, which portrays the raw materials purchasing function of one of Anthony's clients, a medium-size manufacturing company, from the preparation of initial documents through the vouching of invoices for payment in accounts payable. The flowchart was a portion of the work performed on the audit engagement to evaluate internal control.

Required

Identify and explain the internal control weaknesses evident from the flowchart. Include the internal control weaknesses resulting from activities performed or not performed. All documents are prenumbered.

AICPA

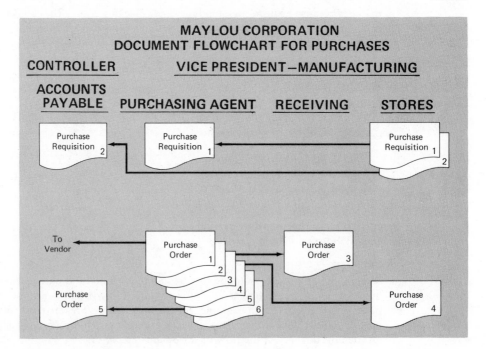

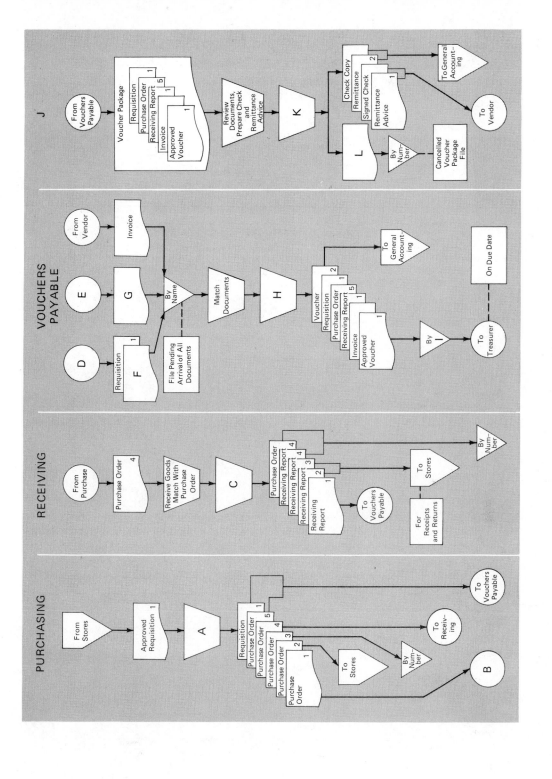

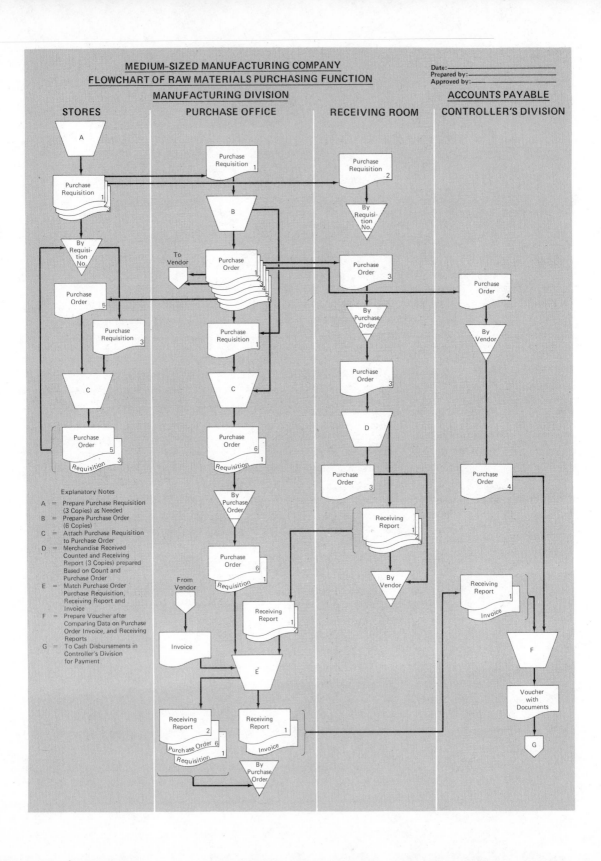

10-33 ConSport Corporation is a regional wholesaler of sporting goods. The systems flow-chart on the next page and the following description present ConSport's cash distribution system.

1. The Accounts Payable Department approves for payment all Invoices (I) for the purchase of inventory. Invoices are matched with the purchase requisitions (PR), purchase orders (PO), and receiving reports (RR). The accounts payable clerks focus on vendor name and skim the documents when they are combined.

2. When all the documents for an invoice are assembled, a two-copy disbursement voucher (DV) is prepared and the transaction is recorded in the voucher register (VR). The disbursement voucher and supporting documents are then filed alphabetically by vendor.

3. A two-copy journal voucher (JV) that summarizes each day's entries in the voucher register is prepared daily. The first copy is sent to the General Ledger Department, and the second copy is filed in the Accounts Payable Department by date.

4. The vendor file is searched daily for the disbursement vouchers of invoices that are due to be paid. Both copies of disbursement vouchers that are due to be paid are sent to the Treasury Department along with the supporting documents. The cashier prepares a check for each vendor, signs the check, and records it in the check register (CR). Copy 1 of the disbursement voucher is attached to the check copy and filed in check number order in the Treasury Department. Copy 2 and the supporting documents are returned to the Accounts Payable Department and filed alphabetically by vendor.

5. A two-copy journal voucher that summarizes each day's checks is prepared. Copy 1 is sent to the General Ledger Department and Copy 2 is filed in the Treasury Department by date.

6. The cashier receives the monthly bank statement with cancelled checks and prepares the bank reconciliation (BR). If an adjustment is required as a consequence of the bank reconciliation, a two-copy journal voucher is prepared. Copy 1 is sent to the General Ledger Department. Copy 2 is attached to Copy 1 of the bank reconciliation and filed by month in the Treasury Department. Copy 2 of the bank reconciliation is sent to the Internal Audit Department.

Required

ConSport Corporation's cash disbursement system has some weaknesses. Review the cash disbursement system and for each weakness in the system

1. Identify where the weakness exists by using the reference number that appears to the left of each symbol.
2. Describe the nature of the weakness.
3. Make a recommendation on how to correct the weakness.

Use the following format in preparing your answer:

Reference Number	Nature of Weakness	Recommendation to Correct Weakness

CMA

Decision Analysis

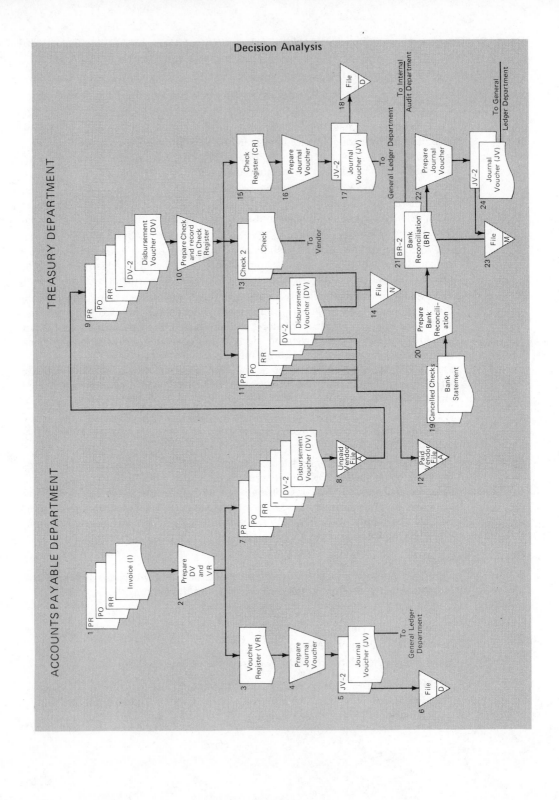

PURCHASING, RECEIVING & CASH DISBURSEMENTS FLOWCHART

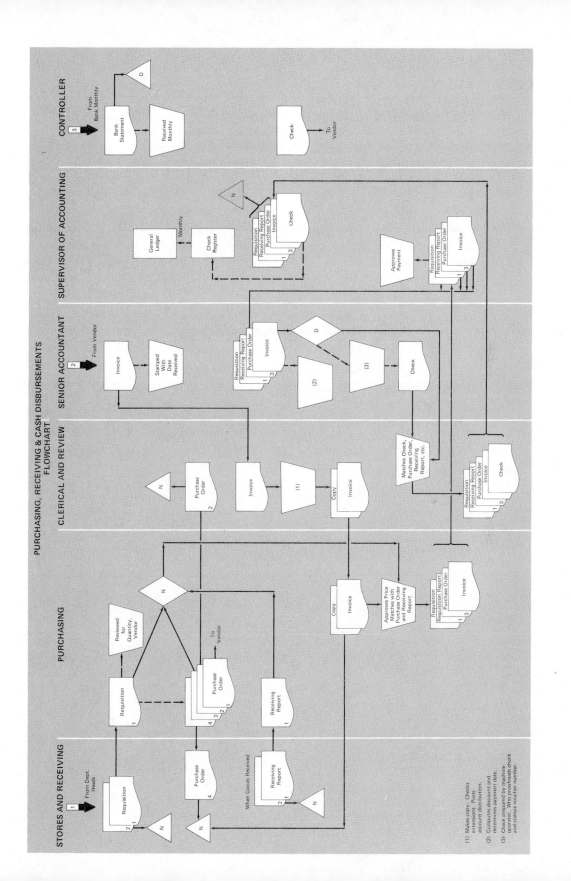

(1) Makes copy. Checks extensions. Posts account distribution.

(2) Computes discount and determines payment date.

(3) Check prepared by machine operator. Who proofreads check and stamps voucher number.

CASE STUDY

10-34 The Daly Company feels that it has definite problems in its internal control functions, particularly in purchasing, receiving, and cash disbursements. Your firm has been engaged to review these areas and to report on its findings.

The company is involved in a highly specialized processing activity with annual gross sales of approximately $25,000,000. The nature of the business is such that not all purchases are received in one shipment and there are many back orders, causing a problem for the production department to meet raw material needs on a timely basis.

It has been agreed that no separation of the receiving and stores department is required.

The flowchart on page 363 (prepared by your assistant) illustrates and describes *all procedures* being performed. The departments are scattered throughout a large plant area.

Required

a. Prepare a listing of the strengths and weaknesses in the system of internal control over purchasing, receiving, and cash disbursements.

b. For each weakness, recommend one or more changes to improve the effectiveness of the control.

Chapter 11

Compliance Tests of Payroll and Production Cycle Transactions

Study Objectives

When you have conscientiously studied this chapter, you should be able to

- Explain the essential features of internal accounting control over payroll and manufacturing transactions.

- Describe the methodology for making a study and evaluation of internal controls pertaining to payroll and manufacturing transactions.

- Prepare and evaluate flowcharts of payroll systems.

- Show how statistical sampling can be used in testing controls over payroll transactions.

- Enumerate the procedures included in an audit program for testing EDP controls over payroll transactions.

- Identify the essential parts of an audit program for testing controls over manufacturing transactions.

This is the fourth and final chapter that pertains exclusively to internal control and compliance testing. Two cycles are covered in the chapter. First, the coverage of the expenditure cycle is completed by focusing on payroll transactions. Second, the production cycle and manufacturing transactions in that cycle are considered.

ADDITIONAL INTERNAL CONTROL ENVIRONMENT CONSIDERATIONS

The internal control environment described in Chapter 10 applies to all transactions in the expenditure cycle. The following additional comments pertain exclusively to payroll transactions. Overall responsibility for payroll administration is generally assigned to a vice president of industrial relations, labor, or manpower management. Departments that are of particular importance to payroll transactions are (1) personnel (2) timekeeping, and (3) payroll. Individuals in these departments should be knowledgeable about laws and regulations applicable to payroll transactions.

Internal auditing exercises surveillance over payroll practices and procedures. Payroll costs usually are subject to budget constraints and periodic reporting of actual and budgeted costs. Sound practices include the use of employee identification badges for employees.

INTERNAL CONTROL OVER PAYROLL TRANSACTIONS

BASIC CONSIDERATIONS

Payroll transactions involve the events and transactions that pertain to executive and employee compensation. This class of transactions includes salaried personnel, hourly and incentive (piecework) wage earners, salespersons' commissions, executive bonuses, pensions and profit-sharing plans, vacation pay, employee benefits (e.g., health insurance), and payroll taxes. Attention in this chapter will be focused on hourly payrolls for employees.

Often, the processing of transactions in this part of the expenditure cycle has evolved into well-organized payroll systems that generally contain effective internal controls. In addition, the auditor is likely to find significant similarities in payroll systems among different companies, including wide application of electronic data processing (EDP).

The following are basic to an understanding of payroll transactions:

Functions

Executing

- Hiring employees.
- Authorizing payroll changes.
- Preparing attendance and timekeeping data.
- Preparing the payroll.
- Paying the payroll.
- Filing and paying payroll taxes.

Recording

- Journalizing and posting payroll transactions.
- Updating employee earnings records.
- Costing time tickets.

Custody

- Protecting payroll funds.
- Protecting payroll records.
- Maintaining correctness of payroll bank account(s).

Common Documents

- *Personnel Authorization.* A memo issued by personnel department indicating the hiring of an employee and each subsequent change in the employee's status for payroll purposes.
- *Clock Card.* A form used by each employer to record hours worked daily during a pay period. It is used with time clocks that record the time on the card.
- *Time Ticket.* A form used in timekeeping to record time worked by an employee on specific jobs. Time worked is often machine-imprinted.
- *Payroll Register.* A report showing each employee's name, gross earnings, payroll deductions, and net pay for a pay period. It provides the basis for paying employees.
- *Payroll Summary.* A report showing total gross earnings, payroll deductions, and net pay for all employees for a pay period. It provides the basis for journalizing the payroll.
- *Payroll Check.* An order drawn on a bank to pay an employee. It is accompanied by a detachable memo indicating gross earnings, payroll deductions, and net pay.
- *Labor (Cost) Distribution Summary.* A report showing the account classifications for gross factory earnings for each pay period.
- *Payroll Tax Returns.* Forms prescribed by taxing authorities for the filing of payroll tax returns.
- *Form W–2.* A form given to the employee and filed with the Internal Revenue Service showing annual earnings, federal income taxes withheld, and FICA taxes withheld.

Accounting Records

- *Books of Original Entry.* General journal, voucher register, and check register or payroll check register.
- *General Ledger Accounts.* Salary and wages expense; factory labor; payroll taxes expense; salaries and wages payable; payroll taxes payable; accounts payable; cash in bank (payroll bank account); manufacturing overhead control.
- *Subsidiary Ledgers.* Manufacturing overhead records and work-in-process records.

File Data

- *Employee Personnel Record.* Holds pertinent employment data for each employee and contains all personnel authorizations issued for the employee, job evaluations, and disciplinary actions, if any.

- *Employee Earnings Record.* Contains each employee's gross earnings, payroll deductions, and net pay for the year by pay periods.

PAYROLL TRANSACTIONS ARE PROPERLY EXECUTED

As in the case of other transactions, the execution of payroll transactions involves a series of functions. The functions, together with the related internal control objectives, are shown below.

Function	Specific Accounting Control Objective
1. Hiring employees	Employees are hired in accordance with management's criteria.
2. Authorizing payroll changes	Pay rates, payroll deductions, changes in job status, and terminations are properly authorized.
3. Preparing attendance and timekeeping data	Appropriate records are maintained and time worked is properly approved.
4. Preparing the payroll	Employee earnings and net pay are accurately determined on the basis of approved time data and authorized deductions.
5. Paying the payroll	Payments of employee compensation are made to bona fide employees on the basis of approved and authorized data.
6. Filing and paying payroll taxes	Payroll tax returns are correctly and promptly filed, and payments are made when due.

Conceptually, the steps in executing payroll transactions are the same as executing the two classes of transactions described in the preceding chapter. For example, hiring of employees is analogous to ordering goods and services, attendance and timekeeping are comparable to receiving, and the vouching and paying functions are similar. The internal control principles applicable to executing payroll transactions are explained below.

Authorization Procedures

The personnel department plays a vital role in the authorization process. Its responsibility extends to each aspect of the employee's status: hiring, job classification, pay rate, payroll deductions, and termination. Authorization procedures should also be established for (1) approving time worked, (2) approving the payroll, and (3) paying the payroll. Time worked should be specifically approved by the employee's supervisor, the payroll should be approved by the head of the payroll department, and the approved payroll, in turn, provides the authorization for payment of the payroll.

Segregation of Functions

The functions involved in executing payroll transactions should be performed by different departments and individuals as shown on the next page.

Function	Department	Related Activities
1. Hiring employees	Personnel	Evaluate qualifications of applicants on basis of job description and hiring policies and issue employment authorization memos.
2. Authorizing payroll changes	Personnel	Issue authorizations for pay rates, payroll deductions, transfers, and terminations, and maintain employee personnel records.
3. Preparing attendance and timekeeping data	Timekeeping	Supervise clock card punching, prepare time tickets, reconcile time ticket and clock card hours, and obtain supervisory approval of time worked.
4. Preparing the payroll	Payroll	Issue clock cards, maintain attendance records, compute employee gross and net earnings, prepare payroll summary and payroll checks, and maintain employee earnings records.
5. Paying the payroll	Vouchers Payable	Prepare voucher for payment of payroll.
	Treasurer	Sign and distribute payroll checks.
6. Filing and paying payroll taxes	Payroll	Prepare and file payroll tax returns.
	Treasurer	Prepare and mail checks in payment of payroll taxes.

A flowchart for the execution of payroll transactions is shown in Figure 11-1.

Documentation Procedures

Each step in executing payroll transactions should be documented. Personnel department authorization forms provide documentation of new hires, pay rates, job reclassifications, and terminations. For hourly employees, many companies use clock cards and time tickets to accumulate time worked.

Preparation of the payroll involves calculating gross earnings, payroll deductions, and net pay for each employee based on authorized pay rates and approved time data. The computed amounts for each employee are then tabulated on a payroll register. When approved by a payroll supervisor, the register provides the basis for

- Posting of gross earnings and payroll deductions to the individual employee's earnings record maintained in payroll.
- Preparing a payroll summary of total gross earnings, payroll deductions, and net pay for the pay period that is sent to general accounting.
- Preparing individual payroll checks that are then sent to the treasurer's office for signature(s) and distribution to employees.

The payroll register constitutes the treasurer department's authority to pay employees. Payment is usually made in the form of prenumbered checks

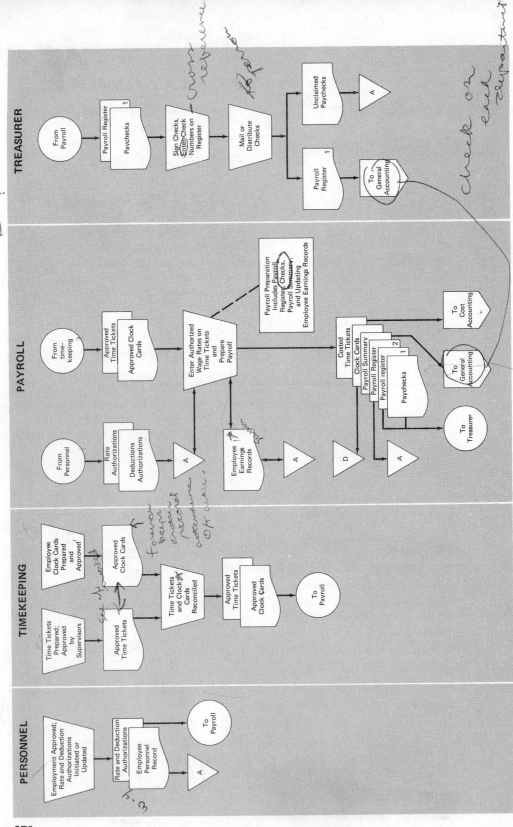

Figure 11-1. MANUAL SYSTEM FOR EXECUTING PAYROLL TRANSACTIONS.

drawn either on the company's regular bank account or a payroll bank account. Payroll checks should be distributed directly to employees, on proper identification, by treasurer department personnel. The checks should not be returned to payroll for distribution since the payroll department would then have control over both preparing and paying the payroll.

A termination notice (authorization) should be issued by the personnel department on completion of an individual's employment. Prompt notification is vital in preventing terminated employees from continuing on the payroll. The subsequent diversion of payroll checks to such unauthorized individuals has characterized a number of payroll frauds.

Every company is expected to comply with legal requirements pertaining to filing payroll tax returns and paying payroll taxes. Ordinarily, the payroll department prepares the tax returns on forms provided by the taxing authority. When payment is due, a voucher is drawn and a check is issued.

Physical Controls and Independent Internal Verification

A common physical control is the use of time clocks for determining total hours worked. When such equipment is used, supervisors or security guards are often designated to observe the punching of the clocks by employees.

Independent internal verification applications include having a second payroll clerk validate (1) the accuracy of the computed payroll data for each employee, (2) the agreement of the amounts on the checks with corresponding amounts in the payroll register, and (3) the agreement of data on the tax returns with the data shown in the employee earnings records.

PAYROLL TRANSACTIONS ARE PROPERLY RECORDED

The functions in recording payroll transactions, an appropriate segregation of duties within the accounting department, and the related internal control objective are shown below.

Function	Department	Specific Accounting Control Objective
1. Journalizing and posting payroll transactions	General Accounting	Payroll data are correctly recorded as to amount, classification, and accounting period.
2. Updating employee earnings records	Payroll Accounting	Employee earnings data for each pay period are correctly posted to the employee's earnings record.
3. Costing time tickets	Payroll Accounting	Proper pay rates are correctly applied to each time ticket.

The internal control principles applicable to the recording of payroll transactions are explained below.

Segregation of Functions

Proper separation of duties in accounting for payrolls in essential. Accounting personnel who record payroll transactions should not prepare or pay the payroll. In addition, personnel who maintain employee earnings records and cost time tickets should not journalize the payroll or post the transactions to the general ledger.

Accounting Records and Procedures

The accounting records consist of books of original entry, the payroll expense and payroll liability accounts in the general ledger, and employee earnings records. Payroll summaries provide the basis for journalizing the payroll, and vouchers and payroll checks furnish the data for recording payment of the payroll. Postings to the employee earnings records are made directly from the payroll registers. A flowchart for the recording of payroll transactions is shown in Figure 11-2.

Independent Internal Verification

There are several opportunities for this internal control principle in recording payroll transactions. Examples include (1) agreeing payroll and labor cost distribution summaries and payroll register totals in general accounting and (2) reconciling costs shown on time tickets with postings to job or production cost records in cost accounting.

CUSTODY OF PAYROLL FUNDS IS PROPERLY MAINTAINED

Assets resulting from payroll transactions consist of payroll bank accounts and unclaimed wages. The following functions and specific accounting control objectives are applicable to maintaining proper custody over these assets:

Function	Department	Specific Accounting Control Objective
1. Protecting payroll funds	Treasurer	Access to payroll bank accounts and unclaimed wages is limited to authorized personnel.
2. Protecting payroll records	Payroll	Access to payroll records is limited to authorized personnel.
3. Maintaining correctness of payroll bank accounts	General Accounting	Recorded bank balances are independently compared with existing assets at reasonable intervals.

The internal control principles applicable to these functions are explained below.

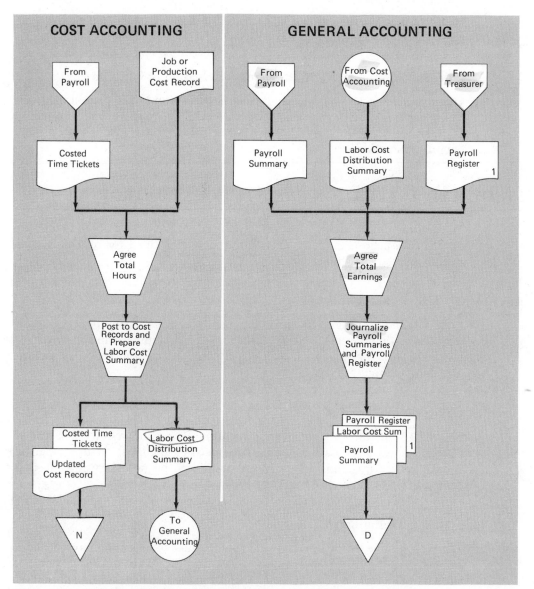

Figure 11-2. MANUAL SYSTEM FOR RECORDING PAYROLL TRANSACTIONS

Physical Controls and Authorization Procedures

Physical controls include the security devices of a bank for the payroll bank account and vaults or safes for the storage of unclaimed wages. Physical controls are also needed to prevent indirect access to payroll funds. Thus, authorization forms, clock cards, and preprinted payroll checks should be stored with a responsible custodian and access should be restricted to authorized personnel. Employee earnings records should be filed in fireproof locked files and access should be restricted to authorized payroll department personnel.

Independent Internal Verification and Segregation of Functions

These principles apply primarily to the reconciliation of the payroll bank account per books with the balance reported on the payroll bank statement. Ordinarily, this is done monthly by personnel not otherwise involved with payroll transactions.

STUDY AND EVALUATION OF INTERNAL CONTROL

The auditor's methodology for meeting the second standard of field work for payroll transactions is identical with the steps described for purchases and cash disbursements transactions in Chapter 10.

REVIEW OF THE PAYROLL SYSTEM

When the auditor intends to rely on the client's control procedures over payroll transactions, it is necessary to perform both the preliminary and the completion phases of the review. The principal steps in the completion phase are explained below.

Gathering Information

Figure 11-3 illustrates an internal control questionnaire for payroll transactions. The questions, which are referenced to specific functions, relate to specific control procedures considered by the auditor to be necessary for effective control.

Making a Preliminary Evaluation

A representative listing of errors and irregularities in executing payroll transactions, and the control procedures necessary to prevent or detect them, is shown in Figure 11-4. Similar listings can be made for the recording of payroll transactions and the custody of payroll funds. From a comparison of the necessary controls with the prescribed controls obtained earlier in the review, the auditor makes a preliminary evaluation of the controls in the payroll system. The auditor's preliminary evaluation should be documented in the working papers.

COMPLIANCE TESTS OF CONTROLS TO BE RELIED ON

When the auditor has identified controls that are expected to be relied on, it is necessary to perform compliance tests on these controls to determine whether

---

CYCLE: Expenditure   **CLASS OF TRANSACTIONS: Payroll**

EXECUTING   Yes | No

1. Are hirings authorized by personnel department? (E1)

2. Are pay rates, payroll deductions, and terminations authorized by the personnel department? (E2)

3. Are time clocks and clock cards used? (E3)

4. Is time clock punching supervised? (E3)

5. Is there supervisory approval of time worked by each employee? (E3)

6. Are time ticket hours reconciled to clock card hours daily? (E3)

7. Is there internal verification of accuracy of payroll computations? (E4)

8. Is there supervisory approval of the payroll? (E4)

9. Is there internal verification of payroll checks with payroll register data? (E5)

10. Are payroll checks signed and distributed by treasurer's office personnel? (E5)

11. Are payroll tax returns reconciled to employees earnings records? (E6)

RECORDING

1. Are personnel who journalize payroll transactions independent of those who prepare and pay the payroll? (R1)

2. Are changes in employee earnings records reconciled with payroll register data? (R2)

3. Are costed time tickets verified for proper rates and mathematical accuracy? (R3)

CUSTODY

1. Are unclaimed wages held by a treasurer's office employee? (C1)

2. Are personnel and employee earnings records kept in locked files? (C2)

3. Is payroll bank account periodically reconciled by an independent person? (C3)

Figure 11-3. INTERNAL CONTROL QUESTIONNAIRE: PAYROLL TRANSACTIONS.

they are operating as planned. An illustrative audit program for testing controls over payroll transactions is shown in Figure 11-5. Observe that the payroll check is used as the sampling unit in testing controls pertaining to the execution of payroll transactions. Alternatively, the line item in the payroll registers may be used in testing when there is a transaction trail of documentary evidence. Compliance tests of payroll transactions should include personnel from each major accounting and functional classification, such as office, sales, factory, and so on. In addition, each of the principal bases for computing compensation—hourly, salaried, and incentive—should be tested.

The witnessing of the distribution of a payroll is an important compliance test. In performing this procedure, the auditor should observe that

- Segregation of functions exists between the preparation and payment of the payroll.

Function	Possible Errors and Irregularities	Necessary Control Procedures	Possible Compliance Tests
EXECUTING			
1. Hiring employees	An unauthorized employee may be added to the payroll records.	Personnel department authorization for new employees.	Examine personnel authorization for new employees.
2. Authorizing payroll changes	Payroll department may not be informed of a pay rate change.	Personnel department authorization of payroll changes.	Examine authorizations of payroll changes.
3. Preparing attendance and timekeeping data	An employee may punch more than one clock card.	Surveillance of time clock punching.	Observe surveillance and inquire of security guard as to number of exceptions.
	Time ticket hours may be incorrect.	Internal verification of agreement of time ticket and clock card hours.	Examine evidence of verification.
		Supervisor approval of hours worked.	Review evidence of approval.
4. Preparing the payroll	Mathematical errors may occur in calculating employee earnings and deductions.	Internal verification of payroll calculations.	Examine evidence of verification.
	Payroll register may be incomplete.	Supervisor approval of payroll register.	Review evidence of approval.
5. Paying the payroll	Checks may be issued for incorrect amounts.	Internal verification of checks with payroll register data.	Review evidence of verification.
	Checks may be distributed to unauthorized recipients.	Segregation of functions between preparation and payment.	Observe segregation of functions.
		Employee identification on distribution.	Witness the distribution of the payroll.
6. Filing and paying payroll taxes	An employee may be omitted from a tax return.	Internal verification of tax return with employee earnings records.	Examine evidence of verification.

Figure 11-4. PRELIMINARY EVALUATION CONSIDERATIONS: EXECUTION OF PAYROLL TRANSACTIONS.

TYPE OF TESTING: Compliance   **PURPOSE:** Study and Evaluation of Internal Control
CYCLE: Expenditure   **CLASS OF TRANSACTIONS:** Payroll

A. CONTROLS IN EXECUTING PAYROLL TRANSACTIONS ARE OPERATING AS PLANNED.

1. For selected payroll checks for the year to date, examine for
   - Authorization of pay rates and deductions. (E2)
   - Supervisory approval of time worked. (E3)
   - Internal verification of payroll calculations. (E4)
   - Internal verification of check with payroll register. (E5)
   - Authorized signatures on check. (E5)
   - Employee endorsement of check. (E5)
2. For pay periods from which checks are drawn, examine payroll registers for supervisory approval of payroll.
3. Witness a distribution of a payroll. (E5)
4. Observe clock card and timekeeping procedures. (E3)
5. Inquire of personnel concerning performance of control procedures.
6. Reperform verification procedures in step 1 on some payroll checks.

B. CONTROLS IN RECORDING PAYROLL TRANSACTIONS ARE OPERATING AS PLANNED.

1. Examine evidence of verification of payroll summaries with payroll entries. (R1)
2. Examine evidence of periodic reconciliations of employee earnings records with payroll register data and tax returns. (R2)
3. Examine sample of time tickets for verification of rates and calculations. (R3)

C. CONTROLS OVER THE CUSTODY OF PAYROLL FUNDS ARE OPERATING AS PLANNED.

1. Observe controls over unclaimed wages. (C1)
2. Observe security over payroll records. (C2)
3. Examine evidence of payroll bank reconciliations. (C3)

Figure 11-5. AUDIT PROGRAM: COMPLIANCE TESTS OF PAYROLL TRANSACTIONS.

- Each employee receives only one check.
- Each employee is identified by badge and/or signature.
- There is proper control and disposition of unclaimed checks.

FINAL EVALUATION OF THE CONTROLS

Based on his preliminary evaluation and the results of compliance testing, the auditor evaluates the reliability of each control expected to be relied on. As previously explained, the analysis of results involves a consideration of both the number and the causes of deviations from prescribed control procedures. The final evaluation is then used to determine the nature, timing, and extent of substantive testing of payroll balances.

STATISTICAL SAMPLING IN COMPLIANCE TESTING

Payroll is another area in which attribute sampling can be utilized in performing compliance tests. The same steps that were illustrated in previous chapters to design, execute, and evaluate the sample are followed.

The objective of the sampling plan may be proper executing or proper recording or both. Sampling units may be payroll checks, clock cards, or line items in the payroll register. When the objective is the proper preparation of the payroll, the following attributes may be of interest in a sampling plan for hourly workers:

- Approval of time worked by supervisor.
- Verification of agreement of time tickets and clock cards.
- Verification of accuracy of payroll calculations.
- Authorization of pay rates and payroll deductions.

The auditor determines a sample size for each attribute by specifying (1) a tolerable deviation rate, based on the extent of reliance to be placed on the related control, (2) an expected population deviation rate, and (3) the desired risk of overreliance. The auditor then proceeds to randomly select the sample, examine the sample items, and statistically and qualitatively evaluate and interpret the sample results.

ELECTRONIC DATA PROCESSING

Electronic data processing of payroll transactions is very common. Since these transactions occur on a regular basis at the end of each payroll period, it is customary to use batch processing. However, it should also be recognized that numerous changes in pay rates, job classifications, and payroll deductions may occur during a payroll period. Accordingly, many companies provide the personnel department with on-line access to the employee's personnel data master file maintained on the computer. A case study of the payroll system that has this on-line access capability is described below.

DESCRIPTION OF THE PAYROLL SYSTEM

In the Hart Company, the batch entry/batch processing method is used to perform three payroll functions: (1) preparing the payroll register, (2) preparing payroll checks, and (3) updating the employee earnings master file. Magnetic tape is used for input data and master files are maintained on magnetic disk. In addition, on-line entry/on-line processing is used to update the personnel data master file. A flowchart of the payroll system is shown in Figure 11-6.

The manual control procedures are similar to those described in earlier EDP case studies. These controls include the batch totals and the batch transmittal

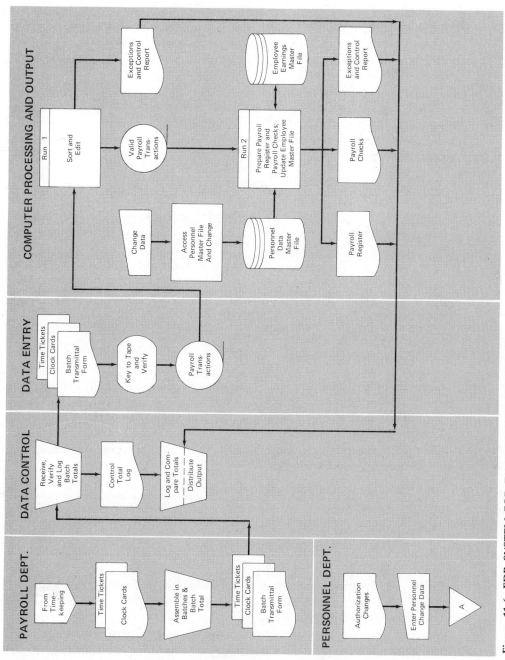

Figure 11-6. EDP SYSTEM FOR PAYROLL TRANSACTIONS.

form in the payroll department, the review and verification of the batch totals in data control, and the verification of keypunched data in data entry.

As shown in Figure 11-6, the system provides for the updating of the personnel data master file by direct access from on-line terminals and two computer runs.

Run 1. In this run, the payroll transactions are sorted by employee number and the data are verified by an *edit check* routine. The outputs consist of a valid payroll transaction tape and a control and exception report that is sent to data control.

Run 2. In this run, the valid transactions data are processed using the Hart Company's payroll application program. The program is run using (1) the personnel data master file which contains current authorized pay rates and payroll deductions, and (2) the employee earnings master file which contains earnings data for the year to date. The output of this run consists of an updated earnings master file in machine-readable form and printouts of payroll checks (with accompanying earnings and deductions data), the payroll register, and a control total and exception report. The checks are subsequently forwarded by data control to the treasurer's department for signing.

STUDY AND EVALUATION OF EDP CONTROLS

The methodology for making a study and evaluation of EDP controls in a payroll system is the same as described in earlier case studies. An audit program for testing the EDP application controls in the Hart Company is shown in Figure 11-7.

In testing the program controls in run 1, the auditor uses test data that contains invalid conditions such as:

- Missing or invalid employee number.
- Total hours per clock card not in agreement with hours on time tickets.
- Time tickets with invalid job numbers.
- Total hours that exceed a predetermined limit.

In testing the processing steps in run 2, the auditor uses test data to determine that the program controls are operating as planned for (1) calculating employee earnings and deductions, and (2) reporting as exceptions amounts that exceed predetermined limits.

In both tests, the test data are run using the client's regular programs, and the output of the test runs is manually compared by the auditor with the expected results. The extent of testing of master files is dependent on the effectiveness of EDP general controls pertaining to file security and documentation of program changes. As shown in Figure 11-7, the auditor decides to test these files by using generalized audit software. For the personnel data file, a random sample of employees is obtained. The pay rates and deductions for these employees are printed out and traced to source documents. The

TYPE OF TESTING: Compliance	PURPOSE: EDP Application Controls
CYCLE: Expenditure	CLASS OF TRANSACTIONS: Payroll

A. INPUT CONTROLS ARE PROPERLY FUNCTIONING.

1. Randomly select a sample of employee earnings in the payroll register and trace to source documents.
2. Review, on test basis, reconciliation of batch totals in data control with control totals in run 1.
3. Selectively review error listings of run 1 and investigate items to determine that they have been properly cleared.
4. Design and use test data to test program controls of edit routine in run 1.

B. PROCESSING CONTROLS ARE PROPERLY FUNCTIONING.

1. Observe the procedures for reconciling control totals in runs 1 and 2 and selectively trace control totals to related input controls.
2. Review error lists for run 2 for unusual items and determine the disposition of rejected data.
3. Use test data to test the program logic in run 2.
4. Use generalized audit software to test master file data.

C. OUTPUT CONTROLS ARE PROPERLY FUNCTIONING.

1. Review reconciliation of output controls with input controls.
2. On a test basis, obtain printouts of employee earnings master files used in run 2 and use related payroll register data to reconcile changes in totals and selectively account for changes in individual employee earnings data.

Figure 11-7. AUDIT PROGRAM: COMPLIANCE TESTS OF EDP APPLICATION CONTROLS FOR PAYROLL TRANSACTIONS.

software program also is used to make a reasonableness test on pay rates in the personnel data file. Through use of the computer, the file is searched for abnormal pay rates, rate changes within specified time periods, and rate changes in excess of a specified percentage. The selection criteria are run against the file and the printout is manually traced to source documents by the auditor.

In using generalized audit software to test the employee earnings file for reasonableness, the selection criteria include excessive gross or net earnings, excessive income tax withholdings, and FICA withholdings in excess of the statutory maximum.

From evidence obtained from the compliance tests, the auditor determines the reliance that can be placed on EDP controls and their effect on the nature, timing, and extent of substantive tests of payroll balances.

THE PRODUCTION CYCLE

NATURE OF THE PRODUCTION CYCLE

The production cycle relates to the conversion of raw materials into finished goods. This cycle includes production planning and control of the types and quantities of goods to be manufactured, the inventory levels to be maintained, and the transactions and events pertaining to the manufacturing process. Transactions in this cycle begin at the point where raw materials are requisitioned for production and end with the transfer of the manufactured product to finished goods. The accounting function associated with this cycle embraces a cost accounting system, which may include standard costs and perpetual inventory records.

The production cycle interfaces with both the expenditure and the revenue cycles. The former involves the acquisition of goods and services needed in production; the latter involves the custody and subsequent sale of finished goods.

INTERNAL CONTROL ENVIRONMENT

In the organizational structure of a manufacturing company, an officer with the title vice president of operations, manufacturing, or production usually has overall responsibility for production. This individual has line authority over the production planning and control department and each manufacturing department or division.

Personnel engaged in the production cycle include department or division heads, foremen, and factory workers. Production budgets are used to control the quantity and scheduling of production, and cost budgets and standard costs are frequently used to control manufacturing costs.

MATERIALITY AND AUDIT RISK

In a manufacturing company, inventories and cost of goods sold are usually material to the company's financial position and results of operations. Thus, the auditor seeks to keep audit risk that the financial statements are materially misstated because of production cycle transactions at a relatively low level. This is accomplished by making a study and evaluation of internal controls over production cycle transactions to determine control risk. Based on this assessment, the auditor then sets detection risk for substantive testing at a level that is consistent with desired overall audit risk.

INTERNAL ACCOUNTING CONTROL OBJECTIVES

For the production cycle, the operative objectives of internal accounting control are as follows:

- Production cycle transactions (i.e., manufacturing transactions) are properly executed.
- Production cycle transactions are properly recorded.
- Custody of assets (i.e., work in process and finished goods) is properly maintained.

These three objectives provide the framework for discussing (1) the basic features of accounting control over manufacturing transactions in this cycle and (2) the study and evaluation of internal control over these transactions.

INTERNAL CONTROL OVER MANUFACTURING TRANSACTIONS

BASIC CONSIDERATIONS

The following are basic to an understanding of the events and transactions pertaining to the manufacturing transactions in the production cycle:

Functions

Executing

- Issuing production orders.
- Issuing raw materials.
- Processing raw materials.
- Transferring completed work to finished goods.

Recording

- Journalizing and posting manufacturing transactions.
- Updating work in process and finished goods records.

Custody

- Protecting work in process and finished goods.
- Maintaining correctness of work in process and finished goods records.

Common Documents

- *Production Order.* A form indicating the quantity and kind of goods to be manufactured. An order may pertain to a job order or a continuous process.
- *Bill of Materials.* A listing of raw material components for a production order. In some cases, the listing is included in the production order.
- *Materials Requisition.* A memo to the storeroom requesting the release of materials for use on an approved production order.
- *Routing Ticket.* A notice accompanying the transfer of work in process between departments and to finished goods.
- *Daily Activity Reports.* Separate reports showing raw materials and direct labor used during the day.
- *Completed Production Report.* A report showing that work has been completed on a production order.
- *Quality Control Report.* A report issued by a quality control inspector that completed production meets quality control standards, or conversely that the goods are defective.

Accounting Records

- *Books of Original Entry.* General journal and voucher register.
- *General Ledger Accounts.* Raw materials, work in process, finished goods, manufacturing overhead, over- or underabsorbed overhead, and standard cost variances.
- *Subsidiary Ledgers.* Stores ledger, work in process records, finished goods records, manufacturing overhead records.

MANUFACTURING TRANSACTIONS ARE PROPERLY EXECUTED

The functions and specific accounting control objectives in executing manufacturing transactions are as follows:

Function	Specific Accounting Control Objective
1. Issuing production orders	Orders are issued in accordance with management's established criteria.
2. Issuing raw materials	Materials are issued on the basis of approved materials requisitions.
3. Processing of raw materials	Production is based on authorized production orders.
4. Transferring completed work to finished goods	Transfers are properly authorized.

The internal control principles applicable to these functions are explained below.

Authorization Procedures

The production planning and control department has the responsibility to authorize production. Both general and specific authorizations may occur. The former usually involve production for stock, the latter pertain to tailor-made customer orders. Evidence of authorization is provided by production orders, which then serve as the basis for incurring materials and labor costs.

Before an order for stock items (inventory) is released for production, a supervisor in production control should determine that (1) the quantities requested are compatible with established reorder quantities and production budgets, and (2) existing quantities are at the reorder level.

During the production process, the movement of goods between departments and into the finished goods warehouse should be authorized. On completion of the work, approval should be obtained from quality control that the finished job meets the company's quality control standards.

Segregation of Functions

An appropriate separation of duties for manufacturing transactions is as follows:

Function	Department	Related Activities
1. Issuing production orders	Production Planning and Control	Prepare and approve product specifications, prepare bill of materials, schedule production, and issue production orders.
2. Issuing raw materials	Raw Materials Stores	Release raw materials, obtain materials requisitions for each issue, and prepare batch or daily totals of materials issued.
3. Processing raw materials	Manufacturing (fabricating, enameling, assembling)	Apply direct labor, prepare time tickets and control totals of labor use.
4. Transferring completed work to finished goods	Manufacturing	Prepare completed production report, obtain quality control report, prepare routing ticket, and obtain receipt from finished goods.

Documentation Procedures

The production order is a key document in the production cycle. The orders should be prenumbered and signed by a supervisor. For custom-made items, the orders should be accompanied by a detailed bill of materials. During production, documentation procedures should (1) provide evidence of direct materials and direct labor use, (2) create a basis for physical control of the goods, and (3) permit the determination of accurate production cost data.

Materials requisitions serve as the authorization for the release of materials from the storeroom. For control purposes, they should be prenumbered and storeroom personnel should prepare daily or batch totals of materials issued. *Time tickets* provide the documentation for direct labor use, and timekeeping should prepare daily control totals of hours worked. Manufacturing overhead rates should be based on budgeted overhead costs.

Routing tickets provide the basis for control over the movement of goods through the production process. The tickets should be initialed by the transferring department, signed by the department accepting the goods, and forwarded to accounting. Routing rickets should be prenumbered and filed with the production order. Transfers to finished goods are documented by a completed production report, a quality control report, and a routing ticket signed by personnel in the finished goods warehouse.

Independent Internal Verification

This principle is applicable in accounting for prenumbered documents and comparing the daily activity reports with corresponding materials requisitions and time tickets.

MANUFACTURING TRANSACTIONS ARE PROPERLY RECORDED

The functions and specific accounting control objectives in recording manufacturing transactions are as follows:

Function	Department	Specific Accounting Control Objective
1. Journalizing and posting manufacturing transactions	General Accounting	All manufacturing transactions are correctly recorded as to amount, classification, and accounting period.
2. Updating work in process records	Cost Accounting	Work in process records are accurately updated on a timely basis.
3. Updating finished goods records	Inventory Accounting	Finished goods records are promptly and accurately updated.

The internal control principles applicable to these functions are explained below.

Authorization Procedures

Authorizations are necessary in establishing manufacturing overhead (burden) rates and setting standard costs. Similarly, all revisions of these data should be formally authorized.

Segregation of Functions

Adherence to the assignment of departmental responsibilities indicated above should provide for proper segregation of functions in recording. In addition, there should be a separation of duties between these departments and payroll and inventory accounting.

Accounting Records and Procedures

This principle serves the following purposes in this cycle:

- Costing direct materials and direct labor.
- Assigning manufacturing overhead to production.
- Recording the transfer of costs between departments.
- Determining the cost of work in process and finished goods inventories.

Direct materials costs are obtained through the costing of materials requisitions. Direct labor costs are derived from the costing of time tickets. Manufacturing overhead costs are usually based on predetermined burden rates. When standard costs are used, variance accounts are required. In a job order system, the subsidiary work-in-process ledger consists of individual job cost sheets. Entries for the transfer of costs between departments should parallel the physical movement of the goods through the manufacturing process. The costing of ending work in process is obtained from unfinished job and production cost records. In addition, finished goods records are updated from completed job cost sheets and production cost reports.

Independent Internal Verification

There are two applications of this principle in recording. First, an accounting supervisor should verify the agreement of daily entries for direct materials and direct labor with the data shown on the daily activity reports. Second, there should be independent verification of agreement of total postings to work in process records with the daily activity reports.

CUSTODY OF WORK IN PROCESS AND FINISHED GOODS IS PROPERLY MAINTAINED

This objective pertains to physical controls over work in process and finished goods inventories, and periodic comparisons of finished goods records with existing assets. The functions and specific internal accounting control objectives are as follows:

Function	Department	Specific Accounting Control Objective
1. Protecting work in process	Manufacturing	Access to work in process is limited to authorized personnel.
2. Protecting finished goods	Finished Goods Warehouse	Goods are stored in locked warehouse.
3. Maintaining correctness of work in process records.	Cost Accounting	Recorded balances are independently compared with goods in process at reasonable intervals.
4. Maintaining correctness of finished goods records	Inventory Accounting	Recorded balances are independently compared with goods on hand at reasonable intervals.

The internal control principles applicable to these objectives are explained below.

Physical Controls and Authorization Procedures

Whenever possible, work in process and finished goods should be stored in locked areas and access thereto should be limited to authorized personnel. Physical controls over work in various stages of completion on an assembly line may consist of surveillance by supervisory personnel and tagging of the goods.

Segregation of Functions and Independent Internal Verification

Individuals responsible for the custody of work in process and finished goods should not be involved in the recording of manufacturing transactions. Independent internal verification occurs when work-in-process and finished goods records are compared with goods on hand by individuals who do not maintain the records or have custody of the inventory.

STUDY AND EVALUATION OF INTERNAL CONTROL

The auditor's methodology for meeting the second standard of field work for manufacturing transactions is the same as for other major classes of transactions.

REVIEW OF THE MANUFACTURING SYSTEM

A questionnaire that may be used in gathering information about prescribed controls over manufacturing transactions is shown in Figure 11-8. As in previous examples, the questions relate to necessary control procedures and are referenced to specific functions.

A representative listing of errors and irregularities is shown in Figure 11-9. From a comparison of necessary controls and prescribed controls, the auditor makes a preliminary evaluation of the specific controls in the client's system.

COMPLIANCE TESTS OF CONTROLS TO BE RELIED ON

An audit program for compliance testing of manufacturing transactions is illustrated in Figure 11-10. In this program, the production order is used as the sampling unit. Alternatively, the sampling unit may be the job cost sheet or the production cost report.

FINAL EVALUATION OF THE CONTROLS

Based on his preliminary evaluation and the results of compliance testing, the auditor makes a final evaluation of the controls over manufacturing transactions. The auditor then determines the effects of his evaluation on the nature, timing, and extent of substantive tests of production cycle balances.

CYCLE: Production	CLASS OF TRANSACTIONS: Manufacturing	
EXECUTING	Yes	No

1. Are prenumbered production orders used and accounted for? (E1)
2. Are production orders approved by a supervisor? (E1)
3. Is there a bill of materials for each production order? (E1)
4. Are materials requisitions required before materials can be released for stores? (E2)
5. Are daily totals of direct materials use prepared by stores? (E2)
6. Are time tickets prepared for direct labor incurred? (E3)
7. Are daily totals of direct labor hours prepared and reconciled with time ticket hours? (E3)
8. Are completed production reports prepared? (E4)
9. Is a quality control report issued on finished work? (E4)
10. Do routing tickets accompany the transfer of goods? (E4)
11. Is receipt obtained from transferee when goods are transferred? (E4)

RECORDING

1. Are daily entries for direct materials and direct labor agreed to daily activity reports? (R1)
2. Is there verification of correct application of overhead job cost sheets? (R1)
3. Is there segregation of functions between general accounting and cost accounting? (R1)
4. Are there periodic reconciliations of work in process and finished goods with subsidiary records? (R2, R3)

CUSTODY

1. Is work in process tagged during production? (C1)
2. Are finished goods stored in locked warehouses? (C2)
3. Are perpetual finished goods records periodically compared with goods on hand? (C3)

Figure 11-8. INTERNAL CONTROL QUESTIONNAIRE: MANUFACTURING TRANSACTIONS.

CONCLUDING COMMENTS

The seven chapters pertaining to the study and evaluation of internal control have now been completed. These chapters have explained and illustrated the auditor's responsibilities and methodology for meeting the second standard of field work.

While the study and evaluation of internal control are a vital part of the typical audit engagement, it must be remembered that this auditing standard is not an end in itself. GAAS dictate that a correlation exists between the

Function	Possible Errors and Irregularities	Necessary Control Procedures	Possible Compliance Test
EXECUTING			
1. Issuing production orders	Excessive quantities may be authorized for production.	Supervisory approval of each order.	Review evidence of approval.
2. Issuing raw materials	The wrong materials may be requisitioned.	Bill of materials; supervisory approval of requisitions.	Determine existence of bill of materials; review approval.
3. Processing raw materials	Direct labor time tickets are assigned to overhead.	Daily activity reports of direct labor.	Examine evidence of agreement of activity reports with time tickets.
4. Transferring completed work to finished goods	Goods may be lost during transfer.	Routing ticket and receipt from finished goods.	Examine routing tickets and receipts.
RECORDING			
1. Journalizing and posting manufacturing transactions	Direct materials or direct labor may not be recorded.	Internal verification of daily entries with daily activity reports.	Review evidence of verification.
2. Updating work in process records	Job cost sheets may not be posted.	Periodic reconciliation of work in process with job cost sheets.	Review periodic reconciliations.
3. Updating finished goods records	Perpetual cards may not be posted.	Periodic reconciliations of finished goods with perpetual cards.	Review periodic reconciliations.
CUSTODY			
1. Protecting work in process	Goods may be lost or stolen in production.	Tagging of work and storage in locked areas.	Observe physical controls.
2. Protecting finished goods	Goods may be stolen from warehouse.	Locked warehouse with access only to authorized personnel.	Observe physical controls.
3. Maintaining correctness of finished goods records	Perpetual cards may not agree with goods on hand.	Periodic independent comparisons of records with count of goods on hand.	Review evidence of counts and comparisons.

Figure 11-9. PRELIMINARY EVALUATION CONSIDERATIONS: MANUFACTURING TRANSACTIONS.

TYPE OF TESTING: Compliance   PURPOSE: Study and Evaluation of Internal Control
CYCLE: Production   CLASS OF TRANSACTIONS: Manufacturing

A. CONTROLS IN EXECUTING MANUFACTURING TRANSACTIONS ARE OPERATING AS
   PLANNED.

1. Examine selected production orders for evidence of
   - Proper authorization. (E1)
   - Bill of materials. (E1)
   - Approved materials requisitions. (E2)
   - Approved time tickets. (E3)
   - Use of correct burden rate. (E3)
   - Completed production report. (E4)
   - Quality control report. (E4)
   - Routing tickets. (E4)
   - Signed receipts for goods from finished goods. (E4)
2. Examine evidence of internal verification of daily activity reports of materials and direct labor
   use. (E3)
3. Observe and make inquiries of employees in performance of control procedures.

B. CONTROLS IN RECORDING MANUFACTURING TRANSACTIONS ARE OPERATING AS PLANNED.

1. Review evidence of verification of daily activity reports with daily entries. (R1)
2. Review verification of correct burden rate. (R1)
3. Observe segregation of functions between general accounting and cost accounting. (R2, R3)
4. Examine evidence of periodic reconciliations of control accounts with subsidiary records. (R2,
   R3)

C. CONTROLS OVER THE CUSTODY OF WORK IN PROCESS ARE OPERATING AS PLANNED.

1. Observe physical controls over work in process and finished goods. (C1, C2)
2. Examine evidence of comparisons of finished goods records with goods on hand. (C3)

Figure 11-10. AUDIT PROGRAM: COMPLIANCE TESTS OF MANUFACTURING TRANSACTIONS.

effectiveness of internal controls and the extent to which substantive tests are
to be restricted.

Part III, which follows, considers the substantive tests that may be performed in verifying account balances.

REVIEW QUESTIONS

11-1 Briefly explain the environmental practices associated with payroll transactions.
11-2 What are the functions in (a) executing, (b) recording, and (c) custody of payroll
transactions?
11-3 Indicate the specific internal accounting control objectives in (a) hiring, (b) preparing
the payroll, and (c) paying the payroll.

11-4 What authorizations are required for payroll transactions? For each authorization, identify the department or individual who should make the authorization.

11-5 Explain the primary activities of the (a) timekeeping and (b) payroll departments.

11-6 Distinguish between a payroll summary and a payroll register, and indicate the principal uses of each.

11-7 Diagram the flow of payroll data within (a) the timekeeping and (b) the payroll departments.

11-8 Diagram the flow of payroll data within general accounting.

11-9 What control procedures should be prescribed and followed for proper custody over assets pertaining to payroll transactions?

11-10 Explain the applicability of independent internal verification to (a) executing payroll transactions and (b) custody of payroll funds.

11-11 Describe the steps of the audit program for compliance testing payroll transactions in a manual system that uses a sample of documents.

11-12 What controls should be observed in witnessing the distribution of a payroll?

11-13 What attributes may be identified in using statistical sampling in performing compliance tests of payroll transactions?

11-14 a. Identify the computer runs that are illustrated in Figure 11-6.
b. Which run(s) may be tested by the use of test data?

11-15 Explain the nature of the production cycle.

11-16 Identify the departments reporting to the vice president of operations.

11-17 Enumerate the functions related to the production cycle.

11-18 Indicate the specific accounting control objectives for each function in the execution of manufacturing transactions.

11-19 Indicate the purposes served by production orders in the production cycle.

11-20 What purposes are served by accounting records and procedures in the production cycle?

OBJECTIVE QUESTIONS FROM PROFESSIONAL EXAMINATIONS

Indicate the *best* answer for each of the following multiple-choice questions.

11-21 These questions relate to payroll transactions in the expenditure cycle.

1. The proper use of prenumbered termination notice forms by the payroll department should provide assurance that all
   a. Uncashed payroll checks were issued to employees who have *not* been terminated.
   b. Personnel files are kept up to date.
   c. Employees who have *not* been terminated receive their payroll checks.
   d. Terminated employees are removed from the payroll.

2. For an appropriate segregation of duties, journalizing and posting summary payroll transactions should be assigned to
   a. The treasurer's department.
   b. General accounting.
   c. Payroll accounting.
   d. The timekeeping department.

3. Which of the following internal accounting control procedures could best prevent direct labor from being charged to manufacturing overhead?
   a. Comparison of daily journal entries with factory labor summary.
   b. Examination of routing tickets from finished goods on delivery.
   c. Reconciliation of work in process inventory with cost records.
   d. Recomputation of direct labor based on inspection of time cards.

4. Hitech, Inc., has changed from a conventional to a computerized payroll clock card system. Factory employees now record time in and out with magnetic cards and the EDP system automatically updates all payroll records. Because of this change
   a. The auditor must audit through the computer.
   b. Internal control has improved.
   c. Part of the transaction trail has been lost.
   d. The potential for payroll related fraud has been diminished.

5. In the weekly computer run to prepare payroll checks, a check was printed for an employee who had been terminated the previous week. Which of the following controls, if properly utilized, would have been most effective in preventing the error or ensuring its prompt detection?
   a. A control total for hours worked, prepared from time cards collected by the timekeeping department.
   b. Requiring the treasurer's office to account for the numbers of the prenumbered checks issued to the EDP department for the processing of the payroll.
   c. Use of a check digit for employee numbers.
   d. Use of a header label for the payroll input sheet.

11-22 These questions pertain to manufacturing transactions in the production cycle.

1. A well functioning system of internal control over the inventory/production functions would provide that finished goods are to be accepted for stock only after presentation of a completed production order and a(n)
   a. Shipping order.
   b. Material requisition.
   c. Bill of lading.
   d. Inspection report.

2. A client's physical count of inventories was higher than the inventory quantities per the perpetual records. This situation could be the result of the failure to record
   a. Sales.
   b. Sales discounts.
   c. Purchases.
   d. Purchase returns.

3. The auditor tests the quantity of materials charged to work in process by tracing these quantities to
   a. Cost ledgers.
   b. Perpetual inventory records.
   c. Receiving reports.
   d. Material requisitions.

COMPREHENSIVE QUESTIONS

11-23 The following questions are included in Figure 11-3:

1. Are pay rates, payroll deductions, and terminations authorized by the personnel department?

2. Are time clocks and clock cards used?

3. Is there supervisory approval of time worked by each employee?

4. Is there internal verification of accuracy of payroll computations?

5. Is there supervisory approval of the payroll?

6. Are payroll checks signed and distributed by treasurer office personnel?

7. Is there internal verification of payroll checks with payroll register data?

8. Are costed time tickets verified for proper rates and mathematical accuracy?

9. Are unclaimed wages controlled by a treasurer's office employee?

10. Are personnel and employee earnings records kept in locked files?

11. Are hirings authorized by personnel department?

12. Is time clock punching supervised?

Required

a. Identify the internal accounting control operative objective to which each question relates (i.e., executing, recording, or custody).

b. Identify the function and specific accounting control objective to which the question pertains.

c. Indicate the internal control principle that is involved.

d. Identify an error or irregularity that may result from a "no" answer to each question. (Present your answers in tabular form using separate columns for each part.)

11-24 The following control procedures over payroll transactions are prescribed by the Hahn Company:

1. Operating department requisition for each hiring.

2. Personnel department authorizations for termination of employment.

3. Employee authorizations for payroll deductions.

4. Supervised clock card punching.

5. Internal verification of agreement of payroll checks and payroll register.

6. Distribution of payroll checks by individual who did not prepare payroll.

7. Internal verification of payroll summaries and payroll entries.

8. Supervisor approval of time tickets.

9. Employee identification on distribution of payroll checks.

10. Internal verification of payroll.

Required

a. Indicate the function served by each procedure.

b. Identify an error or irregularity that may be prevented or detected by the control procedure.

c. Indicate a compliance test that may be performed to determine whether each control procedure above is operating as prescribed. (Present your answers in tabular form using separate columns for each part.)

11-25 Assume the following exceptions to prescribed control procedures over payroll transactions occurred in the Haze Company:

1. A fictitious employee is on the payroll.

2. A fictitious pay rate is used in calculating an employee's gross earnings.

3. An employee is paid for unauthorized overtime hours.
4. A mathematical error is made in computing an employee's net earnings.
5. A payroll check is issued for an incorrect amount.
6. A payroll check is distributed to an unauthorized recipient.
7. An employee's time tickets do not agree with clock card hours.
8. A terminated employee is not removed from the payroll.

Required

a. Indicate the function and the specific internal accounting control objective associated with each occurrence.
b. Indicate a control procedure(s) that could prevent or detect the occurrences.
c. Identify a compliance test that would determine whether the controls indicated in b above are operating as planned. (Present your answers in tabular form using separate columns for each part.)

11-26 In the Sumet Company, two employees were terminated for falsifying their time records. The two employees had altered overtime hours on their time cards after their supervisors had approved the hours actually worked.

Several years ago, the company discontinued the use of time clocks. Since then, the plant supervisors have been responsible for manually posting the time cards and approving the hours for which their employees should be paid. The postings are usually entered in pencil by the supervisors or their secretaries. After the postings for the week are complete, the time cards are approved and placed in the mail racks outside the supervisors' offices for pickup by the timekeepers. Sometimes, the timekeepers do not pick up the time cards promptly.

Required

Assuming the company does not wish to return to using time clocks, give three recommendations to prevent recurrence of the situation described above. For each recommendation, indicate how it will deter fraudulent reporting of hours worked.

IIA

11-27 The Kowal Manufacturing Company employs about 50 production workers and has the following payroll procedures.

The factory foreman interviews applicants and on the basis of the interview either hires or rejects the applicants. When the applicant is hired, he prepares a W-4 form (Employee's Withholding Exemption Certificate) and gives it to the foreman. The foreman writes the hourly rate of pay for the new employee in the corner of the W-4 form and then gives the form to a payroll clerk as notice that the worker has been employed. The foreman verbally advises the payroll department of rate adjustments.

A supply of blank time cards is kept in a box near the entrance to the factory. Each worker takes a time card on Monday morning, fills in his name, and notes in pencil on the time card his daily arrival and departure times. At the end of the week, the workers drop the time cards in a box near the door to the factory.

The completed time cards are taken from the box on Monday morning by a payroll clerk. Two payroll clerks divide the cards alphabetically between them, one taking the A to L section of the payroll and the other taking the M to Z section. Each clerk is fully responsible for her section of the payroll. She computes the gross pay, deductions, and net pay, posts the details to the employee's earnings records, and prepares and numbers the payroll checks. Employees are automatically removed from the payroll when they fail to turn in a time card.

The payroll checks are manually signed by the chief accountant and given to the foreman. The foreman distributes the checks to the workers in the factory and arranges for the delivery of the checks to the workers who are absent. The payroll bank account is reconciled by the chief accountant, who also prepares the various quarterly and annual payroll tax reports.

Required

a. Identify the errors or irregularities that may occur in the Kowal Company's procedures.

b. For each error or irregularity in a above, give your recommended improvements.

AICPA (adapted)

11-28 In connection with his examination of the financial statements of the Olympia Manufacturing Company, a CPA is reviewing procedures for accumulating direct labor hours. He learns that all production is by job order and that all employees are paid hourly wages, with time-and-one-half for overtime hours.

Olympia's direct labor hour input process for payroll and job cost determination is summarized in the flowchart on page 397:

Steps A and C are performed in timekeeping, step B in the factory operating departments, step D in payroll audit and control, step E in data preparation (keypunch), and step F in computer operations.

Required

For each input processing step A through F

a. List the possible errors or discrepancies that may occur.

b. Cite the corresponding control procedure for each error or discrepancy.

Note: Your discussion of Olympia's procedures should be limited to the input process for direct labor hours, as shown in steps A through F in the flowchart. Do not discuss personnel procedures for hiring, promotion, termination, and pay rate authorization. In step F do not discuss equipment, computer program, and general computer operational controls.

Organize your answer for each input-processing step as follows:

Step	Possible Errors or Discrepancies	Control Procedures

AICPA

11-29 You are reviewing the working papers containing a narrative description of the Tenney Corporation's factory payroll system. A portion of that narrative is as follows:

Factory employees punch time clock cards each day when entering or leaving the shop. At the end of each week, the timekeeping department collects the time cards and prepares duplicate batch control slips by department showing total hours and number of employees. The time cards and original batch control slips are sent to the payroll accounting section. The second copies of the batch control slips are filed by date.

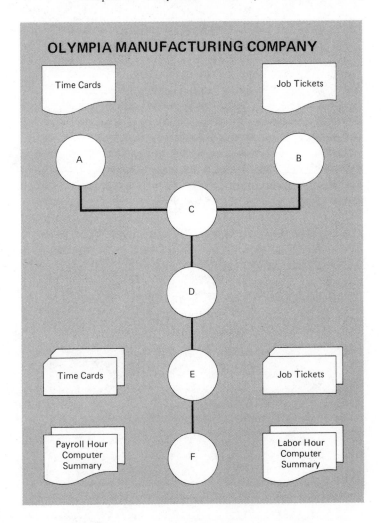

In the payroll accounting section, payroll transaction cards are keypunched from the information on the time cards, and a batch total card for each batch is keypunched from the batch control slip. The time cards and batch control slips are then filed by batch for possible reference. The payroll transaction cards and batch total card are sent to data processing, where they are sorted by employee number within batch. Each batch is edited by a computer program that checks the validity of employee number against a master employee tape file and the total hours and number of employees against the batch total card. A detail printout by batch and employee number is produced which indicates batches that do not balance and invalid employee numbers. This printout is returned to payroll accounting to resolve all differences.

In searching for documentation, you found a flowchart of the payroll system that included all appropriate symbols but was only partially labeled. The portion of this flowchart described by the above narrative appears on page 398.

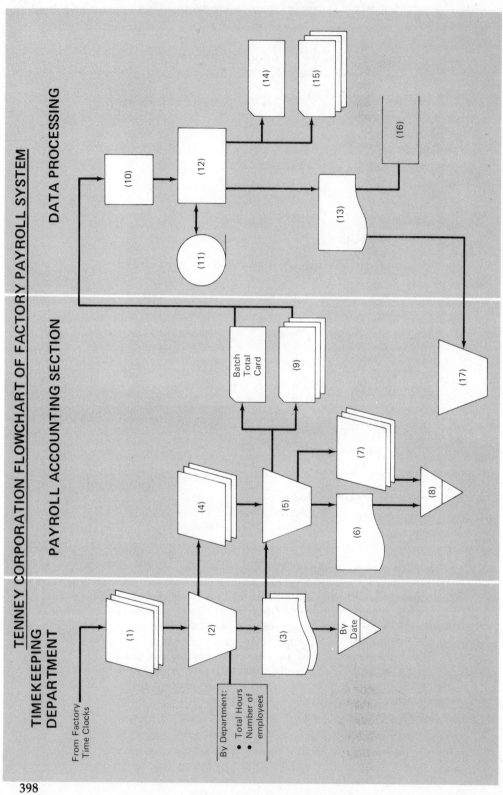

TENNEY CORPORATION FLOWCHART OF FACTORY PAYROLL SYSTEM

TIMEKEEPING DEPARTMENT

PAYROLL ACCOUNTING SECTION

DATA PROCESSING

From Factory Time Clocks

By Department:
• Total Hours
• Number of employees

Batch Total Card

By Date

Required

a. Number your answer 1 through 17. Next to the corresponding number of your answer, supply the appropriate labeling (document name, process description, or file order) applicable to each numbered symbol on the flowchart.

b. Flowcharts are one of the aids an auditor may use to determine and evaluate a client's internal control system. List advantages of using flowcharts in this context.

AICPA

11-30 The Generous Loan Company has 100 branch loan offices. Each office has a manager and four or five subordinates who are employed by the manager. Branch managers prepare the weekly payroll, including their own salaries, and pay employees from cash on hand. The employee signs the payroll sheet signifying receipt of his salary. Hours worked by hourly personnel are inserted in the payroll sheet from time cards prepared by the employees and approved by the manager.

The weekly payroll sheets are sent to the home office along with other accounting statements and reports. The home office compiles employee earnings records and prepares all federal and state salary reports from the weekly payroll sheets.

Salaries are established by home office job evaluation schedules. Salary adjustments, promotions, and transfers of full-time employees are approved by a home office salary committee based on the recommendations of branch managers and area supervisors. Branch managers advise the salary committee of new full-time employees and terminations. Part-time and temporary employees are hired without referral to the salary committee.

Required

a. Based on your review of the system, how might payroll funds be diverted?

b. Indicate your recommendations for improvement.

c. Do you believe any weaknesses in the system are material? Explain.

AICPA (adapted)

11-31 As part of the audit of Manor Company, you are assigned to review and test the payroll transactions of the Galena plant. Your tests show that all numerical items were accurate. The proper hourly rates were used and the wages and deductions were calculated correctly. The payroll register was properly footed, totaled, and posted.

Various plant personnel were interviewed to ascertain the payroll procedures being used in the department. You determine that

1. The payroll clerk receives the time cards from the various department supervisors at the end of each pay period, checks the employee's hourly rate against information provided by the personnel department, and records the regular and overtime hours for each employee.

2. The payroll clerk sends the time cards to the plant's data processing department for compilation and processing.

3. The data processing department returns the time cards with the printed checks and payroll register to the payroll clerk on completion of the processing.

4. The payroll clerk verifies the hourly rate and hours worked for each employee by comparing the detail in the payroll register to the time cards.

5. If errors are found, the payroll clerk voids the computer-generated check, prepares another check for the correct amount, and adjusts the payroll register accordingly.

6. The payroll clerk obtains the plant signature plate from the accounting department and signs the payroll checks.

7. An employee of the personnel department picks up the checks and holds them until they are delivered to the department supervisors for distribution to the employees.

Required

a. Identify the shortcomings in the payroll procedures used in the payroll department of the Galena plant and suggest corrective action.

b. Identify the weaknesses, if any, that you believe are material and the reasons why.

CMA (adapted)

11-32 A CPA's audit working papers contain a narrative description of a segment of the Croyden Factory, Inc. payroll system and the flowchart on page 401.

Narrative

The internal control system with respect to the personnel department is well functioning and is not included in the accompanying flowchart.

At the beginning of each work week, payroll clerk No. 1 reviews the payroll department files to determine the employment status of factory employees and then prepares time cards and distributes them as each individual arrives at work. This payroll clerk, who is also responsible for custody of the signature stamp machine, verifies the identity of each payee before delivering signed checks to the foreman.

At the end of each work week, the foreman distributes payroll checks for the preceding work week. Concurrent with this activity, the foreman reviews the current week's employee time cards, notes the regular and overtime hours worked on a summary form, and initials the aforementioned time cards. The foreman then delivers all time cards and unclaimed payroll checks to payroll clerk No. 2.

Required

a. Based on the narrative and accompanying flowchart, what are the weaknesses in the system of internal control?

b. Based on the narrative and accompanying flowchart, what inquiries should be made with respect to clarifying the existence of possible additional weaknesses in the system of internal control?

Note: Do not discuss the internal control system of the personnel department.

AICPA

11-33 The prescribed control procedures over manufacturing transactions in the Adrian Company are as follows:

1. Bill of materials for each production order.
2. Authorized production order for each job or process.
3. Approved materials requisition slips.
4. Daily activity reports of direct labor.
5. Tagging of work in process.
6. Routing ticket and receipt from finished goods.
7. Periodic reconciliations of work in process with job cost sheets.
8. Storage of finished goods in locked areas.

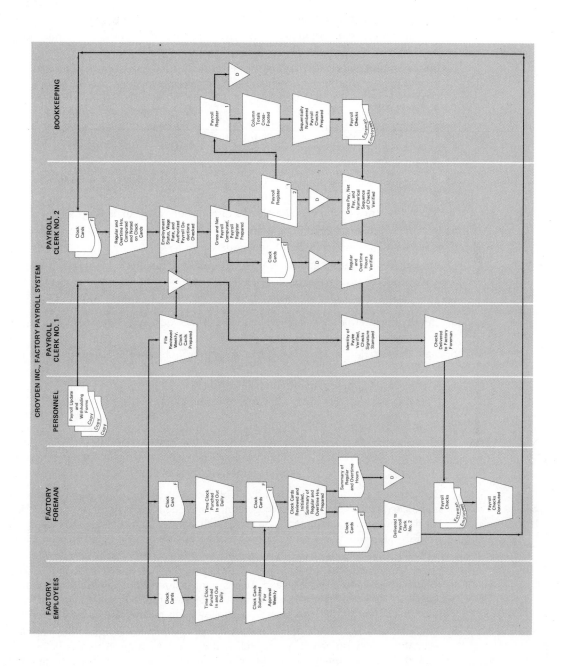

CROYDEN INC., FACTORY PAYROLL SYSTEM

Required

a. Indicate the specific internal accounting control objective served by each procedure.

b. Identify the internal accounting control principle that is involved.

c. Identify an error or irregularity that may be prevented or detected by the control procedure.

d. Indicate a compliance test that may be performed to determine whether each control procedure is operating as prescribed. (Present your answers in tabular form using separate columns for each part.)

11-34 The following questions appear in Figure 11-8:

1. Are production orders approved by a supervisor?
2. Is there verification of correct application of overhead to job cost sheets?
3. Is a quality-control report issued on finished goods?
4. Are daily entries for direct materials and direct labor agreed to daily activity reports?
5. Is work in process tagged during production?
6. Is there a bill of materials for each production order?
7. Are perpetual finished goods records periodically compared with goods on hand?
8. Are completed production reports prepared?

Required

a. Identify the internal control objective to which each question relates (i.e., executing, recording, or custody).

b. State the function and specific accounting control objective to which the question pertains.

c. Indicate an error or irregularity that may result from a "no" answer to each question. (Present your answers in tabular form using separate columns for each part.)

11-35 You have been engaged by the management of Alden, Inc. to review its internal control over the purchase, receipt, storage, and issue of raw materials. You have prepared the following comments that describe Alden's procedures:

1. Raw materials, which consist mainly of high-cost electronic components, are kept in a locked storeroom. Storeroom personnel include a supervisor and four clerks. All are well trained, competent, and adequately bonded. Raw materials are removed from the storeroom only on written or oral authorization of one of the production foremen.

2. There are no perpetual-inventory records; hence, the storeroom clerks do not keep records of goods received or issued. To compensate for the lack of perpetual records, a physical inventory count is taken monthly by the storeroom clerks who are well supervised. Appropriate procedures are followed in making the inventory count.

3. After the physical count, the storeroom supervisor matches quantities counted against a predetermined reorder level. If the count for a given part is below the reorder level, the supervisor enters the part number on a materials requisition list and sends this list to the accounts payable clerk. The accounts payable clerk prepares a purchase order for a predetermined reorder quantity for each part and mails the purchase order to the vendor from whom the part was last purchased.

4. When ordered materials arrive at Alden, they are received by the storeroom clerks. The clerks count the merchandise and agree the counts to the shipper's bill of lading. All vendors' bills of lading are initialed, dated, and filed in the storeroom to serve as receiving reports.

Required

a. Describe the weaknesses in internal control and recommend improvements of Alden's procedures for the purchase, receipt, storage, and issue of raw materials. Organize your answer sheet as follows:

Weaknesses	Recommended Improvements

b. Do you believe any of the weaknesses are material? Explain.

AICPA (adapted)

11-36 The Jameson Company produces a variety of chemical products for use by plastics manufacturers. The plant operates on two shifts, five days per week with maintenance work performed on the third shift and on Saturdays as required.

An audit conducted by the staff of the new corporate internal audit department has recently been completed and the comments on inventory control were not favorable. Audit comments were particularly directed to the control of raw material ingredients and maintenance materials.

Raw material ingredients are received at the back of the plant, signed for by one of the employees of the batching department, and stored near the location of the initial batching process. Receiving tallies are given to the supervisor during the day and he forwards the tallies to the inventory control department at the end of the day. The inventory control department calculates ingredient use using weekly reports of actual production and standard formulas. Physical inventories are taken quarterly. Purchase requisitions are prepared by the inventory control department and rush orders are frequent. In spite of the need for rush orders, the production superintendent regularly gets memos from the controller stating that there must be excess inventory because the ingredient inventory dollar value is too high.

Maintenance parts and supplies are received and stored in a storeroom. There is a storeroom clerk on each of the operating shifts. Storeroom requisitions are to be filled out for everything taken from the storeroom; however, this practice is not always followed. The storeroom is not locked when the clerk is out because of the need to obtain parts quickly. The storeroom is also open during the third shift for the maintenance crews to get parts as needed. Purchase requisitions are prepared by the storeroom clerk and physical inventory is taken on a cycle count basis. Rush orders are frequent.

Required

a. Identify the weaknesses in Jameson Company's internal control procedures used for (1) ingredients inventory and (2) maintenance material and supplies inventory.

b. Recommend improvements that should be instituted for each of these areas.

CMA

11-37 Kent County Grain and Milling Company decided to stimulate the sale of its flour by including a coupon, redeemable for fifty cents (50¢), in every 25- and 50-pound sack of flour produced subsequent to October 1, 19X0. The company contemplates that 150,000 coupons will be in the hands of customers before completion of the promotional campaign on March 31, 19X1.

On commencing your year-end work on January 10, 19X1 for the calendar year ending December 31, 19X0, the controller of Kent County Grain and Milling Company requested that you review the accounting records and the internal accounting controls applicable to the flour coupons.

In your review of the accounting records and the system of internal accounting controls, you learned the following:

1. A perpetual record of coupons received from the printer is entered from a copy of the receiving ticket, damaged coupons are reported orally by a line foreman, and coupons used are entered from a copy of the production report of sacks of flour packed. A summary of the perpetual record as of December 31, 19X0 is as follows:

Coupons received to date	150,000
Coupons damaged and destroyed	(2,000)
Coupons included in 25-pound sacks of flour	(50,000)
Coupons included in 50-pound sacks of flour	(25,000)
On hand per record	73,000

2. Unused coupons are kept in a storeroom with stationery and supplies and are readily accessible. No count of coupons within a package is made as they are received from the printers; however, the number of packages times the indicated amount in each package is recorded on a receiving ticket that is later agreed, in the office, with a copy of the vendor's invoice.

3. Coupons are sometimes damaged by the machinery that mechanically inserts them in the sacks. The production superintendent said that he thought that the line foreman destroyed these coupons. As previously mentioned, the number of damaged coupons is reported to the production superintendent orally each day by the foreman.

4. The line foreman takes a quantity of unused coupons from the storeroom each day based on scheduled production for that day.

5. Correspondence containing coupons mailed to the company for redemption is first opened in the mail department. The coupons are then sent to the cashier's department, where they are redeemed in cash out of a fund especially set up for that purpose. The cashier places a 50 cent piece in a self-addressed envelope, seals the envelope, and returns it to the mail department for ultimate disposition. The cashier stamps the coupon paid with the date of payment.

6. Once each week, the cashier's coupon fund is reimbursed in the same manner as any other imprest fund.

7. Complaints from customers not receiving their 50 cent pieces are sent to the cashier for disposition.

You also learned that a physical inventory of unused coupons was taken on December 31, 19X0. It was found that 71,250 coupons were on hand. As of December 31, 19X0, flour containing 50,000 coupons had been sold to the company's retail outlets. In addition, by December 31, 19X0, 37,500 coupons had been redeemed and paid, and it was estimated that only 50% of the remaining coupons outstanding at that time would be redeemed.

Required

a. Prepare a memorandum to the controller as to weaknesses in his present control procedures in regard to handling redeemable coupons and your recommendations for improvement.

b. Prepare a journal entry setting up the company's liability for unredeemed coupons at December 31, 19X0. Show your method of computing the liability.

c. Identify the weaknesses, if any, you believe are material. Explain fully.

AICPA (adapted)

CASE STUDY

11-38 The Vane Corporation is a manufacturing concern that has been in business for the past 18 years. During this period, the company has grown from a very small family-owned operation to a medium-sized manufacturing concern with several departments. Despite this growth, a substantial number of the procedures employed by Vane Corp. have been in effect since the business was started. Just recently, Vane Corp. has computerized its payroll function.

The payroll function operates in the following manner. Each worker picks up a weekly time card on Monday morning and writes in his name and identification number. These blank cards are kept near the factory entrance. The workers write on the time card the time of their daily arrival and departure. On the following Monday, the factory foremen collect the completed time cards for the previous week and send them to data processing.

In data processing, the time cards are used to prepare the weekly time file. This file is processed with the master payroll file, which is maintained on magnetic tape according to worker identification number. The checks are written by the computer on the regular checking account and imprinted with the treasurer's signature. After the payroll file is updated and the checks are prepared, the checks are sent to the factory foremen, who distribute them to the workers or hold them for the workers to pick up later if they are absent.

The foremen notify data processing of new employees and terminations. Any changes in hourly pay rate or any other changes affecting payroll are usually communicated to data processing by the foremen.

The workers also complete a job time ticket for each individual job they work on each day. The job time tickets are collected daily and sent to cost accounting, where they are used to prepare a cost distribution analysis.

Further analysis of the payroll function reveals the following:

1. A worker's gross wages never exceed $300 per week.
2. Raises never exceed $0.55 per hour for the factory workers.
3. No more than 20 hours of overtime is allowed each week.
4. The factory employs 150 workers in ten departments.

The payroll function has not been operating smoothly for some time, but even more problems have surfaced since the payroll was computerized. The foremen have indicated that they would like a weekly report indicating worker tardiness, absenteeism, and idle time, so they can determine the amount of productive time lost and the reason for the lost time. The following errors and inconsistencies have been encountered in the past few pay periods:

1. A worker's paycheck was not processed properly, because he had transposed two numbers in his identification number when he filled out his time card.

2. A worker was issued a check for $1,531.80 when it should have been $153.81.

3. One worker's paycheck was not written, and this error was not detected until the paychecks for that department were distributed by the foreman.

4. Part of the master payroll file was destroyed when the tape reel was inadvertently mounted on the wrong tape drive and used as a scratch tape. Data processing attempted to reestablish the destroyed portion from original source documents and other records.

5. One worker received a paycheck for an amount considerably larger than he should have. Further investigation revealed that 84 had been punched instead of 48 for hours worked.

6. Several records on the master payroll file were skipped and not included on the updated master payroll file. This was not detected for several pay periods.

7. In processing nonroutine changes, a computer operator included a pay rate increase for one of his friends in the factory. This was discovered by chance by another employee.

Required

Identify the control weaknesses in the payroll procedure and in the computer processing as it is now conducted by the Vane Corp. Recommend the changes necessary to correct the system. Arrange your answer in the following columnar format:

Control Weaknesses	Recommendations

CMA

PART III

VERIFICATION OF ACCOUNT BALANCES

The verification of account balances relates to substantive tests performed by the auditor at or near the balance sheet date. In practice, as in this book, the verification of balances follows the study and evaluation of internal control.

There are five chapters in this section. Chapter 12 describes the use of statistical and nonstatistical sampling in verifying account balances. Chapters 13–15 explain and illustrate the audit objectives and methodology for substantive tests of balances resulting from specific transactions within a given cycle. The final chapter (16) discusses the steps the auditor takes in verifying income statement balances and completing the audit.

Chapter 12

Audit Sampling in Substantive Testing

Study Objectives

After studying this chapter, you should be able to

- Explain the applicability of audit sampling to substantive testing.

- Recognize and define the components of audit risk associated with audit sampling in substantive testing.

- Determine which sampling approach is most appropriate for various sampling application circumstances.

- Explain and apply the essential steps in designing, executing, and evaluating a probability-proportional-to-size sampling plan.

- Enumerate and apply the essential steps for each of the three techniques in classical variables sampling plans.

- Describe the differences between nonstatistical and statistical sampling plans for substantive tests.

The basic concepts of audit sampling and the application of sampling in compliance testing are explained in Chapter 7. This chapter considers the use of audit sampling in substantive testing. The chapter is divided into four sections: (1) basic concepts, (2) probability-proportional-to-size sampling, (3) classical variables sampling, and (4) nonstatistical sampling.

BASIC CONCEPTS

NATURE AND PURPOSE

As explained in Chapter 7, audit sampling is the application of auditing procedures to less than 100% of the items within a population, such as an account balance or class of transactions, for the purpose of evaluating some characteristic of the population. Whereas attribute sampling is used to obtain information about the rate of occurrence of deviations from prescribed controls, the audit sampling methods described in this chapter are used to obtain information about the correctness of monetary amounts. Thus, they serve the purpose of substantive tests, which is to obtain evidence as to the validity and propriety of the accounting treatment of transactions and balances, or conversely, of errors or irregularities therein.

Sampling plans for substantive tests may be designed to (1) test whether an account balance is fairly stated (for example, the book value of accounts receivable) or (2) make an independent estimate of some amount (for example, to price an inventory for which no recorded book value exists). The emphasis in this chapter is on testing the reasonableness of recorded amounts.

UNCERTAINTY AND AUDIT RISK

The auditor is justified in accepting some uncertainty in substantive testing when the cost and time required to make a 100% examination of items in a population are, in his judgment, greater than the adverse consequences of expressing an erroneous opinion from examining only a sample of the data.

Audit sampling in substantive testing is subject to both sampling risk and nonsampling risk. As explained in Chapter 7, the sampling risks associated with substantive testing are

- *Risk of Incorrect Acceptance* (sometimes referred to as the beta risk) is the risk that the sample supports the conclusion that the recorded account balance is not materially misstated when it is materially misstated.
- *Risk of Incorrect Rejection* (sometimes referred to as the alpha risk) is the risk that the sample supports the conclusion that the recorded account balance is materially misstated when it is not materially misstated.[1]

It will be recalled that the risk of incorrect acceptance relates to the effectiveness of the audit, whereas the risk of incorrect rejection relates to audit efficiency.

The risk of incorrect acceptance in audit sampling relates to the detection risk associated with the *specific substantive test of details* that is to be applied to the sample items selected. This risk, therefore, does not refer to the likelihood that *all* substantive tests that may be applied to the account being examined will fail to detect any material errors.

[1] Auditing Standards Board, *Codification of Statements on Auditing Standards* (New York: American Institute of Certified Public Accountants, 1985), Auditing Section 350.12 (hereinafter referred to and cited as AU §).

STATISTICAL SAMPLING APPROACHES

Two statistical sampling approaches may be used by the auditor in substantive testing: (1) probability-proportional-to-size (PPS) sampling and (2) classical variables sampling.

The fundamental difference between the two approaches is that PPS sampling is based on *attribute sampling theory,* while classical variables sampling is based on *normal distribution theory.* Each approach can contribute to obtaining sufficient evidence under the third standard of field work. However, in certain circumstances, as described in this chapter, one approach may be more practical and appropriate in meeting the auditor's objective than the other.

The principal circumstances affecting the choice between the two approaches are tabulated in Figure 12-1. It may be observed for example, that PPS sampling may be more appropriate when (1) the number of units in, and the variability of, the population are unknown, (2) the population contains only debit balances, (3) only a few errors of overstatement are expected, and (4) computer assistance is not available.

PROBABILITY-PROPORTIONAL-TO-SIZE-SAMPLING[2]

PPS sampling is an approach that uses attribute sampling theory to express a conclusion in dollar amounts rather than as a rate of deviations. This form of sampling may be used in the substantive testing of both transactions and balances.

PPS is primarily applicable in testing transactions and balances for overstatement. It may be especially useful in tests of

- Receivables when unapplied credits to customer accounts are insignificant.
- Investment securities.
- Inventory price tests when few differences are anticipated.
- Plant asset additions.[3]

PPS sampling may not be the most cost-effective approach for receivables and inventories when the above conditions are not met and where the primary objective is to independently estimate the value of a class of transactions or balances.

---

[2]There are three variations of PPS sampling: (1) dollar unit sampling (DUS), (2) cumulative monetary amount (CMA), and (3) combined attribute variables (CAV) sampling. The distinctions among these variations are beyond the scope of this text.

[3]Statistical Sampling Subcommittee, *Audit and Accounting Guide: Audit Sampling,* (New York: American Institute of Certified Public Accountants, 1983), p. 69. (Hereinafter referred to as *Audit Sampling Guide.*)

| | Appropriate Sampling Approach | |
Sampling Application Circumstances	PPS	Classical Variables
AVAILABILITY OF INFORMATION		
Book values for sampling units not available		X
Number of units in population unknown at start of sampling	X	
Variability of population unknown	X	
CHARACTERISTICS OF POPULATION UNITS		
Existence of zero or credit balances		X
EXPECTATIONS REGARDING ERRORS		
Expect few errors of overstatement only	X	
Expect many errors or errors of both under- and overstatement		X
EASE OF APPLICATION		
Computer assistance not available	X	

Figure 12-1. CIRCUMSTANCES AFFECTING SELECTION OF SAMPLING APPROACH FOR SUBSTANTIVE TESTING.

SAMPLING PLAN

The steps in a PPS sampling plan are similar but not identical to those used in attribute sampling. The steps are:

- Determine the objectives of the plan.
- Define the population and sampling unit.
- Determine the sample size.
- Determine the sample selection method.
- Execute the sampling plan.
- Evaluate the sample results.

The considerations involved in executing these steps are explained below and a case study is used to illustrate each step. The auditor should document each step in his working papers.

DETERMINE THE OBJECTIVES OF THE PLAN

The most common objective of PPS sampling plans is to test the fairness of a recorded account balance. To illustrate this application, it is assumed that the auditor's objective is to obtain evidence about the book value of trade accounts receivable of the Harris Company.

DEFINE THE POPULATION AND SAMPLING UNIT

The population consists of the class of transactions or the account balance to be tested. For each population, the auditor should decide whether all of the items should be included. For example, four populations are possible when the population is based on account balances in the customers' ledger: that is all balances, debit balances, credit balances, and zero balances.

The sampling unit in PPS sampling is the individual dollar, and the population is considered to be a *number* of dollars equal to the total dollar amount of the population. Each dollar in the population is given an equal chance of being selected in the sample. While individual dollars are the basis for sample selection, the auditor does not actually examine individual dollars in the population. Rather he examines the account, transaction, document, or line item associated with the dollar selected. Individual dollars selected for a sample are sometimes thought of as hooks that upon selection snag or bring in the entire item with which they are associated. The item snagged (account, document, etc.) is known as a *logical sampling unit.*

It is this feature that gives PPS sampling its name. The more dollars associated with a logical unit, the greater its chance of being snagged. Thus, the likelihood of selection is proportional to its size. This feature is also responsible for two limitations of PPS sampling. In testing assets, zero and negative balances should be excluded from the population because such balances have no chance of being selected in the sample. Similarly, PPS sampling is not suitable in testing liabilities for understatement since the more a balance is understated the less is its chance of being included in the sample.

The auditor chooses a logical sampling unit compatible with the nature of the audit procedures to be performed. Accordingly, if the auditor intends to seek confirmation of customer account balances, he would ordinarily choose the customer account as the logical unit. Alternatively, the auditor might choose to seek confirmation of specific transactions with customers. In that case he might choose customer invoices as the logical unit. The auditor then selects the sample items from a physical representation of the population, such as a computer printout of customer balances, or computer audit software may be used to select the sample items directly from a machine-readable form of the physical representation. Before selecting the sample, the auditor should determine that the physical representation is complete. This may be done by manually reconciling the printout to a control account balance, or by using the computer to reconcile a machine-readable file to a control total.

For the Harris Company, (1) the population is defined as customer accounts with debit balances, (2) the aggregate book value of these accounts is $600,000, (3) the customer account is defined as the logical sampling unit, and (4) the printout from which the accounts are to be selected has been reconciled to the control account balance of $600,000 referred to above.

DETERMINE SAMPLE SIZE

The formula for determining sample size in PPS sampling is

$$n = \frac{BV \times RF}{TE - (AE \times EF)}$$

where

BV = book value of population tested.

RF = reliability factor for the specified risk of incorrect acceptance.

TE = tolerable error.

AE = anticipated error.

EF = expansion factor for anticipated error.

Each of these factors is explained below.

Book Value of Population Tested

The book value specified in determining sample size must relate precisely to the definition of the population as described in the preceding section. The amount of the book value has a direct effect on sample size—the larger the book value being tested, the larger the sample size.

Reliability Factor for Specified Risk of Incorrect Acceptance

In specifying an acceptable level of risk of incorrect acceptance, the auditor should consider (1) the level of audit risk that he is willing to take that a material error in the account will go undetected, (2) the degree of assurance obtained from reliance on internal accounting controls, and (3) the results of other auditing procedures including analytical review. For example, if he concludes that substantial reliance can be placed on internal controls, and if other auditing procedures provide some assurance about the fairness of the book value being tested, he will be willing to accept a higher risk of incorrect acceptance for the PPS sample, perhaps up to 30 percent. If little reliance can be placed on the controls, and if other procedures provide little assurance about the account being tested, then greater assurance must be obtained from the test and the auditor will specify a low risk of incorrect acceptance, perhaps as low as 5 percent. Experience and professional judgment must be used in making these determinations.[4] The risk of incorrect acceptance has an inverse effect on sample size—the lower the specified risk, the larger the sample size.

[4]A model for relating the risk components in an audit is presented in Appendix A of this chapter.

The reliability factor (RF) for this risk is obtained from Figure 12-2. It is based on the risk of incorrect acceptance specified by the auditor and *zero number of overstatement errors*, regardless of the number of errors anticipated. In the Harris Company, the auditor specifies a 5% risk of incorrect acceptance. Thus, the reliability factor is 3.0.

Tolerable Error

Tolerable error is the maximum error that can exist in an account before it is considered to be materially misstated. Some auditors use the term *materiality* (or material amount) as an alternative to tolerable error. In specifying this factor, the auditor should realize that errors in individual accounts, when aggregated with errors in other accounts, may cause the financial statements as a whole to be materially misstated.

RELIABILITY FACTORS FOR ERRORS OF OVERSTATEMENT

Number of Over-statement Errors	Risk of Incorrect Acceptance								
	1%	5%	10%	15%	20%	25%	30%	37%	50%
0	4.61	3.00	2.31	1.90	1.61	1.39	1.21	1.00	.70
1	6.64	4.75	3.89	3.38	3.00	2.70	2.44	2.14	1.68
2	8.41	6.30	5.33	4.72	4.28	3.93	3.62	3.25	2.68
3	10.05	7.76	6.69	6.02	5.52	5.11	4.77	4.34	3.68
4	11.61	9.16	8.00	7.27	6.73	6.28	5.90	5.43	4.68
5	13.11	10.52	9.28	8.50	7.91	7.43	7.01	6.49	5.68
6	14.57	11.85	10.54	9.71	9.08	8.56	8.12	7.56	6.67
7	16.00	13.15	11.78	10.90	10.24	9.69	9.21	8.63	7.67
8	17.41	14.44	13.00	12.08	11.38	10.81	10.31	9.68	8.67
9	18.79	15.71	14.21	13.25	12.52	11.92	11.39	10.74	9.67
10	20.15	16.97	15.41	14.42	13.66	13.02	12.47	11.79	10.67
11	21.49	18.21	16.60	15.57	14.78	14.13	13.55	12.84	11.67
12	22.83	19.45	17.79	16.72	15.90	15.22	14.63	13.89	12.67
13	24.14	20.67	18.96	17.86	17.02	16.32	15.70	14.93	13.67
14	25.45	21.89	20.13	19.00	18.13	17.40	16.77	15.97	14.67
15	26.75	23.10	21.30	20.13	19.24	18.49	17.84	17.02	15.67
16	28.03	24.31	22.46	21.26	20.34	19.58	18.90	18.06	16.67
17	29.31	25.50	23.61	22.39	21.44	20.66	19.97	19.10	17.67
18	30.59	26.70	24.76	23.51	22.54	21.74	21.03	20.14	18.67
19	31.85	27.88	25.91	24.63	23.64	22.81	22.09	21.18	19.67
20	33.11	29.07	27.05	25.74	24.73	23.89	23.15	22.22	20.67

Figure 12-2. RELIABILITY FACTORS FOR PPS SAMPLING. (SOURCE: *Audit Sampling Guide, op. cit.,* p. 117.)

Tolerable error has an inverse effect on sample size—the smaller the tolerable error, the larger the sample size. For the Harris Company, the auditor specifies a tolerable error equal to 5% of book value, or $30,000.

Anticipated Error and Expansion Factor

In PPS sampling, the auditor does not quantify the risk of incorrect rejection. This risk is controlled indirectly, however, by specifying the anticipated error that is inversely related to the risk of incorrect rejection and directly related to sample size.

The auditor uses his prior experience and knowledge of the client and professional judgment in determining an amount for anticipated error. He must bear in mind that an excessively high anticipated error will unnecessarily increase sample size, while too low an estimate will result in a high risk of incorrect rejection. For the Harris Company, the auditor specifies anticipated error of $6,000.

The expansion factor is required only when errors are anticipated. It is obtained from Figure 12-3 using the auditor's specified risk of incorrect acceptance. The smaller the specified risk of incorrect acceptance, the larger the expansion factor. Like anticipated error, the expansion factor has a direct effect on sample size. In the Harris case study, the expansion factor for anticipated error is 1.6. The combined effect of anticipated error (*AE*) and this factor (*EF*) is then subtracted from tolerable error in determining sample size.

Calculation of Sample Size

The factors for determining sample size in the Harris Company are $BV = \$600,000$; $RF = 3.0$; $TE = \$30,000$; $AE = \$6,000$; and $EF = 1.6$. Thus, sample size is 88, computed as follows:

$$n = \frac{\$600,000 \times 3.0}{\$30,000 - (\$6000 \times 1.6)} = 88$$

EXPANSION FACTORS FOR EXPECTED ERRORS

	Risk of Incorrect Acceptance								
	1%	5%	10%	15%	20%	25%	30%	37%	50%
Factor	1.9	1.6	1.5	1.4	1.3	1.25	1.2	1.15	1.0

Figure 12-3. EXPANSION FACTORS FOR PPS SAMPLING. (Source: *Audit Sampling Guide, op. cit.,* p. 118.)

The effect on sample size of a change in the value of one factor, while holding the other factors constant, may be summarized as follows:

Factor	Relationship to Sample Size
Book value	Direct
Risk of incorrect acceptance	Inverse
Tolerable error	Inverse
Anticipated error	Direct
Expansion factor for anticipated error	Direct

[handwritten annotation: higher 20 of not lower sample]

It may be noted that specifying a low risk of incorrect acceptance makes sample size larger in two ways: (1) by increasing the value of the numerator in the formula through the *RF* factor and (2) by decreasing the value of the denominator through the expansion factor (*EF*).

DETERMINE THE SAMPLE SELECTION METHOD

The most common selection method used in PPS sampling is systematic selection. This method divides the total population of dollars into equal intervals of dollars. A logical unit is then systematically selected from each interval. Thus, a sampling interval (*SI*) must be calculated as follows:

$$SI = \frac{BV}{n}$$

In the Harris Company, the sampling interval is $6,818 ($600,000 ÷ 88).

The initial step in the selection process is to pick a starting random number between 1 and 6,818. The sample will then include each logical unit that contains every 6,818th dollar thereafter in the population. In the selection process, it is necessary to determine the cumulative balance of the book values of the logical units in order to determine which logical units are hooked or snagged by the individual dollar units selected. The process is illustrated for the Harris Company in Figure 12-4 where (1) the customer account number is used to identify the logical units and (2) the starting random number is 5,000. Note that the amounts in the dollar unit selected column represent every 6,818th dollar after 5,000. The dollar unit selected causes the entire book value of the related logical sampling unit to be included in the sample. It may be observed that the selection process will result in the selection of *all* logical units with book values equal to or greater than the sampling interval. The use of a computer program facilitates the selection process. However, it is also possible to select manually with the aid of an adding machine.

Logical Unit (Customer Number)	Book Value	Cumulative Balance	Dollar Unit Selected	Book Value of Sample Item
01001	$1,200	$ 1,200		
01025	6,043	7,243	5,000	$6,043
01075	2,190	9,433		
01140	3,275	12,708	11,818	3,275
01219	980	13,688		
01365	1,647	15,335		
01431	4,260	19,595	18,636	4,260
01592	480	20,075		
01667	7,150	27,225	25,454	7,150
.				
.				
.				
Total	$600,000			

Figure 12.-4. SYSTEMATIC SELECTION PROCESS.

EXECUTE THE SAMPLING PLAN

In this phase of the plan, the auditor applies appropriate auditing procedures to determine an audit value for each logical unit included in the sample. In the Harris sample, this includes obtaining confirmations for as many sample units as possible and applying alternative procedures when no response is received to the confirmation request.

When differences occur, the auditor records both the book and audit values in his working papers. This information is then used to project the total error in the population as explained in the next section.

EVALUATE THE SAMPLE RESULTS

In evaluating the results of the sample, the auditor considers (1) the projected error determined from the sample, (2) the allowance for sampling risk, and (3) the upper error limit. Item (3) is the sum of items (1) and (2). These factors are analogous to the sample deviation rate, allowance for sampling risk, and upper deviation limit used in evaluating the results of an attribute sampling plan, as discussed in Chapter 7. However, in PPS sampling, each factor is expressed as a dollar amount rather than as a percentage. The evaluation process differs depending on whether any errors are found in the sample.

No Errors

The error results of the sample are used to project the error in the population. When no errors are discovered in the sample, the projected error is zero dollars. Moreover, the allowance for sampling risk is equal to the upper error limit, which always is equal to or less than the tolerable error specified in designing the sample. Accordingly, when no errors are found, the auditor can ordinarily conclude, without making additional calculations, that the book value of the population is not overstated by more than the tolerable error at the specified risk of incorrect acceptance.

If no errors are found in the sample when some were anticipated in the sample design, the auditor may wish to express a more precise conclusion about the population by calculating the allowance for sampling risk. When no errors are found, this factor consists of one component sometimes referred to as *basic precision* (*BP*). The amount is obtained by multiplying the reliability factor (*RF*) for zero errors at the specified risk of incorrect acceptance times the sampling interval (*SI*). In the Harris Company, basic precision is $20,454 computed as follows:

$$BP = RF \times SI$$
$$= 3.0 \times \$6,818$$
$$= \$20,454$$

Since projected error is zero, this amount is also equal to the upper error limit, which is less than the $30,000 tolerable error specified in the sample design. Thus, the auditor may now state that the book value for the population is not overstated by more than $20,454 at a 5% risk of incorrect acceptance.

Some Errors

If errors are found in the sample, the auditor must calculate both the projected error in the population and the allowance for sampling risk in order to determine the upper error limit for overstatement errors. The upper error limit is then compared with tolerable error.

Projected Population Error. A projected error amount is calculated for each logical unit containing an error. These amounts are then summed to arrive at the projected error for the entire population. The projected error is calculated differently for (1) logical units with book values less than the sampling interval and (2) logical units with book values equal to or greater than the sampling interval.

For *each* logical unit with a book value less than the sampling interval that contains an error, a tainting percentage and projected error are calculated as follows:

Tainting Percentage = (book value − audit value) ÷ book value
Projected error   = tainting percentage × sampling interval

The calculations recognize that each logical unit included in the sample represents one sampling interval of the dollars in the population book value. Thus, the degree to which a logical unit is "tainted" with error is projected to all of the dollars in the sampling interval it represents.

For each logical unit for which the book value is equal to or greater than the sampling interval, the projected error is the amount of error found in the unit (book value − audit value). Since the logical unit itself is equal to or greater than the sampling interval, a tainting percentage to project the error to the interval is unnecessary. Rather, the actual amounts of such errors are used in arriving at the projected error for the population as a whole.

To illustrate, assume the PPS sample of the Harris Company's accounts receivable revealed the following errors:

Book Value (BV)	Audit Value (AV)	Tainting Percentage (TP = (BV − AV)/BV)	Sampling Interval (SI)	Projected Error (TP × SI) or (BV − AV)
$ 950	$ 855	10	$6,818	$ 682
2,500	−0−	100	6,818	6,818
7,650	6,885	N/A*	N/A*	765
5,300	5,035	5	6,818	341
8,000	−0−	N/A*	N/A*	8,000
$24,400	$12,775			$16,606

*Logical unit is greater than sampling interval; therefore, projected error equals actual error (BV − AV).

Note that the first, second, and fourth logical units containing errors have book values less than the sampling interval. Accordingly, tainting percentages have been calculated and used to determine the projected errors. The third and fifth units have book values greater than the sampling interval. Therefore, the projected error for each is the difference between the book value and the audit value. The total error in the sample is $11,625 ($24,400 − $12,775) and the total projected error in the population is $16,606.

Allowance for Sampling Risk. The allowance for sampling risk for samples containing errors has two components: (1) basic precision and (2) an incremental allowance resulting from the errors. The calculation of basic precision is the same as explained previously for no errors. Thus, in the Harris Company, the amount of this component is again $20,454.

To calculate the incremental allowance for sampling risk, the auditor must consider separately the logical units with book values less than the sampling interval and those with book values equal to or greater than the sampling interval. Since *all* logical units equal to or greater than the sampling interval will have been examined, there is no sampling risk associated with them. Consequently, the calculation of the incremental allowance involves only errors related to logical units with book values less than the sampling interval.

The calculation of the incremental allowance involves the following steps:

- Determine the appropriate incremental change in reliability factors.
- Rank the projected errors for *logical units less than the sampling interval* from highest to lowest.

- Multiply the ranked projected errors by the appropriate factor and sum the products.

The following tabulation illustrates the first step:

5% Risk of Incorrect Acceptance

Number of Overstatement Errors	Reliability Factor	Incremental Change in Reliability Factor	Incremental Change in Reliability Factor Minus One
0	3.00	—	—
1	4.75	1.75	.75
2	6.30	1.55	.55
3	7.76	1.46	.46
4	9.16	1.40	.40

The data in the first two columns above are taken from Figure 12-2 for the specified risk of incorrect acceptance (5% in this illustration). Each entry in the third column is the reliability factor on the same line less the reliability factor on the previous line. The column four factors are obtained by subtracting one from each of the column three factors.

The second and third steps are illustrated below.

Ranked Projected Errors	Incremental Change in Reliability Factor Minus One	Incremental Allowance for Sampling Risk
$6,818	.75	$5,114
682	.55	375
341	.46	157
		$5,646

Observe that (1) only the projected errors for logical units less than the sampling interval are ranked and (2) the appropriate reliability factor is obtained from column four of the preceding tabulation. The incremental allowances for the projected errors are then added to determine the total incremental allowance of $5,646. Thus, the total allowance for sampling risk in the Harris Company is $26,100 computed as follows:

Basic precision	$20,454
Incremental allowance for sampling risk	5,646
Total allowance for sampling risk	$26,100

Upper Error Limit for Overstatement Errors. The upper error limit equals the sum of the projected errors plus the allowance for sampling risk. For the

Harris sample, the upper error limit is

Projected errors	$16,606
Allowance for sampling risk	26,100
Upper error limit	$42,706

Thus, the auditor may conclude that there is a 5% risk that the book value is overstated by $42,706 or more.

Generally, if the upper error limit is less than the tolerable error, the sample results support the conclusion that the population book value is not misstated by more than the tolerable error at the specified risk of incorrect acceptance. In the Harris sample, the upper error limit exceeds the tolerable error of $30,000 specified in designing the sample. When this occurs, the auditor should consider several possible reasons and alternative courses of action. These matters are discussed below in the section on *Reaching an Overall Conclusion*. However, whether the upper error limit is less than, equal to, or greater than the tolerable error, certain qualitative considerations should be made prior to reaching an overall conclusion.

Qualitative Considerations. As in attribute sampling, the auditor should consider the qualitative aspects of the monetary misstatements. He should realize that the misstatements may be due to (1) differences in principle or application, or (2) errors or irregularities. He should also consider the relationship of the misstatements to other phases of the audit. For example, if misstatements are discovered in substantive tests in amounts or frequency greater than implied by the degree of reliance initially placed on internal accounting control, the auditor should consider whether the planned reliance is still appropriate.

Reaching an Overall Conclusion. The auditor uses professional judgment in combining evidence from several sources to reach an overall conclusion on the fairness of an account balance. When (1) the results of a PPS sample reveal the upper error limit to be less than the tolerable error, (2) the results of other substantive tests do not contradict this finding, and (3) analysis of the qualitative considerations reveals no evidence of irregularities, the auditor can generally conclude that the population is fairly stated. When any of these conditions do not hold, further evaluation of the circumstances is necessary.

For example, if the upper error limit is greater than the tolerable error, the auditor should consider the following possible reasons and actions:

- The sample is not representative of the population. The auditor might suspect this is the case when all other related evidence suggests the population is fairly stated. In this case, the auditor might examine additional sampling units or perform alternative procedures to determine whether the population is misstated.[5]

- The amount of anticipated error specified in designing the sample may not have been large enough relative to tolerable error to adequately limit the allowance for sampling risk. That is, the population may not be misstated by more than the tolerable error, but because the amount of error in the population is greater than anticipated, more precise information is needed from the sample. If the auditor believes this situation pertains, he may examine additional sampling units and reevaluate or perform alternative auditing procedures to determine whether the population is misstated by more than the tolerable error.

- The population may be misstated by more than the tolerable error. If the auditor believes this to be the case, he may request the client to investigate the errors and, if appropriate, adjust the book value.

As a result of any of these courses of action, the client's book value might be adjusted. If the upper error limit after adjustment is less than the tolerable error, the sample results would support the conclusion that the population, as adjusted, is not misstated by more than the tolerable error at the specified risk of incorrect acceptance. For example, in the Harris sample, two receivables with book values of $2,500 and $8,000 were found to have audit values of zero. If these accounts were written off, the projected error for the population would be reduced by $6,818 + $8,000 = $14,818. Additionally, the incremental allowance for sampling risk related to the $2,500 receivable would be eliminated, further reducing the upper error limit below the $30,000 tolerable error specified in designing the sample.

Figure 12-5 illustrates how the application of PPS sampling in the audit of the Harris Company's receivables may be documented in a microcomputer-generated working paper.

ADVANTAGES AND DISADVANTAGES OF PPS SAMPLING

In making a decision as to the use of this approach in audit sampling, the auditor should be aware of the advantages and disadvantages of PPS sampling. The advantages of PPS sampling are

- It is generally easier to use than classical variables sampling because the auditor can calculate sample sizes and evaluate sample results by hand or with the assistance of tables.

- The size of a PPS sample is not based on any measure of the estimated variation of audit values.

- PPS sampling automatically results in a stratified sample because items are selected in proportion to their dollar values.

[5]A simple method of expanding the sample is to divide the sampling interval in half. This will produce a sample containing all of the units in the original sample plus an equal number of additional units. Other methods of expanding the sample size are beyond the scope of this text.

OBJECTIVE:	TO TEST FAIRNESS OF AGGREGATE BOOK VALUE OF CUSTOMER ACCOUNTS WITH DEBIT BALANCES AS OF 12/31/X1.
POPULATION AND SAMPLING UNIT:	TOTAL BOOK VALUE OF ACCOUNTS WITH DEBIT BALANCES PER MASTER FILE PRINTOUT. LOGICAL SAMPLING UNIT = CUSTOMER ACCOUNT

SAMPLE SIZE:
BOOK VALUE OF POPULATION	600,000 (BV)		
RISK OF INCORRECT ACCEPTANCE	5 %	RF=	3.0
TOLERABLE ERROR	30,000 (TE)		
ANTICIPATED ERROR	6,000 (AE)	EF=	1.6
n = (BV * RF)/(TE - (AE * EF))	88		

SAMPLE SELECTION:
SAMPLING INTERVAL = BV/n	6,818 (SI)
RANDOM START	5,000
LOGICAL SAMPLING UNITS SELECTED LISTED ON W/P	B-3

EXECUTION OF SAMPLING PLAN:
AUDIT PROCEDURES APPLIED LISTED ON W/P B-1
BOOK AND AUDIT VALUES FOR SAMPLE ITEMS WITH ERRORS LISTED BELOW

EVALUATION OF SAMPLE RESULTS:

PROJECTED ERROR:

	BOOK VALUE (BV)	AUDIT VALUE (AV)	TAINTING % (TP) = ((BV - AV)/BV)	SAMPLING INTERVAL (SI)	PROJECTED ERROR (TP * SI) OR (BV - AV)
1	950	855	10	6,818	682
2	2,500	0	100	6,818	6,818
3	7,650	6,885	N/A	N/A	765
4	5,300	5,035	5	6,818	341
5	8,000	0	N/A	N/A	8,000
	24,400	12,775		TOTAL	16,606

ALLOWANCE FOR SAMPLING RISK:

BASIC PRECISION (BP) = RF * SI		20,454

INCREMENTAL ALLOWANCE:

	RANKED PROJECTED ERRORS	INCREMENTAL CHANGE IN RELIABILITY FACTOR MINUS ONE	INCREMENTAL ALLOWANCE FOR SAMPLING RISK
1	6,818	0.75	5,114
2	682	0.55	375
3	341	0.46	157
		TOTAL	5,646

ALLOW FOR SAMP RISK = BP + INCREMENTAL ALLOW   26,100

UPPER ERROR LIMIT:
UEL = PROJECTED ERROR + ALLOWANCE FOR SAMPLING RISK   42,706   UEL > TE

CONCLUSION: UEL of $42,706 exceeds TE of $30,000. Client subsequently agreed to write off two accounts with book values of $2,500 and $8,000, respectively, and audit values of zero. This reduces UEL to $22,774, which is below TE. See adjusting entry on W/P AE-1. Total of customer accounts with debit balances, as adjusted, is fairly stated.

Figure 12-5. PPS SAMPLING PLAN WORKING PAPER.

- PPS systematic sample selection automatically identifies any item that is individually significant if its value exceeds an upper monetary cutoff.
- If the auditor expects no errors, PPS sampling will usually result in a smaller sample size than under classical variables sampling.
- A PPS sample can be designed more easily and sample selection may begin before the complete population is available.

In contrast, PPS sampling has the following disadvantages:

- It includes an assumption that the audit value of a sampling unit should not be less than zero or greater than book value. When understatements or audit values of less than zero are anticipated, special design considerations may be required.
- If understatements are identified in the sample, the evaluation of the sample may require special considerations.
- The selection of zero balances or balances of a different sign requires special consideration.
- PPS evaluation may overstate the allowance for sampling risk when errors are found in the sample. As a result, the auditor may be more likely to reject an acceptable book value for the population.
- As the expected number of errors increases, the appropriate sample size increases. Thus a larger sample size may result than under classical variables sampling.[6]

Professional judgment should be exercised by the auditor in determining the appropriateness of this approach in a given audit circumstance.

CLASSICAL VARIABLES SAMPLING

As explained earlier, the auditor may use a classical variables sampling approach in substantive testing. Under this approach, normal distribution theory is used in evaluating the characteristics of a population based on the results of a sample drawn from the population.

Classical variables sampling may be useful to the auditor when the audit objective relates to either the possible under- or overstatement of an account balance and other circumstances when PPS sampling is not appropriate or cost-effective.

TYPES OF SAMPLING TECHNIQUES

There are three techniques (or methods) that may be used in classical variables sampling: (1) mean-per-unit (MPU), (2) difference, and (3) ratio. All three techniques require the determination of the total number of units in the pop-

[6]*Audit Sampling Guide, op. cit.,* pp. 68–69.

ulation and an audit value for each item in the sample. The auditor should consider the following constraints in selecting the technique that is most appropriate in the circumstances.

- *The Ability to Design a Stratified Sample.* Stratification may significantly reduce sample size under the MPU method but may not materially affect sample size under the difference or ratio techniques.
- *The Expected Number of Differences Between Audit and Book Values.* A minimum number of differences must exist between these values in the sample to use either the difference or ratio techniques.
- *The Available Information.* Book values must be available for each sampling unit in ratio and difference estimation. Book values are not required with the MPU technique.[7]

When all of the constraints can be satisfied by any of the methods, the auditor ordinarily will prefer either difference or ratio estimation because these methods generally require a smaller sample size than the MPU method. Thus, they are more cost efficient in meeting the auditor's objectives.

The sampling plan for each technique involves the same steps required in PPS sampling. However, as explained below, there is some variation in the way some of the steps are performed among the three techniques.

MEAN-PER-UNIT (MPU) ESTIMATION[8]

This technique involves determination of an audit value for each item in the sample. An average of these audit values is then calculated and multiplied by the number of units in the population to obtain an estimate of the total population value. An allowance for sampling risk associated with this estimate is then calculated for use in evaluating the sample results.

Determine the Objectives of the Plan

The objective of an MPU sampling plan may be to test the fairness of a recorded account balance or develop an independent estimate of an amount when no recorded book value is available. For illustrative purposes, it is assumed that a test is to be made of the fairness of the book value of loans receivable in the Ace Finance Company.

Define the Population and Sampling Unit

In defining the population, the auditor should consider the nature of the items comprising the population and whether all items should be eligible for inclusion in the sample. It is not necessary, however, to verify that the book values

---

[7] *Audit Sampling Guide, op. cit.*, pp. 90–91 (adapted).

[8] This technique is sometimes referred to as the *simple extension* method.

for the individual items sum to the total recorded book value of the population because the individual book values are not a variable in MPU calculations.

The sampling unit should be compatible with the audit objective and the audit procedures to be performed. For example, if the objective is to determine whether the recorded balance for accounts receivable is fairly stated and evidence is to be obtained by seeking confirmation of account balances from customers, then the *customer account* should be the sampling unit. Alternatively, if the objective is to determine whether the sales account is fairly stated and evidence is to be obtained by examining documents supporting recorded sales transactions, then *line entries* in the sales journal would be an appropriate sampling unit. A physical representation of all units comprising the population, such as a list of customer accounts, facilitates the process of selecting units for the sample.

For the Ace Finance Company: (1) the population is defined as 3,000 small loans receivable, (2) the recorded book value of these receivables is $1,340,000, (3) individual loans are defined as the sampling unit, and (4) the physical representation from which sample items are selected is a computer printout listing all loans receivable.

Determine the Sample Size

The following factors determine sample size in an MPU estimation sample:

- Population size (number of units).
- Estimated population standard deviation.
- Tolerable error.
- Risk of incorrect rejection.
- Risk of incorrect acceptance.
- Allowance for sampling risk.

Population Size. It is critical to have accurate knowledge of the number of units in the population since this factor enters into the calculation of both the sample size and sample results. Population size directly affects sample size—that is, the larger the population, the larger the sample size. As noted above, the population for the Ace Finance Company consists of 3,000 loans receivable.

Estimated Population Standard Deviation. In MPU estimation, the sample size required to achieve specified statistical objectives is related directly to the variability of the values of the population items. The measure of variability used is the standard deviation. Since an audit value is not obtained for every population item, the *standard deviation* of the audit values for the items in the sample is used as an estimate of the population standard deviation. But since the sample standard deviation is not known before the sample is selected, it also must be estimated.

There are three ways of estimating this factor. First, in a recurring engagement, the standard deviation found in the preceding audit may be used to estimate the standard deviation for the current year. Second, the standard deviation can be estimated from available book values. Third, the auditor can take a small presample of 30 to 50 items and base the estimate of the current year's population standard deviation on the audit values of these sample items. When this is done, the presample may be made a part of the final sample. Computer programs for MPU estimation sampling include a routine to calculate the estimated standard deviation.

The formula for calculating the standard deviation is

$$S_{x_j} = \sqrt{\sum_{j=1}^{n} \frac{(x_j - \bar{x})^2}{n - 1}}$$

where

$\displaystyle\sum_{j=1}^{n}$ = *sum of sample values;* $j = 1$ means summary should begin with first item and n means that the summary should end with the last item in the sample.

x_j = audit values of individual sample items.

$\bar{x}$ = mean of the audit values of sample items.

n = number of items audited.

A primary concern of the auditor in MPU sampling is whether the population should be stratified. Stratified sampling involves dividing the population into relatively homogeneous groups or strata. A homogeneous group in this context is one that has little variability in the values of the items comprising the group or stratum. Sampling is performed separately on each stratum and sample results for each stratum are subsequently combined to evaluate the total sample.

Stratification may be advantageous because the combined sample size often will be significantly less than a single sample size based on an unstratified population. This follows from the fact that sample size decreases as the variability of the population decreases. In fact, a change in the variability of a population affects sample size by the square of the relative change. Consequently, when the variation in the population changes from 200 to 100 (i.e., halved), the sample size required to meet the same statistical objectives is decreased by a factor of 4 (one-half squared equals one fourth).

The optimal number of strata depends on the pattern of variation in the population values and the additional costs associated with designing, executing, and evaluating each stratified sample. Because of the complexity of the procedure, stratification is generally used only when appropriate computer software is available. To simplify subsequent illustrations in this chapter, unstratified samples are used. In practice, when population values are highly variable and stratification is not feasible, the auditor may be able to use either difference or ratio estimation to achieve a reduction from the sample size that MPU sampling would require.

The Ace Finance Company limits loans to a maximum of $500 per customer. Thus, variability is low and the auditor concludes there is no need to stratify the population. Based on last year's audit, the auditor estimates a standard deviation of $100.

Tolerable error.   The considerations applicable to tolerable error are the same in MPU sampling as in PPS sampling. For the Ace Finance Company, the auditor specifies a tolerable error of $60,000.

Risk of Incorrect Rejection.   This factor permits the auditor to control the risk that the sample results will support the conclusion that the recorded account balance is materially misstated when it is not. The principal consequence of this risk is the potential incurrence of additional costs associated with expanded audit procedures following the initial rejection. However, the additional auditing procedures should ultimately result in the conclusion that the balance is not materially misstated.

In contrast to PPS sampling, the auditor must quantify the risk of incorrect rejection in MPU sampling. This risk has an inverse effect on sample size. If the auditor specifies a very low risk of incorrect rejection, the size and cost of performing the initial sample will be larger. Therefore, the auditor should use his experience and knowledge of the client to specify an appropriate risk of incorrect rejection to balance the costs associated with the initial sample and the potential costs of later expanding the sample.

In some computer software programs, the auditor inputs the risk of incorrect rejection directly as a percentage figure. Other programs require the auditor to input a *confidence* or *reliability* level, which is the complement of the risk of incorrect rejection. In either case, the computer then converts the percentage into an appropriate standard normal deviate or U_R factor for use in calculating the sample size. If the sample size is being calculated manually, a U_R factor for the specified risk of incorrect rejection is obtained from a table like the one illustrated in Figure 12-6.

The auditor decides to specify a 5% risk of incorrect rejection in the Ace Finance Company. Thus, the U_R factor is 1.96.

Risk of Incorrect Acceptance.   The factors to be considered in specifying this risk are the same as in PPS sampling. The risk of incorrect acceptance of a materially misstated balance is ordinarily specified in the range of from 5 to 30 percent, depending on the auditor's reliance on internal control and the results of other substantive tests. The risk of incorrect acceptance has an inverse effect on sample size—the lower the specified risk, the larger the sample size. In Ace Finance, the auditor specifies a 20% risk of incorrect acceptance.

Allowance for Sampling Risk.   The allowance for sampling risk (sometimes referred to as "desired precision") is derived from the following formula:

$$A = R \times TE$$

Risk of Incorrect Rejection	Standard Normal Deviate (U_R Factor)	Corresponding Confidence or Reliability Level*
.30	±1.04	.70
.25	±1.15	.75
.20	±1.28	.80
.15	±1.44	.85
.10	±1.64	.90
.05	±1.96	.95
.01	±2.58	.99

*For information purposes only.

Figure 12-6. SELECTED RISK OF INCORRECT REJECTION PERCENTAGES AND CORRESPONDING STANDARD NORMAL DEVIATES OR U_R FACTORS.

where

A = desired or planned allowance for sampling risk.

R = ratio of desired allowance for sampling risk to tolerable error.

TE = tolerable error.

The ratio for the R factor is based on the specified risks of incorrect acceptance and incorrect rejection. The amount of the ratio is obtained from the table shown in Figure 12-7. For example, if the aforementioned risks are set at 20 and 10%, respectively, the R factor is .661. In the Ace Finance Company, the foregoing risks have been specified at 20 and 5%. Thus, the R factor is

Risk of Incorrect Acceptance	Risk of Incorrect Rejection			
	.20	.10	.05	.01
.01	.355	.413	.457	.525
.025	.395	.456	.500	.568
.05	.437	.500	.543	.609
.075	.471	.532	.576	.641
.10	.500	.561	.605	.668
.15	.511	.612	.653	.712
.20	.603	.661	.700	.753
.25	.653	.708	.742	.791
.30	.707	.756	.787	.829
.35	.766	.808	.834	.868
.40	.831	.863	.883	.908
.45	.907	.926	.937	.952
.50	1.000	1.000	1.000	1.000

Figure 12-7. RATIO OF DESIRED ALLOWANCE FOR SAMPLING RISK TO TOLERABLE ERROR.
(Source: *Audit Sampling Guide, op. cit.,* p. 115.)

.70. This factor is then multiplied by the tolerable error of $60,000 to produce an allowance for sampling risk of $42,000.

Sample Size Formula.   The following formula is used to determine sample size for an MPU estimation sample:

$$n = \left(\frac{N \cdot S_{x_j} \cdot U_R}{A}\right)^2$$

where

N = population size.
S_{x_j} = estimated population standard deviation.
U_R = the standard normal deviate for the desired risk of incorrect rejection.
A = desired or planned allowance for sampling risk.

In the Ace Finance Company, these four factors are 3,000, $100, 1.96, and $42,000, respectively. Thus, sample size is 196 computed as follows:

$$n = \left(\frac{3,000 \times \$100 \times 1.96}{\$42,000}\right)^2 = 196$$

This formula assumes sampling with replacement (i.e., an item once selected is put back into the population and is eligible for selection again). When sampling without replacement, a finite correction factor is recommended when the relationship between n (sample size) and N (population size) is greater than .05. The adjusted sample size (n') is determined as follows:

$$n' = \frac{n}{1 + \dfrac{n}{N}}$$

Since n/N is greater than .05 (196 ÷ 3000 = .065) in Ace Finance, the adjusted sample size is

$$n' = \frac{196}{1 + \dfrac{196}{3000}} = 184$$

Determine the Sample Selection Method

Either the simple random number selection method or the systematic selection method discussed in Chapter 7 may be used in selecting the sample under the MPU technique. In the Ace Finance Company, the auditor decides to use a computer random number generator to identify the 184 loan receivable accounts to be examined.

Execute the Sampling Plan

The execution phase of an MPU estimation sampling plan includes the following steps:

- Perform appropriate auditing procedures to determine an audit value for each sample item.
- Calculate the following statistics based on the sample data:
  - the average of the sample audit values ($\bar{x}$).
  - the standard deviation of the sample audit values (S_{x_j}).

The average and standard deviation statistics for the sample may be computed manually or by a computer.

For the Ace Finance sample, the sum of the audit values is assumed to be $81,328, resulting in an average audit value of $442 ($81,328 ÷ 184). The standard deviation of the audit values is assumed to be $90.

Evaluate the Sample Results

In this, the final step of the sampling plan, the auditor makes both a quantitative and a qualitative assessment of the results and then reaches an overall conclusion.

Quantitative Assessment. In making this evaluation in an MPU sampling plan, the auditor calculates

- The estimated total population value.
- The achieved allowance for sampling risk, sometimes referred to as *achieved precision.*
- A range for the estimated total population value, sometimes referred to as the *precision interval.*

The *estimated total population value* ($\hat{X}$) is calculated as follows:

$$\hat{X} = N \cdot \bar{x}$$

Thus, the estimated total population value for Ace Finance Company's 3,000 loans receivable is

$$\hat{X} = 3,000 \times \$442 = \$1,326,000$$

The basic formula for calculating the *achieved allowance for sampling risk* is

$$A' = N \cdot U_R \cdot \frac{S_{x_j}}{\sqrt{n}}$$

where S_{x_j} is the standard deviation of the sample audit values. When the finite correction factor has been used in determining sample size, the formula is modified as follows:

$$A' = N \cdot U_R \cdot \frac{S_{x_j} \cdot \sqrt{1 - \dfrac{n'}{N}}}{\sqrt{n'}}$$

Therefore, the achieved allowance for sampling risk for Ace Finance is

$$A' = 3{,}000 \times 1.96 \times \frac{\$90 \sqrt{1 - \dfrac{184}{3000}}}{\sqrt{184}} = \$37{,}803$$

The *range for the estimated population value* is derived from the estimated population value and the achieved allowance for sampling risk. The formula is

$$\hat{X} \pm A'$$

In Ace Finance Company, the calculation is as follows:

$$\begin{aligned} \hat{X} \pm A' &= \$1{,}326{,}000 \pm \$37{,}803 \\ &= \$1{,}288{,}197 \text{ to } \$1{,}363{,}803 \end{aligned}$$

If the book value falls within this range, the sample results support the conclusion that the book value is fairly stated. This conclusion is valid in the case study as the book value of $1,340,000 falls within the range.

It should be recognized that the sample results may support fair presentation of the book value, but not within the level of risk of incorrect acceptance specified by the auditor. This occurs when A' is greater than A, which will be the case when the standard deviation of the sample audit values is greater than the estimated standard deviation used to determine sample size. In order to hold this risk to the planned level, the auditor computes the *adjusted achieved allowance for sampling risk* from the following formula:

$$A'' = A' + TE \left(1 - \frac{A'}{A}\right)$$

A'' is then substituted for A' in the formula used to calculate the range for the estimated population value. To illustrate, if A' had been $43,000 in Ace Finance, A'' is $41,571 as shown below.

$$\begin{aligned} A'' &= \$43{,}000 + \$60{,}000 \left(1 - \frac{\$43{,}000}{\$42{,}000}\right) \\ &= \$41{,}571 \end{aligned}$$

Note that A'', $41,571, is less than A, $42,000. Using A'', the estimated population range is $1,326,000 ± $41,571 or $1,284,429 to $1,367,571. Since the book value $1,340,000 falls within the range, the sample results indicate that the book value is fairly stated at the planned risk of incorrect acceptance.

The book value may fall outside the range because the achieved allowance for sampling risk is significantly smaller than the planned allowance. When this occurs, the auditor (1) calculates the difference between the book value and the far end of the range and (2) compares the difference to tolerable error. If the difference is equal to or less than tolerable error, the sample results indicate that the book value is fairly stated. For example, if the achieved allowance in Ace Finance Company is $12,000, the range becomes $1,314,000 to $1,338,000 and the book value ($1,340,000) falls outside the precision interval. The difference between the book value and the far end of the range is $26,000 ($1,340,000 − $1,314,000). Since this is less than the tolerable error of $60,000, the book value is supported.

Qualitative Assessment. Prior to reaching an overall conclusion, the auditor should consider the qualitative aspects of the sample results. These considerations are the same in MPU sampling as in PPS sampling.

Reaching an Overall Conclusion. When either the auditor's quantitative (statistical) or qualitative assessments of sample results do not support the conclusion that the population is fairly stated, he should use professional judgment in deciding on an appropriate course of action. The possible causes and actions are as follows:

Causes	Actions
1. The sample is not representative of the population.	Expand the sample and reevaluate the results.
2. The achieved allowance for sampling risk may be larger than the desired allowance because the sample size was too small.	Same as above.
3. The population book value may be misstated by more than tolerable error.	Have client investigate and, if warranted, adjust the book value and reevaluate the sample results.

Figure 12-8 summarizes the steps performed in designing, executing, and evaluating the MPU sampling plan to test the book value of Ace Finance Company's loans receivable. It also illustrates how these steps can be documented in a microcomputer generated working paper.

DIFFERENCE ESTIMATION

In difference estimation sampling, a difference is calculated for each sample item equal to the item's audit value minus its book value. The average of the differences is then used to obtain an estimate of the total population value, and the variability of the differences is used in determining the achieved

```
ACE FINANCE COMPANY                                              W/P REF: B-4
MPU SAMPLE - LOANS RECEIVABLE                    PREPARED BY: W.C.B. DATE 1/28/X2
DECEMBER 31, 19X1                                REVIEWED BY: REZ   DATE 2/5/X2
```

OBJECTIVE:	TO TEST FAIRNESS OF THE BOOK VALUE FOR LOANS RECEIVABLE AS OF 12/31/X1.

POPULATION AND SAMPLING UNIT:	3000 LOANS RECEIVABLE ON COMPUTER LISTING PREPARED FROM MASTER FILE. SAMPLING UNIT = INDIVIDUAL LOAN RECEIVABLE	

SAMPLE SIZE:	POPULATION SIZE	3,000 (N)
	ESTIMATED STANDARD DEVIATION	100 (Sxj)
	TOLERABLE ERROR	60,000 (TE)
	RISK OF INCORRECT REJECTION	5 % Ur = 1.96
	RISK OF INCORRECT ACCEPTANCE	20 %
	RATIO OF DESIRED ALLOWANCE FOR SAMPING RISK (A) TO TE	0.70 (R)
	DESIRED ALLOWANCE FOR SAMPLING RISK = R * TE	42,000 (A)
	$n = ((N * Sxj * Ur)/A)^2$	196
	$n' = n/(1 + (n/N))$	184

SAMPLE SELECTION:	SIMPLE RANDOM USING COMPUTER GENERATED RANDOM NUMBER LIST TO CORRESPOND TO LOAN NUMBERS. SAMPLING UNITS SELECTED LISTED ON W/P	B-5

EXECUTION OF SAMPLING PLAN:	AUDIT PROCEDURES APPLIED LISTED ON W/P	B-1
	AUDIT VALUES OF SAMPLE ITEMS SHOWN ON W/P	B-5
	AVERAGE OF SAMPLE AUDIT VALUES	442.00 (x)
	STANDARD DEVIATION OF SAMPLE AUDIT VALUES	90.00 (Sxj)

EVALUATION OF SAMPLE RESULTS:	ESTIMATED TOTAL POPULATION VALUE:		
	$X^\wedge = N * x$		1,326,000 (X^)
	ACHIEVED ALLOWANCE FOR SAMPLING RISK:		
	$A' = N * Ur * (Sxj * \sqrt{1-(n'/N)} / \sqrt{n'})$		37,803 (A')
	RANGE:		
	$X^\wedge +- A' =$ 1,288,197 TO 1,363,803		

CONCLUSION:	*Total book value of $1,340,000 falls within calculated range for estimated total population value. Sample results support conclusion that loans receivable are not misstated by more than tolerable error.*

Figure 12-8. MEAN-PER-UNIT SAMPLING PLAN WORKING PAPER.

allowance for sampling risk. Three conditions are indispensable in using this technique:

- The book value of each population item must be known.
- The total book value of the population must be known and correspond to the sum of the book values of the individual items.
- More than a few differences between audit and book values must be expected.

As explained below, the calculation of the allowance for sampling risk in difference estimation is based on the *variability of the differences* in the sample. Without a sufficient number of differences, the variability measure is unreliable. Among statisticians, the minimum number of differences required to ensure reliability varies considerably, ranging from 20 to 50.

The steps in performing difference estimation are explained in the following sections. The Ace Finance Company loans receivable case study is used again to highlight the similarities and differences between the MPU and difference estimation techniques.

Determine the Objectives and Define the Population and Sampling Unit

Since book values must be known in difference estimation, this method can be used only to test the fairness of a recorded balance. Other considerations relevant to these steps are the same as in MPU sampling. Accordingly, the following assumptions for the Ace Finance Company in the MPU illustration are continued: (1) population = 3,000 loans receivable, (2) book value of population = $1,340,000, and (3) sampling unit = the individual loan.

Determine the Sample Size

The same factors are required in determining sample size for MPU and difference estimation samples, with one exception. In difference estimation, the estimated standard deviation of the differences between audit and book values is used rather than the estimated standard deviation of the audit values themselves. The auditor may base this estimate on the results of the prior year's sample, or on the differences found in a presample in the current audit. As stated above, the estimate may be unreliable if it is based on too few differences.

Changes are required in the formulas used earlier in MPU estimation for computing the standard deviation and sample size. In the standard deviation formula (p. 428), the following substitutions in symbols are required:

- S_{d_j} (estimated standard deviation of population differences) for S_{x_j}.
- d_j (differences between audit and book values of individual sample items) for x_j.
- $\bar{d}$ (mean of the differences between audit and book values for the sample items) for $\bar{x}$.

In the sample size formula (p. 431), S_{d_j} is substituted for S_{x_j}.

For the Ace Finance Company, the auditor estimates that S_{d_j} is $70. Other assumptions continued from the MPU illustration are: $N = 3,000$; $TE = \$60,000$; risk of incorrect rejection $= .05$ ($U_R = 1.96$); risk of incorrect acceptance $= .20$; and $A = \$42,000$. Therefore, sample size is 96 items, computed as follows:

$$n = \left(\frac{N \cdot U_R \cdot S_{d_j}}{A}\right)^2 = \left(\frac{3,000 \times 1.96 \times \$70}{\$42,000}\right)^2 = 96$$

Observe that the sample size is considerably smaller than the sample size of 196 in the MPU example. This is due to the fact that the estimated standard deviation of the differences between audit and book values ($70) is smaller than the estimated standard deviation of the audit values used in the MPU illustration ($100). In this example, an adjustment of the sample size by a finite correction factor is unnecessary because n/N is less than .05 (96 ÷ 3,000 = .032).

Determine the Sample Selection Method

The performance of this step is the same in both MPU and difference estimation.

Execute the Sampling Plan

The initial step in executing the sampling plan is to determine the audit value for each sample item. Thus, this is the same as in MPU sampling. However, then the following steps occur:

- Calculate a difference for each sample item equal to the item's audit value minus its book value. The difference may be positive (audit value exceeds book value), negative (audit value is less than book value), or zero (audit value equals book value). Note that a positive difference indicates understatement of the book value and a negative difference means the book value is overstated.
- Sum the differences of the individual samples items (Σ_{d_j}).
- Divide the sum of the differences by the number of items in the sample to obtain the average (or mean) difference ($\bar{d}$).
- Compute the standard deviation of the sample differences (S_{d_j}).

In our case study, the following sample results are assumed: $\Sigma_{d_j} = \$-480$, $\bar{d} = \$-5$, and $S_{d_j} = \$68$.

Evaluate the Sample Results

As in MPU sampling, both quantitative and qualitative assessments are made in reaching an overall conclusion based on the sample results.

In making the quantitative assessment, in difference estimation the *estimated total projected difference* ($\hat{D}$) in the population is first determined as follows:

$$\hat{D} = N \times \bar{d}$$

Therefore, in the Ace Finance Company, $\hat{D}$ is

$$\hat{D} = 3,000 \times (\$-5) = \$-15,000$$

The negative sign indicates the projected error is an overstatement (audit value is less than book value).

The *estimated total population value* is then determined as follows:

$$\hat{X} = BV + \hat{D}$$

Thus, the estimated total population value is

$$\hat{X} = \$1,340,000 + (\$-15,000) = \$1,325,000$$

The second step in making the quantitative assessment is computing the *achieved allowance for sampling risk*. In making this calculation, it is necessary to substitute the estimated standard deviation of the population differences (S_{d_j}) for the estimated standard deviation of the population values (S_{x_j}). Since the finite correction factor was not used in determining sample size in this case study, the formula is

$$A' = N \cdot U_R \cdot \frac{S_{d_j}}{\sqrt{n}}$$

In this case study, the achieved allowance is $40,809 computed as follows:

$$A' = 3,000 \times 1.96 \times \frac{\$68}{\sqrt{96}} = \$40,809$$

Since A' ($40,809) is less than A ($42,000), it is not necessary to calculate A''.

The final step in the quantitative assessment is to calculate the *range for the estimated population value* and determine whether the book value falls within the range. As in the case of MPU sampling, the range is equal to $\hat{X} \pm A'$. The range, therefore, is $1,284,191 to $1,365,809. Since the book value falls within the range, the quantitative assessment supports the conclusion that the book value is fairly stated. Note this is the same conclusion that was supported by the MPU technique.

Finally, the same *qualitative considerations* that were explained previously for MPU sample results should be made prior to reaching an overall conclusion. Figure 12-9 shows a difference estimation sampling plan working paper.

RATIO ESTIMATION

In ratio estimation sampling, the auditor determines an audit value for each item in the sample. A ratio is calculated next by dividing the sum of the audit values by the sum of the book values for the sample items. This ratio is multiplied by the total book value to arrive at an estimate of the total population

```
ACE FINANCE COMPANY                                         W/P REF: B-4
DIFFERENCE ESTIMATION SAMPLE - LOANS RECEIVABLE    PREPARED BY: W.C.B  DATE 1/28/x2
DECEMBER 31, 19X1                                   REVIEWED BY: R.E.Z  DATE 2/5/x2
```

OBJECTIVE:	TO TEST FAIRNESS OF THE BOOK VALUE FOR LOANS RECEIVABLE AS OF 12/31/X1.

POPULATION AND SAMPLING UNIT:	3000 LOANS RECEIVABLE ON COMPUTER LISTING PREPARED FROM MASTER FILE. SAMPLING UNIT = INDIVIDUAL LOAN RECEIVABLE	
	TOTAL BOOK VALUE OF POPULATION	1,340,000 (BV)

SAMPLE SIZE:	POPULATION SIZE	3,000 (N)	
	ESTIMATED STANDARD DEVIATION OF DIFFERENCES	70 (Sdj)	
	TOLERABLE ERROR	60,000 (TE)	
	RISK OF INCORRECT REJECTION	5 %	Ur = 1.96
	RISK OF INCORRECT ACCEPTANCE	20 %	
	RATIO OF DESIRED ALLOWANCE FOR SAMPING RISK (A) TO TE	0.70 (R)	
	DESIRED ALLOWANCE FOR SAMPLING RISK = R $\ast$ TE	42,000 (A)	
	$n = ((N \ast Ur \ast Sdj)/A)^2$	96	

SAMPLE SELECTION:	SIMPLE RANDOM USING COMPUTER GENERATED RANDOM NUMBER LIST TO CORRESPOND TO LOAN NUMBERS.
	SAMPLING UNITS SELECTED LISTED ON W/P B-5

EXECUTION OF SAMPLING PLAN:	AUDIT PROCEDURES APPLIED LISTED ON W/P	B-3
	BOOK AND AUDIT VALUES OF SAMPLE ITEMS SHOWN ON W/P	B-5
	SUM OF DIFFERENCES OF SAMPLE ITEMS	(480.00)
	AVERAGE OF DIFFERENCES	(5.00) (d)
	STANDARD DEVIATION OF SAMPLE DIFFERENCES	68.00 (Sdj)

EVALUATION OF SAMPLE RESULTS:	ESTIMATED TOTAL PROJECTED DIFFERENCE	
	$\quad D^\wedge = N \ast \bar{d}$	(15,000) (D^)
	ESTIMATED TOTAL POPULATION VALUE:	
	$\quad X^\wedge = BV + D^\wedge$	1,325,000 (X^)
	ACHIEVED ALLOWANCE FOR SAMPLING RISK:	
	$\quad A' = N \ast Ur \ast (Sdj / \sqrt{n})$	40,809 (A')
	RANGE:	
	$\quad X^\wedge \mathbin{+\mkern-8mu-} A' = \quad\quad 1,284,191 \quad TO \quad 1,365,809$	

CONCLUSION:	*Total book value of $1,340,000 falls within Calculated range for estimated total population value. Sample results support conclusion that loans receivable are not misstated by more than tolerable error.*

Figure 12-9. DIFFERENCE ESTIMATION SAMPLING PLAN WORKING PAPER.

value. An allowance for sampling risk is then calculated based on the variability of the ratios of the audit and book values for the individual sample items.

The conditions for using ratio estimation are the same as those for difference estimation. The choice between ratio and difference estimation depends primarily on whether there is any correlation between the amount of the individual differences and their book values. When the differences are closely proportional to book value (i.e., the amount of the differences tend to increase as book values increase), ratio estimation will require a smaller sample size and therefore be more efficient. Computer programs are available that permit the auditor to input book and audit values for a presample to determine the sample size under both difference and ratio estimation. The auditor can then choose the technique that appears most efficient in the circumstances.

The steps in ratio estimation are the same as in difference estimation except as explained below.

Execute the Sampling Plan

After an audit value for each sample item has been determined, it is necessary in ratio estimation to

- Calculate the ratio of the audit and book value for each item.
- Calculate the ratio of the sums of the audit and book values for the sample items. (R)
- Compute the standard deviation of the individual ratios of the sample items. (S_{r_i})

Evaluate the Sample Results

In ratio estimation, the *estimated total population value* is derived from the following formula:

$$\hat{X} = BV \times R$$

Consequently, if the sums of the audit and book values of the sample items in the Ace Finance Company are $196,000 and $200,000, respectively, the R factor is 98% and the estimated value of the population is $1,313,200 ($1,340,000 × 98%).

The formula for determining the *achieved allowance for sampling risk* is the same as in difference estimation, except the standard deviation of the individual ratios in the sample is substituted for the standard deviation of the differences. The standard deviation of ratios is an extremely cumbersome calculation, and it is rarely done in practice without the assistance of a computer. Accordingly, manual calculation of this factor is not illustrated.

Once the estimated total population value and achieved allowance for sampling risk are computed, the range for the estimated total population value is determined. The sample results are then assessed quantitatively and qualitatively in the same manner as for MPU or difference estimation.

ADVANTAGES AND DISADVANTAGES OF CLASSICAL VARIABLES SAMPLING

Now that the three techniques of classical variables sampling have been explained, it is possible to evaluate this statistical approach. The principal advantages of this approach in audit sampling are

- The samples may be easier to expand than PPS samples, if that becomes necessary.
- Zero balances and different sign balances do not require special design considerations.
- If there are a large number of differences between book and audit values, the auditor's objectives may be met with a smaller sample size than in PPS sampling.[9]

The disadvantages of classical variables sampling should also be recognized. They consist primarily of the following:

- Classical variables sampling is more complex than PPS sampling; generally, an auditor needs the assistance of computer programs to design an efficient sample and evaluate sample results.
- To determine sample size, the auditor must have an estimate of the standard deviation of the characteristic of interest in the population.[10]

The auditor should use professional judgment in selecting the approach that is most appropriate in the circumstances.

NONSTATISTICAL SAMPLING IN SUBSTANTIVE TESTING

As explained earlier, the auditor may choose to use nonstatistical sampling in certain substantive testing applications. The major differences between statistical and nonstatistical sampling are in the steps for determining sample size and evaluating sample results. These steps are often perceived as being more objective or rigorous in statistical sampling and more subjective and judgmental in nonstatistical samples. However, judgment is also required in statistical applications, and certain relationships considered explicitly in statistical samples may be helpful in designing and evaluating nonstatistical samples.

DETERMINE THE SAMPLE SIZE

Careful consideration of sample design must be made to achieve efficient and effective samples. This is accomplished in statistical samples through explicit specification of key factors and relating them through mathematical models.

---

[9]*Audit Sampling Guide, op. cit.,* p. 87.
[10]*Audit Sampling Guide, op. cit.,* p. 87.

Consideration of the same factors in nonstatistical samples may help to produce more efficient and effective samples, even if the factors are not explicitly quantified. For example, the auditor should consider the following relationships:

Factor	Effect on Sample Size
Population size	Direct
Variation in the population	Direct
Tolerable error	Inverse
Expected error	Direct
Risk of incorrect acceptance	Inverse
Risk of incorrect rejection	Inverse

Careful subjective analysis of these factors in a particular circumstance, combined with the auditor's experience and judgment, should result in a sample size that is more appropriate than an arbitrarily determined sample size. The auditor may, but is not required to, consult statistical tables or models in evaluating the appropriateness of judgmentally determined sample sizes.

EVALUATE THE SAMPLE RESULTS

In nonstatistical as well as statistical sampling, the auditor should (1) project the error found in the sample to the population and (2) consider the sampling risk in evaluating sample results.

Two acceptable methods of projecting the error in nonstatistical samples are:

- Divide the total dollar amount of error in the sample by the fraction of total dollars from the population included in the sample.
- Multiply the average difference between audit and book values for sample items by the number of units in the population.

To illustrate, assume the following data for the Norris Company:

Number of items in population	2,500
Total book value of population	$800,000
Number of items in sample	100
Total book value of sample items	$32,000
Total audit value of sample items	$33,600

Under the first method described above, projected error is determined as follows:

$$\frac{\$33,600 - \$32,000}{\$32,000 \div \$800,000} = \frac{\$1,600}{.04} = \$40,000$$

The second method results in the following calculation:

$$\frac{\$33,600 - \$32,000}{100} \times 2,500 = \$40,000$$

Thus, both methods yield a total projected error of $40,000. Since the total audit value of the sample items exceeds their total book value, the projected error represents an understatement.

In nonstatistical samples, the auditor cannot calculate an allowance for sampling risk for specific, measurable levels of risk of incorrect acceptance and rejection. However, he may view the difference between the projected amount and tolerable error as an allowance for sampling risk. If tolerable error exceeds projected error by a large amount, he may be reasonably assured that there is an acceptably low sampling risk that the actual error exceeds tolerable error. For example, if tolerable error is $80,000 in the Norris Company, actual error in the population would have to exceed twice the $40,000 projected error from the sample before exceeding tolerable error. On the other hand, if tolerable error is $42,000, there is only a $2,000 difference between tolerable and projected error. In such case, the auditor may conclude that there is an unacceptably high sampling risk that the actual error exceeds tolerable error.

The number and size of errors found in the sample relative to expected errors are also helpful in assessing sampling risk. When the sample has been carefully designed and the number and size of errors found do not exceed his expectations, the auditor can generally conclude that there is an acceptably low risk that actual error exceeds tolerable error.

When the results of a nonstatistical sample do not appear to support the book value, the auditor may (1) examine additional sample units and reevaluate, (2) apply alternative auditing procedures and reevaluate, or (3) ask the client to investigate and, if appropriate, make an adjustment. As in statistical sampling, prior to reaching an overall conclusion, consideration should be given to the qualitative characteristics of the errors.

CONCLUDING COMMENTS

Audit sampling is widely used in substantive testing. Both statistical and nonstatistical audit sampling can provide the auditor with sufficient evidence to have a reasonable basis for an opinion. The use of statistical sampling has increased significantly in practice in recent years, and this trend can be expected to continue in the future. In the next two chapters, additional applications of PPS and classical variables sampling will be explained and illustrated.

Appendix 12A

Relating the Risk Components in Audit Sampling to Substantive Testing

The appendix to AU § 350 contains the following model for expressing the general relationship of ultimate risk to other risk components in an audit.[11]

$$UR = IC \times AR \times TD$$

where

    $UR =$ the allowable ultimate risk that monetary errors equal to tolerable error might remain undetected in the account balance or class of transactions after the auditor has completed all audit procedures deemed necessary.

    $IC =$ the auditor's assessment of the risk that, given that errors equal to tolerable error occur, the system of internal accounting control fails to detect them.

    $AR =$ the auditor's assessment of the risk that analytical review procedures and other relevant substantive tests would fail to detect the errors, given that the errors occur and are not detected by the system of internal accounting control.

    $TD =$ the allowable risk of incorrect acceptance for the substantive test of details, given that the errors occur and are not detected by the system of internal accounting control or analytical review procedures and other relevant substantive tests.

This model differs from the model presented in the appendix to Chapter 3 in the following respects:

1. *UR*, ultimate risk, is used here whereas *AR*, audit risk, was used earlier. Both terms refer to the auditor's overall risk in expressing an opinion on the financial statements.
2. *IR*, inherent risk, is not explicitly stated in this model whereas it is stated in Chapter 3. In this model, it is implicitly set conservatively at one. Accordingly, it is not a factor in the relationships expressed above.
3. *AR*, analytical review, and *TD*, tests of details in sum equal *DR*, detection risk, used in the earlier model. The symbols used here recognize that substantive tests consist of analytical review procedures and tests of details of transactions and balances.

---

[11] *Auditing Standards Board, op. cit.*, AU § 350, Appendix, par. 4.

This model is not intended to be applied as a mathematical formula in all situations. It may, however, be helpful to the auditor in making his subjective evaluations of the factors in the model and in understanding how they relate to each other. The assessment of the risk for each factor involves a considerable amount of subjectivity and the exercise of professional judgment. Ultimate risk is generally set at 5 or 10%. The following guidelines have been developed to assist the auditor in making explicit judgments of the risk associated with IC and AR.[12]

Internal Accounting Control (*IC*)		Analytical Review and Other Relevant Substantive Tests (*AR*)	
Reliance	**Risk Factor**	**Effectiveness**	**Risk Factor**
Substantial	10–30%	Very	10–40%
Moderate	20–70%	Moderate	30–60%
Limited or none	60–100%	Marginal or none	50–100%

The relationships expressed in the model may be useful to the auditor in planning his substantive tests of details. For example, if the auditor concludes that $UR = 5\%$, $IC = 30\%$, and $AR = 50\%$, the risk of incorrect acceptance for the test of details is 33%, computed as follows:

$$TD = \frac{UR}{IC \times AR} = \frac{(.05)}{(.30)(.50)} = 33\%$$

In analyzing this result, the auditor may decide that the performance of another relevant substantive test may lower the risk for AR to 30%. In such case, the risk of incorrect acceptance for the test of details becomes 55% ((.05)/(.30)(.30)). The auditor then must decide whether the cost of the additional auditing procedure is warranted by the cost saving that will result from the reduction in sample size for the planned test of details.

REVIEW QUESTIONS

12-1 Explain two purposes that may be served in designing substantive tests.

12-2 a. Identify and define the components of sampling risk associated with substantive testing.
   b. How do these components relate to detection risk?

12-3 Identify the two major statistical sampling approaches used in substantive testing and indicate the fundamental difference between them.

12-4 a. What effect does the availability of information about the following have on selecting an appropriate sampling approach for a substantive test?
   1. Book values for population items.

[12]*Audit Sampling Guide, op. cit.*, p. 124–125.

2. Number of units in the population.
3. Variability of the population items.

b. What effects does the auditor's expectations about errors have on selecting a sampling approach?

12-5 Explain the difference between the sampling unit and the logical sampling unit in a PPS sample.

12-6 Explain why units with zero and credit balances require special consideration when using PPS sampling.

12-7 a. Give the formula for calculating sample size in PPS sampling.
b. Explain what each element in the formula represents and how a change in that element, other things constant, affects sample size.

12-8 What role does the specification of anticipated error play in designing a PPS sample?

12-9 What three factors are considered in evaluating a PPS sample?

12-10 What are the two components of the allowance for sampling risk for PPS samples?

12-11 Explain the terms *tainting percentage* and *projected error* as they pertain to individual items in a PPS sample.

12-12 Identify three classical variables sampling techniques used in substantive testing.

12-13 a. Give the formula for determining sample size in a mean-per-unit sampling plan.
b. Explain what each element in the formula represents.
c. How does the formula differ for (1) difference estimation and (2) ratio estimation?

12-14 How is the risk of incorrect acceptance controlled in classical variables sampling plans?

12-15 Explain three ways of estimating the standard deviation for a mean-per-unit sampling plan.

12-16 Explain the role of each of the following in a classical variables sampling plan:
a. Planned allowance for sampling risk.
b. Achieved allowance for sampling risk.
c. Adjusted achieved allowance for sampling risk.

12-17 What alternatives exist when sample results do not support the book value?

12-18 Why do the difference and ratio estimation techniques generally produce more efficient samples than mean-per-unit estimation?

12-19 Describe briefly the technique by which the estimated total population value is determined under (1) mean-per-unit, (2) difference, and (3) ratio estimation sampling.

12-20 a. Describe two acceptable methods for projecting the error found in nonstatistical samples.
b. What may be viewed as the allowance for sampling risk in such samples?

OBJECTIVE QUESTIONS FROM PROFESSIONAL EXAMINATIONS

Indicate the *best* answer for each multiple-choice question.

12-21 The following questions relate to a variety of issues concerning audit sampling in substantive testing.

1. Which of the following sampling plans would be designed to estimate a numerical measurement of a population, such as a dollar value?
a. Numerical sampling.
b. Discovery sampling.

      c. Sampling for attributes.

      d. Sampling for variables.

2. What is the primary objective of using stratification as a sampling method in auditing?

      a. To increase the risk of incorrect acceptance at which a decision will be reached from the results of the sample selected.

      b. To determine the deviation rate for a given characteristic in the population being studied.

      c. To decrease the effect of variance in the total population.

      d. To determine the precision interval of the sample selected.

3. An auditor initially planned to use unrestricted random sampling with replacement in the examination of accounts receivable. Later, the auditor decided to use unrestricted random sampling without replacement. As a result only of this decision, the sample size should

      a. Increase.

      b. Remain the same.

      c. Decrease.

      d. Be recalculated using a binomial distribution.

4. Which of the following is an advantage of monetary (dollar) unit sampling over variables random sampling?

      a. It allows the auditor to control the risk of reliance on the sample.

      b. It permits auditors to optimize the sample size given the statistically measured risk they are willing to accept.

      c. It solves the problem that accounts with zero balances escape selection from the sample.

      d. It provides greater assurance that accounts with large balances will not escape selection for the sample.

12-22 The following questions relate to the relationship between risk and audit sampling.

1. If the achieved allowance for sampling risk of a statistical sample at a given risk level is greater than the desired allowance, this is an indication that the

      a. Standard deviation was larger than expected.

      b. Standard deviation was less than expected.

      c. Population was larger than expected.

      d. Population was smaller than expected.

2. Which of the following models expresses the general relationship of risks associated with the auditor's evaluation of internal accounting controls (IC), analytical review procedures and other relevant substantive tests (AR), and ultimate audit risk (UR) that would lead the auditor to conclude that additional substantive tests of details of an account balance are not necessary?

	AR	IC	UR
a.	20%	40%	10%
b.	20%	60%	5%
c.	10%	70%	$4\frac{1}{2}\%$
d.	30%	40%	$5\frac{1}{2}\%$

3. An advantage of using statistical sampling techniques is that such techniques

      a. Mathematically measure risk.

      b. Eliminate the need for judgmental decisions.

      c. Define the values of tolerable error and risk of incorrect acceptance required to provide audit satisfaction.

      d. Have been established in the courts to be superior to judgmental sampling.

12-23 The following questions relate to the difference and ratio estimation techniques of variables sampling.

1. The major reason that the difference and ratio estimation methods would be expected to produce audit efficiency is that the
   a. Number of members of the populations of differences of ratios is smaller than the number of members of the population of book values.
   b. Beta risk may be completely ignored.
   c. Calculations required in using difference or ratio estimation are less arduous and fewer than those required when using MPU estimation.
   d. Variability of the populations of differences or ratios is less than that of the populations of book values or audit values.

2. Use of the ratio estimation sampling technique to estimated dollar amounts is *inappropriate* when
   a. The total book value is known and corresponds to the sum of all the individual book values.
   b. A book value for each sample item is unknown.
   c. There are some observed differences between audit values and book values.
   d. The audit values are nearly proportional to the book values.

3. Using statistical sampling to assist in verifying the year-end accounts payable balance, an auditor has accumulated the following data:

	Number of Accounts	Book Balance	Balance Determined by the Auditor
Population	4,100	$5,000,000	?
Sample	200	$ 250,000	$300,000

With the ratio estimation technique, the auditor's estimate of year-end accounts payable balance would be

a. $6,150,000
b. $6,000,000
c. $5,125,000
d. $5,050,000

COMPREHENSIVE QUESTIONS

12-24 A recent Statement on Auditing Standards entitled "Audit Sampling" establishes concepts applicable to both statistical and nonstatistical sampling but does not explicitly endorse either approach as being superior. The Statement refers to uncertainty in an audit engagement and states that ultimate risk is a combination of two factors

1. The probability that a material error will occur during the accounting process.
2. The probability that a material error will not be discovered by the auditor.

The second factor of ultimate risk is controlled, to a degree, by the auditor's quality of performance in conducting substantive tests (i.e., tests of details of transactions and balances) and analytical review procedures. The quality of substantive tests is affected by both sampling and nonsampling risk.

Required

a. Distinguish between sampling and nonsampling risk and give two examples of nonsampling risk.

b. Explain under what conditions audit sampling would be considered an appropriate alternative to a 100% examination of all the items in the balance of an account or a class of transactions.

c. Identify three factors that should be considered in determining sample size for substantive tests. For each factor identified, explain what conditions should lead to a smaller sample size.

d. Briefly explain each of the following four sample selection techniques including comments as to whether each will result in a sample that is representative of the population being tested.
   1. Random number sampling.
   2. Systematic sampling.
   3. Haphazard selection.
   4. Block sampling.

CMA

12-25 An auditor employs monetary-unit (probability-proportional-to-size) sampling in testing the valuation of physical inventory. The book value of inventory is $500,000 and represents the cumulative value of 2,000 vouchers. The maximum tolerable error (or level of materiality) is determined to be $25,000 and the auditor decides on a 5% risk of incorrect acceptance. This completes the auditor's design specifications for the sample.

The test revealed one voucher that was on the books at $100 but had an audit value of $70. No other errors were found.

Required

a. What sample size and sampling interval were used by the auditor?

b. Under the assumption that the auditor wrote a conclusion based on the data presented, what would the conclusion state?

c. Critique the auditor's sampling plan and describe what actions the auditor might take given the sample results.

d. What are the advantages of using monetary-unit (probability-proportional-to-size) sampling as an audit tool?

IIA (adapted)

12-26 You have completed a pricing test of the Grapefruit Computer Company's inventory using a PPS sampling plan. The sample design for your test of the $5,000,000 inventory (book value) specified a risk of incorrect acceptance of 10% and a tolerable error of $400,000. You anticipated not more than $50,000 of error in the inventory due to excellent internal controls.

Required

a. What size sample should you have examined?

b. What was your sampling interval?

c. If you assume no errors were found in the sample, what is your conclusion (state as precisely as possible)?

d. If you assume the sample yielded a projected error of $35,000, and an incremental allowance for sampling risk of $18,200, what conclusion might you draw from the sample?

12-27 Assume the following errors were found in a PPS sample:

Sample Item	Book Value	Audit Value
1	$ 550	0
2	640	$ 576
3	1,800	0
4	2,400	1,800
5	2,700	2,430

Required

a. Calculate the projected error assuming
   1. The sampling interval was $2,000.
   2. The sampling interval was $2,500.

b. If a risk of incorrect acceptance of 10% was specified in the sample design, the sampling interval was $2,000, and five errors were found as enumerated above, calculate
   1. Basic precision.
   2. The incremental allowance for sampling risk.
   3. The upper error limit.

c. If tolerable error was $45,000 and anticipated error was $5,000, what conclusion would you reach based on your results in b above?

12-28 You decide to use statistical sampling to test the reasonableness of the recorded book value of the Key West Company's accounts receivable. Because the company's internal accounting controls over accounts receivable have been evaluated by you as excellent and you believe few errors will be found, you decide to use probability-proportional-to-size sampling. The company has 2,000 customer accounts with a total book value of $1,500,000. You decide $75,000 is the maximum tolerable misstatement and anticipate that there may be $15,000 of error in the population. You wish to limit the risk of incorrect acceptance to 10%. It is your intention to seek positive confirmation of accounts included in your sample and to apply alternative procedures to accounts for which no reply is received.

Required

a. Compute the sample size.

b. Compute the sampling interval.

c. Assume the following errors were found in the sample:

Sample Item	Book Value	Audit Value
1	$ 800	$ 720
2	500	0
3	16,000	15,200
4	14,000	0

Calculate
1. Projected error.
2. Allowance for sampling risk.
3. Upper error limit.

d. State your conclusion based on the results in c above.

12-29 An audit client has an inventory of 10,000 head of beef cattle (steers). The steers were purchased at various dates and varying prices. In view of the dollar amounts involved, $200,000 is considered to be a material amount. A risk of incorrect rejection of 5% and a risk of incorrect acceptance of 10% are acceptable. The estimated standard deviation of the population is $105. The book value is $2,840,000.

Required

a. Compute the sample size for a mean-per-unit sample.
b. Assume that the sample produced an average audit value of $275 with a standard deviation of $100. What conclusion is supported by the sample?

12-30 A contractor has 1,515 homes in various states of construction. From a random pre-sample of 50 homes, you determine that the estimated population standard deviation is $2,000. On the basis of audit risk and other factors, you set desired allowance for sampling risk at $250,000 and desired risk of incorrect rejection at 10%.

Required

a. Determine sample size, assuming mean-per-unit sampling with replacement.
b. What would sample size be if the standard deviation was increased to $3,000?
c. Assume the auditor elects to limit sample size to 330 in the interest of cost efficiencies. What risk of incorrect rejection can be achieved if desired allowance for sampling risk remains at $250,000 and the standard deviation remains at $2,000?
d. What allowance for sampling risk results if the risk of incorrect rejection is held at 10% and sample size is 330?
e. Redo part a above assuming sampling without replacement.

12-31 This question is designed to test your knowledge of sampling risks in classical variables sampling plans.

Required

a. Will your resulting sample size be larger or smaller if the risk of internal control not detecting material errors is 10% rather than 50%, when all other factors are equal?
b. Will your sample be larger or smaller if you specify a risk of incorrect acceptance of 50% for a test of details rather than 11%?

c. If you desire risk of incorrect rejection of 5% and risk of incorrect acceptance of 15%, what amount should your planned allowance for sampling risk be when tolerable error is $100,000?

d. If the achieved allowance for sampling risk is greater than the planned allowance, then the actual risk of incorrect acceptance is (greater/less) than the planned risk?

e. Assuming tolerable error is $200,000, the planned risks of incorrect rejection and acceptance are 5 and 20%, respectively, and the achieved allowance for sampling risk is $155,000, calculate the adjusted achieved allowance for sampling risk.

12-32 Data relative to three MPU sampling plans are presented below:

	1	2	3
Tolerable error	$120,000	$150,000	$180,000
Size of population	5,000	6,000	8,000
Risk of incorrect rejection	5%	10%	5%
Estimated population standard deviation	$75	$100	$120
Risks that errors accumulating to greater than tolerable error will not be detected by:			
Internal control	40%	50%	40%
Analytical review and other substantive procedures (excluding test of details)	85%	25%	50%
Desired ultimate risk	5%	5%	5%

Required

a. Using the model in Appendix A, determine an appropriate risk of incorrect acceptance for each population.

b. Calculate sample size in each of the plans. Show computations.

12-33 The following facts pertain to a difference estimation sampling plan:

1. Objective is to determine whether book value is fairly stated.
2. Population consists of 4,000 customer accounts.
3. Book value of accounts receivable is $2.65 million.
4. The preliminary estimated standard deviation of the differences used to determine sample size is $140.
5. Tolerable error is $80,000.
6. Ultimate risk is 5%.
7. Risk of incorrect rejection is 5%.
8. Risk of incorrect acceptance is 25%.
9. Sample size is 315.
10. Audit value of the sample items is $206,955 and book value is $208,687.50.
11. The standard deviation of the sample differences is $160.

Required

a. Verify the sample size indicated above in item 9.

b. Compute achieved allowance for sampling risk. Is this consistent with the planned risk of incorrect acceptance? Why or why not? If not, compute the adjusted allowance.

c. Is book value fairly stated? Explain.

12-34 The Hard Finance Company has 3,000 loans outstanding at a recorded book value of $980,000. As the auditor on this engagement, Mary Jones selects a sample of 300 loans for vouching. These loans have a reported book value of $96,000 and an audited value of $94,000.

Required

Compute the estimated total value of the loans by (1) means-per-unit estimation, (2) difference estimation, and (3) ratio estimation.

12-35 Walker Corporation has two operating divisions that manufacture industrial products. Walker's management believes that diversification is long overdue and, in particular, wants to diversify into high-technology areas.

Walker's Board of Directors has decided to diversify by means of business combination and has identified Newstrand Laboratories, a closely held corporation, as an acquisition candidate. Newstrand's stockholders are not opposed to a takeover, and its President has encouraged Walker to audit Newstrand's financial statements for the fiscal year ended November 30, 19X1.

Walker's Internal Audit Department was instructed by the Audit Committee of the Board to perform an audit examination of Newstrand's financial statements and this assignment was given to Donna Robinson, an Audit Manager in the department. Because accounts receivable represented over 20% of Newstrand's reported total assets at November 30, 19X1, Robinson decided to perform that segment of the audit herself.

Robinson obtained Newstrand's accounts receivable trial balance of 5,000 debit balances that total $6,250,000 as shown on Newstrand's Statement of Financial Position at November 30, 19X1. She decided to use ratio estimation sampling without replacement in determining the accuracy of the accounts receivable balance. Robinson desires to hold the risk of incorrect acceptance to 5% and the risk of incorrect rejection to 10%. Her estimate of the standard deviation of the ratios is $100. She has concluded that an over- or understatement of the account by more than $100,000 would constitute a material misstatement.

Required

a. Calculate the size of the sample (number of accounts) that Donna Robinson should select in her examination of Newstrand's accounts receivable.

b. Without prejudice to your answer to requirement a, assume Robinson selected 320 accounts with a total book value of $400,000 and a total audit value of $392,000.
   1. Calculate the estimated total audit value (point estimate) of Newstrand's accounts receivable at November 30, 19X1 by using the ratio estimation technique.
   2. Explain how the estimated total audit value (point estimate) is used in the evaluation of sample results.

c. Without prejudice to your answers to requirements a and b, assume Donna Robinson, in her evaluation of the sample results, determined that the planned allowance for sampling risk was not achieved at the desired risk level.
   1. Give possible reasons why the planned allowance was not achieved.
   2. What additional audit steps would Robinson take in determining the accuracy of the accounts receivable balance?

CMA (adapted)

12-36 Wheeler and Jones, CPAs, are examining the December 31, 19X1 inventory of Better Parts, Inc., a distributor of electronic parts. They have already performed procedures to satisfy themselves that (1) a computer printout listing inventory at year-end in ascending sequence by stock number and lot number is complete, (2) the quantities shown thereon are correct, (3) the extensions of quantity times price are accurate, (4) the listing is properly footed, and (5) the total agrees to the general ledger ending inventory account balance.

As the next step, Wheeler and Jones decide to use a nonstatistical sample to test the pricing of the inventory. They plan to perform this test by checking prices to (1) vendors' invoices and (2) current price lists provided by vendors. The ending inventory consists of 2,500 stock items with a total recorded value of $1,900,000. A perpetual inventory record is maintained for each stock item. Additionally, an inventory tag showing the quantity on hand at year-end is on file for each item.

Wheeler and Jones agree that a misstatement of $75,000 or more in the inventory balance, when combined with error in other accounts, might result in material misstatement of the financial statements.

Required

a. To what component of audit risk does the inventory pricing test relate?

b. What factors should influence Wheeler and Jones' determination of sample size?

c. What should the sampling unit be and how should the sample items be selected?

d. Assume that a sample of the pricing of 125 stock items was examined. The total recorded value for these items was $95,000. Six of the items in the sample had pricing errors resulting in those items being overstated by $3,600. How should Wheeler and Jones interpret the sample results?

12-37 In planning the audit of accounts receivable, you decide to select accounts for confirmation using a variables estimation sampling plan. A major reason for your decision is the advantage of being able to measure and control the risks involved. You recall that auditing literature describes ultimate risk as a combination of two separate risks: (1) that material errors will occur in the accounting process by which the financial statements are developed and (2) that any material errors that occur will not be detected in the auditor's examination.

Required

a. How does this description of risk relate to the following expression in the context of the variables sampling application described above?

$$UR = IC \times TD \times AR$$

b. What guidelines are available for specifying the amount of ultimate risk?

CASE STUDY

12-38* Fairview Publishing Company, incorporated in 19X4, is a small, closely held publisher of high school textbooks. A local accounting firm has reviewed the preparation of the financial statements, performed certain audit procedures, and prepared the tax returns for many years. The accountants' report has always contained a disclaimer of opinion, because the stockholders would not permit confirmation of receivables or observation of inventories.

The company plans to "go public" in about three years. In anticipation of this, they engaged you in May to perform an audit for the year ended June 30.

The company's first fiscal quarter is usually the most profitable; the last quarter is usually a break-even situation.

The company has a job order cost system for determining its unit cost prices for each textbook. If a book has not been ordered by any customer for 12 months, it is "no valued," scrapped, and discontinued. Only a minimal quantity is maintained of each title until a firm order is received. The company expects that it has no more than a $3,000 inventory of any one title.

You have completed your year-end inventory work and found the client's perpetual records were remarkably accurate with respect to quantities, unit prices, and extensions. No errors were located, and it was concluded that the perpetual records can be relied on for beginning inventory quantities.

However, as to the beginning inventory amount, the client is not able to produce a listing with detail sufficient to provide a transaction trail. They can find only an adding machine tape to support the recorded amount, $1,405,165. The tape is in no particular order.

At June 30 of the prior year, the company had exactly 1,000 different titles in inventory. This agrees with the number of entries on the tape and the number of perpetual records having a quantity at the beginning of the current year.

In this case, $150,000 is considered the tolerable error.

The risks that errors accumulating to greater than tolerable error will not be detected by (1) internal controls and (2) by analytical review and substantive tests other than this test of details are 25 and 50%, respectively. The ultimate risk is 5%.

A 5% risk of incorrect rejection is also viewed as acceptable. Based on this year's inventory, the standard deviation should approximate $635 and you have decided to use one stratum.

Required

a. What is the nature and objective of the test?
b. Compute the risk of incorrect acceptance.
c. What planned allowance for sampling risk should be used in determining sample size?
d. Calculate sample size (without replacement) using the estimated standard deviation of $635 and the planned allowance determined in c above.
e. Assuming the sample produces an audit value of sample items of $118,000 and a standard deviation of $662, calculate (1) the estimated total population value and (2) the achieved allowance for sampling risk.
f. Compute adjusted achieved allowance.
g. Interpret the results of the sample.

Chapter 13

Substantive Tests of Cash and Revenue Cycle Balances

Study Objectives

After you have completed a careful study of this chapter, you should be able to

- Explain the nature, scope, and timing of substantive tests of balances.

- Describe the audit objectives for substantive tests of balances.

- Design and execute an audit program for verifying cash balances.

- Prepare a proof of cash.

- Develop and execute an audit program for receivables balances.

- Indicate the auditor's responsibilities in performing the required auditing procedure of confirming accounts receivable.

- Recognize the applicability of statistical sampling and electronic data processing in verifying accounts receivable balances.

Specific substantive tests of account balances are considered in this chapter. First, attention is given to the verification of year-end cash balances that result from the revenue and expenditure cycles. Second, the verification of receivables balances resulting from the revenue cycle is discussed. A brief explanation of tests of balances and audit objectives for these tests precedes the main focus of the chapter.

NATURE AND SCOPE OF TESTS OF BALANCES

To have a reasonable basis for an opinion on the client's financial statements, the auditor must obtain sufficient competent evidential matter. Such evidence is obtained through substantive tests. As explained in Chapter 4, these tests take one of three forms: (1) tests of details of transactions, which often are performed concurrently with compliance tests during interim work, (2) tests of details of balances, and (3) analytical review procedures. When substantive tests are performed at or near the balance sheet date, they are directed primarily at the verification of the account balance. Hence, the single designation "tests of balances" is used in these chapters in referring to year-end substantive tests.

Tests of balances are explained within the context of account balances that result from specific classes of transactions within a single cycle except in the case of cash and inventories. Both of these accounts are affected by more than one cycle. Cash is discussed in this chapter; inventories are considered with expenditure and production cycle balances in Chapter 14. Tests of balances are sometimes referred to as *direct* tests of balances.

In the typical audit engagement, the following approaches are often taken in designing audit programs for tests of balances:

- When control risk over a specific class of transactions is low, tests of balances are applied to resulting balance sheet account balances and reliance is placed primarily on internal controls and analytical review procedures for the related income statement account balances.
- When internal controls over a specific class of transactions are not tested or control risk is high, tests of balances are applied to both resulting balance sheet and income statement account balances.

MATERIALITY AND AUDIT RISK IN TESTS OF BALANCES

In performing substantive tests, the auditor seeks to detect errors in account balances that are large enough, individually or in the aggregate, to be material to the financial statements. It will be recalled that in audit planning, the auditor makes a preliminary judgment about materiality at both the financial statement and account balance levels. This assessment, referred to as *planning materiality*, must be reviewed before performing substantive tests to determine whether it is still appropriate. Often, modification will be necessary because information obtained from other aspects of field work may be significantly different from the information available at the time the audit was planned. Moreover, major changes may have occurred in the company's financial position and operations from such developments as the acquisition (or sale) of a subsidiary company or the introduction (or discontinuance) of an important product line.

Substantive tests pertain to *detection risk* that is a key component of audit risk. As in the case of materiality, it is often necessary for the auditor to modify his planned level of detection risk for an account balance as a result of additional information obtained from other parts of the examination. A critical factor is the auditor's assessment of control risk based on the study and evaluation of internal control pertaining to the account balance. It has been explained earlier, that there is an inverse relationship between control risk and detection risk. When control risk is high for a material account balance, the auditor will need more evidence to determine the propriety of the balance and keep detection risk low. Thus, control risk significantly affects the nature, timing, and extent of substantive tests.

It is essential, therefore, for the auditor to make careful assessments of materiality and audit risk for each material account balance before performing substantive tests. These assessments should be incorporated into the audit program for substantive testing.

SUBSTANTIVE TESTS PRIOR TO THE BALANCE SHEET DATE

An auditor may apply substantive tests to the details of a particular asset or liability account at an interim date. The decision to perform the tests prior to the balance sheet date should be based on whether the auditor can

- Control the added audit risk that errors existing in the account at the balance sheet date will not be detected by the auditor. This risk becomes greater as the time period remaining between the date of the interim tests and the balance sheet date is lengthened.
- Reduce the cost of substantive tests necessary at the balance sheet date to meet planned audit objectives so that testing prior to the balance sheet date will be cost-effective.

The potential added audit risk can be controlled if substantive tests for the remaining period can provide a reasonable basis for extending the audit conclusions from the tests performed at the interim date to the balance sheet date. Conditions that contribute to the control of this risk are (1) internal accounting controls during the remaining period can be relied on, (2) there are no conditions or circumstances that might predispose management to misstate the financial statements in the remaining period, (3) the year-end balances of the accounts examined at the interim date are reasonably predictable as to amount, relative significance, and composition, and (4) the client's accounting system will provide information concerning significant unusual transactions and significant fluctuations that may occur in the remaining period.[1] If these conditions do not exist, the account should be examined at the balance sheet date.

[1] Auditing Standards Board, *Codification of Statements on Auditing Standards* (New York: American Institute of Certified Public Accountants, 1985). Auditing Section 313.05–07 (hereinafter referred to and cited as AU §).

Substantive tests prior to the balance sheet date do not eliminate the need for substantive tests at the balance sheet date. Such tests for the remaining period ordinarily should include

- Comparison of the account balances at the two dates to identify amounts that appear to be unusual and investigation of such amounts.
- Other analytical review procedures or other substantive tests of details to provide a reasonable basis for extending the interim audit conclusions to the balance sheet date.

When properly planned and executed, the combination of substantive tests prior to the balance sheet date and substantive tests for the remaining period should provide the auditor with sufficient competent evidential matter to have a reasonable basis for an opinion on the client's financial statements.

AUDIT OBJECTIVES FOR TESTS OF BALANCES

As explained earlier, assertions are the representations made by management in the financial statements. They can be either explicit or implicit. Financial statement assertions can be classified into the following categories: (1) existence or occurrence, (2) completeness, (3) rights and obligations, (4) valuation or allocation, and (5) statement presentation and disclosure.[2]

Management's assertions can be translated into corresponding categories of audit objectives. In addition, in this text, one additional audit objective will be recognized: *clerical accuracy*. An explanation of the six categories of audit objectives that will be used in this textbook for tests of balances is as follows.

Clerical Accuracy

The objective of clerical accuracy pertains to the mathematical correctness of the accounting records and the client's supporting schedules. The audit procedures involved in meeting this objective include: (1) footing and cross-footing journals, registers, and schedules; (2) agreeing the beginning account balances with the final balances on last year's working papers; (3) proving the mathematical accuracy of all client-prepared schedules appearing in the working papers; (4) tracing postings from the journals to the general ledger accounts; (5) agreeing the totals of schedules with the ledger balances; and (6) agreeing control accounts and subsidiary ledgers. Attention is focused on the latter two procedures in tests of balances in these chapters. Many auditors regard this objective as a prerequisite for meeting the other objectives.

Existence or Occurrence

This objective is two-dimensional. First, it relates to management's explicit assertions that specific assets and liabilities exist at the balance sheet date. Second, it pertains to the assertion that recorded transactions represent eco-

---

[2]Auditing Standards Board, *op. cit.*, AU § 326.03.

nomic events that occurred during the year. Management's assertions about existence extend to assets with physical substance, such as cash, inventories, and plant assets, and to accounts without physical substance such as accounts receivable and accounts payable.

The audit objective of existence or occurrence is often referred to as the *validity* objective. It is primarily concerned with the *overstatement* of account balances and recorded transactions. Accordingly, in meeting this objective, the auditor works from the financial statements and accounting records to supporting evidence. For tangible assets held by the company, the most reliable evidence of existence is direct personal knowledge that is obtained from inspecting and counting the assets. For tangible assets held for the client by others and assets that do not have physical properties, the auditor usually seeks evidence directly from outside independent sources by confirming the existence of the assets. The review of such documents as invoices, cancelled checks, and contracts also provides evidence about existence or occurrence.

Completeness

The purpose of this objective is to determine whether all transactions and accounts that should be presented in the financial statements are included therein. For example, management asserts that all claims against customers are reported in accounts receivable on the balance sheet and that all sales for the year are shown on the income statement. In meeting the completeness objective, the auditor obtains corroborating information that the accounting records are not *understated* by omissions that are material, either individually or in the aggregate, in relation to the financial statements take as a whole.

Account balances and recorded data may be incomplete because of (1) errors of omission, (2) errors resulting from recording transactions in the wrong accounting period, and (3) deliberate misstatement. The completeness objective extends only to transactions and accounts that the auditor believes may be understated based on his knowledge of the client. This objective is the complement of the existence or occurrence objective.

The completeness objective is generally the most difficult audit objective to satisfy. To meet this objective, it often is necessary for the auditor to perform *tests of details of related populations*. Consequently, the auditor may test shipping documents for evidence of unrecorded sales, and cash disbursements made in a subsequent period for the omission of accounts payable at the balance sheet date. The use of analytical review procedures is also helpful in meeting this objective. As explained in an earlier chapter, analytical review procedures involve a comparison and study of relationships among data. Thus, a significant decline in the gross profit rate compared with prior years may indicate the possibility of unrecorded sales. Similarly, an unexpected decrease in the debt to equity ratio compared to preceding years may indicate that recorded liabilities are understated. In these instances, the auditor would be expected to investigate the matters further when he believes they may have a material effect on the financial statements.

Rights and Obligations

This objective relates to management's implicit assertions that the company has rights to existing assets and that reported liabilities are obligations of the entity. Ordinarily, rights to assets result from ownership and creditors' claims are legal obligations. However, a lessee has the right to use leased property even though ownership resides with the lessor, and earned but unfunded pension costs are liabilities but not legal obligations.

Documentary evidence, such as title certificates and legal contracts, are important in meeting this objective. Inspection of title registrations will verify the company's ownership of delivery trucks and inspection of purchase contracts will reveal the amount owed. Confirmations also are useful in verifying rights and obligations. For instance, the auditor can confirm the ownership of a note receivable by communicating with the debtor. Similarly, confirmation with a bond trustee establishes the amount of bonds payable that are outstanding at the balance sheet date.

Valuation or Allocation

In assigning dollar amounts to financial statement components, management asserts that the amount has been properly determined in accordance with GAAP. This audit objective, therefore, focuses on whether the company has followed the cost, matching, and consistency principles of accounting. It is concerned with such matters as original cost, net book value, net realizable value, cost allocations, accruals, and estimates.

The valuation objective is frequently met through a review of documentation created when the transactions occurred. Recalculation is often used to obtain evidence as to the propriety of allocations.

Statement Presentation and Disclosure

In the financial statements, management asserts that the components are properly presented and accompanying disclosures are adequate. The statement presentation and disclosure objective relates to these assertions. Presentation pertains to the identification, classification, and arrangement of the components in a financial statement. Disclosure involves the description of material and relevant facts in the body of the statements and the accompanying notes. Disclosures may be required by authoritative pronouncements or by circumstances pertaining to the client's financial position and results of operations.

The auditor obtains evidence about his objective through such procedures as examining contracts, reading the minutes of board of directors meetings, and making inquiries about contingencies to the client's legal counsel.

Summary of Audit Objectives

A summary of the six audit objectives for tests of balances is shown in Figure 13-1.

Audit Objective	Purpose of Objective
Clerical accuracy	Establish the mathematical accuracy of accounting records and agreement of records with supporting schedules.
Existence or occurrence	Determine the existence of balance sheet items and the occurrence of recorded transactions.
Completeness	Determine that all transactions that should have been recorded are recorded in the accounts.
Rights and obligations	Verify client rights to existing assets and the validity of creditor claims on existing assets.
Valuation or allocation	Ascertain that statement items are stated at proper amounts.
Statement presentation and disclosure	Determine appropriateness of the presentation of statement items and the adequacy of accompanying disclosures.

Figure 13-1. NATURE AND PURPOSE OF AUDIT OBJECTIVES.

It should be recognized that some objectives are interrelated. For example, establishing the existence of cash on hand also contributes to the rights and completeness objectives. Similarly, satisfying the completeness objective for accounts payable provides evidence that the payables represent obligations of the entity and are properly valued.

Audit programs are generally designed and executed to meet these six audit objectives.

TESTS OF CASH BALANCES

The starting point in the design of the audit program for testing cash balances is the auditor's evaluation of internal control procedures over cash receipts and cash disbursements transactions. As described in Chapters 9 and 10, the auditor's reliance on controls over these two classes of transactions will affect the nature, timing, and extent of the tests of cash balances.

Cash balances include cash on hand, cash in bank, and miscellaneous balances such as plant expansion funds and bond sinking funds. Attention here is centered on the first two types of cash balances.

An audit program for tests of cash balances is shown in Figure 13-2. Some of the tests shown in the program may satisfy more than one audit objective, but they are listed alongside the primary objective that they satisfy. Some of the audit objectives are combined because of the nature of cash.

The audit procedures for cash result in evidential matter that has a high degree of reliability because much of the corroborating information is obtained through (1) the auditor's direct personal knowledge and (2) direct commu-

---

TYPE OF TEST: Substantive   **PURPOSE: Validity and Propriety of Balances**
CYCLE: Revenue and Expenditure   **ACCOUNTS: Cash on Hand and Cash in Bank**

A. CLERICAL ACCURACY

1. Foot cash journals and schedules.
2. Reconcile schedules with ledger balances.

B. EXISTENCE OR OCCURRENCE, RIGHTS AND OBLIGATIONS, AND VALUATION OR ALLOCATION

1. Count cash on hand.
2. Confirm bank balances.

C. COMPLETENESS

1. Perform cash cutoff test.
2. Examine or prepare bank reconciliations.
3. Obtain and use bank cutoff statements.
4. Trace bank transfers.
5. Prepare proof of cash.
6. Make analytical review.

D. STATEMENT PRESENTATION AND DISCLOSURE

1. Make inquiries and review documentation for cash restrictions and liens.
2. Compare statement presentation and disclosures with GAAP.

Figure 13-2. AUDIT PROGRAM: CASH BALANCES.

nication from independent sources outside the enterprise. Each procedure is explained below within the framework of the six audit objectives.

CLERICAL ACCURACY

The starting point in the verification of cash is to determine the mathematical accuracy of the cash journals and cash balances. Two tests of balances are used in meeting this objective: (1) the cash journals are footed and cross-footed and postings traced to general ledger accounts and (2) all cash schedules prepared by the client are footed and the totals reconciled to account balances. The footing of a bank reconciliation schedule includes the recalculation of any subtotals, such as outstanding checks.

EXISTENCE OR OCCURRENCE, RIGHTS AND OBLIGATIONS, AND VALUATION OR ALLOCATION

The auditor's primary concern under these objectives is whether the client has all the cash it claims to have. This involves the comparison of recorded cash balances with cash on hand and cash in banks. As shown in the audit program, two tests of balances are directed at these objectives.

Count Cash on Hand

Undeposited cash receipts, change funds, and petty cash funds are ordinarily considered to be cash on hand. To properly perform this test, the auditor should

- Control all cash and negotiable instruments held by the client until all funds have been counted.
- Insist that the custodian of the cash be present throughout the count.
- Obtain a signed receipt from the custodian on the return of the funds to the client.
- Ascertain that all undeposited checks are payable to the order of the client, either directly or through endorsement.

The control of all funds is designed to prevent transfers by the client of counted funds to uncounted funds. The sealing of funds and the use of additional auditors are often required when cash is held in many locations. The safeguards pertaining to the custodian serve to minimize the possibility, in the event of a shortage, of the client claiming that all cash was intact when released to the auditor for counting.

Confirm Bank Balances

It is customary for the auditor to confirm cash on deposit with banks as of the balance sheet date. A completed standard bank confirmation request form used in this test is illustrated in Figure 13-3. It may be noted that the request includes not only the cash balances on deposit, but also direct and indirect obligations to the bank, contingent liabilities, and security agreements.

The confirmation request is prepared in duplicate and signed by an authorized check signer of the client. Both copies are sent to the bank, and the original is returned to the auditor. To enhance the competency of the evidence from this procedure, the auditor should personally mail the request in his own return address envelope and the response should be returned directly to the auditor by the bank.

Bank confirmation requests should be sent to all banks in which the client has an account, including those that may have a zero balance at the end of the year. Such communication may disclose the existence of a balance in the account and/or obligations and contingencies to the bank. The auditor uses the confirmation responses in reconciling bank and book balances, verifying loans, and determining the existence of restrictions on cash and contingencies such as notes receivable discounted.

The terms of bank loans and the establishment of a line of credit with a bank may require the borrower to maintain a cash balance equal to an agreed-

> ORIGINAL
> To be mailed to accountant

December 20 19 *X1*

Your completion of the following report will be sincerely appreciated. IF THE ANSWER TO ANY ITEM IS "NONE," PLEASE SO STATE. Kindly mail it in the enclosed stamped, addressed envelope *direct* to the accountant named below.

Report from

Yours truly, *Bates Company*

(ACCOUNT NAME PER BANK RECORDS)

(Bank) *City Bank*

10 Monroe Street

Midtown, Indiana

By *CA. Merten, Tres.*

Authorized Signature

Bank customer should check here if confirmation of bank balances only (item 1) is desired. ☐

NOTE—If the space provided is inadequate, please enter totals hereon and attach a statement giving full details as called for by the columnar headings below.

Accountant *Beddy + Abel*
4 Court Street
Urban, Michigan

1. At the close of business on *December 31* 19 *X1* our records showed the following balance(s) to the **credit** of the above named customer. In the event that we could readily ascertain whether there were any balances to the credit of the customer not designated in this request, the appropriate information is given below.

AMOUNT	ACCOUNT NAME	ACCOUNT NUMBER	Subject to Withdrawal by Check?	Interest Bearing? Give Rate
$ *120,262.47*	*General*	*12345-642*	*yes*	*no*
$ *5,000.00*	*Payroll*	*12345-643*	*yes*	*no*

2. The customer was directly liable to us in respect of loans, acceptances, etc., at the close of business on that date in the total amount of $_____, as follows:

AMOUNT	DATE OF LOAN OR DISCOUNT	DUE DATE	INTEREST Rate	INTEREST Paid to	DESCRIPTION OF LIABILITY, COLLATERAL, SECURITY INTERESTS, LIENS, ENDORSERS, ETC.
$ *120,000*	*8/1/X1*	*2/1/X2*	*15*	*N/A*	*Unsecured*
$ *80,000*	*12/1/X1*	*6/1/X2*	*15*	*N/A*	*Unsecured*

3. The customer was contingently liable as endorser of notes discounted and/or as guarantor at the close of business on that date in the total amount of $ *None*, as below:

AMOUNT	NAME OF MAKER	DATE OF NOTE	DUE DATE	REMARKS
$				

4. Other direct or contingent liabilities, open letters of credit, and relative collateral, were

None

5. Security agreements under the Uniform Commercial Code or any other agreements providing for restrictions, not noted above, were as follows (if officially recorded, indicate date and office in which filed):

None

Yours truly, (Bank) *City Bank*

Date *January 9* 19 *X2*

By *Nancy L. Springer, V.P.*

Authorized Signature

Additional copies of this form are available from the American Institute of CPAs, 1211 Avenue of the Americas, New York, N. Y. 10036

Figure 13-3. STANDARD BANK CONFIRMATION REQUEST FORM.

on percentage of the amount borrowed or a specified dollar amount. The required minimum balance is referred to as a *compensating balance*. The American Institute of Certified Public Accountants (AICPA) has developed a special form for confirming compensating balance agreements. Because of the specific data requested, the confirmation should be sent separately to the loan officer of the bank and not be included with the regular bank confirmation request.

COMPLETENESS

This objective relates to whether the client's cash balances include all cash transactions that should be recorded. As shown in Figure 13-2, there are six tests of balances that pertain to completeness.

Perform Cash Cutoff Test

A proper cutoff of cash receipts and cash disbursements at the end of the year is essential to the proper statement of cash on the balance sheet and the overall fairness of the client's financial statements. Evidence concerning the accuracy of the cutoff can be obtained by personal observation and a review of internally created documentation. If auditors can be present at all client locations on the balance sheet date, it is possible by personal observation to ascertain that all cash received prior to the close of business is included in cash on hand or in deposits in transit. Furthermore, the auditor can personally determine the last check written and mailed by the client. Subsequent tracing of this evidence to the accounting records will verify the accuracy of the cash cutoff.

As an alternative to physical observation, the auditor can generally obtain satisfactory evidence of a prompt cutoff by (1) reviewing the source documents pertaining to cash receipts and cash disbursements for several days before and after the balance sheet date and (2) determining whether they are recorded in the proper accounting period. The use of a bank cutoff statement, described below, is also helpful in determining whether a proper cash cutoff has been made.

Examine or Prepare Bank Reconciliations

Most companies reconcile their bank and book balances monthly. When the reconciliations are done independently and reviewed by internal auditors, the auditor may only need to review the client's reconciliation at the end of the year. The review should include

- Tracing bank balances to the bank confirmation responses.
- Verifying the validity of the reconciling items such as deposits in transit and outstanding checks.
- Scanning the bank statements for erasures and alterations and investigating any occurrences.

- Establishing the propriety of any adjusting entries and determining that the client has recorded them.

A client-prepared reconciliation is shown in Figure 13-4.

When internal accounting control is weak, the auditor may prepare the bank reconciliation. Normally, the bank statement and accompanying data (e.g., paid checks, debit memos, etc.) will be in the possession of the client and therefore some alterations could have been made. To eliminate this possibility, the client can be asked to instruct the bank to send the year-end bank statement directly to the auditor.

The evidence provided by a bank reconciliation alone is generally not considered to be sufficient to verify the balance of cash in bank because of the uncertainties concerning two of the most important reconciling items: (1) deposits in transit and (2) outstanding checks. Such evidence is obtainable only by tracing these items to the bank statement in the next accounting period. The procedure of obtaining a bank cutoff statement is designed, in part, for this purpose. When the cutoff statement validates these and other reconciling items, the reliance that an auditor can place on a bank reconciliation is significantly enhanced.

Obtain and Use Bank Cutoff Statements

A bank cutoff statement is a bank statement as of a date subsequent to the date of the balance sheet. The date should be at a point in time that will permit most of the year-end outstanding checks to clear the bank. Usually, the date is seven to ten business days following the end of the client's fiscal year in areas where most of the banks are members of the Federal Reserve System and ten days or longer in areas where this is not the case.

The client must request the cutoff statement from the bank and instruct that it be sent directly to the auditor. On receipt of the cutoff statement, with enclosed canceled checks and bank memoranda, the auditor should

- Trace all prior year dated checks to the outstanding checks listed on the bank reconciliation.
- Trace deposits in transit on the bank reconciliation to deposits on the cutoff statement.
- Scan the cutoff statement and enclosed data for unusual items.

The tracing of checks is designed to verify the list of outstanding checks. In this step, the auditor may also find that a prior period check not on the list of outstanding checks has cleared the bank and that some of the checks listed as outstanding have not cleared the bank. The former may be indicative of an irregularity known as kiting, which is explained on page 470; the latter may be due to delays in (1) mailing the checks by the payer, (2) depositing the checks by the payees, and (3) processing the checks by the bank. The auditor should investigate any unusual circumstances.

Prepared by: C.J.A Date: 1/15/x2
Reviewed by: a.c.e. Date: 1/18/x2

Bates Company
(PBC)   Bank Reconciliation - City Bank - General
Acc. # 110   12/31/x1   A-1

Bank Acc. No. 12345-642

Balance per bank   120262 47 ᴪ

Deposits in transit: Per books   Per bank
                          12-30   1-2   842515 √
                          12-31   1-7   1784479 √
                                                                    2626994 ᴪ

Outstanding checks: 1047   22594 √
                                         1429   2160000 √
                                         1435   4725 √
                                         1436   142814 √
                                         1437   100000 √
                                         1440   83208 √
                                         1441   4108 √   (251749) ᴪ
Add NSF check - RZIM - 12/29   20000 ∅

Balance per books   1215592 ᴪ
Adjusting Entry - AJE ④   20000
Balance as adjusted   1213592
                                                                    To A

                          Adjusting Entry
Dr. Accounts Receivable ZIM   200
   Cr. Cash in Bank   200
NSF check charged by bank $200

ᴪ   Agreed to bank statement and bank confirmation
√   Traced to cut off bank statement
ᴪ   Footed
∅   Traced to statement and debit memoranda
ᴪ   Traced to general ledger

Figure 13-4. CLIENT-PREPARED BANK RECONCILIATION.

When the aggregate effect of uncleared checks is material, it may be indicative of an irregularity known as *window dressing*, which is a deliberate attempt to overstate a company's short-term solvency.[3] In such case, the auditor should

[3] Assume at the balance sheet date, the client's balances show current assets of $800,000 and current liabilities of $400,000. If $100,000 of checks to short-term creditors have been prematurely entered, the correct totals are current assets of $900,000 and current liabilities of $500,000, which results in a 1.8:1 current ratio instead of the reported 2:1.

trace the uncleared checks to the check register and supporting documentation and, if necessary, make inquiries of the treasurer.

The tracing of deposits in transit to the cutoff statement is normally a relatively simple matter since the first deposit on the cutoff statement should be the deposit in transit shown on the reconciliation. When this is not the case, the auditor should determine the underlying circumstances for the time lag from the treasurer and corroborate his explanations.

In scanning the cutoff statement for unusual items, the auditor should be alert for such items as unrecorded bank debits and credits and bank errors and corrections.

Inasmuch as the cutoff statement is obtained directly by the auditor from an independent source outside the client's organization, it provides a high degree of competent corroborating information about the validity of the year-end bank reconciliation and the amount of cash in bank at the statement date.

Trace Bank Transfers

Many entities maintain accounts with more than one bank. A company with multiple bank accounts may make authorized transfers of money between bank accounts. For example, money may be transferred from a general bank account to a payroll bank account for payroll checks that are to be distributed on payday. When a bank transfer occurs, several days (called the *float period*) generally will elapse before the check clears the bank on which it is drawn. Thus, cash on deposit per bank records will be overstated during this period because the check will be included in the balance of the bank in which it is deposited and will not be deducted from the bank on which it is drawn. Bank transfers many also result in a misstatement of the bank balance per books if the disbursement and receipt are not recorded in the same accounting period.

Intentionally recording a bank transfer as a deposit in the receiving bank while failing to show a deduction from the bank account on which the transfer check is drawn is an irregularity known as *kiting*. Kiting may be used to conceal a cash shortage or overstate cash in bank at the statement date.

An auditor requires evidence on the validity of bank transfers or conversely, of errors or irregularities therein. This is obtained by preparing a schedule of these checks issued at or near the end of the client's fiscal year. Data for the schedule are obtained from an analysis of the cash entries per books and applicable bank and cutoff bank statements. The schedule lists all transfer checks and shows the dates that the checks were recorded by the client and the bank, as illustrated in Figure 13-5.

If we assume all checks are dated and issued on December 31, check 4100 in Figure 13-5 has been handled properly since both book entries were made in December and both bank entries occurred in January. This check would be listed as an outstanding check in reconciling the general bank account at December 31 and as a deposit in transit in reconciling the payroll bank account. Check 4275 illustrates a transfer check in transit at the closing date. Cash per

Check Number	Bank Accounts		Amount of Check	Disbursement Date		Receipt Date	
	From	To		Per Books	Per Bank	Per Books	Per Bank
4100	General	Payroll	$50,000	12/31	1/3	12/31	1/2
4275	General	Branch #1	$10,000	12/31	1/4	1/2	1/2
4280	General	Branch #2	$20,000	1/2	1/2	12/31	12/31
B403	Branch #4	General	$5,000	1/2	1/3	1/3	12/31

Figure 13-5. BANK TRANSFER SCHEDULE.

books is understated $10,000 since the check has been deducted from the balance per books by the issuer in December, but has not been added to the Branch #1 account per books by the depositor until January. Thus, an adjusting entry is required at December 31 to increase the branch balance per books.

Checks 4280 and B403 illustrate the likelihood of kiting because these December checks were not recorded as disbursements per books until January even though they were deposited in December. Check 4280 results in a $20,000 overstatement of cash in bank because the receipt per books occurred in December, but the corresponding book deduction was not made until January. Check B403 may illustrate an attempt to conceal a cash shortage since the bank deposit occurred in December presumably to permit reconcilement of bank and book balances, and all other entries were made in January.

Kiting is possible when weaknesses in internal accounting control allow one individual to issue and record checks (i.e., improper segregation of functions), or there is collusion between the individuals who are responsible for the two functions. In addition to tracing bank transfers, kiting may be detected by (1) obtaining and using a bank cutoff statement because the kited check clearing in January will not appear on the list of outstanding checks for December and (2) performing a cash cutoff test since the last check issued in December will not be recorded in the check register.

Prepare Proof of Cash

A *proof of cash* is a simultaneous reconciliation of bank transactions and balances with corresponding data per books for a specified period of time. This substantive test is generally prepared only when the auditor has concluded that internal control over cash is weak. As illustrated in Figure 13-6, a proof of cash permits a reconciliation of four bank and book items: beginning balances, cash receipts transactions, cash disbursements transactions, and ending balances. The illustrated format may be extended to show the "true cash" balance by adding (or subtracting) book adjustments from the ending balance per books.

Prepared by: *W.C.R.*   Date: *1/12/X2*
Reviewed by: *W.K.S.*   Date: *1/16/X2*

Bates Company
Proof of Cash for December

Acc. # 110 City Bank - General   12/31/X1   A-3

	Balance 11/30/X1	Receipts	Disbursements	Balance 12/31/X1
Per bank statement	11,526.40	91,227.60	90,727.53	12,026.47 C
Deposit in transit:				
Beginning (11/30)	2,132.08 √	(2,132.08)		
Ending (12/31)		2,626.94		2,626.94 Θ
Outstanding checks:				
Beginning (11/30)	(2,726.45) Θ		(2,726.45)	
Ending (12/31)			2,517.49 Θ	(2,517.49)
Other items:				
NSF Check			(200.00) ↳	200.00
Per books	10,931.776 ↙	91,722.373 √	90,498.357 ↙	12,155.792 √
	F	F	F	FF

C Traced to bank confirmation
√ Traced to December bank statement
↙ Traced to cash in bank account
↳ Examined debit memo
Θ Agrees with list of outstanding checks
F Footed
FF Footed and crossfooted
Θ Traced to January cutoff bank statement

Figure 13-6. PROOF OF CASH WORKING PAPER.

The following steps are helpful in preparing a proof of cash:

- Obtain the bank and book totals from the bank statement and cash in bank account, respectively.
- Obtain the beginning and ending balance reconciling items from the bank reconciliations at the designated dates.
- Determine the reconciling items for the two middle columns by analysis.

All reconciling items in the schedule are attributable to either negating (for purposes of reconciliation only) items recorded by the bank that have not been recorded on the books or recognizing items recorded on the books that have not been recorded by the bank. In Figure 13-6, for instance, the deposit in transit on November 30 is subtracted from December bank receipts because that deposit is not included in the December receipts per books. In contrast, deposits in transit on December 31 are added to receipts per bank and to the ending bank balance because this amount has been recorded on the books but not by the bank.

The occurrence of a dishonored customer check sometimes proves to be troublesome in preparing a proof of cash. When the bank receives notice of "not sufficient funds" (NSF) from the customer's bank, it issues a debit memorandum (often referred to as an *NSF charge*) that is posted as a debit on the depositor's bank statement to cancel the credit that was made when the check was originally deposited. The action taken by the depositor on notification of dishonor determines the effect on the proof of cash. The disposition of the NSF check in Figure 13-6 is based on the fact that the depositor made no entry on notification and that the check was not redeposited prior to December 31.

The failure of any of the four columns of a proof of cash to reconcile is indicative of an unexplained error or irregularity that should be investigated by the auditor.

Make Analytical Review

Relationships that may be used in applying analytical review procedures to cash balances include: (1) the amount of each cash balance, (2) the percentage of total current assets represented by cash, and (3) the number of days cash requirements on hand. Any significant fluctuations and unusual results obtained in comparing the relationships with prior years, budget expectations, and industry data normally will require further investigation to determine whether all cash transactions have been recorded.

STATEMENT PRESENTATION AND DISCLOSURE

Cash should be properly presented in the balance sheet and appropriate disclosure should be made of any restrictions on the use of cash.

When compensating balances exist, any cash balances legally restricted under loan or line of credit agreements should be segregated on the balance sheet and classified according to the appropriate classification of the related debt. In addition, supplementary disclosures, in the form of notes to the financial statements, must be made of pertinent provisions of the agreement such as the rate of interest, maximum limit of short-term borrowing, and repayment terms. A bank overdraft is normally reported as a current liability.

The auditor determines the appropriateness of the statement presentation from a review of the draft of the client's statements and the evidence obtained from the foregoing substantive tests. For example, the response from a bank confirmation may indicate the existence of restrictions on the use of cash funds. In addition, the auditor should review the corporate minutes and loan agreements for evidence of cash restrictions, and make inquiry of management.

TESTS OF RECEIVABLES BALANCES

The nature, timing, and extent of substantive tests of receivables balances depend on the auditor's evaluation of internal controls of sales and cash receipts transactions in the revenue cycle, as described in Chapters 8 and 9.

Accordingly, if the auditor has determined that controls over credit approval are weak, additional tests of the allowance for uncollectibles account may be necessary. In contrast, when controls over billings are strong, the auditor may confirm accounts receivable one or two months prior to the balance sheet date. An audit program for receivables and the allowance for uncollectibles is illustrated in Figure 13-7. In this program, the audit objectives of existence or occurrence and rights and obligations are combined.

The auditor relies primarily on evidential matter obtained from confirmations in meeting these two objectives. Corroborating information for the other objectives is obtained largely from documentation originating within the client organization.

CLERICAL ACCURACY

The starting point for tests of accounts receivable and the allowance for uncollectible accounts is an aged trial balance of individual customer balances prepared by the client. The components (transactions) comprising the balance are aged by the length of time the receivable has been outstanding (unpaid) at the balance sheet date. An aged trial balance, which is illustrated in Figure 13-8, is generally manually or electronically prepared by the client.

The auditor should verify the accuracy of the aged trial balance. This is done by recalculating the totals of the schedule, tracing selected customer balances to the subsidiary ledger, and selectively tracing unpaid invoices to sales transaction dates.

Since all customer balances are included, the aged trial balance is used extensively in performing other tests of balances. For instance, as shown in Figure 13-8, it may be used in confirming accounts receivable. The aged trial balance may also enable the auditor to identify balances that should be reclassified, such as customers with credit balances and amounts due from officers and affiliated companies.

EXISTENCE OR OCCURRENCE AND RIGHTS AND OBLIGATIONS

These objectives relate to whether recorded receivables are owned by the client and represent valid claims against customers. Four auditing procedures apply to these objectives.

Inspect Notes on Hand

The auditor should inspect all notes in the possession of the client. This procedure should occur simultaneously with the count of cash and marketable

TYPE OF TEST: Substantive	**PURPOSE:** Validity and Propriety of Balances
	ACCOUNTS: Notes and Accounts Receivable and
CYCLE: Revenue	**Allowable for Uncollectible Accounts**

A. CLERICAL ACCURACY

1. Foot supporting schedules.
2. Reconcile general ledger balances with schedules and subsidiary ledger totals.

B. EXISTENCE OR OCCURRENCE AND RIGHTS AND OBLIGATIONS

1. Inspect notes on hand.
2. Confirm accounts receivable.
3. Confirm notes receivable.
4. Review documentation in client's files.

C. COMPLETENESS

1. Perform sales and sales returns cutoff test.
2. Make analytical review.

D. VALUATION OR ALLOCATION

1. Examine subsequent collections.
2. Review documentation and schedules pertaining to collectibility.
3. Recalculate interest earned and accrued.

E. STATEMENT PRESENTATION AND DISCLOSURE

1. Make inquiries and review documentation concerning assigning, pledging, or factoring (selling) accounts receivable, and the discounting of notes receivable.
2. Compare statement presentation and disclosures with GAAP.

Figure 13-7. AUDIT PROGRAM: RECEIVABLES BALANCES.

securities. In examining notes receivable, the auditor compares the terms and face value of the instrument with the client's records and with the schedule of notes and interest that normally is prepared by the client for the auditor. The auditor should also be alert for notes held beyond their maturity dates, notes bearing abnormal interest rates, and nontrade notes such as those issued by officers and affiliated companies. The existence of any of these factors should be indicated in the working papers in determining the collectibility of the notes and the appropriate statement presentation.

The auditor is expected to ascertain that the notes are made out to the client or are endorsed to the client. Similarly, the auditor also inspects any collateral held by the client as security for a note. If the collateral is in the form of securities, it should be examined to obtain evidence that the debtor has legal title.

BATES COMPANY
AGED TRIAL BALANCE - ACCOUNTS RECEIVABLE - TRADE
DECEMBER 31, 19X1

W/P REF: *B-1*
PREPARED BY: *a.C.E.* DATE *1/15/X2*
REVIEWED BY: *P.A.R.* DATE *1/20/X2*

ACCT. 120

(PBC)

ACCOUNT NAME	OVER 90 DAYS	OVER 60 DAYS	OVER 30 DAYS	CURRENT	CONF. NO.	BALANCE PER BOOKS 12/31/X1	ADJUSTMENTS	BALANCE PER AUDIT 12/31/X1	CASH RECEIVED 1/1/X2 TO 1/15/X2
ACE ENGINEERING		2,529.04	2,016.14	11,875.90	1 C	16,421.08 n ✓		16,421.08	12,621.93 ⊕
APPLIED DEVICES			15,938.89	27,901.11	2 C	43,840.00 n ✓		43,840.00	29,464.00 ⊕
BARRY MANUFACTURING	1,088.92	743.12	3,176.22	8,993.01		14,001.27 n ✓		14,001.27	1,003.36
BRANDT ELECTRONICS	501.10	7,309.50	30,948.01	24,441.25	3 C	63,199.86 n ✓		63,199.86	26,810.60 ⊕
CERMETRICS, INC.			3,813.76	8,617.30		12,431.06 n ✓		12,431.06	3,813.76 ⊕
COLUMBIA COMPONENTS				4,321.18		4,321.18 n ✓		4,321.18	
DRAKE MANUFACTURING			739.57	2,953.88		3,693.45 n ✓		3,693.45	
EMC		1,261.01	1,048.23	16,194.76	4 C	18,504.00 n ✓		18,504.00	17,248.24 ⊕
GROTON ELECTRIC	(4,611.91)	12,411.27	20,006.63	89,017.15	5 C	116,823.14 n ✓		116,823.14	76,328.41 ⊕
HARVEY INDUSTRIES		1,709.16	6,111.25	18,247.31		26,067.72 n ✓		26,067.72	8,134.41
JED INC.	2,615.87	12,098.00	15,434.46	56,536.88	6 Ⓔ	86,685.21 n ✓	(1,416.21)	85,269.00	27,532.87 ⊕
JERICO ELECTRIC		1,198.72	13,123.14			14,321.86 n ✓		14,321.86	1,198.72
KEYSTONE INDUSTRIES		3,012.45	4,363.68	17,167.04	7 C	24,543.17 n ✓		24,543.17	3,963.54 ⊕
LEDDER ELECTRONICS	1,315.10	7,273.63	15,331.91	10,106.15	8 C	34,026.79 n ✓		34,026.79	9,568.56
OAK CITY ELECTRONICS	3,821.49	4,778.08	5,936.89	21,432.25	9 C	35,968.71 n ✓		35,968.71	8,599.57 ⊕
NATIONAL PRODUCTS			905.45	9,500.68		10,406.13 n ✓		10,406.13	905.45
PROGRESS ELECTRONICS				3,017.90		3,017.90 n ✓		3,017.90	
RIKER CORP.		571.02	6,201.62	9,724.14	10 U	16,496.78 n ✓		16,496.78	7,124.18 ⊕
S.E.G. INC.		1,656.80	3,210.16	8,565.85		13,432.81 n ✓		13,432.81	6,312.00
W & M MANUFACTURING CORP.		1,904.65	2,166.78	28,389.69	11 C	32,461.12 n ✓		32,461.12	16,109.13 ⊕
YANCEY CORP.	814.98	2,861.05	9,874.13	13,561.80	12 C	27,111.96 n ✓		27,111.96	11,168.98 ⊕
MISCELLANEOUS			190.36	1,571.18		1,761.54 n ✓		1,761.54	
	5,545.55	61,317.50	160,537.28	392,136.41		619,536.74	(1,416.21)	618,120.53	267,907.71
	✓	✓	✓	✓		B	B	B	

C   Confirmed
n   Traced to Subledger - Verified aging
✓   Footed or Crossfooted
⊕   Traced to C/R Journal and examined remittance advices
U   Unable to confirm

Ⓔ   Credit memo issued 1/12/X2
AJE ⑦ See EE6
　　Dr. Sales Returns   1,416.21
　　Cr. Accounts Rec.   1,416.21

Figure 13-8. AGED TRIAL BALANCE WORKING PAPER.

Confirm Accounts Receivable

Confirmation of accounts receivable involves direct written communication between the individual customers and the auditor. Through confirmation, the auditor obtains evidence about the existence of the customer and the accuracy of the balance due from the customer. A confirmation is not a request for payment. Consequently, this procedure is not directed at evidence on the collectibility or net realizable value of the claim. Confirmation responses, however, may reveal previously paid items and disputed items that affect the proper valuation of the claim. Relevant considerations in performing this procedure are as follows.

Practicability and Reasonableness.   The confirmation of accounts is a generally accepted auditing procedure whenever (1) the receivables are material to a company's financial position or results of operations and (2) it is practicable and reasonable to do so. In auditing, *practicable* means capable of being done with available means or with reason or prudence; *reasonable* means sensible in the light of prevailing circumstances. In virtually all cases, it will be practicable and reasonable for the auditor to perform this procedure.

However, there are two circumstances in which the auditor may be unable to confirm accounts receivable. First, debtors may be unable to confirm if they use voucher systems that show the amount owed on individual transactions, but not the total amount owed to one creditor. This is generally true of governmental agencies. In some cases, the auditor may be able to overcome this problem by confirming individual transactions rather than balances. Second, the client may prohibit the auditor from confirming any or certain accounts receivable. Complete prohibition represents a serious limitation on the scope of the auditor's examination that generally will result in a disclaimer of opinion on the financial statements. The effect of partial prohibition should be evaluated on the basis of management's reasons therefor and whether the auditor can satisfy himself by other auditing procedures.

Form of Confirmation.   There are two forms of confirmation request: (1) the *positive* form, which requires the debtor to respond whether or not the balance shown is correct and (2) the *negative* form, which requires the debtor to respond only when the amount shown is incorrect. The two forms are illustrated in Figures 13-9 and 13-10. The positive confirmation request is usually made in the form of a separate letter, but it may be in the form of a stamp on the customer's monthly statement. In contrast, the negative request is usually in the form of a stamp. The positive form generally produces the better evidence, because under the negative form, the failure to receive a response can only lead to a presumption that the balance is correct, whereas the customer may have overlooked the request or neglected to return an exception.

The form of the confirmation request rests with the auditor. In reaching this decision, the auditor considers the effectiveness of the client's internal accounting controls and the composition of the customers' accounts. The positive form is preferred when control risk is high (i.e., there appears to be opportunity for errors or irregularities to occur) or individual account balances are relatively large. When the reverse is true, the negative form may be used.

Frequently, a combination of the two forms is used in a single engagement. For example, in the audit of a public utility, the auditor may elect to use the negative form for residential customers and the positive form for commercial customers. When the positive form is used, the auditor should generally follow up with a second and sometimes an additional request to those debtors that fail to reply.[4]

Timing and Extent of Requests.   The confirmation date and the number of responses to be requested are decisions that must be made by the auditor. Confirmation may be requested as of the balance sheet date or a month or two before the statement date, if internal controls are effective. In the latter

---

[4]Auditing Standards Board, *op. cit.*, AU § 331.08.

Bates Company
P.O. Box 1922
Sandusky, Ohio 44870

Ace Engineering Service
Box 131
Indiana, Pennsylvania 15701

    This request is being sent to you to enable our independent auditors to confirm the correctness of our records. It is not a request for payment.

    Our records on <u>December 31, 19X1</u> showed an amount of <u>$16,421.08</u> receivable from you. Please confirm whether this agrees with your records on that date by signing and returning this form direct to our auditors. An addressed envelope is enclosed for this purpose. If you find any difference please report details direct to our auditors in the space provided below.

A. C. Martin

_____
Controller

The above amount is correct ☐. The above amount is incorrect for the following reasons: _____

_____

_____

                                    _____

                                      (Individual or Company Name)

             By: _____

Conf. No. 1.

Figure 13-9. POSITIVE CONFIRMATION REQUEST: LETTER FORM.

Please examine this monthly statement carefully
and advise our auditors

Reddy & Abel
465 City Center Bldg.
Marian, New York 11748

_____

Certified Public Accountants

_____

_____

as to any exceptions.

A self-addressed stamped envelope is enclosed
for your convenience.

THIS IS NOT A REQUEST FOR PAYMENT

Figure 13-10. NEGATIVE CONFIRMATION REQUEST: STAMP FORM.

case, the auditor is expected to perform other substantive tests of transactions from the confirmation date to the balance sheet date. In addition, the auditor may elect to reconfirm balances at year end that have changed significantly since the confirmation date. Accounts to be confirmed may be selected by the computer, chosen from random number tables, or selected by the auditor on a judgmental basis. The sample should be sufficiently representative to justify valid generalization about the entire population of receivables.

Controlling the Requests.   The auditor must control every step in the confirmation process. This means

- Ascertaining that the amount, name, and address on the confirmation agree with the corresponding data in the customer's account.
- Maintaining custody of the confirmations until they are mailed.
- Using his own return address envelopes for the confirmations.
- Personally depositing the requests in the mail.
- Insisting that the returns be sent directly to the auditor.

Client assistance can be used in the preparation of the requests provided the foregoing controls are observed.

Disposition of Exceptions.   Confirmation responses will inevitably contain some exceptions. The auditor should describe all exceptions in the working papers. Exceptions may be attributable to in-transit items at the confirmation date, items in dispute, errors, and irregularities. All differences should be investigated by the auditor, and their resolution indicated in the working papers.

Evaluating the Results.   The auditor's working papers should contain a summary of the results from confirming accounts receivable. The summary should show the number of confirmations sent for each form (positive and negative) and the number of replies received. For positive confirmations, the summary should show (1) the percentage in dollars of accounts confirmed and (2) the percentage in dollars of accounts with no responses and errors. For negative confirmations, the summary should show the percentage in dollars of returns with exceptions. From the summary data, the auditor can determine the sufficiency of the evidence obtained from this test of details.

When insufficient responses are received or numerous exceptions are found, the auditor may be unable to issue a standard audit report, unless the auditing procedures of reviewing documentation in the customer's account file and examining collections subsequent to the examination date are more extensively applied. These procedures are explained later in the chapter.

Applicability to Audit Objectives.   The confirmation of accounts receivable balances is the *primary* source of evidence in determining that accounts receivable exist at the balance sheet date. This test of balances is also a *secondary* source of evidence in meeting the following audit objectives:

Audit Objective	Explanation
Clerical accuracy	The correctness of individual customer balances contributes to the correctness of the accounts receivable balance.
Occurrence	Acknowledged indebtedness by the debtor indicates that the related sales transactions took place.
Completeness	A confirmed balance indicates that all revenue cycle transactions have been recorded; exceptions in responses may indicate that some transactions have not been recorded or recorded in the wrong accounting period.
Rights	Acknowledgment of indebtedness indicates that the client has a legal claim on the customer for payment.
Valuation or allocation	The correctness of customer balances contributes to the determination of gross claims on customers at the balance sheet date; exceptions in responses may affect the net realizable value of accounts receivable.

The primary sources of evidence for each of the foregoing audit objectives are obtained from the tests of balances shown in the audit program in Figure 13-7.

Confirm Notes Receivable

The auditor normally uses the positive form of confirmation for notes and acceptances receivable. Confirmations are sent to both the maker of the instrument and any party that is currently holding the note for the client. The request to the maker should include verification of the terms, last interest payment date, balance due, and a description of any collateral. The confirmation to holders is designed to determine the existence of the note and the attendant circumstances pertaining thereto. Notes may be held by others for collection or because they have been discounted, sold, renewed, dishonored, or pledged.

Review Documentation in Client's Files

The customer account file maintained by the client should contain such documents as customer orders, shipping documents, sales invoices, credit memoranda, and correspondence. These documents provide evidence on the existence of the receivable. This procedure may be used to supplement confirmation procedures when no response is obtained from a positive confirmation or the negative form of confirmation is used.

COMPLETENESS

This objective relates to whether all accounts receivable transactions that should be recorded are recorded in the proper period. The substantive tests applicable to this objective consist of the cash cutoff test described earlier in this chapter and the following procedures.

Perform Sales and Sales Returns Cutoff Test

The sales cutoff test is designed to obtain reasonable assurance that (1) sales and accounts receivable are recorded in the accounting period in which the goods are shipped and (2) the corresponding entries for inventories and cost of goods sold are made in the same period.

The basis for recognizing sales normally is the date of shipment, but when goods are shipped F.O.B. (free on board) destination, the seller may arbitrarily add several days to the shipping date, since legal title does not pass in such case until the buyer receives the goods. The sales cutoff test usually is made as of the balance sheet date. The test involves

- Examining shipping documents for several days before and after the cutoff date to determine the date and terms of shipment.
- Tracing shipping documents to the sales and inventory records to establish that the entries were made in the correct accounting period.
- Inspecting invoices for a period of time before and after the cutoff date to ascertain the validity and propriety of the shipments and corresponding entries.
- Inquiring of management about any direct shipments by outside suppliers to customers and determining the appropriateness of related entries.

If internal control is weak, the auditor should be alert for the possibility of fictitious sales. For example, unordered goods may be shipped to a regular customer shortly before the statement date, with the subsequent return not made and booked until the following period. When evidence obtained from the sales cutoff indicates material errors in recording year-end sales, the auditor should request the client to make the necessary adjustments.

The sales returns cutoff test involves: (1) reviewing the receiving report on goods returned and (2) retracing the credit memos to recorded entries shortly before and after the balance sheet date. Sales shipped prior to the end of the year but returned after year-end should be deducted from sales.

Make Analytical Review

The reasonableness of the balances in accounts receivable, sales, and uncollectible accounts expense should be tested by analytical review procedures. The following financial relationships are often used:

Financial Relationship	Formula
Accounts receivable turnover	Net sales ÷ Average accounts receivable
Accounts receivable to total current assets	Accounts receivable ÷ Total current assets
Rate of return on net sales	Net income ÷ Net sales
Uncollectible accounts expense to net credit sales	Uncollectible accounts expense ÷ Net sales
Uncollectible accounts expense to actual uncollectibles	Uncollectible accounts expense ÷ Actual uncollectibles

The absence of significant fluctuations in comparing each relationship with prior years, expected results, and industry data provides evidential matter that supports the reasonableness of the related account balance. In contrast, a significant fluctuation requires further investigation by the auditor. For example, an unexpected decrease in the rate of return on net sales may indicate that some sales have not been recorded or have been recorded in the wrong accounting period.

VALUATION OR ALLOCATION

For receivable balances, this objective includes verifying (1) gross claims against debtors, (2) collectibility of receivables, (3) uncollectible accounts expense, and (4) interest earned on notes receivable. There are three tests of balances that are applicable to this objective.

Examine Subsequent Collections

The best evidence of collectibility is the receipt of payment from the customer. Prior to actual receipt, the collectibility of an account can only be estimated. Between the balance sheet date and the conclusion of the auditor's examination, collections on the prior year's receivables may be received by the client. The matching of such collections back to balances outstanding at the statement date establishes the collectibility of the accounts.

In performing this test, the auditor should recognize the possible adverse implications of collections that cannot be matched to specific transactions or balances. For example, a round sum amount may, on investigation, reveal items in dispute, and token payments on large balances may indicate financial instability on the part of the customer.

Review Documentation and Schedules Pertaining to Collectibility

Receivables should be stated on the balance sheet at net realizable value. This value for notes receivable is determined by the collectibility of the instrument or, in the event of default, by the value of the collateral held. In evaluating collectibility, the auditor usually looks for evidence that might adversely affect the client's ability to obtain collection at the due date. One source is to examine the schedule of notes receivable for past due notes and notes that have been frequently renewed. Inquiry of the credit manager may also be helpful.

The schedule of notes should indicate the existence of any collateral that may be in the form of securities or negotiable warehouse receipts. The auditor should ascertain the current realizable value of the collateral at the statement date. When securities are widely traded current market prices can be obtained from published prices or a broker. Similarly, the value of the warehouse receipts may be obtained from market quotations of the merchandise pertaining thereto.

For accounts receivable, the aged trial balance is the starting point in determining the adequacy of the allowance account. The auditor should review the percentages used for each of the current and past-due categories for reasonableness. In addition, for past-due accounts, the auditor should

- Examine correspondence in the debtor's file.
- Review published annual financial statements.
- Make inquiries of outside agencies, such as Dun & Bradstreet, about the customer's credit rating.
- Review correspondence between the client and outside collection agencies about the status of accounts turned over for collection.
- Discuss the collectibility of the account with appropriate management personnel.

From the foregoing, it should be apparent that substantial evidence is generally available to the auditor in making a determination of the reasonableness of the allowance for uncollectible accounts. It is neither necessary nor desirable for the auditor to place too much reliance on the opinion of the credit manager or other client personnel in making this decision. An analysis of an allowance account is illustrated in Figure 13-11.

Recalculate Interest Earned and Accrued

The auditor obtains evidence of interest rates and interest dates by inspecting the notes. Verification of interest earned and accrued is achieved by reperformance of the client's interest calculations shown on the schedule of notes receivable. When a client, such as a financial institution, has numerous notes, the recomputations can be made on a test basis. The auditor should also verify accrued interest receivable and interest collected. The former requires recourse to the date and terms of the note. The latter involves a review of cash receipts records and supporting documentation.

STATEMENT PRESENTATION AND DISCLOSURE

The auditor is required to determine whether receivables are properly identified, classified, and disclosed in the financial statements. The existence of contingencies and pledges of notes should be disclosed in the statements. Data pertaining to these matters are obtained from confirming notes held by others, bank confirmation responses, and inquiries of management.

For accounts receivable, a scanning of the aged trial balance may reveal items that may require separate identification and classification. For example, credit balances may warrant reclassification as current liabilities and receivables from employees, officers, affiliated companies, and related parties should be specifically identified if material. Evidence of the existence of liens and assignments may be obtained from a review of the minutes and inquiry of management.

Equal consideration must be given by the auditor to the client's presentation of sales and net sales. Proper presentation of sales may include reporting of sales by segments.

Prepared by: M.Q.Y. Date: 1/18/X2
Reviewed by: P.A.R. Date: 1/20/X2

Bates Company
Allowance for Uncollectible Accounts
12/31/X1

Acc. # 122 B-3

	Balance 1/1/X1			5000	Ø
	Accounts Written Off:				
	Penn Central	535 10	И		
	Dudley Inc.	460 90	И		
	P+L Corp.	287 09			
				⟨1283 09⟩	
	Balance Per Books 12/31/X1			3716 91	L
	Add AJE (8) See Below			1283 09	
	Audited Balance 12/31/X1			5000 00	
				Ta B	
	Possible Uncollectible Accounts				
1.	Barry Mfg. - Amount has been in dispute since 6/10. Resolution unsure. Customer claims goods not mfgd. to specifications.			1088 92	
2.	Progress Electronics - Co. filed for Chap 11 bankruptcy on 1/10/X1. Examined corresp. and it appears maximum recoverable will be 10% and that is doubtful.			3017 90	
3.	Miscellaneous small amounts on which Bates has decided they will not pursue collection.			190 36	
	Total possible uncollectible accounts			4297 18	
	Based on the above information, it appears that an allowance for uncollectible accounts of $5000 is reasonable and should cover any potential losses on outstanding A/R at 12/31/X1 the following adjustment is proposed. (8)				
DR	General and Admin. Expenses (420)	1283 09			
CR	Allowance for uncollectible A/C's (122)			1283 09	
	To adjust allowance to required amount A5				
И	Examined correspondence - companies currently in chapter 11 bankruptcy - expected return is max. of 5% per discussion with client + copies of plans of arrangement.				
Ø	Agrees with ending balance in prior year W/P's.				

Figure 13-11. ALLOWANCE FOR UNCOLLECTIBLE ACCOUNTS WORKING PAPER.

STATISTICAL SAMPLING OF RECEIVABLES BALANCES

Both probability-proportional-to-size and classical variables sampling plans are frequently used in the audit of receivable balances and may also be used in the audit of sales, sales adjustments, and other revenue accounts such as interest or lease income. The remainder of this section presents a case study involving the use of statistical sampling in the audit of the Porter Company's trade accounts receivable. Through use of the approach developed in Chapter 12, each step in designing, executing, and evaluating the sample is explained.

Determine the Objectives of the Plan

The objective of the sample is to test the fairness of the total recorded book value of Porter's receivables. Because the evaluation of related internal controls and the results of other substantive tests suggest that errors of both under and overstatement may occur with some frequency, it is decided to use the difference estimation technique.

Define the Population and Sampling Unit

The population consists of 1,000 customer accounts with a total recorded book value of $985,500. The auditor obtains a computer listing of these accounts and satisfies himself as to its completeness and that the individual book values sum to the total recorded book value. Since confirmation of customer account balances will be the primary audit procedure performed on the sample items, the individual customer account is designated as the sampling unit.

Determine Sample Size

To determine sample size, the auditor specifies the following:

- Population size (N) = 1,000.
- Estimated standard deviation of the differences (S_{d_j}) = $105.
- Risk of incorrect rejection = .05.
- Risk of incorrect acceptance = .05.
- Tolerable error = $40,000.

The estimated standard deviation is based on the results of the prior year's audit. The risks of incorrect rejection and acceptance are set at a low level because, as noted above, little assurance is available from other procedures. The specified tolerable error represents the maximum misstatement allowable in the control account that will still permit the auditor to conclude that the balance is fairly stated.

For the specified risks of incorrect rejection and acceptance, the auditor determines the ratio, R, of desired allowance for sampling risk to tolerable error, TE, from a table like the one in Figure 12-7. In this case, the ratio is .543. The desired allowance for sampling risk, A, is then calculated as follows:

$$A = R \times TE$$
$$= .543 \times \$40,000$$
$$= \$21,720$$

After determining the appropriate U_R factor for the specified risk of incorrect rejection (U_R = $1.96 for .05 from Figure 12-6), the auditor determines sample size as follows:

$$n = \left(\frac{N \times U_R \times S_{d_j}}{A}\right)^2 = \left(\frac{1,000 \times 1.96 \times \$105}{\$21,720}\right)^2 = 90$$

Since n/N (90/1,000) is greater than .05, the adjusted sample size for sampling without replacement is determined as follows:

$$n' = \frac{n}{1 + \dfrac{n}{N}} = \frac{90}{1 + \dfrac{90}{1,000}} = 83$$

Determine the Sample Selection Method

The auditor uses a random number table to obtain 83 random numbers to use in manually selecting a simple random number sample from the customer accounts listing.

Execute the Sampling Plan

First and second confirmation requests are sent and alternative auditing procedures are performed for all non-replies to obtain an audit value for each of the 83 sample items. The difference between the audit and book value for each item as well as the average difference, $\bar{d}$, and the standard deviation of the differences, Sdj, are calculated. In this case study, $\bar{d}$ is assumed to be $\$-35$ and Sdj is assumed to be $\$112$. These statistics are then used in evaluating the sample results.

Evaluate the Sample Results

The auditor calculates (1) the total projected error, $\hat{D}$, (2) the total estimated population value, $\hat{X}$, and (3) the achieved allowance for sampling risk, A'. He then calculates the range about the estimated total value. These computations are shown below.

Estimated Total Projected Error

$$\hat{D} = N \times \bar{d} = 1,000 \times \$-35 = \$-35,000$$

Estimated Total Population Value

$$\hat{X} = BV + \hat{D} = \$985,500 + (\$-35,000)$$
$$= \$950,500$$

Achieved Allowance for Sampling Risk

$$A' = N \times U_R \times \frac{Sdj \sqrt{1 - \dfrac{n}{N}}}{\sqrt{n}} = 1,000 \times 1.96 \times \frac{\$112 \sqrt{1 - \dfrac{83}{1,000}}}{\sqrt{83}}$$
$$= \$23,073$$

Since A' ($23,073) is greater than A ($21,720), the auditor calculates an adjusted achieved allowance for sampling risk as follows:

$$A'' = A' + TE\left(1 - \frac{A'}{A}\right)$$

$$= \$23,073 + \$40,000\left(1 - \frac{\$23,073}{\$21,720}\right)$$

$$= \$20,581$$

He then calculates the range.

$$\hat{X} \pm A'' = \$950,500 \pm \$20,581$$
$$= \$929,919 \text{ to } \$971,081$$

Since the total book value, $985,500, does not fall within the computed range, the sample results support the conclusion that the account is misstated by more than tolerable error.

After reviewing the nature and amounts of differences in the sample and considering the results of other tests and the qualitative aspects of the errors, the auditor concludes that the client should investigate the errors and prepare an adjustment to the account. The auditor will then reevaluate the sample results and all other relevant evidence to reach a conclusion about whether the adjusted account balance is fairly stated.

COMPUTER-ASSISTED TESTS OF ACCOUNTS RECEIVABLE BALANCES

When a client maintains its accounts receivable records by EDP, the auditor may use the computer to assist in performing substantive tests on the accounts receivable balances. This is possible if the auditor has appropriate generalized audit software or a program tailor-made for the client.

In this illustration, it is assumed that the client's master file of accounts receivable is maintained in magnetic tape form. In addition to updating the file for revenue cycle transactions, the client's program provides for monthly printouts of an aged trial balance and monthly statements for customers.

There are two widely used computer-assisted applications in testing accounts receivable balances: (1) verifying the accuracy of the accounts receivable aged trial balance and (2) preparing confirmation requests. These applications, which are illustrated in Figure 13-12, are explained below.

Verify Accuracy of Aged Trial Balance

The auditor may use a generalized audit software package to verify the accuracy of the aged trial balance. To accomplish this objective, the auditor first inputs the audit selection criteria in Figure 13-12 that are desired in the test. The auditor then runs a program that copies the accounts receivable master file and converts it onto a tape in a format that is compatible with the software package. The auditor proceeds to process the tape with the specified audit

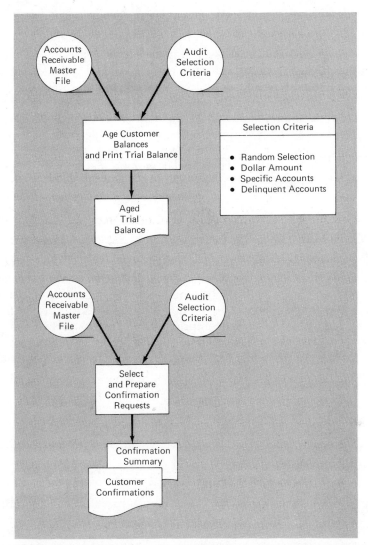

Figure 13-12. COMPUTER-ASSISTED TESTS OF ACCOUNTS RECEIVABLE BALANCES.

selection criteria using the software package. The printed output is compared by the auditor with accounts receivable control and the aged trial balance is analyzed as part of the auditor's input in determining the adequacy of the allowance for doubtful accounts.

A further test is to compare the details of the aged trial balance from the auditor's run with the details of the client's EDP aged trial balance for the same date. The auditor may also trace individual balances shown on the auditor's trial balance to documentation in the customer's account file such as invoices and customer monthly statements.

Prepare Confirmation Requests

In this application, a generalized software package is used to select the customer accounts for confirmation. As in the preceding example, the auditor must input the desired audit selection criteria, convert the master file to tape in a format compatible with the software package, and process the data using the software program. The printouts of this application are the confirmation requests and summary data used by the auditor for control purposes.

In addition to these two applications, the computer may be used to accumulate other data that may be of interest to the auditor such as account balances that have (1) new large dollar volume amounts and (2) unusual activity, such as the payment of a recent bill before paying an earlier billing.

CONCLUDING COMMENTS

The audit objectives in performing substantive tests of account balances apply to all cycles. These objectives consist of (1) clerical accuracy, (2) existence or occurrence, (3) completeness, (4) rights and obligations, (5) valuation or allocation, and (6) statement presentation and disclosure. The verification of cash and receivables balances comprises an important part of the auditor's substantive tests of balances in a typical audit engagement. Simultaneous cash counts, bank confirmations, and cash cutoff procedures are essential audit procedures for cash balances. In addition, the confirmation of receivables is a required auditing procedure under GAAS.

REVIEW QUESTIONS

13-1 a. Describe the nature and scope of tests of balances.
b. What approaches are generally used for tests of balances.

13-2 Indicate the effects of materiality and audit risk on substantive tests of balances.

13-3 a. What factors should be considered in deciding whether to perform tests of balances prior to the balance sheet date.
b. Substantive tests prior to the balance sheet date can be considered as substitutes for tests at the balance sheet date. Do you agree? Why or why not?

13-4 Identify and briefly explain the purpose of each of the audit objectives that are applicable to tests of balances.

13-5 Indicate the procedures the auditor may use in meeting the completeness objective and the type of evidence that may be obtained.

13-6 What precautions should be taken by the auditor in (a) counting cash on hand and (b) confirming bank balances?

13-7 Identify the five types of information included in a standard bank confirmation.

13-8 a. What safeguards must be taken by the auditor in obtaining and using a bank cutoff statement?
b. What steps should be taken by the auditor after he has received a cutoff statement?

13-9 What procedures are involved in performing a cash cutoff test?

13-10 a. Define and illustrate *kiting*.

     b. How can kiting be prevented and detected?

13-11 a. Explain the purpose of a proof of cash.

     b. What circumstance generally results in the preparation of a proof of cash?

13-12 Identify the audit procedures in tests of receivable balances that satisfy the audit objectives of (a) existence or occurrence and (b) completeness.

13-13 In confirming receivables, what conditions (a) may make it impracticable or unreasonable for the auditor to perform this test, (b) should be considered by the auditor in determining the form of the confirmation request, and (c) are relevant to the auditor in determining the timing and extent of the requests?

13-14 a. What precautions should the auditor take in confirming accounts receivables?

     b. Indicate the circumstances when the confirmation of accounts receivable is a secondary source of evidence in meeting specific audit objectives.

13-15 When the auditor is unable to confirm accounts receivable, indicate (a) the alternative procedures he may perform and (b) the effects on his audit report.

13-16 For an aged trial balance prepared by the client, explain (a) the auditor's responsibilities and (b) the specific types of data he may obtain therefrom.

13-17 How does the auditor perform a sales cutoff test?

13-18 What is the best evidence of the collectibility of an account?

13-19 How does the auditor establish the reasonableness of the allowance for uncollectible accounts?

13-20 What specific assistance can a computer provide in verifying accounts receivable balances?

OBJECTIVE QUESTIONS FROM PROFESSIONAL EXAMINATIONS

Indicate the *best* answer for each of the following multiple-choice questions.

13-21 These questions pertain to substantive tests of cash balances.

  1. As one of the year-end audit procedures, the auditor instructed the client's personnel to prepare a standard bank confirmation request for a bank account that had been closed during the year. After the client's treasurer had signed the request, it was mailed by the assistant treasurer. What is the major flaw in this audit procedure?

    a. The confirmation request was signed by the treasurer.

    b. Sending the request was meaningless because the account was closed before the year-end.

    c. The request was mailed by the assistant treasurer.

    d. The CPA did *not* sign the confirmation request before it was mailed.

  2. An unrecorded check issued during the last week of the year would most likely be discovered by the auditor when the

    a. Check register for the last month is reviewed.

    b. Cut-off bank statement procedures are performed.

    c. Bank confirmation is reviewed.

    d. Search for unrecorded liabilities is performed.

3. To gather evidence regarding the balance per bank in a bank reconciliation, an auditor would examine all of the following *except*
   a. Cutoff bank statement.
   b. Year-end bank statement.
   c. Bank confirmation.
   d. General ledger.
4. A "proof of cash" used by an auditor
   a. Proves that the client's year-end balance of cash is fairly stated.
   b. Confirms that the client has properly separated the custody function from the recording function with respect to cash.
   c. Validates that the client's bank did not make an error during the period being examined.
   d. Attests that the auditor has complied with generally accepted auditing standards.
   e. Determines if there were any unauthorized disbursements or unrecorded deposits for the given time period.

13-22 These questions relate to the verification of accounts receivable balances.

1. Auditors may use positive and/or negative forms of confirmation requests for accounts receivable. An auditor most likely will use
   a. The positive form to confirm all balances regardless of size.
   b. A combination of the two forms, with the positive form used for large balances and the negative form for the small balances.
   c. A combination of the two forms, with the positive form used for trade receivables and the negative form for other receivables.
   d. The positive form when controls related to receivables are satisfactory, and the negative form when controls related to receivables are unsatisfactory.
2. In the confirmation of accounts receivable, the auditor would most likely
   a. Request confirmation of a sample of the inactive accounts.
   b. Seek to obtain positive confirmations for at least 50% of the total dollar amount of the receivables.
   c. Require confirmation of all receivables from agencies of the federal government.
   d. Require that confirmation requests be sent within one month of the fiscal year-end.
3. During the process of confirming receivables as of December 31, 19X2, a positive confirmation was returned indicating the "balance owed as of December 31 was paid on January 9, 19X3". The auditor would most likely
   a. Determine whether there were any changes in the account between January 1 and January 9, 19X3.
   b. Determine whether a customary trade discount was taken by the customer.
   c. Reconfirm the zero balance as of January 10, 19X3.
   d. Verify that the amount was received.
4. An auditor reconciles the total of the accounts receivable subsidiary ledger to the general ledger control account, as of October 31, 19X2. By this procedure, the auditor would be most likely to learn of which of the following?
   a. An October invoice was improperly computed.
   b. An October check from a customer was posted in error to the account of another customer with a similar name.
   c. An opening balance in a subsidiary ledger account was improperly carried forward from the previous accounting period.
   d. An account balance is past due and should be written off.

COMPREHENSIVE QUESTIONS

13-23 As the senior auditor on the audit of the Elles Company for the year ending December 31, you discover the following errors in cash working papers prepared by your assistants:

1. Compensating bank balances were overlooked

2. Kiting was missed.

3. Several December 31 checks were not recorded as disbursements until January. These checks are not listed as outstanding on the December 31 bank reconciliation.

4. The petty cash on hand was $25 short of the imprest fund balance.

5. The December cash disbursements journal included the checks issued January 2 and 3.

6. Several mathematical errors were made in the client's December bank reconciliation schedule.

7. The December 31 bank balance shown on the reconciliation schedule was incorrect.

8. A contingent liability on a discounted note receivable was missed.

Required

a. Identify the test of balances that should have detected each error.

b. For each error, indicate the applicable audit objective.

c. Indicate the type of evidence obtained by each audit procedure.

13-24 Lingham Company's fiscal year ends on April 30, and the company's certified public accountant, Sanders & Stein, conducts the annual audit during May and June . Sanders & Stein has prepared audit procedures for the different phases of the audit engagement with Lingham Company. Included among the audit program steps for cash on deposit with the Union State Bank are the following:

1. Obtain a bank confirmation as of April 30, 19X0, directly from Union State Bank.

2. Prepare a proof of cash for the month of April 19X0.

3. Obtain a cutoff bank statement directly from Union State Bank for a 15-day period (May 15) subsequent to the close of operations on April 30, 19X0.

Required

a. Why should Sanders & Stein obtain a bank confirmation directly from the Union State Bank?

b. What is a "proof of cash" and why is it important in the audit of the cash in the bank account?

c. What is the purpose of obtaining a cutoff bank statement for a 15-day period after the end of Lingham Company's fiscal year?

CMA

13-25 The Patricia Company had poor internal control over its cash transactions. Facts about its cash position at November 30, 19X0 were as follows:

The cashbook showed a balance of $18,901.62, which included undeposited receipts. A credit of $100 on the bank's records did not appear on the books of the company. The balance per bank statement was $15,550. Outstanding checks were: #62 for $116.25,

#183 for $150, #284 for $253.25, #8621 for $190.71, #8623 for $206.80, and #8632 for $145.28.

The cashier abstracted all undeposited receipts in excess of $3,794.41 and prepared the following reconciliation:

Balance per books, November 30, 19X0		$18,901.62
Add: Outstanding checks:		
8621	$190.71	
8623	206.80	
8632	145.28	442.79
		$19,344.41
Less: Undeposited receipts		3,794.41
Balance per bank, November 30, 19X0		$15,550.00
Deduct: Unrecorded credit		100.00
True cash, November 30, 19X0		$15,450.00

Required

a. Prepare a working paper showing how much the cashier abstracted.

b. How did he attempt to conceal his theft?

c. Using only the information given, name two specific features of internal control which were apparently lacking.

AICPA

13-26 You are the in-charge accountant examining the financial statements of the Gutzler Company for the year ended December 31, 19X0. During late October 19X0 you, with the help of Gutzler's controller, completed an internal control questionnaire and prepared the appropriate memoranda describing Gutzler's accounting procedures. Your comments relative to cash receipts are as follows.

All cash receipts are sent directly to the accounts receivable clerk with no processing by the mail department. The accounts receivable clerk keeps the cash receipts journal, prepares the bank deposit slip in duplicate, posts from the deposit slip to the subsidiary accounts receivable ledger, and mails the deposit to the bank.

The controller receives the validated deposit slips directly (unopened) from the bank. He also receives the monthly bank statement directly (unopened) from the bank and promptly reconciles it.

At the end of each month, the accounts receivable clerk notifies the general ledger clerk by journal voucher of the monthly totals of the cash receipts journal for posting to the general ledger.

Each month, with regard to the general ledger cash account, the general ledger clerk makes an entry to record the total debits to cash from the cash receipts journal. in addition, the general ledger clerk on occasion makes debit entries in the general ledger cash account from sources other than the cash receipts journal (e.g., funds borrowed from the bank).

Certain standard auditing procedures that are listed below have already been performed by you in the audit of cash receipts. The extent to which these procedures were performed is not relevant to the question.

1. Total and cross-total all columns in the cash receipts journal.

2. Trace postings from the cash receipts journal to the general ledger.

3. Examine remittance advices and related correspondence to support entries in the cash receipts journal.

Required

Considering Gutzler's internal control over cash receipts and standard auditing procedures already performed, list all other auditing procedures and reasons therefore that should be performed to obtain sufficient audit evidence regarding cash receipts. Do not discuss the procedures for cash disbursements and cash balances. Also, do not discuss the extent to which any of the procedures are to be performed. Assume adequate controls exist to assure that all sales transactions are recorded. Organize your answer sheet as follows:

Other Audit Procedures	Reason for Other Audit Procedures

AICPA

13-27 The LMN Company maintains three bank accounts: City Bank–Regular, City Bank–Payroll, and Metro Bank–Special. Your analysis of cash disbursements records for the period June 23 to July 6 reveals the bank transfers:

Check No	Date of Check	Bank Drawn On	Payee	Amount
2476	June 23	Regular	Payroll	$100,000
2890	June 25	Regular	Payroll	200,000
3140	June 28	Regular	Special	100,000
A1006	June 29	Special	Payroll	50,000
A1245	June 30	Special	Regular	25,000
3402	June 30	Regular	Special	125,000

You determine the following facts about each of the first five checks: (1) the date of the cash disbursements journal entry is the same as the date of the check, (2) the payee receives the check two days later, (3) the payee records and deposits the check on the day it is received, and (4) it takes five days for a deposited check to clear banking channels and be paid by the bank on which it is drawn. Check 3402 was not recorded as a disbursement until July 1. This check was picked up by the payee on the date it was issued and it was included in the payee's after-hours bank deposit on June 30.

Required

a. What are the purposes of the audit of bank transfers?
b. Prepare a bank transfer schedule as of June 30 using the format illustrated in Figure 13-5.
c. Prepare separate adjusting entries for any checks that require adjustment.
d. In the reconciliations for the three bank accounts, indicate the check numbers that should appear as (1) an outstanding check or (2) a deposit in transit.
e. Which check(s) may be indicative of kiting?

13-28 The following information was obtained in an audit of the cash account of Tuck Company as of December 31, 19X0. Assume that the CPA has satisfied himself as to the validity of the cash book, the bank statements, and the returned checks, except as noted.

1. The bookkeeper's bank reconciliation at November 30, 19X0.

Balance per bank statement		$ 19,400
Add deposit in transit		1,100
Total		$ 20,500
Less: Outstanding checks		
#2540	$140	
1501	750	
1503	480	
1504	800	
1505	30	2,300
Balance per books		$ 18,200

2. A summary of the bank statement for December 19X0:

Balance brought forward	$ 19,400
Deposits	148,700
	$168,100
Charges	132,500
Balance, December 31, 19X0	$ 35,600

3. A summary of the cash book for December 19X0 before adjustments.

Balance brought forward	$ 18,200
Receipts	149,690
	$167,890
Disbursements	124,885
Balance, December 31, 19X0	$ 43,005

4. Included with the canceled checks returned with the December bank statement were the following:

Number	Date of Check	Amount of Check	Comment
1501	November 28, 19X0	$ 75	This check was in payment of an invoice for $750 and was recorded in the cash book as $750.
1503	November 28, 19X0	$580	This check was in payment of an invoice for $580 and was recorded in the cash book as $580.

Number	Date of Check	Amount of Check	Comment
1523	December 5, 19X0	$150	Examination of this check revealed that it was unsigned. A discussion with the client disclosed that it had been mailed inadvertently before it was signed. The check was endorsed and deposited by the payee and processed by the bank even though it was a legal nullity. The check was recorded in the cash disbursements.
1528	December 12, 19X0	$800	This check replaced 1504 that was returned by the payee because it was mutilated. Check 1504 was not cancelled on the books.
——	December 19, 19X0	$200	This was a counter check drawn at the bank by the president of the company as a cash advance for travel expense. The president overlooked informing the bookkeeper about the check.
——	December 20, 19X0	$300	The drawer of this check was the Tucker Company.
1535	December 20, 19X0	$350	This check had been labeled NSF and returned to the payee because the bank had erroneously believed that the check was drawn by the Luck Company. Subsequently, the payee was advised to redeposit the check.
1575	January 5, 19X0	$10,000	This check was given to the payee on December 30, 19X0 as a postdated check with the understanding that it would not be deposited until January 5. The check was not recorded on the books in December.

5. The Tuck Company discounted its own 60-day note for $9,000 with the bank on December 1, 19X0. The discount rate was 6%. The bookkeeper recorded the proceeds as a cash receipt at the face value of the note.

6. The bookkeeper records customers' dishonored checks as a reduction of cash receipts. When the dishonored checks are redeposited, they are recorded as a regular cash receipt. Two NSF checks for $180 and $220 were returned by the bank during December. The $180 check was redeposited but the $220 check was still on hand at December 31. Cancellations of Tuck Company checks are recorded by a reduction of cash disbursements.

7. December bank charges were $20. In addition, a $10 service charge was made in December for the collection of a foreign draft in November. These charges were not recorded on the books.

8. Check 2540 listed in the November outstanding checks was drawn three years ago. Since the payee cannot be located, the president of Tuck Company agreed to the CPA's suggestion that the check be written back into the accounts by a journal entry.

9. Outstanding checks at December 31, 19X0 totaled $4,000 excluding checks 2540 and 1504.

10. The bank had recorded a deposit of $2,400 on January 2, 19X1. The bookkeeper had recorded this deposit on the books on December 31, 19X0 and then mailed the deposit to the bank.

Required

Prepare a four-column reconciliation ("proof of cash") of the cash receipts and cash disbursements recorded on the bank statement and on the company's books for the month of December 19X0. Use the format illustrated in this chapter.

AICPA (adapted)

13-29 Dodge, CPA, is examining the financial statements of a manufacturing company with a significant amount of trade accounts receivable. Dodge is satisfied that the accounts are properly summarized and classified and that allocation, reclassifications, and valuations are made in accordance with GAAP. Dodge is planning to use accounts receivable confirmation requests to satisfy the third standard of field work as to trade accounts receivable.

Required

a. Identify and describe the two forms of accounts receivable confirmation requests and indicate what factors Dodge will consider in determining when to use each.

b. Assume Dodge has received a satisfactory response to the confirmation requests. Describe how Dodge could evaluate collectibility of the trade accounts receivable.

AICPA

13-30 The following situations were not discovered in the audit of Pars Company by an inexperienced staff assistant:

1. Several accounts were incorrectly aged on the client's aging schedule.

2. Interest earned on notes receivable was incorrectly accrued.

3. A note reported to be held by a bank for collection is fictitious.

4. Four year-end sales are recorded in the wrong accounting period.

5. The customers' ledger totals are correct but balances in some individual customer accounts are incorrect.

6. Errors were made in journalizing sales invoices.

7. The allowance for uncollectible accounts is understated.

8. Two notes on hand were not owned or endorsed to Pars Company.

9. The accounts receivable turnover ratio is unreasonable.

10. The contingent liability pertaining to the discounting of a note receivable was not disclosed.

Required

a. Identify the test of balances that should have detected each situation.

b. For each situation indicate the relevant audit objective.

c. Indicate the type of corroborating information obtained by each audit procedure.

13-31 Jerome and Gerard, CPAs, are preparing for the annual audit of the Fordham Office Machine Company. Several procedures that are included in the audit program pertaining to accounts receivable and sales are summarized below:

1. Evaluate internal controls relating to accounts receivable and sales.

2. Obtain and analyze an aged trial balance of accounts receivable; indicate any collections subsequent to the balance sheet date.

3. Confirm accounts receivable by direct written communication with customers.

4. Evaluate the adequacy of the allowance for uncollectible accounts.

5. Review the year-end cutoff of sales and cash collections.

6. Examine all phases of several sales transactions and subsequent cash collections selected at random.

Required

a. What are the auditor's objectives in performing each procedure?

b. What is meant by "year-end cutoff of sales" (5 in the summarized audit program above), and why is it important that the "year-end cutoff of sales" be reviewed by the auditor?

CMA (adapted)

13-32 You have been assigned to the first examination of the accounts of The Chicago Company for the year ending March 31, 19X1. The accounts receivable were circularized at December 31, 19X0 and at that date, the receivables consisted of approximately 200 accounts with balances totaling $956,750. Seventy-five of these accounts with balances totaling $650,725 were selected for circularization. All but 20 of the confirmation requests have been returned; 30 were signed without comments, 14 had minor differences that have been cleared satisfactorily while 11 confirmations had the following comments:

1. We are sorry but we cannot answer your request for confirmation of our account as the PDQ Company uses as accounts payable voucher system.

2. The balance of $1,050 was paid on December 23, 19X0.

3. The above balance of $7,750 was paid on January 5, 19X1.

4. The above balance has been paid.

5. We do not owe you anything at December 31, 19X0 as the goods, represented by your invoice dated December 30, 19X0, number 25,050, in the amount of $11,550, were received on January 5, 19X1 on FOB destination terms.

6. An advance payment of $2,500 made by us in November 19X0 should cover the two invoices totaling $1,350 shown on the statement attached.

7. We never received these goods.

8. We are contesting the propriety of this $12,525 charge. We think the charge is excessive.

9. Amount okay. As the goods have been shipped to us on consignment, we will remit payment on selling the goods.

10. The $10,000, representing a deposit under a lease, will be applied against the rent due to us during 19X3, the last year of the lease.

11. Your credit dated December 5, 19X0 in the amount of $440 cancels the above balance.

Required

What steps would you take to clear satisfactorily each of the above 11 comments?

AICPA

13-33 The Fox Company has been using 0.05% of net sales in providing for uncollectible accounts. The provision, however, has been inadequate since the allowance account shows a debit balance of $1,772 on December 31, 19X0 before making the annual provision for bad debts.

On December 31, 19X0, the Fox Company decides to switch to the aging method. On this date, the trial balance shows accounts receivable of $84,000. This total includes $15,000 of past-due accounts and $4,000 of customer credit balances. Further investigation reveals that $4,000 of past-due accounts represent advances to officers and $2,000 of past-due accounts are worthless. In addition, it is found that the cashbook was held open until January 2, 19X1 with the result that $5,000 of January collections on current accounts were entered as December cash receipts. Management estimates that past-due accounts are 20% uncollectible and current accounts are 3% uncollectible.

Required

a. Compute the bad debt provision at December 31, 19X0 under the aging method. Show computations.

b. Prepare the adjusting entries required at December 31, 19X0.

c. Indicate the evidence an auditor may obtain about past-due accounts. Comment on the competency of the evidence.

13-34 You are engaged to perform an audit of the Wilcox Corp. For the year ended December 31, 19X0.

Only merchandise shipped by the Wilcox Corporation to customers up to and including December 30,19X0 has been eliminated from inventory. The inventory as determined by physical inventory count has been recorded on the books by the company's controller. No perpetual inventory records are maintained. All sales are made on an FOB shipping point basis. You are to assume that all purchase invoices have been correctly recorded.

The following lists of sales invoices are entered in the sales journal for the months of December 19X0 and January 19X1, respectively.

	Sales Invoice Amount	Sales Invoice Date	Cost of Merchandise Sold	Date Shipped
			December	
a.	$ 3,000	Dec. 21	$2,000	Dec. 31
b.	2,000	Dec. 31	800	Nov. 3
c.	1,000	Dec. 29	600	Dec. 30
d.	4,000	Dec. 31	2,400	Jan. 3

	Sales Invoice Amount	Sales Invoice Date	Cost of Merchandise Sold	Date Shipped
e.	10,000	Dec. 30	5,600	Dec. 29 (shipped to consignee)
		January		
f.	$ 6,000	Dec. 31	$4,000	Dec. 30
g.	4,000	Jan. 2	2,300	Jan. 2
h.	8,000	Jan. 3	5,500	Dec. 31

Required

Record necessary adjusting journal entries at December 31, in connection with the foregoing data.

AICPA

13-35 As the in-charge auditor, you begin your field work to examine the December 31, financial statements of a client on January 5, knowing that you must leave temporarily for another engagement on January 7 after outlining the audit program for your assistant. Before leaving, you inquire about the assistant's progress in his examination of notes receivable. Among other things, he shows you a working paper listing the makers' names, the due dates, the interest rates, and amounts of 17 outstanding notes receivable totaling $100,000. The working paper contains the following notations:

1. Reviewed system of internal control and found it to be satisfactory.
2. Total of $100,000 agrees with general ledger control account.
3. Traced listing of notes to sales journal.

   The assistant also informs you that he is preparing to request positive confirmation of the amounts of all outstanding notes receivable and that no other audit work has been performed in the examination of notes receivable and interest arising from equipment sales. There were no outstanding accounts receivable for equipment sales at the end of the year.

   You ask your assistant to examine all notes receivable on hand before you leave. He returns in 30-minutes from the office safe where the notes are kept and reports that notes on hand total only $75,000.

Required

List the possible explanations that you would expect from the client for the $25,000 difference. (Eliminate fraud or misappropriation from your consideration.) Indicate beside each explanation the audit procedures you would apply to determine if each explanation is correct.

AICPA

13-36 Data relevant to the audit of accounts receivable in two companies are tabulated below:

	Company X	Company Y
Client's book value	$90,000	$200,000
Population size	1,000	2,000
Desired risk of incorrect acceptance	20%	30%
Desired risk of incorrect rejection	10%	5%
Tolerable error	$ 9,000	$ 10,000
Estimated standard deviation	$ 50	$ 25

Required

a. Compute the required sample size for each company with replacement.

b. Compute the required sample size for each company without replacement.

c. Assume the total audited value of the X Company sample calculated in b above is $13,600 and its standard deviation is $52. May the auditor conclude that the book value is fairly stated?

d. Assume that the mean of the sample audit values of the Y Company sample calculated in part b above is $90 and the sample standard deviation is $30. May the auditor conclude that Y's book value for receivables is fairly stated?

13-37 An auditor is conducting an examination of the financial statements of a wholesale appliance distributor. The distributor supplies appliances to hundreds of individual customers in the metropolitan area. The distributor maintains detail accounts receivable records on a computer disk. At the end of each business day, the customer account file is updated. Each customer record in the computer file contains the following data:

1. Customer account number.

2. Address.

3. Open (unpaid) invoices at the beginning of the month, by invoice number and date.

4. Sales during the current month, by invoice number and date.

5. Individual cash receipts during the current month.

6. Date of last sale.

7. Date of last cash receipt.

8. Total sales during the year.

The auditor is planning to confirm selected accounts receivable as of the end of the current month. The auditor will have available a computer tape of the data on the accounts receivable master file on the date that the company regularly sends monthly statements to its customers. The auditor also has a general purpose software package.

Required

The auditor is planning to perform the customary audit procedures involved in the verification of accounts receivable. Identify the basic procedures to be performed and describe how the use of the general-purpose software package and the tape of the accounts receivable file data might be helpful to the auditor in performing such auditing procedures. Organize your answer as follows:

Basic Receivable Auditing Procedure	How General-Purpose Computer Software Package and Tape of Accounts Receivable Data Might Be Helpful

AICPA

CASE STUDY

13-38* The Ohio River Authority is an instrumentality of the state created to control, store, and preserve the waters of the Ohio River within its reservoirs and to regulate the flow therefrom to develop hydroelectric energy and to provide water for irrigation and to conserve and protect the soil along its watershed.

The board of directors of the authority has selected us as auditors for the year ended June 30, 19X1. The interim work is completed in March and the review of operating procedures and tests of internal control have enabled us to determine the following:

1. The Authority has three branch offices, all located within a 300-mile radius of the home office, to conduct operations in their respective districts. The functions of these branches include the installation and servicing of power facilities, meter reading, billing, maintaining detail customers' ledgers, receiving collections on accounts receivable, and the preparation of various daily reports that are forwarded to the home office accounting department for entry to the general ledger accounts.

2. The Authority maintains separate departments under the supervision of responsible employees for each of the following functions: (a) meter installation (b) meter reading, (c) billing and posting receivables ledgers, (d) cash collections, (e) credit approval and follow-up, (f) accounting.

3. The employees of the home office accounting department function as internal auditors and perform an audit of each branch office at least once every two years. The internal audits are comprehensive but do not include circularization of accounts receivable, bank balances, or outstanding liabilities.

4. Sales of primary power at wholesale rates and power sales to most of the larger commercial and industrial customers are billed at rates established under contracts with the customers. All sales of irrigation water are charged to customers at contract rates.

5. The number of customers served, classified according to major income statement captions, are: wholesale 50, retail-residential 9,000, retail-commercial 1,600, and water 150.

6. Revenues from irrigation water contracts are based on a standard rate per acre as stated in the contract, regardless of the amount of water used for irrigation during the growing season from April to September. The Authority accrues this income monthly and bills the farmer at the end of the growing season.

7. The Authority requires all power customers to put up a deposit prior to installation of the power meters. Residential consumers must deposit $5; deposits of other customers range from $5 to $100. Bad debts are infrequent and, after deducting deposits, have been minor in the past.

8. Total kilowatt hours of electric energy sales are accounted in the same classifications used for revenue in the income statement.

9. Accounts receivable substantially turn over every month.

10. Our internal control work did not disclose any significant exceptions in recording transactions or safeguarding assets.

11. Excerpts from financial statements audited by another CPA firm one year ago are as follows:

Balance Sheet		Income Statement	
Cash	$277,710	Sales primary power:	
Accounts Receivable:		Wholesale	
Customer electrical	401,823	Municipalities	$1,802,516
Accrued irrigation		Rural co-ops	954,919
contracts	141,825	Other utilities	759,160

Balance Sheet		Income Statement	
Notes receivable	484	Retails	
Allowance for		Commercial	771,565
uncollectible		Residential	345,045
accounts	(584)	Other operating	
Total assets	37,306,309	revenues	
Customer deposits	(57,226)	Sales of water	280,460
		Fees—operating	
		co-ops	131,699
		Other	32,209
		Net income	1,263,700

These data are comparable to the current year's statements prepared by the Authority.

Required

1. What procedures will be used in confirming accounts receivable? Indicate when confirmations will be mailed, what type of confirmations will be used, how many accounts will be circularized, and how control of detail account balances will be established.

2. What methods should be utilized to determine the adequacy of the bad debt allowance?

3. What audit steps should be performed to determine that the revenue reported on the income statement is reasonable?

Chapter 14

Substantive Tests of Expenditure and Production Cycle Balances

Study Objectives

After completing a careful study of this chapter, you should be able to

- Prepare and execute audit programs for inventories, plant assets, and current liability balances.

- Describe the auditor's responsibilities in observing the client's inventory taking.

- Apply statistical sampling and EDP in testing inventory balances.

- Explain the major differences between the verification of current assets and plant assets.

- Identify the differences in audit risk between current assets and current liabilities.

- Contrast the confirmation of accounts payable and the confirmation of accounts receivable.

The explanation of substantive tests of balances is continued in this chapter. Attention is focused primarily on three types of accounts as being representative of material account balances resulting from transactions in the expenditure and production cycles. These accounts are (1) inventories, (2) plant assets, and (3) accounts payable. The form and arrangement of the chapter are similar to that used in Chapter 13.

TESTS OF INVENTORY BALANCES

Inventories include goods held for sale to customers, goods in the process of production, and materials and supplies expected to be used or consumed in production. The term *merchandise inventory* is usually applied to goods held for sale by a retailer or wholesaler when such goods have been acquired in a condition for resale. The terms *raw materials, work in process, finished goods,* and *factory supplies* are generally used in referring to the inventories of a manufacturing company. In this chapter, the term *inventories* will be used as an all-inclusive designation for all of the foregoing terms.

The examination of inventories requires careful planning and a very substantial investment in audit time, cost, and effort. The audit program for tests of inventory balances is directly related to the results of the auditor's tests of internal accounting control procedures in the revenue, expenditure, and production cycles. For example, weak physical controls over inventory storage may lead to more extensive tests of quantities on hand at the statement date. Conversely, effective controls over the costing of perpetual inventory records may result in a reduction of inventory pricing tests during year-end work. The primary tests of inventory balances are shown in Figure 14-1. Each of the tests is explained below within the framework of the audit objectives.

CLERICAL ACCURACY

Tests for mechanical accuracy include footing of inventory schedules and summaries. In addition, the balances in inventory accounts are reconciled with the totals of inventory summaries and perpetual inventory records. The accuracy of pricing extensions on the inventory summaries is also verified as part of this objective.

EXISTENCE OR OCCURRENCE

This objective relates to management's assertions on the physical existence of the inventory and the occurrence of purchases and manufacturing transactions. Tests of balances are the primary source of evidence for existence, whereas reliance on internal accounting control generally constitutes the major support for occurrence. There are two tests of balances for this objective.

Observe Client's Inventory Taking

The observation of inventories has been a generally accepted auditing procedure for over 40 years. This procedure is required whenever inventories are material to a company's financial statements and it is practicable and reasonable to do so. The observation of inventories may prove to be inconvenient,

TYPE OF TEST: Substantive	**PURPOSE: Validity and Propriety of Balances**
CYCLE: Expenditure and Production	**ACCOUNTS: Inventories**

A. CLERICAL ACCURACY

1. Verify accuracy of inventory schedules and summaries.
2. Reconcile general ledger control with inventory records and schedules.

B. EXISTENCE OR OCCURRENCE

1. Observe client's inventory taking.
2. Confirm inventories in public warehouses.

C. COMPLETENESS

1. Perform purchases and purchases returns cutoff tests.
2. Make analytical review.

D. RIGHTS AND OBLIGATIONS

1. Make inquiries of management regarding ownership.
2. Examine consignment agreements.
3. Review purchase commitments.

E. VALUATION OR ALLOCATION

1. Review data pertaining to inventory quality.
2. Vouch and test inventory pricing.
3. Review entries to cost of goods sold.

F. STATEMENT PRESENTATION AND DISCLOSURE

1. Make inquiries of management as to pledging of inventories.
2. Compare statement presentation and disclosure with GAAP.

Figure 14-1. AUDIT PROGRAM: INVENTORY BALANCES.

time-consuming, and difficult for the auditor but it is seldom impracticable and unreasonable.

In performing this auditing procedure, the auditor is expected to (1) observe the taking of the inventory by the client, (2) make some test counts of inventory quantities, and (3) make inquiries of the client concerning the inventories. The auditor has no responsibility to take or supervise the taking of the inventory. From this auditing procedure, the auditor obtains direct knowledge of the effectiveness of the client's inventory taking and the measure of reliance that may be placed on management's assertions as to the quantities and physical condition of the inventories.[1] In some cases, outside inventory specialists may

[1]Auditing Standards Board, *Codification of Statements on Auditing Standards* (New York: American Institute of Certified Public Accountants, 1985), Auditing Section 331.09 (hereinfter referred to and cited as AU §).

be hired by the client to take the inventory. When this occurs, the auditor must also be present to observe their counts because from an auditing standpoint, the specialists are basically the same as company employees. The primary audit considerations applicable to this required procedure are as follows:

Timing and Extent of the Test. The timing of an inventory observation depends on the client's inventory system and the effectiveness of internal accounting control. In a periodic inventory system, quantities are determined by a physical count, and all counts are made as of a specific date. The date should be at or near the balance sheet date, and the auditor should ordinarily be present on the specific date.

In a perpetual inventory system, physical counts may be taken and compared to inventory records at interim dates. When the perpetual records are well kept and comparisons with physical counts are made periodically by the client, the auditor should be present to observe a representative sample of such counts. In such case, this procedure may occur either during or after the end of the period under audit. In companies where inventories are at multiple locations, the auditor's observations ordinarily should encompass all significant inventory locations.

Inventory-Taking Plans. The taking of a physical inventory by a client is usually done according to a plan or a list of instructions. The client's instructions should include such matters as the

- Names of employees responsible for supervising the inventory taking.
- Date of the counts.
- Locations to be counted.
- Detailed instructions on how the counts are to be made.
- Use and control of prenumbered inventory tags and summary (compilation) sheets.
- Provisions for handling the receipt, shipment, and movement of goods during the counts if such activity is unavoidable.
- Segregation or identification of goods not owned.

The auditor should review and evaluate the client's inventory-taking plans well in advance of the counting date. With ample lead time, the client should be able to respond favorably to suggested modifications in the plans before the count is begun. It is common for the auditor to assist the client in designing an inventory-taking plan that will facilitate both the taking and the observing of the inventory.

Advance planning must be done by the auditor if an inventory observation is to be done efficiently and effectively. An experienced auditor usually has the responsibility for (1) planning the procedure, (2) determining the manpower needs, and (3) assigning members of the audit team to specific locations. Each observer should be provided with a copy of the client's inventory plans and written instructions of his duties.

Performing the Test.   In observing inventories, the auditor should

- Scrutinize the care with which client employees are following the inventory plan.
- See that all merchandise is tagged and no items are double tagged.
- Determine that prenumbered inventory tags and compilation sheets are properly controlled.
- Make some test counts and trace quantities to compilation sheets.
- Be alert for empty containers and hollow squares (empty spaces) that may exist when goods are stacked in solid formations.
- Watch for damaged and obsolete inventory items.
- Appraise the general condition of the inventory.
- Identify the last receiving and shipping documents used and determine that goods received during the count are properly segregated.
- Inquire about the existence of slow-moving inventory items.

The extent of the auditor's test counts depends, in part, on the care exercised by client employees in taking the inventory and the nature and composition of the inventory. Ordinarily, the auditor will stratify the inventory items in order to include the items of highest dollar value in the count and take a representative sample of other items. Recourse to perpetual inventory records is helpful in identifying the high-value items and selecting the sample items.

In making test counts, the auditor should record the count and give a complete and accurate description of the item (identification number, unit of measurement, location, etc.) in the working papers as shown in Figure 14-2. Such data are essential for the auditor's comparison of the test counts with the client's counts, and the subsequent tracing of the counts to inventory summary sheets and perpetual inventory records. Any differences in any of the comparisons should be investigated by the auditor. The test counts and related comparisons provide the auditor with evidence of the existence of the inventory and the accuracy of the client's counts, inventory compilation sheets, and perpetual inventory records.

On conclusion of the observation procedure, a designated member of the audit team should prepare an overall summary. The summary should include a description of such matters as (1) departures from the client's inventory-taking plan, (2) the extent of test counts and any material discrepancies resulting therefrom, and (3) conclusions on the accuracy of the counts and the general condition of the inventory.

When inventories are material and the auditor does not observe the inventory at or near the year-end

- Tests of the accounting records alone will not be sufficient as to quantities.
- It will always be necessary for the auditor to make, or observe, some physical counts of the inventory and to apply appropriate tests of intervening transactions.[2]

---

[2]Auditing Standards Board, *op. cit.,* AU § 331.12.

Highlift Company
Raw Materials Test Counts
12/31/X1
F-2

Tag No.	Inventory Sheet No.	Inventory Number	Description	Count Client		Audit	Difference
6531	15	1-42-003	Back Plate	125 ✓		125	
8340	18	1-83-012	1/4" Copper Plate	93 ✓		93	
1483	24	2-11-004	Single End Wire	1321 yds ✓		1325 yds.	4 yds.
4486	26	2-28-811	Copper Tubing	220 ft ✓		220 ft.	
3334	48	4-26-204	Side Plate	424 ✓		424	
8502	64	7-44-310	1/2" Copper Wire	276 ft. ✓		276 ft.	
8844	68	7-72-460	3/8" Copper Wire	419 ft. ✓		419 ft.	
6295	92	3-48-260	Front Plate	96 ✓		69	27 units

Each difference was corrected by the client. The net effect of the corrections was to increase inventory by $840. Total inventory values for which test counts were made and traced to inventory summaries without exception = $26,460 or 22% of the total. In my opinion, errors were immaterial.

✓ = Traced to client's inventory summary sheets (F-4) noting corrections for all differences.

Figure 14-2. INVENTORY TEST COUNTS WORKING PAPER.

This language is unequivocal; the observation (or counting) of the inventory can be postponed, but it cannot be eliminated. The auditor must obtain some physical evidence pertaining to ending inventories in order to comply with generally accepted auditing standards (GAAS). In addition, the auditor should review the records of any counts made by the client.

Inventories Determined by Statistical Sampling. A company may have inventory controls or use methods of determining inventories, such as statistical sampling, that do not require an annual physical count of every item of inventory. Such methods do not relieve the auditor of the responsibility to observe the taking of inventories. It is still necessary to observe such counts as deemed necessary in the circumstances. In addition, the auditor must obtain evidence on the appropriateness of the method used to determine inventory quantities. When statistical sampling methods are used by the client, the auditor must ascertain that (1) the sampling plan has statistical validity, (2) it has been properly applied, and (3) the results in terms of precision and reliability are reasonable in the circumstances.[3]

Observation of Beginning Inventories. In order to express an unqualified opinion on the income statement, the auditor must observe the taking of both the beginning and ending inventories. On a continuing audit engagement, this requirement is met by observing the ending inventory of each year. However, in the initial audit of an established company, the auditor may either be appointed after the beginning inventory has been taken or be asked to report on the financial statements of one or more prior periods. In such circumstances, it is clearly impracticable and unreasonable for the auditor to have observed the inventory taking, and GAAS permit the auditor to verify the inventories by other auditing procedures.

When the client has been audited by another firm of independent auditors in the prior period(s), the other procedures may include a review of the predecessor auditor's report and/or working papers and a review of the client's inventory summaries for the prior period(s). If the client has not been audited previously, the auditor may be able to obtain audit satisfaction by reviewing the summaries of any client counts, testing prior inventory transactions, and applying gross profit tests to the inventories. Such procedures are only appropriate when the auditor is able to verify the validity and propriety of the ending inventory for the period under audit.[4]

Effects on Auditor's Report. When inventories have been observed, the auditor may be able to issue a standard audit report. This is also permissible when the auditor has used alternative substantive tests to verify the existence of the beginning inventory. However, when sufficient evidence has not been obtained as to the existence of beginning inventories or the auditor is unable to observe the taking of ending inventories, the auditor is precluded from issuing a standard audit report. The specific effects on the auditor's report are considered in Chapter 17.

Applicability to Audit Objectives. Like the confirmation of accounts receivable, the observation of inventories applies to more than one audit objective. As explained above, this procedure is the *primary* source of evidence that inventories exist at the balance sheet date. This test of balances is also a *secondary* source of evidence for the following objectives:

[3] Auditing Standards Board, *op. cit.*, AU § 331.11.
[4] Auditing Standards Board, *op. cit.*, AU § 331.13.

Audit Objective	Explanation
Clerical accuracy	Quantities observed provide the basis for compiling the total dollar amount of the inventory on the inventory summaries.
Occurrence	Because the goods are on hand, the purchase transactions must have taken place.
Completeness	All goods on hand at the balance sheet date are included in inventory.
Rights and obligations	Quantities included in inventory are owned by the client and related obligations are owed.
Valuation or allocation	Quantities on hand provide the basis for determining the inventory value at the balance sheet date; damaged and obsolete goods can be valued at net realizable value.

The tests of balances associated with each objective in the audit program in Figure 14-1 generally provide the primary source of evidence for the specified objective.

Confirm Inventories in Public Warehouses

When client inventories are stored in public warehouses or with other outside custodians, the auditor should obtain evidence as to the existence of the inventory by direct communication with the custodian. This type of evidence is deemed to be sufficient except when the amounts involved represent a significant proportion of current or total assets. When this is the case, the auditor should apply one or more of the following procedures:

- Review and test the owner's control procedures for investigating the warehouseman and evaluating the warehouseman's performance.
- Obtain an independent accountant's report on the warehouseman's system of internal accounting control relevant to custody of goods and, if applicable, pledging of receipts, or apply alternative procedures at the warehouse to gain reasonable assurance that information received from the warehouseman is reliable.
- Observe physical counts of the goods, if practicable and reasonable.
- If warehouse receipts have been pledged as collateral, confirm with lenders pertinent details of the pledged receipts (on a test basis, if appropriate).[5]

Inspection of warehouse receipts held by the client may also provide evidence of goods stored in a public warehouse, but such evidence alone is not sufficient.

---

[5]Auditing Standards Board, *op. cit.*, AU § 331.14.

COMPLETENESS

This objective is directed at whether all of the company's inventories are recorded. The following tests of balances are used to obtain evidence on the completeness of inventory balances.

Perform Purchases and Purchases Returns Cutoff Tests

A purchase cutoff test is performed to obtain evidence that all goods owned by the client at the balance sheet date are included in inventory and that the related liability is recorded. Legal title to goods in transit is determined by whether shipping terms are F.O.B. (free on board) shipping point or destination.

The cutoff period extends from several days before the balance sheet date to several days after. For this five- to seven-day period, the auditor examines evidence that year-end purchases have been recorded in the proper accounting period. The test involves tracing of receiving reports to voucher register entries and vouching recorded entries to receiving reports and vendors' invoices.

Any material cutoff errors should be proposed for correction by the client. This test should include inventory in transit from branches, divisions, and affiliates of the client as well as shipments from vendors.

A similar test is made of purchases returns to determine that inventory and the related payables are relieved of the cost of the returned goods in the proper period.

Make Analytical Review

The application of analytical review procedures to inventories frequently involves the following financial relationships:

Financial Relationship	Formula
Rate of gross profit	Gross profit ÷ Net sales
Inventory turnover	Cost of goods sold ÷ Average inventory
Number of days sales in inventory	365 ÷ Inventory turnover
Inventory to total current assets	Inventory ÷ Total current assets

When comparisons with other data, such as prior years, budget expectations, and industry statistics, produce normal or expected results, the auditor has additional corroborating evidence on the reasonableness and completeness of inventory balances. In contrast, if unusual fluctuations or results are obtained, the auditor should make further investigation. For example, an abnormally low gross profit rate could occur from an understatement of ending inventory.

RIGHTS AND OBLIGATIONS

This objective relates to whether inventories are owned by the client and whether any binding commitments exist for the future purchase of goods. Three auditing procedures are applicable to this objective.

Make Inquiries of Management Regarding Ownership

Since title to goods purchased passes to the buyer no later than when the goods are received, there is a presumption that goods on hand are owned by the client. Support for this presumption is obtained by tracing purchases to vendors' invoices, payment vouchers, and paid checks.

However, goods on hand may be held for customers, at their request, after a sale has occurred, and goods may be held on consignment. Thus, management is requested to segregate goods not owned during the inventory taking. In addition, the auditor usually requests a written assertion on ownership of inventories in the client representation letter. This letter is illustrated in Chapter 16.

Examine Consignment Agreements

Under consignment agreements, title to the goods remains with the owner (i.e., the consignor). Thus, goods held on consignment should not be included in the holder's (i.e., the consignee's) physical inventory count or reported as inventory in its balance sheet.

The auditor should inquire of management as to any goods held on consignment. When consignments exist, the agreement should be examined for terms and conditions. If the client has shipped goods on consignment, the auditor should review the documentation to determine that goods held by the consignee are included in the consignor's inventory at the balance sheet date.

Review Purchase Commitments

Inquiry of management is used to determine the existence of binding contracts for future purchases of goods. When such commitments exist, the auditor should examine the terms of the contracts and evaluate the propriety of the company's accounting and reporting thereof. An important test is to compare the contract prices with the supplier's current selling price for the items. If the former exceeds the latter and the difference is not covered by a binding sales contract on the items, a loss has occurred. When material losses exist on purchase commitments, they should be recognized in the statements, together with a disclosure of the attendant circumstances.

VALUATION OR ALLOCATION

The proper valuation of inventories and cost of goods sold is vital to the overall fairness of financial statements. This objective relates to the cost and net realizable value of the inventory. Three tests of balances are applicable to the valuation of inventories and cost of goods sold.

Review Data Pertaining to Inventory Quality

The auditor's responsibility for quality is limited to that of a reasonably informed observer. This means that the auditor is expected to determine whether the inventory appears to be in condition for sale, use, or consumption and whether there are any obsolete, slow-moving, or damaged goods. The auditor obtains evidence of general condition or obsolescence by

- Observing the client's inventory taking.
- Scanning perpetual inventory records for slow-moving items.
- Reviewing quality control production reports.
- Making inquiries of client.

When the evidence suggests a decline in the utility of the goods, appropriate write-down below cost is required by GAAP.

When client assertions about the nature of the inventory pertain to highly technical matters, the auditor may require the assistance of an outside expert. This might occur, for example, in an oil company with different grades of gasoline and motor oil, or in a jewelry store with different carat diamonds and different jeweled watches. As explained in Chapter 4, the auditor may use the work of a specialist as an audit procedure to obtain competent evidential matter, providing he is satisfied about the qualifications and independence of the expert.

Vouch and Test Inventory Pricing

This verification procedure consists of two steps

- Determining the propriety and consistency of the client's pricing (costing) of inventory quantities.
- Tracing unit costs used by the client to supporting documentation.

A review of perpetual inventory records and inquiry of the client should enable the auditor to determine both the basis (historical cost) and costing methods [first in, first out (FIFO), last in, first out (LIFO), etc.] used in pricing inventory quantities. The consistency of the pricing, in turn, can be established by recourse to last year's working papers on a recurring audit and/or to the prior year's financial statements. This step in the verification of pricing includes a review of the pricing of obsolete and damaged goods to ascertain that they are not valued in excess of net realizable value at the statement date.

Evidence in support of unit costs varies with the nature of the inventory. For items purchased for resale, use, or consumption (merchandise inventory, raw materials, and supplies), costs should be traced to representative vendor invoices. When the lower of cost or market method is used, the auditor must verify both cost and market. The current replacement cost of an item may be obtained (1) from purchases made at or near the balance sheet date or (2) by inquiries of suppliers.

The nature and extent of the auditor's pricing tests of work in process and finished goods depend on the reliability of the client's cost accounting records and the methods used by the client in accumulating such costs. The methods should be reviewed by the auditor for propriety and the accuracy and consistency of application.

Review Entries to Cost of Goods Sold

Considerable evidence on the propriety, accuracy, and consistency of costs assigned to cost of goods sold is obtained from tests of sales, purchases, and manufacturing transactions and by substantive tests of inventory balances. Direct tests of cost of goods may be limited to (1) scanning entries for possible errors and (2) performing analytical review procedures. When the client uses standard costs, the auditor should determine the underlying causes of variances in order to evaluate the propriety of the accounting treatment. In some cases, an overall adjustment of cost of goods sold and ending inventory may be warranted.

STATEMENT PRESENTATION AND DISCLOSURE

It is customary to identify the major inventory categories in the balance sheet and the cost of goods sold in the income statement. In addition, there should be disclosure of the inventory costing method(s) used, the pledging of inventories, and the existence of major purchase commitments.

Evidence pertaining to statement presentation and disclosure is provided by the substantive tests described above. Further evidence may be obtained, as needed, from a review of the minutes of board of directors meetings, and inquiries of management. Based on the evidence and a comparison of the client's financial statements with applicable accounting pronouncements, the auditor determines the propriety of the presentation and disclosures.

STATISTICAL SAMPLING OF INVENTORY BALANCES

The expenditure and production cycles offer many opportunities for implementing statistical sampling. A primary application chosen for illustration in the following case study is an audit of inventory balances. Each step in designing, executing, and evaluating the sampling plan for the audit of the Henson Company's inventory balance is explained.

Determining the Objectives of the Plan

The objective is to test the fairness of the recorded book value for Henson's inventory. Having already tested quantities, the auditor is concerned primarily with testing prices and extensions in this sample. Internal controls over inventory transactions have been found to be strong, and prior year's audits have revealed few errors in the inventory balance. Because of this and since the auditor is concerned primarily with overstatement errors, he decides to use probability-proportional-to-size (PPS) sampling.

Defining the Population and Sampling Unit

The population consists of 2,000 different inventory items, with a total recorded book value of $4,500,000. A computer listing is obtained showing quantity, price, and extended dollar value for each item. As a test of the completeness of the listing, it is footed and agreed to the total recorded book value. The logical sampling unit is lines on the inventory listing representing different stock items.

Determining Sample Size

To determine an appropriate sample size, the auditor specifies the risk of incorrect acceptance, tolerable error, and anticipated error. He sets the risk of incorrect acceptance at .20, which reflects the good internal control situation and assurance gained from other audit procedures including analytical review. He decides tolerable error is $45,000. While he expects few errors, he wishes to hold down the risk of incorrect rejection; therefore, he specifies an anticipated error of $10,000. He next obtains the reliability factor for the .20 risk of incorrect acceptance and zero errors from Figure 12-2 and the corresponding expansion factor for the anticipated error from Figure 12-3. These are 1.61 and 1.3, respectively. He then calculates sample size as follows:

$$n = \frac{BV \times RF}{TE - (AE \times EF)} = \frac{\$4,500,000 \times 1.61}{\$45,000 - (\$10,000 \times 1.3)} = 226$$

Determining the Sample Selection Method

Systematic selection is used based on a sampling interval calculated as follows:

$$SI = \frac{BV}{n} = \frac{\$4,500,000}{226} = \$19,911$$

Thus, the logical unit associated with every 19,911th dollar will be included in the sample.

Executing the Sampling Plan

The primary auditing procedures performed on the sample items are (1) testing the price to recent invoices and (2) testing the accuracy of the extension of quantity times price. A list of errors showing both book and audited values is made. Only two errors are found.

Evaluating Sample Results

To evaluate the sample, the auditor calculates the projected error and an allowance for sampling risk. He then compares the sum of these to tolerable error. The calculation of the projected errors is shown below.

Book Value (BV)	Audit Value (AV)	Tainting Percentage [TP = (BV − AV)/BV]	Sampling Interval (SI)	Projected Error (TP × SI) or (BV − AV)
$10,000	$9,000	10	$19,911	$1,991
8,000	7,600	5	19,911	996
			Total	$2,987

The calculation of the allowance for sampling risk includes two components: basic precision and incremental allowance for sampling risk. Basic precision is $32,057 (sampling interval, $19,911, × reliability factor, 1.61). The incremental allowance is calculated as follows:

Ranked Projected Errors	Incremental Change in Reliability Factor Minus One	Incremental Allowance for Sampling Risk
$1,991	.39 (3.00 − 1.61 − 1)	$ 776
996	.28 (4.28 − 3.00 − 1)	274
		$1,055

Thus, the total allowance for sampling risk is $33,112 ($32,057 + $1,055). Adding this to the total projected error of $2,987 produces an achieved upper error limit of $36,099. Since this amount is less than the tolerable error of $45,000, the sample results support the conclusion that the recorded book value of the inventory is fairly stated at the levels of risk specified.

COMPUTER-ASSISTED TESTS OF INVENTORY BALANCES

When the client maintains perpetual inventory records by electronic data processing (EDP), the auditor may use the computer to perform substantive tests of inventory balances. This is possible if the auditor has the appropriate software.

In this illustration, it is assumed that the client's master file of merchandise inventory is maintained on magnetic tape. The file includes the inventory part number, warehouse location, unit cost, and the quantity on hand. In addition to updating the file for sales in the revenue cycle and purchases in the expenditure cycle, the client's programs provide for a monthly printout of the quantity, unit cost, and total cost for each inventory item and the total cost of inventories on hand.

There are two widely used computer-assisted applications in testing inventory balances: (1) selecting items for test counts and (2) verifying inventory pricing. These applications, which are illustrated in Figure 14-3, are explained below.

Select Items for Test Counts

In order to use the computer in performing this substantive test, the auditor inputs the desired audit selection criteria, such as (1) all inventory items with a balance over a specified dollar amount and (2) a random selection of remaining items. With the appropriate software program, the criteria are then run with the client's master file to obtain a printout of items for test count.

Verify Inventory Pricing

Computer assistance in performing this test of inventory balances extends to the verification of both the total cost of the inventory and the cost of selected individual units. The first objective is achieved by using a software package that performs a price-time-quantity calculation for each inventory item and computes a total dollar value for goods on hand. If inventory is stored in different locations, the audit criteria may specify totals for each location. The auditor then compares the totals with the client's data and differences are investigated.

The procedure for verifying the cost of individual units of inventory is similar to the technique described above for test counts. Audit selection criteria in this case may also include slow-moving items and items normally subject to frequent price fluctuations. The printout of this run is a listing of individual

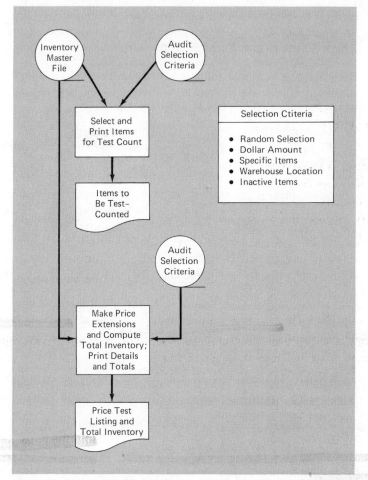

Figure 14-3. COMPUTER-ASSISTED TESTS OF INVENTORY BALANCES.

items of inventory that are traced to source documents for verification of unit costs.

The computer may also be used to identify excess quantities, compare inventory balances between two points in time, and determine the effects of possible changes in inventory costing methods.

TESTS OF PLANT ASSET BALANCES

Plant assets consist of tangible resources that are held for use in operations. This category on the balance sheet includes: (1) land, buildings, equipment, furniture, and fixtures; (2) leaseholds; and (3) accumulated depreciation. The principal related income accounts are depreciation expense, repairs expense, and rent on operating leases.

Plant assets often represent the largest component of total assets on the balance sheet, and expenses associated with plant assets are material factors in the determination of net income.

COMPARISON WITH AUDIT OF CURRENT ASSETS

The time required to perform substantive tests of plant assets is significantly less than the time required to verify current assets. This is due to the following factors:

- Fewer transactions occur.
- Plant assets are less vulnerable to misappropriation.
- Confirmation of plant assets and observation of inventories of plant assets are not required.

The auditor also has considerably more flexibility in scheduling tests of plant asset balances as they do not need to be performed at or near the balance sheet date.

INITIAL AUDIT ENGAGEMENT

The auditor's substantive tests will be much more extensive in his initial audit of a client than in a repeat engagement. In the first audit, evidence must be obtained on the propriety of the beginning balances in the accounts and the ownership of the assets comprising the balances. When the client has previously been audited by another independent auditor, the acquisition of such evidence is facilitated when the successor auditor is able to review the predecessor auditor's working papers. However, if the client has not been previously audited, the auditor must undertake the investigation of the balances and the ownership of major units of plant currently in service. Information concerning beginning balances in an initial audit is usually summarized and kept in the auditor's permanent working papers.

RECURRING AUDIT ENGAGEMENT

The extent of substantive testing depends on whether any reliance is to be placed on internal accounting control. When there are few plant asset transactions, the auditor may decide to make only a preliminary review of internal controls and perform extensive tests of plant asset balances. In contrast, when there are numerous plant asset transactions, the auditor normally will complete his review of the controls and perform compliance tests of the controls expected to be relied on. This may be done as part of evaluating the controls over purchases transactions in the expenditure cycle or separately within that cycle. Ordinarily, the auditor will use separate testing because plant asset acquisitions will not occur with enough frequency to assure satisfactory audit coverage through the testing of purchases transactions.

TYPE OF TESTS: Substantive   **PURPOSE:** Validity and Propriety of Balances
CYCLE: Expenditure   **ACCOUNTS:** Plant Assets

A. CLERICAL ACCURACY

1. Foot plant asset schedules.
2. Reconcile general ledger balances with subsidiary ledgers and supporting schedules.

B. EXISTENCE OR OCCURRENCE

1. Inspect plant additions.
2. Review documentation in client's files.

C. COMPLETENESS

1. Make plant tour.
2. Make analytical review.

D. RIGHTS AND OBLIGATIONS

1. Inspect documentation of ownership.
2. Examine lease contracts.

E. VALUATION OR ALLOCATION

1. Vouch plant asset additions.
2. Vouch plant asset disposals.
3. Analyze entries to repairs expense.
4. Review entries to accumulated depreciation.

F. STATEMENT PRESENTATION AND DISCLOSURE

1. Make inquiries of management and review documentation for pledging of plant assets.
2. Compare statement presentation and disclosures with GAAP.

Figure 14-4. AUDIT PROGRAM: PLANT ASSET BALANCES.

In a recurring engagement, the auditor concentrates on the current year's transactions because the balances at the beginning of the year have been validated through the preceding year's audit. Heavy reliance is placed on documentary evidence in verifying asset balances and on mathematical evidence in verifying accumulated depreciation. An audit program for plant assets is shown in Figure 14-4.

CLERICAL ACCURACY

This objective is met by footing plant asset and depreciation schedules and reconciling general ledger balances with subsidiary ledgers and supporting schedules. An auditor's schedule for plant assets and accumulated depreciation is illustrated in Figure 14-5.

```
HIGHLIFT COMPANY                                                                    W/P REF: G
PROPERTY, PLANT AND EQUIPMENT AND ACCUMULATED DEPRECIATION              PREPARED BY: C.J.A. DATE 3/4/X2
LEAD SCHEDULE                                                          REVIEWED BY: R.C.P. DATE 3/12/X2
DECEMBER 31, 19X1
```

W/P REF	ACCT. NO.	ACCOUNT TITLE	..................ASSET COST..................					..............ACCUMULATED DEPRECIATION..............				
			BALANCE 12/31/X0	ADDITIONS	DISPOSALS	ADJUSTMENTS DR/(CR)	BALANCE 12/31/X1	BALANCE 12/31/X0	PROVISIONS	DISPOSALS	ADJUSTMENTS (DR)/CR	BALANCE 12/31/X1
G-1	301	LAND	450,000 √				450,000					
G-2	302	BUILDINGS	2,108,000 √	125,000		(2l) (25,000)	2,208,000	379,440	84,320		(2l) (1,000)	462,760
G-3	303	MACHINERY AND EQUIPMENT	3,757,250 √	980,000	370,000	(2l) 25,000	4,392,250	1,074,210	352,910	172,500	(2l) 1,000	1,255,620
G-4	304	FURNITURE AND FIXTURES	853,400 √	144,000	110,000		887,400	217,450	43,250	21,000		239,700
			7,168,650	1,249,000	480,000	0	7,937,650	1,671,100	480,480	193,500	0	1,958,080
			F	F	F	F	FF	F	F	F	F	FF

√ Traced to general ledger and 12/31/X0 working papers
F Footed
FF Crossfooted and footed

Figure 14-5. PLANT ASSET AND ACCUMULATED DEPRECIATION LEAD SCHEDULE.

EXISTENCE OR OCCURRENCE

This objective relates to the physical existence of plant assets at the balance sheet date and the occurrence of related income statement transactions. The auditing procedures of physical inspection and examination of documents are used in completing the two tests of balances applicable to this objective.

Inspect Plant Additions

Information on plant additions may be obtained from an analysis of plant accounts, an examination of plant asset schedules, a review of the minutes of board of directors meetings, and inquiry of management. The inspection of plant assets acquired during the year enables the auditor to obtain direct personal knowledge of their existence.

Physical inspection may allow the auditor to acquire other corroborating information. For example, during the inspection, the auditor can make inquiries concerning the disposition of a retired unit, if any, and the incurrence of installation, testing, and other costs to make a new facility ready for its intended use.

When a complete physical inventory of plant assets is taken by the client, the auditor is not required to observe it. However, a review of the inventory compilation may reveal the existence of unrecorded plant assets or the failure to remove retired assets from the records.

Review Documentation in Client's Files

The client's files should contain numerous documents that relate to this objective. Evidence of existence may take the form of completed construction contracts, receiving reports, certificates of title, tax bills, and insurance policies. Support for occurrence may be found in vendor invoices, vouchers, "paid" checks, and work orders pertaining to repairs expense.

COMPLETENESS

The completeness objective is designed to determine that all plant asset transactions are recorded. This objective is met through (1) making cash disbursements and purchases cutoff tests and (2) performing the following tests of plant assets.

Make Plant Tour

The auditor generally makes a tour of the client's operating facilities. Through a plant tour, the auditor obtains direct personal knowledge of the types of machinery and equipment in use and the condition of the plant. The auditor should be alert for obsolete or damaged units, major new additions, and construction, betterments, and repair work in progress. Such items should be noted and traced to the accounting records.

Make Analytical Review

The following financial relationships are often used in applying analytical review procedures to plant assets:

Financial Relationship	Formula
Plant asset turnover	Net sales ÷ Average plant assets
Rate of return on plant assets	Net income ÷ Average plant assets
Plant assets to stockholders' equity	Plant assets ÷ Stockholders' equity
Repairs expense to net sales	Repairs expense ÷ Net sales

When comparisons of these relationships with other data reveal normal or expected results, the auditor obtains additional corroborating evidence on the completeness of the account balance. However, an abnormal result should be investigated. For example, an extreme decrease in the ratio of repairs expense to net sales may indicate that some maintenance expenditures have not been recorded or that the expenditures have been incorrectly debited to plant asset accounts.

RIGHTS AND OBLIGATIONS

Rights to plant assets may exist through ownership and from lease contracts. Lease contracts, in turn, may represent an obligation of the entity. Two tests are applicable to this objective.

Inspect Documentation of Ownership

The ownership of vehicles may be established by examining certificates of title, registration certificates, and insurance policies. For equipment, furniture, and fixtures, the "paid" invoice may be the best evidence of ownership. Evidence of ownership in real property is found in deeds, title insurance policies, property tax bills, mortgage payment receipts, and fire insurance policies. Verification of ownership in real property can also be substantiated by a review of public records. When this form of additional evidence is desired, the auditor may seek the help of an attorney.

Examine Lease Contracts

Lease agreements convey to a lessor the right to use property, plant, or equipment, usually for a specified period of time. For accounting purposes, leases may be classified as either capital leases or as operating leases. The auditor should read the lease agreement to determine the proper accounting classification of the lease in accordance with *Financial Accounting Standards Board* pronouncements. When a capital lease exists, both an asset and a liability should be recognized in the accounts and statements.

VALUATION OR ALLOCATION

This objective pertains to the cost and net book value of plant assets on the balance sheet, and the amounts reported for depreciation and related plant asset expenses in the income statement. Vouching, recalculation, and scanning are the primary audit procedures used in performing the three tests of balances applicable to valuation or allocation.

Vouch Plant Asset Additions

All additions should be supported by documentary evidence in the form of authorizations in the minutes, vouchers, invoices, contracts, and canceled checks. The recorded amounts should be vouched to supporting documentation. If there are numerous transactions, the vouching may be done on a test basis. In performing this test, the auditor ascertains that appropriate accounting recognition has been given to installation, freight, and similar costs. For construction in progress, the auditor may review the contract and documentation in support of construction costs.

When plant assets are acquired under a capital lease, the cost of the property and the related liability should be recorded at the present value of the future minimum lease payments. The accuracy of the client's determination of the present value of the lease liability should also be verified by recomputation.

Vouch Plant Asset Disposals

Evidence of sales, retirements, and trade-ins should be available to the auditor in the form of cash remittance advices, written authorization, and sales agreements. Such documentation should be carefully examined to determine the accuracy and propriety of the accounting records, including the recognition of gain or loss, if any.

The following procedures may also be useful to the auditor in determining whether all retirements have been recorded:

- Analyze the miscellaneous revenue account for proceeds from sales of plant assets.
- Investigate disposition of facilities associated with discontinued product lines and operations.
- Trace retirement work orders and authorizations for retirements to the accounting records.
- Review insurance policies for termination or reductions of coverage.
- Make inquiry of management as to retirements.

Analyze Entries to Repairs Expense

The auditor's objectives in performing this test are to determine the propriety and consistency of the charges to repairs expense. Propriety involves a consideration of whether the client has made appropriate distinctions between capital and repair expenditures. Accordingly, the auditor should scan the individual charges to identify those which are sufficiently material to be capitalized. For these items, the auditor should examine supporting documentation, such as the vendor's invoice, company work order, and management authorization to determine the propriety of the charge or the need for an adjusting entry.

Consistency involves a determination of whether the company's criteria for distinguishing between capital and revenue expenditures is the same as in the preceding year.

Review Entries to Accumulated Depreciation

In meeting the valuation or allocation objective for accumulated depreciation, the auditor seeks evidence on the reasonableness, consistency, and accuracy of depreciation charges. An essential starting point for the auditor in making this test is to ascertain the depreciation methods used by the client during the year under examination. The identity of the methods can be obtained from a review of depreciation schedules prepared by the client and inquiry of the client. The auditor must then determine whether the methods currently in use are consistent with the preceding year. On a recurring audit, this can be established by a review of last year's working papers.

Determination of the reasonableness of depreciation provisions involves a consideration of such factors as (1) the client's past history in estimating useful lives and (2) the remaining useful lives of existing assets.

The auditor's verification of accuracy is achieved through recalculation. Ordinarily, this is done on a selective basis by recomputing the depreciation on major assets and testing depreciation taken on additions and retirements during the year.

STATEMENT PRESENTATION AND DISCLOSURE

The financial statements, or the notes thereto, should show the following information for property, plant, and equipment:

- Depreciation expense for the period.
- Balances of major classes of depreciable assets, by nature or function, at the balance sheet date.
- Accumulated depreciation, either by major classes of depreciable assets or in total, at the balance sheet date.
- A general description of the method or methods used in computing depreciation with respect to major classes of depreciable assets.[6]

Property pledged as security for loans should be disclosed. Information on pledging may be obtained from reviewing the minutes and long-term contractual agreements, by confirming debt agreements, and through inquiries of management. The appropriateness of client's disclosures related to assets under lease can be determined by recourse to the authoritative accounting pronouncements and the related lease agreements.

Companies meeting certain size requirements are required to disclose certain information on the effects of changing prices in annual reports to stockholders. The auditor should make inquiries of management and compare the data with other relevant information to determine whether the disclosures are in conformity with GAAP.

TESTS OF CURRENT LIABILITY BALANCES

The expenditure cycle produces many current liability balances including accounts payable, wages payable, and payroll taxes payable. These accounts will be used to illustrate substantive testing of current liability balances.

COMPARISON WITH TESTS OF ASSET BALANCES

Current liabilities are significant in evaluating an entity's short-term solvency. These accounts are as vulnerable to errors and irregularities as current assets. Similarly, deliberate misrepresentation of financial position could occur as frequently with liabilities as with assets. However, the nature of the actions and the techniques of concealment differ significantly. In most misrepresentations, it is presumed that the client desires to report a financial position that

---

[6]Accounting Principles Board, *APB Opinion No. 12, Omnibus Opinion* (New York: American Institute of Certified Public Accountants, 1967).

is better than the true condition. Thus, the client may *overstate assets* and/or *understate liabilities.*

To overstate assets, the client will have to either record a legitimate transaction improperly or create and record a fictitious transaction. In either case, the irregularity is a matter of record and the auditor's examination of assets might detect the impropriety. In contrast, to understate liabilities, personnel can destroy all evidence pertaining to the transaction that created the obligation or can merely forget to record the transaction. In either case, the error is not a matter of accounting record and the auditor's examination may not detect the error. In the design and execution of an audit program for liabilities, the auditor must be constantly alert to the possibility of an understatement of obligations by management.

AUDIT PROGRAM

The nature, timing, and extent of substantive tests of current liability account balances depends on the auditor's reliance on internal control over expenditure cycle transactions. When controls are not tested for compliance, the auditor must perform extensive substantive tests. When controls are tested for compliance, the auditor may reduce the amount of substantive testing. An audit program for testing these balances is shown in Figure 14-6. Primary attention is given in the program to accounts payable.

A comparison of the accounts payable portion of this program with the program for accounts receivable in Chapter 13 will show many similarities. This is understandable since an account payable on the records of the buyer is an account receivable on the books of the seller. However, there is a major difference in executing the two programs. For accounts receivable, the tests of balances focus on the possibility of overstatement, whereas for accounts payable, the auditor is concerned about the possibility of understatement. It should also be recognized that there is more externally created documentation for accounts payable than for accounts receivable. It will be recalled that external sources of evidence are generally assumed to have greater reliability than internally created evidence. The impact of these differences should be recognized in the following explanation of the specific audit procedures.

CLERICAL ACCURACY

The starting point for substantive tests of accounts payable is a schedule of amounts owed to specific creditors. Ordinarily, the schedule is prepared by the client from the unpaid voucher file or the creditors' subsidiary ledger. The auditor must verify the accuracy of the manual or computerized listing by refooting the schedule and reconciling the total with the ledger balance. In addition, the auditor selectively tests the items on the schedule with the unpaid file or creditors' subsidiary ledger.

The auditor scrutinizes the listing of payables for debit balances and amounts owed to subsidiary companies and other nontrade creditors. When material, such items should be identified for subsequent investigation.

TYPE OF TEST: Substantive	PURPOSE: Validity and Propriety of Balances
CYCLE: Expenditure	ACCOUNTS: Accounts Payable, Wages
and Production	Payable, and Payroll Taxes Payable

A. CLERICAL ACCURACY

1. Foot schedule of individual creditor balances.
2. Reconcile accounts payable with supporting schedule and creditors' ledger totals.

B. EXISTENCE OR OCCURRENCE, COMPLETENESS, AND RIGHTS AND OBLIGATIONS

1. Review documentation in client's files.
2. Confirm accounts payable.
3. Examine subsequent payments to creditors.
4. Search for unrecorded accounts payable.
5. Make analytical review.

C. VALUATION OR ALLOCATION

1. Vouch accounts payable schedule.
2. Recalculate accrued wages and payroll taxes payable.

D. STATEMENT PRESENTATION AND DISCLOSURE

1. Make inquiries and review documentation on purchase commitments and contract terms.
2. Compare statement presentation and disclosure with GAAP.

Figure 14-6. AUDIT PROGRAM: CURRENT LIABILITY BALANCES.

EXISTENCE OR OCCURRENCE, COMPLETENESS, AND RIGHTS AND OBLIGATIONS

The auditor's principal concern with these objectives is to determine that all obligations of the entity are reported in the financial statements. In addition to the purchase cutoff test described earlier in this chapter, there are five procedures that pertain to these objectives.

Review Documentation in Client's Files

The client's files should contain various documents that support the validity of creditor claims against assets. These include documentation required under a voucher system (i.e., purchase order, receiving report, and vendor's invoice). In addition, it should be possible to examine creditor monthly statements received by the client.

Confirm Accounts Payable

Unlike the confirmation of accounts receivable, the confirmation of accounts payable is not required. This procedure is optional because (1) confirmation offers no assurance that unrecorded payables will be discovered and (2) external evidence in the form of invoices and vendor monthly statements should be available to substantiate the balances. Confirmation of accounts payable is recommended when control risk is high, there are individual creditors with relatively large balances, and a company is experiencing difficulties in meeting its obligations.

When confirmation is to be undertaken, accounts with zero or small balances should be among those selected for confirmation because they may be more understated than accounts with large balances. In addition, confirmations should be sent to major vendors who (1) were used in the prior year but not in the current year and (2) do not send monthly statements. The positive form should be used in making the confirmation request as illustrated in Figure 14-7. It may be observed that the confirmation does not specify the amount due. In confirming a payable, the auditor prefers to have the creditor indicate the amount due because that is the amount reconciled to the client's records. As in the case of confirming accounts receivable, the auditor must control the preparation and mailing of the requests and should receive the responses directly from the respondent.

Examine Subsequent Payments to Creditors

This test is similar to the tracing of collections from customers subsequent to the statement date. This test is scheduled toward the end of field work in order to enhance the opportunity of obtaining evidence concerning unrecorded debts that existed at the statement date. The test consists of tracing vouchers or checks issued after the statement date to the list of payables at the balance sheet date. The comparison should enable the auditor to identify

- Large disbursements that clearly relate to the list of payables or to liabilities incurred subsequent to the statement date.
- Large disbursements pertaining to the prior period not included in the list of payables.
- Significant listed balances that remain unpaid.

The latter two items should be investigated by the auditor. A payment not on the list indicates the possibility of unrecorded liabilities, whereas unpaid items may be attributable to items in dispute, misplaced vouchers, errors in recording transactions, or items not due for payment.

Search for Unrecorded Accounts Payable

This test supplements other substantive procedures pertaining to accounts payable. It consists of a specific investigation to discover the existence of any significant vendors' invoices that are unrecorded at the statement date. The search usually occurs after the results of other tests are evaluated. In making a search, the auditor may also obtain evidence that an invoice or voucher has been recorded in the wrong accounting period. The procedures used by the

HIGHLIFT COMPANY
P.O. Box 1777
Cleveland, Ohio 39087

January 4, 19X1

Supplier, Inc.
2001 Lakeview Drive
Cleveland, Ohio 39089

Dear Sir or Madam:

Will you please send directly to our auditors, Reddy & Abel, Certified Public Accountants, an itemized statement of the amount owed to you by us at the close of business December 31, 19X0? Will you please also supply the following information:

Amount not yet due $ _____
Amount past due $ _____
Amount of purchase commitments $ _____
Description of any collateral held _____
_____

A business reply envelope addressed to our auditors is enclosed. A prompt reply will be very much appreciated.

Very truly yours,

D. R. Owens

Controller
Highlift Company

Figure 14-7. ACCOUNTS PAYABLE CONFIRMATION.

auditor in this test may include, but are not necessarily limited to, the following:

- Inquire of accounting and purchasing personnel concerning unrecorded invoices that are being held for approval or further information such as a requested allowance for damaged goods.
- Investigate unmatched purchase orders, receiving reports, and invoices that may indicate the incurrence of a liability as of the balance sheet date.
- Review capital budgets, work orders, and construction contracts for unrecorded amounts.

Any unrecorded liabilities that have a material effect on financial position or the results of operations should be proposed to the client for adjustment.

Make Analytical Review

The application of analytical review procedures to accounts payable involves financial relationships that are similar to those described in Chapter 13 for accounts receivable. For example, individual creditor balances can be aged, the accounts payable turnover can be computed (net credit purchases ÷ accounts payable), and the percentage of current liabilities represented by accounts payable can be determined. An abnormal increase in accounts payable turnover, for example, could be due to unrecorded accounts payable.

VALUATION OR ALLOCATION

The objective of valuation or allocation relates to the amount of the liability and the related cost or expense. Relatively few problems are encountered by the auditor in meeting this objective. There are two procedures that are applicable to this objective.

Vouch Accounts Payable Schedule

Previous procedures in the audit program have established the clerical accuracy, existence, and completeness of amounts owed to creditors at the balance sheet date. This procedure is directed at the proper valuation of the obligation. To achieve this objective, amounts owed to creditors shown in the schedule of accounts payable are vouched to supporting documentation. When a voucher system is used by the client, the documentation should be attached to the voucher in the unpaid voucher file at the balance sheet date. Thus, this audit test is facilitated when it is done at or near the statement date. When such a system is not used, the creditor's account file should contain the supporting documentation.

Recalculate Accrued Wages and Payroll Taxes Payable

A variety of adjusting entries may be made by a company for compensation owed to officers and employees at the balance sheet date. Accruals may pertain to commissions, bonuses, vacation pay, sick leave pay, and other benefits. The auditor seeks evidence on the correctness of the accrual. This is done by reviewing documentation in support of the entry and recalculating the amount accrued.

Similarly, the auditor should trace accrued payroll taxes to tax returns and verify the amount by recalculation.

STATEMENT PRESENTATION AND DISCLOSURE

Each major type of obligation, such as accounts payable, accrued expenses payable, and taxes payable should be identified in the current liability section. For short-term notes payable, there should also be disclosure of interest rates and the existence of any assets pledged as collateral. Evidence pertaining to this objective may be obtained through inquiries of management and a review of debt contracts. The auditor then compares the statement presentation and disclosures with GAAP.

CONCLUDING COMMENTS

Inventory, plant asset, and current liability balances associated with specific transaction cycles offer myriad challenges for the auditor. Observation of the physical inventory is a generally accepted auditing procedure, and pricing and cutoff tests are often extensive. In an initial engagement of an established client, additional work is required for plant assets to establish existence or occurrence, rights and obligations, and valuation or allocation. In recurring audits, primary attention is given to the vouching of entries to plant asset accounts and verifying the reasonableness, accuracy, and consistency of depreciation. For current liabilities, the auditor's primary risk is that credit claims are understated. Considerable reliance is placed on examination of documents in the verification of current liability balances.

REVIEW QUESTIONS

14-1 Identify the audit procedures that enable an auditor to verify the (a) existence or occurrence and (b) valuation or allocation objectives for inventory balances.

14-2 For the observation of inventories, indicate (a) when this test is required, (b) the steps to be performed, and (c) the timing and extent of the test.

14-3 a. Why is it necessary for the auditor to make tests of the client's inventory counts?
b. When statistical sampling methods are used in determining inventories, what additional requirements must be met by the auditor?

14-4 What alternative procedures are available to the auditor when he is unable to observe (a) the ending inventory and (b) the beginning inventory?

14-5 Indicate the applicability of observing inventories to the audit objectives for inventories.

14-6 List the procedures that are required when inventories kept in a public warehouse are material.

14-7 a. What ratios may be used in applying analytical review procedures to inventories?
b. What effects may the comparative results have on the remainder of the auditor's examination?

14-8 a. Explain the auditor's responsibility for the quality and condition of the inventory.
b. Indicate how the auditor can discover obsolete and slow-moving items.

14-9 How does the auditor verify inventory pricing?

14-10 a. What information is required to determine sample size in a PPS variables sampling plan of inventory balances?
b. Assuming the auditor has calculated the projected error in the population, what additional information is required to determine the achieved upper error limit?

14-11 What data and program(s) are needed to use the computer in an inventory pricing test?

14-12 Indicate the principal differences between the audit of plant assets and current assets.

14-13 What audit procedures are performed to determine (a) rights and obligations and (b) valuation or allocation of plant assets?

14-14 Identify the relationships that may be used in making an analytical review of property, plant, and equipment.

14-15 What procedures may be helpful in determining whether all plant asset retirements have been recorded?

14-16 Indicate the matters that should be considered in reviewing entries to accumulated depreciation.

14-17 Identify the principal differences between tests of asset balances and tests of current liability balances.

14-18 a. What audit procedures are used to verify the existence or occurrence and completeness of accounts payable?

b. How may the auditor obtain evidence as to the valuation and completeness of accrued wages payable?

14-19 What purposes are served by examining payments to creditors subsequent to the statement date?

14-20 List the procedures that may be useful searching for unrecorded accounts payable?

OBJECTIVE QUESTIONS FROM PROFESSIONAL EXAMINATIONS

Indicate the *best* answer for each of the following multiple-choice questions.

14-21 These questions relate to the verification of inventory balances.

1. An auditor has accounted for a sequence of inventory tags and is now going to trace information on a representative number of tags to the physical inventory sheets. The purpose of this procedure is to obtain assurance that
   a. The final inventory is valued at cost.
   b. All inventory represented by an inventory tag is listed on the inventory sheets.
   c. All inventory represented by an inventory tag is bona fide.
   d. Inventory sheets do *not* include untagged inventory items.

2. From the auditor's point of view, inventory counts are more acceptable prior to the year end when
   a. Internal control is weak.
   b. Accurate perpetual inventory records are maintained.
   c. Inventory is slow-moving.
   d. Significant amounts of inventory are held on a consignment basis.

3. Purchase cut-off procedures should be designed to test whether or not all inventory
   a. Purchased and received before the year end was recorded.
   b. On the year end balance sheet was carried at lower of cost or market.
   c. On the year end balance sheet was paid for by the company.
   d. Owned by the company is in the possession of the company.

14-22 These questions pertain to substantive tests of plant asset balances.

1. In violation of company policy, Lowell Company erroneously capitalized the cost of painting its warehouse. The auditor examining Lowell's financial statements would most likely detect this when
   a. Discussing capitalization policies with Lowell's controller.
   b. Examining maintenance expense accounts.
   c. Observing, during the physical inventory observation, that the warehouse had been painted.

    d. Examining the construction work orders supporting items capitalized during the year.

2. The auditor is most likely to seek information from the plant manager with respect to the
   a. Adequacy of the provision for uncollectible accounts.
   b. Appropriateness of physical inventory observation procedures.
   c. Existence of obsolete machinery.
   d. Deferral of procurement of certain necessary insurance coverage.

3. The audit procedure of analyzing the repairs and maintenance accounts is primarily designed to provide evidence in support of the audit proposition that all
   a. Expenditures for fixed assets have been recorded in the proper period.
   b. Capital expenditures have been properly authorized.
   c. Noncapitalizable expenditures have been properly expensed.
   d. Expenditures for fixed assets have been capitalized.

14-23 These questions apply to direct tests of accounts payable balances.

1. Unrecorded liabilities are most likely to be found during the review of which of the following documents?
   a. Unpaid bills.
   b. Shipping records.
   c. Bills of lading.
   d. Unmatched sales invoices.

2. Using statistical sampling to assist in verifying the year-end accounts payable balance, an auditor has accumulated the following data:

	Number of Accounts	Book Balance	Balance Determined by the Auditor
Population	4,100	$5,000,000	?
Sample	200	$ 250,000	$300,000

   With the ratio estimation technique, the auditor's estimate of year-end accounts payable balance would be
   a. $6,150,000
   b. $6,000,000
   c. $5,125,000
   d. $5,050,000

3. An auditor would be most likely to identify a contingent liability by mailing a(an)
   a. Standard bank confirmation.
   b. Related party transaction confirmation.
   c. Accounts payable confirmation.
   d. Transfer agent confirmation.

COMPREHENSIVE QUESTIONS

14-24 In performing tests of balances on inventory balances, the auditor should recognize that the following potential errors may occur or exist:

1. All inventory items are not counted or tagged.

2. Extension errors are made on the client's inventory summaries.

3. Purchases received near the balance sheet date may be included in the physical count but may not be booked.

4. Obsolete and damaged goods are not noticed in warehouse.

5. Inventory stored in a public warehouse may not exist.

6. Client personnel may incorrectly count the inventory.

7. The lower of cost or market method may be incorrectly applied.

8. Empty containers or hollow squares may be included in the inventory.

9. Goods held on consignment may be included as inventory.

10. Losses on purchases commitments may not be recognized.

Required

a. Identify the audit procedure that should enable the auditor to detect each error.

b. Indicate the audit objective to which the audit procedure relates.

c. Identify the type of evidential matter obtained by the audit procedure.

14-25 Often, an important aspect of a CPA's examination of financial statements is his observation of the taking of the physical inventory.

Required

a. What are the general objectives or purposes of the CPA's observation of the taking of the physical inventory? (Do not discuss the procedures or techniques involved in making the observation.)

b. For what purposes does the CPA make and record test counts of inventory quantities during his observation of the taking of the physical inventory? Discuss.

c. A number of companies employ outside service companies that specialize in counting, pricing, extending, and footing inventories. These service companies usually furnish a certificate attesting to the value of the inventory.

If we assume that the service company took the inventory on the balance sheet date,

1. How much reliance, if any, can the CPA place on the inventory certificate of outside specialists? Discuss.

2. What effect, if any, would the inventory certificate of outside specialists have on the type of report the CPA would render? Discuss.

3. What reference, if any, would the CPA make to the certificate of outside specialists in his audit report?

AICPA

14-26 In connection with his examination of the financial statements of Knutson Products Co., an assembler of home appliances, for the year ended May 31, 19X0, Ray Abel, CPA, is reviewing with Knutson's controller the plans for a physical inventory at the Company warehouse on May 31. (*Note:* In answering the two parts of this question, do not discuss procedures for the physical inventory of work in process, inventory pricing, or other audit steps not directly related to the physical inventory taking.)

1. Finished appliances, unassembled parts, and supplies are stored in the warehouse, which is attached to Knutson's assembly plant. The plant will operate during the count. On May 30, 19X0, the warehouse will deliver to the plant the estimated

quantities of unassembled parts and supplies required for May 31 production, but there may be emergency requisitions on May 31. During the count, the warehouse will continue to receive parts and supplies and to ship finished appliances. However, appliances completed on May 31 will be held in the plant until after the physical inventory.

2. Warehouse employees will join with accounting department employees in counting the inventory. The inventory takers will use a tag system.

Required

a. What procedures should the company establish to insure that the inventory count includes all items that should be included and that nothing is counted twice?

b. What instructions should the company give to the inventory takers?

AICPA

14-27 Ace Corporation does not conduct a complete annual physical count of purchased parts and supplies in its principal warehouse but uses statistical sampling instead to estimate the year-end inventory. Ace maintains a perpetual inventory record of parts and supplies and believes that statistical sampling is highly effective in determining inventory values and is sufficiently reliable to make a physical count of each item of inventory unnecessary.

Required

a. Identify the audit procedures that should be used by the independent auditor that change or are in addition to normal required audit procedures when a client utilizes statistical sampling to determine inventory value and does not conduct a 100% annual physical count of inventory items.

b. List the normal audit procedures that should be performed to verify physical quantities whenever a client conducts a periodic physical count of all or part of its inventory.

AICPA (adapted)

14-28 Your audit client, Household Appliances, Inc. operates a retail store in the center of town. Because of lack of storage space, Household keeps inventory that is not on display in a public warehouse outside of town. The warehouseman receives inventory from suppliers and, on request from your client by a shipping advice or telephone call, delivers merchandise to customers or the retail outlet.

The accounts are maintained at the retail store by a bookkeeper. Each month, the warehouseman sends to the bookkeeper a quantity report indicating opening balance, receipts, deliveries, and ending balance. The bookkeeper compares book quantities on hand at month-end with the warehouseman's report and adjusts his books to agree with the report. No physical counts of the merchandise at the warehouse were made by your client during the year.

You are now preparing for your examination of the current year's financial statements in this recurring engagement. Last year, you rendered an unqualified opinion.

Required

a. Prepare an audit program for the observation of the physical inventory of Household Appliances, Inc. (1) at the retail outlet and (2) at the warehouse.

b. As part of your examination, would you verify inventory quantities at the warehouse by means of
1. A warehouse confirmation? Why?
2. Test counts of inventory at the warehouse? Why?
c. Since the bookkeeper adjusts books to quantities shown on the warehouseman's report each month, what significance would you attach to the year-end adjustments if they were substantial? Discuss.

AICPA

14-29 Decker, CPA, is performing an examination of the financial statements of Allright Wholesale Sales, Inc., for the year ended December 31, 19X0. Allright has been in business for many years and has never had its financial statements audited. Decker has gained satisfaction with respect to the ending inventory and is considering alternative audit procedures to gain satisfaction with respect to management's representations concerning the beginning inventory, which was not observed.

Allright sells only one product (bottled brand X beer) and maintains perpetual inventory records. In addition, Allright takes physical inventory counts monthly. Decker has already confirmed purchases with the manufacturer and decided to concentrate on evaluating the reliability of perpetual inventory records and performing analytical review procedures to the extent that prior years' unaudited records will enable such procedures to be performed.

Required

What are the audit tests, including analytical review procedures, that Decker should apply in evaluating the reliability of perpetual inventory records and gaining satisfaction with respect to the January 1, 19X0 inventory?

AICPA

14-30 As auditor for the Court Company, you decide to use variables sampling to estimate the total cost of an inventory of 1,250 items that has a net book value of $280,400. The auditor decides to use a sampling plan that will provide a risk of 5% that a fairly stated book value is not rejected as being materially misstated. Based on past experience, it is believed that the standard deviation of the population is $120. The audit estimate is to be made with a tolerable error of $30,000 and a risk of incorrect acceptance of 10%.

Required

a. Calculate the required sample size, assuming MPU sampling without replacement.
b. Assume the sample from part (a) has a mean audit value of $225 and a standard deviation of $110. Compute the achieved allowance for sampling risk.
c. Is the book value fairly stated? Explain.

14-31 In auditing the annual physical inventory being taken by employees in the Sutter Company, you decide to use PPS sampling for variables to estimate the cost of the inventory. Thus far, the following information has been compiled:

Book value of inventory	$2,960,000
Tolerable error	$200,000
Population size	6,511
Estimated standard deviation	$100
Desired risk of incorrect acceptance	5%
Anticipated error	$50,000

Required

a. Calculate sample size and the sampling interval.

b. Assume that three items in the sample contained errors as follows:

Part Number	Book Value	Audit Value
40965	$15,700	$12,560
41139	56,000	50,400
47622	23,200	22,040

Calculate the projected error and the allowance for sampling risk.

c. What conclusion is supported by the sample results? Explain.

14-32 An auditor is conducting an examination of the financial statements of a wholesale cosmetics distributor with an inventory consisting of thousands of individual items. The distributor keeps its inventory in its own distribution center and two public warehouses. An inventory computer file is maintained on a computer disk and at the end of each day the file is updated. Each record of the inventory file contains the following data:

1. Item number.
2. Location of item.
3. Description of item.
4. Quantity on hand.

5. Cost per item.
6. Date of last purchase.
7. Date of last sale.
8. Quantity sold during year.

The auditor is planning to observe the distributor's physical count of inventories as of a given date. The auditor will have available a computer tape of the data on the inventory file on the date of the physical count and a general-purpose computer software package.

Required

The auditor is planning to perform basic inventory auditing procedures. Identify the basic inventory auditing procedures and describe how the use of the general-purpose software package and the tape of the inventory file data might be helpful to the auditor in performing such auditing procedures. Organize your answer as follows:

Basic Inventory Auditing Procedure	How General-Purpose Computer Software Package and Tape of the Inventory File Data Might Be Helpful
1. Observe the physical count, making and recording test counts when applicable.	Determining which items are to be test counted by selecting a random sample of a representative number of items from the inventory file as of the date of the physical count.

AICPA

14-33 Rivers, CPA, is the auditor for a manufacturing company with a balance sheet that includes the caption "Property, Plant & Equipment." Rivers has been asked by the company's management if audit adjustments or reclassifications are required for the following material items that have been included in or excluded from "Property, Plant & Equipment":

1. A tract of land was acquired during the year. The land is the future site of the client's new headquarters, which will be constructed in the following year. Commissions were paid to the real estate agent used to acquire the land, and expenditures were made to relocate the previous owner's equipment. These commissions and expenditures were expensed and are excluded from "Property, Plant & Equipment."

2. Clearing costs were incurred to make the land ready for construction. These costs were included in "Property, Plant & Equipment."

3. During the land clearing process, timber and gravel were recovered and sold. The proceeds from the sale were recorded as other income and are excluded from "Property, Plant & Equipment."

4. A group of machines was purchased under a royalty agreement that provides royalty payments based on units of production from the machines. The cost of the machines, freight costs, unloading charges, and royalty payments were capitalized and are included in "Property, Plant & Equipment."

Required

a. Identify the audit objectives for "Property, Plant & Equipment." Do not indicate the principal audit procedures pertaining to each.

b. Indicate whether each of the items numbered 1 to 4 above requires one or more audit adjustments or reclassifications, and explain why such adjustments or reclassifications are required or not required. Organize your answers as follows:

Item Number	Is Audit Adjustment or Reclassification Required? Yes or No	Reasons Why Audit Adjustment or Reclassification Is Required or Not Required

AICPA (adapted)

14-34 Pierce, an independent auditor, was engaged to examine the financial statements of Mayfair Construction Incorporated for the year ended December 31, 19X3. Mayfair's financial statements reflect a substantial amount of mobile construction equipment used in the firm's operations. The equipment is accounted for in a subsidiary ledger. Pierce performed a study and evaluation of internal accounting control and found it satisfactory.

Required

Identify the substantive audit procedures that Pierce should utilize in examining mobile construction equipment and related depreciation in Mayfair's financial statements.

AICPA

14-35 You are engaged in the examination of the financial statements of the Ute Corporation for the year ended December 31, 19X3. The following schedules for the property, plant, and equipment and related allowance for depreciation accounts have been prepared by the client. You have checked the 12/31/X2 balances to your prior year's audit working papers.

Ute Corp.
Analysis of Property, Plant, and Equipment and Related
Allowance for Depreciation Accounts
Year Ended December 31, 19X3

Assets

Description	Final 12/31/X2	Additions	Retirements	Per Books 12/31/X3
Land	$ 22,500	$ 5,000		$ 27,500
Buildings	120,000	17,500		137,500
Machinery and equipment	385,000	40,400	$26,000	399,400
	$527,500	$62,900	$26,000	$564,400

Allowance for Depreciation

Description	Final 12/31/X2	Additions*	Retirements	Per Books 12/31/X3
Buildings	$ 60,000	$ 5,150		$ 65,150
Machinery and equipment	173,250	39,220		212,470
	$233,250	$44,370		$277,620

* Depreciation expense for the year.

Your examination reveals the following information:

1. All equipment is depreciated on the straight line basis (no salvage value taken into consideration) based on the following estimated lives: buildings, 25 years; all other items, 10 years. The company's policy is to take one-half year's depreciation on all asset acquisitions and disposals during the year.

2. On April 1, the company entered into a ten-year lease contract for a die casting machine with annual rentals of $5,000 payable in advance every April 1. The lease is cancellable by either party (60 days' written notice is required) and there is no option to renew the lease or buy the equipment at the end of the lease. The estimated useful life of the machine is ten years with no salvage value. The company recorded the die casting machine in the machinery and equipment account at $40,400, the present discounted value at the date of the lease, and $2,020, applicable to the machine, has been included in depreciation expense for the year.

3. The company completed the construction of a wing on the plant building on June 30. The useful life of the building was not extended by this addition. The lowest construction bid received was $17,500, the amount recorded in the Buildings account. Company personnel were used to construct the addition at a cost of $16,000 (materials, $7,500; labor, $5,500; and overhead, $3,000).

4. On August 18, $5,000 was paid for paving and fencing a portion of land owned by the company and used as a parking lot for employees. The expenditure was charged to the Land account.

5. The amount shown in the machinery and equipment asset retirement column represents cash received on September 5 on disposal of a machine purchased in July 19X1 for $48,000. The bookkeeper recorded depreciation expense of $3,500 on this machine in 19X3.

6. Crux City donated land and building appraised at $10,000 and $40,000, respectively, to the Ute Corporation for a plant. On September 1, the company began operating the plant. Since no costs were involved, the bookkeeper made no entry for the above transaction.

Required

a. Prepare the formal adjusting journal entries that you would suggest at December 31, 19X3 to adjust the accounts for the above transactions. Disregard income tax implications. The books have not been closed. Computations should be rounded off to the nearest dollar.

b. Prepare a schedule for property, plant, and equipment and accumulated depreciation using the working paper reference *P*.

AICPA (adapted)

14-36 Mincin, CPA, is the auditor of the Raleigh Corporation. Mincin is considering the audit work to be performed in the accounts payable area for the current year's engagement.

The prior year's papers show that confirmation requests were mailed to 100 of Raleigh's 1,000 suppliers. The selected suppliers were based on Mincin's sample that was designated to select accounts with large dollar balances. A substantial number of hours were spent by Raleigh and Mincin resolving relatively minor differences between the confirmation replies and Raleigh's accounting records. Alternate audit procedures were used for those suppliers who did not respond to the confirmation requests.

Required

a. Identify the accounts payable audit objectives that Mincin must consider in determining the audit procedures to be followed.

b. Identify situations when Mincin should use accounts payable confirmations and discuss whether Mincin is required to use them.

c. Discuss why the use of large dollar balances as the basis for selecting accounts payble for confirmation might not be the most efficient approach and indicate what more efficient procedures could be followed when selecting accounts payable for confirmation.

AICPA

14-37 You were in the final stages of your examination of the financial statements of Ozine Corporation for the year ended December 31, 19X0 when you were consulted by the Corporation's president who believes there is no point in your examining the 19X1 voucher register and testing data in support of 19X1 entries. He stated that (a) bills pertaining to 19X0 that were received too late to be included in the December voucher register were recorded as of the year-end by the Corporation by journal entry, (b) the internal auditor made tests after the year-end, and (c) he would furnish you with a letter certifying that there were no unrecorded liabilities.

Required

a. Should a CPA's test for unrecorded liabilities be affected by the fact that the client made a journal entry to record 19X0 bills that were received late? Explain.

b. Should a CPA's test for unrecorded liabilities be affected by the fact that a letter is obtained in which a responsible management official certifies that to the best of his knowledge all liabilities have been recorded? Explain.

c. Should a CPA's test for unrecorded liabilities be eliminated or reduced because of the internal audit tests? Explain.

d. Assume that the Corporation, which handled some government contracts, had no internal auditor but that an auditor for a federal agency spent three weeks auditing the records and was just completing his work at this time. How would the CPA's unrecorded liability test be affected by the work of the auditor for a federal agency?

e. What sources in addition to the 19X1 voucher register should the CPA consider to locate possible unrecorded liabilities?

AICPA

14-38 Taylor, CPA, is engaged in the audit of Rex Wholesaling for the year ended December 31, 19X2. Taylor performed a proper study of the system of internal accounting control relating to the purchasing, receiving, trade accounts payable, and cash disbursement cycles and has decided not to proceed with compliance testing. Based on analytical review procedures, Taylor believes that the trade accounts payable balance on the balance sheet as of December 31, 19X2 may be understated.

Taylor requested and obtained a client-prepared trade accounts payable schedule listing the total amount owed to each vendor.

Required

What additional substantive audit procedures should Taylor apply in examining the trade accounts payable?

AICPA

14-39 Finney, CPA, was engaged to conduct an audit of the financial statements of Clayton Realty Corporation for the month ending January 31, 19X4. The examination of monthly rent reconciliations is a vital portion of the audit engagement.

The following rent reconciliation was prepared by the controller of Clayton Realty Corporation and was presented to Finney who subjected it to various audit procedures:

Clayton Realty Corporation
Rent Reconciliation
for the Month Ended
January 31, 19X4

Gross apartment rents (Schedule A)	$1,600,800*
Less vacancies (Schedule B)	20,500*
Net apartment rentals	1,580,300
Less unpaid January rents (Schedule C)	7,800*
Total	1,572,500
Add prepaid rent collected (Apartment 116)	500*
Total cash collected	$1,573,000*

Schedules A, B, and C are available to Finney but have not been illustrated. Finney has conducted a study and evaluation of the system of internal control and found that it could be relied on to produce reliable accounting information. Cash receipts from rental operations are deposited in a special bank account.

Required

What substantive audit procedures should Finney employ during the audit in order to substantiate the validity of each of the dollar amounts marked by an asterisk?

AICPA

CASE STUDY

14-40* Your firm has been engaged to examine the financial statements of Brown Appliances, Inc. for the year ended December 31. The company manufactures major appliances sold to the general public through dealers and distributors.

You are to audit the trade accounts payable of a division of Brown Appliances, Inc. The trade accounts payable of this division aggregate $2.5 million, which is 60% of total accounts payable. Accounts payable total 40% of total liabilities and 30% of total liabilities and stockholders' equity. Net income for the year is $3 million.

Excerpts from the internal control memorandum follow:

"Invoices from suppliers are received in the purchasing department, where they are matched with receiving reports and checked to the applicable purchase order for quantities and pricing. Invoices and receiving reports are then forwarded to the accounting department for clerical checking and final approval for payment.

"On the payment date (the seventh working day of the month), invoices with attached receiving reports are separated into two groups: one group of invoices with receiving reports dated in the prior month, the other group with receiving reports dated in the current month. The check register is then prepared, with each group having a separate total and check number sequence. The accounts payable for monthly financial statement purposes is the total of the check register for invoices with receiving reports dated in the prior month. A voucher register is not maintained.

"The purchasing department holds unmatched receiving reports and unmatched invoices.

"Cutoff procedures as established by the company appear adequate; however, the company makes it a practice not to record inventory in transit.

"Vendors' statements received by the company are forwarded to a clerk in the accounting department. The clerk does not check all charges appearing on the vendors' statements, but does reconcile all old outstanding charges appearing thereon."

An accounts payable listing has been prepared by the company for the auditors. As explained above, this listing was prepared from the check register of December charges paid in January, and shows vendor, check number, invoice date, date paid, and amount. A quick review of the listing reveals the following:

1. January-dated invoices amounting to $200,000 appear on the listing payable to Talley and Park Advertising Agency, for advertising to appear in *Better Homes and Gardens* magazine in February and March. This was included in the year-end accounts payable listing at the request of the vice-president of advertising because he said he wanted to more closely match advertising department budgeted expenses with actual expenditures for the year. The distribution was made to advertising expense.

2. Amounts appear on the listing as payments for payrolls, payroll taxes, other taxes, and profit-sharing plans.

3. No amounts appear on the listing for legal or accounting services.

Required

Discuss the problems and procedures involved in auditing this company's accounts payable. Specifically discuss (a) the auditing procedures you would use in your examination and (b) the adjustments you would recommend to be made to the accounts payable listing.

Chapter 15

Auditing the Investing and Financing Cycles

Study Objectives

On completing a thorough study of this chapter, you should be able to

- Describe the events and transactions that pertain to the investing cycle and the financing cycle.

- State the functions and specific internal accounting control objectives for transactions in these cycles.

- Explain the applicability of the second standard of field work to these cycles.

- Design audit programs for substantive tests of investing and financing cycle balances.

- Execute audit programs for verifying account balances resulting from these two cycles.

Three cycles have been discussed in this book: revenue, expenditure, and production. The remaining cycles to be considered are the investing cycle and the financing cycle. These cycles embrace the major nonoperating activities of many companies.

The format of this chapter differs from the preceding tests of balances chapters. First, brief consideration is given to internal control principles and the study and evaluation of internal control. Then, comprehensive attention is directed to substantive tests of account balances. Each cycle is discussed separately.

THE INVESTING CYCLE

An entity's investing cycle pertains to the activities relating to the ownership of securities issued by other entities. The securities may be in the form of certificates of deposit (CDs), preferred and common stock, or corporate and government bonds. Consideration will be given here only to investments in common stock and corporate bonds held either as a short- or long-term investment.

BASIC CONSIDERATIONS

The following are basic to an understanding of the events and transactions in this cycle:

Functions

Executing

- Purchasing securities.
- Receiving periodic revenue.
- Selling securities.

Recording

- Journalizing and posting investing transactions.
- Updating investment ledger.

Custody

- Protecting securities.
- Maintaining correctness of investment balances.

Common Documents

- *Stock Certificate.* An engraved form showing the number of shares of stock owned by a shareholder in a corporation.
- *Bond Certificate.* An engraved form showing the number of bonds owned by a bondholder.
- *Bond Indenture.* A contract stating the terms of the bond issue between the bondholder and the issuing entity.
- *Broker's Advice.* A statement from a broker specifying the details of an investing transaction.

Accounting Records

- *Books of Original Entry.* General journal, cash receipts journal, voucher register, and check register.
- *General Ledger Accounts.* Marketable securities, investments in stock (or bonds), interest revenue, dividend revenue, earnings from investments under equity method, gains (losses) on sales of securities.[1]
- *Subsidiary Ledger.* Investments (or securities).

MATERIALITY AND AUDIT RISK

Marketable securities held as short-term investments often are material to a company's short-term solvency, but income from such securities is seldom

---

[1]Additional accounts are required when marketable equity securities are reported at the lower of aggregate cost or market.

significant to the results of operations of an industrial or commercial company. Securities held as long-term investments may be material to both the balance sheet and income statement.

The auditor should be able to keep audit risk for investing cycle transactions and balances at a very low level. Control risk is generally low because in most commercial enterprises (1) these transactions occur infrequently and (2) effective controls can be maintained at relatively little cost. The auditor can also keep detection risk low as it is usually possible to obtain evidential matter from independent sources outside the enterprise and acquire direct personal knowledge concerning the balances.

The following discussion of internal control, compliance tests, and substantive tests applies equally to marketable securities and long-term investments in securities, except as specifically indicated.

INTERNAL ACCOUNTING CONTROL OBJECTIVES

The three operative objectives of internal accounting control are applicable to the investing cycle. It will be recalled that these objectives consist of proper (1) executing of transactions, (2) recording of transactions, and (3) custody of assets. The assignment of departmental responsibility and specific control objectives for each function in this cycle are as follows:

Function	Department	Specific Accounting Control Objective
EXECUTING		
Purchasing securities	Treasurer	Purchases are made in accordance with management's authorizations.
Receiving periodic revenue	Cashier	Dividend and interest checks are promptly deposited intact.
Selling securities	Treasurer	Sales are made in accordance with management's authorizations.
RECORDING		
Journalizing and posting transactions	General Accounting	Transactions and events are correctly recorded as to amount, classification, and accounting period.
Updating investment ledger	Investment Ledger Accounting	Transactions are promptly and correctly posted to individual investment accounts.
CUSTODY		
Protecting securities	Treasurer	Access to securities is restricted to authorized personnel.
Maintaining correctness of investment balances	General Accounting	Recorded balances are compared with existing assets at reasonable intervals.

The basic features of internal accounting control are explained below.

Securities Transactions Are Properly Executed

Three principles of internal control are applicable in executing these transactions.

Authorization Procedures. The purchase and sale of securities may be executed on specific authorization of the board of directors. In such case, the corporate minutes should include the authorization. If authorization is delegated by the board of directors, it usually is assigned to a corporate officer, such as the treasurer or vice president of finance. Evidence of such authorizations should be in writing and signed by the officer.

Segregation of Functions. The separation of duties in executing transactions is illustrated above. Controls over the receipt of periodic revenue follow the procedures described for cash receipts in Chapter 9.

Documentation Procedures. Documentation of purchases of securities includes authorizations, broker's advices, paid vouchers, canceled checks, and the stock or bond certificates. The latter should be in the name of the company rather than in the name of the custodian. For sales of securities, authorizations, broker's advices, and cash remittance advices should be available. The latter form of documentation should also be present for the receipt of cash dividends and interest.

Securities Transactions Are Properly Recorded

The internal control principles applicable to this objective are as follows.

Segregation of Functions. Accounting personnel who record investment transactions should not perform any other functions pertaining to such transactions. In addition, personnel who journalize and post transactions to the general ledger should not update the investment ledger.

Accounting Records and Procedures. When a client has an investment portfolio, it is preferable to have an investment subsidiary ledger with an account for each security. For large portfolios, the subsidiary ledger may be maintained by electronic data processing (EDP).

Custody of Securities Is Properly Maintained

There are four internal control principles that apply to this objective.

Physical Controls and Authorization Procedures. Because securities are vulnerable to theft and misappropriation, physical controls should be used in protecting these assets. Securities should be kept in a safe place, such as in a bank safety deposit box or with an independent custodian. Direct access to storage areas should be limited to authorized personnel only. Many companies also require the presence of two responsible persons when there is direct access to a safety deposit box in order to prevent unauthorized removal of securities. To minimize the likelihood of unauthorized indirect access to securities, every withdrawal request should be in writing and signed by two company officers, each acting within the scope of his authority.

Independent Internal Verification and Segregation of Functions. The principle of independent internal verification is also applicable to this objective. Periodically, securities owned by a company should be counted and compared with the accounting records by personnel who do not have other duties pertaining to the securities.

STUDY AND EVALUATION OF INTERNAL CONTROL

As in the case of other major classes of transactions, the auditor must make a preliminary review of the flow of transactions through the accounting system. When there are few investment transactions, the auditor may decide to proceed directly to substantive tests of investment balances after meeting this requirement. This decision may be based on cost-benefit considerations, rather than on the absence of effective controls. When a client has an extensive investment portfolio and numerous transactions, the auditor may decide to complete his review of internal control and perform compliance tests on the controls expected to be relied on.

SUBSTANTIVE TESTS OF INVESTMENT BALANCES

An audit program for testing account balances in the investing cycle is shown in Figure 15-1. A discussion of the audit procedures is given below.

Clerical Accuracy

As in the case of other account balances, this objective is met by verifying the mechanical accuracy of supporting schedules and reconciling data on the schedules with ledger data. A client-prepared schedule for the investing cycle is a listing of securities owned at the statement date.

Existence or Occurrence and Rights and Obligations

The auditor is expected to obtain evidence of the (1) existence of securities at or near the balance sheet date, (2) ownership of the securities, and (3) occurrence of securities transactions during the year. The audit procedures applicable to this objective are as follows.

Inspect and Count Securities on Hand. This test ordinarily is performed simultaneously with the auditor's count of cash and other negotiable instruments. As in the case of cash, (1) the custodian of the securities should be

| TYPE OF TEST: Substantive | PURPOSE: Validity and Propriety of Balances |
| CYCLE: Investing | ACCOUNTS: Marketable Securities, Long-Term Investments, and Related Income Statement Accounts |

A. CLERICAL ACCURACY

1. Foot schedules of securities.
2. Reconcile general ledger balances with data on schedules.

B. EXISTENCE OR OCCURRENCE AND RIGHTS AND OBLIGATIONS

1. Inspect and count securities on hand.
2. Confirm securities held by others.

C. COMPLETENESS

1. Make analytical review.

D. VALUATION OR ALLOCATION

1. Vouch entries in investment accounts.
2. Recalculate revenue earned.
3. Review documentation concerning market values.

E. STATEMENT PRESENTATION AND DISCLOSURE

1. Make inquiries of management and review documentation on pledging of securities.
2. Compare statement presentation with GAAP.

Figure 15-1. AUDIT PROGRAM: INVESTMENT CYCLE BALANCES.

present throughout the count, (2) a receipt should be obtained from the custodian when the securities are returned, and (3) all securities should be controlled by the auditor until the count is completed.

In inspecting securities, the auditor should observe such matters as the certificate number on the document, name of owner (which should be the client, either directly or through endorsement), description of the security, number of shares (or bonds), and name of issuer. These data should be recorded as part of the auditor's analysis of the investment account. Figure 15-2 illustrates an audit working paper for marketable equity securities. For securities purchased in prior years, the data should be compared with those shown on last year's working papers. A lack of agreement between the certificate numbers may be indicative of unauthorized transactions for those securities.

Securities on hand may be stored for safekeeping in several different locations. In such case, either simultaneous counts should be made at the locations or the securities should be kept under seal until all locations have been counted. For example, banks will generally seal a safety deposit box at the

```
WILLIAMS COMPANY                                                              W/P REF: H-2
MARKETABLE EQUITY SECURITIES                                   PREPARED BY: Q.E.R DATE 1/3/X2
DECEMBER 31, 19X1                                              REVIEWED BY: R.C.22 DATE 1/10/X2
                                        ACCTS. 115 AND 425
```

DESCRIPTION	CTF. NO.	DATE ACQUIRED	NO. OF SHARES	COST PER SHARE	BALANCE 1/1/X1	PURCHASES	SALES	BALANCE 12/31/X1	MARKET PRICE AT 12/31/X1 PER SHARE	TOTAL	DIVIDEND INCOME
GENERAL MANUFACTURING CO.	C2779	4/21/X0	900	22.00	19,800 ✓			19,800 ✗∧	24.50 ✚	22,050 ∧	675 ⊗
METROPOLITAN EDISON CO.	M82931	9/21/X0	500	33.20	16,600 ✓		16,600 φ	∧			127 ⊗
PACIFIC PAPERS, INC.	54942	2/14/X1	200	18.50		3,700 φ		3,700 ✗∧	17.00 ✚	3,400 ∧	
WARRENTON CORP.	7336	7/19/X0	400	27.25	10,900 ✓			10,900 ✗∧	29.25 ✚	11,700 ∧	120 ⊗
					47,300 ✓	3,700	16,600	34,400 ✗		37,150	922
					F	F	F	FF To H-1		F To R-1	F

η Examined stock ctf. at Federal Trust Co.
✓ Traced to prior year's working papers
✓✗ Traced to general ledger balance
F Footed
FF Footed and crossfooted
∧ Extension checked
φ Vouched to broker's advices and board of directors authorization
✚ Per market quotation in 1/2/X2 Wall Street Journal
⊗ Dividend rates checked to Standard and Poors;
     dividends received traced to cash receipts journal.

Aggregate market value exceeded aggregate cost of
securities at both beginning and end of year.
Therefore, no allowance for decline in market value.

Figure 15-2. MARKETABLE EQUITY SECURITIES WORKING PAPER.

client's request and will confirm to the auditor that there was no access to the box during the counting period. When the count is not made on the balance sheet date, the auditor should prepare a reconciliation from the date of count to the statement date by reviewing any intervening security transactions.

Confirm Securities Held by Others. Securities held by outsiders for safe-keeping must be positively confirmed by the auditor. Confirmations should be requested as of the date securities held by the client are counted. The confirmation process for securities is identical with the steps required in confirming receivables. Thus, the auditor must control the mailings and receive the responses directly from the custodian. The data confirmed are the same as the data that should be noted by the auditor when he is able to inspect the securities.

Securities may also be held by creditors as collateral against loans or be placed in escrow by court order. In such cases, the confirmation should be sent to the indicated custodian.

Completeness

All investing cycle transactions that have occurred should be recorded in the accounts and statements. The auditor generally relies on cutoff tests of cash transactions to meet this objective. In some cases, the auditor may also use analytical review.

Make Analytical Review.   Analytical review procedures may involve the interrelationship of specific accounts and ratio analysis. Account relationships include the reconciliation of bond interest revenue with interest rates on bonds held as an investment. Two widely used ratios are (1) investments as a percentage of total assets and (2) the rate of return on investments. The investigation of unreconcilable items and unusual fluctuations in the financial relationships may reveal unrecorded transactions.

Valuation or Allocation

This audit objective relates to the cost and carrying value of short- and long-term investments and the propriety of related income statement amounts. The tests of balances in meeting the valuation or allocation objective are explained below.

Vouch Entries in Investment Accounts.   A variety of entries may be made to investment accounts. Acquisition of securities should be vouched to brokers' advices and canceled checks. Similarly, sales should be supported by bank or brokers' advices. Authorizations for purchases and sales should be found in the minutes of board of directors meetings.

For investments in stock accounted for by the equity method of accounting, it is necessary for the auditor to obtain evidence that the client's management can exercise significant influence over the investee. This is done through inquiry of management and by a review of the circumstances that support management's conclusion. When an investor owns more than 20% of the voting stock of an investee and does not use the equity method of accounting, the auditor should (1) obtain evidence that the investor cannot exert significant influence over the investee and (2) determine that appropriate disclosure is made in the financial statements.

For investments accounted for under the equity method, audited financial statements of the investee generally constitute sufficient evidential matter regarding the underlying net assets and the results of operations of the investee. Audited financial statements also represent competent evidence for investments in bonds and similar debt obligations.[2]

---

[2]Auditing Standards Board, *Codification of Statements on Auditing Standards* (New York: American Institute of Certified Public Accountants, 1985), Auditing Section 332.05 (hereinafter referred to and cited as AU §).

Recalculate Revenue Earned. Income from investments is verified by documentary evidence and recalculation. Dividends on all stocks listed on stock exchanges and many others are included in dividend record books published by many investment services. The auditor can independently verify the dividend revenue by reference to the declaration date, amount, and payment date shown in the record book.

Interest earned and interest collected on investments in bonds can be verified by examining the interest rates and payment dates indicated in the bond indenture. In addition, the auditor also reviews the client's amortization schedule for bond premium and discount and recalculates the amount amortized, if any. The verification of these accounts is usually incorporated into the schedule of investments, as illustrated in Figure 15-2.

Review Documentation Concerning Market Values. Marketable equity securities, such as common stock, should be valued at the lower of aggregate cost or market, and marketable debt securities, such as government and corporate bonds, should be stated at the lower of cost or a permanent decline in market value. The value of securities at the balance sheet date may be obtained from market quotations. The auditor should verify market quotations by reference to published security prices on stock exchanges. If published data are not available, the auditor should obtain direct confirmation from an independent broker.

When market quotations are based on a reasonably broad and active market, they ordinarily constitute sufficient competent evidential matter on the current market value of the securities.

Statement Presentation and Disclosure

The proper presentation of investments in securities in the financial statements requires

- Identification and classification of the different types of investments in the balance sheet.
- Recognition of realized revenues, gains, and losses in the income statement.
- Recognition of allowance for market declines and unrealized gains and losses associated therewith.
- Disclosure of the basis and methods of accounting used.
- Disclosure of liens, if any.

The substantive tests described above should provide evidence of the first four items. The inspection of the minutes and loan agreements should reveal the existence of liens. In addition, the auditor should make inquiries of management regarding its intent in holding the securities. On the basis of the evidence obtained, the auditor determines whether the proposed statement presentations and disclosures are appropriate.

THE FINANCING CYCLE

An entity's financing cycle consists of transactions pertaining to the acquisition of capital funds through issuance of long-term debt and capital stock and the subsequent redemption or reacquisition of these securities. Long-term debt includes borrowings from notes, mortgages, and bonds; capital stock includes preferred and common stock. The issuance of bonds and common stock typically represents the primary sources of capital funds. Accordingly, attention will be directed primarily on these two sources of financing.

BASIC CONSIDERATIONS

The following are basic to an understanding of the events and transactions in the financing cycle:

Functions

Executing

- Issuing bonds and capital stock.
- Paying bond interest and cash dividends.
- Redeeming and reacquiring bonds and capital stock.

Recording

- Journalizing and posting financing transactions.
- Updating subsidiary ledgers.

Custody

- Protecting bondholder and stockholder ledgers.
- Maintaining correctness of bondholder and stockholder records.

Accounting Records

- *General Ledger Accounts.* Bonds payable, premium (discount) on bonds, interest expense, gain (loss) on retirement of bonds, preferred stock, common stock, treasury stock, paid-in capital, retained earnings, dividends, and dividends payable.
- *Subsidiary Ledgers.* Bondholders and stockholders.

The common documents and books of original entry pertaining to the financial cycle are similar to those described for the investing cycle.

MATERIALITY AND AUDIT RISK

There is considerable variation in the importance of long-term debt to the fair presentation of financial position. In some major corporations, long-term debt is immaterial to total liabilities and stockholders' equity, whereas in many public utilities such liabilities may represent more than 50% of the total claims on corporate assets. Stockholders' equity clearly is a material component of a balance sheet. The income statement effects of financing cycle transactions for a manufacturing company are generally immaterial, whereas the effect of dividends on the retained earnings statement may be material. The disclosure requirements for long-term debt and stockholders' equity are usually significant.

Audit risk is similar to the risk described earlier for investing cycle transactions and balances. Ordinarily, control risk is low, and the auditor can also keep detection risk at a low level.

INTERNAL ACCOUNTING CONTROL OBJECTIVES

Each of the operative objectives of internal accounting control is applicable to the financing cycle. In order to meet these objectives, it is useful to identify the following specific accounting control objectives and assignment of responsibility for each function in the cycle:

Function	Department	Specific Accounting Control Objective
EXECUTING		
Issuing bonds and capital stock	Treasurer	Issues are made in accordance with board of directors authorizations and legal requirements, and proceeds are promptly deposited intact.
Paying bond interest and cash dividends	Treasurer	Payments are made to proper payees in accordance with board of directors or management authorizations.
Redeeming and reacquiring bonds and capital stock	Treasurer	Transactions are executed in accordance with board of directors authorizations.
RECORDING		
Journalizing and posting transactions	General Accounting	Transactions are correctly recorded as to amount, classification, and accounting period.
Updating subsidiary ledgers	Corporate Secretary	Transactions are correctly posted to individual accounts.
CUSTODY		
Protecting bondholder and stockholder ledgers	Subsidiary Ledger Accounting	Ledgers are kept in locked files and access is limited to authorized personnel.
Maintaining correctness of bondholder and stockholder records	Subsidiary Ledger Accounting	Recorded balances are periodically verified with bondholders and stockholders.

Bond and Capital Stock Transactions Are Properly Executed

The following internal control principles are applicable to this objective.

Authorization Procedures.   Formal authorization procedures are followed in the issuance of bonds and capital stock. Board-of-directors authorization is required in each case; in addition, stockholder approval is usually required for new stock issues. The certificates must be signed by one or two corporate officers. Board-of-directors authorization also precedes the reacquisition of bonds that is not in accordance with the terms of the issue, reacquisition of capital stock, and the declaration of dividends.

Payments of interest and dividends ordinarily are subject to the controls over cash disbursements procedures described in Chapter 10.

Segregation of Functions.   Full adherence to this internal control principle should occur in executing financing cycle transactions. Responsibility for executing the authorizations frequently is assigned to a corporate officer, such as the treasurer, who does not participate in the recording of the transactions.

For bond issues, a trustee, usually either a bank or a trust company, frequently acts as an independent third party to protect the respective interests of the bondholders and the issuing corporation.

For a publicly held company, additional compliance with this principle exists through the use of an outside registrar and transfer agent for capital stock issues and transfers. These agents are usually banks or trust companies that have the experience, competent personnel, and facilities to assure maximum efficiency and control over capital stock transactions. The primary responsibility of a registrar is to verify that stock is issued in accordance with the articles of incorporation, statutory requirements, and the formal authorizations of the board of directors. When a registrar is not used, these responsibilities are assumed by corporate legal staff or counsel. The registrar maintains records of total shares authorized, issued, and canceled. Every new certificate is prepared and recorded by the registrar.

A stock transfer agent maintains detailed records of each shareholder's stock ownership and records the transfers of stock ownership among shareholders. The transfer agent assists corporate officers in seeing that each stock transfer meets regulatory requirements. Another arrangement that contributes to effective internal control is the use of an outside independent agent, such as a bank, for the payment of bond interest and dividends.

Documentation Procedures.   Documentation of financing cycle transactions takes a variety of forms. Each type of security issue is based on a formal written contract that stipulates the terms of the issue. Evidence of authorizations is found in the minutes. Proceeds of issues are evidenced by brokers' advices and cash remittance advices. Payments of interest and dividends are supported by paid vouchers and canceled checks. These forms of evidence are also available for reacquisitions of bonds and capital stock.

In addition, the redemption of bonds should be evidenced by a cremation certificate that signifies the original certificate has been destroyed. The stock certificates and stubs for stock retired should be clearly marked canceled and the canceled certificate attached to the stub.

Bond and Capital Stock Transactions Are Properly Recorded

The internal control principles applicable to this objective are as follows.

Segregation of Functions. Accounting personnel who record financing transactions should not execute them. For bond issues, a bond register should be maintained showing the bonds held by each bondholder. The register may be kept by the issuing corporation or a bond registrar. For capital stock issues, a stockholders' ledger should be maintained. In a small company, the corporate secretary has this responsibility; in a large company, a stock transfer agent performs this function.

Accounting Records and Procedures. As indicated above, subsidiary ledgers should be maintained for both bonds and capital stock. In recording capital stock transactions, a proper distinction must be maintained between paid-in and accumulated capital.

Independent Internal Verification. When bondholder and stockholder ledgers are maintained by the issuer, there should be independent verification of the agreement of the subsidiary ledgers with the general ledger control accounts. If these records are kept by outside parties, the total number of bonds and shares of stock outstanding should be periodically verified through reports submitted by the outside parties.

Custody of Assets Is Properly Maintained

The internal control principles applicable to this objective are the same as those described for the investing cycle.

Physical Controls and Authorization Procedures. Physical controls in the form of safes and safety deposit boxes should be used to store bond cremation certificates, treasury stock, and the stock certificate book. Such facilities may also be employed to safeguard unissued bond and stock certificates from unauthorized use. Responsibility for restricting access should be assigned to a company officer.

Independent Internal Verification and Segregation of Functions. These principles involve the comparison of recorded subsidiary balances with supporting evidence. The comparisons should be made by individuals who do not have any other responsibilities for financing cycle transactions. Bonds and capital stock outstanding should be compared periodically with certificate stubs and other supporting documentation.

STUDY AND EVALUATION OF INTERNAL CONTROL

The auditor's responsibilities under the second standard of field work for the financing cycle are comparable to those described earlier in this chapter for the investing cycle. Thus, the auditor may elect to forego completing the review of the system and rely entirely on substantive tests in verifying financial cycle balances. The use of outside independent agents in keeping the subsidiary ledgers and paying interest and dividends often reduces the need for the auditor to rely on the client's controls.

SUBSTANTIVE TESTS OF LONG-TERM DEBT BALANCES

From an auditing standpoint, notes payable, mortgages payable, and bonds payable have similar characteristics. Generally, these forms of debt (1) involve interest-bearing contractual agreements, (2) require approval by the board of directors, and (3) may be secured by the pledging of collateral. Ordinarily, a company will have infrequent transactions pertaining to long-term debt, but the amount per transaction may be material. Tests of balances may occur before or after the balance-sheet date. The primary tests of long-term debt balances and the audit objectives to which they pertain are shown in Figure 15-3. The tests are explained below within the framework of the audit objectives.

Clerical Accuracy

The starting point in the testing of balances is to verify the mathematical accuracy of supporting schedules by footing the schedules and reconciling data on the schedules with general ledger balances. A common schedule is a listing of the number of bonds held by registered owners prepared by the bond trustee. The schedule is footed and the total compared with bonds issued and outstanding.

Existence or Occurrence and Rights and Obligations

Tests of balances for these audit objectives are designed to provide evidence that (1) recorded long-term debt exists at the balance sheet date, (2) long-term debt transactions have actually occurred, and (3) long-term debt represents a legal obligation. The following tests of balances are applicable to these objectives:

Review Authorizations and Contracts. The authority of a corporation to enter into a contractual agreement to borrow money through the issuance or incurrence of long-term debt rests with the board of directors. Accordingly, evidence of authorizations should be found in the minutes of board meetings. Normally, the auditor only reviews the authorizations that have occurred during the year under audit, since evidence of the authorizations for debt outstanding at the beginning of the year should be in the permanent working paper file.

Authorization for the debt issue should include reference to the applicable sections of the corporate bylaws that pertain to such financing. It may also include the opinion of the company's legal counsel on the legality of the debt.

TYPE OF TEST: Substantive	PURPOSE: Validity and Propriety of Balances
CYCLE: Financing	ACCOUNTS: Long-term Debt and Interest Expense

A. CLERICAL ACCURACY

1. Foot supporting schedules.
2. Reconcile general ledger with supporting schedules.

B. EXISTENCE OR OCCURRENCE AND RIGHTS AND OBLIGATIONS

1. Review authorizations and contracts.
2. Confirm debt.

C. COMPLETENESS

1. Make analytical review.

D. VALUATION OR ALLOCATION

1. Vouch entries to long-term debt accounts.
2. Recalculate interest expense.

E. STATEMENT PRESENTATION AND DISCLOSURE

1. Make inquiries and review documentation for restrictions and liens.
2. Compare statement presentation with GAAP.

Figure 15-3. AUDIT PROGRAM: TESTS OF LONG-TERM DEBT BALANCES.

Further support for existence is obtained by a review of debt contracts and periodic reports received from trustees.

Vouchers, paid checks, and reports of independent paying agencies provide evidence of the occurrence of interest transactions.

Confirm Debt. The auditor is expected to confirm the existence and terms of long-term debt by direct communication with lenders and bond trustees. Notes payable to banks in which the client has an account are confirmed as part of the confirmation of bank balances. Other notes are confirmed with the holders by separate letter. Such requests should be made by the client and mailed by the auditor. The existence of mortgages and bonds payable normally can be confirmed directly with the trustee. Each confirmation should include a request for the current status of the debt and current year's transactions. All confirmation responses should be compared to the records and any differences should be investigated.

Completeness

This objective focuses on the possible understatement of long-term debt and interest expense. The audit tests for completeness include the confirmation of long-term debt, described above, and analytical review.

Make Analytical Review.   Three ratios are often used in making an analytical review of long-term debt: (1) debt to equity, (2) interest expense to average debt, and (3) number of times bond interest is earned. Each ratio can be compared internally with prior year results and budget expectations. In addition, they can be used for external comparisons with industry data. Any unusual fluctuations should be investigated.

Valuation or Allocation

The points of concern in this objective are the carrying value of long-term debt and the accuracy of interest expense. Two tests of balances are applicable to this objective.

Vouch Entries to Long-Term Debt Accounts.   For bonds, the auditor should obtain evidence on both the face value and net proceeds of the obligation at the date of issue. Issuances of debt instruments should be traced to cash receipts as evidenced by brokers' advices. Payments on principal of long-term debt can be verified by an examination of vouchers and canceled checks; payments in full can be validated by an inspection of the canceled instrument and, in the case of bonds, a cremation certificate. When installment payments are involved, their propriety can be traced to repayment schedules. Bonds may also be converted into stock. Evidence of such transactions is available in the form of canceled bond certificates and the issuance of related stock certificates.

From the evidence obtained, the auditor should be able to determine the validity and propriety of the accounting treatment of the transactions. Special care should be exercised in ascertaining that net proceeds were properly allocated to principal, accrued interest, and discount or premium. Similarly, the auditor must determine that gains or losses and carrying values were properly recognized on payment.

Recalculate Interest Expense.   Evidence of interest expense and accrued interest payable is easily obtainable by the auditor. The auditor reperforms the client's interest calculations and traces interest payments to supporting vouchers, canceled checks, and confirmation responses. Accrued interest, in turn, is verified by identifying the last interest payment date and recalculating the amount booked by the client.

When bond interest coupons are involved, the auditor can examine the canceled coupons and reconcile them to the amount paid. When bonds were originally sold at a premium or discount, the auditor should review the client's amortization schedule and verify the recorded amount of amortization by recalculation.

Audit working papers, such as the analysis of notes payable and interest in Figure 15-4, are used in verifying long-term debt balances.

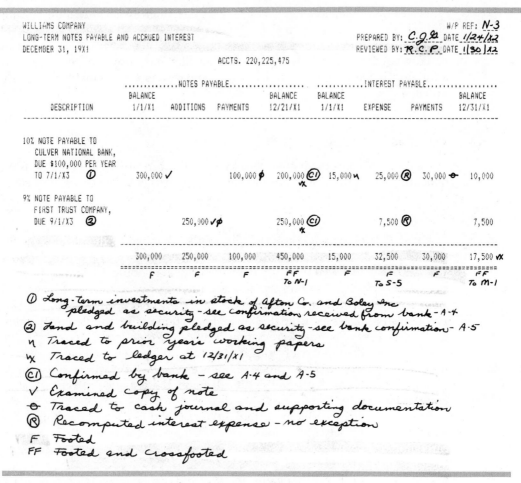

Figure 15-4. NOTES AND INTEREST PAYABLE WORKING PAPER.

Statement Presentation and Disclosure

In evaluating the appropriateness of the client's classification of long-term debt, the auditor should be aware of applicable Financial Accounting Standards Board (FASB) pronouncements. The auditor meets this objective through inspection of the debt contract, confirmation with trustees, and inquiry of management.

SUBSTANTIVE TESTS OF STOCKHOLDERS' EQUITY BALANCES

As in the case of long-term debt, capital stock transactions in the financing cycle may be verified at any convenient time during the audit engagement. An audit program for tests of these balances is shown in Figure 15-5. As in the case of bonds, the verification of the current year's capital stock transactions receives priority in executing the audit program.

TYPE OF TEST: Substantive	PURPOSE: Validity and Propriety of Balances
CYCLE: Financing	ACCOUNTS: Stockholders' Equity

A. CLERICAL ACCURACY

1. Foot supporting schedules.
2. Reconcile data on schedules to ledger balances.

B. EXISTENCE OR OCCURRENCE

1. Review authorizations and terms of stock issues.
2. Confirm shares outstanding with registrar and transfer agent.
3. Inspect stock certificate book.
4. Inspect certificates of shares held in treasury.

C. COMPLETENESS

1. Make analytical review.

D. RIGHTS AND OBLIGATIONS

1. Make inquiries of legal counsel.
2. Review articles of incorporation and bylaws.

E. VALUATION OR ALLOCATION

1. Vouch capital stock entries.
2. Vouch dividend entries.
3. Vouch entries to retained earnings.

F. STATEMENT PRESENTATION AND DISCLOSURE

1. Review minutes of board of directors meetings for stock options and dividend restrictions.
2. Compare statement presentation with GAAP.

Figure 15-5. AUDIT PROGRAM: STOCKHOLDERS' EQUITY BALANCES.

Clerical Accuracy

The accuracy of supporting schedules is established by footing the schedules and reconciling the data on the schedules to the ledger balances. For a small company without a registrar and transfer agent, a common schedule is a trial balance of the stockholders' ledger. Total shares shown in the schedule should agree with the shares outstanding in the capital stock account.

Existence or Occurrence

For account balances, this objective relates to the validity of recorded stockholders' equity balances; for transactions, such as those pertaining to the issuance of stock, the acquisition of treasury stock, and the payment of dividends, the objective is to determine whether the transactions actually occurred. Several tests of balances are used by the auditor in meeting this objective.

Review Authorizations and Terms of Stock Issue. All stock issues, stock reacquisitions, and dividend declarations should be authorized by the board of directors. Accordingly, a review of the minutes should provide evidence of stockholders' equity transactions authorized during the year. In some cases, the minutes also contain information about the legality of the authorized action.

Different classes of stock may contain restriction provisions or convey preferences in dividend declarations and liquidation. The auditor should examine each issue for such terms and make appropriate notation in the working papers.

Confirm Shares Outstanding with Registrar and Transfer Agent. When the client uses a registrar, the auditor should confirm total shares authorized, issued, and outstanding at the balance sheet date with the registrar. Confirmation with the transfer agent, in turn, provides evidence of shares held by each stockholder. The confirmation responses are then compared with the capital stock accounts and the stockholders' ledger.

Inspect Stock Certificate Book. This test is required when the client serves as its own transfer agent. Several steps are involved in the test. First, the auditor should examine the stock certificate book to determine that (1) stubs for shares issued and outstanding have been properly filled out, (2) canceled certificates are attached to original stubs, and (3) all unissued certificates are intact.

Second, the auditor should ascertain that the changes during the year have been correctly recorded in the individual stockholders' accounts in the subsidiary ledger. When there are numerous issuances and cancellations, this comparison may be done on a test basis.

Third, the auditor should reconcile the total shares issued and outstanding as shown in the stock certificate book with total shares reported in the stockholders' ledger and capital stock accounts.

Inspect Certificates of Shares Held in Treasury. If capital stock is held in the treasury, the auditor should count the certificates at the same time other securities are counted. Ideally, the count should be made at the balance sheet date. If this is not possible, there must be a reconciliation from the date of the count to the balance sheet date. The number of shares held should also be agreed to the shares shown in the treasury stock account. In inspecting the certificates, the auditor should note in the working papers the number of shares acquired during the year for subsequent tracing to the cash records.

Completeness

The completeness objective is directed at whether recorded stockholders' equity accounts reflect all data that should be recorded. Evidence for this objective ordinarily is obtained from the tests of balances previously described under existence or occurrence. Analytical review procedures are also helpful in meeting this objective.

Make Analytical Review. The following ratios may be helpful in establishing the completeness of capital stock accounts: (1) book value per share, (2) return on shareholders' equity, (3) equity ratio, (4) dividend payout ratio, and (5) the price-earnings ratio. Each ratio can be compared with both internal and external data to determine when unreasonable or unexpected relationships exist. When the analysis reveals unusual fluctuations or questionable items, they should be investigated by the auditor.

Rights and Obligations

Management's assertions about the rights and obligations pertain to whether capital stock was legally issued and shareholders have a legal claim on corporate assets at the balance sheet date. Evidence of the legality of a stock issue and any changes in capitalization may be obtained through inquiry of the client's legal counsel. The attorney's response preferably should be in writing. A review of the articles of incorporation and bylaws should also reveal the right of the entity to authorize and execute the stockholders' equity transactions.

Valuation or Allocation

This objective pertains to the proper statement amounts for stockholders' equity balances. For these balances, the valuation objective includes maintaining a proper distinction between paid-in capital and retained earnings in recording stock transactions. Evidence concerning this objective is obtained primarily through the vouching of recorded entries.

Vouch Capital Stock Entries. Each change in a capital stock account should be vouched to supporting documentation. For a new issue of stock, the auditor can examine remittance advices of the cash proceeds from the issue. The proceeds should be traced to the cash receipt records and capital stock and other paid-in capital accounts. If the consideration for the shares was other than cash, the auditor should carefully examine the basis for the valuation, such as the market value of the consideration received or given. For the shares issued, market quotations may be useful in determining the propriety of the valuation; when the value of the property received is used, an appraisal may

Prepared by: *A.E.R.* Date: *1/12/x2*
Reviewed by: *R.C.P.* Date: *1/19/x2*

Willens Company P-2
Capital Stock $100 par
Acc. # 600 12/31/x1

	Shares			
	Authorized	Issued and Outstanding	Amount	
Balances, 1/1/x1	100,00 √	5000 √	500,000 √	
Shares issued at par for cash on 4/1/x1		1000 ¥	100,000 n ∅	
Balances, 12/31/x1	10000	6000 C	600,000	To-P/1

√ - Traced to prior years working papers
¥ - Traced to approval per minutes of Board of Directors meeting on 3/20/x1
∅ - Traced proceeds to cash receipts
C - Confirmed by First Trust Company, transfer agent for the company—See P-3

Reviewed minutes of all Board of Directors meetings for evidence of capital stock transactions. Only reference was to transaction of 4/1/x1 as per above.

Figure 15-6. CAPITAL STOCK WORKING PAPER.

be necessary. An analysis of a capital stock account is illustrated in Figure 15-6. Similar analyses are prepared for treasury stock and other stockholders' equity accounts.

The auditor should exercise care in determining the propriety of the accounting treatment for shares issued as part of stock option, stock warrant, or stock conversion plans or in connection with a stock split. Documentation of the cost of treasury stock should be available to the auditor in the form of authorizations in the minutes, disbursement vouchers, and canceled checks.

Vouch Dividend Entries.   All dividend distributions should be authorized by the board of directors. The auditor should inspect the minutes for authorization and note the amount per share and relevant dates. In determining the propriety of the distribution, the auditor should

- Establish that preferential or other rights of stockholders and any restrictions on dividend distributions have been recognized.
- Establish the number of shares outstanding on the date of record and verify the accuracy of the total dividend declaration by recalculation.
- Ascertain the propriety of the entry to record the declaration.
- Trace dividend payments to canceled checks and other documentation.

Vouch Entries to Retained Earnings.   Each entry to retained earnings except the posting of net income (or net loss) should be vouched to supporting documentation. Entries for dividend declarations and retained earnings appropriations are traced to the minute book. The client is also expected to furnish support for any prior-period adjustments. Vouching enables the auditor to ascertain whether (1) a proper distinction has been made between paid-in capital and retained earnings and (2) applicable legal and contractual requirements have been met.

Statement Presentation and Disclosure

APB Opinion No. 12 provides that disclosure of changes in the separate accounts comprising stockholders' equity is required to make the financial statements sufficiently informative. Such disclosure may be made in the basic statements and notes thereto or be presented in a separate statement.

Disclosures related to the equity section include details of stock option plans, dividends in arrears, par or stated value, and dividend and liquidation preferences. The auditor meets this audit objective by a review of evidence obtained from the foregoing tests and from a review of the corporate minutes for provisions and agreements affecting the stockholders' equity accounts. In reviewing the minutes, the auditor should note whether any shares of stock have been reserved for stock option or similar plans, commitments for future issuance of stock in the purchase of or merger with another company, and restrictions limiting dividend payments or requiring minimum working capital requirements. Relevant evidence may also be obtained from discussions and communications with legal counsel.

CONCLUDING COMMENTS

Internal accounting controls over transactions in the investing and financing cycles are generally strong because of infrequent transactions, officer participation in the transactions, and the use of outside custodians and independent agents. In the typical audit engagement, it is relatively easy for the auditor to obtain sufficient competent evidential matter concerning investment, long-term debt, and stockholders' equity accounts by direct tests of such balances.

REVIEW QUESTIONS

15-1 Indicate the functions associated with the investing cycle.

15-2 Evaluate the materiality and audit risk for investing cycle balances.

15-3 Explain the specific internal accounting control objectives for the functions identified in 1 above.

15-4 What internal accounting control principles are applicable to (a) executing and (b) recording securities transactions?

15-5 Identify the internal control principles that relate to the custody of securities.

15-6 Indicate the alternative decision paths the auditor may take in making a study and evaluation of internal control over investment transactions, and explain the circumstances when each choice is justified.

15-7 What precautions should be taken by the auditor in inspecting and counting securities on hand?

15-8 What data should be shown in the working papers concerning securities?

15-9 Indicate the form and timing of confirming securities held by outside custodians.

15-10 Indicate the audit procedures that are useful in verifying the (a) existence or occurrence and rights and obligations and (b) valuation or allocation objectives for investment balances.

15-11 What evidence is available to the auditor in determining (a) "market" when securities are accounted for on the cost basis and (b) the value of underlying net assets when securities are accounted for under the equity method?

15-12 Indicate the statement presentation and supplemental disclosures that are required for investments in securities.

15-13 Identify (a) the functions and (b) the specific internal accounting control objectives for financing cycle transactions.

15-14 Briefly explain the application of (a) authorization procedures and (b) segregation of functions to the proper execution of transactions in the financing cycle.

15-15 What audit procedures are useful in verifying (a) existence or occurrence, (b) completeness, and (c) valuation or allocation of long-term debt balances?

15-16 Indicate the purposes served in confirming debt with holders.

15-17 Identify the specific relationships that may be determined in making an analytical review of long-term debt balances.

15-18 What audit procedures may be employed to establish the (a) existence or occurrence and (b) rights and obligations of stockholders' equity balances?

15-19 List the procedures that are required in vouching dividend payments.

15-20 What procedures are used in determining whether there is proper statement presentation and disclosure of stockholder equity items?

OBJECTIVE QUESTIONS FROM PROFESSIONAL EXAMINATIONS

Indicate the *best* answer for each of the following multiple-choice questions.

15-21 These questions pertain to the investing cycle.

1. Of the following, which is the most efficient audit procedure for verification of interest earned on bond investments?
   a. Tracing interest declarations to an independent record book.
   b. Recomputing interest earned.
   c. Confirming interest rate with the issuer of the bonds.
   d. Vouching the receipt and deposit of interest checks.

2. The auditor can best verify a client's bond sinking fund transactions and year-end balance by
   a. Confirmation with individual holders of retired bonds.
   b. Confirmation with the bond trustee.
   c. Recomputation of interest expense, interest payable, and amortization of bond discount or premium.
   d. Examination and count of the bonds retired during the year.

3. Which of the following is *not* one of the auditor's primary objectives in an examination of marketable securities?
   a. To determine whether securities are authentic.
   b. To determine whether securities are the property of the client.
   c. To determine whether securities actually exist.
   d. To determine whether securities are properly classified on the balance sheet.

15-22 These questions relate to financing cycle transactions and balances.

1. All corporate capital stock transactions should ultimately be traced to the
   a. Minutes of the board of directors.
   b. Cash receipts journal.
   c. Cash disbursements journal.
   d. Numbered stock certificates.

2. The auditor's program for the examination of long-term debt should include steps that require the
   a. Verification of the existence of the bondholders.
   b. Examination of any bond trust indenture.
   c. Inspection of the accounts payable subsidiary ledger.
   d. Investigation of credits to the bond interest income account.

3. Several years ago, Conway, Inc., secured a conventional real estate mortgage loan. Which of the following audit procedures would be *least* likely to be performed by an auditor examining the mortgage balance?
   a. Examine the current year's cancelled checks.
   b. Review the mortgage amortization schedule.
   c. Inspect public records of lien balances.
   d. Recompute mortgage interest expense.

4. An audit program for the examination of the retained earnings account should include a step that requires verification of the

    a. Market value used to charge retained earnings to account for a two-for-one stock split.

    b. Approval of the adjustment to the beginning balance as a result of a write-down of an account receivable.

    c. Authorization for both cash and stock dividends.

    d. Gain or loss resulting from disposition of treasury shares.

COMPREHENSIVE QUESTIONS

15-23 You have been assigned to the examination of the "investments" account of one of your firm's older clients, the *D* Co. During the prior year, your client received more than $1 million from the sale of all of its stock in a subsidiary. The proceeds from this sale were promptly invested in time certificates of deposit (CDs) having various maturities. More than one year has elapsed since the sale of the stock, and your client continues to invest the funds in CDs. Investment decisions are made by the company treasurer, who also is responsible for custody of the CDs.

During the current year, *D*'s treasurer obtained $100,000 from the surrender of a CD at maturity and invested the proceeds in another six-month certificate having an interest rate of 10%. This transaction was recorded on the books of the company as being for a CD bearing an interest rate of 8%. At the end of the six months, the treasurer redeemed this CD for its $105,000 maturity value. On the books of the company, the transaction was recorded as having been for $104,000, and the treasurer deposited that amount in the company's bank account prior to reinvesting the proceeds in another security.

Required

    a. What internal controls could have prevented or permitted detection of the treasurer's action?

    b. What audit procedures could you perform to discover this irregularity?

15-24 In verifying investing cycle balances, the auditor should recognize that the following errors may occur or exist:

    1. A mathematical error is made in accruing interest earned.

    2. A 25% common stock investment in an affiliated company is accounted for on the cost basis.

    3. Securities held by an outside custodian are in the treasurer's name.

    4. Securities on hand at the beginning of the year are diverted to personal use in July and are replaced in December.

    5. An authorized purchase is recorded at cost and the broker's fee is expensed.

    6. Ten shares of stock reported to be on hand are missing.

    7. Marketable equitable securities are reported at cost, which is above market.

    8. The schedule of marketable securities does not reconcile to the general ledger accounts.

    9. Gain on a sale of securities is reported net of taxes.

    10. Securities pledged as collateral on a bank loan are not disclosed.

Required

a. Identify the substantive tests that should enable the auditor to detect each error.

b. Indicate the audit objective to which the audit procedure relates.

c. Identify the type of evidential matter obtained by the audit procedure.

15-25 Cassandra Corporation, a manufacturing company, periodically invests large sums in marketable equity securities. The investment policy is established by the Investment Committee of the Board of Directors, and the treasurer is responsible for carrying out the Investment Committee's directives. All securities are stored in a bank safe deposit vault.

The independent auditor's internal control questionnaire with respect to Cassandra's investments in marketable equity securities contains the following three questions:

- Is investment policy established by the Investment Committee of the Board of Directors?
- Is the treasurer solely responsible for carrying out the Investment Committee's directives?
- Are all securities stored in a bank safe deposit vault?

Required

In addition to the above three questions, what questions should the auditor's internal control questionnaire include with respect to the company's investments in marketable equity securities?

AICPA

15-26 As a result of highly profitable operations over a number of years, Eastern Manufacturing Corporation accumulated a substantial investment portfolio. In his examination of the financial statements for the year ended December 31, 19X0, the following information came to the attention of the corporation's CPA:

1. The manufacturing operations of the corporation resulted in an operating loss for the year.

2. In 19X0, the corporation placed the securities making up the investment portfolio with a financial institution that will serve as custodian of the securities. Formerly, the securities were kept in the corporation's safe deposit box in the local bank.

3. On December 22, 19X0, the corporation sold and then repurchased on the same day a number of securities that had appreciated greatly in value. Management stated that the purpose of the sale and repurchase was to establish a higher cost and book value for the securities and to avoid the reporting of a loss for the year.

Required

a. List the objectives of the CPA's examination of the investment account.

b. Under what conditions would the CPA accept a confirmation of the securities on hand from the custodian in lieu of inspecting and counting the securities himself?

c. What disclosure, if any, of the sale and repurchase of the securities would the CPA recommend for the financial statements?

AICPA

15-27 In connection with his examination of the financial statements of Belasco Chemicals, Inc., Kenneth Mack, CPA, is considering the necessity of inspecting marketable securities on the balance sheet date, May 31, 19X1 or at some other date. The marketable securities held by Belasco include negotiable bearer bonds, which are kept in a safe in the treasurer's office, and miscellaneous stocks and bonds kept in a safe deposit box at The Merchants Bank. Both the negotiable bearer bonds and the miscellaneous stocks and bonds are material to proper presentation of Belasco's financial position.

Required

a. What are the factors that Mr. Mack should consider in determining the necessity for inspecting these securities on May 31, 19X1, as opposed to other dates?

b. Assume that Mr. Mack plans to send a member of his staff to Belasco's offices and The Merchants Bank on May 31, 19X1, to make the securities inspection. What instructions should he give to his staff member as to the conduct of the inspection and the evidence to be included in the audit working papers? (*Note:* Do not discuss the valuation of securities, the income from securities, or the examination of information contained in the books and records of the company.)

c. Assume that Mack finds it impracticable to send a member of his staff to Belasco's offices and The Merchants Bank on May 31, 19X1. What alternative procedures may he employ to assure himself that the company had physical possession of its marketable securities on May 31, 19X1, if the securities are inspected (1) May 28, 19X1? (2) June 5, 19X1?

AICPA

15-28 As part of his examination of the financial statements of the Marlborough Corporation for the year ended March 31, 19X1, Marion Romito, CPA, is reviewing the balance-sheet presentation of a $1.2 million advance to Franklin Olds, Marlborough's president. The advance, which represents 50% of current assets and 10% of total assets, was made during the year ended March 31, 19X1. It has been described in the balance sheet as "miscellaneous accounts receivable" and classified as a current asset.

Olds informs the CPA that he has used the proceeds of the advance to purchase 35,000 shares of Marlborough's common stock, in order to forestall a take-over raid on the company. He is reluctant to have his association with the advance described in the financial statements because he does not have voting control and fears that this will "just give the raiders ammunition."

Olds offers the following four-point program as an alternative to further disclosure:

1. Have the advance approved by the board of directors. (This can be done expeditiously because a majority of the board members are officers of the company.)

2. Prepare a demand note payable to the company with interest of 7.5% (the average bank rate paid by the company).

3. Furnish an endorsement of the stock to the company as collateral for the loan. (During the year under audit, despite the fact that earnings did not increase, the market price of Marlborough common rose from $20 to $40 per share. The stock has maintained its $40 per share market price subsequent to year-end.)

4. Obtain a written opinion from the company attorney supporting the legality of the company's advance and the use of the proceeds.

Required

a. Discuss the proper balance-sheet classifications of the advance to Olds and other appropriate disclosures in the financial statements and footnotes.

b. Discuss each point of Olds' four-point program as to whether or not it is desirable and as to whether or not it is an alternative to further disclosure.

c. If Olds refuses to permit further disclosure, what action(s) should the CPA take? Discuss.

d. In his discussion with the CPA, Olds warns that the raiders, if successful, probably will appoint new auditors. What consideration should the CPA give to this factor? Explain.

AICPA

15-29 The schedule on page 572 was prepared by the controller of World Manufacturing Inc. for use by the independent auditors during their examination of World's year-end financial statements. All procedures performed by the audit assistant were noted in the "Legend" section at the bottom. The schedule was properly initialed, dated, and indexed, and then submitted to a senior member of the audit staff for review. Internal control was reviewed and is considered to be satisfactory.

Required

a. What information that is essential to the audit of marketable securities is missing from this schedule?

b. What are the essential audit procedures that were not noted as having been performed by the audit assistant?

AICPA

15-30 You were engaged to examine the financial statements of Ronlyn Corporation for the year ended June 30.

On May 1, the Corporation borrowed $500,000 from Second National Bank to finance plant expansion. The long-term note agreement provided for the annual payment of principal and interest over five years. The existing plant was pledged as security for the loan.

Due to unexpected difficulties in acquiring the building site, the plant expansion had not begun at June 30. To make use of the borrowed funds, management decided to invest in stocks and bonds, and on May 16, the $500,000 was invested in securities.

Required

a. What are the audit objectives in the examination of long-term debt?

b. Prepare an audit program for the examination of the long-term note agreement between Ronlyn and Second National Bank.

c. How could you verify the security position of Ronlyn at June 30?

d. In your audit of investments, how would you
   1. Verify the dividend or interest income recorded?
   2. Determine market value?
   3. Establish the authority for security purchases?

AICPA

15-31 The following transactions and events relate to financing cycle transactions:

1. Declare cash dividend on common stock.
2. Issue bonds.
3. Pay bond interest.

World Manufacturing Inc. Marketable Securities Year Ended December 31, 19X1

Description of Security	YR. DUE	%	Serial No.	Face Value of Bonds	Gen. Ledger 1/1	Purch. in 19X1	Sold in 19X1	Cost	Gen. Ledger 12/31	12/31 Market	Pay Date(s)	Amt. Rec.	Accruals 12/31
CORP. BONDS													
A	91	6	21-7	10,000	9,400a				9,400	9,100	1/15 7/15	300b, d 300b, d	275
D	83	4	73-0	30,000	27,500a				27,500	26,220	12/1	1,200b, d	100
G	98	9	16-4	5,000	4,000a				4,000	5,080	8/1	450b, d	188
Rc	85	5	08-2	70,000	66,000a		57,000b	66,000					
Sc	99	10	07-4	100,000		100,000e			100,000	101,250	7/1	5,000b, d	5,000
					106,900	100,000	57,000	66,000	140,900	141,650		7,250	5,563
					a, f	f	f	f	f, g	f		f	f
STOCKS													
P 1,000 shs. Common			1,044		7,500a				7,500	7,600	3/1 6/1 9/1 12/1	750b, d 750b, d 750b, d 750b, d	250
U 50 shs. Common			8,530		9,700a				9,700	9,800	2/1 8/1	800b, d 800b, d	667
					17,200				17,200	17,400		4,600	917
					a, f				f, g	f		f	f

Legends and comments relative to above:
a = Beginning balances agreed to 19X0 working papers.
b = Traced to cash receipts.
c = Minutes examined (purchase and sales approved by the board of directors).
d = Agreed to 1099 (tax form).
e = Confirmed by tracing to broker's advice.
f = Totals footed.
g = Agreed to general ledger.

4. Purchase 500 shares of treasury stock.
5. Pay cash dividend declared in 1 above.
6. Issue additional common stock for cash.
7. Accrue bond interest payable at year-end.
8. Redeem outstanding bonds.
9. Establish appropriation for bond retirement.
10. Announce a 2-for-1 stock split.

Required

a. Identify the substantive test(s) that will be useful in verifying each transaction or event.
b. For each procedure in (a) indicate the type of audit evidence obtained.

15-32 The following covenants are extracted from the indenture of a bond issue. The indenture provides that failure to comply with its terms in any respect automatically advances the due date of the loan to the date of noncompliance (the regular due date is 20 years hence):

1. "The debtor company shall endeavor to maintain a working capital ratio of 2 to 1 at all times, and, in any fiscal year following a failure to maintain said ratio, the company shall restrict compensation of officers to a total of $100,000. Officers for this purpose shall include Chairman of the Board of Directors, President, all Vice Presidents, Secretary, and Treasurer."
2. "The debtor company shall keep all property that is security for this debt insured against loss by fire to the extent of 100% of its actual value. Policies of insurance comprising this protection shall be filed with the trustee."
3. "The debtor company shall pay all taxes legally assessed against property that is security for this debt within the time provided by law for payment without penalty, and shall deposit receipted tax bills or equally acceptable evidence of payment of same with the trustee."
4. "A sinking fund shall be deposited with the trustee by semiannual payments of $300,000, from which the trustee shall, in his discretion, purchase bonds of this issue."

Required

a. Indicate the audit procedures you would perform for each covenant.
b. Comment on any disclosure requirements that you believe are necessary.

AICPA

15-33 Andrews, CPA, has been engaged to examine the financial statements of Broadwall Corporation for the year ended December 31, 19X1. During the year, Broadwall obtained a long-term loan from a local bank pursuant to a financing agreement which provided that the

1. Loan was to be secured by the company's inventory and accounts receivable.
2. Company was to maintain a debt to equity ratio not to exceed two to one.
3. Company was not to pay dividends without permission from the bank.
4. Monthly installment payments were to commence July 1, 19X1.

In addition, during the year the company also borrowed, on a short-term basis, from the president of the company, including substantial amounts just prior to the year end.

Required

a. For purposes of Andrews' audit of the financial statements of Broadwall Corporation, what procedures should Andrews employ in examining the described loans? *Do not discuss internal control.*

b. What are the financial statement disclosures that Andrews should expect to find with respect to the loans from the president?

AICPA

15-34 The Eaton Company was incorporated July 10, 19X0, with an authorized capital as follows:

1. Common stock, Class A, 20,000 shares, par value $25 per share.
2. Common stock, Class B, 100,000 shares, par value $5 per share.

The capital stock account in the general ledger is credited with only one item in the year 19X0. This represents capital stock sold for cash, at par, as follows:

1. Class A, 12,000 shares.
2. Class B, 60,000 shares.

The sum of open certificate stubs in the stock certificate books at December 31, 19X0 indicates that 82,000 shares of stock were outstanding.

Required

a. State possible explanations for this apparent discrepancy.
b. State the procedures you would perform to determine the cause of the discrepancy.

AICPA

15-35 You are engaged in doing the audit of a corporation whose records have not previously been audited by you. The corporation has both an independent transfer agent and a registrar for its capital stock. The transfer agent maintains the record of stockholders and the registrar checks that there is no overissue of stock. Signatures of both are required to validate certificates.

It has been proposed that confirmations be obtained from both the transfer agent and the registrar as to the stock outstanding at balance-sheet date. If such confirmations agree with the books, no additional work is to be performed as to capital stock.

Required

If you agree that obtaining the confirmations as suggested would be sufficient in this case, give the justification for your position. If you do not agree, state specifically all additional steps you would take and explain your reason for taking them.

AICPA

15-36 You are a CPA engaged in an examination of the financial statements of Pate Corporation for the year ended December 31, 19X3. The financial statements and records of Pate Corporation have not been audited by a CPA in prior years.

The stockholders' equity section of Pate Corporation's balance sheet at December 31, 19X3 follows:

Stockholders' Equity

Capital stock—10,000 shares at $10 par value authorized; 5,000 shares issued and outstanding	$ 50,000
Capital contributed in excess of par value of capital stock	32,580
Retained earnings	47,320
Total stockholders' equity	$129,900

Pate Corporation was founded in 19X0. The corporation has ten stockholders and serves as its own registrar and transfer agent. There are no capital stock subscription contracts in effect.

Required

a. Prepare the detailed audit program for the examination of the three accounts comprising the Stockholders' Equity section of Pate Corporation's balance sheet. (Do not include in the audit program the verification of the results of the current year's operations.)

b. After every other figure on the balance sheet has been audited by the CPA, it might appear that the retained earnings figure is a balancing figure and requires no further verification. Why does the CPA verify retained earnings as he does the other figures on the balance sheet? Discuss.

AICPA

CASE STUDY

15-37* The Jones Company, located in Chicago, has been your client for many years. The company manufactures light machinery and has a calendar year closing. At December 31, 19X1 and 19X0, the following items appeared in the accounts applicable to marketable and investment securities. All investments in securities are carried on the books at cost and represent approximately 8% of total assets. Income from securities represents approximately 3% of income before federal income tax.

Balance Sheet Accounts	19X0	19X1
U.S. government certificates of indebtedness, 3% series D dated May 15, 19X0, due May 15, 19X2	$300,000	$300,000
Marketable securities:		
50 shares of AP Company	5,000	5,000
100 shares of UC Corporation	—	8,000
75 shares of IC Corporation	12,000	—
Investment in a 60% owned subsidiary—SUB, Inc.	50,000	50,000
Accrued interest income	1,125	1,125
Income Statement Accounts		
Interest income	9,000	9,000
Gain (loss) on sale of securities	(2,000)	3,000
Dividend income	13,000	14,000

During 19X1, there were 14 purchases and sales of marketable securities. The U.S. Government securities shown above are held at the Utah Banking Company. The AP Company securities are held in the Jones Company's safe and the UC Corporation securities are in a safety deposit box at the Chicago Bank Company, which is the company's bank. Access to the company's safe is limited to the treasurer or his assistant. Access to the safety deposit box is limited to any two of the treasurer, the assistant treasurer, or the controller. The securities of SUB, Inc. are also held by the Chicago Bank Company as collateral for a loan that the Jones Company has outstanding. SUB, Inc. has a June 30 closing and is audited by your firm.

Your tests of internal control indicate unusual strengths in the areas of cash receipts and cash disbursements. The treasurer is responsible for the physical control of securities, while the controller is responsible for the recording of all transactions affecting securities. An assistant to the assistant controller maintains an investment ledger that shows the name of each investment, the number of shares held or the face value of bonds, the date of purchase and sale, if applicable, the cost, the physical location of the securities and the income thereon. This person prepares monthly statements of securities on hand showing their description and cost. All purchases and sales of securities are authorized by the company's finance committee. The following audit program has been prepared for the examination of securities at December 31, 19X1.

1. *U.S. Government Securities:*
   a. Prepare a schedule of the securities at December 31, 19X1.
   b. Obtain direct confirmation from the Utah Banking Company as to description and amount of securities held.
   c. Trace the confirmation to the schedule and so indicate.
   d. Verify the interest earned for the year and accrued interest receivable at December 31, 19X1.
   e. Trace the appropriate totals to the general ledger accounts.
2. *Marketable Securities:*
   a. Prepare an analysis of the securities account for the year under audit, including the market value of the securities at December 31, 19X1.
   b. Count AP Company securities at the company's office at the close of business on December 31, 19X1. Inspection of the securities should be in the presence of client's representative. Note the time of count, name of client's representative, and name of the auditor on the count sheet. Accompanied by the client's representative, inspect the UC Corporation securities at the Chicago Bank Company. Inspection should be completed at the close of business on December 31, 19X1. The same information should be shown on this count sheet as is indicated to be appropriate for the count sheet mentioned above. The count sheets should show the number of shares, the full name of security, and the type of security (preferred or common shares).
   c. Vouch purchases and sales by reference to brokers' advices. Compare authorizations of the finance committee to the schedule.
   d. Compare dividends received for the year with a published dividend record.
   e. Verify the recorded gain or loss on sale of securities.
   f. Trace the appropriate totals on the schedule to the general ledger accounts.
3. *Investment in 60% Owned Subsidiary—SUB, Inc.:*
   a. Request the Chicago Bank Company to confirm that it holds the securities for SUB, Inc. as collateral for a loan. The amount payable to the bank may be confirmed concurrently.

b. Review the monthly statements of SUB, Inc. since your latest examination and compare them with the audited statements at June 30. Obtain an explanation of all unusual transactions and fluctuations.

c. Discuss the December 31, 19X1 financial statements with the management of the company. Inquire as to material amounts not recorded.

d. Establish that the intercompany accounts are in agreement at December 31.

e. Record the company's equity in the net assets and net income of SUB, Inc. at December 31, 19X1.

Required

a. List the audit procedures that you believe are appropriate and identify the audit objective(s) to which each procedure relates.

b. List the audit procedures that you believe are inappropriate and give the reasons for your conclusion.

Chapter 16

Substantive Tests of Income Statement Balances/Completing the Audit

Study Objectives

When you have concluded your study of this chapter, you should be able to

- Indicate the applicability of materiality and audit risk in verifying income statement balances.

- Describe the audit objectives for income statement accounts.

- Explain the application of analytical review procedures and tests of details to income statement balances.

- Enumerate the steps in completing the field work phase of the examination.

- Identify the steps involved in evaluating audit findings.

- State the nature and extent of the auditor's postaudit responsibilities.

As the title suggests, this chapter consists of two major sections. The first involves substantive tests of revenue and expense account balances; the second covers specific responsibilities that must be met by the auditor in completing the audit examination. In the chapter, brief consideration is also given to the auditor's postaudit responsibilities.

SUBSTANTIVE TESTS OF REVENUE AND EXPENSE BALANCES

Generally accepted auditing standards (GAAS) apply equally to both the income statement and balance sheet. Thus, the auditor must have a reasonable basis for expressing an opinion on the fairness of management's income statement representations and disclosures as well as the balance sheet.

MATERIALITY AND AUDIT RISK

Materiality levels for the income statement may be based on operating income, pretax income, or net income. The audit risk associated with the income statement relates to the likelihood that the auditor will unknowingly fail to modify his opinion when the statement is materially mistated. As explained earlier, the assessment of audit risk requires consideration of each of the components of audit risk (i.e., inherent risk, control risk, and detection risk). In making this assessment, it is often helpful to recognize that income statement balances may result from (1) routine processing of regular transactions such as purchases and sales; (2) nonroutine transactions, such as officers' bonuses and extraordinary events; and (3) management judgments, such as those for product warranties and bad debts. For routine transactions, control risk is a vital concern. This risk is inversely related to the effectiveness of the client's system of internal control. For nonroutine transactions and management judgments, both inherent and control risk may be involved depending on whether any control procedures are applicable. Based on his assessment of inherent and control risks, the auditor determines the appropriate level of detection risk that can be accepted in performing substantive tests of income statement balances. As explained previously, the auditor wants to keep audit risk at a relatively low level.

In assessing the appropriate level of detection risk for year-end substantive tests, the auditor may again elect to use the analytical review procedures employed in planning the audit. At this point in the examination, more actual financial and operating company data and more industry data should be available to the auditor. A comparison and study of the data may enable the auditor to (1) reevaluate the audit program planned for accounts targeted for additional audit effort and (2) identify new unusual relationships and unexpected fluctuations that warrant investigation.

AUDIT OBJECTIVES

As in the case of substantive tests of balance sheet accounts, it is necessary to identify audit objectives in verifying income statement accounts. Five of the audit objectives for balance sheet accounts are applicable to revenue and expense accounts as shown on the next page:

Audit Objective	Applicability to Income Statement Accounts
Clerical accuracy	Schedules supporting revenue and expense balances are mathematically correct and agree with ledger balances.
Existence or occurrence	Transactions affecting statement accounts actually occurred during the year.
Completeness	Income statement balances include all transactions that should be recorded.
Valuation or allocation	Income statement items are stated at proper amounts.
Statement presentation and disclosure	Income statement items are properly identified, presented, and classified, and accompanying disclosures are adequate.

Note that only the rights and obligations objective does not apply. In meeting these objectives, the auditor may use both analytical review procedures and tests of details of transactions and balances.

ANALYTICAL REVIEW PROCEDURES

Analytical review procedures are a powerful audit tool in obtaining audit evidence about income statement balances. This type of substantive testing may be used directly or indirectly. Direct tests occur when a revenue or an expense account is compared with other relevant data to determine the reasonableness of its balance. For example, the ratio of sales commissions to sales can be compared with the results of prior years and budget data for the current year.

In applying analytical review procedures to income statement accounts, there are many opportunities to compare the financial information with nonfinancial information as illustrated below.

Account	Analytical Review Procedure
Hotel room revenue	Number of rooms × occupancy rate × average room rate.
Tuition revenue	Number of equivalent full-time students × tuition rate for a full-time student.
Wages expense	Average number of employees per pay period × average pay per period × the number of pay periods.
Gasoline expense	Number of miles driven ÷ average miles per gallon × average per gallon cost.

In some cases, the auditor may elect to use analytical review procedures as the only direct test of some income statement balances. For example, if control risk over expenditure cycle transactions is low, expenses such as those for utilities, gasoline, and property taxes may only be examined through analytical review procedures. Similarly, if controls over revenue cycle transactions are reliable, only analytical review procedures may be applied to sales returns and allowances.

Indirect tests occur when evidence concerning income statement balances can be derived from analytical review procedures applied to related balance sheet accounts. For example, accounts receivable turnover may be used in verifying accounts receivable, and the findings may impact on whether bad debts expense is fairly stated.

The quality of the evidence provided by analytical review procedures depends primarily on the reliability of the comparative data. When outside independent relevant data are used, the evidence can be persuasive. Analytical review procedures are designed to (1) confirm normal relationships and expected fluctuations among data and (2) identify data that are abnormal or unexpected. When the former occurs, the auditor has obtained evidence as to the reasonableness of the account. When the latter occurs, it signals to the auditor that further investigation and additional evidence may be needed for the account.

The auditor's investigation will include (1) inquiry of management, (2) evaluating management's responses, and (3) where there is need, corroborating management's replies through other substantive tests. If management's replies do not provide sufficient explanation or they cannot be corroborated, the nature and extent of the auditor's investigation will be influenced by

- *Nature of the Item.* A significant fluctuation in sales in a merchandising company will receive more attention than a fluctuation in insurance expense in the same company.

- *Auditor's Knowledge of the Client's Business.* Knowledge of a prolonged labor strike may satisfactorily explain an unexpected downward fluctuation in sales.

- *Results of Other Substantive Tests.* A review of the client's aging schedule may indicate a material lengthening of the age of accounts receivable. This test may explain a significant fluctuation in bad debts expense.

- *Auditor's Study and Evaluation of Internal Accounting Control.* The extent of the auditor's investigation of an unexpected fluctuation in sales returns and allowances may vary depending on the company's internal controls over these transactions.[1]

TESTS OF DETAILS OF INCOME STATEMENT BALANCES

When control risk is low, the auditor hopes to obtain sufficient competent evidential matter concerning these balances from (1) corroborating information provided by tests of details of related balance sheet accounts and (2) analytical

---

[1]Auditing Standards Board, *Codification of Statements on Auditing Standards* (New York: American Institute of Certified Public Accountants, 1985), Auditing Section 318.09 (adapted) (hereinafter referred to and cited as AU §).

review procedures. Direct tests of details of income statement balances may be necessary when

- *Inherent Risk is High.* This may occur in the case of nonroutine transactions and management's judgments and estimates.
- *Control Risk is High.* This situation may occur when (1) internal controls for nonroutine and routine transactions are ineffective or (2) the auditor elects not to rely on the internal controls.
- *Analytical Review Procedures Reveal Unusual Relationships and Unexpected*

Prepared by: *A.E.R.* Date: 1/5/X3
Reviewed by: *R.C.P.* Date: 1/18/X3

Ragel Company
Officers' Salaries
PBC   12/31/X2   Acc #500

	Gross Salaries		
	19X2	19X1	19X0
F.J. Curtis, President	85000 ✓	80000	75000
J.W. Nielson, V.P. Purchasing	65000 ✓	58000	50000
S.A. Powers, Secretary	34000 ✓	25000	20000
R.M. Nichols, Controller	52000 ✓	44000	40000
E.J. Jarvis, Treasurer	50000 ✓	42000	36000
Total charged to General and Administrative Exp. (S-3)	286000 ✓	249000	221000
P.J. Spencer, V.P. Sales charged to Selling Exp. (S-2)	58000 ✓	52000	45000
J.E. Sperry, V.P. Production charged to Factory Ovhd. (S-1)	65000 ✓	58000	50000
Totals	409000 ⋎	359000	316000
	F	F	F

✓ = Agreed to salaries approved by Board of Directors per minutes of meeting held on 12/20/X0.

F = Footed

⋎ = Traced to General Ledger

Figure 16-1. OFFICERS' SALARIES WORKING PAPER.

Fluctuations. These circumstances were explained in the preceding section.

- *The Account Requires Analysis.* Analysis is usually required for accounts that (1) require special disclosure in the income statement, (2) contain information needed in preparing tax returns and reports for regulatory agencies such as the SEC, and (3) general account titles that suggest the likelihood of misclassifications and errors.

Accounts requiring separate analysis generally include

Legal expense and   Taxes, licenses, and fees
professional fees
                                     Rents and royalties
Maintenance and repairs
                                     Contributions
Travel and entertainment
                                     Advertising[2]
Officers' salaries and expenses

An audit working paper for officers' salaries is illustrated in Figure 16-1. Schedules of income statement accounts are usually prepared by the client.

COMPLETING THE AUDIT

Many facets of interim and year-end field work have been discussed in the previous chapters of this book. Attention here is focused on the procedures that the auditor normally performs in completing the audit. For convenience of discussion, the material is subdivided into two categories: (1) completing the field work and (2) evaluating the findings. The completion of field work involves additional substantive tests. The evaluation of findings includes the review of working papers and formulating an opinion on the financial statements. The specific steps in each category are tabulated below:

Completion of Field Work	Evaluation of Findings
• Make subsequent events review.	• Make final assessment of materiality and audit risk.
• Make inquiries of client's lawyer.	
• Identify and examine related party transactions.	• Formulate an opinion on financial statements.
• Obtain client representation letter.	• Complete review of working papers.
• Make overall analytical review.	• Make technical review of financial statements.
• Make general review of statement of changes in financial position.	• Make required communication of material weaknesses in internal accounting control.
	• Prepare and issue management letter.

[2]AICPA Audit and Accounting Manual (New York: American Institute of Certified Public Accountants, 1984), Section 6500.690.

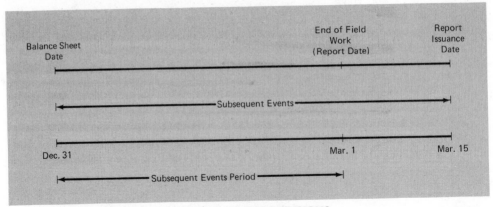

Figure 16-2. SUBSEQUENT EVENTS TIME DIMENSIONS.

SUBSEQUENT EVENTS REVIEW

The auditor's responsibility for assessing the fairness of the client's financial statements is not limited to an examination of events that occur prior to the date of the balance sheet. The auditor also has specified responsibilities for events that occur after the balance sheet date. These events are called *subsequent events*. As shown in Figure 16-2, the time frame for a subsequent event extends from the balance sheet date to the issuance of the auditor's report. Figure 16-2 also identifies a *subsequent events period*, which extends from the balance sheet date to the end of field work. During this period, the auditor is required under GAAS to apply certain procedures to discover the occurrence of any subsequent events that may have a material effect on the financial statements being reported on. As explained more fully later in the chapter, the auditor has no responsibility to discover subsequent events that occur between the end of field work and the issuance of the audit report.

Types of Events

There are two types of subsequent events.

- *Type 1* consists of those events that provide additional evidence with respect to conditions that existed at the date of the balance sheet and affect the estimates inherent in the process of preparing financial statements.

- *Type 2* consists of those events that provide evidence with respect to conditions that did not exist at the date of the balance sheet but arose subsequent to that date.[3]

Type 1 events require *adjustment* of the financial statements; Type 2 events require *disclosure* in the statements, or in very material cases, by attaching pro-

[3]Auditing Standards Board, *op. cit.,* AU § 560.03 and .05.

forma (as if) data to the financial statements. The following examples are illustrative of the two types of events:

Type 1	Type 2
Realization of recorded year-end assets, such as receivables and inventories, at a different amount than recorded.	Issuance of long-term debt or equity capital stock.
	Purchase of a business.
Settlement of recorded year-end estimated liabilities, such as litigation and product warranties, at a different amount than recorded.	Casualty losses resulting from fire or flood.

An example may help in distinguishing between the two types of events. Assume that a major customer becomes bankrupt on February 1, 19X1 and that the client considered the customer's balance to be totally collectible in making its estimate of potential uncollectible accounts in its December 31, 19X0 statements. If, on review of the subsequent event, the auditor determines that the bankruptcy was attributable to the customer's deteriorating financial position that existed (but was unknown to the client) at the balance sheet date, the client should be requested to adjust the December 31, 19X0 statements for the loss. If, on the other hand, the auditor determines that the customer was financially sound at December 31 and the bankruptcy resulted from a fire or similar catastrophe that occurred after the balance sheet date, only disclosure in the notes to the December 31 statements is needed. Ordinarily, Type 1 events require adjustment because they typically represent conditions that have accumulated over an extended period of time.

Auditor's Responsibility for Subsequent Events

The auditor should identify and evaluate subsequent events up to the date of the auditor's report that should be as of the end of field work. This responsibility is discharged in two ways: (1) by being alert for subsequent events in performing year-end substantive tests such as cutoff tests and the search for unrecorded liabilities and (2) by performing the following specific auditing procedures at or near the completion of field work:

- Read the latest available interim financial statements and compare them with the statements being reported on and make other comparisons appropriate in the circumstances.
- Inquire of management having responsibility for financial and accounting matters as to
  - Any substantial contingent liabilities or commitments listed at the balance sheet date or date of inquiry.
  - Any significant changes in capital stock, long-term debt, or working capital to the date of inquiry.

○ The current status of items previously accounted for on the basis of tentative, preliminary, or inconclusive data.

○ Whether any unusual adjustments have been made since the balance sheet date.

- Read minutes of meetings of directors, stockholders, and other appropriate committees.
- Inquire of client's legal counsel concerning litigation, claims, and assessments.
- Obtain letter of representation from client about subsequent events that would, in its opinion, require adjustment or disclosure.
- Make additional inquiries or perform additional procedures considered necessary in the circumstances.[4]

The procedures pertaining to legal counsel and the representation letter are explained later in the chapter.

Effects on Auditor's Report

Improper treatment of subsequent events will require modification of the auditor's standard report when the effect on the financial statements is material. Depending on materiality, either a qualified or adverse opinion should be issued, as is explained in Chapter 17.

INQUIRIES OF CLIENT'S LAWYERS

Litigation, claims, and assessments (LCA) may have a material affect on a company's financial statements. Thus, in performing an examination in accordance with GAAS, the auditor must determine whether LCA are reported in conformity with GAAP. Each of these matters is included under the term *loss contingencies* in *FASB Statement No. 5, Accounting for Contingencies*. Loss contingencies should be recorded in the financial statements when (1) the loss is *probable* and (2) the amount of the loss can be reasonably estimated. Only disclosure may be required when there is just a *possibility* of a loss to the enterprise or the amount of the probable loss cannot be reasonably estimated.

Audit Considerations

With respect to LCA, the auditor should obtain evidential matter on

- The existence of a condition, situation, or set of circumstances indicating an uncertainty as to the possible loss to an entity arising from litigation, claims, and assessments.
- The period in which the underlying cause for legal action occurred.
- The degree of probability of an unfavorable outcome.
- The amount or range of potential loss.[5]

---

[4] Auditing Standards Board, *op. cit.*, AU § 560.12. (adapted)

[5] Auditing Standards Board, *op. cit.*, AU § 337.04.

LCA should be under the direct purview of management. In such cases, management represents the primary source of information about the existence of such matters. Hence, the auditor should obtain from management (1) a description and evaluation concerning LCA that existed at the balance sheet date and (2) assurance from management, preferably in writing, of the existence of any unasserted claims. Other auditing procedures such as the reading of the minutes of directors' meetings and a review of contracts and loan agreements may also disclose LCA.

The auditor should examine supporting documentation in the client's files pertaining to all such matters that have come to his attention. It should be recognized, however, that the auditor normally does not possess sufficient legal skills to make an informed judgment on all such matters. Accordingly, the auditor needs the assistance of an outside specialist. A letter of audit inquiry to the client's outside legal counsel is the auditor's primary means of obtaining corroborating information on management's assertions concerning LCA.

Form and Content of Inquiry

A letter of audit inquiry is illustrated in Figure 16-3. It should be sent by management to each lawyer who has been engaged and has devoted substantive attention during the year to either (1) pending or threatened LCA or (2) unasserted claims and assessments that management believes would result in an unfavorable outcome if asserted. The letter should ask the lawyer to respond directly to the auditor. When the lawyer refuses to respond, or if he has not given enough attention to items to be able to respond, it may be necessary for the auditor to modify his report.

RELATED PARTY TRANSACTIONS

A related party transaction occurs when the relationship between the transacting parties may not permit one of the parties to pursue fully its own separate interests. Examples include transactions (1) between a parent company and its subsidiary, (2) between or among subsidiaries of a common parent, or (3) between a company and its executive officers. An examination made in accordance with GAAS cannot assure that all related party transactions will be discovered. However, the auditor is required to

- Be aware of the possibility that material related party transactions may have occurred.
- Apply procedures that may identify such transactions.
- Determine whether identified related party transactions are properly accounted for, including the appropriateness of financial statement disclosures.

Related party transactions may be discovered through auditing procedures normally performed in an examination. In addition, the auditor should consider applying additional procedures that are specifically directed to related

---

XYZ Corporation
Midtown, Texas 48100

[Name and Address of Legal Counsel]

Dear Sirs:

In connection with an examination of our financial statements at [balance sheet date] and for the [period] then ended, management of the Company has prepared, and furnished to our auditors [name and address of auditors], a description and evaluation of certain contingencies, including those set forth below involving matters with respect to which you have been engaged and to which you have devoted substantive attention on behalf of the Company in the form of legal consultation or representation. These contingencies are regarded by management of the Company as material for this purpose. Your response should include matters that existed at [balance sheet date] and during the period from that date to the date of your response.

Pending or Threatened Litigation
[Description Provided]

Unasserted Claims and Assessments
[Description Provided]

Please furnish to our auditors such explanation, if any, that you consider necessary to supplement the foregoing information, including an explanation of those matters as to which your views may differ from those stated and an identification of the omission of any contingencies or a statement that the list of such matters is complete.

We understand that whenever, in the course of performing legal services for us with respect to a matter recognized to involve an unasserted possible claim or assessment that may call for financial statement disclosure, if you have formed a professional conclusion that we should disclose or consider disclosure concerning such possible claim or assessment, as a matter of professional responsibility to us, you will so advise us and will consult with us concerning the question of such disclosure and the applicable requirements of *Statement of Financial Accounting Standards No. 5*. Please specifically confirm to our auditors that our understanding is correct.

Please specifically identify the nature of and reasons for any limitation on your response. A return envelope is enclosed for your reply.

Very truly yours,

_____
Signature of Client

Figure 16-3. LETTER OF AUDIT INQUIRY. (Source: Auditing Standards Board, *op. cit.*, AU § 337A.01.)

party transactions. These include reviewing (1) the board of director minutes for the authorization of such transactions, (2) conflict-of-interest statements obtained by the company from its management, and (3) related party information submitted in filings with regulatory commissions such as the SEC.[6]

---

[6]Auditing Standards Board, *op. cit.*, AU § 334.08.

In examining identified related party transactions, the auditor is not expected to determine whether a particular transaction would have occurred if the parties had not been related, or assuming the transaction did take place, what the exchange price and terms would have been.[7] He is required, however, to determine the substance of the transactions and their effects on the financial statements. To obtain sufficient competent evidential matter about related party transactions, the auditor's procedures should extend beyond inquiry of management.

CLIENT REPRESENTATION LETTER

The auditor is required to obtain certain written representations from management in meeting the third standard of field work. Client representations are commonly referred to as *rep letters*. The objectives of written representations from management are to

- Confirm oral representations given to the auditor.
- Document the continuing appropriateness of such representations.
- Reduce the possibility of misunderstandings concerning management's representations.
- Impress on management that it has the primary responsibility for the financial statements.

A rep letter complements other auditing procedures, and it may bring to light matters not otherwise discovered by the auditor.

Written representations from management may be limited to matters that either individually or collectively are considered to be material to the financial statements. Such representations should be prepared on the client's stationery, addressed to the auditor, signed by appropriate officers and employees, and dated as of the date of the auditor's report. In many audits, the auditor will draft the representations that subsequently become the responsibility of the individual who signs the letter.

Content of Representation Letter

The professional literature identifies 20 items that may be included in a rep letter. A partial listing is as follows:

- Acknowledgment of management's responsibility for the financial statements.
- Completeness and availability of the accounting records and minutes of meetings of stockholders, directors, and audit committees.

---

[7]Auditing Standards Board, *op. cit.*, AU § 334.12.

- Absence of unrecorded transactions and errors and irregularities in the financial statements.
- Compliance with (or violations of) laws and regulations.
- Existence (or nonexistence) of compensating balances, related party transactions, contingencies, and losses from contractual commitments.
- Information concerning subsequent events.
- Management's plans or intentions that may affect the carrying value or classification of assets and liabilities.[8]

(Date of Auditor's Report)

(To the Independent Auditor)

In connection with your examination of the (identification of financial statements) or (name of client) as of (date) and for the (period of examination) for the purpose of expressing an opinion as to whether the (consolidated) financial statements present fairly the financial position, results of operations, and changes in financial position of (name of client) in conformity with generally accepted accounting principles (other comprehensive basis of accounting), we confirm, to the best of our knowledge and belief, the following representations made to you during your examination.

1. We are responsible for the fair presentation in the (consolidated) financial statements of financial position, results of operations, and changes in financial position in conformity with generally accepted accounting principles (other comprehensive basis of accounting).

2. We have made available to you all
   a. Financial records and related data.
   b. Minutes of the meetings of stockholders, directors, and committees of directors, or summaries of actions of recent meetings for which minutes have not yet been prepared.

3. There have been no
   a. Irregularities involving management or employees who have significant roles in the system of internal accounting control.
   b. Irregularities involving other employees that could have a material effect on the financial statements.
   c. Communications from regulatory agencies concerning noncompliance with, or deficiencies in, financial reporting practices that could have a material effect on the financial statements.

4. We have no plans or intentions that may materially affect the carrying value or classification of assets and liabilities.

5. The following have been properly recorded or disclosed in the financial statements:
   a. Related party transactions and related amounts receivable or payable, including sales, purchases, loans, transfers, leasing arrangements, and guarantees.
   b. Capital stock repurchase options or agreements or capital stock reserved for options, warrants, conversions, or other requirements.
   c. Arrangements with financial institutions involving compensating balances or other arrangements involving restrictions on cash balances and line-of-credit or similar arrangements.

---

[8] Auditing Standards Board, *op. cit.*, AU § 333.04.

d. Agreements to repurchase assets previously sold.

6. There are no

 a. Violations or possible violations of laws or regulations whose affects should be considered for disclosure in the financial statements or as a basis for recording a loss contingency.

 b. Other material liabilities or gain or loss contingencies that are required to be accrued or disclosed by *Statement of Financial Accounting Standards No. 5.*

7. There are no unasserted claims or assessments that our lawyer has advised us are probable of assertion and must be disclosed in accordance with *Statement of Financial Accounting Standards No. 5.*

8. There are no material transactions that have not been properly recorded in the accounting records underlying the financial statements.

9. Provision, when material, has been made to reduce excess or obsolete inventories to their estimated net realizable value.

10. The company has satisfactory title to all owned assets, and there are no liens or encumbrances on such assets nor has any asset been pledged.

11. Provision has been made for any material loss to be sustained in the fulfillment of, or from inability to fulfill, any sales commitments.

12. Provision has been made for any material loss to be sustained as a result of purchase commitments for inventory quantities in excess of normal requirements or at prices in excess of the prevailing market prices.

13. We have complied with all aspects of contractual agreements that would have a material effect on the financial statements on the event of noncompliance.

14. No events have occurred subsequent to the balance sheet date that would require adjustment to, or disclosure in, the financial statements.

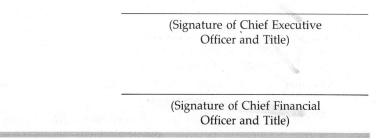

                         (Signature of Chief Executive
                               Officer and Title)

                         (Signature of Chief Financial
                               Officer and Title)

Figure 16-4. CLIENT REPRESENTATION LETTER: (Source: Auditing Standards Board, *op. cit.,* AU § 333A.05).

Representations concerning the foregoing matters normally should be signed by the chief executive officer and the chief financial officer. A rep letter is illustrated in Figure 16-4.

Effects of Representation Letter

A rep letter is not a substitute for any auditing procedures necessary to provide a reasonable basis for an opinion on the financial statements. Such evidence is judged to have relatively low reliability because of possible management bias.

The refusal of management to furnish a written representation constitutes a limitation on the scope of the auditor's examination that may preclude the issuance of a standard audit report. A scope limitation may also exist when the auditor is not able to perform audit procedures considered necessary in the circumstances to verify essential data in the management representation letter.

OVERALL ANALYTICAL REVIEW

The objective of the typical audit engagement is the expression of an opinion on the fairness of the financial statements taken as a whole. It is essential therefore for the auditor to apply overall analytical review procedures to the final draft of the client's financial statements. In making overall analytical review tests, the auditor may emphasize statement categories and totals. Analytical review procedures that may be performed at the end of the year include the following:

- Compare financial statement subtotals and totals with corresponding prior period amounts and current year budget data.
- Calculate relevant ratios and compare with (1) prior year and current year budgeted ratios and (2) current year ratios of major competitors or composite industry data.
- Compare nonfinancial data, such as sales volume, production volume, and number of employees by location, with prior year and current year planned activity.
- Compare common-size statements to similar statements of prior years.

Both systematic comparison (i.e., comparison of current-year data with budgeted or forecast data for the same period and with actual results of one or more preceding periods) and an analysis of interrelationships should be made. In addition, comparisons of data, such as gross profit margin and net income, with similar industry data may be helpful in judging the fairness of the overall results. Key financial relationships, such as the current ratio, debt-to-equity ratio, book value per share of common stock, and rates of return on assets and common stock equity, are often calculated and systematically compared with other data.

The overall analytical review should extend to the working papers to determine that there are adequate explanations of unusual fluctuations found in making comparative analyses of individual account balances. An overall analytical review provides the auditor with a final opportunity to evaluate the fairness of the financial statements and investigate any unusual fluctuations and questionable items.

General Review of Statement of Changes in Financial Position

1. Verify the clerical accuracy of the statement by recalculation.

2. Ascertain that the statement format (e.g., concept of funds) is the most informative in the circumstances.

3. Ascertain that the statement discloses all important aspects of the company's financing and investing activities.

4. Determine that the statement discloses the important sources and uses of cash (or working capital).

5. Ascertain that the format correctly and prominently shows funds provided from or used by operations and funds provided from or used by extraordinary items.

6. Verify that the statement is based on the balances shown in the audited financial statements at the beginning and end of the period covered by the audit.

7. Establish that a statement of changes in financial position is presented for each period for which an income statement is presented.

8. Trace, match, or agree statement amounts to like amounts in other financial statements and/or in the working papers.

9. Ascertain that the term "funds" used in the presentation is consistent with prior years.

10. Establish that a comparative schedule of working capital elements is presented.

Figure 16-5. AUDIT PROGRAM: STATEMENT OF CHANGES IN FINANCIAL POSITION.

GENERAL REVIEW OF STATEMENT OF CHANGES IN FINANCIAL POSITION

The statement of changes in financial position is a basic financial statement. Thus, the auditor is required to express an opinion on the fairness of its presentation. Ordinarily, it is not necessary for the auditor to perform substantive tests on specific items in the statement because the evidence from tests of income statement and balance sheet accounts should provide sufficient verification for the items. It is usually necessary,however, for the auditor to perform the general steps shown in Figure 16-5.

The auditor should recognize that substantial flexibility in form, content, and terminology is permitted in the statement of changes in financial position. For example, replacing working capital with cash in expressing the changes in financial position is considered to be a reclassification rather than a change in an accounting principle.[9] When changes in the method of presentation materially affect the comparability of the statements, they should be disclosed in the statements and the prior year's statements should be restated using the new method. If this is done, the auditor can issue a standard audit report.

[9]Auditing Standards Board, *op. cit.*, AU § 420.15.

FINAL ASSESSMENT OF MATERIALITY AND AUDIT RISK

In formulating an opinion on the financial statements, the auditor should assimilate all the evidence gathered during his examination. An essential prerequisite in deciding on the opinion to express is a final assessment of materiality and audit risk. The starting point in this process is to aggregate errors that were found in examining each account that were not corrected by the client. In some cases, the uncorrected errors may have been individually immaterial so that no correction was requested by the auditor. In other cases, the client may have been unwilling to make the corrections that were requested. The next step in the process is to determine the effects of the aggregate errors on net income and other financial statement categories to which the errors pertain, such as current assets or current liabilities.

The auditor's determination of the aggregate errors in the current period should include the following components:

- Uncorrected errors specifically identified through substantive tests of details of transactions and balances (referred to as *known errors*).
- Projected uncorrected errors estimated through audit sampling techniques.
- Estimated errors detected through analytical review procedures and quantified by other auditing procedures.

The total of these components is referred to as *likely error*. The auditor's assessment of aggregate likely error may also include the effect on the current period's financial statements of any uncorrected likely errors from a prior period when including them may lead to the conclusion that the statements are materially misstated. A working paper illustrating one approach to analyzing aggregate error is shown in Figure 16-6.

The data that have been accumulated are then compared to the auditor's preliminary judgments concerning materiality that were made in planning the audit. It will be recalled that planning materiality extended to both the individual account and the financial statement levels. If any adjustments in planned materiality have been made during the course of the examination they should, of course, be included in this assessment.

In planning the audit, the auditor specified an acceptable level of audit risk. Likely error directly affects audit risk. As aggregate likely error increases, the risk that the financial statements may be materially misstated also increases.[10] When the auditor concludes that audit risk is at an acceptable level, he can proceed to formulate the opinion supported by his findings. However, if the auditor believes audit risk is not acceptable, he should either (1) perform additional substantive tests or (2) convince the client to make the corrections necessary to reduce the risk of material misstatement to an acceptable level.

[10]Auditing Standards Board, *op. cit.*, AU § 312.32.

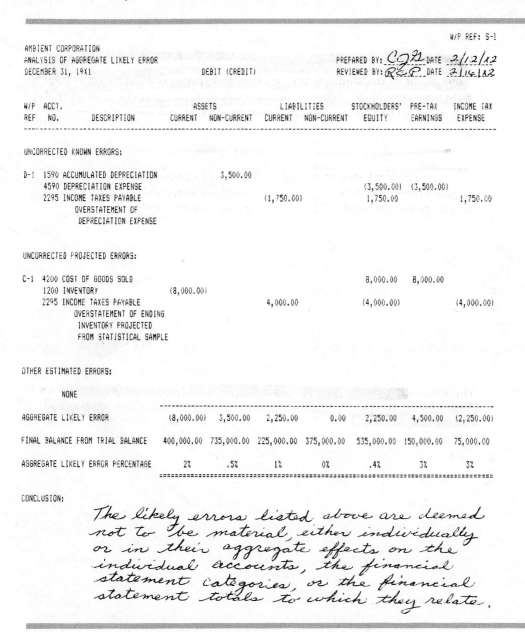

AMBIENT CORPORATION
ANALYSIS OF AGGREGATE LIKELY ERROR
DECEMBER 31, 19X1   DEBIT (CREDIT)

PREPARED BY: CJ2   DATE 2/12/12
REVIEWED BY: R&P   DATE 3/14/12

W/P REF	ACCT. NO.	DESCRIPTION	ASSETS CURRENT	ASSETS NON-CURRENT	LIABILITIES CURRENT	LIABILITIES NON-CURRENT	STOCKHOLDERS' EQUITY	PRE-TAX EARNINGS	INCOME TAX EXPENSE
		UNCORRECTED KNOWN ERRORS:							
D-1	1590	ACCUMULATED DEPRECIATION		3,500.00					
	4590	DEPRECIATION EXPENSE					(3,500.00)	(3,500.00)	
	2295	INCOME TAXES PAYABLE			(1,750.00)		1,750.00		1,750.00
		OVERSTATEMENT OF DEPRECIATION EXPENSE							
		UNCORRECTED PROJECTED ERRORS:							
C-1	4200	COST OF GOODS SOLD					8,000.00	8,000.00	
	1200	INVENTORY	(8,000.00)						
	2295	INCOME TAXES PAYABLE			4,000.00		(4,000.00)		(4,000.00)
		OVERSTATEMENT OF ENDING INVENTORY PROJECTED FROM STATISTICAL SAMPLE							
		OTHER ESTIMATED ERRORS:							
		NONE							
		AGGREGATE LIKELY ERROR	(8,000.00)	3,500.00	2,250.00	0.00	2,250.00	4,500.00	(2,250.00)
		FINAL BALANCE FROM TRIAL BALANCE	400,000.00	735,000.00	225,000.00	375,000.00	535,000.00	150,000.00	75,000.00
		AGGREGATE LIKELY ERROR PERCENTAGE	2%	.5%	1%	0%	.4%	3%	3%

CONCLUSION:

The likely errors listed above are deemed not to be material, either individually or in their aggregate effects on the individual accounts, the financial statement categories, or the financial statement totals to which they relate.

Figure 16-6. ANALYSIS OF AGGREGATE LIKELY ERROR WORKING PAPER.

OPINION ON FINANCIAL STATEMENTS

During the course of an audit engagement, a variety of audit tests are performed. These tests often are performed by staff personnel whose participation in the audit may be limited to a few areas or accounts. As the tests for each functional area or statement item are completed, the staff auditor is expected to summarize his findings.

It is necessary in completing the audit for the separate findings to be summarized and evaluated for the purpose of expressing an opinion on the financial statements taken as a whole. The ultimate responsibility for these steps rests with the partner in charge of the engagement. In some cases, the audit manager makes the initial determinations that are then carefully reviewed by the partner.

Before reaching a final decision on the opinion, a conference generally is held with the client. At this meeting, the auditor reports his findings orally and attempts to provide rationale for proposed adjustments and/or additional disclosures. Management, in turn, may attempt to defend its position. In the end, some agreement is generally reached on the changes to be made and the auditor can proceed to issue a standard audit report. When such an agreement is not obtained, the auditor may not be able to issue an unqualified opinion.

Communication of the auditor's opinion is made through an audit report. Audit reports are explained in Chapters 17 and 18.

REVIEW OF WORKING PAPERS

In Chapter 4, the first-level review of working papers by a supervisor was explained. It will be recalled that the review is made to evaluate the work done, the evidence obtained, and the conclusions reached by the preparer of the working paper. Additional reviews of the working papers are made at the end of field work by members of the audit team. The levels of review that may be made in completing the audit are:

Reviewer	Nature of Review
Manager	Reviews working papers prepared by seniors and reviews some or all of the working papers reviewed by seniors.
Partner in charge of engagement	Reviews working papers prepared by managers and reviews other working papers on a selective basis.

The partner's review of the working papers is designed to obtain assurance that

- The work done by subordinates has been accurate and thorough.
- The judgments exercised by subordinates were reasonable and appropriate in the circumstances.
- The audit engagement has been completed in accordance with the conditions and terms specified in the engagement letter.

- All significant accounting, auditing, and reporting questions raised during the examination have been properly resolved.
- The working papers support the auditor's opinion.
- Generally accepted auditing standards have been met.

A checklist may be used in reviewing working papers. The checklist consists of a series of relevant questions and spaces for answers. A common format is illustrated in Figure 16-7. In some cases, the checklist also includes space for comments.

Some firms require an independent "cold" review of the working papers by a partner who did not participate in the audit. The rationale for this review is based on the objectivity of the reviewer who may challenge matters approved by earlier reviewers. Thus, this review provides additional assurance that all GAAS have been met in the engagement.

TECHNICAL REVIEW OF FINANCIAL STATEMENTS

Many public accounting firms have detailed financial statement checklists that are completed by the auditor who performs the initial review of the financial statements. The completed checklist is then reviewed by the manager and partner in charge of the engagement. Prior to the release of the audit report on a publicly held client, there may also be a technical review of the statements by a partner who was not a member of the audit team.

The checklists include matters pertaining to the form and content of each of the basic financial statements as well as to required disclosures. Most firms now have separate checklists for SEC and non-SEC clients. The completed checklist and the findings of the reviewers should be included in the working papers.

	Yes	No	N/A
Do the working papers contain evidence of proper planning and supervision?	☐	☐	☐
Are all open points cleared and all questions answered?	☐	☐	☐
Are overall evaluations of internal controls included in the working papers?	☐	☐	☐
Is there documentation of tests and evaluation of the internal audit function, and of the nature and extent of reliance thereon?	☐	☐	☐
Are written conclusions as to the audit work for each significant account or group of related accounts included in the working papers?	☐	☐	☐
Do the working papers contain a summary of significant matters relative to audit procedures or financial statement presentation that were brought to the attention of the partner or principal by the manager?	☐	☐	☐

Figure 16-7. PARTIAL WORKING PAPER REVIEW CHECKLIST.

COMMUNICATION OF MATERIAL WEAKNESSES

As briefly explained in Chapter 5, the auditor is required to communicate material weaknesses in internal accounting control to senior management and the board of directors (or its audit committee). It will be recalled that a *material weakness* is a condition in which there is more than a relatively low risk that errors or irregularities, in amounts material to the financial statements, may occur and not be detected within a timely period by employees in the normal course of performing their assigned functions.

The communication, which may be oral or written, should be made at the earliest practicable date following the completion of the auditor's study and evaluation of internal accounting control. A suggested form of written communication is illustrated in Chapter 18.

In the absence of material weaknesses, the auditor is not required to communicate that fact. When there are material weaknesses for which management believes corrective action is not practicable, the auditor may limit his communication to a summary of such weaknesses and a statement to the effect that correction is impracticable. The auditor may also include comments on corrective action that has been taken or is in process. In addition, an auditor may elect to disclose immaterial weaknesses in internal accounting control. The auditor's communication on material weaknesses in internal accounting control may be issued separately or be incorporated in a management letter. The auditor's communication on internal accounting control may be useful to management in its evaluation of compliance with the internal accounting control provisions of the Foreign Corrupt Practices Act. Because of its importance in this regard, extra care should be exercised by the auditor in identifying a weakness as material.

MANAGEMENT LETTER

During the course of an audit engagement, auditors observe many facets of the client's business organization and operations. At the conclusion of an examination, many auditors believe it is desirable to write a letter to management that contains recommendations for improving the efficiency and effectiveness of those matters that were noticed during the course of the audit. The issuance of such letters has become an integral part of the services rendered by many auditors to their clients. A management letter tangibly demonstrates the auditors' continuing interest in the welfare and future of the client.

Matters that are relevant to management letters should be noted in the audit working papers as the audit progresses to insure that they are not overlooked. Subsequently, the working papers should provide adequate documentation of the management letter comments. Such support will also be useful in any discussions with management about the comments.

Management letters should be carefully prepared, well-organized, and written in a constructive tone. Prompt issuance of the letters creates a favorable impression and may encourage both an early and positive response by management.

Management letters may include comments on

- Internal accounting control weaknesses that are not considered to be material.
- The accounting and information system, including EDP.
- Administrative controls pertaining to achieving the objectives of the organization.
- Management of resources such as cash, inventories, and investments.
- Tax-related matters.

An example of a management letter is shown in Figure 16-8.

POSTAUDIT RESPONSIBILITIES

This section pertains to the auditor's responsibilities following the completion of field work. It includes a consideration of

- Subsequent events occurring between the date and issuance of the auditor's report.
- The discovery of existing facts.
- The discovery of omitted procedures.

EVENTS BETWEEN DATE AND ISSUANCE OF REPORT

As shown in Figure 16-2, a time interval of one to two weeks may elapse between the end of field work and the actual issuance of the audit report. The auditor has no responsibility to make any inquiries or to perform any auditing procedures during this time period to discover any material subsequent events.[11] However, if knowledge of such an event comes to the auditor's attention, he should consider whether there should be disclosure in or adjustment of the financial statements for the event. When adjustment is required and management appropriately modifies the statements, the auditor may issue a standard audit report. When required disclosure is made by management, the auditor may also issue a standard report providing the reports is *redated* to coincide with the date of the subsequent event. Alternatively, the auditor may *dual date* the audit report. Under this course of action, the original date is retained except for the dating of the subsequent event. For example, dual dating might say

February 28, 19X1, except for the information in Note A for which the date is March 7, 19X1.

[11] Auditing Standards Board, *op. cit.,* AU § 530.02.

Reddy & Abel
Certified Public Accountants
465 City Center Building
Marian, New York 11748

March 31, 19X1

Dear Mr. Jones:

Our examination of the financial statements of OYE Inc. for the year ended December 31, 19X0 has disclosed certain opportunities for improvements in your organization and operations. Items that we believe should be brought to your attention are set forth below.

Internal Accounting Control

One individual is both the cashier and the custodian of marketable securities. We believe these duties should be segregated between two employees in order to minimize the possibility of unauthorized purchases and sales of marketable securities.

Data Processing

Because of the size of the Company and the widespread geographic location of its operating entities, we believe you should begin to develop a long-range data processing plan. Without such a plan, the Company might find itself in the position of utilizing several service bureaus, developing noncoordinated procedures, or possibly acquiring small pieces of equipment at outlying locations that are not compatible.

Administrative Controls

Common Stock

As in the prior years, there is no effective means to control the number of stock certificates outstanding. We recommend that all stock certificates outstanding be assigned a permanent number and that new certificates be issued from a stub-type stock book using prenumbered certificates. Periodically, the open stubs in the stock book should be reconciled to shares outstanding.

Insurance Coverage

The Company presently carries life insurance coverage on the President. We recommend that life insurance coverage be considered for other executives vital to the Company's continued success.

Tax Matters

Sales Tax on Property and Equipment Purchases

Sales taxes paid on purchases of property and equipment are capitalized in the financial statements and tax returns. Such taxes can be deducted for tax purposes.

This letter is issued solely for the information of the Company's management; it should not be presented or quoted to anyone outside the Company. We would be pleased to discuss the matters reported or to answer any questions you may have at your convenience.

Yours very truly,

Ivan M. Reddy

Reddy & Abel
Certified Public Accountants

Figure 16-8. MANAGEMENT LETTER.

Dual dating is the most common practice because redating of the entire report extends the auditor's overall responsibility beyond the completion of field work. Under redating, the auditor should extend his subsequent events review procedures to the later date. If management refuses to make the necessary changes for the event, the auditor should qualify his opinion and dual-date his report.

DISCOVERY OF EXISTING FACTS

The auditor has no responsibility for the postaudit discovery of facts existing (but unknown) at the date of the audit report. However, if (1) the auditor becomes aware of such facts and (2) the facts may have affected the report that was issued, the auditor is required to ascertain the reliability of the information. When the investigation confirms the existence of the fact and the auditor believes the information is important to those relying or likely to rely on the financial statements, the auditor should take steps to prevent future reliance on the audit report.

The preferred result is the preparation of revised statements by the client and the issuance of a revised audit report as soon as practicable. If the client refuses to disclose the newly discovered facts, the auditor should notify each member of the board of directors of such refusal and take the following steps to prevent futher reliance on his report:

- Notify the client that the audit report must no longer be associated with the financial statements.
- Notify the regulatory agencies having jurisdiction over the client that the report should no longer be relied on.
- Notify (generally vià the regulatory agency) each individual known to be relying on the statements that the report should no longer be relied on.[12]

DISCOVERY OF OMITTED PROCEDURES

After the date of the audit report, the auditor may conclude that one or more auditing procedures considered necessary in the circumstances was omitted from his examination. Auditing standards do not require the auditor to conduct any postaudit reviews of his work. However, discovery of an omitted procedure may result from a post-engagement review performed during a firm's quality-control inspection program or during an outside peer review.

On discovery of an omitted procedure, the auditor should assess its importance to his ability to currently support the opinion expressed on the financial statements. A review of the working papers and a reevaluation of the overall scope of the audit may enable the auditor to conclude that he can still support his previously expressed opinion. Alternatively, if he decides that

[12]Auditing Standards Board, *op. cit.*, AU § 561.08.

the opinion cannot be supported and he believes persons are currently relying on his report, the auditor should promptly perform the omitted procedures or alternative procedures that would provide a satisfactory basis for his opinion.[13]

When a satisfactory basis for an opinion is obtained and the evidence supports the opinion expressed, the auditor has no further responsibility. However, if the performance of the omitted procedures reveals facts existing at the report date that would have changed his previously expressed opinion, the auditor should follow the notification procedures described in the last paragraph of the preceding section to prevent further reliance on his report. If the auditor is unable to perform the omitted or alternative procedures, he should consult his attorney to determine an appropriate course of action concerning his responsibilities.

CONCLUDING COMMENTS

This chapter completes the explanation of substantive tests of account balances and the auditor's responsibilities in completing the audit. When considered in concert with Parts I and II of this book, six of the ten GAAS have been explained. We now proceed to Part IV, where in-depth consideration is given to the four reporting standards and other auditor responsibilities.

REVIEW QUESTIONS

16-1 Evaluate income statement balances as to materiality and audit risk.

16-2 Indicate the applicability of the audit objectives to income statement accounts.

16-3 a. How important are analytical review procedures in verifying income statement balances?
b. What factors affect the auditor's investigation of unusual relationships and fluctuations?

16-4 a. What are the auditor's primary means of obtaining evidence about revenue and expense accounts?
b. When may the auditor elect to perform detailed tests of income statement balances?

16-5 Enumerate the steps involved in completing field work.

16-6 a. What is meant by the term *subsequent events?*
b. Identify the two types of subsequent events and the criteria used in distinguishing between them.

16-7 a. Explain the auditor's responsibility for subsequent events.
b. How does he discharge this responsibility?

16-8 a. What information should be verified about litigation, claims, and assessments (LCA)?
b. Contrast the value of (1) management's responses and (2) lawyer's responses to the auditor's inquiries about LCA?

---

[13] Auditing Standards Board, *op. cit.*, AU § 390.05.

16-9 a. Can an examination in accordance with GAAS be expected to discover all related party transactions? Discuss.

b. What approach is followed by the auditor in discovering related party transactions?

16-10 a. List the objectives that are met by a client representation letter.

b. What effect may a "rep" letter have on the auditor's examination and audit report?

16-11 a. What factors should be emphasized in making an overall analytical review?

b. State the purposes served by an overall analytical review.

16-12 The auditor must examine the specific items in the statement of changes in financial position. Do you agree? Why or why not?

16-13 a. What are the purposes of the auditor's final assessment of materiality and audit risk?

b. Distinguish between known error and likely error.

16-14 a. How and by whom is the opinion on the financial statements formulated?

b. How may proposed adjustments and disclosures be handled?

16-15 a. Identify the reviewer and the nature of his review of working papers.

b. What are the objectives of the partner's review of working papers?

16-16 a. Who are the principal recipients of the auditor's required communication of material weaknesses in internal control?

b. Indicate the form and timing of the communication.

16-17 a. What purpose is served by management letters?

b. List the types of data that may be included in management letters.

16-18 a. Explain the auditor's responsibility for subsequent events occurring after completion of field work but before issuance of his audit report.

b. What is meant by dual dating an audit report?

16-19 a. What responsibility does the auditor have for the postaudit discovery of facts existing at the date of his report?

b. Identify the steps the auditor should take when the client refuses to make disclosure of the newly discovered facts.

16-20 a. What responsibility does the auditor have for omitted audit procedures after the report date?

b. Indicate the possible consequences of the auditor's investigations of omitted procedures.

OBJECTIVE QUESTIONS FROM PROFESSIONAL EXAMINATIONS

Indicate the *best* answer for each of the following multiple choice questions.

16-21 These questions pertain to subsequent events.

1. Which of the following subsequent events will be *least* likely to result in an adjustment to the financial statements?

a. Culmination of events affecting the realization of accounts receivable owned as of the balance sheet date.

b. Culmination of events affecting the realization of inventories owned as of the balance sheet date.

c. Material changes in the settlement of liabilities that were estimated as of the balance sheet date.

     d. Material changes in the quoted market prices of listed investment securities since the balance sheet date.

2. Which of the following material events occurring subsequent to the December 31, 19X3, balance sheet would *not* ordinarily result in an adjustment to the financial statements before they are issued on March 2, 19X4?

     a. Write-off of a receivable from a debtor who had suffered from deteriorating financial condition for the past six years. The debtor filed for bankruptcy on January 23, 19X4.

     b. Acquisition of a subsidiary on January 23, 19X4. Negotiations had begun in December of 19X3.

     c. Settlement of extended litigation on January 23, 19X4 in excess of the recorded year-end liability.

     d. A 3 for 5 reverse stock split consummated on January 23, 19X4.

16-22 These questions relate to inquiries of client's lawyers.

1. The letter of inquiry that is ordinarily sent to lawyers with whom management consulted concerning litigation, claims, and assessments is the auditor's method of

     a. Identifying all possible unasserted claims.

     b. Obtaining admissions of irregularities that are safeguarded by privileged communications laws.

     c. Obtaining corroboration of information furnished by the client.

     d. Identifying impaired assets and incurred liabilities.

2. An attorney is responding to an independent auditor as a result of the audit client's letter of inquiry. The attorney may appropriately limit the response to

     a. Asserted claims and litigation.

     b. Matters to which the attorney has given substantive attention in the form of legal consultation or representation.

     c. Asserted, overtly threatened, or pending claims and litigation.

     d. Items that have an extremely high probability of being resolved to the client's detriment.

3. A lawyer limits a response concerning a litigated claim because the lawyer is unable to determine the likelihood of an unfavorable outcome. Which type of opinion should the auditor express if the litigation is adequately disclosed and the range of potential loss is material in relation to the client's financial statements considered as a whole?

     a. Adverse.

     b. Unaudited.

     c. Qualified.

     d. Unqualified.

16-23 These questions involve client representation letters.

1. If managment refuses to furnish certain written representations that the auditor believes are essential, which of the following is appropriate?

     a. The auditor can rely on oral evidence relating to the matter as a basis for an unqualified opinion.

     b. The client's refusal does *not* constitute a scope limitation that may lead to a modification of the opinion.

     c. This may have an effect on the auditor's ability to rely on other representations of management.

     d. The auditor should issue an adverse opinion because of management's refusal.

2. A written representation from a client's management that, among other matters, acknowledges responsibility for the fair presentation of financial statements, should normally be signed by the
   a. Chief executive officer and the chief financial officer.
   b. Chief financial officer and the chairman of the board of directors.
   c. Chairman of the audit committee of the board of directors.
   d. Chief executive officer, the chairman of the board of directors, and the client's lawyer.
3. Which of the following expressions is *least* likely to be included in a client's representation letter?
   a. No events have occurred subsequent to the balance sheet date that require adjustment to, or disclosure in, the financial statements.
   b. The company has complied with all aspects of contractual agreements that would have a material effect on the financial statements in the event of noncompliance.
   c. Management acknowledges responsibility for illegal actions committed by employees.
   d. Management has made available all financial statements and related data.

16-24 These questions pertain to the auditor's post-audit responsibilities.

1. After issuance of the auditor's report, the auditor has *no* obligation to make any further inquiries with respect to audited financial statements covered by an auditor's report unless a
   a. Contingency is resolved.
   b. Development occurs that may affect the client's ability to continue as a going concern.
   c. Material defalcation ensues.
   d. History of significant non-arms-length related party transactions is discovered.
2. Jones, CPA, examined the 19X3 financial statements of Ray Corp. and issued an unqualified opinion on March 10, 19X4. On April 2, 19X4, Jones became aware of a 19X3 transaction that may materially affect the 19X3 financial statements. This transaction would have been investigated had it come to Jones' attention during the course of the examination. Jones should
   a. Take *no* action because an auditor is *not* responsible for events subsequent to the issuance of the auditor's report.
   b. Contact Ray's management and request their cooperation in investigating the matter.
   c. Request that Ray's management disclose the possible effects of the newly discovered transaction by adding an unaudited footnote to the 19X3 financial statements.
   d. Contact all parties who might rely on the financial statements and advise them that the financial statements are misleading.

COMPREHENSIVE QUESTIONS

16-25 Windek, a CPA, is nearing the completion of an examination of the financial statements of Jubilee, Inc., for the year ended December 31, 19X0. Windek is currently concerned with ascertaining the occurrence of subsequent events that may require adjustment or disclosure essential to a fair presentation in conformity with generally accepted accounting principles.

Required

a. Briefly explain what is meant by the phrase "subsequent event."

b. How do those subsequent events that require financial statement adjustment differ from those that require financial statement disclosure?

c. What are the procedures that should be performed in order to ascertain the occurrence of subsequent events?

AICPA

16-26 In connection with your examination of the financial statements of Olars Manufacturing Corporation for the year ended December 31, 19X0, your post-balance-sheet-date review disclosed the following items:

1. January 3, 19X1: The state government approved a plan for the construction of an express highway. The plan will result in the appropriation of a portion of the land area owned by Olars Manufacturing Corporation. Construction will begin in late 19X1. No estimate of the condemnation award is available.

2. January 4, 19X1: The funds for a $25,000 loan to the corporation made by Mr. Olars on July 15, 19X0 were obtained by him by a loan on his personal life insurance policy. The loan was recorded in the account Loan from Officers. Mr. Olars' source of the funds was not disclosed in the company records. The corporation pays the premiums on the life insurance policy and Mrs. Olars, wife of the president, is the beneficiary of the policy.

3. January 7, 19X1: The mineral content of a shipment of ore en route on December 31, 19X0 was determined to be 72%. The shipment was recorded at year end at an estimated content of 50% by a debit to Raw Material Inventory and a credit to Accounts Payable in the amount of $20,600. The final liability to the vendor is based on the actual mineral content of the shipment.

4. January 15, 19X1: Culminating a series of personal disagreements between Mr. Olars, the president, and his brother-in-law, the treasurer, the latter resigned, effective immediately, under an agreement whereby the corporation would purchase his 10% stock ownership at book value as of December 31, 19X0. Payment is to be made in two equal amounts in cash on April 1 and October 1, 19X1. In December, the treasurer had obtained a divorce from his wife, who was Mr. Olars' sister.

5. January 31, 19X1: As a result of reduced sales, production was curtailed in mid-January and some workers were laid off. On February 5, 19X1, all the remaining workers went on strike. To date, the strike is unsettled.

6. February 10, 19X1: A contract was signed whereby Mammoth Enterprises purchased from Olars Manufacturing Corporation all of the latter's fixed assets (including rights to receive the proceeds of any property condemnation), inventories, and the right to conduct business under the name "Olars Manufacturing Division." The effective date of the transfer will be March 1, 19X1. The sale price was $500,000 subject to adjustment following the taking of a physical inventory. Important factors contributing to the decision to enter into the contract were the policy of the board of directors of Mammoth Industries to diversify the firm's activities and the report of a survey conducted by an independent market appraisal firm that revealed a declining market for Olars products.

Required

Assume that the above items came to your attention prior to completion of your audit work on February 15, 19X1 and that you will render an audit report. For *each* of the above items,

a. Give the audit procedures, if any, that would have brought the item to your attention. Indicate other sources of information that may have revealed the item.

b. Discuss the disclosure that you would recommend for the item, listing all details that you would suggest should be disclosed. Indicate those items or details, if any, that should not be disclosed. Give your reasons for recommending or not recommending disclosure of the items or details.

AICPA

16-27 In connection with his examination of Flowmeter, Inc., for the year ended December 31, 19X0, Hirsch, CPA, is aware that certain events and transactions that took place after December 31, 19X0, but before he issues his report dated February 28, 19X1 may affect the company's financial statements.

The following material events or transactions have come to his attention:

1. On January 3, 19X1, Flowmeter, Inc., received a shipment of raw materials from Canada. The materials had been ordered in October 19X0 and shipped FOB shipping point in November 19X0.

2. On January 15, 19X1, the company settled and paid a personal injury claim of a former employee as the result of an accident that occurred in March 19X0. The company had not previously recorded a liability for the claim.

3. On January 25, 19X1, the company agreed to purchase for cash the outstanding stock of Porter Electrical Co. The acquisition is likely to double the sales volume of Flowmeter, Inc.

4. On February 1, 19X1, a plant owned by Flowmeter, Inc., was damaged by a flood resulting in an uninsured loss of inventory.

5. On February 5, 19X1, Flowmeter, Inc., issued and sold to the general public $2,000,000 in convertible bonds.

Required

For each of the above events or transactions, indicate the audit procedures that should have brought the item to the attention of the auditor and the form of disclosure in the financial statements including the reasons for such disclosures. Organize your answer in the following format:

Item No.	Audit Procedures	Required Disclosure or Entry and Reasons

AICPA

16-28 During an audit engagement, an auditor is expected to communicate with lawyers concerning claims, litigation, and assessments. Listed below are five situations regarding LCA. The last clause or sentence of each case states a conclusion:

1. If the client's lawyer is silent on certain aspects of an attorney's letter request, the auditor may infer the response is complete.

2. Letters of audit inquiry ask for the lawyer's evaluation of the probable outcome of matters reported in his response. If the lawyer's response does not contain this evaluation, the auditor should conclude the scope of his examination has been restricted.

3. The Top Dollar Corporation is involved in litigation for which the potential liability is so great that an unfavorable judgment at or near the claimed amount would seriously impair its operations. This is how the company's attorneys answered the legal confirmation request:

   > While no assurance can be given as to the outcome of this action, based on the facts known by us to date, in the confidence of the attorney/client relationship and otherwise, and our understanding of the present law, we believe the company has good and meritorious defense to the claims asserted against it and should prevail.

   On this basis, the independent auditor may issue an unqualified opinion.

4. In situations where the auditor has orally discussed matters involving litigation with the client's legal counsel and obtained his oral opinion on the outcome of disputed matters, it is not necessary to obtain written confirmation of these oral opinions if the auditor has summarized the attorney's opinion in a memo to the working papers.

5. For the past ten years, XYZ Company has used the services of JJH&I for its primary legal advice and in many significant matters of litigation. Ninty-five% of JJH&I's legal fees originate from services performed for XYZ Company. At December 31, JJH&I was handling litigation involving great potential liability to the company and has now responded to the auditor's letter of inquiry. If we assume full disclosure, complete reliance can be placed on this response.

Required

For each case, indicate whether you agree or disagree with the conclusion and the reason(s) therefor.

16-29 During an audit engagement, Harper, CPA, has satisfactorily completed an examination of accounts payable and other liabilities and now plans to determine whether there are any loss contingencies arising from litigation, claims, or assessments.

Required

What are the audit procedures that Harper should follow with respect to the existence of loss contingencies arising from litigation, claims, and assessments? Do not discuss reporting requirements.

AICPA

16-30 During the examination of the annual financial statements of Amis Manufacturing, Inc., the company's president, R. Alderman, and Luddy, the auditor, reviewed matters that were supposed to be included in a written representation letter. Upon receipt of the following client representation letter, Luddy contacted Alderman to state that it was incomplete.

To E. K. Luddy, CPA

In connection with your examination of the balance sheet of Amis Manufacturing, Inc. as of December 31, 19X5, and the related statements of income, retained earnings, and changes in financial position for the year then ended, for the purpose of expressing an opinion as to whether the financial statements present fairly the financial position, results of operations, and changes in financial position of Amis Manufacturing, Inc. in conformity with generally accepted accounting principles, we confirm, to the best of our knowledge and belief, the following representations made to you during your examination. There were no

- Plans or intentions that may materially affect the carrying value or classification of assets and liabilities.
- Communications from regulatory agencies concerning noncompliance with, or deficiencies in, financial reporting practices.
- Agreements to repurchase assets previously sold.
- Violations or possible violations of laws or regulations whose effects should be considered for disclosure in the financial statements or as a basis for recording a loss contingency.
- Unasserted claims or assessments that our lawyer has advised are probable of assertion and must be disclosed in accordance with Statements of Financial Accounting Standards No. 5.
- Capital stock repurchase options or agreements or capital stock reserved for options, warrants, conversions, or other requirements.
- Compensating balance or other arrangements involving restrictions on cash balances.

R. Alderman, President
Amis Manufacturing, Inc.

March 14, 19X6

Required

Identify the other matters that Alderman's representation letter should specifically confirm.

AICPA

16-31 In your audit of the Lerner Corporation, you request a management "rep" letter. You are particularly interested in management's representations on

1. Irregularities involving management or employees.
2. Minutes of directors' meetings.
3. Compliance with laws and regulations.
4. Completeness of the accounting records.
5. Net realizable value of inventories.
6. Ownership of assets.

Required

Using Figure 16-4 as an example, prepare a rep letter in good form covering the points listed above.

16-32 In auditing the financial statements of a manufacturing company that were prepared from data processed by electronic data processing equipment, the CPA has found that his traditional "audit trail" has been obscured. As a result, the CPA may place increased emphasis on overall checks of the data under audit. These overall checks, which are also applied in auditing visibly posted accounting records, include the computation of ratios, which are compared to prior year ratios or industrywide norms. Examples of such overall checks or ratios are the computation of the rate of inventory turnover and the computation of the number of days' sales in receivables.

Required

a. Discuss the advantages to the CPA of the use of ratios as overall checks in an audit.

b. In addition to the computations given above, list the ratios that a CPA may compute during an audit as overall checks on balance sheet accounts and related nominal accounts. For each ratio listed, name the two (or more) accounts used in its computation.

c. When a CPA discovers that there has been a significant change in a ratio when compared to the prior year's ratio, he considers the possible reasons for the change. Give the possible reasons for the following significant changes in ratios:

1. The rate of inventory turnover (ratio of cost of sales and average inventory) has decreased from the prior year's rate.

2. The number of days' sales in receivables (ratio of average daily accounts receivable and sales) has increased over the prior year.

AICPA

16-33 Annette, CPA, is conducting the 19X5 audit of the financial statements of Johnson Company and has been given the following statement of changes in financial position:

Johnson Company
Statement of Changes in Financial Position
For the Year Ended December 31, 19X5
(in thousands)

Funds Provided from Operations

New income from operations	$46,000
Add or (deduct) items not requiring outlay of working capital in the current period:	
Depreciation	5,500
Deferred income taxes	1,500
Investment in unconsolidated subsidiary (net of cash dividends paid)	(1,700)*
From operations prior to extraordinary loss	51,300
Extraordinary loss	(13,000)
From operations after extraordinary loss	38,300
Proceeds from exercise of stock options	2,700*
Total	$41,000

Johnson Company (*Continued*)
Funds Used

Cash dividends paid on common and preferred stock	$15,000*
Increase in long-term investments (net of allowance)	3,000 ⎫
Allowance for unrealized losses on noncurrent marketable equity securities	5,000 ⎭ *
Increase in working capital	18,000
Total	$41,000

Changes in Working Capital—Increase (Decrease)

Cash and short-term investments	$(9,000)
Accounts receivable	17,000
Inventories	18,000
Accounts payable and accrued liabilities	(7,000)
Other current assets and liabilities	(1,000)
Increase in working capital	$18,000

Annette has completed necessary auditing procedures on the balance sheet, income statement, and statement of stockholders' equity and is satisfied that these statements are fairly presented with adequate disclosures in the statements and the footnotes. Annette has not yet examined the statement of changes in financial position.

Required

a. What general steps should be followed by Annette to examine the statement of changes in financial position of the Johnson Company? Do not discuss the presentation or verification of any specific item on the statement.

b. What additional specific steps should be followed by Annette to verify each of the four items marked with an asterisk on the statement of changes in financial position of the Johnson Company?

AICPA

16-34 The major result of a financial audit conducted by an independent accountant is the expression of an opinion by the auditor on the fairness of the financial statements. While the auditor's report containing the opinion is the best known report issued by the independent auditor, other reports are often prepared during the course of a normal audit. One such report is the management letter (informal report).

Required

a. What is the purpose of a management letter?

b. Identify the major types of information that are likely to be covered in a management letter. Support your answer with a detailed example of one of the types identified above.

CMA

16-35 On June 15, you were assigned to the current year's audit of Castle Petroleum Company. The company is a large, progressive oil company operating in the United States and 15 foreign countries. Last year, gross sales were $600 million and net income was $60 million. Total assets approximated $850 million at December 31 of the preceding year.

The controller is responsible for maintaining the financial records of the company, preparing and interpreting financial statements, preparing federal and state tax returns, studying and establishing systems and procedures, formulating depreciation policies, coordinating matters between the company and the independent public accountants, and certain other matters. The treasurer's department is the custodian of cash and securities and is responsible for collecting cash receipts, disbursing funds, preparing cash forecasts and budgets, and maintaining friendly relations with bankers and underwriters.

Your review and tests of internal control during interim work disclose the following:

1. No accounting manual is maintained to provide descriptions of the approximately 450 accounts. However, a chart of accounts showing account number, name, and subcodings is used. Periodically, bulletins on special accounting problems are issued. A suggestion that a descriptive accounting manual be maintained was incorporated in your firm's management letter two years ago. The controller has indicated that such a manual is probably desirable, but you find that no effort has been made to develop one.

2. No listing is prepared of checks received in the mailroom and subsequently forwarded to the cash receipts section. All letters are opened by the mailroom unless it is obvious that a check is enclosed. If an envelope appears to contain a check, it is forwarded to the cash receipts section unopened. Approximately 250 check remittances are received each day. Receipts in cash are minor.

3. During your several visits to the treasurer's department, you note that the check signing machines are left unlocked at noon. Virtually all checks are signed by machine. The number of signatures recorded by the machines are investigated. At all times, blank checks are locked in a filing cabinet located in the same room with the check signing machines; the key to the cabinet is hidden in an unlocked desk drawer.

4. The company generally attempts to do most of its purchasing through the purchasing department located at the home office. However, to prevent the closing down of plants or drilling sites, field personnel are authorized to make emergency purchases. Company policy requires that the employee making the purchase obtain a counter order slip (COS). The COS then is routed to the district supervisor for approval and submission to the purchasing department at the home office. The purchasing department then prepares a confirming purchase order (CPO) for each COS instructing the vendor to invoice Castle Petroleum Company. The CPO is mailed to the vendor. Approximately 125,000 CPOs are prepared each year.

5. For years, the company has prepared annual budgets for each operating department, and at year-end the actual results have been compared and variances investigated. The budgets are prepared by the treasurer and are reviewed and approved by the board of directors.

6. Capital expenditure proposals are accompanied by a calculation of the payback period. Subsequent savings are compared to those forecast in an effort to improve forecasting ability.

Required

Prepare a draft of a management letter that you believe is appropriate. If you exclude any of the above, give your reasons.

16-36 The fiscal year of the Edie Company ends on December 31. Your audit report, dated February 26, is to be delivered to the client on March 9. Listed below are events that occur or are discovered from the date of the balance sheet to June 30 of the following year:

1. Jan. 15   Inventory is sold at a price below December 31 net realizable value.
2. Jan. 20   A major customer becomes bankrupt from ongoing net losses.
3. Jan. 31   The board of directors authorizes the acquisition of a company as a subsidiary.
4. Feb. 10   A fire destroys a major company warehouse.
5. Feb. 25   A lawsuit is decided against the company for an accident that occurred on October 10. The damages are three times higher than estimated on December 31.
6. Feb. 28   The board of directors authorizes a 2-for-1 stock split.
7. Mar. 7   A foreign government expropriates a major foreign subsidiary following the unexpected overthrow of the government.
8. Mar. 31   A court rules that a minority group is the rightful legal owner of land on which an operating division is located.

Required

a. Identify each event as a (1) subsequent event requiring adjustment, (2) subsequent event requiring disclosure, (3) subsequent event occurring after field work but before issuance of report, or (4) postaudit discovery of facts existing at date of report.
b. Explain your audit responsibilities for each of the categories in (a).
c. Indicate how you would obtain knowledge of each of the eight items.
d. What additional responsibilities does an auditor have for the postaudit discovery of facts if the client refuses to make required disclosures?

CASE STUDY

16-37 Tuloak Manufacturing Company is a small manufacturer of oak porch swings. It was organized as a proprietorship by its current president and majority stockholder, Samuel Lawten. Tuloak was incorporated in 19X0 when growth of the company necessitated the raising of additional capital.

The accounting system of Tuloak is quite simple. The system has evolved over the years in response to external reporting requirements, and a strong emphasis has not been placed on internal control. The firm's relatively small size (49 employees) also makes effective internal control more difficult than in a larger firm.

The CPA firm of Deber & Associates has been hired to perform the audit of Tuloak for fiscal year ending October 31, 19X0. This is the first time that Deber has been engaged to audit Tuloak's financial statements. The partner in charge of the audit has reminded his staff that material weaknesses in internal control must be communicated to audit clients. The partner has concluded that a management letter should be issued to Tuloak following the audit for the year ended October 31, 19X0. The management letter sent by Deber to Tuloak is reproduced below.

On receipt of the managment letter, Mr. Lawten asked his chief accountant, Charles Earl, to respond to the management letter. The response prepared by Mr. Earl is shown on the next page.

Deber & Associates, CPAs
Oak Park, North Carolina

Samual Lawten, *President*
Tuloak Manufacturing Company

In connection with our audit of the financial statements of Tuloak Manufacturing Company of October 31, 19X0, we reviewed various internal procedures and controls of the company in order to plan the scope of the audit. We did not make a comprehensive review for the purpose of submitting detailed recommendations. However, as a result of our review, we did observe certain areas where material weaknesses in internal controls and procedures exist. These weaknesses are itemized below and should be corrected.

Cash. Control over cash disbursements for purchases of materials is inadequate due to the fact that creditor checks are prepared by the accounts payable bookkeeper, later signed by the treasurer, then returned to the accounts payable bookkeeper for mailing to creditors.

We recommend that the checks be mailed by the treasurer rather than by the accounts payable bookkeeper.

Accounts Receivable. The extension of credit to customers is approved by the sales manager, who also authorizes the write-off of delinquent accounts.

We recommend that the write-off of delinquent accounts be approved by the chief accountant.

Inventory. Purchases of raw materials are made only on receipt of a purchase requisition signed by the production supervisor. When shipments of raw materials are received, a receiving report is signed by any available production worker in the vicinity of the receiving dock.

We recommend that the production supervisor be the only employee permitted to sign the receiving report; then, the supervisor will know that the materials requisitioned have arrived.

Marketable Securities. Stock certificates related to marketable securities are kept in Mr. Lawten's office desk drawer to facilitate prompt settlement when the expected holding period is relatively short.

We recommend that all stock certificates be held in a bank safety deposit box accessible only to Mr. Lawten.

Payroll. Hourly production workers are required to punch in on a mechanical time clock each morning, then punch out at the end of the day. Presumably, they take a one-hour lunch break. Occasionally, a worker might not return from lunch, have a friend punch his card at the end of the day, and receive a full day's pay for a half-day's work.

To prevent this from happening in the future, we recommend that each employee be required to punch out and back in for lunch and that each supervisor initial the daily time cards of each employee under his/her control, thereby verifying the presence of workers for the full day.

Sincerely,

Deber & Associates

Memorandum

TO: Samuel Lawten, President
FROM: Charles Earl, Chief Accountant
SUBJECT: Response to management letter from Deber & Associates

Pursuant to your request, I am writing this memo in response to the management letter of our independent accountants, Deber & Associates. My comments related to each of their recommendations are presented below.

Cash. I do not believe that the change in procedure recommended is necessary because the accounts payable bookkeeper cannot possibly benefit from handling the signed checks made payable to our material suppliers. Each check is supported by an approved purchase requisition, purchase order, receiving report, and vendor's invoice.

Accounts Receivable. The current system of having the sales manager approve the write-off of delinquent accounts is preferable because the sales manager is more familiar with each of the customers having delinquent accounts and thus can more accurately determine the appropriate time to write off their accounts. In addition, as chief accountant, I should not be required to approve the write-off of accounts that I am responsible for maintaining.

Inventory. The auditors' recommendation that the production supervisor alone sign receiving reports is impractical because the supervisor is often supervising employees physically removed from the vicinity of the receiving dock. Such a requirement would reduce the production supervisor's effectiveness. I suggest we continue with the present system of receiving report approvals.

Marketable Securities. All stock certificates related to marketable securities are registered in the company name, so putting such certificates in a bank safety deposit box is unnecessary. In addition, your desk drawer may be locked, and the advantage of convenient access more than offsets any improvement in control.

Payroll. The recommendation that hourly production workers punch out and back in for their lunch breaks would necessitate new time cards to accommodate twice as many clock entries as are currently required. In addition, if an employee is going to miss a half day's work by having a friend punch his or her card at the end of the day under the current system, only one additional erroneous entry will be required by the friend after lunch under the proposed system.

Required

For each of the weaknesses of internal controls and procedures identified by Deber & Associates, discuss whether

a. The weakness identified by Deber & Associates is substantive and should be brought to Tuloak's attention.

b. The recommendation proposed by Deber & Associates is a reasonable and appropriate solution.

c. The response of Charles Earl of Tuloak Manufacturing Company is satisfactory under the circumstances.

CMA

PART IV

REPORTING AND OTHER RESPONSIBILITIES

In this, the concluding part of this book, attention is directed at the reporting standards and the responsibilities imposed on the auditor by the profession, the courts, and the Securities and Exchange Commission. There are five chapters in this part.

The first two chapters relate to the auditor's reporting function. Chapter 17 focuses exclusively on audit reports in the typical audit engagement. Chapter 18 considers other types of audit reports and communications resulting from other types of professional services.

The final three chapters explain the responsibilities of the auditor in (1) meeting the code of professional ethics established by the public accounting profession, (2) recognizing the potential legal liabilities in the practice of public accounting, and (3) complying with the requirements of the Securities and Exchange Commission in rendering professional services to SEC clients.

Chapter 17

Reporting on Audited Financial Statements

Study Objectives

When you have completed your study of this chapter, you should be able to

- Explain the meaning of each of the four reporting standards.

- Enumerate the circumstances that result in a departure from the auditor's standard report.

- Describe the effects of each circumstance on the form and content of the auditor's report.

- Identify and correct substandard audit reports.

- Discuss the auditor's responsibilities in reporting on comparative statements.

- State the auditor's reporting responsibilities for information accompanying audited financial statements.

The final phase of an audit engagement is reporting the findings. In the preparation and issuance of a report on audited financial statements, the auditor must comply with the four reporting standards. Each of these generally accepted auditing standards (GAAS) is explained and illustrated in this chapter. In addition, consideration will be given to circumstances that may cause the auditor to modify the standard audit report.

Throughout this chapter, it will be assumed that management is asserting that the financial statements are prepared in conformity with generally accepted accounting principles (GAAP). This chapter expands on the explanation of auditor's reports in Chapter 2.

STANDARDS OF REPORTING

The ten GAAS include the following four reporting standards.

- The report shall state whether the financial statements are presented in accordance with generally accepted accounting principles.
- The report shall state whether such principles have been consistently observed in the current period in relation to the preceding period.
- Informative disclosures in the financial statements are to be regarded as reasonably adequate unless otherwise stated in the report.
- The report shall contain either an expression of opinion regarding the financial statements, taken as a whole, or an assertion to the effect that an opinion cannot be expressed. When an overall opinion cannot be expressed, the reasons therefor should be stated. In all cases where an auditor's name is associated with financial statements, the report should contain a clear-cut indication of the character of the auditor's examination, if any, and the degree of responsibility he is taking.[1]

The first three reporting standards are discussed in due course. For the present, attention is focused on the fourth reporting standard.

FOURTH REPORTING STANDARD

The objective of the fourth standard is to prevent misinterpretation of the degree of responsibility the auditor is assuming when his name is associated with financial statements.[2] This standard directly influences the form, content, and language of the auditor's report.

Expressing or Denying an Opinion

This standard requires the auditor to express an opinion or assert that an opinion cannot be expressed. In the latter case, the reasons therefor should be stated in the auditor's report.

Financial Statements

The financial statements referred to in this standard apply to a single statement, such as a balance sheet, as well as to a complete set of basic statements (balance sheet, income statement, retained earnings statement, and statement of changes in financial position). In some cases, the basic statements may be accompanied by a statement of changes in stockholders' equity accounts. The financial statements may be individual company statements, consolidated

---

[1] Auditing Standards Board, *Codification of Statements on Auditing Standards* (New York: American Institute of Certified Public Accountants, 1985), Auditing Section 150.02 (hereinafter referred to and cited as AU §).

[2] Auditing Standards Board, *op. cit.*, AU § 509.05.

statements, and statements of one or more prior periods that are presented on a comparative basis with those of the current period. The auditor's opinion must be expressed (or denied) in terms of the financial statement(s) that have been examined as set forth in the scope paragraph of the auditor's report.

Reference in the fourth standard of reporting to the statements "taken as a whole" is important to the auditor in several ways. First, it means that the auditor's opinion should pertain to what the individual statement, in its entirety, purports to present. For the balance sheet, this is financial position; for the income statement, it is results of operations, and so on. The auditor is not expected to express an opinion on individual components or categories of the individual statement in the ordinary audit engagement. Second, "taken as a whole" does not mean that the auditor is prohibited from expressing different opinions on the statements included in a complete set of financial statements. It is possible, for example, to express an unqualified opinion on the balance sheet and another type of opinion on the income statement and the statement of changes in financial position. Different opinions within a given set of basic financial statements are rare.

Character of Auditor's Examination

Along with the expression (or denial) of an opinion regarding the financial statements, the auditor is required to include in his report a clear-cut indication of the character of the examination. The nature of the examination is described in the second sentence of the scope paragraph of the auditor's report through the phrases "in accordance with generally accepted auditing standards," "tests of the accounting records," and "such other auditing procedures as we considered necessary in the circumstances." In lay terms, these phrases can be interpreted to mean that the examination was made according to established professional standards, which included selective testing of the accounting records and the application of appropriate auditing procedures.

The primary frame of reference for an examination is GAAS, and any departures from these standards must be indicated in the scope paragraph of the auditor's report. When an examination has not been made, the scope paragraph should clearly indicate this fact and there should be no reference to auditing standards.

Association with Financial Statements

A certified public accountant may be associated with audited or unaudited financial statements. The concern in this chapter is with audited financial statements. A CPA is associated with audited financial statements when he has been engaged to examine the statements in accordance with GAAS and has applied auditing procedures to such statements. Association also exists when a CPA consents to the use of his name in a report, document, or written communication containing audited financial statements.

Degree of Responsibility

The final requirement of the fourth reporting standard is that the auditor must indicate the degree of responsibility that is being taken for the examination and the opinion. This is done through such wording as "we have examined," "our examination," and "in our opinion." The use of these words without qualification means that the auditor is assuming full or complete responsibility for the work done and the opinion rendered. When more than one auditor is involved in the examination and each auditor assumes responsibility only for his own work and his own opinion, both the scope and opinion paragraphs must indicate the divided responsibility that exists.

AUDITOR'S STANDARD REPORT

The auditor's standard report was introduced in Chapter 2. Recall that it consisted of a scope (or opening) paragraph, an opinion (or closing) paragraph, and standardized language. The language of the report varies slightly depending on whether the auditor is reporting on financial statements for one year or for two or more years. A standard report is illustrated in Figure 17-1.

The wording of the standard report contains two implicit assertions. First, the existence of audit risk is implicit in the phrase "In our opinion." As explained earlier, audit risk is the risk that the auditor may unknowingly fail to appropriately modify his opinion on the financial statements that are materially misstated.[3] Second, the phrase "present fairly in conformity with generally accepted accounting principles" implicitly indicates the auditor's belief that the financial statements taken as a whole are not *materially* misstated.[4]

The report is normally addressed to the individuals or groups that appointed the auditors. For a corporate client, this is the board of directors and/or stockholders; for unincorporated clients, the addressee is the partners or proprietor. The auditor's standard report should be dated as of the completion of field work. The signature on the report is generally in the firm name because the firm assumes responsibility for the work and the findings of its professional staff.

TYPES OF OPINIONS

As explained in Chapter 2, there are four types of opinions that may be expressed on audited financial statements:

- An *unqualified opinion* states that the financial statements present fairly financial position, results of operations, and changes in financial position in conformity with GAAP consistently applied.

- A *qualified opinion* states that, "except for" or "subject to" the effects of the matter to which the qualification relates, the financial statements present fairly . . . consistently applied.

[3]Auditing Standards Board, *op. cit.*, AU § 312.02.
[4]Auditing Standards Board, *op. cit.*, AU § 327.05.

To the Shareholders and Board of Directors of Sears, Roebuck and Co.:

We have examined the Consolidated Statements of Financial Position of Sears, Roebuck and Co. as of December 31, 1984 and 1983, and the related Consolidated Statements of Income. Shareholders' Equity and Changes in Financial Position for each of the three years in the period ended December 31, 1984. Our examinations were made in accordance with generally accepted auditing standards and, accordingly, included such tests of the accounting records and such other auditing procedures as we considered necessary in the circumstances.

In our opinion, the financial statements referred to above present fairly the financial position of Sears, Roebuck and Co. as of December 31, 1984 and 1983, and the results of its operations and the changes in its financial position for each of the three years in the period ended December 31, 1984, in conformity with generally accepted accounting principles applied on a consistent basis.

Touche Ross & Co.

Chicago, Illinois
March 19, 1985

Figure 17-1. AUDITOR'S STANDARD REPORT: FINANCIAL STATEMENTS FOR TWO OR MORE YEARS.

- An *adverse opinion* states that the financial statements do not present fairly . . . in conformity with GAAP.

- A *disclaimer of opinion* states that the auditor does not express an opinion on the financial statements.

The auditor's judgment concerning the "fairness" of the overall presentation of financial statements is applied within the framework of generally accepted accounting principles. Without that framework, the auditor would not have a uniform standard for making a judgment.[5]

In deciding on the appropriate opinion, the auditor considers the following questions:

- Was (were) the examination(s) made in accordance with GAAS?
- Are the financial statements prepared in conformity with GAAP, which include adequate disclosures (first and third standards of reporting)?
- Have GAAP been applied on a consistent basis (second standard of reporting)?
- Are the financial statements unaffected by any unusual uncertainties?

Materiality should be considered in answering these questions. A negative answer should be given only when an exception pertains to a matter that has a material effect on the financial statements. With due recognition to materiality, the auditor is able to express an unqualified opinion when affirmative answers are given to all of the questions. However, the following opinions are appropriate for negative answers to these questions:

[5]Auditing Standards Board, *op. cit.,* AU § 411.03.

Exception	Qualified	Adverse	Disclaimer
Examination not in accordance with generally accepted auditing standards	X*		X
Nonconformity with GAAP, which includes adequate disclosure	X	X	
Inconsistency	X		
Unusual uncertainties	X		X

*If the auditor is not independent in making the examination, a disclaimer of opinion is required.

EFFECTS OF OTHER THAN UNQUALIFIED OPINIONS

The issuance of a qualified, adverse, or disclaimer of an opinion on the fairness of a client's financial statements is a significant development that requires a change in both the form and content of the auditor's standard report. Except for an opinion qualified because of inconsistency, the auditor should use one or more explanatory paragraphs to explain the substantive reasons for the opinion being expressed (or denied). The additional paragraph(s) should be between the scope and opinion paragraphs and be referred to in the opinion paragraph.

When the auditor issues other than an unqualified opinion, the following changes in the wording of the opinion paragraph are required:

Opinion	Language
Qualified • Other than for inconsistency and uncertainties	In our opinion, *except for* . . .
• For inconsistency	*except for* . . . (inserted at end of paragraph)
• For uncertainties	In our opinion, *subject to* . . .
Adverse	In our opinion, *because of* . . . , the financial statements *do not* present fairly . . .
Disclaimer	*Because of* . . . , *we are* unable to *express an opinion on the fairness of* . . .

When a qualified opinion or disclaimer of opinion is due to noncompliance with GAAS, the scope paragraph is modified by adding the following in the second sentence: "except as explained in the following paragraph."

CIRCUMSTANCES RESULTING IN DEPARTURE FROM THE AUDITOR'S STANDARD REPORT

A departure from the auditor's standard report occurs when there is a substantive change in the wording or form of the report. The following circumstances will result in substantive changes in the standard report:

- The scope of the auditor's examination is affected by conditions that preclude the application of one or more auditing procedures he considers necessary in the circumstances.

- The auditor's opinion is based in part on the report of another auditor.

- The financial statements are affected by a departure from a generally accepted accounting principle.

- The financial statements are affected by a departure from an accounting principle promulgated by the body designated by the AICPA Council to establish such principles.

- Accounting principles have not been applied consistently.

- The financial statements are affected by uncertainties concerning future events, the outcome of which is not susceptible of reasonable estimation at the date of the auditor's report.

- The auditor wishes to emphasize a matter regarding the financial statements.[6]

Each of the circumstances is explained below and a number of actual audit reports are illustrated.

SCOPE LIMITATION

In an examination made in accordance with GAAS, the auditor is able to perform all auditing procedures considered necessary in the circumstances. From these procedures, it is expected that the auditor will obtain sufficient competent evidential matter to have a reasonable basis for expressing an opinion on the financial statements. When the auditor cannot perform the necessary procedures or the procedures do not provide sufficient evidence, the auditor is said to have a *scope limitation*.

Causes of Scope Limitations

A scope limitation may be imposed by the client or result from circumstances. Client restrictions may include refusal to (1) permit confirmation of receivables, (2) sign a client representation letter, or (3) give the auditor access to the minutes of board of directors meetings. Restrictions attributable to circumstances may extend to the timing of procedures, such as appointment too late to perform procedures considered necessary in the circumstances, and inadequate client records.

A scope limitation does not exist when the auditor is engaged to make an examination on only one financial statement and not the others, provided he can perform all the procedures he considers necessary in the circumstances. Such an engagement simply involves limited reporting objectives. For example, if the engagement extends only to the balance sheet and the auditor examines that statement in accordance with GAAS, a standard audit report may be issued on the balance sheet.

---

[6]Auditing Standards Board, *op. cit.*, AU § 509.09.

Effects on Auditor's Report

When a scope limitation exists, the auditor should

- Indicate the scope limitation in the scope paragraph of his report.
- Give the substantive reasons for the limitation in an explanatory paragraph.
- Express a qualified opinion or a disclaimer of opinion in the opinion paragraph.

The importance of the missing evidence and the materiality of the effects of the item(s) in question on the financial statements are factors the auditor should consider in deciding whether to qualify or disclaim an opinion. When the scope limitation extends to many financial statement items, there is a greater probability that a disclaimer of opinion will be necessary. Generally, the auditor disclaims an opinion when there is a client-imposed restriction.

The wording of the opinion paragraph should refer to the potential effects on the financial statements of the items for which the auditor has not obtained audit satisfaction, rather than to the scope limitation itself, because the auditor's opinion relates to the financial statements. A scope limitation resulting in a qualified opinion is illustrated in Figure 17-2.

To the Board of Directors and Shareholders of Atlas Incorporated:

We have examined the consolidated balance sheets of Atlas Incorporated and subsidiaries as of December 31, 1985 and 1984, and the related consolidated statements of operations, stockholders' equity, and changes in financial position for each of the three years in the period ended December 31, 1985. Our examinations were made in accordance with generally accepted auditing standards and, accordingly, included such tests of the accounting records and such other auditing procedures as we considered necessary in the circumstances, except as explained in the following paragraph.

As discussed in Note 4 of the Notes to Consolidated Financial Statements, Atlas Incorporated recognized certain adjustments, principally a $4.2 million inventory write-down in 1985. Sufficient documentary evidence could not be examined, or other reliable tests made, to determine the full extent to which these adjustments in the aggregate may affect prior years.

In our opinion, except for the effect on the consolidated statements of operations, stockholders' equity, and changes in financial position of the matter described in the preceding paragraph, the consolidated financial statements referred to above present fairly the financial position of Atlas Incorporated and subsidiaries at December 31, 1985 and 1984, and the results of their operations and the changes in their financial position for each of the three years in the period ended December 31, 1985, in conformity with generally accepted accounting principles applied on a consistent basis.

Reddy & Abel

February 27, 1986

Figure 17-2. AUDITOR'S REPORT QUALIFIED BECAUSE OF SCOPE LIMITATION.

PART OF EXAMINATION MADE BY ANOTHER AUDITOR

When a client has one or more subsidiaries, divisions, or branches, it may be necessary for more than one auditing firm to participate in the examination. Assume, for example, that a client with its major operations located in the Midwest has a foreign subsidiary that is audited by a foreign firm. When two or more auditing firms are involved in an examination, one firm should be the principal auditor. This decision should be based on such factors as the relative amount and significance of the work done and the extent of the firms' knowledge of the overall statements. In this example, the firm auditing the Midwest operations would be the principal auditor.

The principal auditor must then decide whether he is willing to assume responsibility for the work of the other auditors insofar as it relates to the client's statements taken as a whole. If the principal auditor accepts this responsibility, no reference should be made in the audit report to the other auditors' examination. However, if the principal auditor is not willing to assume this responsibility, the fourth standard of reporting requires that reference be made to the other auditors in the auditor's report. Such action is necessary to indicate the shared responsibility that exists among the auditors for both the examination and the expression of an opinion on the financial statements.

Decision Not to Make Reference

If the principal auditor is able to obtain satisfaction as to the (1) independence and professional reputation of the other auditors and (2) scope and quality of the other auditors' examination, reference to the other auditors ordinarily is not made. The principal auditor would be able to reach this decision when

- The other auditors are associated or correspondent firms whose work is well known to the principal auditor.
- The work is performed under the principal auditor's guidance and control.
- The principal auditor reviews the audit programs and working papers of the other auditors.

The principal auditor may also elect not to make reference to another auditor if the portion of the financial statements examined by the other auditor is not material to the financial statements taken as a whole.

Decision to Make Reference

The principal auditor may decide to make reference to another auditor when one or more of the foregoing factors are not present. The principal auditor may also decide to make reference whenever the portion of the financial statements examined by another auditor is material to the financial statements taken as a whole.

The principal auditor is required under this decision to make inquiries concerning the professional reputation of the other auditor and to obtain a representation from the other auditor that he is independent of the client. In cases where the other firm's primary practice is in a foreign country, the principal auditor should also communicate with the other auditor to ascertain his familiarity with GAAS and GAAP in the United States.

Effects on Auditor's Report

A standard audit report is issued when the principal auditor decides not to make reference to the other auditor(s). Mention of the other auditor(s) in such case is inappropriate since the principal auditor is assuming full responsibility for the examination and the opinion.

When the auditor decides to make reference to another auditor, the report should indicate clearly the division of responsibility that exists between the auditors. This is accomplished by modifying the auditor's standard report as follows:

- In the scope paragraph, the magnitude of the portion of the financial statements examined by the other auditor should be indicated.
- In the opinion paragraph, reference should be made to the other auditor.

These modifications do not result in either a three-paragraph report or a qualified opinion. Reference to the other auditor in the opinion paragraph only indicates the divided responsibility among the auditors. This form of reporting should not be regarded as being inferior to a report in which no reference is made to another auditor. An example of a report in which reference is made to another auditor is shown in Figure 17-3.

If the principal auditor concludes that reliance cannot be placed on the other auditor's work and the work done by the other auditor is material to the financial statements taken as a whole, a scope limitation exists. In such cases, the considerations described earlier in this chapter for scope limitations should be followed in modifying the auditor's standard report.

NONCONFORMITY WITH GAAP

The first standard of reporting requires the auditor to explicitly state whether the financial statements are presented in conformity with GAAP. This standard requires the expression of an opinion rather than a statement of fact. For purposes of this standard, GAAP include not only accounting principles, such as the cost principle, but also the methods of applying them, such as the first in, first out (FIFO) and last in, first out (LIFO) methods for inventories, and the straight line and sum-of-the-years'-digits methods for depreciation.

In reaching a decision as to conformity with GAAP, the auditor must obtain evidence concerning whether

- The accounting principles used have general acceptance.
- The accounting principles are appropriate in the circumstances.

Board of Directors and Shareholders
Mobil Corporation

We have examined the accompanying consolidated balance sheet of Mobil Corporation at December 31, 1984 and 1983, and the related consolidated statements of income, changes in shareholders' equity and changes in financial position for each of the three years in the period ended December 31, 1984. Our examinations were made in accordance with generally accepted auditing standards and, accordingly, included such tests of the accounting records and such other auditing procedures as we considered necessary in the circumstances. The consolidated financial statements of Marcor Inc., Montgomery Ward & Co., Incorporated and Container Corporation of America, consolidated subsidiaries, have been examined by other independent public accountants, and we were furnished with their reports thereon. The assets of these consolidated subsidiaries represent approximately 14% and 16% of the consolidated totals for 1984 and 1983 and revenues represent approximately 15%, 14%, and 12% of the consolidated totals for the years ended December 31, 1984, 1983, and 1982.

In our opinion, based upon our examinations and the reports of other independent public accountants, the statements mentioned above present fairly the consolidated financial position of Mobil Corporation at December 31, 1984 and 1983, and the consolidated results of operations and changes in financial position for each of the three years in the period ended December 31, 1984, in conformity with generally accepted accounting principles applied on a consistent basis during the period.

Arthur Young & Company

March 1, 1985

Figure 17-3. AUDITOR'S REPORT INDICATING RELIANCE ON OTHER AUDITORS.

- The financial statements, including the related notes, are informative of matters that may affect their use, understanding, and interpretation.
- The information presented in the financial statements is classified and summarized in a reasonable manner.
- The statements reflect the underlying events and transactions in a manner that presents financial position, results of operations, and changes in financial position within reasonable and practicable limits.[7]

The third and fourth items relate to the adequacy of informative disclosures.

The phrase *generally accepted accounting principles* includes broad guidelines as well as specific conventions, rules, and procedures. There is no single compilation of all established accounting principles. Pronouncements of the Financial Accounting Standards Board are considered to be the primary source of GAAP. In the absence of FASB pronouncements, the auditor should look to the following order of authoritative sources in determining whether an accounting principle is generally accepted:

- Pronouncements of other bodies composed of expert accountants that follow a due-process procedure, such as the AICPA Accounting Stan-

---

[7]Auditing Standards Board, *op. cit.*, AU § 411.04.

dards Executive Committee. Publications in this category include AICPA Statements of Position and AICPA Industry Audit Guides and Accounting Guides.

- Practices or pronouncements that are widely recognized as being generally accepted because they represent prevalent practice. Publications in this category include FASB Technical Bulletins, AICPA Accounting Interpretations, and prevailing industry practices.
- Other accounting literature. This category includes APB Statements, AICPA Issues Papers, FASB Statements of Financial Accounting Concepts, pronouncements of trade associations or regulatory agencies, and accounting textbooks and articles.[8]

Inadequate Disclosure

The third standard of reporting provides that informative disclosures in the financial statements are to be regarded as reasonably adequate unless otherwise stated in the report.

Informative disclosures involve material matters relating to the form, arrangement, and content of the financial statements and the accompanying notes. Authoritative bodies, such as the FASB and the SEC, frequently include disclosure requirements in their pronouncements. Informative disclosure extends to subsequent events and reporting segment information. The auditor's responsibility for segment information is discussed on page 639. In previous chapters of this book, many specific disclosure requirements have been enumerated under the caption "Statement Presentation and Disclosure," such as the basis and methods of inventory costing, market values of securities, liens on assets, and contingencies.

Effects on Auditor's Report

When a departure from a GAAP has a material effect on the financial statements, the auditor should explain the basis and effects of the departure in an explanatory paragraph, if reasonably determinable, and express a qualified or adverse opinion. In deciding whether to express a qualified or adverse opinion, the auditor should consider such factors as the (1) dollar magnitude of the effects, (2) significance of the item to the client, (3) number of statement items affected, and (4) impact of the misstatement on the statements taken as a whole.[9] The issuance of an adverse opinion normally occurs only when the departure from GAAP has a very material effect on the financial statements. Because the consistency standard implies the application of GAAP, no reference should be made to consistency when an adverse opinion is issued.

When the client refuses to make adequate disclosure of data essential to a fair presentation in conformity with GAAP, the auditor is required to

[8]Auditing Standards Board, *op. cit.*, AU § 411.05–08.
[9]Auditing Standards Board, *op. cit.*, AU § 509.16.

- Provide the necessary information in an explanatory paragraph, if practicable, unless its omission from the auditor's report is recognized as appropriate by a specific Statement on Auditing Standards.
- Express either a qualified opinion or an adverse opinion.

Two omissions have been specifically allowed in Statements on Auditing Standards. The auditor is not required to present (1) a statement of changes in financial position when that statement is omitted by a client, or (2) omitted segment information. In both instances, however, the auditor should identify the omitted data in the explanatory paragraph and appropriately modify his opinion.

Modifications of the auditor's report because of inadequate disclosure occur infrequently. Since the necessary data, in most cases, are going to be disclosed, management ordinarily prefers to make the disclosures that will permit a standard audit report.

NONCONFORMITY WITH PROMULGATED ACCOUNTING PRINCIPLES

Rule 203 of the American Institute of Certified Public Accountants' (AICPA) Code of Professional Ethics requires the auditor to determine whether the principles used by the client comply with promulgated accounting principles.[10] Acting under the provisions of this rule, the Council of the AICPA designated the Financial Accounting Standards Board (FASB) as the body to establish accounting principles.

Authoritative Pronouncements

The Council has formally recognized three sets of authoritative pronouncements: (1) statements and interpretations issued by the FASB, (2) Accounting Principles Board (APB) opinions, and (3) AICPA accounting research bulletins. Rule 203 specifies that the client's financial statements must comply with these pronouncements, unless due to unusual circumstances compliance with the pronouncements would cause the financial statements to be misleading.[11] The unusual circumstances contemplated by the rule consist primarily of new legislation or the evolution of a new form of business transaction.

Alternative accounting principles, such as different depreciation methods and inventory costing methods, may be applicable in the circumstances. Unless the promulgating body has established criteria for selecting among alternative principles, the auditor may recognize that more than one principle is acceptable.

Effects on Auditor's Report

A departure from a promulgated principle that has a material effect on the financial statements may occur in the absence of unusual circumstances or because of unusual circumstances. The effects on the auditor's standard report

[10]Rule 203 is fully explained in Chapter 19.
[11]Auditing Standards Board, *op. cit.*, AU § 509.18.

To the Shareholders and Board of Directors of The Advertising Agency:

We have examined the consolidated balance sheets of The Advertising Agency and consolidated subsidiaries as of December 31, 19X5 and December 31, 19X4 and the related consolidated statements of income, shareholders' equity, and changes in financial position for each of the three years in the period ended December 31, 19X5. Our examinations were made in accordance with generally accepted auditing standards and, accordingly, included such tests of the accounting records and such other auditing procedures as we considered necessary in the circumstances.

The Company's treatment of its investment in the common stock of A. D., Inc., a wholly-owned, unconsolidated subsidiary, is at variance with Opinion No. 18 of the Accounting Principles Board of the American Institute of Certified Public Accountants. This Opinion states that an investment in the common stock of an unconsolidated subsidiary should be accounted for by the equity method in consolidated financial statements. The Company carries its investment in the common stock of A. D., Inc., at cost. If the Accounting Principles Board Opinion had been followed, income would have been increased by $200,000 ($2.00 per share) in 19X5 and $125,000 ($1.25 per share) in 19X4 and the amount of retained earnings at December 31, 19X5 would have been increased by $975,000.

In our opinion, except for the investment in common stock of the unconsolidated subsidiary which has not been accounted for in accordance with generally accepted accounting principles as described in the preceding paragraph, the financial statements referred to above present fairly the consolidated financial position of The Advertising Agency and consolidated subsidiaries at December 31, 19X5 and 19X4, and the consolidated results of their operations and changes in their financial position for each of the three years in the period ended December 31, 19X5, in conformity with generally accepted accounting principles applied on a consistent basis.

Reddy & Abel

February 20, 19X6

Figure 17-4. AUDITOR'S REPORT QUALIFIED BECAUSE OF DEPARTURE FROM PROMULGATED GAAP.

depend on the underlying cause of the departure. When unusual circumstances do not exist, the auditor will be required to give all of the substantive reasons in an explanatory paragraph and express either a qualified or an adverse opinion. An appropriate audit report based on assumed data is shown in Figure 17-4.

When there are unusual circumstances, the client may have to depart from a promulgated principle in order to prevent the financial statements from being misleading. Assuming the client uses an established principle from other sources that is applicable to the unusual circumstances, the auditor is permitted under the first reporting standard to issue an unqualified opinion concerning conformity with GAAP. In such case, the report should describe the approximate effects thereof, if practicable, and the reasons why compliance with the promulgated principle would result in a misleading statement.

INCONSISTENT APPLICATION OF GAAP

The second standard of reporting requires the auditor to state whether accounting principles have been consistently applied. The objectives of this standard are: (1) to give assurance that the comparability of financial statements between accounting periods has not been materially affected by changes in accounting principles and (2) to require appropriate reporting by the auditor when comparability has been materially affected by such changes. The consistency standard does not extend to the effects on comparability of changed business conditions, such as the acquisition (or disposal) of a subsidiary company, the introduction of a new product line, and acts of God (e.g. fires, floods, and similar occurrences).

Accounting Changes

A change in an accounting principle results from the adoption of a GAAP different from the one previously used in the preparation of financial statements. As used in the consistency standard, a change in an accounting principle includes:

- A change in the principle itself such as a change from a sales basis to a production basis in recording farm revenue.
- A change in the method of applying a principle, such as a change from the straight-line method of depreciation to the sum-of-the-years'-digits method.
- A change in the reporting entity such as presenting consolidated statements in place of individual company statements or changes in specific subsidiaries comprising the consolidated group.
- The correction of an error in principle, as, for example, a change from a principle not generally accepted to one that is generally accepted.
- A change in principle inseparable from a change in estimate, such as a change from capitalizing and amortizing a cost to recording it as an expense when incurred because future benefits are now doubtful.

Accounting changes involving accounting estimates, corrections of errors not involving a principle, classifications and reclassifications, variations in the format of the statement of changes in financial position, and substantially different transactions or events are not covered by the consistency standard. Such matters, however, may require disclosure under the third standard of reporting.

Effects on Auditor's Report

When the auditor is reporting only on the current year, the period to which the consistency standard relates is the preceding year. In contrast, when the auditor is reporting on two or more years, this standard relates to the consistency of principles between such years and also to the consistency with the immediately preceding year if it is presented with the financial statements being reported on. The consistency standard does not apply in the first year's examination of a new company.

When a report is qualified because of an inconsistency, the auditor must (1) explicitly express his concurrence by using the expression *with which we concur*, and (2) use "qualifying" language in the consistency wording. Figure 17-5 illustrates a report for a change in accounting principle reported as a cumulative effect in the current year's income statement. An audit report for an accounting change requiring restatement of prior years is included in Figure 17-6. Lack of consistency in the application of generally accepted accounting principles is the primary cause of qualified opinions.

The auditor is required to comply with the second standard of reporting in his first examination of an established client. Where adequate accounting records are kept by the client, it ordinarily is possible for the auditor to obtain satisfaction as to the consistency of the application of accounting principles between the current and the preceding year. However, when the auditor is not able to do so and the amounts involved are material, he would be unable to express an unqualified opinion on the results of operations and changes in financial position for the current period, but he could give an unqualified opinion on the balance sheet without reference to consistency. In such case, the circumstances would be explained in an explanatory paragraph.

To the Shareholders and Board of Directors of The Singer Company:

We have examined the balance sheet of The Singer Company and consolidated subsidiaries as of December 31, 1984 and 1983, and the related statements of income, additional paid-in capital, retained earnings and changes in financial position for each of the years in the three-year period ended December 31, 1984. Our examinations were made in accordance with generally accepted auditing standards and, accordingly, included such tests of the accounting records and such other auditing procedures as we considered necessary in the circumstances.

In our opinion, the aforementioned financial statements present fairly the financial position of The Singer Company and consolidated subsidiaries at December 31, 1984 and 1983, and the results of their operations and the changes in their financial position for each of the years in the three-year period ended December 31, 1984, in conformity with generally accepted accounting principles consistently applied during the period except for the change, with which we concur, in the method of accounting for foreign currency translation, as described in Note 1 to the financial statements.

Peat, Marwick, Mitchell & Co.

New York, New York
February 6, 1985

Figure 17-5. AUDITOR'S REPORT QUALIFIED FOR INCONSISTENT APPLICATION OF GAAP.

UNCERTAINTIES

The term *uncertainties* applies to the outcome of any statement items or disclosures that are not susceptible of reasonable estimation prior to issuance of the statements. Uncertainties differ from accounting estimates in that the latter are capable of reasonable determination by the client in the preparation of financial statements. Uncertainties may range from a single event in which the effect on the financial statements can be isolated and understood to multiple events whose possible effects on the financial statements are complex and difficult to assess. The former include the outcome of a lawsuit or an IRS audit of a tax return; the latter include recurring operating losses and major financial problems that affect the ability of the company to continue in existence.

Uncertainties present a special problem for the auditor because evidence of their resolution does not exist prior to completing the examination. On the basis of evidence that is available, the auditor has the responsibility of determining whether the uncertainties are properly accounted for and disclosed. The auditor is not expected to predict the outcome of the uncertainties.

Continued Existence of Entity

In a typical audit, the auditor assumes the entity will continue as a going concern. However, when his normal auditing procedures reveal information contrary to that assumption, the auditor should consider and evaluate such data. Contrary information may pertain to

- Solvency problems such as working capital shortages and defaults on loan agreements.
- Internal matters such as the loss of key management personnel and work stoppages.
- External matters such as legal proceedings and the loss of important customers[12]

In evaluating the significance of the contrary information, the auditor should (1) weigh any mitigating factors, (2) consider management plans for dealing with the problems, and (3) perform such substantive tests as are reasonable and practicable.

Effects on Auditor's Report

The effects of uncertainties on the auditor's report depend on the auditor's professional judgment. When the auditor concludes that the resolution of an uncertainty will not have a material effect on the financial statements, a standard report may be issued. However, when the uncertainty may have a ma-

---

[12]Auditing Standards Board, *op. cit.*, AU § 340.04.

To the Board of Directors and Shareholders of Allis-Chalmers Corporation

We have examined the consolidated financial statements of Allis-Chalmers Corporation and its subsidiaries (the "Company") appearing on pages 6 through 17 of this report at December 31, 1984 and 1983, and the results of their operations and changes in their financial position for each of the three years in the period ended December 31, 1984. Our examinations of these statements were made in accordance with generally accepted auditing standards and accordingly included such tests of the accounting records and such other auditing procedures as we considered necessary in the circumstances.

As more fully described in the Financing note on pages 13 and 14, neither the Company nor Allis-Chalmers Credit Corporation will be able to pay debt due upon expiration of credit override agreements which have most recently been extended until May 31, 1985 and the Company will not be able to comply with the original covenants of its loan agreements. The Company's continuation in its present form is dependent upon the ability of the Company and of Allis-Chalmers Credit Corporation to refinance such debt or otherwise restructure capitalization and upon the ability of the Company to ultimately return to profitability. The financial statements do not include adjustments relating to the recoverability and classification of recorded asset amounts or the amounts and classification of liabilities that might be necessary should the Company be unable to continue in its present form.

In our opinion, subject to the effects on the 1984 financial statements of such adjustments, if any, as might have been required had the outcome of the uncertainties referred to in the preceding paragraph been known, the Company's consolidated financial statements appearing on pages 6 through 17 of this report present fairly the financial position of the Company and its subsidiaries at December 31, 1984 and 1983 and the results of their operations and the changes in their financial position for each of the three years in the period ended December 31, 1984, in conformity with generally accepted accounting principles applied on a consistent basis after restatement for the change, with which we concur, in the method of accounting for certain inventories as described in the Inventories note on pages 10 and 11.

Price Waterhouse

March 28, 1985

Figure 17-6. AUDITOR'S REPORT QUALIFIED BECAUSE OF AN UNCERTAINTY. (*Authors' Note:* This report also includes a consistency exception.)

terial effect on the financial statements, the auditor should (1) describe the uncertainty in the explanatory paragraph and (2) express a qualified opinion, using "subject to" language, as illustrated in Figure 17-6. The auditor may also disclaim an opinion when a material uncertainty exists.

EMPHASIS OF A MATTER

In some situations, the auditor may wish to emphasize in his report a matter that is properly accounted for and adequately disclosed while still expressing an unqualified opinion. To do so, the auditor should (1) use standard wording in the scope and opinion paragraphs, (2) describe the matter being emphasized in an explanatory paragraph, and (3) make no reference to the explanatory material in the opinion paragraph. Reference in the opinion paragraph to the matter being emphasized is prohibited because a phrase "with the foregoing explanation" could be misconstrued as a qualification of the auditor's opinion. Items that may merit emphasis in a given case include related party transactions, a change in an accounting estimate, and changes in operating conditions.

SUMMARY OF DEPARTURES FROM AUDITOR'S STANDARD REPORT

The effects of the circumstances discussed in this chapter on the auditor's standard report are tabulated in Figure 17-7. It may be observed that the effects do not always result in a three-paragraph report. Moreover, it should be noted that some of the circumstances permit the expressing of an unqualified opinion.

OTHER REPORTING CONSIDERATIONS

The auditor has a variety of other reporting responsibilities as explained below.

COMPARATIVE STATEMENTS

As indicated earlier in this chapter, the fourth standard of reporting applies not only to the financial statements of the current period, but also to statements of any prior periods presented on a comparative basis with those of the current period. During his examination for the current year, the auditor should be alert to circumstances and events relating to prior-period financial statements.

The auditor's current examination may produce evidence that the opinion on the prior year's statements should be different than the opinion originally expressed. This could result from such events as (1) subsequent resolution of an uncertainty that existed in the prior year, (2) discovery of an uncertainty applicable to the prior year that was not known when the opinion on the prior year's statements was rendered, and (3) restatement of prior-period statements to bring them into conformity with GAAP. In such cases, the auditor should indicate in the explanatory paragraph of his current year's report that a different opinion is being expressed on the prior year's financial statements and explain the substantive reasons therefor. The following paragraph from the audit report on the financial statements of Basic Earth Services, Inc. for the fiscal year ending March 31, 1985 is illustrative.

In our auditors' report dated June 15, 1984, our opinion on the fiscal year 1984 consolidated financial statements was qualified, subject to the effect of such adjustments, if any, as might have been required had the

Circumstance	Scope Paragraph Modification	Explanatory Paragraph	Opinion Paragraph Modification	Type of Opinion
Scope limitation	Yes	Yes	Yes	Qualified or disclaimer
Other auditors:				
• Make reference	Yes	No	Yes	Unqualified
• Do not make reference	No	No	No	Unqualified
Departure from GAAP	No	Yes	Yes	Qualified or adverse
Departure from promulgated principle:				
• Justified	No	Yes	No	Unqualified
• Not justified	No	Yes	Yes	Qualified or adverse
Inconsistency	No	No	Yes	Qualified
Uncertainties	No	Yes	Yes	Qualified (subject to) or disclaimer
Emphasis of a matter	No	Yes	No	Unqualified

Figure 17-7. SUMMARY OF EFFECTS OF CIRCUMSTANCES ON AUDITOR'S STANDARD REPORT.

outcome of the consolidated class action lawsuit been known. As explained in note 6 to the consolidated financial statements, the class action lawsuit was settled on June 21, 1985 subject to hearing and court approval, and the cost to Basic has been recorded in the 1985 consolidated financial statements. Accordingly, our present opinion on the fiscal year 1984 consolidated financial statements, as presented herein, is no longer qualified as subject to the class action lawsuit.

There are no changes in the scope and opinion paragraphs when an opinion is updated.

Additional reporting requirements must be met when there has been a change in auditors during the periods covered by the comparative statements. If the predecessor auditor's report of a prior year is not presented, which is the usual case, the successor auditor should indicate in the scope paragraph of his report on the current year

- That the financial statements of the prior period were examined by other auditors.
- The date of their report.

- The type of opinion rendered by the predecessor auditor.
- The substantive reasons, therefor, if it (the opinion) was other than unqualified.[13]

The scope paragraph shown below illustrates the wording when the predecessor auditor expressed an unqualified opinion

> We have examined the consolidated balance sheet of Pan Am Corporation and Subsidiaries as of December 31, 1984, and the related consolidated statement of operations, stockholder equity and changes in financial position for the year then ended. Our examination was made in accordance with generally accepted auditing standards and, accordingly, included such tests of the accounting records and such other auditing procedures as we considered necessary in the circumstances. The consolidated financial statements at December 31, 1983 and for each of the two years in the period then ended were examined by other auditors whose report dated February 24, 1984 expressed an unqualified opinion on those statements.

No additional changes are required in the remainder of the auditor's report. If the predecessor auditor agrees to reissue his report or consents to the reuse of his report, he should perform procedures to determine whether his previous opinion on the financial statements is still appropriate.

SEGMENT INFORMATION

FASB Statement No. 14, "Financial Reporting for Segments of a Business Enterprise," requires certain companies to include specified information about an entity's operations in different industries, its foreign operations and export sales, and its major customers in annual financial statements prepared for stockholders. Such information is referred to as segment information, and it is considered to be an integral part of the financial statements.

The objective of applying auditing procedures to segment information is to provide the auditor with a reasonable basis for concluding whether the information is presented in conformity with *FASB Statement No. 14*. From an auditing point of view, segment information is considered to be a matter of informative disclosure under generally accepted accounting principles (GAAP). The auditor should inquire of management, test the entity's application of the percentages specified in *FASB Statement No. 14*, and apply analytical review procedures in examining segment information.

The auditor's standard report should not make any reference to segment information when the data have been presented in conformity with GAAP. Modification of the report is required for (1) inadequate disclosure when the

[13]Auditing Standards Board, *op. cit.*, AU § 505.12.

segment information is either misstated or omitted or (2) a scope limitation when the auditor is unable to apply the procedures considered necessary in the circumstances.[14] As explained earlier, the auditor is not required to present the omitted information in his report.

INFORMATION ACCOMPANYING AUDITED FINANCIAL STATEMENTS

Information accompanying audited financial statements consists of: (1) supplementary information required by the FASB, (2) voluntary information provided by management, and (3) additional information provided by the auditor. The auditor is not required by GAAS to examine any of the information because the data are outside the basic financial statements. However, the auditor has some responsibilities concerning the information as explained below.

Required Supplementary Information

The FASB has determined that certain supplementary information is an essential part of a company's financial reporting. As a result of FASB pronouncements, the presentation of supplementary information is currently required on (1) the effects of changing prices, (2) oil and gas reserves, and (3) mineral reserves. The Auditing Standards Board (ASB) has issued an SAS on the auditor's basic responsibilities for such information and separate SASs on the information that is currently required.

The auditor is required to apply certain limited procedures to the information and report any deficiencies in or omissions of such information. The limited procedures involve inquiry of management regarding the methods of preparing the information, and comparison of the information for consistency with other available data. The auditor's reporting responsibility is referred to as *exception reporting*. Since the information is not audited and not a required part of the basic financial statements, a standard audit report should be issued except in the following circumstances:

- The supplementary information required in the circumstances is omitted.
- The auditor has concluded that the measurement or presentation of the supplementary information departs materially from guidelines prescribed by the FASB.
- The auditor is unable to complete the prescribed procedures.[15]

These circumstances should be described in one or more explanatory paragraphs of the auditor's report. The auditor need not present the supplementary information when it is omitted by the entity. *The foregoing circumstances have no effect on either the scope or opinion paragraphs of the auditor's report.*

---

[14]Auditing Standards Board, *op. cit.,* AU § 435.08.
[15]Auditing Standards Board, *op. cit.,* AU § 553.08.

Voluntary Information Provided by Management

The audited financial statements of a client are usually presented in a document called an *annual report*. This document includes such information as financial highlights, a letter from the president and/or chairman of the board, comparative financial statistics, schedules, and graphic presentations of financial data that is voluntarily provided by management. The auditor is required to read this information to determine whether the data, or the manner of presentation, is materially inconsistent with the financial statements on which an opinion is being expressed.

For example, in referring to per-share earnings in the president's letter, a client may only state earnings per share before an extraordinary loss when the income statement shows earnings per share data in accordance with *APB Opinion No. 15*. When a material inconsistency appears to exist, the auditor should determine whether the statements, the audit report, or the other information should be revised. If it is the latter and the client refuses to make the necessary changes, the auditor may elect to (1) include an explanatory paragraph in the audit report on the matter, (2) withhold his audit report, or (3) withdraw from the engagement.[16]

In reading the voluntary information, the auditor may also believe there is a material misstatement of fact. If the matter is not resolved to the auditor's satisfaction, the auditor should notify the client in writing and consult with his legal counsel on the matter.

Additional Information Provided by the Auditor

At the conclusion of an audit engagement, the auditor gives the client a document that contains the client's basic financial statements and the auditor's report thereon. The auditor may include additional information he has prepared that pertains to the basic statements. The information, such as details and historical summaries of selected statement items and statistical data, is intended to facilitate the analysis and interpretation of the basic financial statements. It is important to recognize that the additional information in the *auditor-submitted document* is presented outside the basic statements and is not necessary for a fair presentation of the statements. Like the basic financial statements, the data in the additional information are representations of management because they are derived from the basic statements.

The auditor is required by the fourth standard of reporting to report on all the information included in an auditor-submitted document. Thus, he must describe the character of his examination, if any, and either express or disclaim an opinion. In expressing an opinion, the auditor should indicate whether the additional information is fairly stated *in all material respects in relation to the basic financial statements taken as a whole* as shown in Figure 17-8. The report may be added to the auditor's standard report or appear separately in the document. When the information is not audited, it should either be marked

---

[16]Auditing Standards Board, *op. cit.*, AU § 550.04.

Our examination was made for the purpose of forming an opinion on the basic financial statements taken as a whole. The (identify accompanying information) is presented for purposes of additional analysis and is not a required part of the basic financial statements. Such information has been subjected to the auditing procedures applied in the examination of the basic financial statements and, in our opinion, is fairly stated in all material respects in relation to the basic financial statements taken as a whole.

Figure 17-8. AUDITOR'S REPORT ON ADDITIONAL INFORMATION SUBMITTED WITH AUDIT REPORT. (SOURCE: Auditing Standards Board, *op. cit.*, AU § 551.12.)

unaudited or include a reference to the disclaimer of opinion in the auditor's report on the information.

A summary of the auditor's reporting responsibilities for information accompanying audited financial statements is given in Figure 17-9.

CONDENSED FINANCIAL STATEMENTS AND SELECTED FINANCIAL DATA

The auditor may be engaged to report on condensed financial statements and selected financial data (e.g. a five-year financial summary) derived from financial statements that he has audited. Because such information does not constitute a fair presentation of financial position, results of operations, and changes in financial position in conformity with GAAP, the auditor's report should differ from his report on the complete financial statements. The report should indicate

- That the auditor has examined and expressed an opinion on the complete financial statements.
- The date of the auditor's report and type of opinion expressed on the complete financial statements.

Accompanying Information	Reporting Responsibility	
	Extent	Comment
Supplementary information required by FASB	Exception reporting only	Exceptions described in explanatory paragraph.
Voluntary information provided by management	None	Consider disclosure of exceptions in explanatory paragraph.
Additional information provided by auditor	Full	Report may be added to standard report or may be separate.

Figure 17-9. REPORTING RESPONSIBILITIES FOR INFORMATION ACCOMPANYING AUDITED FINANCIAL STATEMENTS.

- Whether, in the auditor's opinion, the information set forth in the condensed financial statements (or the selected financial data) is fairly stated in all material respects in relation to the complete financial statements from which it has been derived.[17]

Condensed financial statements are usually presented separately from the complete financial statements, whereas selected financial data are presented in a document (e.g. an annual report) that includes the complete financial statements. Thus, the auditor's report on condensed financial statements ordinarily is a separate report, whereas his report on selected financial data is generally presented as an additional paragraph in his report on the complete financial statements.

CONCLUDING COMMENTS

This chapter completes the coverage of an audit engagement when the auditor is engaged to make an examination of financial statements prepared in conformity with GAAP. Each of the four reporting standards plays a vital role in reporting on audited financial statements. When circumstances occur that prevent the issuance of a standard report, the auditor must modify his report and express the type of opinion that is justified by the findings.

REVIEW QUESTIONS

17-1 a. What aspects of a company's financial statements are covered in the first three reporting standards?
  b. State the objective of the fourth standard of reporting.

17-2 Explain the reference in the fourth standard of reporting to (a) financial statements, (b) character of the examination, and (c) the degree of responsibility the auditor is taking.

17-3 Identify and explain the four types of opinions an auditor may render.

17-4 What conditions must be met to warrant the expression of an unqualified opinion?

17-5 Identify the circumstances that may warrant the expression of (a) a qualified opinion, (b) an adverse opinion, and (c) a disclaimer of opinion.

17-6 What are the effects on the form of the auditor's report of (a) a qualified opinion and (b) a disclaimer of opinion?

17-7 Indicate the changes in language in the opinion paragraph for each opinion that is other than unqualified.

17-8 What circumstances may cause substantive changes in the auditor's standard report?

17-9 a. Indicate the factors that may cause a scope limitation.
  b. Explain the report modifications that result from a scope limitation.

[17]Auditing Standards Board, *op. cit.*, AU § 552.05 and 552.09.

17-10 What factors should be considered by an auditor in determining (a) whether he can serve as the principal auditor, and (b) whether, as principal auditor, he should make reference to the work of another auditor?

17-11 Explain the effects on the auditor's standard report of the decision to (a) make reference and (b) not make reference to another auditor.

17-12 When are financial statements presumed to be in conformity with GAAP?

17-13 What effect does inadequate disclosure have on the auditor's report?

17-14 a. What body is authorized by the AICPA to issue pronouncements on GAAP?
b. Which pronouncements are recognized as being authoritative under Rule 203?

17-15 Indicate the possible effects on the auditor's report of a departure from (a) a promulgated principle and (b) a GAAP.

17-16 Enumerate the types of changes that are covered by the consistency standard.

17-17 a. State the meaning of the term *uncertainties*.
b. Indicate the effects on the auditor's report of an uncertainty when the resolution of the matter may have a material effect on the financial statements.

17-18 What reporting requirements apply when the auditor wishes to emphasize a matter in his report?

17-19 In reporting on comparative statements, what are the continuing auditor's reporting responsibilities when an opinion on a prior year is changed and
a. There has been no change in auditors.
b. The prior year was reported on by a predecessor auditor and his report is not presented with the current year.

17-20 a. Identify the three types of information that may accompany audited financial statements.
b. Describe the nature of the auditor's reporting responsibility for each type of information identified in (a) above.

OBJECTIVE QUESTIONS FROM PROFESSIONAL EXAMINATIONS

Indicate the *best* answer choice for each of the following multiple choice questions.

17-21 These questions relate to the four reporting standards.

1. The fourth reporting standard requires the auditor's report to contain either an expression of opinion regarding the financial statements, taken as a whole, or an assertion to the effect that an opinion cannot be expressed. The objective of the fourth standard is to prevent
a. The CPA from reporting on one basic financial statement and *not* the others.
b. Misinterpretations regarding the degree of responsibility the auditor is assuming.
c. The CPA from expressing different opinions on each of the basic financial statements.
d. Management from reducing its final responsibility for the basic financial statements.

2. The first standard of reporting requires that "the report shall state whether the financial statements are presented in accordance with generally accepted accounting principles." This should be construed to require
a. A statement of fact by the auditor.
b. An opinion by the auditor.

   c. An implied measure of fairness.

   d. An objective measure of compliance.

3. The objective of the consistency standard is to provide assurance that

   a. There are *no* variations in the format and presentation of financial statements.

   b. Substantially different transactions and events are *not* accounted for on an identical basis.

   c. The auditor is consulted before material changes are made in the application of accounting principles.

   d. The comparability of financial statements between periods is *not* materially affected by changes in accounting principles without disclosure.

17-22 These questions relate to the type of opinion that an auditor should express.

1. An auditor's report included an additional paragraph disclosing that there is a difference of opinion between the auditor and the client for which the auditor believed an adjustment to the financial statements should be made. The opinion paragraph of the auditor's report most likely expressed a(n)

   a. Unqualified opinion.

   b. "Except for" opinion.

   c. "Subject to" opinion.

   d. Disclaimer of opinion.

2. If the auditor believes there is minimal likelihood that resolution of an uncertainty will have a material effect on the financial statements, the auditor would issue a(n)

   a. "Except for" opinion.

   b. Adverse opinion.

   c. Unqualified opinion.

   d. "Subject to" opinion.

3. When the client fails to include information that is necessary for the fair presentation of financial statements in the body of the statements or in the related footnotes, it is the responsibility of the auditor to present the information, if practicable, in the auditor's report and issue a(n)

   a. Qualified opinion or a disclaimer of opinion.

   b. Qualified opinion or an adverse opinion.

   c. Adverse opinion or a disclaimer of opinion.

   d. Qualified opinion or an unqualified opinion.

17-23 These questions involve the effects of circumstances on the form and content of the auditor's report.

1. The principal auditor is satisfied with the independence and professional reputation of the other auditor who has audited a subsidiary. To indicate the division of responsibility, the principal auditor should modify

   a. Only the scope paragraph of the report.

   b. Only the opinion paragraph of the report.

   c. Both the scope and opinion paragraphs of the report.

   d. Only the opinion paragraph of the report and include an explanatory middle paragraph.

2. An auditor's standard report expresses an unqualified opinion and includes a middle paragraph that emphasizes a matter included in the notes to the financial statements. The auditor's report would be deficient if the middle paragraph states that the entity

   a. Is a component of a larger business enterprise.

   b. Has changed from the completed-contract method to the percentage of completion method for accounting for long-term construction contracts.

c. Has had a significant subsequent event.

d. Has accounting reclassifications that enhance the comparability between years.

3. In which of the following circumstances may the auditor issue the standard audit report?

a. The principal auditor assumes responsibility for the work of another auditor.

b. The financial statements are affected by a departure from a generally accepted accounting principle.

c. The auditor's report covers the company's first year of operations.

d. The auditor wishes to emphasize a matter regarding the financial statements.

17-24 These questions are based on the "other considerations" section of this chapter.

1. When comparative financial statements are presented but the predecessor auditor's report is *not* presented, the current auditor should do which of the following in the audit report?

a. Disclaim an opinion on the prior year's financial statements.

b. Identify the predecessor auditor who examined the financial statements of the prior year.

c. Make *no* comment with respect to the predecessor auditor's examination.

d. Indicate the type of opinion expressed by the predecessor auditor.

2. When an auditor submits a document containing audited financial statements to a client, the auditor has a responsibility to report on

a. Only the basic financial statements included in the document.

b. The basic financial statements and only that additional information required to be presented in accordance with provisions of the Financial Accounting Standards Board.

c. All of the information included in the document.

d. Only that portion of the document that was audited.

3. When auditing a public entity's financial statements that include segment information, the auditor should

a. Make certain the segment information is labeled unaudited and determine that the information is consistent with audited information.

b. Make certain the segment information is labeled unaudited and perform only analytical review procedures on the segment information.

c. Audit the segment information and, if the information is adequate and in conformity with GAAP, *not* make reference to the segment information in the auditor's report.

d. Audit the segment information and, if the information is adequate and in conformity with GAAP, refer to the segment information in the auditor's report.

COMPREHENSIVE QUESTIONS

17-25 On completion of the examination of his client's financial statements, the CPA, in his report, must either express an opinion or disclaim an opinion on the statements taken as a whole. His opinion may be unqualified, qualified, or adverse.

Required

a. Under what general conditions may a CPA express an unqualified opinion on his client's financial statements?

b. Define and distinguish among (1) a qualified opinion, (2) an adverse opinion, and (3) a disclaimer of opinion on the statements taken as a whole.

c. Indicate the effect of the opinions in (b) above on the form of the auditor's report.

d. Indicate the proper qualifying language for the opinions in (b) above.

17-26 Assume that the following separate circumstances are sufficiently material to cause a departure from the auditor's standard report:

1. Change from LIFO to FIFO, necessitating a restatement of prior years' statements.

2. Other auditors, Jones and Jones, audited a subsidiary company that accounts for 5% of the consolidation's total assets and 10% of total revenues.

3. Replacement cost is used in the basic financial statements for inventories, cost of sales, plant assets, and depreciation.

4. The continuation of the company as a going concern is in doubt.

5. Pensions are properly recorded, but the total pension expense of $532,000 and the company's policy to fund accrued pension costs are not disclosed in the notes as required by *APB Opinion No. 8*.

6. The fact that 25% of the company's inventories result from related party transactions is disclosed in the notes to the statements but the auditor decides to indicate this fact in the audit report.

7. Finished goods stored in a foreign country were not observed or test counted. The items constitute 15% of ending inventory.

8. The lease provisions of *FASB Statement No. 13* were not properly followed in accounting for leases.

Required

a. Indicate the type of circumstance and its effects on the auditor's standard report using the format illustrated on page 638 of this chapter.

b. Prepare the parts of the auditor's standard report that are changed by each circumstance.

17-27 The following report was drafted by an audit assistant at the completion of an audit engagement and was submitted to the auditor with client responsibility for review. The auditor has reviewed matters thoroughly and has properly concluded that the scope limitation was not client-imposed and sufficiently material to warrant a disclaimer of opinion although a qualified opinion was appropriate.

To Carl Corporation Controller

We have examined the accompanying financial statements of Carl Corporation as of December 31, 19X2. Our examination was made in accordance with generally accepted auditing standards, and accordingly included such auditing procedures as we considered necessary in the circumstances.

On January 15, 19X3, the company issued debentures in the amount of $1,000,000 for the purpose of financing plant expansion. As indicated in note 6 to the financial statements, the debenture agreement restricts the payment of future cash dividends to earnings after December 31, 19X2.

The company's unconsolidated foreign subsidiary did not close down production during the year under examination for physical inventory purposes and took no physical inventory during the year. We made extensive tests of book inventory figures for accuracy of calculation and reasonableness of pricing. We did not make physical tests of inventory quantities. Because of this, we are unable to express an unqualified opinion on the financial statements taken as a whole. However:

Except for the scope limitation regarding inventory, in our opinion the accompanying balance sheet presents the financial position of Carl Corporation at December 31, 19X2, subject to the effect of the inventory on the carrying value of the investment. The accompanying statements of income and retained earnings present the incomes and expenses and the result of transactions affecting retained earnings in accordance with generally accepted accounting principles.

December 31, 19X2

Pate & Co., CPAs

Required

Identify all of the deficiencies in the above draft of the proposed report.

17-28 You are newly engaged by the James Company, a New England manufacturer with a sales office and warehouse located in a western state. The James Company audit must be made at the peak of your busy season when you will not have a senior auditor available for travel to the western outlet. Furthermore, the James Company is reluctant to bear the travel expenses of an out-of-town auditor.

Required

a. Under what conditions would you, the principal auditor, be willing to accept full responsibility for the work of another auditor?

b. What would be your requirements with respect to the integrity of the other auditor? To whom would you direct inquiries about the other auditor?

c. What reference, if any, would you make to the other auditor in your report if you were
   1. Assuming full responsibility for his work?
   2. Not assuming responsibility for his work?

AICPA

17-29 Presented below is an independent auditor's report that contains deficiencies. The corporation being reported on is profit oriented and publishes general-purpose financial statements for distribution to owners, creditors, potential investors, and the general public.

We have examined the consolidated balance sheet of Belleno Corporation and subsidiaries as of December 31, 19X0, and the related consolidated statements of income and retained earnings and changes in financial position for the year then ended. Our examination was made in accordance with generally accepted auditing standards and accordingly included such tests of the accounting records and such other auditing procedures as we considered necessary in the circumstances.

We did not examine the financial statements of Seidel Company, a major consolidated subsidiary. These statements were examined by other auditors whose report thereon has been furnished to us, and our opinion expressed herein, insofar as it relates to Seidel Company, is based solely on the report of the other auditors.

In our opinion, except for the report of the other auditors, the accompanying consolidated balance sheet and consolidated statements of income and retained earnings and changes in financial position present fairly the financial position of Belleno Corporation and subsidiaries at December 31, 19X0, and the results of its operations and the changes in its financial position for the year then ended, in conformity with generally accepted accounting principles applied on a basis consistent with that of the preceding year.

Required

Describe the reporting deficiencies, explain the reasons therefor, and briefly discuss how the report should be corrected. Do not discuss the addressee, signature, and date. Also, do not write the foregoing auditor's report. Organize your answer sheet as follows:

Deficiency	Reason	Correction

AICPA (adapted)

17-30 Lancaster Electronics produces electronic components for sale to manufacturers of radios, television sets, and phonographic systems. In connection with his examination of Lancaster's financial statements for the year ended December 31, 19X1, Don Olds, CPA, completed field work two weeks ago. Olds now is evaluating the significance of the following items prior to preparing his auditor's report. Except as noted, none of these items has been disclosed in the financial statements or footnotes.

Item 1

Recently, Lancaster interrupted its policy of paying cash dividends quarterly to its stockholders. Dividends were paid regularly through 19X0, discontinued for all of 19X1 in order to finance equipment for the company's new plant and resumed in the first quarter of 19X2. In the annual report, dividend policy is to be discussed in the president's letter.

Item 2

A ten-year loan agreement, which the company entered into three years ago, provides that dividend payments may not exceed net income earned after taxes subsequent to the date of the agreement. The balance of retained earnings at the date of the loan agreement was $298,000. From that date through December 31, 19X1, net income after taxes has totaled $360,000 and cash dividends have totaled $130,000. Based on these data, the staff auditor assigned to this review concluded that there was no retained earnings restriction at December 31, 19X1.

Item 3

The company's new manufacturing plant building, which cost $600,000 and has an estimated life of 25 years, is leased from the Sixth National Bank at an annual rental of $100,000. The company is obligated to pay property taxes, insurance, and maintenance. At the conclusion of its ten-year noncancelable lease, the company has the option of purchasing the property for $1. In Lancaster's income statement, the rental payment is reported on a separate line.

Item 4

A major electronics firm has introduced a line of products that will compete directly with Lancaster's primary line, now being produced in the specially designed new plant. Because of manufacturing innovations, the competitor's line will be of comparable quality but priced 50% below Lancaster's line. The competitor announced its new line during the week following completion of field work. Olds read the announcement in the newspaper and discussed the situation by telephone with Lancaster executives. Lancaster will meet the lower prices that are high enough to cover variable manufacturing and selling expenses but will permit recovery of only a portion of fixed costs.

Required

For each item 1 to 4 above, discuss the following:

a. Any additional disclosure in the financial statements and footnotes that the CPA should recommend to his client.

b. The effect of this situation on the CPA's report on Lancaster's financial statements. For this requirement, assume that the client did not make the additional disclosure recommended in a above.

Complete your discussion of each item (both a and b above) before beginning discussion of the next item. The effects of each item on the financial statements and the CPA's report should be evaluated independently of the other items. The cumulative effects of the four items should not be considered.

AICPA

17-31 Nancy Miller, CPA, has completed field work for her examination of the financial statements of Nickles Manufacturers, Inc. for the year ended March 31, 19X1, and now is preparing her auditor's report. Presented below are three independent, unrelated assumptions concerning this examination.

Assumption 1

The CPA was engaged on April 15, 19X1, to examine the financial statements for the year ended March 31, 19X1 and was not present to observe the taking of the physical inventory on March 31, 19X1. Her alternative procedures included examination of shipping and receiving documents with regard to transactions during the year under review as well as transactions since the year end, extensive review of the inventory count sheets, and discussion of the physical inventory procedures with responsible Company personnel. She has also satisfied herself as to inventory valuation and consistency in valuation method. Inventory quantities are determined solely by means of physical count. (*Note:* Assume that the CPA is properly relying on the examination of another auditor with respect to the beginning inventory.)

Assumption 2

As of April 1, 19X1, Nickles has an unused balance of $1,378,000 of federal income tax net operating loss carryover that will expire at the end of the Company's fiscal years as follows: $432,000 in 19X2, $870,000 in 19X3, and $76,000 in 19X4. Nickles' management expects that the Company will have enough taxable income to use the loss carryover before it expires.

Assumption 3

On February 28, 19X1, Nickles paid cash for all of the outstanding stock of Ashworth, Inc., a small manufacturer. The combination was consummated as of that date and has been appropriately accounted for as a purchase.

Required

For each assumption described above, discuss the following:

a. In detail, the appropriate disclosures, if any, in the financial statements and accompanying footnotes.
b. The effect, if any, on the auditor's standard report. For this requirement, assume that Nickles makes the appropriate disclosures.

Note: Complete your discussion of each assumption (both a and b above) before beginning discussion of the next assumption. In considering each independent assumption, assume that the other two situations did not occur. Organize your answer sheet as follows.

Assumption Number	(a) Financial Statements and Footnotes	(b) Auditor's Report

AICPA (adapted)

17-32 Sturdy Corporation owns and operates a large office building in a desirable section of New York City's financial center. For many years, the management of Sturdy Corporation has modified the presentation of their financial statements by

1. Reflecting a write-up to appraisal values in the building accounts.
2. Accounting for depreciation expense on the basis of such valuations.

Wyley, a successor CPA, was asked to examine the financial statements of Sturdy Corporation, for the year ended December 31, 19X0. After completing the examination, Wyley concluded that, consistent with prior years, an adverse opinion would have to be expressed because of the materiality of the apparent deviation from the historical-cost principle.

Required

a. Describe in detail the form of presentation of the middle paragraph of the auditor's report on the financial statements of Sturdy Corporation for the year ended December 31, 19X0, clearly identifying the information contained in the paragraph. Do not discuss deferred taxes.
b. Write a draft of the opinion paragraph of the auditor's report on the financial statements of Sturdy Corporation for the year ended December 31, 19X0.

AICPA

17-33 The CPA must comply with the GAAS of reporting when he prepares his opinion on the client's financial statements. One of the reporting standards relates to consistency.

Required

a. Discuss the statement regarding consistency that the CPA is required to include in his opinion. What is the objective of requiring the CPA to make this statement about consistency?
b. Discuss what mention of consistency, if any, the CPA must make in his opinion

relating to his first audit of the financial statements of the following companies:

1. A newly organized company ending its first accounting period.
2. A company established for a number of years.

c. Discuss whether the changes described in each of the cases below would require recognition in the CPA's opinion as to consistency. (Assume the amounts are material.)

1. The company disposed of one of its subsidiaries that had been included in its consolidated statements for prior years.
2. After two years of computing depreciation under the declining balance method for income tax purposes and under the straight line method for reporting purposes, the declining balance method was adopted for reporting purposes.
3. The estimated remaining useful life of plant property was reduced because of obsolescence.

AICPA

17-34 The following tentative auditor's report was drafted by a staff accountant and submitted to a partner in the accounting firm of Better & Best, CPAs:

To the Audit Committee of American Widgets, Inc.

We have examined the consolidated balance sheets of American Widgets, Inc., and subsidiaries as of December 31, 19X2 and 19X1, and the related consolidated statements of income, retained earnings, and changes in financial position, for the years then ended. Our examinations were made in accordance with generally accepted auditing standards as we considered necessary in the circumstances. Other auditors examined the financial statements of certain subsidiaries and have furnished us with reports thereon containing no exceptions. Our opinion expressed herein, insofar as it relates to the amounts included for those subsidiaries, is based solely on the reports of the other auditors.

As discussed in Note 4 to the financial statements, on January 8, 19X3, the company halted the production of certain medical equipment as a result of inquiries by the Food and Drug Administration, which raised questions as to the adequacy of some of the company's sterilization equipment and related procedures. Management is not in a position to evaluate the effect of this production halt and the ensuing litigation, which may have an adverse effect on the financial position of American Widgets, Inc.

As fully discussed in Note 7 to the financial statements, in 19X2 the company extended the use of the last-in, first out (LIFO) method of accounting to include all inventories. In examining inventories, we engaged Dr. Irwin Same (Nobel Prize winner 19X0) to test check the technical requirements and specifications of certain items of equipment manufactured by the company.

In our opinion, except for the effects, if any, on the financial statements of the ultimate resolution of the matter discussed in the second preceding paragraph, the financial statements referred to above present fairly the financial position of American Widgets, Inc., as of December 31, 19X2, and the results of operations for the years then ended, in conformity with generally accepted accounting principles applied on a basis consistent with that of the preceding year.

To be signed by
Better & Best, CPAs

March 1, 19X3, except
for Note 4 as to which
the date is January 8, 19X3

Required

Identify deficiencies in the staff accountant's tentative report that constitute departures from the generally accepted standards of reporting. Do not consider any AICPA exposure drafts that are currently outstanding.

AICPA

17-35 The following auditor's report was drafted by an assistant at the completion of an audit engagement of Cramdon, Inc., and was submitted to the partner with client responsibility for review. The partner has examined matters thoroughly and has properly concluded that the opinion on the 19X4 financial report should be modified only for the change in the method for computing sales. Also, due to an uncertainty, a "subject to" opinion was issued on the 19X3 financial statements that are included for comparative purposes. The 19X3 auditor's report was dated March 3, 19X4. In 19X4, the litigation against Cramdon, which was the cause of the 19X3 "subject to" opinion, was resolved in favor of Cramdon.

To Board of Directors of Cramdon, Inc.

We have examined the financial statements that are the representations of Cramdon, Inc., incorporated herein by reference, for the years ended December 31, 19X4 and 19X3. Our examinations were made in accordance with generally accepted auditing standards and, accordingly, included such auditing procedures as we considered necessary in the circumstances.

As discussed in Note 7 to the financial statements, our previous opinion on the 19X3 financial statements was other than unqualified pending the outcome of litigation. Due to our attorney's meritorious defense in this litigation, our opinion on these financial statements is different from that expressed in our previous report.

In our opinion, based on the preceding, the accompanying financial statements referred to above present fairly the financial position, results of operations, and changes in financial position for the period ended December 31, 19X4, in conformity with generally accepted accounting principles consistently applied, except for the change in the method of computing sales as described in Note 14 to the financial statements.

CPA

March 5, 19X5

Required

Identify the deficiencies contained in the auditor's report as drafted by the audit assistant in the (a) scope paragraph, (b) middle paragraph, and (c) opinion paragraph. Rewriting the auditor's report is not an acceptable solution.

17-36 Roscoe, CPA, has completed the examination of the financial statements of Excelsior Corporation as of and for the year ended December 31, 19X1. Roscoe also examined and reported on the Excelsior financial statements for the prior year. Roscoe drafted the following report for 19X1.

We have examined the balance sheet and statements of income and retained earnings of Excelsior Corporation as of December 31, 19X1. Our examination was made in accordance with generally accepted accounting standards and accordingly included such tests of the accounting records as we considered necessary in the circumstances.

In our opinion, the above-mentioned financial statements are accurately and fairly presented in accordance with generally accepted accounting principles in effect at December 31, 19X1.

Roscoe, CPA
(Signed)
March 15, 19X2

Other information:

1. Excelsior is presenting comparative financial statements for 19X1 and 19X0.

2. Excelsior does not wish to present a statement of changes in financial position for either year.

3. During 19X1, Excelsior changed its method of accounting for long-term construction contracts and properly reflected the effect of the change in the current year's financial statements and restated the prior-year's statements. Roscoe is satisfied with Excelsior's justification for making the change. The change is discussed in footnote number 12.

4. Roscoe was unable to perform normal accounts receivable confirmation procedures but alternate procedures were used to satisfy Roscoe as to the validity of the receivables.

5. Excelsior Corporation is the defendant in a litigation, the outcome of which is highly uncertain. If the case is settled in favor of the plaintiff, Excelsior will be required to pay a substantial amount of cash that might require the sale of certain fixed assets. The litigation and the possible effects have been properly disclosed in footnote number 11.

6. Excelsior issued debentures on January 31, 19X0, in the amount of $10 million. The funds obtained from the issuance were used to finance the expansion of plant facilities. The debenture agreement restricts the payment of future cash dividends to earnings after December 31, 19X6. Excelsior declined to disclose this essential data in the footnotes to the financial statements.

Required

Consider all facts given and rewrite the auditor's report in acceptable and complete format incorporating any necessary departures from the standard report.

Do not discuss the draft of Roscoe's report but identify and explain any items included in *"Other Information"* that need not be part of the auditor's report.

AICPA

17-37 Ross, Sandler & Co., CPAs, completed an examination of the 19X2 financial statements of Fairfax Corporation on March 17, 19X3, and concluded that an unqualified opinion was warranted. Because of a scope limitation arising from the inability to observe the January 1, 19X1 inventory, the predecessor auditors, Smith, Ellis & Co., issued a report that contained an unqualified opinion on the December 31, 19X1 balance sheet and a qualified opinion with respect to the statements of income, retained earnings, and changes in financial position for the year then ended.

The management of Fairfax Corporation has decided to present a complete set of comparative (19X2 and 19X1) financial statements in their annual report.

Required

Prepare an auditor's report, assuming the March 1, 19X2 auditor's report of Smith, Ellis & Co. is not presented.

AICPA

17-38 The annual reports of three major United States corporations contained departures from the auditor's standard report because of the following notes to financial statements:

R.J. Reynolds Industries, Inc.

Notes to Financial Statements

Note C—Commitments and Contingencies

In July 19X2, two civil actions purporting to be class actions were brought against the six major United States cigarette manufacturers, including the Company, and others, by certain tobacco farmers alleging violations of the antitrust laws and seeking damages aggregating approximately $2.5 billion plus attorneys' fees and costs. Both actions are in their early stages and investigation of the facts is not complete. Counsel has advised the Company, based on its investigation and the formal discovery to date, that in its opinion these cases are not proper class actions and the Company has substantial factual and legal defenses to the charges made. Accordingly, the Company has made no provision for this matter in its financial statements.

Dow Chemical Company

Notes to Financial Statements

B. Inventories—In 19X2, the Company abandoned its historical worldwide practice of valuing inventories on the first-in, first-out basis in favor of the last-in, first-out basis in order to more effectively match current costs and revenues. If the LIFO method had not been adopted, inventories at December 31, 19X2 would have been $993 million, or $271 million greater than the carrying value at that date. The effect of the change was to reduce earnings per share by $1.53.

The Goodyear Tire and Rubber Company

Accounting Change

In accordance with a recent ruling of the Financial Accounting Standards Board, research and development expenses were excluded as an element of cost used for pricing inventory. This has been done on a retroactive basis and consequently prior years have been restated. Inventories and taxes have been decreased by $20,853,000 and $9,692,000, respectively at December 31, 19X2 and 19X1. The effect of this change on 19X2, 19X1, and 19X0 income was not significant.

Required

a. Write the explanatory and opinion paragraphs of the auditor's report for each company. Cover the balance sheets at December 31, 19X2 and 19X1, and the statements of income, retained earnings, and changes in financial position for each of the three years ended December 31, 19X2.

b. Write the explanatory paragraph of the audit report for R. J. Reynolds in the succeeding year. Assume the lawsuits were settled in 19X3 in favor of the company.

CASE STUDY

17-39 Devon Incorporated engaged Smith to examine its financial statements for the year ended December 31, 19X3. The financial statements of Devon Incorporated for the year ended December 31, 19X2, were examined by Jones whose March 31, 19X3 auditor's report expressed an unqualified opinion. This report of Jones is not presented with the 19X3–19X2 comparative financial statements.

Smith's working papers contain the following information that does not appear in footnotes to the 19X3 financial statements as prepared by Devon Incorporated

- One director appointed in 19X3 was formerly a partner in Jones' accounting firm. Jones' firm provided financial consulting services to Devon during 19X9 and 19X8, for which Devon paid approximately $1,600 and $9,000, respectively.
- The company refused to capitalize certain lease obligations for equipment acquired in 19X3. Capitalization of the leases in conformity with generally accepted accounting principles would have increased assets and liabilities by $312,000 and $387,000, respectively, and decreased retained earnings as of December 31, 19X3, by $75,000, and would have decreased net income and earnings per share by $75,000 and $.75, respectively, for the year then ended. Smith has concluded that the leases should have been capitalized.
- During the year, Devon changed its method of valuing inventory from the first-in, first-out method to the last-in, first-out method. This change was made because management believes LIFO more clearly reflects net income by providing a closer matching of current costs and current revenues. The change had the effect of reducing inventory at December 31, 19X3 by $65,000 and net income and earnings per share by $38,000 and $.38, respectively, for the year then ended. The effect of the change on prior years was immaterial; accordingly, there was no cumulative effect of the change. Smith firmly supports the company's position.

After completion of the field work on February 29, 19X4, Smith concludes that the expression of an adverse opinion is not warranted.

Required

Prepare the body of Smith's report dated February 29, 19X4, and addressed to the Board of Directors to accompany the 19X3–19X2 comparative financial statements.

AICPA

Chapter 18

Other Reports and Services

Study Objectives

When you have completed the study of this chapter, you should be able to

- Distinguish among the three types of services a CPA may render to a client.

- Identify the types of special reports that may be issued.

- Describe the auditor's report when financial statements are prepared on a comprehensive basis other than GAAP.

- Differentiate between the reports that may be issued on internal accounting control.

- Explain the objectives and reporting requirements of the Single Audit Act.

- Contrast the review report on interim financial information and the report on interim financial statements.

- Prepare the accountant's standard report on a compilation engagement.

As an auditor and accountant in a firm, a certified public accountant (CPA) may render three types of services to a client: audit, review, or accounting. This chapter has two primary objectives: to describe and illustrate additional types of reports pertaining to audit engagements and to explain the objectives, standards, procedures, and reports relating to performing review and accounting services for a client.

AUDITING SERVICES

The audit or attest function has been and continues to be the central purpose of this book. In rendering audit services, the auditor is expected to make the examination and report his findings in accordance with generally accepted auditing standards (GAAS). In Chapter 17, reporting is directed solely on audit reports issued on financial statements prepared in conformity with generally accepted accounting principles (GAAP). Now, it is appropriate to consider other reports that may result from audit engagements. These include special reports, reports on personal financial statements, and reports on internal accounting control.

SPECIAL REPORTS

Reports issued in connection with the following criteria constitute special reports:

- Financial statements prepared in accordance with a comprehensive basis of accounting other than GAAP.
- Specific elements, accounts, or items of a financial statement.
- Compliance with aspects of contractual agreements or regulatory requirements related to audited financial statements.
- Financial information presented in prescribed forms or schedules that require a prescribed form of auditor's report.[1]

The responsibilities of the auditor for the first three types of special reports are explained below.

Comprehensive Basis Other than GAAP

The basis of accounting used by the client is considered to be comprehensive when it is (1) a basis prescribed by a regulatory body, (2) a basis used in filing its income tax return, (3) the cash or modified cash basis, or (4) a basis having substantial support, such as the price level or replacement cost basis.

The use of these alternative bases is common. Many companies subject to regulatory bodies keep their accounts solely on the basis prescribed by the agency. For example, railroads conform with the requirements of the Interstate Commerce Commission (ICC), public utilities use the basis set forth by the Federal Energy Regulatory Commission, and insurance companies follow state insurance commission accounting requirements. In addition, many small companies and individual practitioners, such as doctors, lawyers, and CPAs, use the income tax, cash, or modified cash basis of accounting. When an entity

---

[1] Auditing Standards Board, *Codification of Statements on Auditing Standards* (New York: American Institute of Certified Public Accountants, 1985), Auditing Section 621.01 (hereinafter referred to and cited as AU §).

uses a basis other than GAAP, the notes to the financial statements should indicate the basis and how it differs from GAAP.

All of the GAAS are applicable whenever the auditor examines and reports on any financial statement regardless of the basis of accounting used in preparing the statement. The major difference in this case is that the statements are not intended to present fairly financial position, and so forth, in conformity with GAAP. However, the first standard of reporting is satisfied by indicating whether the statements are presented fairly in conformity with the basis of accounting used.[2]

In reporting on statements prepared on a comprehensive basis other than GAAP, the auditor should issue a three-paragraph report that contains

- A *scope paragraph* that may be standard except that more distinctive titles should be used for each statement, such as statement of assets and liabilities (cash basis) for the balance sheet and statement of revenue collected and expenses paid for the income statement.

- An *explanatory paragraph* that should (1) refer to the note to the financial statements that describes the basis of accounting and how it differs from GAAP and (2) indicate that the statements are not intended to be in conformity with GAAP.

- An *opinion paragraph* that indicates whether (1) the financial statements are fairly presented on the basis described and (2) the disclosed basis has been applied on a consistent basis.

When the auditor concludes that the financial statements are not presented fairly, a qualified or adverse opinion should be expressed as explained in the preceding chapter. A special report for financial statements prepared on a cash basis is illustrated in Figure 18-1.

Specified Elements, Accounts, or Items of a Financial Statement

An auditor may report on these data when he has been engaged to express an opinion or apply agreed-upon procedures. The standards applicable to each type of engagement are explained below.

Expression of Opinion. This category of special reports includes the expression of an opinion on rentals, royalties, profit participation plans, or provisions for income taxes. An engagement to express an opinion on one or more of these items may be made in conjunction with an examination of financial statements or it may be done in a separate engagement. In such an engagement, all of the GAAS apply except the first and second standards of reporting. The first standard of reporting is not applicable because the specified items do not constitute a financial statement. The consistency standard applies only if the items have, in fact, been stated in conformity with GAAP.

---

[2]Auditing Standards Board, *op. cit.*, AU § 621.01.

BOARD OF DIRECTORS
XYZ CORPORATION

We have examined the statement of assets and liabilities arising from cash transactions of XYZ Company as of December 31, 19XX, and the related statement of revenue collected and expenses paid for the year then ended. Our examination was made in accordance with generally accepted auditing standards and, accordingly, included such tests of the accounting records and such other auditing procedures as we considered necessary in the circumstances.

As described in Note X, the Company's policy is to prepare its financial statements on the basis of cash receipts and disbursements; consequently, certain revenue and the related assets are recognized when received rather than when earned, and certain expenses are recognized when paid rather than when the obligation is incurred. Accordingly, the accompanying financial statements are not intended to present financial position and results of operations in conformity with generally accepted accounting principles.

In our opinion, the financial statements referred to above present fairly the assets and liabilities arising from cash transactions of XYZ Company as of December 31, 19XX, and the revenue collected and expenses paid during the year then ended, on the basis of accounting described in Note X, which basis has been applied in a manner consistent with that of the preceding year.

Figure 18-1. AUDITOR'S REPORT ON FINANCIAL STATEMENTS PREPARED ON CASH BASIS.
(SOURCE: Auditing Standards Board, *op. cit.*, AU § 621.08.)

In reporting, the auditor may use either a two- or a three-paragraph report. In the scope paragraph, the specific elements, accounts, or items should be identified and the character of the examination indicated. The latter is done by reference to GAAS. In addition, the report should indicate (1) the basis on which the items are presented, (2) whether they are presented fairly on that basis, and if applicable, (3) whether the basis was applied in a manner consistent with the preceding period. An example of a three-paragraph report is illustrated in Figure 18-2. A special report on specific items should not be issued if the auditor has expressed an adverse opinion or disclaimed an opinion on the financial statements taken as a whole.

Application of Agreed-Upon Procedures. A CPA may accept an engagement to apply agreed-upon procedures to specified elements, accounts, or items of a financial statement. For example, in a proposed acquisition, the prospective purchaser may only ask the accountant to reconcile the bank balances and confirm the accounts receivable of the entity that may be acquired. This type of engagement is permitted provided (1) the parties involved have a clear understanding of the procedures to be performed and (2) distribution of the report is restricted to named parties involved.

An engagement to perform agreed-upon procedures does not constitute an examination in accordance with GAAS. Only the three general standards and the first standard of field work are applicable. The CPA's report on the results of agreed-upon procedures should

- Indicate the elements, accounts, or items to which the procedures were applied.

BOARD OF DIRECTORS
XYZ CORPORATION

We have examined the schedule of royalties applicable to engine production of the Q Division of XYZ Corporation for the year ended December 31, 19XX, under the terms of a license agreement dated May 14, 19XX, between ABC Company and XYZ Corporation. Our examination was made in accordance with generally accepted auditing standards and, accordingly, included such tests of the accounting records and such other auditing procedures as we considered necessary in the circumstances.

We have been informed that, under XYZ Corporation's interpretation of the agreement referred to above, royalties were based on the number of engines produced after giving effect to a reduction for production retirements that were scrapped, but without a reduction for field returns that were scrapped, even though the field returns were replaced with new engines without charge to customers. This treatment is consistent with that followed in prior years.

In our opinion, the schedule of royalties referred to above presents fairly the number of engines produced by the Q Division of XYZ Corporation during the year ended December 31, 19XX, and the amount of royalties applicable thereto under the license agreement referred to above, on the basis indicated in the preceding paragraph.

Figure 18-2. AUDITOR'S REPORT ON SPECIFIED ELEMENTS, ACCOUNTS, OR ITEMS OF A FINANCIAL STATEMENT. (SOURCE: Auditing Standards Board, *op. cit.*, AU § 621.14.)

- State the intended distribution of the report.
- Enumerate the procedures performed.
- State the findings.
- Disclaim an opinion with respect to the elements, accounts, or items.
- State that the report relates only to the specified items and does not extend to the entity's financial statements taken as a whole.[3]

When the agreed-upon procedures indicate that no adjustments are needed, it is permissible for the CPA to express *negative assurance* on the specified elements, accounts, or items. This is done in the report by stating: "No matters came to our attention that caused us to believe that the specified items should be adjusted."

Compliance Reports Related to Audited Financial Statements

This type of special report pertains to contractual agreements, such as bond indentures, and regulatory requirements of such agencies as the Federal Home Loan Mortgage Corporation. The auditor's involvement with such reports arises from the desire by the lender or agency to obtain assurance from an independent party concerning compliance. In such circumstances, the auditor is not required to audit the data for compliance. However, if the auditor has audited the related financial statements, it is permissible for the auditor to

[3]Auditing Standards Board, *op. cit.*, AU § 622.04.

BOARD OF DIRECTORS
XYZ COMPANY

We have examined the balance sheet of XYZ Company as of December 31, 19X1, and the related statements of income, retained earnings, and changes in financial position for the year then ended, and have issued our report thereon dated March 5, 19X2. Our examination was made in accordance with generally accepted auditing standards and, accordingly, included such tests of the accounting records and such other auditing procedures as we considered necessary in the circumstances.

In connection with our examination, nothing came to our attention that caused us to believe that the Company had failed to comply with the limitation and increased investment requirement in section 993(d)(2) and (3) of the Internal Revenue Code of 1954. However, it should be noted that our examination was not directed primarily toward obtaining knowledge of noncompliance with such requirements.

Figure 18-3. AUDITOR'S REPORT ON COMPLIANCE WITH REGULATORY REQUIREMENTS. (SOURCE: Auditing Standards Board, *op. cit.*, AU § 621.19.)

give negative assurance on compliance by stating that "nothing came to our attention which would indicate that these amounts [or items] are not fairly presented [stated]."

Compliance reports may be issued as a separate report, or they may be included as an "add on" to the auditor's report on the accompanying financial statements. In the latter, an explanatory third paragraph is often added after the opinion paragraph. Such positioning serves to keep intact the two-paragraph standard auditor's report. A separate report on compliance is illustrated in Figure 18-3.

REPORTS ON PERSONAL FINANCIAL STATEMENTS

Personal financial statements present the assets, liabilities, estimated income taxes, and net worth of an individual or groups of individuals, such as a family, at a specified date. The basic personal financial statement is a *statement of financial condition*.[4] Guidelines for this statement are

- Assets should be recorded at their estimated current values, and liabilities should be stated at their estimated current amounts.
- Assets and liabilities and changes in them should be reported on the accrual basis of acounting.
- The statements should include sufficient disclosures to make them informative.

Optional personal financial statements consist of (1) a statement of changes in net worth and (2) comparative statements.

Personal financial statements are no different from any other financial statements concerning the applicability of GAAS. The auditor is required, for

---

[4]Personal Financial Statements Task Force, *Personal Financial Statements Guide* (New York: American Institute of Certified Public Accountants, 1983), p. 50.

I (we) have examined the statement of financial condition of James and Jane Person as of [*date*], and the related statement of changes in net worth for the [*period*] then ended. My (our) examination was made in accordance with generally accepted auditing standards and, accordingly, included such tests of the accounting records and such other auditing procedures as I (we) considered necessary in the circumstances.

In my (our) opinion, the financial statements referred to above present fairly the financial condition of James and Jane Person as of [*date*], and the changes in their net worth for the [*period*] then ended, in conformity with generally accepted accounting principles applied on a basis consistent with that of the preceding [*period*].

Figure 18-4. AUDITOR'S STANDARD REPORT ON PERSONAL FINANCIAL STATEMENTS.
(SOURCE: Personal Financial Statements Task Force, *op. cit.*, p. 24.)

instance, to have a reasonable basis for expressing an opinion on the statements. In achieving this objective, the auditor may have to rely primarily, if not exclusively, on substantive tests, because internal controls may be nonexistent or known, on the basis of a preliminary review, to be ineffective. In examining personal financial statements, the auditor should obtain corroborating evidence of reported amounts and perform the procedures necessary to determine that all assets and liabilities have been recorded.

The auditor's standard report on personal financial statements includes references to both GAAS and GAAP. However, special wording is required in the scope and opinion paragraphs as illustrated in Figure 18-4. The auditor may, when circumstances warrant, express a qualified, adverse, or disclaimer of opinion on personal financial statements as described in Chapter 17.

REPORTS ON INTERNAL ACCOUNTING CONTROL

A CPA issues a report on internal accounting control (IAC) when he is engaged to

- Express an opinion on the entity's system of IAC in effect as of a specified date.
- Report on the entity's system based solely on the study and evaluation of IAC made as part of an audit of the entity's financial statements in accordance with GAAS.
- Report on all or part of an entity's system based on preestablished criteria of regulatory agencies.
- Issue other special-purpose reports on all or part of an entity's system.[5]

Consideration will be given below to each circumstance.

Engagement to Express an Opinion

The study and evaluation of IAC for the purpose of expressing an opinion may be made separately from or in conjunction with an audit of the entity's

[5] Auditing Standards Board, *op. cit.*, AU § 642.02.

financial statements. In the latter case, it generally will be necessary for the accountant to expand the scope of his study in order to have a reasonable basis for an opinion of the internal accounting control system as a whole. For example, all control procedures should be reviewed and tested for compliance, not just the controls that are to be relied on to determine the extent to which other auditing procedures are to be restricted.

In making a study for the purpose of expressing an opinion, the CPA should (1) plan the scope of the engagement, (2) review the design of the system, (3) test compliance with prescribed procedures, and (4) evaluate the results of his review and tests. These steps are analogous to those described in Chapter 5 when the study and evaluation of IAC were made as part of a financial statement audit. In addition, the CPA should obtain a written representation from management that acknowledges management's responsibility for establishing and maintaining the system of internal control and states that management has disclosed to the CPA all material weaknesses in the system of which it is aware. When the study is made as part of a financial statement audit, the auditor is not required to duplicate any procedures that may be performed in the audit.

The CPA's report in this type of engagement should include:

- A description of the scope of the engagement.
- The date to which the opinion relates.
- A statement that the establishment and maintenance of the system are the responsibility of management.
- A brief explanation of the broad objectives and inherent limitations of IAC.
- The accountant's opinion on whether the system taken as a whole was sufficient to meet the broad objectives of IAC insofar as those objectives pertain to the prevention or detection of errors or irregularities in amounts that would be material in relation to the financial statements.[6]

An illustrative report containing an unqualified opinion is shown in Figure 18-5. There are no restrictions on the distribution of the accountant's report in this type of engagement. An unqualified opinion does not indicate whether a company is in compliance with the IAC provisions of the Foreign Corrupt Practices Act. However, it may be useful to management's own evaluation of compliance.

Modifications of the standard report are required when material weaknesses exist or a scope limitation has occurred. Material weaknesses should be described in the report and either a qualified or an adverse opinion should be expressed on the system as a whole. The treatment of a scope limitation is the same as in a report on audited financial statements.

[6] Auditing Standards Board, *op. cit.*, AU § 642.38.

TO THE BOARD OF DIRECTORS AND SHAREHOLDERS OF XYZ COMPANY

We have made a study and evaluation of the system of internal accounting control of XYZ Company and subsidiaries in effect at December 31, 19XX. Our study and evaluation was conducted in accordance with standards established by the American Institute of Certified Public Accountants.

The management of XYZ Company is responsible for establishing and maintaining a system of internal accounting control. In fulfilling this responsibility, estimates and judgments by management are required to assess the expected benefits and related costs of control procedures. The objectives of a system are to provide management with reasonable, but not absolute, assurance that assets are safeguarded against loss from unauthorized use or disposition, and that transactions are executed in accordance with management's authorization and recorded properly to permit the preparation of financial statements in accordance with generally accepted accounting principles.

Because of inherent limitations in any system of internal accounting control, errors or irregularities may nevertheless occur and not be detected. Also, projection of any evaluation of the system to future periods is subject to the risk that procedures may become inadequate because of changes in conditions, or that the degree of compliance with the procedures may deteriorate.

In our opinion, the system of internal accounting control of XYZ Company and subsidiaries in effect at December 31, 19XX, taken as a whole, was sufficient to meet the objectives stated above insofar as those objectives pertain to the prevention or detection of errors or irregularities in amounts that would be material in relation to the consolidated financial statements.

Figure 18-5. REPORT ON INTERNAL CONTROL BASED ON ENGAGEMENT TO EXPRESS AN OPINION. (SOURCE: Auditing Standards Board, *op. cit.*, AU § 642.39.)

Engagement Based Solely on Financial Statement Audit

A study and evaluation of IAC made as part of a financial statement audit is not sufficient for an expression of an opinion on the system taken as a whole. The auditor may report on the system provided the report

- Indicates that it is intended solely for management, a specified regulatory agency, or other specified third party.
- Describes the limited purpose of the study and evaluation.
- Disclaims an opinion on the system taken as a whole.[7]

The standard report contains a scope paragraph, two middle paragraphs that are identical with the corresponding paragraphs of the report illustrated in Figure 18-5, a conclusions paragraph, and a paragraph restricting the distribution of the report. The wording of the standard report is illustrated in Figure 18-6.

Observe that the conclusions paragraph contains

- A statement that the examination (of the financial statements) would not necessarily disclose all material weaknesses in the system.
- A disclaimer of opinion on the system taken as a whole.
- A statement that the examination disclosed no material weaknesses.

[7]Auditing Standards Board, *op. cit.*, AU § 642.48.

As indicated previously, the auditor is required to communicate material weaknesses in internal control to senior management and the board of directors. When the communication is in writing, the fourth paragraph of the report in Figure 18-6 should (1) contain a description of the material weaknesses that have come to the auditor's attention and (2) state that the weaknesses were considered in determining the substantive tests to be applied in the examination of the financial statements.

Engagement Based on Preestablished Criteria

Some governmental and regulatory agencies require reports on IAC of entities under their jurisdiction. In such cases, specific criteria may be provided for evaluating the adequacy of the controls. When the criteria are set forth in reasonable detail and in terms susceptible to objective application, a CPA may accept an engagement to review and report on the entity's system.

TO THE BOARD OF DIRECTORS OF *XYZ* COMPANY

We have examined the financial statements of *XYZ* Company for the year ended December 31, 19X1, and have issued our report thereon dated February 23, 19X2. As part of our examination, we made a study and evaluation of the Company's system of internal accounting control to the extent we considered necessary to evaluate the system as required by generally accepted auditing standards. The purpose of our study and evaluation was to determine the nature, timing, and extent of the auditing procedures necessary for expressing an opinion on the Company's financial statements. Our study and evaluation were more limited than would be necessary to express an opinion on the system of internal accounting control taken as a whole.

The management of *XYZ* Company is responsible for establishing and maintaining a system of internal accounting control. In fulfilling this responsibility, estimates and judgments by management are required to assess the expected benefits and related costs of control procedures. The objectives of a system are to provide management with reasonable, but not absolute, assurance that assets are safeguarded against loss from unauthorized use or disposition, and that transactions are executed in accordance with management's authorization and recorded properly to permit the preparation of financial statements in accordance with generally accepted accounting principles.

Because of inherent limitations in any system of internal accounting control, errors or irregularities may nevertheless occur and not be detected. Also, projection of any evaluation of the system to future periods is subject to the risk that procedures may become inadequate because of changes in conditions, or that the degree of compliance with the procedures may deteriorate.

Our study and evaluation made for the limited purpose described in the first paragraph would not necessarily disclose all material weaknesses in the system. Accordingly, we do not express an opinion on the system of internal accounting control of *XYZ* Company taken as a whole. However, our study and evaluation disclosed no condition that we believed to be a material weakness.

This report is intended solely for the information of management (or specified regulatory agency or other specified third party) and should not be used for any other purpose.

Figure 18-6. REPORT ON INTERNAL CONTROL BASED SOLELY ON AUDIT ENGAGEMENT.
(SOURCE: Auditing Standards Board, *op. cit.,* AU § 642.49.)

The CPA's report should (1) clearly identify the matters covered by his study (2) indicate whether the study included tests of compliance with the procedures covered by his study, (3) describe the objectives and limitations of IAC and of accountants' evaluations of it, (4) state the accountant's conclusion based on the agency's criteria, concerning the adequacy of the procedures studied, with an exception as to any material weaknesses, and (5) state it is intended for use in connection with the grant or other purpose to which the report refers and that it should not be used for any other purpose.[8]

Engagement to Issue a Special-Purpose Report

An auditor may be asked to issue a special-purpose report on the system of internal accounting control in a service organization. Service organizations include (1) bank trust departments that maintain custody of pension plan assets for customers and (2) EDP service centers that process transactions for customers. In such cases, the auditor for the customer may desire a report on the service organization's internal accounting control to assist him in determining the scope of his audit of the customer's financial statements. The service organization's auditor may issue a special-purpose report on internal accounting control on

- The design of the system.
- Both the design of the system and compliance tests of the system.
- The system of the segment of the service organization that pertains to the customer's transactions.[9]

The auditor's report on the first two types of special reports is similar to the report on internal accounting control based solely on a financial statement audit. Thus, the report should contain a disclaimer of opinion on the system and state that the report is intended solely for use by the management of the service center, the service center's customers, and the auditors of the customers. The auditor's report on the third type of special report is similar to a report on internal accounting control based on an engagement to express an opinion. Accordingly, this report should contain an opinion on the system of the segment of the service organization (see Figure 18-5) and there is no restriction on the distribution of the special report.

THE SINGLE AUDIT OF STATE AND LOCAL GOVERNMENTS

The Single Audit Act of 1984 enacted into law the concept of organization-wide financial and compliance audits, the "Single Audit". A major provision of the Act is that any state or local government receiving $100,000 or more in Federal financial assistance either directly from a federal agency or indirectly

[8]Auditing Standards Board, *op. cit.,* AU § 642.56.
[9]Auditing Standards Board, *op. cit.,* AU § 324.27.

through another state or local government in any fiscal year must have an annual audit.[10] The audit must be made by independent public accountants or independent state or local government auditors. It is estimated that the Act will affect 20,000 governmental entities who receive almost $100 billion annually in federal financial assistance. The Single Audit eliminates the need for various federal agencies to conduct separate financial and compliance audits on their grants to state and local governments.

The objectives of the Single Audit Act are to

- Improve the financial management of state and local governments with respect to federal financial assistance programs.
- Establish uniform requirements for audits of federal financial assistance provided to state and local governments.
- Promote the efficient and effective use of audit resources.
- Ensure that federal departments and agencies, to the maximum extent practicable, rely upon and use audit work done pursuant to the requirements of the Single Audit Act.[11]

The Director of the Office of Management and Budget (OMB) (1) prescribes policies, procedures, and guidelines to implement the law and (2) designates cognizant audit agencies to monitor compliance with the Act.

The scope of a single audit extends to the entire state or local government's operations excluding public hospitals, colleges and universities. In performing the audit, the independent auditor must meet the Government Accounting Office (GAO) audit standards for financial and compliance audits enumerated in Chapter 1 of this text. These standards include, but are not limited to, the AICPA's generally accepted auditing standards. In each audit the auditor is required to determine and report whether

- The financial statements of the organization present fairly its financial position and the results of its financial operations in accordance with generally accepted accounting principles and that the organization has complied with laws and regulations that may have a material effect on the financial statements;
- The organization has internal control systems to provide reasonable assurance that it is managing federal financial assistance programs in compliance with applicable laws and regulations; and
- The organization has complied with laws and regulations that may have a material effect upon each major federal assistance program.[12]

---

[10]A governmental unit that receives $25,000 or more but less than $100,000 in any fiscal year has the option to have a single audit or have audits according to other federal statutes and regulations. In addition, states that have a biennial audit requirement may continue to have audits on a two year basis.

[11]The Single Audit Act of 1984, Public Law 98-502, Section 1.

[12]Single Audit Act 7502.

In order to meet the reporting requirements of the Act, it is necessary for the auditor to issue three separate but interrelated reports on (1) the financial statements of the recipient of federal assistance, (2) internal accounting controls of the recipient organization including internal controls used to manage federal financial assistance programs, and (3) the recipient organization's compliance with laws and regulations applicable to the federal assistance programs.[13] These components may be bound together and issued as a single audit report.

In reporting on the financial statements, the independent auditor should use standard report language. The report on internal control is similar to the report based solely on an audit engagement shown in Figure 18-6. In the scope paragraph, however, the auditor must also refer to applicable GAO standards which go beyond GAAS. The GAO standards require the auditor to identify among other things:

- the entity's significant internal accounting controls,
- the controls identified that were evaluated,
- the controls identified that were not evaluated (the auditor may satisfy this requirement by identifying any significant classes of transactions and related assets not included in the study and evaluation), and
- the material weaknesses identified as a result of the evaluation.[14]

The auditor's report on compliance consists of (1) comments on the work done, (2) a statement of positive assurance on those items tested for compliance, (3) a statement of negative assurance regarding items not tested for compliance, and (4) disclosure of any material instances of non-compliance.[15] The report should contain wording restricting its use to satisfying the single audit requirement. However, upon acceptance by the auditee, the report is a matter of public record. A compliance report is illustrated in Appendix 18A.

REVIEW SERVICES

Review services are a relatively new development in the public accounting profession. This activity resulted from the profession's efforts to be responsive to the needs of clients, regulatory agencies, and the investing public for a service that would provide some form of limited assurance about the reliability of financial data without requiring an examination in accordance with GAAS.

---

[13]Task Force on Single Audits of Federal Financial Assistance, Proposed Audit Guide, *Audits of Federal Financial Assistance to State and Local Governmental Units*, (New York: American Institute of Certified Public Accountants, 1984), p. 59 (5.1) (hereinafter referred to as Proposed Audit Guide).

[14]Comptroller General of the United States, *Standards for Audit of Governmental Organizations, Programs, Activities, and Functions* (Washington, D.C.: U.S. Government Printing Office, 1981 Revision), p. 29.

[15]Proposed Audit Guide, *op. cit.*, p. 62 (adapted).

A review differs significantly from an audit as to procedures and objectives. For example, a review generally is limited to two types of procedures: inquiry and analytical review; and a review does not result in the expression of an opinion. In addition, the individual making the review should not be referred to as an auditor. It is possible, however, for a CPA to render both auditing and review services to the same client. The major types of review engagements and the AICPA group authorized to establish guidelines for the service are as follows:

Type of Review	AICPA Group
Interim financial information of a public entity[16]	Auditing Standards Board
Financial statements of a nonpublic entity[16]	Accounting and Review Services Committee
Financial forecasts	Financial Forecasts and Projections Task Force

The guidelines for each type of review service are described below.

INTERIM FINANCIAL INFORMATION FOR PUBLIC ENTITIES

Interim financial information (IFI) includes current data during a fiscal year on financial position, results of operations, and changes in financial position. Such information may be issued on a monthly or quarterly basis or at other intervals. IFI may take the form of either complete financial statements, summarized financial statements, or summarized financial data.[17] IFI may be presented alone or in a note to audited financial statements.

In this type of a review, the accountant is expected to (1) possess (or acquire) a level of knowledge of the accounting principles and practices of the industry in which the entity operates and (2) have (or obtain) an understanding of the entity's business and accounting practices. The knowledge and understanding are ordinarily obtained through prior experience with the entity or its industry and from inquiry of entity personnel.

Objective and Procedures

The objective of the review of IFI is to provide the accountant with a basis for reporting whether material modifications should be made for such information to conform with GAAP.[18] This objective differs significantly from the objective

---

[16]The distinction between public and nonpublic entities is based primarily on whether the entity's securities are traded either on a stock exchange or in the over-the-counter market.

[17]APB Opinion No. 28, *Interim Financial Reporting* (New York: American Institute of Certified Public Accountants, 1973).

[18]Auditing Standards Board, *op. cit.,* AU § 722.03.

of an audit which is to have a basis for expressing an opinion on the fairness of the financial statements. The review program for IFI should include:

- Inquiry concerning (1) the accounting system, to obtain an understanding of the manner in which transactions are recorded, classified, and summarized in the preparation of interim financial information and (2) any significant changes in the system of internal accounting control, to ascertain their potential effect on the preparation of interim financial information.

- Application of analytical review procedures to interim financial information to identify and provide a basis for inquiry about relationships and individual items that appear to be unusual.

- Reading the minutes of meetings of stockholders, board of directors, and committees of the board of directors to identify actions that may affect the interim financial information.

- Reading the interim financial information to consider, on the basis of information coming to the accountant's attention, whether the information to be reported conforms with GAAP.

- Obtaining reports from other accountants, if any, who have been engaged to make a review of the interim financial information of significant segments of the reporting entity, its subsidiaries, or other investees.

- Inquiry of officers and other executives having responsibility for financial and accounting matters concerning (1) whether the interim financial information has been prepared in conformity with GAAP consistently applied, (2) changes in the entity's business activities or accounting practices, (3) matters as to which questions have arisen in the course of applying the foregoing procedures, and (4) events subsequent to the date of the IFI that would have a material effect on the presentation of such information.

- Obtain written representations from management concerning its responsibility for the information, completeness of the minutes, subsequent events and other matters.[19]

Note that the accountant is not required to make a study and evaluation of internal control or obtain corroborating evidence needed in an audit. The extent of these procedures will be influenced by the accountant's knowledge of (1) the client's accounting and reporting practices, (2) weaknesses in internal accounting control, (3) changes in nature or volume of the client's business activities, and (4) the effects of new accounting pronouncements on the client.

Accountant's Report

The report on IFI should contain the following elements:

- A statement that the review was made in accordance with the standards for such reviews.

---

[19]Auditing Standards Board, *op. cit.*, AU § 722.06.

We have made a review of [describe the information or statements reviewed] of *ABC* Company and consolidated subsidiaries as of September 30, 19X1, and for the three-month and nine-month periods then ended, in accordance with standards established by the American Institute of Certified Public Accountants.

A review of interim financial information consists principally of obtaining an understanding of the system for the preparation of interim financial information, applying analytical review procedures to financial data, and making inquiries of persons responsible for financial and accounting matters. It is substantially less in scope than an examination in accordance with generally accepted auditing standards, the objective of which is the expression of an opinion regarding the financial statements taken as a whole. Accordingly, we do not express such an opinion.

Based on our review, we are not aware of any material modification that should be made to the accompanying financial (information or statements) for them to be in conformity with generally accepted accounting principles.

Figure 18-7. ACCOUNTANT'S REPORT ON REVIEW OF INTERIM FINANCIAL INFORMATION FOR A PUBLIC ENTITY. (SOURCE: Auditing Standards Board, *op. cit.*, AU § 722.18.)

- An identification of the IFI reviewed.
- A description of the procedures for a review of IFI.
- A statement that a review is significantly less in scope than an examination in accordance with GAAS and, accordingly, no opinion is expressed.
- A statement as to whether the accountant is aware of any material modifications that should be made to the information to make it conform with GAAP.[20]

The report should be addressed and dated in the same manner as the auditor's standard report. In addition, each page of the interim financial information should be clearly marked "unaudited." An illustrative report is presented in Figure 18-7.

FINANCIAL STATEMENTS OF A NONPUBLIC ENTITY

A CPA may be engaged to review interim and/or annual financial statements of a nonpublic entity. The objective, procedures, and reporting for this type of review service for a nonpublic entity are similar to those described above for a public entity, but they are not identical. The objective of a review for a nonpublic entity includes *other comprehensive bases of accounting* as well as GAAP.[21] This addition recognizes that smaller companies may use a cash or income tax basis of accounting.

[20] Auditing Standards Board, *op. cit.*, AU § 722.17.

[21] Accounting and Review Services Committee, *Statement on Standards for Accounting and Review Services No. 1, Compilation and Review of Financial Statements* (New York: American Institute of Certified Public Accountants, 1978), para. 4 (hereinafter referred to and cited as *SSARS No. 1*).

I [we] have reviewed the accompanying balance sheet of *XYZ* Company as of December 31, 19*XX*, and the related statements of income, retained earnings, and changes in financial position for the year then ended, in accordance with standards established by the American Institute of Certified Public Accountants. All information included in these financial statements is the representation of the management [owners] of *XYZ* Company.

A review consists of inquiries of company personnel and analytical procedures applied to financial data. It is substantially less in scope than an examination in accordance with generally accepted auditing standards, the objective of which is the expression of an opinion regarding the financial statements taken as a whole. Accordingly, I [we] do not express such an opinion.

Based on my [our] review, I am [we are] not aware of any material modifications that should be made to the accompanying financial statements in order for them to be in conformity with generally accepted accounting principles.

Figure 18-8. ACCOUNTANT'S REPORT ON REVIEW OF FINANCIAL STATEMENTS FOR A NON-PUBLIC ENTITY. (Source: *SSARS No. 1, op. cit.*, para. 35.)

The principal differences in review procedures are that it is not necessary to inquire about changes in internal accounting control or to obtain a representation letter from management.

There is one substantive change in reporting: the report should state that all information in the financial statements is the representation of the management (owners) of the entity.[22] In addition, each page of the financial statements reviewed by the accountant should include a reference such as "See Accountant's Review Report." A review report is illustrated in Figure 18-8. If the accountant is unable to perform the review considered necessary in the circumstances, a review report should not be issued.

FINANCIAL FORECASTS

A financial forecast for an entity is an estimate of the most probable financial position, results of operations, and changes in financial position for one or more future periods of time. Financial forecasts have been an important tool of management in internal planning and decision making for many years. They have also been used externally by companies in obtaining loans and in the private and public placement of debt and equity securities.

In recent years, some companies have started to include financial forecasts in their annual reports, and the inclusion of sales and earnings forecasts in filings with the SEC is now permissible. In an effort to add credibility to forecasts, some companies have CPAs review and report on them. Standards for such engagements have been established by the AICPA through a Financial Forecasts and Projections Task Force. The recommendations of this group were reviewed by the Auditing Standards Board prior to issuance. The guidelines of the task force are authoritative, but they do not have the same status as a Statement on Auditing Standards.

[22]*SSARS No. 1., op. cit.*, para. 32.

Objective and Guidelines

The objective of the accountant's review of a forecast is to provide a basis for reporting whether

- The forecast is properly prepared on the basis of management's stated assumptions.
- The forecast is properly prepared on a basis consistent with the accounting principles expected to be used in the historical financial statements covering the forecast period.
- The underlying assumptions provide a reasonable basis for the forecast.

Ten guidelines are given for the preparation of a financial forecast. These guidelines are presented in Appendix 18B.

Procedures

As in other review engagements, the accountant relies primarily on inquiry and analytical review procedures in making the review. The accountant's working papers should include written representations from management acknowledging its responsibility for both the forecast and the underlying assumptions. The scope of the accountant's review is influenced by (1) the accountant's knowledge of the business, (2) management's record in previous forecasts, (3) the length of the forecast period, and (4) the complexity of the forecasting process.

Accountant's Report

The accountant's standard report on a review of a financial forecast should include

- An identification of the forecast information presented by management and a description of what it is intended to represent.
- A statement that the review was made in accordance with applicable AICPA guidelines for a review of a financial forecast and a brief description of the nature of such a review.
- A statement that the accountant assumes no responsibility to update the report for events and circumstances occurring after the date of the report.
- A statement regarding whether the accountant believes that the financial forecast is presented in conformity with applicable AICPA guidelines for presentation of a financial forecast and whether the underlying assumptions provide a reasonable basis for management's forecast.
- A caveat regarding the ultimate attainment of the forecast results.[23]

---

[23]Financial Forecasts and Projections Task Force, *Guide for a Review of a Financial Forecast*, (New York: AICPA, 1980), p. 21 (hereinafter referred to as *Forecast Guide*).

The accompanying forecast balance sheet, statements of income, retained earnings, and changes in financial position, and summary of significant forecast assumptions of XYZ Company as of December 31, 19XX, and for the year then ending, is management's estimate of the most probable financial position, results of operations, and changes in financial position for the forecast period. Accordingly, the forecast reflects management's judgment, based on present circumstances, of the most likely set of conditions and its most likely course of action.

We have made a review of the financial forecast in accordance with applicable guidelines for a review of a financial forecast established by the American Institute of Certified Public Accountants. Our review included procedures to evaluate both the assumptions used by management and the preparation and presentation of the forecast. We have no responsibility to update this report for events and circumstances occurring after the date of this report.

Based on our review, we believe that the accompanying financial forecast is presented in conformity with applicable guidelines, for presentation of a financial forecast established by the American Institute of Certified Public Accountants. We believe that the underlying assumptions provide a reasonable basis for management's forecast. However, some assumptions inevitably will not materialize and unanticipated events and circumstances may occur; therefore, the actual results achieved during the forecast period will vary from the forecast, and the variations may be material.

Figure 18-9. STANDARD REPORT ON REVIEW OF A FINANCIAL FORECAST. (SOURCE: *Forecast Guide, op. cit.*, p. 22.)

The standard report is illustrated in Figure 18-9. When the accountant concludes that a qualification of his report is required, an adverse opinion generally should be issued in order to minimize possible misinterpretations of the qualification.

ACCOUNTING SERVICES

Attention in this section is directed at two types of accounting services: services pertaining to unaudited financial statements of a public entity and compilation services (i.e., preparation of financial statements) for a nonpublic entity. Accounting services may also include (1) preparing a working trial balance; (2) assisting in adjusting the books of account; (3) consulting on accounting, tax, and similar matters; (4) preparing tax returns; (5) providing various manual or automated bookkeeping or data processing services unless the output is in the form of financial statements; and (6) processing financial data for clients of other accounting firms.[24] The responsibility for setting standards for accounting services is shared by two AICPA groups: the Auditing Standards Board for public entities and the Accounting and Review Services Committee for nonpublic entities.

[24]*SSARS No. 1., op. cit.*, para. 02.

UNAUDITED FINANCIAL STATEMENTS FOR A PUBLIC ENTITY

A CPA may be associated with the financial statements of a public company even though he has not audited them. For example, he may assist the company in preparing its unaudited (and unreviewed) interim financial statements for inclusion in certain SEC filings.

A CPA is associated with financial statements when he (1) has consented to the use of his name in a report, document, or written communication containing the statements, or (2) submits to clients or others financial statements that he has prepared or assisted in preparing even though his name is not appended to the statements.[25]

When accountants are associated with unaudited financial statements of public entities, they are required to

- Include a disclaimer of opinion.
- State that an audit was not made.
- Mark each page of the statements as unaudited.

The first two requirements are illustrated in Figure 18-10.

The accountant is not required to perform any auditing procedures in an accounting service engagement. If any procedures are performed, they should not be described in the accountant's report. When a CPA knows, from knowledge about the client or the work done, that the unaudited statements are not in conformity with generally accepted accounting principles, the client should be requested to make the necessary revisions in the statements. If the client refuses, the accountant should clearly state his reservations on the statements along with a disclaimer of opinion. If, in such case, the client will not accept the accountant's report, the CPA should refuse to be associated with the statements and, if necessary, withdraw from the engagement.

COMPILATION OF FINANCIAL STATEMENTS FOR A NONPUBLIC ENTITY

Many nonpublic entities only desire accounting services from a CPA. This frequently occurs when the owners are able to personally supervise business operations, and audited or reviewed financial statements are not required to obtain a loan from the local bank. The rendering of accounting services is a major part of the practice of some small CPA firms.

Small enterprises may ask a CPA to prepare or assist in preparing its financial statements in order to obtain more accurate and reliable statements. This type of accounting service for a nonpublic entity is referred to as a *compilation engagement*. As in other engagements, the CPA should establish a clear understanding with the client as to the service to be performed. The understanding should be set forth in an engagement letter describing (1) the nature of the service, (2) the limitations of the service (i.e., cannot be relied

---

[25]Auditing Standards Board, *op. cit.*, AU § 504.03.

The accompanying balance sheet of *X* Company as of December 31, 19X1, and the related statements of income, retained earnings, and changes in financial position for the year then ended were not audited by us and, accordingly, we do not express an opinion on them.

Date: _____ Signature

Figure 18-10. ACCOUNTANT'S REPORT ON UNAUDITED STATEMENTS. (SOURCE: Auditing Standards Board, *op. cit.*, AU § 504.05.)

upon to disclose errors and irregularities), and (3) the nature of the compilation report.[26]

Objective and Nature

The objective of this type of accounting service is to present, in the form of financial statements, information supplied by an entity without giving any assurance about the conformity of the statements with generally accepted accounting principles or another comprehensive basis of accounting. In completing a compilation engagement, the CPA is expected to be knowledgeable of the client and the accounting principles and practices of the industry in which the client operates. He should also have a general understanding of its accounting records, the qualifications of its accounting personnel, and the form and content of its financial statements. Such knowledge is ordinarily obtained from experience with the client and inquiry of client personnel.

The CPA is not required to verify information furnished by the client. However, he may deem it necessary to perform other accounting services during the compilation engagement. Before issuing his report, the accountant should read the compiled statements to determine that they are appropriate in form and free from obvious material errors.

Accountant's Report

The CPA should issue a report stating that

- A compilation has been performed in accordance with standards established by the AICPA.
- A compilation is limited to presenting in the form of financial statements information that is the representation of management (owners).
- The statements have not been audited or reviewed and, accordingly, the accountant does not express an opinion or any other form of assurance on them.[27]

---

[26]*SSARS No. 1., op. cit.*, Para. 8.

[27]Accounting and Review Services Committee, *Statement on Standards for Accounting and Review Services No. 5, Reporting on Compiled Financial Statements* (New York: American Institute of Certified Public Accountants, 1982), para 1 (hereinafter referred to and cited as *SSARS No. 5*).

I (we) have compiled the accompanying balance sheet of *XYZ* Company as of December 31, 19XX, and the related statements of income, retained earnings, and changes in financial position for the year then ended, in accordance with standards established by the American Institute of Certified Public Accountants.

A compilation is limited to presenting in the form of financial statements information that is the representation of management [owners]. I [we] have not audited or reviewed the accompanying financial statements and, accordingly, do not express an opinion or any other form of assurance on them.

Figure 18-11. ACCOUNTANT'S REPORT ON COMPILATION OF FINANCIAL STATEMENTS.
(SOURCE: *SSARS No. 5, op. cit.,* para. 2.)

In addition, each page of the financial statements should include a reference to the accountant's compilation report. The standard report for this type of service is illustrated in Figure 18-11.

Modifications of the standard report are required in the following circumstances:

- *The Financial Statements Are Not in Conformity with Generally Accepted Accounting Principles.* When the accountant becomes aware of this fact and the client is unwilling to change the statements, the CPA should indicate the departure by adding the following sentence to the second paragraph of his report:

    However, I did become aware of a departure from generally accepted accounting principles that is described in the following paragraph.[28]

- *The Financial Statements Omit Substantially All Disclosures.* When the accountant concludes that the omissions were not intended to mislead users, the only change from the standard report is the addition of the following paragraph.

    Management has elected to omit substantially all of the disclosures (and the statement of changes in financial position) required by generally accepted accounting principles. If the omitted disclosures were included in the financial statements, they might influence the user's conclusions about the company's financial position, results of operations, and changes in financial position. Accordingly, these financial statements are not designed for those who are not informed about such matters.[29]

- *The CPA Is Not Independent of the Client.* The only change from the standard report is the addition of a paragraph with the following wording:

    I am not independent with respect to XYZ Company.[30]

[28]*SSARS No. 1, op. cit.,* para. 18.
[29]*SSARS No. 1, op. cit.,* para. 21.
[30]*SSARS No. 1, op. cit.,* para. 22.

CHANGE OF ENGAGEMENT

In the course of rendering professional services, a CPA may be asked to change from one type of service to another. A change is a *"step-up"* when it results in a higher level of assurance than originally agreed to (e.g., change from a compilation to a review or from a review to an audit). The CPA can agree to this type of change when (1) there appears to be sufficient evidence to support the higher level of assurance and (2) it seems likely that the revised engagement can be completed in accordance with professional standards. Constraining factors for the CPA may be the availability of personnel and practical considerations relating to the timing of the work.

In contrast, a change in engagement is a *"step-down"* when a lower level of assurance is requested by the client. This change may be accepted by the CPA if there has been a misunderstanding concerning the original engagement or client circumstances have changed. For example, the client's potential loan grantors may conclude that reviewed financial statements will suffice instead of audited statements as initially requested. However, a CPA is precluded from agreeing to a "step-down" change when the client has imposed restrictions on the CPA's work at the higher level of assurance. The restrictions may include refusing to furnish a client representation letter or prohibiting the CPA from making inquiry with the client's outside legal counsel.

CONCLUDING COMMENTS

A CPA should tailor his communication to the type of service that has been performed. For audit services, the auditor may issue (1) special reports, (2) reports on personal financial statements, and (3) reports on internal accounting controls. For review services, the accountant may issue reports on (1) interim financial information for public entities, (2) financial statements of nonpublic entities, and (3) financial forecasts. For accounting services, the accountant may issue reports on (1) unaudited financial statements of public entities and (2) the compilation of financial statements of nonpublic companies.

In issuing these reports, it is imperative that the CPA clearly indicate the nature of the work done and express the findings in a manner that is appropriate to the service rendered.

Appendix 18A

Compliance Report under Single Audit Act[31]

September 21, 19XX

TO THE HONORABLE MEMBERS OF THE CITY COUNCIL, CITY OF X

We have examined the general purpose financial statements of the City of X, for the year ended June 30, 19XX, and have issued our report thereon dated September 21, 19XX. Our examination was made in accordance with generally accepted auditing standards; the provisions of *Standards for Audit of Governmental Organizations, Programs, Activities, and Functions,* promulgated by the U.S. Comptroller General, as they pertain to financial and compliance audits; the Single Audit Act of 1984 (Pub. L. No. 98–502); the provisions of the Office of Management and Budget's *Compliance Supplement for Single Audits of Grants to State and Local Governments** (the *Compliance Supplement*), and accordingly, included such tests of the accounting records and such other auditing procedures as we considered necessary in the circumstances.

In connection with the examination referred to above, a representative number of transactions from each major federal assistance program were selected to determine if federal funds are being expended in accordance with the terms of applicable agreements and those provisions of federal law or regulations that could have a material effect on the financial statements or on each major federal assistance program tested. The results of our tests indicate that for the items tested, the City of X complied with the material terms and conditions of the federal assistance agreements, except as described in the schedule of findings and questioned costs. Further, for the items not tested, based on our examination and the procedures referred to above, nothing came to our attention to indicate that the City of X had not complied with the significant compliance terms and conditions of the programs referred to above beyond the findings and questioned costs noted above.

This report is intended solely for the use of the City of X, the cognizant audit agency, and other federal audit agencies. This restriction is not intended to limit the distribution of this report, which, upon acceptance by the City of X, is a matter of public record.

---

*If the auditor, using professional judgment, decides not to use the *Compliance Supplement*, he would not refer to it in the report. Instead, reference would be made to the appropriate statutes, regulations, or agreements governing the assistance programs.

[31]Proposed Single Audit Guide, p. 73.

Appendix 18B

AICPA Guidelines for Preparation of Financial Forecasts[32]

1. *Single Most Probable Result.* A financial forecasting system should provide a means for management to determine what it considers to be the single most probable forecast result. In addition, determination of the single most probable result generally should be supplemented by the development of ranges or probabilistic statements.

2. *Accounting Principles Used.* The financial forecasting system should provide management with the means to prepare financial forecasts using the accounting principles that are expected to be used when the events and transactions envisioned in the forecast occur.

3. *Appropriate Care and Qualified Personnel.* Financial forecasts should be prepared with appropriate care by qualified personnel.

4. *Best Information Available.* A financial forecasting system should provide for seeking out the best information, from whatever source, reasonably available at the time.

5. *Reflection of Plans.* The information used in preparing a financial forecast should reflect the plans of the enterprise.

6. *Reasonable Assumptions Suitably Supported.* The assumptions utilized in preparing a financial forecast should be reasonable and appropriate and should be suitably supported.

7. *Relative Effect of Variations.* The financial forecasting system should provide the means to determine the relative effect of variations in the major underlying assumptions.

8. *Adequate Documentation.* A financial forecasting system should provide adequate documentation of both the forecast and the forecasting process.

9. *Regular Comparison with Attained Results.* A financial forecasting system should include the regular comparison of the forecast with attained results.

10. *Adequate Review and Approval.* The preparation of a financial forecast should include adequate review and approval by management at the appropriate levels.

REVIEW QUESTIONS

18-1 What criteria are necessary for a report to be considered a "special report"?

18-2 a. Indicate the applicability of generally accepted auditing standards to an examination of financial statements prepared on a comprehensive basis other than GAAP.

   b. Explain the primary requirements in reporting on such statements.

[32]Forecast Guide, *op. cit.,* p. 47.

18-3 In reporting on specific elements, accounts, or items of a financial statement, what are (a) the applicability of GAAS and (b) the primary reporting requirements?

18-4 a. What type of assurance is an auditor permitted to give in a compliance report?
b. Identify the alternative ways in which this type of special report may be issued.

18-5 a. Describe the essential characteristics of personal financial statements.
b. How does the auditor's standard report on personal financial statements differ from the report on other financial statements?

18-6 a. What steps are required in an engagement to express an opinion on internal accounting control?
b. Enumerate the content of an opinion report on internal accounting control.

18-7 a. What conditions must be met to issue a report on internal accounting control based solely on a financial statement audit?
b. Identify the key points that should be included in the conclusions paragraph of this type of report.

18-8 a. What conditions are required for an auditor to accept an engagement based on preestablished criteria?
b. Indicate the points to be included in a report based on preestablished criteria.

18-9 a. Indicate the types of special reports that may be issued on the system of internal accounting control in a service organization.
b. Which type of report is most reliable? Why?

18-10 a. Identify the objectives of the single audit of state and local governments.
b. Indicate the three reporting requirements of the Single Audit Act.

18-11 Identify the three reports that are issued in a single audit and indicate the type of opinion (or conclusion) contained in each report.

18-12 a. Contrast a review engagement from an audit engagement as to procedures and objectives.
b. Indicate the AICPA group authorized to establish guidelines for rendering review services to (1) interim financial information (IFI) of a public entity and (2) financial statements of a nonpublic entity.

18-13 a. State the objective of the review of IFI of a public entity.
b. Enumerate the elements that should be included in a report on IFI of a public entity.

18-14 Identify the major differences in objectives, procedures, and reporting between a review of financial data for a nonpublic entity and a public entity.

18-15 a. Explain the objective of the accountant's review of a forecast.
b. What types of evaluations can an accountant make about the underlying assumptions of a forecast?

18-16 List the essential elements of the accountant's report on a forecast.

18-17 a. State the activities that may be rendered when an accountant performs accounting services for a client.
b. What AICPA group has the authority to set standards for accounting services?

18-18 Explain the accountant's reporting requirements when he is associated with unaudited financial statements for a public entity.

18-19 a. What is a CPA expected to do in completing a compilation engagement for a nonpublic entity?
b. Enumerate the essential aspects of the accountant's standard report on a compilation service.

18-20 Distinguish between a "step-up" and a "step-down" change of engagement and explain the circumstances when each change may be acceptable or unacceptable.

OBJECTIVE QUESTIONS FROM PROFESSIONAL EXAMINATIONS

Indicate the *best* answer choice for each of the following multiple choice questions.

18-21 These questions relate to special reports and reporting on internal accounting control.

1. When reporting on financial statements prepared on a comprehensive basis of accounting other than generally accepted accounting principles, the independent auditor should include in the report a paragraph that
   a. States that the financial statements are *not* intended to be in conformity with generally accepted accounting principles.
   b. Justifies the comprehensive basis of accounting being used.
   c. Refers to the authoritative pronouncements that explain the comprehensive basis of accounting being used.
   d. States that the financial statements are *not* intended to have been examined in accordance with generally accepted auditing standards.

2. Auditors' reports issued in connection with which of the following are generally *not* considered to be special reports or special-purpose reports?
   a. Specified elements, accounts, or items of a financial statement.
   b. Compliance with aspects of contractual agreements related to audited financial statements.
   c. Financial statements prepared in conformity with the price-level basis of accounting.
   d. Compiled financial statements prepared in accordance with appraised liquidation values.

3. The accountant's report expressing an opinion on an entity's system of internal accounting control would *not* include a
   a. Description of the scope of the engagement.
   b. Specific date that the report covers, rather than a period of time.
   c. Brief explanation of the broad objectives and inherent limitations of internal accounting control.
   d. Statement that the entity's system of internal accounting control is consistent with that of the prior year after giving effect to subsequent changes.

4. A CPA's study and evaluation of the system of internal accounting control in an audit
   a. Is generally more limited than that made in connection with an engagement to express an opinion on the system of internal accounting control.
   b. Is generally more extensive than that made in connection with an engagement to express an opinion on the system of internal accounting control.
   c. Will generally be identical to that made in connection with an engagement to express an opinion on the system of internal accounting control.
   d. Will generally result in the CPA expressing an opinion on the system of internal accounting control.

18-22 These questions pertain to either a review or a compilation engagement.

1. The objective of a review of interim financial information is to provide the CPA with a basis for
   a. Expressing a limited opinion that the financial information is presented in conformity with generally accepted accounting principles.

b. Expressing a compilation opinion on the financial information.
c. Reporting whether material modifications should be made to such information to make it conform with generally accepted accounting principles.
d. Reporting limited assurance to the board of directors only.

2. Which of the following procedures is *not* included in a review engagement of a nonpublic entity?
a. Inquiries of management.
b. Inquiries regarding events subsequent to the balance sheet date.
c. Any procedures designed to identify relationships among data that appear to be unusual.
d. A study and evaluation of internal control.

3. A CPA's report on a forecast should include all of the following *except*
a. A description of what the forecast information is intended to represent.
b. A caveat as to the ultimate attainment of the forecasted results.
c. A statement that the CPA assumes *no* responsibility to update the report for events occurring after the date of the report.
d. An opinion as to whether the forecast is fairly presented.

4. Each page of the financial statements compiled by an accountant should include a reference such as
a. See accompanying accountant's footnotes.
b. Unaudited, see accountant's disclaimer.
c. See accountant's compilation report.
d. Subject to compilation restrictions.

5. Compiled financial statements should be accompanied by a report stating all of the following *except*
a. The accountant does *not* express an opinion or any other form of assurance on them.
b. A compilation has been performed.
c. A compilation is limited to presenting in the form of financial statements information that is the representation of management.
d. A compilation consists principally of inquiries of company personnel and analytical procedures applied to financial data.

COMPREHENSIVE QUESTIONS

18-23 Jiffy Clerical Services is a corporation that furnishes temporary office help to its customers. Billings are rendered monthly based on predetermined hourly rates. You have examined the company's financial statements for several years. Following is an abbreviated statement of assets and liabilities on the modified cash basis as of December 31, 19X0:

Assets:	
Cash	$20,000
Advances to employees	1,000
Equipment and autos, less accumulated depreciation	25,000
Total assets	$46,000

Liabilities:

Employees' payroll taxes withheld	$ 8,000
Bank loan payable	10,000
Estimated income taxes on cash basis profits	10,000
Total liabilities	$28,000
Net assets	$18,000

Represented by:

Common stock	$ 3,000
Cash profits retained in the business	15,000
	$18,000

Unrecorded receivables were $55,000 and payables were $30,000.

Required

a. Prepare the report you would issue covering the statement of assets and liabilities as of December 31, 19X0, as summarized above, and the related statement of cash revenue and expenses for the year ended that date.

b. Briefly discuss and justify your modifications of the conventional report on accrual basis statements.

AICPA

18-24 Young and Young, CPAs, completed an examination of the financial statements of XYZ Company, Inc., for the year ended June 30, 19X3, and issued a standard unqualified auditor's report dated August 15, 19X3. At the time of the engagement, the Board of Directors of XYZ requested a special report attesting to the adequacy of the provision for federal and state income taxes and the related accruals and deferred income taxes as presented in the June 30, 19X3, financial statements.

Young and Young submitted the appropriate special report on August 22, 19X3.

Required

Prepare the special report that Young and Young should have submitted to XYZ Company, Inc.

AICPA

18-25 Rose & Co., CPAs, have satisfactorily completed the examination of the financial statements of Bale & Booster, a partnership, for the year ended December 31, 19X0. The financial statements that were prepared on the entity's income tax (cash) basis include footnotes which indicate that the partnership was involved in continuing litigation of material amounts relating to alleged infringement of a competitor's patent. The amount of damages, if any, resulting from this litigation could not be determined at the time of completion of the engagement. The prior years' financial statements were not presented.

Required

Based on the information presented, prepare an auditor's report that includes appropriate explanatory disclosure of significant facts.

AICPA

18-26 In addition to examining the financial statements of the *ABC* Company at December 31, 19X0, the auditor agrees to review the loan agreement dated July 1, 19X0 with the Main Street Bank to determine whether the borrower is complying with the terms, provisions, and requirements of sections 14 to 30 inclusive. The auditor finds that the *ABC* Company is in full compliance with the loan agreement.

Required
a. Prepare a report on compliance with contractual provisions, assuming it is to be a separate report.
b. Indicate how the report on compliance would differ if it were included as part of the auditor's report on the financial statements.

18-27 In order to obtain information that is necessary to make informed decisions, management often calls on the independent auditor for assistance. This may involve a request that the independent auditor apply certain audit procedures to specific accounts of a company that is a candidate for acquisition and report on the results. In such an engagement, the agreed-upon procedures may constitute a scope limitation.

At the completion of an engagement performed at the request of Uclean Corporation that was limited in scope as explained above, the following report was prepared by an audit assistant and submitted to the auditor for review:

To the Board of Directors of Ajax Corporation

We have applied certain agreed-upon procedures, as discussed below, to accounting records of Ajax Corporation, as of December 31, 19X1, solely to assist Uclean Corporation in connection with the proposed acquisition of Ajax Corporation.

We have examined the cash in banks and accounts receivable of Ajax Corporation as of December 31, 19X1, in accordance with generally accepted auditing standards and, accordingly, included such tests of the accounting records and such other auditing procedures as we considered necessary in the circumstances.

In our opinion, the cash and receivables referred to above are fairly presented as of December 31, 19X1, in conformity with generally accepted accounting principles applied on a basis consistent with that of the preceding year. We therefore recommend that Uclean Corporation acquire Ajax Corporation pursuant to the proposed agreement.

[signature]

Required
Comment on the proposed report describing those assertions that are

a. Incorrect or should otherwise be deleted.
b. Missing and should be inserted.

AICPA

18-28 As part of your annual audit of Fall Camper Company, you have the responsibility for preparing a report on internal control. Your workpapers include a completed internal control questionnaire and documentation of other tests of the internal control system that you have reviewed. This review identified a number of material weaknesses; for some of these, corrective action by management is not practicable in the circumstances.

Required

a. Discuss the form and content of the report on internal control based on your annual audit.

b. Write the first, fourth, and fifth paragraphs of your report.

c. Discuss the differences in the form and content of the report if it were based on preestablished criteria of a regulatory agency.

18-29 The financial statements of the Liber Company have never been audited by an independent CPA. Recently, Liber's management asked John Burns, CPA, to conduct a special study of Liber's internal accounting controls for the purpose of expressing an opinion on the system. The study will not include an examination of Liber's financial statements. Following completion of his special study, Burns plans to prepare a report that is consistent with the requirements of the engagement.

Required

a. Describe the responsibility of management for internal control and the broad objectives, and inherent limitations of internal accounting control as set forth in a report on internal accounting control.

b. Explain and contrast the study of internal control that Burns might make as part of an examination of financial statements with his engagement to express an opinion as to (1) objectives of review or study, (2) scope of review or study, and (3) nature and content of reports. Organize your answer for b as follows:

Examination of Financial Statements	Special Study to Express Opinion
1. Objective	1. Objective
2. Scope	2. Scope
3. Report	3. Report

c. Write the first and fourth paragraphs of the report based (1) on a special study to express an opinion and (2) solely on a financial statement audit.

AICPA (adapted)

18-30 NorBor Solar Systems is a privately owned manufacturer of passive solar heating systems. There has been increased consumer demand for NorBor's products due to expanded public awareness of energy self-sufficiency and attractive federal tax energy credits. NorBor needs a major expansion of production facilities in order to meet this increased demand. However, management cannot finance this expansion program from internally generated funds. Furthermore, the continued high interest rates have discouraged management from incurring additional debt. Therefore, NorBor is reviewing the option of a public offering of its securities.

NorBor's financial statements have been audited by the external audit firm of Jones & Mattengly since NorBor's creation seven years ago. Each year, the firm has issued NorBor an unqualified opinion on its financial statements.

The managing partner of Jones & Mattengly has reminded NorBor's management that a public offering of NorBor's stock would make the company subject to the internal accounting control provisions of the Foreign Corrupt Practices Act. NorBor's management has decided to engage its external audit firm to conduct an examination of

NorBor's internal accounting control system. The external auditor is expected to issue a report that should assist NorBor's management in determining whether it is in compliance with the federal law. Jones & Mattengly's examination will follow the procedures expressed in AU § 642, "Reporting on Internal Accounting Control."

Required

a. What role should the management of NorBor Solar Systems play in the examination of the internal accounting control system by the external auditor? Explain your answer.

b. Describe the general content of the report that will be issued by Jones & Mattengly, assuming that the standard form of report is used.

c. Identify the types of opinions Jones & Mattengly could render on NorBor's internal accounting control system as well as the underlying conditions that would make each type of opinion appropriate. Use the following format in preparing your answer:

Type of Opinion	Underlying Conditions

CMA

18-31 Loman, CPA, who has examined the financial statements of the Broadwall Corporation, a publicly held company, for the year ended December 31, 19X0 was asked to perform a limited review of the financial statements of Broadwall Corporation for the period ending March 31, 19X0. The engagement letter stated that a limited review does not provide a basis for the expression of an opinion.

Required

a. Explain why Loman's limited review will not provide a basis for the expression of an opinion.

b. What are the review procedures that Loman should perform, and what is the purpose of each procedure? Structure your response as follows:

Procedure	Purpose of Procedure

AICPA

18-32 For the year ended December 31, 19X0, Novak & Co., CPAs, audited the financial statements of Tillis Ltd., and expressed an unqualified opinion dated February 27, 19X1.

For the year ended December 31, 19X1, Novak & Co., were engaged by Tillis Ltd., to review Tillis Ltd.'s financial statements, that is, "look into the company's financial statements and determine whether there are any obvious modifications that should be made to the financial statements in order for them to be in conformity with generally accepted accounting principles."

Novak made the necessary inquiries, performed the necessary analytical procedures, and performed certain additional procedures that were deemed necessary to achieve the requisite limited assurance. Novak's work was completed on March 3, 19X2, and the financial statements appeared to be in conformity with generally accepted accounting principles that were consistently applied. The report was prepared on March 5, 19X2. It was delivered to Jones, the controller of Tillis Ltd., on March 9, 19X2.

Required

Prepare the properly addressed and dated report on the comparative financial statements of Tillis Ltd., for the years ended December 31, 19X0 and 19X1.

AICPA

18-33 You have been engaged to perform a review service for the partnership of Reed and Wright. Your review does not uncover any material errors of omission or commission in the company's financial statements.

Required

a. Indicate the nature of the review that was performed.

b. Explain the references to standards and management in the first paragraph of the accountant's standard report on a review.

c. Write the second and third paragraphs of the accountant's report that would be applicable for Reed and Wright.

18-34 A CPA was engaged by the Alba Nursing Home to prepare, on the CPA's stationery and without audit, financial statements for 19X0 and its 19X0 income tax return. From the accounting and other records, he learned the following information about the Nursing Home:

1. The Alba Nursing Home is a partnership that was formed early in 19X0. The Nursing Home occupies a large old mansion that stands on a sizable piece of ground beside a busy highway. The property was purchased by the partnership from an estate that out-of-state heirs wanted to settle. The heirs were unfamiliar with the local real estate market and sold the property at the bargain price of $10,000 for the house and $5,000 for the land.

2. A few weeks after the purchase, the partnership employed a competent independent appraisal firm that appraised the house at $100,000 and the land at $50,000.

3. The property was then written up on the partnership books to its appraisal value, and the partners' capital accounts were credited with the amount of the write-up.

4. Additional funds were invested to convert the mansion to a nursing home, purchase the necessary equipment and supplies, and provide working capital.

Required

a. Assume that the CPA prepared the financial statements of the Alba Nursing Home from the accounting records, placed them on his stationery, and labeled each page "Prepared Without Audit." In accordance with the client's preference, the assets were reported only at appraisal values. Under the circumstances presented, what is the CPA's responsibility, if any, to disclose the method of valuation of the assets? Discuss.

b. In this situation, how does the CPA's responsibility for disclosure of the valuation basis of the assets differ, if at all, from the responsibility he would have had if he had made a typical examination of the financial statements?

AICPA (adapted)

18-35 The limitations on the CPA's professional responsibilities when he is associated with unaudited financial statements are often misunderstood. These misunderstandings can be substantially reduced by carefully following professional pronouncements in the course of his work and taking other appropriate measures.

Required

The following list describes seven situations the CPA may encounter or contentions he may have to deal with in his association with and preparation of unaudited financial statements. Briefly discuss the extent of the CPA's responsibilities and, if appropriate, the actions he should take to minimize any misunderstandings. Number your answers to correspond with the numbering in the following list:

1. The CPA was engaged by telephone to perform write-up work including the preparation of financial statements. His client believes that the CPA has been engaged to audit the financial statements and examine the records accordingly.

2. A group of businessmen who own a farm that is managed by an independent agent engage a CPA to prepare quarterly unaudited financial statements for them. The CPA prepares the financial statements from information given to him by the independent agent. Subsequently, the businessmen find the statements were inaccurate because their independent agent was embezzling funds. The businessmen refuse to pay the CPA's fee and blame him for allowing the situation to go undetected, contending that he should not have relied on representations from the independent agent.

3. In comparing the trial balance with the general ledger, the CPA finds an account labeled "audit fees" in which the client has accumulated the CPA's quarterly billings for accounting services including the preparation of quarterly unaudited financial statements.

4. Unaudited financial statements were accompanied by the following letter of transmittal from the CPA:

   We are enclosing your company's balance sheet as of June 30, 19X0, and the related statements of income and retained earnings and changes in financial position for the six months then ended that we have reviewed.

5. To determine appropriate account classification, the CPA reviewed a number of the client's invoices. He noted in his working papers that some invoices were missing but did nothing further because he felt they did not affect the unaudited financial statements he was preparing. When the client subsequently discovered that invoices were missing, he contended that the CPA should not have ignored the missing invoices when preparing the financial statements and had a responsibility to at least inform him that they were missing.

6. The CPA has prepared a draft of unaudited financial statements from the client's records. While reviewing this draft with his client, the CPA learns that the land and building were recorded at appraisal value.

7. The CPA is engaged to review without audit the financial statements prepared by the client's controller. During this review, the CPA learns of several items that by generally accepted accounting principles would require adjustment of the statements and footnote disclosure. The controller agrees to make the recommended adjustments to the statements but says that he is not going to add the footnotes because the statements are unaudited.

AICPA

18-36 An inexperienced staff assistant issued the following report on a financial forecast prepared by the management of Melina Corporation.

The accompanying forecast balance sheet, statements of income, retained earnings, and changes in financial position, and summary of (1) significant forecast conclusions of Melina Corporation as of December 31, 19X6, and for the year then ending, is management's (2) best approximation of the (3) actual financial position, results of operations, and changes in financial position for the forecast period. Accordingly, the forecast reflects (4) management's guarantee based on (5) anticipated circumstances of (6) the actual conditions and actions to be taken.

We have (7) examined the accompanying financial forecast of Melina Corporation in accordance with (8) professional standards established by (9) the American Institute of Certified Public Accountants. Our review included procedures to evaluate (10) management's conclusion and (11) the preparation and accuracy of the forecast. We have no responsibility to update this report (12) unless significant changes in circumstances occur during the forecast period.

(13) In our opinion, the accompanying financial forecast is presented in conformity with (14) generally accepted principles for presentation of a financial forecast established by the American Institute of Certified Public Accountants. We (15) attest that the underlying assumptions provide (16) a verifiable basis for management's forecast. However, (17) some assumptions will not materialize and (18) extraordinary events and circumstances may occur; therefore, the actual results (19) may differ from the forecast results, (20) but the variations should not be material.

Required

For each numbered part of the report, (a) identify the incorrect wording, if any, and (b) give the correct wording. *Note:* It is not necessary to repeat any wording that is correct in your answer to part (b).

18-37 Ann Martin, CPA, has been asked by Harry Adams, owner of Adams Cleaners, to prepare the company's annual financial statements from the company's records. Adams, who is unfamiliar with the services of a CPA, also requests Ms. Martin to add as much prestige to the statements as possible in the form of an opinion or some type of assurance.

Required

a. Explain the nature and limitations of an engagement to compile financial statements.
b. Write the accountant's report on a compilation of financial statements.
c. Explain the type of assurance that may be given if Martin is engaged to review Adams's financial statements.
d. Explain why an opinion cannot be expressed.

CASE STUDY

18-38 Brown, CPA, received a telephone call from Calhoun, the sole owner and manager of a small corporation. Calhoun asked Brown to prepare the financial statements for the corporation and told Brown that the statements were needed in two weeks for external financing purposes. Calhoun was vague when Brown inquired about the intended use of the statements. Brown was convinced that Calhoun thought Brown's work would constitute an audit. To avoid confusion, Brown decided not to explain to Calhoun that the engagement would only be to prepare the financial statements. Brown, with the understanding that a substantial fee would be paid if the work were completed in two weeks, accepted the engagement and started the work at once.

During the course of the work, Brown discovered an accrued expense account labeled "professional fees" and learned that the balance in the account represented an accrual for the cost of Brown's services. Brown suggested to Calhoun's bookkeeper that the account name be changed to "fees for limited audit engagement." Brown also reviewed several invoices to determine whether accounts were being properly classified. Some of the invoices were missing. Brown listed the missing invoice numbers in the working papers with a note indicating that there should be a follow-up on the next engagement. Brown also discovered that the available records included the fixed asset values at estimated current replacement costs. Based on the records available, Brown prepared a balance sheet, income statement, and statement of stockholders' equity. In addition, Brown drafted the footnotes but decided that any mention of the replacement costs would only mislead the readers. Brown suggested to Calhoun that readers of the financial statements would be better informed if they received a separate letter from Calhoun explaining the meaning and effect of the estimated replacement costs of the fixed assets. Brown mailed the financial statements and footnotes to Calhoun with the following note included on each page:

> The accompanying financial statements are submitted to you without complete audit verification.

Required

Identify the inappropriate actions of Brown and indicate what Brown should have done to avoid each inappropriate action. Organize your answer sheet as follows:

Inappropriate Action	What Brown Should Have Done to Avoid Inappropriate Action

AICPA

Chapter 19

Professional Ethics

Study Objectives

After studying this chapter, you should be able to

- Explain the nature and importance of professional ethics.
- Describe the four categories in the AICPA Code of Professional Ethics.
- Indicate the groups that enforce the rules of conduct.
- Identify and explain the essence of each of the rules of conduct.
- Compare the codes of ethics of the Institute of Internal Auditors and the AICPA.

One of the distinguishing characteristics of any profession is the existence of a code of ethics for its members. Just as there are codes of ethics in the legal and medical professions, there is also a code of ethics in the public accounting profession. The primary purpose of this chapter is to explain the code of ethics that is applicable to certified public accountants (CPAs) engaged in the practice of public accounting.

BASIC CONSIDERATIONS

Ethics consist of moral principles and standards of conduct. In general use, the word *ethics* relates to the philosophy of human conduct and principles of human morality and duty. *Morality,* in turn, focuses on the "right" and "wrong" of human behavior.

PROFESSIONAL ETHICS

Professional ethics extend beyond moral principles. They include standards of behavior for a professional person that are designed for both practical and idealistic purposes. While ethics may be designed in part to encourage ideal behavior, they must be both practical and enforceable. To be meaningful, ethics should be above the law but below the ideal. In summary, professional ethics may be regarded as

> a mixture of moral and practical concepts, with a sprinkling of exhortation to ideal conduct designed to invoke "right action" on the part of members of the profession concerned—all reduced to rules which are intended to be enforceable, to some extent at least, by disciplinary action.[1]

Professional ethics are imposed by a profession on its members, who voluntarily accept standards of professional behavior more rigorous than those required by law. A code of ethics significantly affects the reputation of a profession and the confidence in which it is held. Professional ethics have evolved over time and continue to be in the process of change as the practice of public accounting changes.

The following excerpts from the AICPA's Code of Professional Ethics emphasize the importance of ethical standards for CPAs:

> A distinguishing mark of a professional is his acceptance of responsibility to the public. All true professions have therefore deemed it essential to promulgate codes of ethics and to establish means for ensuring their observance.
>
> The reliance of the public, the government and the business community on sound financial reporting and advice on business affairs, and the importance of these matters to the economic and social aspects of life impose particular obligations on certified public accountants.
>
> Ordinarily those who depend upon a certified public accountant find it difficult to assess the quality of his services; they have a right to expect, however, that he is a person of competence and integrity. A man or woman who enters the profession of accountancy is assumed to accept an obligation to uphold its principles, to work for the increase of knowledge in the art and for the improvement of methods, and to abide by the profession's ethical and technical standards.
>
> The ethical Code of the American Institute emphasizes the profession's responsibility to the public, a responsibility that has grown as the number

---

[1]John L. Carey and William O. Doherty, *Ethical Standards of the Accounting Profession* (New York: American Institute of Certified Public Accountants, 1966), p. 6.

of investors has grown, as the relationship between corporate managers and stockholders has become more impersonal and as government increasingly relies on accounting information.

The Code also stresses the CPA's responsibility to clients and colleagues, since his behavior in these relationships cannot fail to affect the responsibilities of the profession as a whole to the public.

The Institute's Rules of Conduct set forth minimum levels of acceptable conduct and are mandatory and enforceable. However, it is in the best interests of the profession that CPAs strive for conduct beyond that indicated merely by prohibitions. Ethical conduct, in the true sense, is more than merely abiding by the letter of explicit prohibitions. Rather it requires unswerving commitment to honorable behavior, even at the sacrifice of personal advantage.[2]

CODES OF PROFESSIONAL ETHICS

More than one code of ethics exists in the public accounting profession. A CPA typically is required to comply with at least three codes: (1) the code promulgated by the AICPA, (2) the code established by the state society of CPAs of which the CPA is a member, and (3) the code prescribed by the state board of accountancy that has granted the CPA a license to practice. Because the AICPA Code is the most comprehensive of the codes, it frequently serves as the model for the others. Accordingly, attention will be directed primarily at the AICPA Code of Ethics in this chapter.

One other code, the Code of Ethics promulgated by the Institute of Internal Auditors, is included in this chapter. Subsequently, in Chapter 20, the regulations of the SEC that relate to the AICPA Code of Ethics will be discussed.

AICPA PROFESSIONAL ETHICS DIVISION

The bylaws of the AICPA provide that there shall be a Professional Ethics Division. This division is headed by a director, who is responsible to the vice president of regulation and review of the AICPA. The division consists of a relatively small full-time staff, active volunteer members, and ad hoc investigatory volunteers, as needed. The division functions through an executive committee, which also serves as the ethics committee of the AICPA, and three subcommittees. The executive committee is responsible for

- Planning the programs of the division's subcommittees and supervising their implementation.

  Issuing formal policy statements and pronouncements of the division.

[2]AICPA Professional Standards, Volume B (New York: American Institute of Certified Public Accountants, 1985), Ethics Section 51.01–06 (hereinafter referred to and cited as ET §).

- Establishing *prima facie*[3] violations of the code or bylaws for possible disciplinary action, including hearings before joint trial boards.
- Proposing changes in the code.

COMPOSITION OF THE AICPA CODE OF PROFESSIONAL ETHICS

There are four categories of ethical standards in the AICPA Code.

Concepts of Professional Ethics. Are positive assertions of behavior to which a CPA should strive beyond the minimum level of acceptable conduct. There are five concepts each stated as an affirmative *Ethical Principle.* The concepts represent the ideal standards of ethical conduct, and they constitute the philosophical foundation for the Code of Ethics. The concepts are not enforceable.

Rules of Conduct. Set forth the minimal level of acceptable conduct. Currently, there are 13 rules. Each rule represents an enforceable standard. Amendments of the rules require a two-thirds vote by the membership of the AICPA.

Interpretations of Rules of Conduct. Provide guidelines about the scope and applicability of the rules. They are adopted and issued by the Professional Ethics Division after exposure to state societies of CPAs and state boards of accountancy. Currently, there are 27 interpretations. Interpretations do not represent enforceable standards, but CPAs are expected to justify any departures from them.

Ethics Rulings. Indicate the applicability of the Rules of Conduct and Interpretations to specific cases and circumstances. They also are issued by the Professional Ethics Division. Over 185 rulings have been issued. Like interpretations, rulings are not enforceable, but CPAs are expected to justify any departures.

A summary of the four categories of the AICPA Code is shown in Figure 19-1.

The rules and interpretations are written in technical language. The following definitions are applicable whenever these two categories are involved.

Client. The person(s) or entity which retains a member or his firm, engaged in the practice of public accounting, for the performance of professional services.

Council. The Council of the American Institute of Certified Public Accountants.

Enterprise. Any person(s) or entity, whether organized for profit or not, for which a CPA provides services.

---

[3] *Prima facie* means true or valid at first impression. Legally, such evidence is sufficient to establish a fact or a case unless disproved.

Category	Nature	Enforceable
Concepts	Ideal standards that constitute the philosophical foundation for the Code	No.
Rules of Conduct	Minimum standards of acceptable conduct	Yes.
Interpretations	Guidelines about the scope and applicability of the Rules of Conduct	No, but the CPA must justify any departure.
Rulings	Explanations of the applicability of the rules and interpretations to specific cases and circumstances	No, but the CPA must justify any departure.

Figure 19-1. COMPOSITION OF THE CODE OF PROFESSIONAL ETHICS.

Firm. A proprietorship, partnership, or professional corporation or association engaged in the practice of public accounting, including individual partners or shareholders thereof.

Institute. The American Institute of Certified Public Accountants.

Member. A member, associate member or international associate of the American Institute of Certified Public Accountants.

Practice of public accounting. Holding out to be a CPA or public accountant and at the same time performing for a client one or more types of services rendered by public accountants. The term shall not be limited by a more restrictive definition which might be found in the accountancy law under which a member practices.

Professional services. One or more types of services performed in the practice of public accounting.[4]

APPLICABILITY OF RULES OF CONDUCT

The following excerpts from the AICPA Code of Professional Ethics indicate the applicability of the Rules of Conduct:

> The Rules of Conduct apply to all services performed in the practice of public accounting, including tax and management advisory services, except (a) where the wording of the rule indicates otherwise and (b) that a member who is practicing outside the United States will not be subject to discipline for departing from any of the rules stated herein so long as his conduct is in accord with the rules of the organized accounting profession in the country in which he is practicing. However, where a member's name is associated with financial statements in such a manner as to imply that he is acting as an independent public accountant and under circumstances that

[4]AICPA Professional Standards, *op. cit.,* ET § 91.11.

would entitle the reader of the statements to assume that United States practices were followed, he must comply with Rules 202 and 203.[5]

A member may be held responsible for compliance with the Rules of Conduct by all persons associated with him in the practice of public accounting who either are under his supervision or are his partners or shareholders in the practice.

A member engaged in the practice of public accounting must observe all the Rules of Conduct. A member not engaged in the practice of public accounting must observe only Rules 102 and 501, since all other Rules of Conduct relate solely to the practice of public accounting.[6]

A member shall not permit others to carry out on his behalf, either with or without compensation, acts which, if carried out by the member, would place him in violation of the Rules of Conduct.[7]

When applicable, a member is also expected to observe the ethical standards of state CPA societies, state boards of accountancy, and other governmental agencies.

ENFORCEMENT OF RULES OF CONDUCT

A member can only be charged with a violation of the Rules of Conduct. However, in the event of an alleged violation of a rule, a member may have to justify any departures from applicable ethics interpretations and rulings. Instances of alleged violations of the Rules of Conduct result from (1) complaints by members and nonmembers; (2) review of newspapers and publications, such as the *SEC Docket* and the *IRS Bulletin*, by personnel in the Professional Ethics Division; and (3) transmittal of possible violations to the AICPA by certain federal agencies.

ENFORCEMENT GROUPS

Enforcement of the Rules of Conduct rests with three groups: the AICPA, state societies of CPAs, and state boards of accountancy. Each group has the authority to make investigations of complaints, conduct disciplinary hearings, and impose sanctions on those who have violated the Rules.

The AICPA's enforcement machinery resides in its Professional Ethics Division and Joint Trial Board Division. The former operates through subcommittees; the latter functions through a system of regional trial boards and a national review board, with the decision of the national board being final.

[5]Rules 202 and 203 are explained on pages 709 and 710.
[6]Rules 102 and 501 are explained on pages 707 and 713.
[7]AICPA Professional Standards, *op. cit.*, ET § 92.05.

The maximum sanction that the AICPA can impose is to expel the member from the Institute.

State CPA society enforcement is achieved through each state's ethics committee and the system of trial boards described above. As in the case of the AICPA, the most severe sanction to be imposed by a state society is loss of membership in the society.

State board of accountancy enforcement is accomplished through its own administrative and investigative staffs. The board has the power to revoke the CPA's license to practice. Thus, the board can terminate a CPA's professional career.

Each of the foregoing groups may act independently on an alleged violation of the Rules of Conduct. This means, for example, that the AICPA and a state society could each conduct its own Trial Board proceedings, and different sanctions may be imposed.

JOINT ETHICS ENFORCEMENT PROCEDURE

In an effort to make enforcement of its Rules of Conduct more effective, the AICPA has developed a Joint Ethics Enforcement Program (JEEP). Slightly over 80% of the state societies have signed enabling agreements to participate in joint enforcement. Under the plan, complaints against a member may be filed with either the state society or the AICPA. The complaints are then channeled to either the AICPA ethics division or the state society ethics committee. As shown in Figure 19-2, the AICPA has jurisdiction over cases involving more than one state, litigation, and issues of broad national concern. The jurisdictional groups may act independently or jointly. Acting within its authority, a group may

- Issue a constructive letter of comment.
- Close the inquiry.
- Determine on the basis of prima facie evidence (1) to issue an administrative reprimand or (2) to refer the case to a regional Trial Board.

In a reprimand, the member is requested to terminate the unethical practice, and he may also be asked to meet specific continuing professional education requirements. Referral of a prima facie case to the trial board is reserved for serious cases in which the jurisdictional group believes there should be public disclosure of the misconduct if the member is found guilty.

The AICPA professional ethics division reports semiannually to the membership on the disposition of ethics investigations processed under JEEP. Figure 19-3 summarizes the activities for a recent six months period.

On completion of the disciplinary hearing(s), the Trial Board may decide to either acquit, censure, suspend, or expel a member. The Board is required to publish the names of all members found guilty of ethics violations.

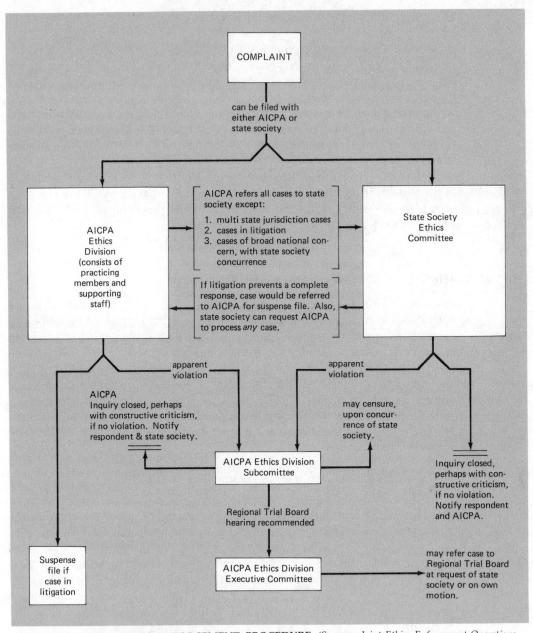

Figure 19-2. JOINT ETHICS ENFORCEMENT PROCEDURE. (SOURCE: *Joint Ethics Enforcement Operations Manual*, AICPA Ethics Division, 1982.)

SEMIANNUAL REPORT OF JOINT ETHICS ENFORCEMENT PROGRAM ACTIVITY

Ethics Committee Activities

		Totals
Investigations open at start of period	462	
Investigations opened during period	309	
Total Investigations		771
Administrative Reprimands issued	42	
Minor Violations issued	16	
No Violation findings	124	
Prima Facie cases in preparation for submission to Joint Trial Board Division	1	
Cases Referred to Joint Trial Board Division:		
Prima Facie cases for Trial Board Hearings	29	
For action under automatic provisions of bylaws	14	
Total Disposition of Case Investigations		226
Remaining Investigations as of December 31, 1984:		
Investigations held pending outcome of litigation:		
State Society Ethics Committees	82	
AICPA Professional Ethics Division	91	
Cases under investigation:		
State Society Ethics Committees	298	
AICPA Professional Ethics Division	74	
Total Remaining Investigations		545
Total Investigations		771

Joint Trial Division Activities

Members Expelled under automatic provision of bylaws	12	
Members Suspended under automatic provision of bylaws	2	
		14
Trial Board Hearings:		
Members Admonished	5	
Members Expelled	8	
Members Suspended	1	
Guilty—CPE Required	1	
Not Guilty	2	
Cases Scheduled, not yet heard	12	29
Total Joint Trial Board Division Cases		43

Figure 19-3. AICPA REPORT ON ETHICS CASES. [SOURCE: *The CPA Letter* (New York: American Institute of Certified Public Accountants, July 1985, Vol. 65, No. 12), p. 4.]

AUTOMATIC DISCIPLINARY PROVISIONS

The bylaws of the AICPA contain several provisions that result in automatic suspension or termination of membership without a hearing. Suspension results when the Secretary of the Institute is notified that a judgment or conviction has been imposed on a member for

- A crime punishable by imprisonment for more than one year.
- Willful failure to file any income tax return that he, as an individual taxpayer, is required by law to file.
- The filing of a false or fraudulent income tax return on his or a client's behalf.
- Willful aiding in the preparation and presentation of a false and fraudulent income tax return of a client.[8]

Termination of membership occurs when the member has exhausted all legal appeals on the judgment or conviction.

Under the automatic disciplinary provisions of the bylaws, membership in the AICPA shall be terminated without a hearing should a member's certificate as a CPA be revoked, withdrawn, or canceled as a disciplinary measure by any governmental agency. This provision also applies when a member's last or only certificate is revoked by a state board of accountancy for failing to meet continuing professional education requirements, unless the member is retired or disabled.

FRAMEWORK FOR DISCUSSION OF RULES OF CONDUCT

Consideration will now be given to each of the specific Rules of Conduct. The discussion will be organized around the five ethical concepts: (1) independence, integrity, and objectivity, (2) general and technical standards, (3) responsibilities to clients, (4) responsibilities to colleagues, and (5) other responsibilities and practices. The format will be as follows:

- The ethical principle for each concept will be stated.
- The nature and purpose of the principle will be explained.
- The applicable Rules of Conduct will be stated.
- Commentary will be given on each of the rules based, in part, on published interpretations and rulings.

In addition, interpretations applicable to each Rule of Conduct are listed in Appendix 19A.

---

[8]AICPA Professional Standards, *op. cit.*, Bylaws Section 7.3.1.

INDEPENDENCE, INTEGRITY, AND OBJECTIVITY

ETHICAL PRINCIPLE

> *A certified public accountant should maintain his integrity and objectivity and, when engaged in the practice of public accounting, be independent of those he serves.*[9]

Independence is the cornerstone of the philosophical structure of the Code of Ethics. A CPA's opinion on financial statements is of little or no value if he is not independent of the client. Independence may be defined as the ability to act with integrity and objectivity. Although neither of these character traits is precisely measurable, both are fundamental to reliance on a CPA. Integrity means being honest and trustworthy, whereas objectivity refers to the CPA's ability to have an impartial attitude on all matters pertaining to a professional engagement.

In establishing rules on independence, the profession uses the criterion of whether reasonable persons having knowledge of all the facts and, taking into consideration normal strength of character and normal behavior under the circumstances, would conclude that a specified relationship between a CPA and a client poses an unacceptable threat to the CPA's integrity and objectivity.[10]

RULES OF CONDUCT

Two Rules of Conduct have been issued on this aspect of the code.

Rule 101. INDEPENDENCE.* A member or a firm of which he is a partner or shareholder shall not express an opinion on financial statements of an enterprise unless he and his firm are independent with respect to such enterprise. Independence will be considered to be impaired if, for example:

A. During the period of his professional engagement, or at the time of expressing his opinion, he or his firm
   1. a. Had or was committed to acquire any direct or material indirect financial interest in the enterprise; or
      b. Was a trustee of any trust or executor or administrator of any estate if such trust or estate had or was committed to acquire any direct or material indirect financial interest in the enterprise, or
   2. Had any joint closely held business investment with the enterprise or any officer, director or principal stockholder thereof which was material in relation to his or his firm's net worth; or

*Each rule is taken from a corresponding ET section in AICPA Professional Standards, *op. cit.*

[9]AICPA Professional Standards, *op. cit.*, ET § 52.
[10]AICPA Professional Standards, *op. cit.*, ET § 52.09.

3. Had any loan to or from the enterprise or any officer, director or principal stock-holder thereof. This latter proscription does not apply to the following loans from a financial institution when made under normal lending procedures, terms, and requirements:

   a. Loans obtained by a member or his firm which are not material in relation to the net worth of such borrower.

   b. Home mortgages.

   c. Other secured loans, except loans guaranteed by a member's firm which are otherwise unsecured.

B. During the period covered by the financial statements, during the period of the professional engagement or at the time of expressing an opinion, he or his firm

   1. Was connected with the enterprise as a promoter, underwriter or voting trustee, a director or officer or in any capacity equivalent to that of a member of management or of an employee; or

   2. Was a trustee for any pension or profit-sharing trust of the enterprise.

The above examples are not intended to be all-inclusive.

Rule 101 requires the CPA to be independent in fact and to avoid circumstances that may appear to impair independence. Several aspects of Rule 101 merit comment.

He and His Firm.   For purposes of Rule 101, "he and his firm" include (1) all partners in the firm, (2) all full- and part-time professional employees of a firm participating in the engagement, and (3) all full- and part-time managerial employees of a firm located in an office participating in a significant portion of the engagement.

The term, he and his firm, includes spouses (whether or not dependent) and dependent persons (whether or not related). However, nondependent close kin such as children, siblings, grandparents, parents, parents-in-law, and their spouses, are excluded from this term, except as specifically noted below.

Time Periods.   Three time periods are identified in Rule 101:

- The period of the auditor's professional engagement, which includes both interim and year-end audit work.
- The period covered by the financial statements, which is the client's fiscal year.
- The time of expressing the auditor's opinion, which is the date of the auditor's report.

The prohibitions pertaining to financial interest (101A) relate to the period of the engagement and the time of expressing an opinion since the member's holdings would seem to a reasonable observer to adversely affect his objectivity. In contrast, the prohibitions relating to business relationships (101B) extend from the beginning of the client's fiscal year to the time of expressing the auditor's opinion because the member would be examining and reporting on decisions he participated in had he been serving in those capacities.

Financial Interest

The prohibitions on financial interest are very explicit.

First, the member or his firm cannot have (or be committed to have) any direct financial interest in the client. The prohibition against a *direct financial interest* is absolute. Thus, a member may not directly own or have an option to buy even one share of stock in the client. *Indirect financial interest* exists, for example, when (1) a member or his firm own stock in a mutual fund that, in turn, owns stock in the client, or (2) a member's nondependent close relative has a financial interest in the client. The restriction against indirect financial interest is based on materiality. Independence is impaired in the foregoing examples only if the mutual fund's holdings in the client are extensive and the relative's financial interest is material to his own net worth.

Second, a member is not allowed to have a joint closely held business investment with a client company or officers, directors, or principal stockholders of such enterprise that is material to either the member's or the firm's net assets. Such a situation would exist when the CPA and an officer of the client each contributed a third of the capital needed to finance (and organize) the company if the amounts were material.

Third, a member is not permitted to have any loan to or from a client, or its officers, directors, or principal stockholders, which is not made under normal lending procedures, terms, and requirements. Any evidence of favoritism in such a transaction could be regarded by a reasonably informed individual as impairing the auditor's independence.

Business Relationships

The purpose of the prohibitions against business relationships (Rule 101B), among other considerations, is to avoid circumstances in which the member or his firm (1) has significant influence over the operating, financial, or accounting policies of the client or (2) is involved in "audit-sensitive" activities within the client's organization. A member who participates in board of director decisions on material transactions and a member serving in a fiduciary capacity for a funded pension plan would have significant influence over the client's policies.

Activities are considered to be "audit-sensitive" if they are normally an element of or subject to significant internal accounting controls. Such positions in the client as cashier, internal auditor, and purchasing agent are considered to be audit-sensitive.

A CPA who performs manual or automated bookkeeping services for an audit client must meet the following requirements to retain the appearance that he is not an employee and therefore lacking in independence in the eyes of a reasonable observer:

- He must not have any other relationships, such as a financial interest, which would impair his integrity and objectivity.
- The client must accept full responsibility for his financial statements.
- The CPA must not assume the role either of an employee or management in the client's operations.

Management Advisory Services

Concern has been expressed in some segments of government and academia that the rendering of management advisory services (MAS) to an audit client by the client's auditor impairs the auditor's independence. This position is based on the belief that the auditor would be reviewing his own work and might be biased in doing so.

The AICPA has consistently maintained that MAS are entirely compatible with independence as long as the CPA serves only as an adviser to management in making the business decision. If the auditor is the decision maker, audit independence is impaired because the auditor would then be acting in "a capacity equivalent to that of a member of management."

To date, there have been no known instances when management advisory services have compromised independence.[11] However, a CPA firm that is a member of the SEC Practice Section, described in Chapter 1, is required to refrain from performing the following MAS for its SEC audit clients:

- Psychological testing.
- Public opinion polls.
- Merger and acquisition assistance for a finder's fee.
- Executive recruitment.
- Actuarial services to insurance companies.[12]

Litigation

Litigation involving CPAs and their clients raises questions about a member's independence. In general, independence is impaired whenever the existence or expressed threat of litigation has significantly altered or is expected to materially change the normal relationship between a client and a CPA. Litigation that results in an adversary position between a client and a CPA, or which links management and the CPA as co-conspirators in withholding information from stockholders, would impair the CPA's independence. In con-

---

[11]Commission on Auditors' Responsibilities, *Report, Conclusions, and Recommendations* (New York: American Institute of Certified Public Accountants, 1978), p. 102.

[12]SEC Practice Section, Division for CPA Firms, *Peer Review Manual,* Revised Edition (New York: American Institute of Certified Public Accountants, 1981), pp. 1-9.

trast, litigation brought by stockholders against a CPA would not necessarily affect independence.

At the present time, there are seven interpretations and 54 rulings in effect on Rule 101. The initial publication in each category is as follows:

Interpretation 101-1: Honorary Directorships and Trusteeships

Members are often asked to lend the prestige of their names to not-for-profit organizations that limit their activities to those of a charitable, religious, civic or similar nature by being named a director or a trustee. A member who permits his name to be used in this manner and who is associated with the financial statements of the organization would not be considered lacking in independence under Rule 101 so long as (1) his position is purely honorary, (2) it is identified as honorary in all letterheads and externally circulated materials in which he is named as a director or trustee, (3) he restricts his participation to the use of his name, and (4) he does not vote or otherwise participate in management functions.

It is presumed that organizations to which members lend only the prestige of their names will have sufficiently large boards of directors or trustees to clearly permit the member to limit his participation consistent with the foregoing restriction.[13]

Ruling 1: Acceptance of a Gift

Question: Would the independence of a member's firm be considered to be impaired if an employee or partner accepts a gift or other unusual consideration from a client?

Answer: If an employee or partner accepts more than a token gift from a client, even with the knowledge of the member's firm, the appearance of independence may be lacking.[14]

The concept of independence is not limited to Rule 101. It also is applicable to six other rules—Rules 102, 202, 302, 502, 503, and 504—that are explained later in the chapter.

Rule 102 INTEGRITY AND OBJECTIVITY. A member shall not knowingly misrepresent facts, and when engaged in the practice of public accounting, including the rendering of tax and management advisory services, shall not subordinate his judgment to others. In tax practice, a member may resolve doubt in favor of his client as long as there is reasonable support for his position.

Whereas Rule 101 applies only to auditing engagements, Rule 102 is applicable to all aspects of the practice of public accounting, including tax and

---

[13] AICPA Professional Standards, *op. cit.*, ET § 101.02.
[14] AICPA Professional Standards, *op. cit.*, ET § 191.01.

management advisory services (MAS). The MAS standards distinguish between two categories of MAS services: (1) *engagements* that involve applying an analytical approach and process in a study or project for an extended time period such as the installation of an EDP system, and (2) *consultations* that consist of informal advice during a short time frame such as a recommendation to use a collection agency to collect past due receivables. Standards of professional practice in rendering tax and MAS services are presented in Appendices 19B and 19C.

GENERAL AND TECHNICAL STANDARDS

ETHICAL PRINCIPLE

> *A certified public accountant should observe the profession's general and technical standards and strive continually to improve his competence and the quality of his services.*[15]

Because of the importance of verifiable accounting data to all segments of the public, CPAs should perform their work at a high level of professionalism. CPAs must constantly strive to improve their competence and always attempt to meet applicable technical standards. Observance of this principle requires subjective determination by the CPA of his ability to meet the complexities of each engagement.

RULES OF CONDUCT

There are four rules on general and technical standards.

Rule 201. GENERAL STANDARDS.   A member shall comply with the following general standards as interpreted by bodies designated by Council, and must justify any departures therefrom.

  a. Professional competence. A member shall undertake only those engagements which he or his firm can reasonably expect to complete with professional competence.
  b. Due professional care. A member shall exercise due professional care in the performance of an engagement.
  c. Planning and supervision. A member shall adequately plan and supervise an engagement.
  d. Sufficient relevant data. A member shall obtain sufficient relevant data to afford a reasonable basis for conclusions or recommendations in relation to an engagement.
  e. Forecasts. A member shall not permit his name to be used in conjunction with any forecast of future transactions in a manner which may lead to the belief that the member vouches for the achievability of the forecast.

---

[15] AICPA Professional Standards, *op. cit.*, ET § 53.

Rule 201 contains five general standards that are meant to be applicable to all types of services performed in professional engagements. Because of its scope, three AICPA groups have been authorized to interpret Rule 201. They are the Accounting and Review Services Committee, the Auditing Standards Board, and the Management Advisory Services Executive Committee. Rule 201a, *Professional competence,* involves not only the technical qualifications of the member and the member's staff, but also the CPA's ability to supervise and evaluate the quality of the work performed by others. This part of Rule 201 is specifically directed at the member's decision-making process when the CPA is deciding whether to accept or decline an engagement. If, on the basis of facts known at the time, the CPA believes he has the capability to complete the assignment in accordance with professional standards, it is ethically permissible to accept the engagement. However, if the member knows, for example, that neither he nor the firm has the computer expertise required to audit a client with a sophisticated electronic data processing (EDP) system, it is not ethically proper to accept the engagement.

Due professional care, planning and supervision, and sufficient relevant data codify practices followed by most members. Adherence to these requirements contributes to the quality of performance of professional engagements for the benefit of the public and the profession.

Rule 201e, *forecasts,* does not prohibit a CPA from being associated with a financial forecast. It only prescribes the manner of the association. A CPA cannot be associated with a forecast in a way that would lead a reader to assume that the CPA is attesting, vouching, or guaranteeing the achievability of the forecast. In order to eliminate any uncertainty about the responsibility that is being taken in connection with a forecast, a CPA should, in describing the association, clearly state that he does not express an opinion on the achievability of the forecast, as is explained and illustrated in Chapter 18.

Rule 202. AUDITING STANDARDS.   A member shall not permit his name to be associated with financial statements in such a manner as to imply that he is acting as an independent public accountant unless he has complied with the applicable generally accepted auditing standards promulgated by the Institute. Statements on Auditing Standards issued by the Institute's Auditing Standards Board are, for purposes of this rule, considered to be interpretations of the generally accepted auditing standards, and departures from such statements must be justified by those who do not follow them.

Rule 202 officially incorporates the Statements on Auditing Standards (SASs) into the Rules of Conduct and requires adherence in every audit engagement to the ten generally accepted auditing standards. This rule enhances the prestige and influence of the Auditing Standards Board and strengthens the authority of the AICPA over its members who provide auditing services for clients. Each member should take seriously the need to justify any departures from these statements since they represent the views of the members of the AICPA's senior technical committee in this area of practice. Rule 202 does not preclude a member being associated with unaudited financial statements.

Rule 203. ACCOUNTING PRINCIPLES. A member shall not express an opinion that financial statements are presented in conformity with generally accepted accounting principles if such statements contain any departure from an accounting principle promulgated by the body designated by Council to establish such principles which has a material effect on the statements taken as a whole, unless the member can demonstrate that due to unusual circumstances the financial statements would otherwise have been misleading. In such cases his report must describe the departure, the approximate effects thereof, if practicable, and the reasons why compliance with the principle would result in a misleading statement.

Rule 203 is discussed in some detail in Chapter 17. It will be recalled that the Financial Accounting Standards Board (FASB) has been designated by the Council of the AICPA as the promulgating body for purposes of this rule. This rule contributes to greater uniformity in the application of generally accepted accounting principles and significantly strengthens the authority of the FASB.

Rule 204. OTHER TECHNICAL STANDARDS. A member shall comply with other technical standards promulgated by bodies designated by Council to establish such standards, and departures therefrom must be justified by those who depart from them.

At the present time, there are three types of other technical standards:

- The FASB is recognized as the body to promulgate standards of disclosure for financial information outside the basic financial statements in published financial reports containing financial statements.
- The Accounting and Review Services Committee is designated as the body to promulgate standards with respect to unaudited financial statements or other unaudited financial information of nonpublic entities.
- The Management Advisory Services Executive Committee is recognized as the group that promulgates standards for management advisory services.[16]

RESPONSIBILITIES TO CLIENTS

ETHICAL PRINCIPLE

A certified public accountant should be fair and candid with his clients and serve them to the best of his ability, with professional concern for their best interests, consistent with his responsibilities to the public.[17]

A CPA has a responsibility to both his client and the public. In discharging the responsibility, a CPA must serve the client with competence. However,

[16]AICPA Professional Standards, *op. cit.,* ET Appendix D.
[17]AICPA Professional Standards, *op. cit.,* ET § 54.

his interest in the welfare of his client must be subordinate to his obligation to the public to maintain his independence, integrity, and objectivity. The relationship between a CPA and a client should be based on mutual respect that permits a frank and straightforward discussion of honest differences of opinion.

RULES OF CONDUCT

Two Rules of Conduct apply to a member's responsibilities to clients.

Rule 301 CONFIDENTIAL CLIENT INFORMATION.   A member shall not disclose any confidential information obtained in the course of a professional engagement except with the consent of the client.

This rule shall not be construed (a) to relieve a member of his obligation under Rules 202 and 203, (b) to affect in any way his compliance with a validly issued subpoena or summons enforceable by order of a court, (c) to prohibit review of a member's professional practices as a part of voluntary quality review under Institute authorization or (d) to preclude a member from responding to any inquiry made by the ethics division or Trial Board of the Institute, by a duly constituted investigative or disciplinary body of a state CPA society, or under state statutes.

Members of the ethics division and Trial Board of the Institute and professional practice reviewers under Institute authorization shall not disclose any confidential client information which comes to their attention from members in disciplinary proceedings or otherwise in carrying out their official responsibilities. However, this prohibition shall not restrict the exchange of information with an aforementioned duly constituted investigative or disciplinary body.

It is fundamental that a CPA hold in strict confidence all information about a client's business affairs. Confidentiality is indispensable in establishing a basis of mutual trust between a CPA and his client.

Rule 301 should not override a CPA's other professional responsibilities. For example, a CPA must still comply with the third standard of reporting that requires disclosure of financial information necessary for fair presentation. In addition, a member can fully respond to a court order or inquiry by the Professional Ethics Division.

Rule 301 prohibits a predecessor auditor from allowing a successor auditor access to working papers without the client's permission. Similarly, a CPA who sells his practice to another CPA cannot transfer the working papers to the new owner without the express permission of each client.

Some states grant privileged communication to auditors that gives the CPA the right to withhold confidential information in a court of law. However, this privilege should not be used by a CPA as an excuse to remain silent when a client has participated or is participating in an illegal or deceitful act. This rule does not apply to disclosure of any confidential information required to properly discharge the member's responsibility under the profession's own standards.

Rule 302 CONTINGENT FEES. Professional services shall not be offered or rendered under an arrangement whereby no fee will be charged unless a specified finding or result is attained, or where the fee is otherwise contingent upon the findings or results of such services. However, a member's fees may vary depending, for example, on the complexity of the service rendered.

Fees are not regarded as being contingent if fixed by courts or other public authorities or, in tax matters, if determined based on the results of judicial proceedings or the findings of governmental agencies.

Rule 302 allows the auditor to charge a fee based on the number of days required to do the job. A member may also elect to lower per diem billing rates for a financially troubled client or perform services without charge for a charitable organization.

However, it is not permissible, by prearrangement, for the member to receive a specified financial return that is conditioned on the results of the work. For example, an audit fee should not be based on a percentage of net income or the amount of the loan obtained from a lender's reliance on audited financial statements. Such a contractual arrangement could impair the CPA's objectivity and hence his independence since the member would have a direct financial interest in the outcome of the audit.

The rule against contingent fees is not applicable when the member bases the fee on the findings or results fixed (or determined) by a court or governmental agency such as the Internal Revenue Service (IRS). In such case, there are recognized constraints against possible bias by the member. However, a member cannot base his fee in preparing a tax return on the amount of taxes he can save his client because the member's duty is to determine the proper tax liability. Thus, there is no basis for computing a saving. It is also unethical for a member to indicate that professional services will be performed for a stated fee, estimated fee, or fee range when at the time of the representation, the member believes such fees will likely be substantially increased and the prospective client is not advised of this likelihood.

RESPONSIBILITIES TO COLLEAGUES

ETHICAL PRINCIPLE

A certified public accountant should conduct himself in a manner that will promote cooperation and good relations among members of the profession.[18]

The development and growth of a profession depend, in large measure, on the ability of individual members to work together for the common good. It is important therefore that a CPA support the efforts of the AICPA and

---

[18] AICPA Professional Standards, *op. cit.*, ET § 55.

state societies of CPAs and seek to have and to maintain good relations with fellow practitioners.

It is understandable that a CPA may wish to expand his practice. In doing so, however, the member should not seek to displace another CPA in a client relationship or act in a manner that would impinge on the integrity, objectivity, or competency of another CPA.

RULES OF CONDUCT

Currently, there are no rules of conduct pertaining to this ethical principle. The AICPA has had to rescind its rules in this category because they were deemed to be in restraint of trade.

OTHER RESPONSIBILITIES AND PRACTICES

ETHICAL PRINCIPLE

A certified public accountant should conduct himself in a manner that will enhance the stature of the profession and its ability to serve the public.[19]

A CPA is a representative of his profession. Accordingly, the member should avoid personal and professional conduct that might reduce public respect and confidence. A CPA is expected to have a professional attitude that places public service above financial reward.

RULES OF CONDUCT

There are five Rules of Conduct pertaining to this aspect of the code.

> **Rule 501 ACTS DISCREDITABLE.**   A member shall not commit an act discreditable to the profession.

Rule 501 relates to acts by a member that may damage or otherwise impinge on the reputation and integrity of the profession. This rule enables disciplinary action to be taken against a member for unethical acts not specifically covered by other rules. Discreditable acts include the actions discussed earlier that result in automatic disciplinary provisions, and they also include failing to comply with continuing professional education requirements.

In separate ethics interpretations, the following acts have been designated as discreditable: (1) retention of client records and auditor working papers, such as adjusting entries, necessary to complete the client's records; (2) discrimination in employment; (3) failure to follow standards and/or other procedures or other requirements in governmental audits; and (4) negligence in

---

[19] AICPA Professional Standards, *op. cit.,* ET § 56.

the preparation of financial statements. A member who commits a discreditable act usually is suspended or expelled from the AICPA.

Rule 502 ADVERTISING AND OTHER FORMS OF SOLICITATION. A member shall not seek to obtain clients by advertising or other forms of solicitation in a manner that is false, misleading, or deceptive. Solicitation by the use of coercion, overreaching, or harassing conduct is prohibited.

This rule is a compromise between members who believe all advertising and solicitation should be banned because it is unprofessional, and members who want to avoid possible legal action by the United States Department of Justice for prohibitions on these activities.

False, misleading, or deceptive advertising includes statements that

- Create false or unjustified expectations of favorable results.
- Imply the ability to influence any court, tribunal, regulatory agency, or similar body or official.
- Consist of self-laudatory statements that are not based on verifiable facts.
- Make comparisons with other CPAs that are not based on verifiable facts.
- Contain testimonials or endorsements.[20]

These statements are prohibited because they may mislead the public and thereby reduce or destroy the profession's usefulness to society. In contrast, advertising that is informative, objective, and in good taste is permitted. For example, a firm may disclose factual information in an advertisement that is verifiable, such as the number of partners and offices in the firm.

Other forms of solicitation include offers made by letter, telephone, or in person to perform professional services. The use of any of the prohibited types of conduct may lessen the CPA's professional effectiveness and independence toward any client obtained through such means.

Rule 503 COMMISSIONS. A member shall not pay a commission to obtain a client, nor shall he accept a commission for a referral to a client of products or services of others. This rule shall not prohibit payments for the purchase of an accounting practice or retirement payments to individuals formerly engaged in the practice of public accounting or payments to their heirs or estates.

Rule 503 on commissions is designed to prevent (1) the client from paying a fee for which commensurate service was not received and (2) the member from becoming involved in conflict-of-interest situations that may impair his independence.

The first situation pertains to the payment of a commission (or fee) by a member to another party to obtain a client. In such case, it is presumed that

---

[20]AICPA Professional Standards, *op. cit.,* ET § 502.03 (adapted).

the member will pass the commission on to the client, and thus the client will be paying for a service that was not received. The second condition involves the receipt of a commission by a CPA from vendors and others in making recommendations to a client. For instance, a computer manufacturer may offer the member a commission for equipment purchased by a client on the CPA's recommendation. The acceptance of a commission under such circumstances would cause the client to doubt whether the equipment was the best or whether it was recommended on the basis of the member's personal financial reward. The conflict of interest is not reduced, in the eyes of a reasonable observer, even if the client should approve the acceptance of the commission. This rule does not prevent the member from charging the client a fee for services rendered in making such recommendations.

Rule 504 INCOMPATIBLE OCCUPATIONS. A member who is engaged in the practice of public accounting shall not concurrently engage in any business or occupation which would create a conflict of interest in rendering professional services.

The thrust of Rule 504 is to discourage a member from engaging in secondary occupations that pertain to the financial affairs of clients or prospective clients. The AICPA has never published a list of incompatible occupations, but prefers to evaluate each case on its merits. Such positions as tax assessor, or a broker in insurance, real estate, or securities, are examples of potentially incompatible occupations that could create a conflict of interest for a member in the practice of public accounting and lessen his independence.

Rule 505 FORM OF PRACTICE AND NAME. A member may practice public accounting, whether as an owner or employee, only in the form of a proprietorship, a partnership or a professional corporation whose characteristics conform to resolutions of Council.

A member shall not practice under a firm name which includes any fictitious name, indicates specialization or is misleading as to the type of organization (proprietorship, partnership or corporation). However, names of one or more past partners or shareholders may be included in the firm name of a successor partnership or corporation. Also, a partner surviving the death or withdrawal of all other partners may continue to practice under the partnership name for up to two years after becoming a sole practitioner.

A firm may not designate itself as "Members of the American Institute of Certified Public Accountants" unless all of its partners or shareholders are members of the Institute.

Rule 505 permits a CPA to practice as an individual, a partnership, or a *professional* corporation. To qualify as a professional corporation, it is necessary to meet certain characteristics established by the Council of the AICPA. These include (1) all shareholders must be engaged in the practice of public accounting, (2) the principal executive officer shall be a shareholder and director, and (3) stockholders shall be jointly and severally liable for the acts of the corporation or its employees except where professional liability insurance is carried or capitalization is maintained in amounts deemed sufficient to offer adequate protection to the public.

INTERNAL AUDITOR CODE OF ETHICS

The Institute of Internal Auditors has adopted the following Code of Ethics for Certified Internal Auditors (CIAs).

CERTIFIED INTERNAL AUDITOR CODE OF ETHICS[21]

Introduction:

The Certified Internal Auditor has an obligation to the profession, management, and stockholders and to the general public to maintain high standards of professional conduct. In recognition of this obligation, The Institute of Internal Auditors, Inc., adopted this Code of Ethics for Certified Internal Auditors.

Adherence to this Code, which is based on the Code of Ethics for members of The Institute, is a prerequisite to maintaining the designation Certified Internal Auditor. A Certified Internal Auditor who is judged by the Board of Directors of The Institute to be in violation of the provisions of the Code shall forfeit the Certified Internal Auditor designation.

Interpretation of Principles:

The provisions of this Code of Ethics cover basic principles in the various disciplines of internal auditing practice. Certified Internal Auditors shall realize that their individual judgment is required in the application of these principles. They have a responsibility to conduct themselves in a manner so that their good faith and integrity should not be open to question. Furthermore, they shall use the "Certified Internal Auditor" designation with discretion and in a dignified manner, fully aware of what the designation denotes and in a manner consistent with all statutory requirements. While having due regard for the limit of their technical skills, they will promote the highest possible internal auditing standards to the end of advancing the interest of their company or organization.

Articles:

I. Certified Internal Auditors shall have an obligation to exercise honesty, objectivity and diligence in the performance of their duties and responsibilities.

II. Certified Internal Auditors, in holding the trust of their employer, shall exhibit loyalty in all matters pertaining to the affairs of the employer or to whomever they may be rendering a service. However, a Certified Internal Auditor shall not knowingly be a party to any illegal or improper activity.

III. Certified Internal Auditors shall refrain from entering into any activity which may be in conflict with the interest of their employer or which would prejudice their ability to carry out objectively their duties and responsibilities.

IV. Certified Internal Auditors shall not accept a fee or a gift from an employee, a client, a customer or a business associate of their employer without the knowledge and consent of senior management.

V. Certified Internal Auditors shall be prudent in their use of information acquired in the course of their duties. They shall not use confidential information for any personal gain or in a manner which would be detrimental to the welfare of their employer.

[21]*Certified Internal Auditor Code of Ethics*, (Altamonte Springs, Fla: The Institute of Internal Auditors Inc., 1972).

VI. Certified Internal Auditors, in expressing an opinion, shall use all reasonable care to obtain sufficient factual evidence to warrant such expression. In reporting, Certified Internal Auditors shall reveal such material facts known to them which, if not revealed, could either distort the report of the results of operations under review or conceal unlawful practice.

VII. Certified Internal Auditors shall continually strive for improvements in the proficiency and effectiveness of their service.

The Interpretation of Principles corresponds to the Ethical Concepts of the AICPA Code, and the Articles are analogous to the AICPA Rules of Conduct. A study of the Articles shows that articles (I) and (III) relate to independence; article (II) to discreditable acts; article (IV) to contingent fees; article (V) to confidential client information; article (VI) to the general standards of due professional care and sufficient relevant data; and article (VII) to the general standard of competence.

The maximum sanction imposed by the Institute of Internal Auditors for violating the provisions of the Code is to revoke the member's designation as a certified internal auditor. The Institute has this authority because it originally issued the internal auditor's certificate.

CONCLUDING COMMENTS

It is not enough for a member of a profession to only live within the law. The professional person must also adhere to both the letter and spirit of a code of professional ethics. The ethical standards of the accounting profession extend to independence, general and technical standards, and the CPA's responsibilities to clients, colleagues, and particularly the public.

The Code of Professional Ethics, established and enforced by the AICPA, state associations of CPAs, and state boards of accountancy has contributed significantly to the stature and reputation of the accounting profession. For the CPA, the Code assures that other CPAs are following the same rules of conduct. For the public, the Code insures that CPAs are meeting high standards of ethical conduct in each engagement.

Appendix 19A

Interpretations of Rules of Conduct

Rule 101— Independence

101–1 Honorary directorships and trusteeships.

101–2 Retired partners and firm independence.

101–3 Accounting services.

101–5 Meaning of the term "normal lending procedures, terms, and requirements."

101–6 The effect of actual or threatened litigation on independence.

101–8 Effect on independence of financial interests in nonclients having investor or investee relationships with a member's client.

101–9 The meaning of certain independence terminology and the effect of family relationships on independence.

Rule 102— Integrity and Objectivity

102–1 Knowing misrepresentations in the preparation of financial statements or records.

Rule 201— General Standards

201–1 Competence.

201–2 Forecasts.

201–3 Shopping for accounting or auditing standards.

Rule 202— Auditing Standards

202–1 Unaudited financial statements.

Rule 203— Accounting Principles

203–1 Departures from established accounting principles.

203–2 Status of FASB interpretations.

203–3 FASB statements that establish standards for disclosure outside of the basic financial statements.

Rule 301— Confidential Client Information

301–1 Confidential information and technical standards.

Rule 501— Acts Discreditable

501–1 Client's records and accountant's workpapers.

501–2 Discrimination in employment practices.

501–3 Failure to follow standards and/or procedures or other requirements in governmental audits.

501–4 Negligence in the preparation of financial statements or records.

Rule 502— Advertising and Other Forms of Solicitation

502–1 Informational advertising.

502–2 False, misleading, or deceptive acts.

502–5 Engagements obtained through efforts of third parties.

Rule 503— Commissions

503–1 Fees in payment for services.

Rule 505— Form of Practice and Name

505–1 Investment in commercial accounting corporation.

505–2 Application of Rules of Conduct to members who operate a separate business.

Details of these interpretations and information concerning all ethics rulings that are in effect are presented in Volume B of the AICPA Professional Standards.

Appendix 19B

Standards for Management Advisory Services Practice[22]

1. The following general standards apply to both MAS engagements and MAS consultations. They are contained in rule 201 of the AICPA Rules of Conduct, and apply to all services performed in the practice of public accounting.[23]

   - *Professional Competence.* A member shall undertake only those engagements which he or his firm can reasonably expect to complete with professional competence.

---

[22]AICPA Professional Standards, *op. cit.*, Management Advisory Services Section 11 and 21.

[23]The use of the terms "MAS engagement" and "MAS consultation" to differentiate the two recognized forms of MAS is not intended to exclude MAS consultations from the meaning of the term "engagement" as it is used in Rule 201.

- *Due Professional Care.* A member shall exercise due professional care in the performance of an engagement.
- *Planning and Supervision.* A member shall adequately plan and supervise an engagement.
- *Sufficient Relevant Data.* A member shall obtain sufficient relevant data to afford a reasonable basis for conclusions or recommendations in relation to an engagement.
- *Forecasts.* A member shall not permit his name to be used in conjunction with any forecast of future transactions in a manner that may lead to the belief that the member vouches for the achievability of the forecast.

2. The following technical standards apply to MAS engagements. . . . They are established under Rule 204 of the AICPA Rules of Conduct.

- *Role of MAS Practitioner.* In performing an MAS engagement, an MAS practitioner should not assume the role of management or take any positions that might impair the MAS practitioner's objectivity.
- *Understanding with Client.* An oral or written understanding should be reached with the client concerning the nature, scope, and limitations of the MAS engagement to be performed.
- *Client Benefit.* Since the potential benefits to be derived by the client are a major consideration in MAS engagements, such potential benefits should be viewed objectively and the client should be notified of reservations regarding them. In offering and providing MAS engagements, results should not be explicitly or implicitly guaranteed. When estimates of quantifiable results are presented, they should be clearly identified as estimates and the support for such estimates should be disclosed.
- *Communication of Results.* Significant information pertinent to the results of an MAS engagement, together with any limitations, qualifications, or reservations needed to assist the client in making its decision, should be communicated to the client orally or in writing.

Appendix 19C

Statements on Responsibilities in Tax Practice[24]

1. *Answers to Questions on Returns.* A CPA should sign the preparer's declaration on a federal tax return only if he is satisfied that reasonable effort has been made to provide appropriate answers to the questions on the

[24]AICPA Professional Standards, *op. cit.*, Tax Practice Section 131–201 (adapted).

return which are applicable to the taxpayer. Where such a question is left unanswered, the reason for such omission should be stated. The possibility that an answer to a question might prove disadvantageous to the taxpayer does not justify omitting an answer or a statement of the reason for such omission.

2. *Recognition of Administrative Proceeding of a Prior Year.* The selection of the treatment of an item in the course of the preparation of a tax return should be based upon the facts and the rules as they are evaluated at the time the return is prepared. Unless the taxpayer is bound as to treatment in the later year, such as by a closing agreement, the disposition of an item as a part of concluding an administrative proceeding by the execution of a waiver for a prior year does not govern the taxpayer in selecting the treatment of a similar item in a later year's return.

3. *Use of Estimates.* A certified public accountant may prepare tax returns involving the use of estimates if such use is generally acceptable or, under the circumstances, it is impracticable to obtain exact data. When estimates are used, the CPA should be satisfied that estimated accounts are not unreasonable under the circumstances.

4. *Knowledge of Error: Return Preparation.*

   a. A CPA shall advise his client promptly upon learning of an error in a previously filed return, or upon learning of a client's failure to file a required return. His advice should include a recommendation of the measures to be taken.

   b. If the CPA is requested to prepare the current year's return and the client has not taken appropriate action to rectify an error in a prior year's return that has resulted or may result in a material understatement of tax liability, the CPA should consider whether to proceed with the preparation of the current year's return.

5. *Knowledge of Error: Administrative Proceedings.* When the CPA is representing a client in an administrative proceeding in respect of a return in which there is an error known to the CPA that has resulted or may result in a material understatement of tax liability, he should request the client's agreement to disclose the error to the Internal Revenue Service. Lacking such agreement, the CPA may be under a duty to withdraw from the engagement.

6. *Advice to Clients.* In providing tax advice to his client, the CPA must use judgment to assure that his advice reflects professional competence and appropriately serves the client's needs.

7. *Certain Procedural Aspects of Preparing Returns.* In preparing a return, the CPA ordinarily may rely on information furnished by his client. He is not required to examine or review documents or other evidence supporting the client's information in order to sign the preparer's declaration. Although the examination of supporting data is not required, the CPA should encourage his client to provide him with supporting data where appropriate.

8. *Positions Contrary to Treasury Department or Internal Revenue Service Interpretations of the Code.* In preparing a tax return a CPA may take a position contrary to Treasury Department or Internal Revenue Service interpretations of the Code without disclosure, if there is reasonable support for the position.

   In preparing a tax return a CPA may take a position contrary to a specific section of the Internal Revenue Code where there is reasonable support for the position. In such a rare situation, the CPA should disclose the treatment in the tax return.

   In no event may a CPA take a position that lacks reasonable support, even when this position is disclosed in a return.

REVIEW QUESTIONS

19-1 Explain the essence of the term *professional ethics.*

19-2 What are the responsibilities of the executive committee of the AICPA Ethics Division?

19-3 Identify and describe the four parts of the Code of Professional Ethics.

19-4 What is the applicability of the Rules of Conduct to the practice of public accounting in (a) the United States and (b) a foreign country?

19-5 a. What groups are responsible for enforcement of the Rules of Conduct?
b. Indicate the penalties that may be imposed by each group.

19-6 a. Identify the two groups that may receive complaints under the Joint Ethics Enforcement Program.
b. How is jurisdiction decided between the groups?
c. What actions may each group take?

19-7 a. What criterion is used in determining whether to refer a case to the joint trial board?
b. Indicate the types of decisions the trial board may render.
c. Identify the circumstances when automatic disciplinary provisions may be invoked.

19-8 a. In Rule 101—Independence, identify the time periods that are applicable to financial interests.
b. Distinguish between direct and indirect financial interest as it pertains to a member and his family.

19-9 a. In Rule 101—Independence, identify the time periods that are applicable to business relationships.
b. Indicate the types of business relationships that are prohibited by Rule 101.

19-10 a. What type of action by a CPA is prohibited in a management advisory services engagement?
b. What types of MAS engagements must be avoided by firms that are members of the SEC Practice Section?

19-11 Enumerate the five subcategories of Rule 201—General Standards.

19-12 What is the impact of Rule 202—Auditing Standards on the auditor?

19-13 a. Which groups are authorized to promulgate technical standards under Rule 204—Other Technical Standards?
b. Indicate the types of standards each group may issue.

19-14 a. What is the essence of Rule 301—Confidential Client Information?

b. Indicate three exceptions to this rule.

19-15 a. Explain the objective of Rule 302—Contingent Fees.

b. What exceptions are permitted under this rule?

19-16 Identify the acts that are prohibited under Rule 501—Acts Discreditable.

19-17 Briefly explain what is permissible and what is prohibited under Rule 502—Advertising and Other Forms of Solicitation.

19-18 a. What is prohibited by Rule 503—Commissions?

b. Explain the rationale of this rule.

19-19 a. Why is a member required to avoid incompatible occupations?

b. Give examples of occupations that potentially are incompatible.

19-20 a. List the forms of business organization that are permitted under Rule 505—Form of Practice and Firm Name.

b. What requirements must be met to operate as a professional corporation?

OBJECTIVE QUESTIONS FROM PROFESSIONAL EXAMINATIONS

Indicate the *best* answer choice for each of the following multiple choice questions.

19-21 These questions relate to Rules of Conduct.

1. According to the AICPA Code of Professional Ethics, a CPA who has a financial interest in a partnership that invests in a potential client is considered to have
   a. An indirect financial interest in the client.
   b. A direct financial interest in the client.
   c. No financial interest in the client.
   d. A partial financial interest in the client.

2. The AICPA Code of Professional Ethics states that a CPA shall not disclose any confidential information obtained in the course of a professional engagement except with the consent of the client. This rule should be understood to preclude a CPA from responding to an inquiry made by
   a. The trial board of the AICPA.
   b. A CPA-shareholder of the client corporation.
   c. An investigative body of a state CPA society.
   d. An AICPA voluntary quality review body.

3. Inclusion of which of the following in a promotional brochure published by a CPA firm would be most likely to result in a violation of the AICPA rules of conduct?
   a. Reprints of newspaper articles that are laudatory with respect to the firm's expertise.
   b. Services offered and fees for such services, including hourly rates and fixed fees.
   c. Educational and professional attainments of partners.
   d. Testimonials and endorsements.

4. A CPA's retention of client records as a means of enforcing payment of an overdue audit fee is an action that is
   a. *Not* addressed by the AICPA Code of Professional Ethics.
   b. Acceptable if sanctioned by the state laws.
   c. Prohibited under the AICPA rules of conduct.
   d. A violation of generally accepted auditing standards.

19-22 These questions relate to the rendering of tax and management advisory services and involve material in the appendix of this chapter.

1. The CPA who undertakes the performance of a management advisory service engagement should bear in mind that the results should
   a. Increase the client's earnings capabilities.
   b. Be communicated in quantitative terms.
   c. Not be set forth as quantitative estimates.
   d. Not be explicitly or implicitly guaranteed.

2. A CPA engaged in tax practice
   a. May take a position contrary to a specific section of the IRS Code without disclosure.
   b. May take a position contrary to Internal Revenue Service interpretations of the IRS Code without disclosure.
   c. Must disclose any position contrary to Treasury Department regulations concerning the IRS Code.
   d. Must *not* take a position contrary to Internal Revenue Service interpretations of the IRS Code without disclosure.

3. In performing MAS engagements, CPAs should *not* take any positions that might
   a. Constitute advice and assistance.
   b. Provide technical assistance in implementation.
   c. Result in new organizational policies and procedures.
   d. Impair their objectivity.

4. A CPA who is engaged to prepare an income tax return has a duty to prepare it in such a manner that the tax is
   a. The legal minimum.
   b. Computed in conformity with generally accepted accounting principles.
   c. Supported by the client's audited financial statements.
   d. Not subject to change on audit.

COMPREHENSIVE QUESTIONS

19-23 An auditor must not only appear to be independent; he must also be independent in fact.

Required

a. Explain the concept of an "auditor's independence" as it applies to third party reliance on financial statements.

b. 1. What determines whether or not an auditor is independent in fact?
   2. What determines whether or not an auditor appears to be independent?

c. Explain how an auditor may be independent in fact but not appear to be independent.

d. Would a CPA be considered independent for an examination of the financial statements of a
   1. Church for which he is serving as treasurer without compensation? Explain.
   2. Women's club for which his wife is serving as treasurer-bookkeeper if he is not to receive a fee for the examination? Explain.

AICPA (adapted)

19-24 An auditor's report was appended to the financial statements of Worthmore, Inc. The statements consisted of a balance sheet as of November 30, 19X0 and statements of income and retained earnings for the year then ending. The first two paragraphs of the report contained the wording of the standard unqualified report, and a third paragraph read as follows:

The wives of two partners of our firm owned a material investment in the outstanding common stock of Worthmore, Inc. during the fiscal year ending November 30, 19X0. The aforementioned individuals disposed of their holdings of Worthmore, Inc. on December 3, 19X0 in a transaction that did not result in a profit or a loss. This information is included in our report in order to comply with certain disclosure requirements of the Code of Professional Ethics of the American Institute of Certified Public Accountants.

BELL & DAVIS
Certified Public Accountants

Required

a. Was the CPA firm of Bell & Davis independent with respect to the fiscal 19X0 examination of Worthmore, Inc.'s financial statements? Explain.

b. Do you find Bell & Davis' auditor's report satisfactory? Explain.

c. Assume that no members of Bell & Davis or any members of their families held any financial interests in Worthmore, Inc. during 19X0. For each of the following cases, indicate if independence would be lacking on behalf of Bell & Davis, assuming that Worthmore, Inc. is a profit-seeking enterprise. In each case, explain why independence would or would not be lacking.

   1. Two directors of Worthmore, Inc. became partners in the CPA firm of Bell & Davis on July 1, 19X0, resigning their directorships on that date.

   2. During 19X0, the former controller of Worthmore, now a Bell & Davis partner, was frequently called on for assistance by Worthmore. He made decisions for Worthmore's management regarding fixed asset acquisitions and the company's product marketing mix. In addition, he conducted a computer feasibility study for Worthmore.

AICPA

19-25 The attribute of independence has been traditionally associated with the CPA's function of auditing and expressing opinions on financial statements.

Required

a. What is meant by "independence" as applied to the CPA's function of auditing and expressing opinions on financial statements? Discuss.

b. CPAs have imposed on themselves certain rules of professional conduct that induce their members to remain independent and to strengthen public confidence in their independence. Which of the rules of professional conduct are concerned with the CPA's independence? Discuss.

c. The Wallydrug Company is indebted to a CPA for unpaid fees and has offered to issue to him unsecured interest-bearing notes. Would the CPA's acceptance of these notes have any bearing on his independence in his relations with the Wallydrug Company? Discuss.

d. The Rocky Hill Corporation was formed on October 1, 19X0 and its fiscal year will end on September 30, 19X1. You audited the corporation's opening balance sheet and rendered an unqualified opinion on it. A month after rendering your report, you are offered the position of secretary of the Company because of the need for a complete set of officers and for convenience in signing various documents. You will have no financial interest in the company through stock ownership or otherwise, will receive no salary, will not keep the books, and will not have any influence on its financial matters other than occasional advice on income tax matters and similar advice normally given a client by a CPA.

1. Assume that you accept the offer but plan to resign the position prior to conducting your annual audit with the intention of again assuming the office after rendering an opinion on the statements. Can you render an independent opinion on the financial statements? Discuss.

2. Assume that you accept the offer on a temporary basis until the corporation has gotten under way and can employ a secretary. In any event, you would permanently resign the position before conducting your annual audit. Can you render an independent opinion on the financial statements? Discuss.

AICPA

19-26 Lakeview Development Corporation was formed on January 2, 19X0, to develop a vacation-recreation area on land purchased the same day by the corporation for $100,000. The corporation also purchased for $40,000 an adjacent tract of land that the corporation plans to subdivide into 50 buildings lots. When the area is developed, the lots are expected to sell for $10,000 each.

The corporation borrowed a substantial portion of its funds from a bank and gave a mortgage on the land. A mortgage covenant requires that the corporation furnish quarterly financial statements.

The quarterly financial statements prepared at March 31 and June 30 by the corporation's bookkeeper were unacceptable to the bank officials. The corporation's president now offers you the engagement of preparing unaudited quarterly financial statements. Because of limited funds, your fee would be paid in Lakeview Development Corporation common stock rather than in cash. The stock would be repurchased by the corporation when funds become available. You would not receive enough stock to be a major stockholder.

Required

a. Discuss the ethical implications of your accepting the engagement and the reporting requirements that are applicable if you should accept the engagement.

b. Assume that you accept the engagement to prepare the September 30 statements. What disclosures, if any, would you make of your prospective ownership of Corporation stock in the quarterly financial statements?

c. The president insists that you present the 50 building lots at their expected sales price of $500,000 in the September 30 unaudited statements as was done in prior statements. The write-up was credited to Contributed Capital. How would you respond to the president's request?

d. After accepting your unaudited September 30 financial statements, the bank notified the corporation that the December 31 financial statements must be accompanied by a CPA's opinion. You were asked to conduct the audit and told that your fee would be paid in cash. Discuss the ethical implications of your accepting the engagement.

AICPA (adapted)

19-27 PART I: During 19X0 your client, Nuesel Corporation, requested that you conduct a feasibility study to advise management of the best way the corporation can utilize electronic data processing equipment and which computer, if any, best meets the corporation's requirements. You are technically competent in this area and accept the engagement. On completion of your study, the corporation accepts your suggestions and installs the computer and related equipment that you recommended.

Required

a. Discuss the effect of the acceptance of this management services engagement would have on your independence in expressing an opinion on the financial statements of the Nuesel Corporation.

b. A local printer of data processing forms customarily offers a commission for recommending him as supplier. The client is aware of the commission offer and suggests that Mackey accept it. Would it be proper for Mackey to accept the commission with the client's approval? Discuss.

PART II: Alex Pratt, a retired partner of your CPA firm, has just been appointed to the board of directors of Palmer Corporation, your firm's client. Pratt is also a member of your firm's income tax committee that meets monthly to discuss income tax problems of the partnership's clients. The partnership pays Pratt $100 for each committee meeting he attends and a monthly retirement benefit of $1,000.

Required

Discuss the effect of Pratt's appointment to the board of directors of Palmer Corporation on your partnership's independence in expressing an opinion on the Palmer Corporation's financial statements.

AICPA (adapted)

19-28 Savage, CPA, has been requested by an audit client to perform a nonrecurring engagement involving the implementation of an EDP information and control system. The client requests that in setting up the new system and during the period prior to conversion to the new system, Savage

- Counsel on potential expansion of business activity plans.
- Search for and interview new personnel.
- Hire new personnel.
- Train personnel.

In addition, the client requests that during the three months subsequent to the conversion, Savage

- Supervise the operation of new system.
- Monitor client-prepared source documents and make changes in basic EDP generated data as Savage may deem necessary without concurrence of the client. Savage responds that he may perform some of the services requested, but not all of them.

Required

a. Which of these services may Savage perform and which of these services may Savage not perform?

b. Before undertaking this engagement, Savage should inform the client of all significant matters related to the engagement. What are these significant matters?

c. If Savage adds to his staff an individual who specializes in developing computer systems, what degree of knowledge must Savage possess in order to supervise the specialist's activities?

AICPA

19-29 There currently are 13 Rules of Conduct. Listed below are circumstances pertaining to some of these rules:

1. A member shall exercise due professional care in the performance of an engagement.
2. In rendering tax services, a member shall not subordinate his judgment to others.
3. A member shall not engage in any business that would create a conflict of interest in rendering professional service.
4. A member shall not accept a commission for a referral to a client of products or services of others.
5. A member's fees may vary depending on the complexity of the service rendered.
6. A member is not precluded from responding to an inquiry by a Trial Board of the AICPA.
7. A member may not serve as a trustee for any pension trust of the client during the period covered by the financial statements.
8. A member shall adequately plan and supervise an engagement.
9. A member may not have or be committed to having any direct financial interest in the client.
10. A member shall not practice under a fictitious firm name.

Required
a. Identify the rule to which each circumstance relates.
b. Indicate one other circumstance that pertains to each rule mentioned in a above.

19-30 In the practice of public accounting, an auditor is expected to comply with the Rules of Conduct set forth in the Code of Ethics. Listed below are circumstances that raise a question about an auditor's ethical conduct:

1. The auditor has a bank loan with a bank that is an audit client.
2. An unqualified opinion is expressed when financial statements are prepared according to existing AICPA *Accounting Research Bulletins* without any attendant unusual circumstances.
3. An auditor retains client's records as a means of enforcing payment of an overdue audit fee.
4. A CPA vouches for the achievability of a forecast.
5. An auditor sells her shares of stock in a client company in April prior to beginning work on the audit for the year ending December 31.
6. An auditor accepts an engagement knowing that he does not have the expertise to do the audit.
7. A CPA quotes a client a fee but also states that the actual fee will be contingent on the amount of work done.
8. A CPA firm states in a newspaper ad that it has had fewer lawsuits than its principal competitors.

9. A CPA resigns his position as secretary-treasurer to the client on May 1, prior to beginning the audit for year ending December 31.
10. A CPA discloses confidential information about a client to a successor auditor.

Required

a. Indicate for each circumstance whether the effect on the Rule of Conduct is (1) a violation, (2) not a violation, or (3) indeterminate.
b. Identify the rule that is at issue in each case and the reason(s) for your answer.

19-31 The following circumstances may involve violations of the Rules of Conduct:

1. A CPA bases his fee on the findings determined by the IRS in a tax audit case.
2. A CPA discloses confidential information in a peer review of the firm's practice.
3. A CPA issues an unqualified opinion when a client departs from GAAP because of a conceptual disagreement with the FASB.
4. Henson, a CPA who is a resident of West Orange, Wyoming, is a stockholder and treasurer of the WOW Public Accounting Firm.
5. Benson seeks to enlarge his CPA practice by preparing a small brochure showing testimonials from existing clients.
6. Abel, CPA, retains client records pending payment of audit fee.
7. Reddy, CPA, is also an insurance broker.
8. A CPA examines the financial statements of a local bank and also serves on the bank's committee that approves loans.
9. Leon, CPA, pays a commission to an attorney to obtain a client.
10. Jenson, CPA, examines the financial statements of a local bank that holds a mortgage on his home.

Required

a. Indicate for each circumstance whether the effect on the Rule of Conduct is (1) a violation, (2) not a violation, or (3) indeterminate.
b. Identify the rule that is at issue in each case and the reason(s) for your answer.

19-32 The following actions by a CPA may involve violations of the Rules of Conduct:

1. Agrees to be an honorary director for a local fund-raising activity.
2. Serves as an executor and trustee of the estate of an individual who owned the majority stock of a closely held client corporation.
3. Accepts a gift from a client.
4. Fails to follow standards required in a governmental audit.
5. Bases his fee on the amount of taxes that will be saved in preparing the tax return.
6. Discloses confidential client information requested by a disciplinary body of a state CPA society.
7. Assists a client in preparing a financial forecast but does not report on the forecast.
8. Prepares cost projections for submission to a governmental agency as an application for a rate increase, and the fee will be based on the amount of the rate increase.
9. Is convicted of falsifying his income tax return.
10. Accepts a commission from a vendor, with the approval of the client, for recommending the vendor's equipment.

11. Issues an unqualified opinion on the basis that the financial statements are in conformity with FASB exposure drafts.

12. Adopts the name of Test and Check, Inc. for his incorporated firm.

Required

a. Indicate for each circumstance whether the effect on the applicable Rule of Conduct is (1) a violation, (2) not a violation, or (3) indeterminate.

b. Identify the rule that is applicable in each case and the reason(s) for your answer.

19-33 Gilbert and Bradley formed a corporation called Financial Services, Inc., each man taking 50% of the authorized common stock. Gilbert is a CPA and a member of the American Institute of CPAs. Bradley is a CPCU (Chartered Property Casualty Underwriter). The corporation performs auditing and tax services under Gilbert's direction and insurance services under Bradley's supervision. The opening of the corporation's office was announced by a three-inch, two-column "card" in the local newspaper.

One of the corporation's first audit clients was the Grandtime Company. Grandtime had total assets of $600,000 and total liabilities of $270,000. In the course of his examination, Gilbert found that Grandtime's building with a book value of $240,000 was pledged as security for a ten-year-term note in the amount of $200,000. The client's statements did not mention that the building was pledged as security for the ten-year-term note. However, as the failure to disclose the lien did not affect either the value of the assets or the amount of the liabilities and his examination was satisfactory in all other respects, Gilbert rendered an unqualified opinion on Grandtime's financial statements. About two months after the date of his opinion, Gilbert learned that an insurance company was planning a loan to Grandtime of $150,000 in the form of a first-mortgage note on the building. Realizing that the insurance company was unaware of the existing lien on the building, Gilbert had Bradley notify the insurance company of the fact that Grandtime's building was pledged as security for the term note.

Shortly after the events described above, Gilbert was charged with a violation of professional ethics.

Required

Identify and discuss the ethical implication of those acts by Gilbert that were in violation of the AICPA Code of Professional Ethics.

AICPA

19-34 The Institute of Internal Auditors has adopted a Code of Ethics for its members.

Required

a. What requirements are imposed on certified internal auditors by the introduction to the Code of Ethics?

b. Indicate the essence of each of the seven articles in the Code of Ethics.

c. For each of the seven articles, indicate the comparable Rule of Conduct, if any, in the AICPA Code of Professional Ethics.

d. What sanction(s) may be imposed on an internal auditor for violating the Code of Ethics?

19-35† The Management Advisory Committee has promulgated practice standards for MAS.

Required

a. Indicate the two categories of practice standards established for MAS.

b. Identify and briefly describe the four types of technical standards.

c. For each of the following, indicate (1) the specific practice standard that is applicable and (2) whether the specified standard has been violated.
   1. At the request of the client, the MAS practitioner makes the business decision.
   2. The MAS service is completed in June and the report of the findings is communicated to the client in December.
   3. A new MAS practitioner is not supervised on her initial MAS engagement.
   4. An MAS practitioner with proficiency and training in computers accepts an engagement to redesign the client's EDP system.
   5. An MAS practitioner acquires a reasonable basis for his recommendations to the client.
   6. An MAS practitioner implicitly guarantees the results of his engagement.

19-36† The senior tax committee of the AICPA issues statements defining a CPA's responsibilities in federal tax practice.

Required

a. Identify and briefly describe the responsibilities a CPA has in rendering federal tax service to a client.

b. What specific responsibilities does the CPA have when
   1. An error is discovered in a previously filed tax return?
   2. She takes a position contrary to an IRS interpretation of the Revenue Code?
   3. A taxpayer does not answer all applicable questions on a tax return?
   4. A taxpayer uses an unreasonable estimate on the tax return?
   5. A taxpayer refuses to permit the CPA to disclose an error in an administrative proceeding?

CASE STUDY

19-37* The following situations involve Herb Standard, staff accountant with the regional CPA firm of Cash & Green:

1. The bookkeeper of Ethical Manufacturing Company resigned two months ago and has not yet been replaced. As a result, Ethical's transactions have not been recorded and the books are not up to date. To comply with terms of a loan agreement, Ethical needs to prepare interim financial statements but cannot do so until the books are posted. Ethical looks to Cash & Green, their independent auditors, for help and wants to borrow Herb Standard to perform the work. They want Herb because he did their audit last year.

2. Herb Standard discovered that his client, Ethical Manufacturing Company, materially understated net income on last year's tax return. Herb informs his supervisor

†Questions 19–35 and 19–36 relate to material contained in the appendices to this chapter.

about this and the client is asked to prepare an amended return. The client is unwilling to take corrective measures. Herb informs the Internal Revenue Service.

3. While observing the year-end inventory of Ethical Manufacturing Company, the plant manager offers Herb Standard a fishing rod, which Ethical manufactures, in appreciation for a job well done.

4. Herb Standard's acquaintance, Joe Lender, is chief loan officer at Local Bank, an audit client of Cash & Green. Herb approaches Joe for an unsecured loan from Local Bank and Joe approves the loan.

5. Herb Standard is a member of a local investment club composed of college fraternity brothers. The club invests in listed stocks and is fairly active in trading. Last week the club purchased the stock of Leverage Corp., a client of another Cash & Green office. Herb has no contact with the members of this office.

Required

For each situation, (a) identify the ethical issues that are involved, (b) discuss whether there has or has not been any violation of ethical conduct. Support your answers by reference to the Rules of Conduct.

Chapter 20

Accountant's Legal Liability

Study Objectives

After reading and studying this chapter, you should be able to

- Explain the accountant's legal liability to clients under common law.

- Describe the accountant's legal liability to third-party beneficiaries under common law.

- Indicate the accountant's common law defenses.

- Enumerate the principal effects on both the plaintiff and defendant of a legal suit under the 1933 Securities Act.

- State the principal liability provisions of the Securities Exchange Act of 1934.

- Cite the issues and rulings of the legal cases described in the chapter.

- Realize the precautions independent accountants should take to avoid legal liability.

In recent years, there has been a dramatic increase in the number of lawsuits in the United States. Many of these suits have been brought against professionals, including certified public accountants, for malpractice. When viewed as a percentage of all professional engagements, the number of lawsuits brought against accountants is extremely small. For instance, in testimony at congressional oversight hearings pertaining to the public accounting profession, the chairman of the SEC stated: "Out of thousands of audits conducted last year for the more than 10,000 publicly held companies that report to the SEC, less than 1% are alleged audit failures."[1] Nevertheless, litigation and the threat thereof are important factors in the practice of public accounting that affect all firms regardless of their size. The cost of malpractice insurance has risen dramatically for CPA firms in recent years. It is estimated that the cost of such insurance for the largest 20 firms is between \$35–\$50 million annually.

Legal liability may be incurred by an accountant in rendering any professional service. Consideration in this chapter, however, will be limited primarily to the CPA's legal liability in performing auditing services. The most significant legal cases are included in the discussion. In addition, a chronological summary of important legal cases is presented in Appendix 20A.

LIABILITY UNDER COMMON LAW

Common law is frequently referred to as unwritten law. It is based on judicial precedent rather than legislative enactment. Common law is derived from principles based on justice, reason, and common sense rather than absolute, fixed, or inflexible rules. The principles of common law are determined by the social needs of the community. Hence, common law changes in response to society's needs. In a specific case, the accountant's liability is determined by a state or federal court that attempts to apply case law precedents that it feels are controlling. Since there are 51 such independent jurisdictions in the United States, different decisions may result with respect to relatively similar factual circumstances.[2] In a common law case, the judge has the flexibility to consider social, economic, and political factors as well as prior case law doctrines (precedents). Under common law, a CPA's legal liability extends principally to two classes of parties: clients and third parties.

LIABILITY TO CLIENTS

A CPA is in a direct contractual relationship with clients. In agreeing to perform services for clients, the CPA assumes the role of an independent contractor. The specific service(s) to be rendered should preferably be set forth in an engagement letter, as described in Chapter 3. The term *privity of contract* refers to the contractual relationship that exists between two or more contracting parties. In the typical auditing engagement, it is assumed that the audit is to be made in accordance with professional standards (i.e., generally accepted auditing standards) unless the contract contains specific wording to the contrary. An accountant may be held liable to a client under either contract law or tort law.

---

[1]"Late Developments," *Journal of Accountancy* (New York: The American Institute of Certified Public Accountants, April 1985), p. 3.

[2]The 50 states and the District of Columbia comprise the 51 jurisdictions.

Contract Law

An auditor may be liable to a client for breach of contract when he

- Issues a standard audit report when he has not made an examination in accordance with GAAS.
- Does not deliver the audit report by the agreed-on date.
- Violates the client's confidential relationship (Ethics Rule of Conduct 301)

A CPA's liability for breach of contract extends to subrogees. A *subrogee* is a party who has acquired the rights of another by substitution. In Part II of this book, the bonding of employees was considered to be an important part of a company's internal control environment. When an embezzlement occurs, the bonding company reimburses the insured for its losses. Then, under the right of subrogation to the insured's contractual claim, it can bring suit against the CPA for failing to discover the defalcation.

When a breach of contract occurs, the plaintiff usually seeks one or more of the following remedies: (1) specific performance of the contract by the defendant, (2) direct monetary damages for losses incurred due to the breach, and (3) incidental and consequential damages that are an indirect result of nonperformance.

Tort Law

A CPA may also be liable to a client under tort law. A *tort* is a wrongful act that injures another person's property, body, or reputation. A tort action may be based on any one of the following causes:

- *Ordinary Negligence.* Failure to exercise that degree of care a person of ordinary prudence (a reasonable man) would exercise under the same circumstances.
- *Gross Negligence.* Failure to use even slight care in the circumstances.
- *Fraud.* Intentional deception, such as the misrepresentation, concealment, or nondisclosure of a material fact, that results in injury to another.

Under tort law, the injured party normally seeks monetary damages. The auditor's working papers are vital in refuting charges for breach of contract and breach of duty in a tort action.

In many cases, the plaintiff has the option to sue under either contract or tort law. The best course of action in a given case involves legal technicalities that are beyond the scope of this book.

Illustrative Cases

Two cases pertaining to liability to clients are considered below. The first case involves negligence; the second relates to breach of contract.

1136 TENANTS' CORP. V. MAX ROTHENBERG & CO. (1971)
LIABILITY TO CLIENT FOR NEGLIGENCE[3]

The plaintiff, a corporation owning a cooperative apartment house, sued the defendant, a CPA firm, for damages resulting from the failure of the defendant to discover the embezzlement of over $110,000 by the plaintiff's managing agent, Riker. Riker had orally engaged Rothenberg at an annual fee of $600.

The plaintiff maintained that Rothenberg had been engaged to perform all necessary accounting and auditing services. The defendant claimed he was only engaged to do write-up work and prepare financial statements and related tax returns. As evidence of their respective contentions, the plaintiff booked the accountant's fee as auditing expenses and the defendant marked each page of the financial statements as unaudited. In addition, the accountant in a letter of transmittal to the financial statements stated that the statements were (1) prepared from the books and records of the corporation and (2) no independent verifications were undertaken thereon. However, the accountant did not issue a report with a disclaimer of an opinion. The trial court found that the defendant was engaged to perform an audit because Rothenberg admitted that he had performed some limited auditing procedures such as examining bank statements, invoices, and bills. In fact, the CPA's working papers included one entitled "Missing Invoices," which showed over $40,000 of disbursements that did not have supporting documentation. The CPA did not inform the plaintiff of these invoices and no effort was made to find them. The trial court also found the CPA negligent in the performance of the service and awarded damages totaling $237,000. The appellate court affirmed saying

- Regardless of whether the CPA was making an audit or performing write-up work, there was a duty to inform the client of known wrongdoing or other suspicious actions by the client's employees.
- Defendant's work sheets indicate that defendant did perform some audit procedures.
- The record shows that the defendant was engaged to audit the books and records and the procedures performed by the defendant were "incomplete, inadequate, and improperly performed."

The *1136 Tenants'* case has frequently been used to demonstrate the importance of having a written contract (engagement letter) for each professional engagement. A written contract is important, but it was not an issue in this case. The critical issue was the CPA's failure to inform the client of employee wrongdoings, *regardless of the type of service rendered*.

The second case is *Fund of Funds, Ltd.* v. *Arthur Andersen & Co.*[4] In this case, the plaintiff sued the auditors for breach of contract because the auditors failed to disclose irregularities to the client when the auditors' engagement letter contained a specific representation that any irregularities would be revealed. The irregularities, totaling over $120 million, resulted from overcharges on a contract between the plaintiff and King Resources, both audited by Andersen. Andersen admitted discovery of the violation of the contract in auditing King but declined to disclose the irregularities to Fund of Funds because of the

---

[3]*1136 Tenants' Corp., v. Max Rothenberg & Co.* (36 A2d 30 NY2d 804), 319 NYS2d 1007 (1971).

[4]*Fund of Funds, Ltd. v. Arthur Andersen & Co.*, 545 F Supp. 1314 (S.D.N.Y. 1982).

AICPA's Code of Professional Ethics that prohibits disclosure of confidential information. The court ruled for the plaintiff on the grounds that the defendants failed to comply with the terms of their engagement letter. Further consideration is given to other issues in this case later in the chapter.

LIABILITY TO THIRD PARTIES

The common law liability of the auditor to third parties is important in any discussion of the auditor's legal liability. A *third party* may be defined as an individual who is not in privity with the parties to a contract. From a legal standpoint, there are two classes of third parties: (1) a primary beneficiary and (2) other beneficiaries. The former is anyone identified to the auditor by name prior to the audit who is to be the primary recipient of the auditor's report. For example, if at the time the engagement letter is signed, the client informs the auditor that his report is to be used to obtain a loan at the City National Bank, the bank becomes a primary beneficiary. In contrast, other beneficiaries are unnamed third parties, such as creditors, stockholders, and potential investors.

The auditor is liable to *all* third parties for gross negligence and fraud under tort law. In contrast, the auditor's liability for ordinary negligence has traditionally been different between the two classes of third parties.

Liability to Primary Beneficiaries

The privity of contract doctrine extends to the primary beneficiary of the accountant's work. The landmark case, *Ultramares Corp.* v. *Touche*, and its major findings are as follows.

ULTRAMARES CORP. V. *TOUCHE* (1931)
LIABILITY FOR NEGLIGENCE[5]

The defendant auditors, Touche, failed to discover fictitious transactions that overstated assets and stockholders equity by $700,000 in the audit of Fred Stern & Co. On receiving the audited financial statements, Ultramares loaned Stern large sums of money that Stern was unable to repay because it was actually insolvent. Ultramares sued the CPA firm for negligence and fraud.

The court found the auditors guilty of negligence but ruled that accountants should not be liable to any third party for negligence except to a primary beneficiary. Judge Cardozo said

If liability for negligence exists, a thoughtless slip or blunder, the failure to detect a theft or forgery beneath the cover of deceptive entries may expose accountants to a liability in indeterminate amounts, for an indeterminate time, to an indeterminate class. The hazards of a business conducted on these terms are so extreme as to enkindle doubt whether a flaw may not exist in the implication of a duty that exposes to these consequences.

The court also ruled that the finding on negligence does not emancipate accountants from the consequences of fraud. It concluded that gross negligence may constitute fraud.

---

[5]*Ultramares Corp. v. Touche*, 255 N.Y. 170, 174 N.E. 441 (1931).

In essence, Ultramares upheld the privity of contract doctrine. The importance of this case can be attributed to several factors. First, Judge Cardozo was considered to be one of the country's greatest judicial scholars and a leader in the development of tort law. Second, the decision was well developed and explained, thereby enabling later jurists to find it easy to use its language and logic.

An analysis of the decision reveals three significant environmental factors: (1) the judge did not want to discourage individuals from entering the accounting profession and thus deprive society of a valuable service, (2) the judge feared the impact of an adverse decision on other professionals (lawyers and doctors), and (3) the client was considered to be the primary beneficiary of the auditor's service.

Liability to Other Beneficiaries

The Ultramares decision remained virtually unchallenged for 37 years, and it still is followed today in many jurisdictions. However, since 1968 there has been a trend to extend the accountant's liability for ordinary negligence beyond the privity of contract doctrine. The following environmental factors have contributed to this development:

- The concept of liability has evolved significantly, so that the consumer is protected from the wrongdoing of both manufacturers (product–liability) and professionals.
- Businesses and accounting firms have increased in size so that they are better able to shoulder the new threshold of responsibility.
- More individuals and groups are relying on audited financial statements, and the U.S. legal system minimizes a plaintiff's costs in legal suits.

As the plaintiff, the relationship of other beneficiaries to the accountant is separated into two categories.

A Specifically Foreseen Class. The first shift away from Ultramares occurred in the form of judicial acceptance of the specifically foreseen class concept. This concept is explained in Restatement (Second) of Torts § 552 as follows[6]:

(1) One who, in the course of his (her) business, profession, or employment, or in any other transaction in which he (she) has a pecuniary interest, supplies false information for the guidance of others in their business transactions, is subject to liability for pecuniary loss caused to them by their justifiable reliance upon the information, if he (she) fails to exercise reasonable care or competence in obtaining or communicating the information.

[6]*Restatement (Second) of Torts* § 552 (1977).

(2) Except as stated in Subsection(3), the liability stated in Subsection(1) is limited to loss suffered

    (a) by a person or one of a limited group of persons for whose benefit and guidance he (she) intends to supply the information or knows that the recipient intends to supply it; and

    (b) through reliance upon it in a transaction that he (she) intends the information to influence or knows that the recipient so intends or in a substantially similar transaction.

(3) The liability of one who is under a public duty to give the information extends to loss suffered by any of the class of persons for whose benefit the duty is created, in any of the transactions in which it is intended to protect them.

Subsection(2) extends the accountant's liability to "a *limited group of persons* for whose benefit the CPA intends to supply the information." Thus, if the client informs the CPA that his audit report is to be used to obtain a bank loan, all banks are foreseen parties, but trade creditors would not be part of the foreseen class. The liability is limited to loss suffered through reliance on the information in a transaction known by the accountant or a similar transaction. In the above instance, this means that the accountant would not be liable if his audit report was used by a bank to invest capital in the client's business in exchange for common stock.

The specifically foreseen class concept imposes an intermediate level of due care on the accountant. However, it does not extend a duty to all users of the information because liability does not extend to all present and future investors, stockholders, or creditors. Court decisions have not required that the injured party be specifically identified, but the class of parties to which the party belonged had to be limited and known at the time the accountant provided the information.

Foreseeable Parties.   A person or group of persons who lack either or both of the two criteria cited above for specifically foreseen parties may be foreseeable parties. This concept extends the accountant's duty of due care to anyone who suffers a pecuniary loss from relying on the accountant's representation. Foreseeable parties include all creditors, stockholders, and present and future investors. Foreseeability is used extensively by the courts in cases involving physical injury. For example, foreseeability is almost universally used in product liability cases when the manufacturer's negligence causes the physical injury. No court has yet to impose liability for negligence resulting in pecuniary loss to parties who were merely foreseeable. However, in a recent case (*Rosenblum* v. *Adler*), the Supreme Court of New Jersey ruled that a public accounting firm could be tried for ordinary negligence by an injured foreseeable party.

Illustrative Cases

During the period 1968–1983, there were a number of cases in which the accountant's liability for ordinary negligence was extended. The leading cases

---

RUSCH FACTORS INC. V. *LEVIN* (1968)
LIABILITY TO FORESEEN PARTIES[7]

The plaintiff had asked the defendant accountant to audit the financial statements of a corporation seeking a loan. The certified statements indicated that the potential borrower was solvent when, in fact, it was insolvent. Rusch Factors sued the auditor for damages resulting from its reliance on negligent and fraudulent misrepresentations in the financial statements. The defendant asked for dismissal on the basis of lack of privity of contract.

The court ruled in favor of the plaintiff. While the decision could have been decided on the basis of the primary benefit rule set forth in Ultramares, the court instead said

> . . . The accountant should be liable in negligence for careless financial misrepresentations relied upon by *actually foreseen and limited classes of persons*. In this case, the defendant knew that his certification was to be used for *potential financiers of the . . . corporation* (emphasis added).

---

that have extended the accountant's liability to specifically foreseen parties and to foreseeable parties are presented on this and the following page.

COMMON LAW DEFENSES

The accountant generally must use due care as a defense in breach of contract suits involving charges of negligence. In tort actions, his primary defenses are *due care* or *contributory negligence.*

When using due care in a suit pertaining to an audit engagement, the auditor attempts to show that the examination was made in accordance with generally accepted auditing standards. The auditor's working papers are critical in this defense. In addition, the auditor hopes to convince the court that there are inherent limitations in the audit process. Thus, because of selective testing, there is a risk that material errors or irregularities, if they exist, may not be detected.

The *Restatement (Second) of Torts* defines contributory negligence as

(C)onduct on the part of the plaintiff which falls below the standard to which he (she) should conform his (her) own protection, and which is a legally contributing cause co-operating with the negligence of the defendant in bringing about the plaintiff's harm.[8]

---

[7]*Rusch Factors, Inc. v. Levin,* 284 F. Supp. 85(D.C.R.I. 1968).

[8]*Restatement (Second) of Torts* § 465 (1965).

ROSENBLUM V. ADLER (1983)
LIABILITY TO FORESEEABLE PARTIES[9]

The plaintiffs, Harry and Barry Rosenblum, acquired common stock of Giant Stores Corporation, a public traded corporation, in conjunction with the sale of their business to Giant. The stock subsequently proved to be worthless after Giant's audited financial statements were found to be fraudulent. The defendant, Adler, was a partner in Touche Ross & Co. that audited the Giant financial statements.

Plaintiffs claimed negligence in the conduct of the audit and that the auditor's negligence was a proximate cause of their loss. Defendants argued for dismissal of the suit because plaintiffs were not in privity with the auditors and they were not a foreseen party.

The Supreme Court of New Jersey denied dismissal, stating

- When the independent auditor furnishes an opinion with no limitation in the certificate regarding to whom the company (audited) may disseminate the financial statements, he has a duty to all those whom that auditor should reasonably foresee as recipients from the company of the statements for its proper business purposes, provided that the recipients rely on the statements pursuant to those business purposes.

- Certified financial statements have become the benchmark for various reasonably foreseeable business purposes and accountants have been engaged to satisfy these ends. In such circumstances, accounting firms should no longer be permitted to hide within the citadel of privity and avoid liability for their malpractice. The public interest will be served by the rule we promulgate this day.

- Irrespective of whether the defendants had actual knowledge of Giant's proposed use of the audited financial statements in connection with the merger, it was reasonably foreseeable that Giant would use the statements in connection with the merger and its consummation.

In reaching its decision, the court cited several public policy factors: (1) insurance is available to accountants to cover these risks, (2) the CPA has a moral responsibility to anyone relying on his opinion, and (3) more rigid standards will cause accountants to do better work. The case was remanded to the trial court for a determination of whether the auditors were negligent in the conduct of the audit.

Thus, if a plaintiff has contributed to his own injury (loss) by his own negligence, the law considers him to be as responsible as the defendent for the injury. In such case, there is no basis for recovery since the negligence of one party nullifies the negligence of the other party. For example, the plaintiff may have withheld vital information from the CPA during the audit or in the preparation of the tax return.

In most states, contributory negligence is only a defense for the accountant when the negligence directly contributes to the accountant's failure to perform. In a leading case, the fact that the client's system of internal control did not

---

[9]*H. Rosenblum Inc. v. Adler*, 461A 2d 138 (N.J. 1983).

prevent an accounting problem from arising was not sufficient to insulate the accountant from liability.[10]

LIABILITY UNDER STATUTORY LAW

Statutory law is established by state and federal legislative bodies. Most states have "blue sky laws" for the purpose of regulating the issuing and trading of securities within a state. Usually, these statutes require that audited financial statements be filed with a designated regulatory agency. Federal statutes are enacted by Congress. The two most important federal statutes affecting auditors are the Securities Act of 1933 and the Securities Exchange Act of 1934, which are administered by the Securities and Exchange Commission (SEC). The 1933 Act requires audited statements in registration statements and the 1934 Act requires annual statements audited by independent public accountants.

The liability of an auditor is more extensive under statutory law than under common law. Two factors are responsible for this condition: (1) some statutory laws grant unnamed third-party beneficiaries rights against auditors for ordinary negligence, and (2) criminal indictments may be brought against auditors. In-depth consideration is given below to the auditor's legal liability under federal securities laws.

SECURITIES ACT OF 1933

The 1933 Act is known as the *Truth in Securities Act*. It is designed to regulate security offerings to the public through the mails or in interstate commerce. Suits against auditors under this act are usually based on Section 11, Civil Liabilities on Account of False Registration Statement, which states, in part

> In case any part of the registration statement, when such part became effective, contained an untrue statement of a material fact or omitted to state a material fact required to be stated therein or necessary to make the statements therein not misleading, any person acquiring such security (unless it is proved that at the time of such acquisition he knew of such untruth or omission) may . . . sue. . . .

It should be noted that "any person" purchasing or otherwise acquiring the securities may sue. This includes unnamed third-party beneficiaries. The act makes the auditor liable for losses to third parties resulting from ordinary negligence, as well as from fraud and gross negligence, to the effective date of the registration statement, which may be 20 working days after the statement is filed with the agency.

---

[10]*National Surety Corp. v. Lybrand*, 256 AD226, 9 NYS 2d 544 (1939).

Section 11 includes two key terms: a *material* fact and *misleading* financial statement. These terms are defined by the SEC as follows:

> The term "material," when used to qualify a requirement for the furnishing of information as to any subject, limits the information required to those matters about which an average prudent investor ought reasonably to be informed.[11]
>
> Financial statements are presumed to be misleading or inaccurate when a material matter is presented in a financial statement in accordance with an accounting principle that has no authoritative support, or has authoritative support but where the SEC has ruled against its use.[12]

A qualification of the auditor's report and/or disclosure of the circumstances will not overcome the presumption that the statements are misleading.[13] However, disclosure will be accepted in lieu of correction when there is disagreement between the SEC and the registrant about the proper principle of accounting to be followed, providing (1) the principle has substantial authoritative support and (2) the commission has not previously expressed its position through SEC pronouncements. The SEC has ruled that the pronouncements of the Financial Accounting Standards Board (FASB) constitute substantial authoritative support.[14] When the FASB has not issued a pronouncement on the matter, the SEC accepts the other sources of authoritative support for GAAP that are enumerated in Chapter 17.

Under the civil provisions of the 1933 Act, the monetary damages are limited to the difference between (1) the amount the investor paid for the security and (2) the market or sales price at the time of the suit. However, if the security has been sold, the amount recoverable is the difference between the amount paid and the sales price. Criminal penalties provide for penalties on conviction of no more then $10,000 in fines or imprisonment of no more than five years, or both, for *willfully* making an untrue statement or omitting a material fact in a registration statement.

Bringing Suit Under the 1933 Act

The principal effects of this Act on the parties involved in a suit may be summarized as follows:

Plaintiff

- May be any person acquiring securities described in the registration statement, whether or not he is a client of the auditor.

[11]SEC, Rule 1-02, regulation S–X.
[12]SEC, Financial Reporting Release No. 1, Section 101 (1982).
[13]*Ibid.*
[14]*Ibid.*

- Must base his claim on an alleged material false or misleading financial statement contained in the registration statement.
- Does not have to prove that he relied on the false or misleading statement or that the loss he suffered was the proximate result of the statement if purchase was made before the issuance of an income statement covering a period of at least 12 months following the effective date of the registration statement.
- Does not have to prove that the auditors were negligent or fraudulent in certifying the financial statements involved.

Defendant

- Has the burden of establishing his freedom from negligence by proving that he had made a reasonable investigation and accordingly had reasonable ground to believe, and did believe, that the statements he certified were true at the date of the statements and as of the time the registration statement became effective, or
- Must establish, by way of defense, that the plaintiff's loss resulted in whole or in part from causes other than the false or misleading statements.

The reasonable investigation concept is often referred to as the *due diligence defense*. Section 11(c) states that the standard of reasonableness is the care required of a prudent person in the management of his own property. For an auditor, the basis for a reasonable investigation of audited financial statements is GAAS.

The BarChris Case

A major case under the Securities Act of 1933 is the BarChris case. The auditing issues in this case are described on the following page.

As a result of this case, a Statement on Auditing Standards was issued on subsequent events that includes specific review procedures, as is explained in Chapter 16.

THE SECURITIES EXCHANGE ACT OF 1934

This Act was passed by Congress to regulate the public trading of securities. The 1934 Act requires companies included under the act to (1) file a registration statement when the securities are publicly traded on national exchanges and over the counter for the first time and (2) keep the registration statement current through the filing of annual reports, quarterly reports, and other information with the SEC. Certain financial information, including the financial statements, must be audited by independent public accountants. Because of the recurring reporting requirements with the SEC, the act is often referred to as the *Continuous Disclosure Act*. The principal liability provisions of the 1934 Act are set forth in Sections 18 and 10.

ESCOTT V. BARCHRIS CONSTRUCTION CORP. (1968)
CIVIL LIABILITY UNDER SECURITIES ACT OF 1933[15]

BarChris was a company that was in constant need of cash. Purchasers of debentures filed suit under Section 11 when the company filed for bankruptcy, alleging that the registration statement pertaining to the sale of the bonds contained material false statements and material omissions. One of the defendants was a national public accounting firm, Peat, Marwick, Mitchell & Co., which pleaded the due diligence defense.

In certifying the registration statement that preceded the bankruptcy by 17 months, the accounting firm performed a subsequent events review, called an S–1 review by the SEC. The purpose of the review was to ascertain whether, subsequent to the certified balance sheet, any material changes had occurred that needed to be disclosed to prevent the balance sheet from being misleading.

The court concluded that Peat Marwick's written audit program for the review was in conformity with generally accepted auditing standards. However, it also found that the work done by a senior who was performing his first S–1 review was unsatisfactory. In ruling that the accounting firm had not established a due diligence defense, the court said

- The senior's review was useless because it failed to discover a material change for the worse in BarChris's financial position that required disclosure to prevent the balance sheet from being misleading.

- The senior did not meet the standards of the profession because he did not take some of the steps prescribed in the written program.

- The senior did not spend an adequate amount of time on a task of this magnitude and, most important of all, he was too easily satisfied with glib answers.

- There were enough danger signals in the materials examined to require some further investigation.

Section 18 Liability.   Under Section 18(a)

> Any person who shall make or cause to be made any statement in any application, report, or document filed pursuant to this title . . . which . . . was made false or misleading with respect to any material fact, shall be liable to any person (not knowing that such statement was false or misleading) who, in reliance upon such statement, shall have purchased or sold a security at a price which was affected by such statement, for damages caused by such reliance, unless the person sued shall prove that he acted in good faith and had no knowledge that such statement was false or misleading.

Section 18 liability is relatively narrow in scope, since it relates only to a false or misleading statement in documents "filed" with the SEC under the Act. Annual reports issued to shareholders are not deemed to be filed with the SEC.

[15]*Escott v. BarChris Construction Corp.*, 283 F Supp 643 (S.D.N.Y. 1968).

Section 10 Liability. Section 10(b) provides that

> It shall be unlawful for any person, directly or indirectly, by the use of any means or instrumentality of interstate commerce or of the mails, or of any facility of any national securities exchange to use or employ, in connection with the purchase or sale of any security registered on a national securities exchange or any security not so registered, any manipulative or deceptive device or contrivances in contravention of such rules and regulations as the Commission may prescribe as necessary or appropriate in the public interest or for the protection of investors.

Under this section, the SEC promulgated Rule 10b–5, which states that it is unlawful for any person, directly or indirectly, to

- Employ any device, scheme, or artifice to *defraud*.
- Make *any untrue statement* of a material fact or *omit* to state a material fact necessary in order to make the statements made, in the light of the circumstances under which they were made, not misleading.
- Engage in any act, practice, or course of business that operates, or would operate, as a *fraud* or *deceit* on any person in connection with the purchase or sale of any security.

Section 10b and Rule 10b-5 are often referred to as the antifraud provisions of the 1934 Act. Section 10 is broad in scope because it applies both to the public and private trading of securities.

Bringing Suit Under the 1934 Act

There are similarities and differences in the effects of Sections 10 and 18 on the parties involved.

Under both sections, the plaintiff (1) may be any person buying or selling the securities, (2) must prove the existence of a material false or misleading statement, and (3) must prove reliance on such statement and damage resulting from such reliance. However, the responsibility of the plaintiff differs under the two sections in terms of proof of auditor fraud. Under Section 18, the plaintiff does not have to prove that the auditor acted fraudulently, but in a Section 10, Rule 10b-5 action, such proof is required.

The defendant in a Section 18 suit must prove that he (1) acted in good faith and (2) had no knowledge of the false or misleading statement. This means that the minimum basis for liability is gross negligence. Accordingly, the auditor's position under Section 18 is the same as under the common law doctrine of Ultramares in which he may also be held liable to third parties for gross negligence. An injured plaintiff in a Section 18 action is allowed to recover his "out of pocket" losses, which are determined by the difference between the contract price and the real or actual value on the transaction date.

The latter is generally established by the market price when the misrepresentation or omission occurred.

Differences Between the 1933 and 1934 Securities Acts

The securities acts apply to different situations. The 1933 Act applies to the initial distribution of securities (capital stock and bonds) to the public by the issuing corporation, whereas the 1934 Act applies to the initial sale and trading of securities for national security markets. Differences between Section 11 of the 1933 Act and Sections 10 and 18 of the 1934 Act exist as to (1) the plaintiff, (2) proof of reliance on the false or misleading statement, and (3) the accountant's liability for negligence. The plaintiff in a 1933 Act suit is any person acquiring the security, whereas the plaintiff under the 1934 Act may be either the buyer or seller of the security. In a Section 11 suit, the plaintiff does not have to prove reliance on the financial statements, but in a Section 10 or Section 18 suit, proof of reliance on the audited statements is necessary. Under the provisions of the 1933 Act, the auditor clearly is liable for ordinary negligence, whereas a 1976 U.S. Supreme Court decision appears to effectively preclude ordinary negligence as a basis for sustaining a claim against an accountant under Section 10b and Rule 10b-5 of the 1934 Act.

The *Hochfelder* Case

Lawsuits against accountants under the 1934 Act are usually based on Section 10(b) and Rule 10b-5. During the decade of the mid-1960s to the mid-1970s, plaintiffs were able to obtain a number of judgments against CPA firms for ordinary negligence under these provisions. A 1976 decision by the United States Supreme Court in *Ernst & Ernst* (now Ernst & Whinney) v. *Hochfelder* may have marked the end of the accountant's liability for ordinary negligence under Section 10 of the 1934 Act. This landmark case is explained on the following page. Based on this decision, an accountant is no longer liable to third parties under Section 10(b) and Rule 10b-5 of the 1934 Act for ordinary negligence. That is, the auditor has no liability in the absence of any intent to deceive or defraud (legally called *scienter*). The *Hochfelder* decision, however, was based on a relatively narrow circumstance.

The Fund of Funds Case

This case dealt with several legal issues as described on page 749. The decision also included a finding on reckless behavior. The jury found that the requisite of scienter was met through the accountant's recklessness. It said

- A reckless misrepresentation, or reckless omission to state information necessary to make that which is stated not misleading, is one that dis-

ERNST & ERNST V. *HOCHFELDER* (1976)
CIVIL LIABILITY FOR NEGLIGENCE UNDER RULE 10b–5 OF 1934 ACT[16]

The plaintiffs were investors in an escrow account allegedly kept by the president (Lester K. Nay) of First Securities Co., a small brokerage firm, audited by the defendant CPA firm (now Ernst & Whinney).

The escrow account, in which a high rate of return was promised, was a ruse perpetrated by Nay. To prevent detection, all investors were instructed to make their checks payable to Nay and to mail them directly to him at First Securities. Within the brokerage house, Nay imposed a "mail rule" that such mail was to be only opened by himself. The escrow account was not recorded on First Securities' books. The fraud was uncovered in Nay's suicide note.

Plaintiffs sued Ernst for damages under Rule 10b-5 for aiding and abetting the embezzlement. They based their claim entirely on the premise that the accountants were negligent in their audit because they had not challenged or investigated the "mail rule."

Following conflicting lower court decisions, the U.S. Supreme Court ruled in favor of the defendants, saying

> When a statute speaks so specifically in terms of manipulation and deception, and of implementing devices and contrivances—the commonly understood terminology of intentional wrongdoing—and when its history reflects no more expansive intent, we are quite unwilling to extend the scope of the statute to negligent conduct.

The Supreme Court failed to rule on whether reckless behavior is sufficient for liability under Rule 10b-5.

---

regards the truth or falsity of the information disclosed in light of a known danger or patently obvious danger.

- The accountants acted with requisite scienter in disregarding known and obvious risks to FOF in issuing its unqualified opinion.
- We also find support for a finding of gross recklessness as the auditors conspicuously failed to test the arm's length nature of the transactions.

Criminal Liability Under the 1934 Act

Section 32(a) establishes criminal liability for "willfully" and "knowingly" making false or misleading statements in reports filed under the 1934 Act. This section also provides for criminal penalties for violating the antifraud provisions of Section 10(b) consisting of fines of not more than $100,000 or imprisonment for not more than five years, or both.

Accountants are rarely prosecuted for criminal liability. The SEC usually prefers to obtain an injunction against the accounting firm with the expectation that civil suits will soon follow. The leading criminal case is described on page 750.

As a result of this case, a Statement on Auditing Standards was issued on the meaning of "present fairly." A major conclusion of this Statement on Auditing Standards was that the auditor's judgment on fairness should be applied within the framework of GAAP, as is explained in Chapter 17. In

---

[16]*Ernst & Ernst v. Hochfelder*, 425 US 185, 96 S Ct 1375, 47 L Ed 2d 668 (1976).

THE FUND OF FUNDS LIMITED V. ARTHUR ANDERSEN & CO. (1982)
CIVIL LIABILITY UNDER 1934 ACT, COMMON LAW FRAUD,
AND BREACH OF CONTRACT[17]

The Fund of Funds Limited (FOF), a mutual investment fund, entered into an oral contract as part of a diversification program to purchase oil and gas properties from King Resources Corporation (KRC) at prices no *less favorable* than the seller received from other customers.

Arthur Andersen & Co (AA) was the auditor for both companies and the same key audit personnel participated in both engagements. In its engagement letter to FOF, AA made the *specific representation* that any irregularities discovered by the accounting firm would be revealed to the client. In auditing KRC, AA discovered that FOF was being billed at prices that were significantly higher than other customers. AA, however, failed to inform FOF because it did not wish to breach the rule of confidential client information. Plaintiff claimed that AA was required to disclose the overcharge or to resign at least one of the two accounts.

As an open-ended mutual fund, FOF was required to value its investment portfolio, which included its investments in natural resources, on a daily basis. The daily share value was used for redeeming investor shares. In its December 31, 1969 financial statements, FOF booked a significant upward revaluation in certain natural resource interests. Their evaluation was based in part on non-arms length non-bona fide sales of small portions of the same interests by KRC. These sales did not satisfy the guidelines established by AA for issuing an unqualified opinion on KRC's financials, but such an opinion was nevertheless issued. AA claimed that their report on KRC was not the cause of FOF's revaluation and that they had no knowledge of the non-bona-fide sales prior to issuing their report.

The jury found AA liable for aiding and abetting violations of securities laws (Rule 106-5) and common law fraud because of their failure to disclose their knowledge of KRC's wrongdoings to FOF. In addition, the jury found the accounting firm guilty of breach of contract because they did not comply with the specific representation in their engagement letter. Plaintiff was awarded damages of $81 million. The judge in the case subsequently reduced the damages to an undisclosed amount.

addition, an SAS was published on the auditor's responsibilities for related party transactions.

PROFESSIONAL STANDARDS AND LEGAL DECISIONS

A difference of opinion exists among the American Institute of Certified Public Accountants (AICPA), the SEC, and the courts about the relative importance of professional standards in legal decisions. An awareness of these differences may be useful in understanding the present legal climate.

The AICPA has made the following statements concerning the importance of professional standards and the conclusiveness of expert testimony concerning the standards:

- The standard of communication required is measured by specific generally accepted accounting principles (GAAP) and GAAS and, in the absence of specific rules or customs, by the views of experts (professional CPAs).

[17]*Fund of Funds, Ltd. v. Arthur Andersen & Co.,* op. cit.

UNITED STATES V. SIMON (1969)
CRIMINAL LIABILITY[18]

This case, also called the Continental Vending case, involved loans made by Continental Vending to its affiliated company, Valley Commercial Corporation, which subsequently lent the money to the president of Continental (Roth). The loans to Roth were secured primarily by the pledging of Continental common stock owned by Roth. Valley, in turn, pledged this stock as collateral against the loans from Continental. The auditor for Continental did not audit Valley. The defendants (a senior partner, a junior partner, and an audit senior of an international accounting firm) approved the following note:

> The amount receivable from Valley Commercial Corp. (an affiliated company of which Mr. Harold Roth is an officer, director, and stockholder) bears interest at 12% a year. Such amount, less the balance of the notes payable to that company, is secured by the assignment to the Company of Valley's equity in certain marketable securities. As of February 15, 1963, the amount of such equity at current market quotations exceeded the net amount receivable.

The government argued that the note should have said

> The amount receivable from Valley Commercial Corp. (an affiliated company of which Mr. Harold Roth is an officer, director and stockholder), which bears interest at 12% a year, was uncollectible at September 30, 1962, since Valley had loaned approximately the same amount to Mr. Roth who was unable to pay. Since that date, Mr. Roth and others have pledged as security for the repayment of his obligation to Valley and its obligation to Continental (now $3,900,000 against which Continental's liability to Valley cannot be offset) securities which, as of February 14, 1963, had a market value of $2,978,000. Approximately 80% of such securities are stock and convertible debentures of the Company.

Specifically, the government charged that the defendant's note was false and misleading because

- Continental's footnote did not show that Roth obtained the money.
- The nature of the collateral was not disclosed even though 80% of it consisted of unregistered securities issued by Continental.
- The net amount of the Valley receivables was improper because the Valley payable that had been offset represented notes discounted with outsiders.
- Reference to the secured position in February did not disclose the significant increase in the Valley receivables at that date.

The defendants, supported by the testimony of eight leaders in the accounting profession, contended that their note was in conformity with GAAP and that such compliance was a conclusive defense against criminal charges of misrepresentation. However, the trial judge rejected this argument and instructed the jury that the "critical test" was whether the balance sheet fairly presented financial position without reference to generally accepted accounting principles. The jury concluded that the balance sheet did not present fairly, and the three defendants were convicted of the criminal charges. The U.S. court of appeals refused to reverse the decision and held that

> We do not think the jury was . . . required to accept the accountants' evaluation whether a given fact was material to overall fair presentation, at least not when the accountant's testimony was not based on specific rules and prohibitions to which they could point, but only on the need for the auditor to make an honest judgment and their conclusion that nothing in the financial statements themselves negated the conclusion that an honest judgment had been made. Such evidence may be highly persuasive, but it is not conclusive, and so the trial judge correctly charged.

The defendants were found guilty. They were fined $17,000 and their licenses to practice as CPAs were revoked.

---

[18] United States v. Simon [425 F 2d 796 (2d Cir. 1969)].

- The jury (or court in a case of trial without jury) is never authorized to question the wisdom of the professional standard.[19]

In contrast, the SEC has taken the following positions on professional standards and expert testimony of auditors:

- The auditor has an obligation that goes beyond specific GAAP and GAAS or professional custom to effectively communicate material information.
- If GAAP and GAAS are found lacking, the SEC will not hesitate to invoke its authority to establish meaningful standards of performance regardless of expert testimony as to professional standards.[20]

The SEC position requires *effective* communication of material information in order to fairly and meaningfully inform the layperson investor.

An indication of the courts' position on these two matters is as follows:

- Where the profession has established specific GAAS for reasonably dealing with a perceived problem, the professional duty will be limited to conformance with the standard if resulting financial statements fairly and meaningfully inform the investor. Even if the auditor fails to follow professional standards, liability is imposed only when the resulting financials actually cause damage to plaintiffs. However, when misleading financials cause losses, the courts will not hesitate to penalize the auditor despite strong evidence of conformity with GAAP and GAAS.
- Where application of auditing standards requires expertise in evaluating and testing internal controls, statistical sampling of transactions, and obtaining competent evidential matter, expert testimony will be conclusive. However, where communication of findings is involved, expert testimony as to compliance with GAAP will be persuasive but not conclusive.[21]

AVOIDANCE OF LITIGATION

CPAs, like other professionals such as doctors and lawyers, are currently practicing in a climate where national public policy is emphasizing protection for the consumer (general public) from substandard work by professionals. An analysis of court cases reveals the following precautions that a CPA may take to help avoid becoming involved in litigation:

Use Engagement Letters for All Professional Services.   Such letters provide the basis for the contractual arrangements and minimize the risk of misunderstanding about the services that have been agreed on.

---

[19]"AICPA Amicus Brief, Continental Vending Case," *Journal of Accountancy* (New York: The American Institute of Certified Public Accountants, May 1970), pp. 69–73.

[20]Denzil Y. Causey, Jr., *Duties and Liabilities of the Public Accountant* (Homewood, Il.: Dow-Jones Irwin, 1979), p. 8.

[21]*Ibid*, p. 10.

Make a Thorough Investigation of Prospective Clients.   As indicated in Chapter 2, investigation is necessary to minimize the likelihood that the CPA will be associated with a client whose management lacks integrity.

Emphasize Quality of Service Rather than Growth.   The ability of a firm to properly staff an engagement is vital to the quality of the work that will result. Acceptance of new business that will likely lead to excessive overtime, abnormally heavy work loads, and limited supervision by experienced professionals should be resisted.

Comply Fully with Professional Pronouncements.   Strict adherence to GAAS and Statements on Auditing Standards is essential. An auditor must be able to justify any material departures from established guidelines.

Recognize the Limitations of Professional Pronouncements.   Professional guidelines are not all-encompassing. In addition, it should be recognized that subjective tests of reasonableness and fairness will be used by judges, juries, and regulatory agencies in judging the auditor's work. The auditor must use sound professional judgment during the examination and in the issuance of the audit report.

Establish and Maintain High Standards of Quality Control.   As suggested in Chapter 1, both the CPA firm and individual auditors have clearly established responsibilities for quality control. Outside peer reviews provide important independent assurance of both the quality and the continued effectiveness of prescribed procedures.

Exercise Caution in Engagements Involving Clients in Financial Difficulty.   The impending threat of solvency or bankruptcy may lead to intentional misrepresentations in the financial statements. Many lawsuits against auditors have resulted from bankruptcies of companies following the issuance of the auditor's report. The auditor should carefully weigh the sufficiency and competency of the evidence he has obtained in his examination of such companies.

CONCLUDING COMMENTS

Litigation has had a significant impact on the public accounting profession in the past two decades and it seems reasonable to expect that it will continue to do so in the foreseeable future. Litigation has been costly to the auditor and has caused an increased awareness of the need for improved quality control (see Chapter 1) in audit engagements. It also seems clear that society will continue to ask auditors to assume greater responsibilities in financial reporting and in discovering management improprieties. It is essential that auditors be responsive to legitimate requests for extending their service to the public. At the same time, however, there must be adequate recognition by the public of the added legal risks that this additional service may entail.

Appendix 20A

Chronological Summary of Legal Cases under Common and Statutory Law[22]

A wealth of valuable case information documents and defines auditors' continually evolving legal responsibilities. By the end of 1985, approximately 300 decisions involving auditors had been rendered in the United States. The following paragraphs briefly describe additional cases that appear to be significant in identifying legal trends related to auditing that have been expressed by the courts and the SEC.

Many of these findings and ideas represent court "dicta," which are expressions of opinion by a judge. Although dicta do not have the force of rule of law, they appear to be very useful in gaining insight into trends in the legal environment.

CASES PRIOR TO 1940

Prior to 1940, litigation against auditors focused on the auditors' common law liability for failure to perform adequate auditing procedures rather than questions of accounting principles, securities law violations, or criminal liability. The leading case in this period was *Ultramares Corp.* v. *Touche.* The most common complaint against auditors was a breach of contract based on their alleged failure to detect embezzlement. This type of complaint is illustrated by the following cases.

Smith v. *London Assurance Corp.* (1905)

Auditors were found liable to their client for breach of contract for failure to discover an embezzlement of a large sum of money by one of the client's employees. The court noted that

- Public accountants constitute a skilled professional class and are therefore subject to the same risks of liability for negligence in the practice of their

---

[22]The commentary and analysis of all cases through the early 1970s are based in part on data prepared by Peat, Marwick, Mitchell & Co. and published in *Research Opportunities in Auditing* (New York: Peat, Marwick, Mitchell & Co., 1976), pp. 85–91.

profession as are members of other skilled professions. The degree of skill implied by one who holds himself out as a professional is that commonly possessed by others in the same employment.

- The contract expressly called for certain auditing procedures that were not actually carried out with reasonable care and diligence.

State Street Trust Co. v. *Ernst* (1938)

Auditors examined accounts receivable but failed to discover the fact that the receivables were overstated because many of the accounts were uncollectible. The court noted that

- An auditor may be liable to third parties for fraud even where there is no deliberate or active fraud on his part. The court indicated that fraud on the part of the auditor may be inferred from any or all of the following:
  - Certifying as true to the knowledge of the auditor when he possessed insufficient knowledge as a basis for the certification.
  - Reckless misstatement.
  - Flimsy grounds for an opinion.
  - A failure to investigate doubtful facts or circumstances.
  - Heedlessness and reckless disregard of consequences.

National Surety Corp. v. *Lybrand* (1939)

The auditors failed to discover embezzlements of cash that were concealed through lapping and kiting practices. The court rejected the auditor's defense of contributory negligence. It concluded that

- The contract for services explicitly required a determination of the client's cash position and therefore implied that certain auditing procedures should be undertaken.
- Expert testimony established that ordinary professional care and the use of proper auditing methods would have identified well-known danger signals and that follow-up inquiries would have led to discovery of the embezzlement.
- Accountants are commonly employed for the very purpose of detecting defalcations that the employee's negligence has made possible.

CASES IN THE 1940s AND 1950s

Litigation against auditors occurred infrequently during the 1940s and 1950s. However, the following three cases are of significance because they shed light on auditors' criminal liability with respect to securities law violations. In addition, they indicate the courts' and SEC's willingness to challenge the adequacy of the profession's standards.

McKesson & Robbins [SEC Accounting Series Release No. 19 (1940)]

The SEC found that the auditors failed to employ a necessary degree of diligence and inquisitiveness that resulted in their failure to discover an overstatement of assets that management had created through recording and manipulation of fictitious inventories. The SEC noted that

- Numerous auditing procedures required strengthening (e.g., inventory, accounts receivable, accounts payable, investigation of new clients, audit committee review).
- Auditors should be responsible for detecting gross misstatements whether resulting from collusion or otherwise.
- Auditors must recognize their responsibility to the public investor by including management activities in their review.

United States v. *White* (1941)

The auditor was convicted of ciminal fraud under Section 17 of the Securities Act of 1933 for his failure to disclose several instances of questionable accounting practices in connection with a registration statement. The court expressed the following thought with respect to the sufficiency of evidence in a criminal case:

- Items of questionable accounting, which taken individually do not demonstrate knowledge of falsity, may acquire greater significance as proof when considered together.

CASES IN THE 1960s

A barrage of litigation was brought against auditors commencing in the later 1960s. According to a *Wall Street Journal* article (November 15, 1966), nearly 100 lawsuits were pending against auditors in late 1966. Compared to previous legal activity, this number represented explosive growth. In June 1968, *Fortune* estimated that as many suits were filed against auditors in the previous 12 months as in the previous 12 years. Three of the major cases in this decade are discussed in the chapter: Rusch Factors, BarChris, and Continental Vending.

This period is not only distinguished by the growth in the volume of litigation against auditors. As the following cases demonstrate, the courts also continued to extend the concepts of auditors' criminal liability and liability for negligence to third parties. They also defined more precisely auditors' obligations under the securities acts and made more frequent judgments regarding the adequacy of measurement and reporting standards.

United States v. Benjamin (1964)

The auditor was convicted in a criminal action under Section 24 of the 1933 Act for his failure to exercise due diligence that would have revealed misrepresentations in pro forma financial statements used in conjunction with sales of unregistered securities. The court stated:

- In our complex society, the accountant's certificate and the lawyer's opinion can be instruments for inflicting pecuniary loss more potent than the chisel or the crowbar. Of course, Congress did not mean that any mistake of law or misstatement of fact should subject an attorney or an accountant to criminal liability simply because more skilled practitioners would not have made them. But Congress equally could not have intended that men holding themselves out as members of these ancient professions should be able to escape criminal liability on a plea of ignorance when they have shut their eyes to what was plainly to be seen or have represented a knowledge they knew they did not possess.

Fischer v. Kletz (1967)

In this case, commonly known as *Yale Express*, the auditor did not disclose errors in a previously issued audit report that were discovered three months later during a management services engagement. In ruling on the case that involved actions under common law and Section 10(b), Rule 10b-5, and Section 18 of the 1934 Act, the court noted that

- An auditor has a duty to anyone still relying on his report to disclose subsequently discovered errors in the report. This duty exists regardless of the auditor's lack of financial interest in any transactions to which the information relates. The obligation arises because of the auditor's special relationship that provides access to the information.

CASES IN THE 1970s

There was a significant decline in the number of lawsuits brought against accountants in the early 1970s. Later, the landmark Supreme Court decision in Hochfelder occurred and there were several suits on negligence. The major cases are summarized below.

Rhode Island Hospital Trust National Bank v. Swartz, Bresenhoff, Yavner & Jacobs (1972)

The defendant auditors issued a disclaimer of opinion on audited financial statements. The plaintiff bank was a foreseen (but unnamed) party. The suit charged that the auditors were guilty of ordinary negligence because the reasons for the disclaimer in the auditors' report contained wording that was misleading. The reasons stated

Additions to fixed assets were found to include principally warehouse improvements. . . . Practically all of this work was done by company employees. . . . Unfortunately, complete detailed cost records were not kept and no exact determination could be made as to the actual cost of said improvements.

The court found no cost records and the capital expenditures were fictitious. Since the disclaimer only referred to valuation and not existence, the court ruled for the plaintiff saying that a general disclaimer cannot relieve the auditor of liability stemming from the impression conveyed by other statements in his report.

Herzfeld v. Laventhol, Kreckstein, Horwath & Horwath (1974)

This case involved a private placement of securities by a corporation engaged in real estate syndication. The financial statements contained a material misrepresentation pertaining to profit on real estate transactions that were never consummated. The auditors were found liable under Section 10(b), Rule 10b–5 of the 1934 Act for failure to fully disclose the facts and circumstances underlying their qualified (subject to) opinion. The court noted that

- The accountant's professional duty to investors cannot be fulfilled by merely following esoteric norms (generally accepted accounting principles) comprehensible only to the initiate.
- The financial reports must fairly present the true financial position to the "untutored eye of an ordinary investor."
- An auditor's qualified opinion should disclose the reasoning and facts which prompted it.

United States v. Weiner (1975)

Three auditors of Equity Funding Corp. of America were convicted after a jury trial of multiple counts of securities fraud and filing false statements with the SEC. The case involved the auditors' failure to detect that $2.1 billion of the company's $3.2 billion of assets were fraudulently obtained through computer produced bogus insurance policies. The fraud covered several years. In addition to criminal convictions against the three partners, five accounting firms paid $44 million in damages.

United States v. Natelli (1975)

In this case, commonly known as the *National Student Marketing Corporation* case, two auditors were convicted of criminal liability under Section 32 of the 1934 Act for failing to properly disclose the writeoff of uncollectible accounts. In the financial statements of the current year (1969), uncollectible accounts pertaining to 1968 regular sales on advertising contracts, which had only been verified by telephone, were reported in part as a retroactive adjustment against sales acquired by pooling in 1968. The accompanying footnote failed to state that regular sales for 1968 were overstated 20% and that actual net earnings were only 46% of reported earnings. The court concluded that

- The treatment of the retroactive adjustment was done intentionally to conceal the errors in the 1968 statements.

- A professional cannot escape criminal liability on a plea of ignorance when they have shut their eyes to what was plainly to be seen.

CASES IN THE 1980s

During this period, the accountants' common law liability for ordinary negligence was extended to foreseeable parties in *Rosenblum* v. *Adler*. In addition, there was some clarification of the meaning of reckless behavior under the 1934 Act in *Fund of Funds Limited* v. *Arthur Andersen & Co.* There also were several other cases involving accountants' liability.

Howard Sirota v. Solitron Devices, Inc. (1982)

The defendant was involved in government contracts that were subject to assessments on excess profits as determined by the Renegotiations Board. When the Board determined that profits were excessive, management admitted to intentionally overstating profits by more than 30% in two different years.

A jury found the auditor for the defendant company guilty of reckless behavior in the conduct of the audits. The trial judge overturned the jury verdict. However, on appeal, the appeals court affirmed the jury's original verdict. In its ruling, the court stated that proof of recklessness may meet the scienter requirement of Rule 10b–5. Such proof was not an issue in this case because the auditor had knowledge of the misstatement.

Cenco Incorporated v. Seidman & Seidman (1982)

In this case, the U.S. Court of Appeals for the Seventh Circuit in Chicago, Illinois, in a three-judge decision, upheld an earlier jury verdict in favor of the auditors, Seidman & Seidman. The defendants were charged with violating various federal securities laws and SEC rules, notably Rule 10b–5. The case pertained to the auditor's failure to detect a $25 million inventory fraud perpetrated by top management. In the decision, the judges distinguished between management fraud and employee fraud and said

- Auditors are not detectives hired to ferret out fraud.
- Auditors must investigate if they suspect fraud; but in this case, the former management made fraud difficult to detect since top executives turned the company "into an engine of theft against outsiders."

The court also gave the auditors permission to sue Cenco for the amount paid ($3.5 million) as damages to Cenco stockholders in a 1980 class action suit settlement pertaining to the fraud.

REVIEW QUESTIONS

20-1 What is meant by common law?

20-2 Under common law, a CPA may be liable to a client.
  a. Explain the meaning and importance of the term *privity of contract*.
  b. How may an auditor breach a contract?
  c. What causes ordinarily underly a tort action?

20-3 a. Who are the classes of third parties that may sustain suits against auditors under common law?
  b. Under what circumstances may an auditor be held liable to third parties?

20-4 Distinguish between foreseen and foreseeable parties. Give examples of each.

20-5 Indicate the significance of *Ultramares, Rusch Factors,* and the *Rosenblum* v. *Adler* cases on the auditor's liability for negligence.

20-6 What are the accountant's primary defenses in tort actions?

20-7 a. Define contributory negligence.
  b. When does contributory negligence ordinarily represent a valid defense?

20-8 Why is the auditor's liability more extensive under statutory law than under common law?

20-9 a. Who may bring suit under the 1933 Securities Act?
  b. What is the basis for such action?

20-10 Under what circumstances will a financial statement be presumed to be misleading?

20-11 What are the responsibilities of the plaintiff and the defendant in a 1933 Act suit?

20-12 State the issues and the court's conclusions in the *BarChris* case.

20-13 a. Who may bring suit under the 1934 Securities Exchange Act?
  b. Is the basis for action the same as in a 1933 Act suit? Explain.

20-14 Explain the conditions associated with liability under Rule 10b–5 of the 1934 Act.

20-15 What are the responsibilities of the plaintiff and the defendant in a 1934 Act suit?

20-16 Enumerate the principal differences in legal liability between the two securities acts.

20-17 a. What was the basis for the *Hochfelder* case?
  b. What is the significance of the decision in the case?

20-18 a. Indicate the jury's findings in the *Fund of Funds* case.
  b. State the accounting issue and the jury's findings in the *Continental* Vending case.

20-19 Contrast the essence of the relative importance of professional standards in legal cases among the AICPA, the SEC, and the courts.

20-20 Identify actions which the auditor may take to avoid litigation.

OBJECTIVE QUESTIONS FROM PROFESSIONAL EXAMINATIONS

Indicate the *best* answer for each of the following multiple choice questions.

20-21 These questions pertain to the accountant's liability under common law.

1. In a common law action against an accountant, the lack of privity is a viable defense if the plaintiff
   a. Bases his action on fraud.
   b. Is the accountant's client.
   c. Is a creditor of the client who sues the accountant for negligence.
   d. Can prove the presence of gross negligence that amounts to a reckless disregard for the truth.
2. Rhodes Corp. desired to acquire the common stock of Harris Corp. and engaged Johnson & Co., CPAs, to audit the financial statements of Harris Corp. Johnson failed to discover a significant liability in performing the audit. In a common law action against Johnson, Rhodes at a minimum must prove
   a. Gross negligence on the part of Johnson.
   b. Negligence on the part of Johnson.
   c. Fraud on the part of Johnson.
   d. Johnson knew that the liability existed.
3. To recover in a common law action based on fraud against a CPA with regard to an audit of financial statements, the plaintiff must prove among other things
   a. Privity of contract.
   b. Unavailability of any other cause of action.
   c. That there was a sale or purchase of securities within a six-month period that resulted in a loss.
   d. Reliance on the financial statements.
4. If a stockholder sues a CPA for common law fraud based on false statements contained in the financial statements audited by the CPA, which of the following is the CPA's best defense?
   a. The stockholder lacks privity to sue.
   b. The CPA disclaimed liability to all third parties in the engagement letter.
   c. The contributory negligence of the client.
   d. The false statements were immaterial.

20-22 These questions relate to the accountant's liability under statutory law.

1. Hall purchased Eon Corp. bonds in a public offering subject to the Securities Act of 1933. Kosson and Co., CPAs, rendered an unqualified opinion on Eon's financial statements, which were included in Eon's registration statement. Kosson is being

sued by Hall based on misstatements contained in the financial statements. In order to be successful, Hall must prove

	Damages	Materiality of the Misstatement	Kosson's Scienter
a.	Yes	Yes	Yes
b.	Yes	Yes	No
c.	Yes	No	No
d.	No	Yes	Yes

2. Doe and Co., CPAs, issued an unqualified opinion on the 19X3 financial statements of Marx Corp. These financial statements were included in Marx's annual report and form 10K filed with the SEC. Doe did not detect material misstatements in the financial statements as a result of negligence in the performance of the audit. Based on the financial statements, Fitch purchased stock in Marx. Shortly thereafter, Marx became insolvent, causing the price of the stock to decline drastically. Fitch has commenced legal action against Doe for damages based on Section 10(b) and Rule 10b–5 of the Securities Exchange Act of 1934. Doe's best defense to such an action would be that
   a. Fitch lacks privity to sue.
   b. The engagement letter specifically disclaimed all liability to third parties.
   c. There is *no* proof of scienter.
   d. There has been *no* subsequent sale for which a loss can be computed.

3. Lewis & Clark, CPAs, rendered an unqualified opinion on the financial statements of a company that sold common stock in a public offering subject to the Securities Act of 1933. Based on a false statement in the financial statements, Lewis & Clark are being sued by an investor who purchased shares of this public offering. Which of the following represents a viable defense?
   a. The investor has *not* met the burden of proving fraud or negligence by Lewis & Clark.
   b. The investor did *not* actually rely on the false statement.
   c. Detection of the false statement by Lewis & Clark occurred after their examination date.
   d. The false statement is immaterial in the overall context of the financial statements.

4. A requirement of a private action to recover damages for violation of the registration requirements of the Securities Act of 1933 is that
   a. The plaintiff has acquired the securities in question.
   b. The issuer or other defendants commit either negligence or fraud in the sale of the securities.
   c. A registration statement has been filed.
   d. The securities be purchased from an underwriter.

COMPREHENSIVE QUESTIONS

20-23 Watts and Williams, a firm of certified public accountants, audited the accounts of Sampson Skins, Inc., a corporation that imports and deals in fine furs. On completion of the examination, the auditors supplied Sampson Skins with 20 copies of the certified balance sheet. The firm knew that Sampson Skins wanted that number of copies of the auditor's report to furnish to banks and other potential lenders.

The balance sheet in question was in error by approximately $800,000. Instead of having a $600,000 net worth, the corporation was insolvent. The management of Sampson Skins had "doctored" the books to avoid bankruptcy. The assets had been overstated by $500,000 of fictitious and nonexisting accounts receivable and $300,000 of nonexisting skins listed as inventory when, in fact, Sampson Skins had only empty boxes. The audit failed to detect these fraudulent entries. Martinson, relying on the certified balance sheet, loaned $200,000 to Sampson Skins. He seeks to recover his loss from Watts and Williams.

1. If Martinson alleges and proves negligence on the part of Watts and Williams, he would be able to recover his loss.
2. If Martinson alleges and proves constructive fraud, i.e., gross negligence on the part of Watts and Williams, he would be able to recover his loss.
3. Martinson is not in privity of contract with Watts and Williams.
4. Unless actual fraud on the part of Watts and Williams could be shown, Martinson could not recover.
5. Martinson is a third-party beneficiary of the contract Watts and Williams made with Sampson Skins.

Required

Indicate whether each of the foregoing statements is true or false under common law. Give the reason(s) for each answer.

AICPA (adapted)

20-24 Perfect Products Co. applied for a substantial bank loan from Capitol City Bank. In connection with its application, Perfect engaged William & Co., CPAs, to audit its financial statements. William completed the audit and rendered an unqualified opinion. On the basis of the financial statements and William's opinion, Capitol granted Perfect a loan of $500,000.

Within three months after the loan was granted, Perfect filed for bankruptcy. Capitol promptly brought suit against William for damages, claiming that it had relied to its detriment on misleading financial statements and the unqualified opinion of William.

William's audit workpapers reveal negligence and possible other misconduct in the performance of the audit. Nevertheless, William believes it can defend against liability to Capitol based on the privity defense.

Required

Answer the following, setting forth reasons for any conclusions stated.

1. Explain the privity defense and evaluate its application to William.
2. What exceptions to the privity defense might Capitol argue?

AICPA

20-25 a. Jackson was a junior staff member of an accounting firm. He began the audit of the Bosco Corporation, which manufactured and sold expensive watches. In the middle of the audit, he quit. The accounting firm hired another person to continue the audit of Bosco. Due to the changeover and the time pressure to finish the audit, the firm violated certain generally accepted auditing standards when it did not follow adequate procedures with respect to the physical inventory. Had the proper procedures been used during the examination, the firm would have discovered that watches worth more than $20,000 were missing. The employee who was stealing the watches was able to steal an additional $30,000 worth before the thefts were discovered six months after the completion of the audit.

Required

Discuss the legal problems of the accounting firm as a result of the above facts.

b. Walter Young, doing business as Walter Young Fashions, engaged the CPA partnership of Small & Brown to examine his financial statements. During the examination, Small & Brown discovered certain irregularities that would have indicated to a reasonably prudent accountant that James Smith, the head bookkeeper, might be engaged in a fraud. More specifically, it appeared to Small & Brown that serious defalcations were taking place. However, Small & Brown, not having been engaged to discover defalcations, submitted an unqualified opinion in the report and did not mention the potential defalcation problem.

Required

What are the legal implications of the above facts as they relate to the relationship between Small & Brown and Walter Young? Explain.

AICPA (adapted)

20-26 Donald Sharpe recently joined the CPA firm of Spark, Watts, and Wilcox. He quickly established a reputation for thoroughness and a steadfast dedication to following prescribed auditing procedures to the letter. On his third audit for the firm, Sharpe examined the underlying documentation of 200 disbursements as a test of purchasing, receiving, vouchers-payable, and cash disbursement procedures. In the process, he found 12 disbursements for the purchase of materials with no receiving reports in the documentation. He noted the exceptions in his working papers and called them to the attention of the in-charge accountant. Relying on prior experience with the client, the in-charge accountant disregarded Sharpe's comments, and nothing further was done about the exceptions.

Subsequently, it was learned that one of the client's purchasing agents and a member of its accounting department were engaged in a fraudulent scheme whereby they diverted the receipt of materials to a public warehouse while sending the invoices to the client. When the client discovered the fraud, the conspirators had obtained approximately $70,000, $50,000 of which was after the completion of the audit.

Required

Discuss the legal implications and liabilities to Spark, Watts, and Wilcox as a result of the above facts.

AICPA

20-27 Keen, a CPA and sole practitioner, was retained by Arthur & Son, a partnership, to audit the company books and prepare a report on the financial statements for submission to several prospective partners as part of a planned expansion of the firm. Keen's fee was fixed on a per-diem basis. After a period of intensive work, Keen had completed about half of the necessary field work when he suffered a paralyzing stroke. He was forced to abandon all his work and, in fact, retired from the profession. The planned expansion of the firm failed to materialize because the prospective partners would act only on the basis of the report that Keen was to have submitted and lost interest when the report was not available.

Required

a. Arthur & Son sues Keen for breach of his contract. Will it recover? Explain.

b. Keen sues Arthur & Son for his fee for the work he was able to complete or, in the alternative, for the reasonable value of the services performed. Will he recover? Explain.

c. Arthur & Son demands from Keen all of the working papers relative to the engagement including several canceled checks, the articles of copartnership, and some other records of the firm. Will the firm succeed in its demand? Explain.

AICPA

20-28 Barney & Company, CPAs, has been engaged to perform an examination of the financial statements of Waldo, Inc., for several years. The terms of the engagement have been set out in an annual engagement letter signed by both parties. The terms of each engagement included the following:

> This being an ordinary examination, it is not primarily or specifically designed, and cannot be relied upon, to disclose defalcations and other similar irregularities, although their discovery may result.

> Three years ago, Harold Zamp, head cashier of Waldo and an expert in computer operations, devised a previously unheard of method of embezzling funds from his employer. At first, Zamp's thefts were small but increased as time went on. During the current year, before Barney began working on the engagement, the thefts became so large that serious variances in certain accounts came to the attention of the controller. When questioned about the variances, Zamp confessed and explained his unique embezzlement scheme. Investigation revealed that Zamp had stolen $257,550. Zamp has no assets with which to repay the thefts.

> Waldo submitted its claim for $257,550 to Multi-State Surety Company in accordance with the terms of the fidelity bond covering Zamp. Fulfilling its surety obligation, Multi-State paid the claim and now seeks to recover its losses from Barney.

> In defense, Barney asserts, in the alternative, the following defenses:

1. Multi-State has no standing in court to sue because it was not a party to the contract (i.e., lacking in privity) between Barney and its client, Waldo.

2. Even if Multi-State had the standing to sue, its claim should be dismissed because Barney's engagements with Waldo did not specifically include the discovery of defalcations other than those that might arise in the process of an ordinary examination.

3. Even if Barney's contract had made it responsible for discoverable defalcations, it could not have discovered Zamp's defalcations with the exercise of reasonable care. Zamp's technique was so new and novel that no accounting firm could have discovered the defalcations in any event.

Required

In separately numbered paragraphs, discuss the validity of each of Barney's defenses.

AICPA

20-29 The CPA firm of Martinson, Brinks & Sutherland, a partnership, was the auditor for Masco Corporation, a medium-sized wholesaler. Masco leased warehouse facilities and sought financing for leasehold improvements to these facilities. Masco assured its bank that the leasehold improvements would result in a more efficient and profitable operation. Based on these assurances, the bank granted Masco a line of credit.

The loan agreement required annual audited financial statements. Masco submitted to the bank its 19X0 audited financial statements that showed an operating profit of $75,000, leasehold improvements of $250,000, and net worth of $350,000. In reliance thereon, the bank loaned Masco $200,000. The audit report that accompanied the financial statements disclaimed an opinion because the cost of the leasehold improvements could not be determined from the company's records. The part of the audit report dealing with leasehold improvements reads as follows:

> Additions to fixed assets in 19X0 were found to include principally warehouse improvements. Practically all of this work was done by company employees and the cost of materials and overhead were paid by Masco. Unfortunately, fully complete detailed cost records were not kept of these leasehold improvements and no exact determination could be made as to the actual cost of said improvements. The total amount capitalized is set forth in note 4.

In late 19X1, Masco went out of business, at which time it was learned that the claimed leasehold improvements were totally fictitious. The labor expenses charged as leasehold improvements proved to be operating expenses. No item of building material cost had been recorded. No independent investigation of the existence of the leasehold improvements was made by the auditors.

If the $250,000 had not been capitalized, the income statement would have reflected a substantial loss from operations and the net worth would have been correspondingly decreased.

The bank has sustained a loss on its loan to Masco of $200,000 and now seeks to recover damages from the CPA firm, alleging that the accountants negligently audited the financial statements.

Required

Answer the following, setting forth reasons for any conclusions stated:

a. Will the disclaimer of opinion absolve the CPA firm from liability?

b. Are the individual partners of Martinson, Brinks & Sutherland, who did not take part in the audit, liable?

c. Briefly discuss the development of the common law regarding the liability of CPAs to third parties.

20-30 Risk Capital Limited, a Delaware corporation, was considering the purchase of a substantial amount of the treasury stock held by Florida Sunshine Corporation, a closely held corporation. Initial discussions with the Florida Sunshine Corporation began late in 19X0.

Wilson and Wyatt, Florida Sunshine's accountants, regularly prepared quarterly and annual unaudited financial statements. The most recently prepared financial statements were for the year ended September 30, 19X1.

On November 15, 19X1, after protracted negotiations, Risk Capital agreed to purchase 100,000 shares of no par, class A capital stock of Florida Sunshine at $12.50 per share. However, Risk Capital insisted on audited statements for calendar year 19X1. The contract specifically provided:

> Risk Capital shall have the right to rescind the purchase of said stock if the audited financial statements of Florida Sunshine for calendar year 19X1 show a material adverse change in the financial condition of the Corporation.

The audited financial statements furnished to Florida Sunshine by Wilson and Wyatt showed no such material adverse change. Risk Capital relied on the audited statements and purchased the treasury stock of Florida Sunshine. It was subsequently discovered that, as of the balance sheet date, the audited statements were incorrect and that in fact there had been a material adverse change in the financial condition of the Corporation. Florida Sunshine is insolvent and Risk Capital will lose virtually its entire investment.

Risk Capital seeks recovery against Wilson and Wyatt.

Required

a. Discuss each of the theories of liability that Risk Capital will probably assert as its basis for recovery.

b. Assuming that only ordinary negligence is proven, will Risk Capital prevail? State "yes" or "no" and explain.

AICPA

20-31 Arthur & Doyle, CPAs, served as auditors for Dunbar Corp. and Wolfe Corp., publicly held corporations listed on the American Stock Exchange. Dunbar recently acquired Wolfe Corp. pursuant to a statutory merger by issuing its shares in exchange for shares of Wolfe. In connection with that merger, Arthur & Doyle rendered an unqualified opinion on the financial statements and participated in the preparation of the pro forma unaudited financial statements contained in the combined prospectus and proxy statement circulated to obtain shareholder approval of the merger and to register the shares to be issued in connection with the merger. Dunbar prepared a Form 8–K (the current report with unaudited financial statements) and Form 10–K (the annual report with audited financial statements) in connection with the merger. Shortly thereafter, financial disaster beset the merged company that resulted in large losses to the shareholders and creditors. A class action suit on behalf of the shareholders and creditors has been filed against Dunbar and its management. In addition, it names Arthur & Doyle as co-defendants, challenging the fairness, accuracy, and truthfulness of the financial statements.

Required

Answer the following, setting forth reasons for any conclusions stated.

As a result of the CPAs having expressed an unqualified opinion on the audited financial statements of Dunbar and Wolfe and as a result of having participated in the preparation of the unaudited financial statements required in connection with the merger, indicate and briefly discuss the various bases of the CPAs' potential civil liability to the shareholders and creditors of Dunbar under

a. The federal securities acts.

b. Common law.

AICPA

20-32* A number of situations that pertain to the auditor's liability under statutory law are described below. At the end of each case, a statement is made concerning one or more of the parties in the suit.

1. In connection with a filing with the SEC, Elite Corporation engaged the public accounting firm of Turner and Miles to examine the financial statements in the registration statement. Two months after the registration statement became effective, it was discovered that a material fact was omitted from Elite's financial statements. One of the investors who acquired securities covered by the registration statement sued Turner and Miles. To win his lawsuit, the investor must prove Turner and Miles were negligent or fraudulent in reporting on the financial statements.

2. Assume it was established that the accountants in question 1 were negligent in certifying Elite's financial statements. They could avoid or reduce their liability by showing that the investor's loss was not due to the omission of the material fact.

3. Assume that
   a. An auditor issued an unqualified opinion on a set of financial statements containing a material misstatement.
   b. The auditor did not know of the misstatement but failed to observe generally accepted auditing standards in performing his examination.
   c. The owner of another company purchased the firm, although he was aware of the misstatement before doing so. He never apprised the auditor of the misstatement.
   d. After the purchase was completed, the purchaser sued the auditor for damages, asserting the auditor had violated the Federal Securities Laws (Paragraph 10(b) of the Securities Exchange Act of 1934, etc.) and accusing him of common law fraud and negligence. The purchaser would be successful in his suit against the auditor.

4. The *BarChris* decision affirms the proposition, among others, that a court can impose its judgment, *in place of the judgment of the auditor*, on matters of accounting and auditing practices.

Required
Indicate whether you believe the statements made above are true or false. Give reasons in support of your answers.

20-33 The Dandy Container Corporation engaged the accounting firm of Adams and Adams to examine financial statements to be used in connection with a public offering of securities. The audit was completed and an unqualified opinion was expressed on the financial statements that were submitted to the Securities and Exchange Commission along with the registration statement. Two hundred thousand shares of Dandy Container common stock were offered to the public at $11 a share. Eight months later, the stock fell to $2 a share when it was disclosed that several large loans to two "paper" corporations owned by one of the directors were worthless. The loans were secured by the stock of the borrowing corporation that was owned by the director. These facts were not disclosed in the financial report. The director involved and the two corporations are insolvent.

1. The Securities Act of 1933 applies to the above described public offering of securities in interstate commerce.

2. The accounting firm has potential liability to any person who acquired the stock in reliance on the registration statement.

3. An investor who bought shares in Dandy Container would make a prima facie case if he alleges that the failure to explain the nature of the loans in question constituted a false statement or misleading omission in the financial statements.

4. The accountants could avoid liability if they could show they were neither negligent nor fraudulent.

5. The accountants could avoid or reduce the damages asserted against them if they could establish that the drop in price was due in whole or in part to other causes.

6. The Dandy investors would have to institute suit within one year after discovery of the alleged untrue statements or omissions.

7. The SEC would defend any action brought against the accountants in that the SEC examined and approved the registration statement.

Required

Indicate whether each of the above statements is true or false under statutory law. Give the reason(s) for your answer.

20-34 Gordon & Groton, CPAs, were the auditors of Bank & Company, a brokerage firm and member of a national stock exchange. Gordon & Groton examined and reported on the financial statements of Bank that were filed with the SEC.

Several of Bank's customers were swindled by a fraudulent scheme perpetrated by Bank's president, who owned 90% of the voting stock of the company. The facts establish that Gordon & Groton were negligent but not reckless or grossly negligent in the conduct of the audit and neither participated in the fraudulent scheme nor knew of its existence.

The customers are suing Gordon & Groton under the antifraud provisions of Section 10(b) and Rule 10b–5 of the Securities Exchange Act of 1934 for aiding and abetting the fraudulent scheme of the president. The customers' suit for fraud is predicated exclusively on the negligence of the auditors in failing to conduct a proper audit, thereby failing to discover the fraudulent scheme.

Required

Answer the following, setting forth reasons for any conclusions stated:

a. What is the probable outcome of the lawsuit?

b. What other theory of liability might the customers have asserted?

AICPA

20-35 Herbert McCoy is the chief executive officer of McCoy Forging Corporation, a small but rapidly growing manufacturing company. For the past several years, Donovan & Company, CPAs, had been engaged to do compilation work, a systems improvement study, and to prepare the company's federal and state income tax returns. In 19X0, McCoy decided that due to the growth of the company and requests from bankers, it would be desirable to have an audit. Moreover, McCoy had recently received a disturbing anonymous letter that stated: "Beware you have a viper in your nest. The money is literally disappearing before your very eyes! Signed: A friend."

McCoy believed that the audit was entirely necessary and easily justifiable on the basis of the growth and credit factors mentioned above. He decided he would keep the anonymous letter to himself.

Therefore, McCoy on behalf of McCoy Forging engaged Donovan & Company, CPAs, to render an opinion on the financial statements for the year ended June 30, 19X1. He told Donovan he wanted to verify that the financial statements were "accurate and proper." He did not mention the anonymous letter. The usual engagement letter providing for an audit in accordance with generally accepted auditing standards (GAAS) was drafted by Donovan & Company and signed by both parties.

The audit was performed in accordance with GAAS. The audit did not reveal a clever defalcation plan by which Harper, the assistant treasurer, was siphoning off substantial amounts of McCoy Forging's money. The defalcations occurred both before and after the audit. Harper's embezzlement was discovered in October 19X1. Although the scheme was fairly sophisticated, it could have been detected had additional checks and procedures been performed by Donovan & Company. McCoy Forging demands reimbursement from Donovan for the entire amount of the embezzlement, some $20,000 of which occurred before the audit and $25,000 after. Donovan has denied any liability and refuses to pay.

Required

Answer the following, setting forth reasons for any conclusions stated:

a. In the event McCoy Forging sues Donovan & Company, will it prevail in whole or in part?

b. Might there be any liability to McCoy Forging on McCoy's part and if so, under what theory?

AICPA

20-36 The following information applies to both Parts I and II.

James Danforth, CPA, audited the financial statements of the Blair Corporation for the year ended December 31, 19X1. Danforth rendered an unqualified opinion on February 6, 19X2. The financial statements were incorporated into Form 10-K and filed with the Securities and Exchange Commission. Blair's financial statements included as an asset a previously sold certificate of deposit (CD) in the amount of $250,000. Blair had purchased the CD on December 29, 19X1, and sold it on December 30, 19X1, to a third party who paid Blair that day. Blair did not deliver the CD to the buyer until January 8, 19X2. Blair deliberately recorded the sale as an increase in cash and other revenue, thereby significantly overstating working capital, stockholders' equity, and net income. Danforth confirmed Blair's purchase of the CD with the seller and physically observed the CD on January 5, 19X2.

PART I: Assume that on January 18, 19X2, while auditing other revenue, Danforth discovered that the CD had been sold. Further assume that Danforth agreed that in exchange for an additional audit fee of $20,000, he would render an unqualified opinion on Blair's financial statements (including the previously sold CD).

Required

Answer the following, setting forth reasons for any conclusions stated:

1. The SEC charges Danforth with criminal violations of the Securities Exchange Act of 1934. Will the SEC prevail? Include in your discussion what the SEC must establish in this action.

2. Assume the SEC discovers and makes immediate public disclosure of Blair's action with the result that no one relies to his detriment on the audit report and financial statements. Under these circumstances, will the SEC prevail in its criminal action against Danforth?

PART II: Assume that Danforth performed his audit in accordance with generally accepted auditing standards (GAAS) and exercised due professional care, but did not discover Blair's sale of the CD. Two weeks after issuing the unqualified opinion, Danforth discovered that the CD had been sold. The day following this discovery, at Blair's request, Danforth delivered a copy of the audit report, along with the financial statements, to a bank that in reliance thereon made a loan to Blair that ultimately proved uncollectible. Danforth did not advise the bank of his discovery.

Required
Answer the following, setting forth reasons for any conclusions stated:
  If the bank sues Danforth for the losses it sustains in connection with the loan, will it prevail?

AICPA

CASE STUDY

20-37 **PART I:** The common stock of Wilson, Inc. is owned by 20 stockholders who live in several states. Wilson's financial statements as of December 31, 19X5, were audited by Doe & Co., CPAs, who rendered an unqualified opinion on the financial statements. In reliance on Wilson's financial statements, which showed net income for 19X5 of $1,500,000, Peters on April 10, 19X6, purchased 10,000 shares of Wilson stock for $200,000. The purchase was from a shareholder who lived in another state. Wilson's financial statements contained material misstatements. Because Doe did not carefully follow GAAS, it did not discover that the statements failed to reflect unrecorded expenses that reduced Wilson's actual net income to $800,000. After disclosure of the corrected financial statements, Peters sold his shares for $100,000, which was the highest price he could obtain.

Peters has brought an action against Doe under federal securities law and state common law.

Required
Answer the following, setting forth reasons for any conclusions stated:

1. Will Peters prevail on his federal securities law claims?
2. Will Peters prevail on his state common law claims?

PART II: Able Corporation decided to make a public offering of bonds to raise needed capital. On June 30, 19X6, it publicly sold $2,500,000 of 12% debentures in accordance with the registration requirements of the Securities Act of 1933.

The financial statements filed with the registration statement contained the unqualified opinion of Baker & Co., CPAs. The statements overstated Able's net income and net worth. Through negligence Baker did not detect the overstatements. As a result, the bonds, which originally sold for $1,000 per bond, have dropped in value to $700.

Ira is an investor who purchased $10,000 of the bonds. He promptly brought an action against Baker under the Securities Act of 1933.

Required

Answer the following, setting forth reasons for any conclusions stated:

Will Ira prevail on his claim under the Securities Act of 1933?

AICPA

Chapter 21

The Independent Accountant and the Securities and Exchange Commission

Study Objectives

After completing a careful study of this chapter, you should be able to

- Describe the organizational structure of the SEC and the division and office that relate to the independent accountant.

- State the components of the SEC's integrated disclosure system.

- Explain the major types of SEC accounting related pronouncements.

- Enumerate the SEC's requirements for the qualifications of the independent accountant and his reports.

- List the independent accountant's primary responsibilities in filings under the Securities Act of 1933 and the Securities Exchange Act of 1934.

- Indicate the independent accountant's responsibilities in meeting the quarterly and special reporting requirements of the 1934 Act.

- Distinguish between the types of enforcement actions the SEC may take against independent accountants.

In the preceding chapter, the liability of the certified public accountant (CPA) under the securities acts is explained. It is the purpose of this chapter to describe the organization of the Securities and Exchange Commission (SEC), the impact it has on the day-to-day activities of independent CPAs who have clients that are subject to SEC regulations, and the principal financial reporting requirements of the Securities Act of 1933 (the 1933 Act) and the Securities Exchange Act of 1934 (the 1934 Act).

The discussion of the responsibilities of the CPA concerning filings under the federal securities acts is limited to accounting and auditing matters and is not intended to offer legal interpretations of the acts.

In the acts, the term *independent public accountant* is used to describe the individual who is required to perform the audit function. Technically, the individual need not be certified (he may be either a CPA or a public accountant), but, in practically all cases, the individual is a CPA. Throughout this chapter, the terms *independent public accountant* and *independent accountant* are considered to be synonymous with the term *auditor* used in previous chapters of this book.

SECURITIES AND EXCHANGE COMMISSION

The SEC was established by the 1934 Act as an independent federal regulatory agency to administer the federal securities acts. Both the SEC and the 1933 and 1934 Acts, which it administers, resulted from efforts by Congress to restore investor confidence in the securities markets that had been severely shaken during the depression. In the words of the SEC,

> Congress, in enacting the Federal Securities laws, created a continuous disclosure system designed to protect investors and to assure the maintenance of fair and honest securities markets. The Commission, in administering and implementing these laws, has sought to coordinate and integrate this disclosure system. . . . The legislative history of the Securities Act of 1933 indicates that the main concern of Congress was to provide full and fair disclosure in connection with the offer and sale of securities.[1]

AUTHORITY OF THE SEC

The authority of the SEC extends to the offer and initial sale of the securities to the public and to the subsequent trading of such securities on national stock exchanges and over-the-counter markets. Thus, virtually all companies offering securities for sale to the public and all companies that have securities publicly traded are subject to the jurisdiction of the SEC. Currently, approximately 10,000 companies are registered with the SEC.

To aid in assuring the fair and orderly operation of the nation's securities markets, the SEC has regulations affecting brokers, stock exchanges, and

[1]Securities and Exchange Commission, *SEC Docket* (Vol. 4, No. 5, May 7, 1974), p. 155.

publicly held companies. These regulations encompass the monitoring of trading practices, the financial condition of brokers, and overseeing the activities and trading rules of securities exchanges. The Commission also requires the registration of publicly traded securities and continuing disclosure of financial and other information about companies that have issued the securities.

In addition, the SEC encourages shareholder participation in the governance of corporations by requiring corporations to provide proxy ballots to shareholders so that they may vote on certain decisions and hold annual shareholder meetings.

In administering the securities acts, the SEC does not pass on the merit of a security, and federal laws do not prohibit the sale or trading of highly speculative securities provided their speculative characteristics or risks are disclosed in the filing with the Commission. Information filed with the SEC generally is a matter of public record. Information previously considered to be confidential is now available to the general public under the Freedom of Information Act, commonly referred to as the Sunshine Act.

ORGANIZATION OF THE SEC

The SEC is headed by a five-person commission appointed by the President of the United States with the approval of the U.S. Senate. Each commissioner serves for a five-year term with one member's term expiring each year. No more than three commissioners may be from the same political party. Traditionally, most appointees have been from the legal profession. One member of the Commission is designated as chairman by the President. The Commission directs a staff of about 2,000 that includes accountants, lawyers, securities analysts, engineers, examiners, and administrative and clerical personnel. The professional staff is organized into five divisions and numerous offices as illustrated in Figure 21-1. The independent accountant's involvement with the SEC is usually made through the Division of Corporation Finance and the Office of the Chief Accountant.

Division of Corporation Finance

The principal responsibility of this Division is to prevent (1) fraudulent offerings of securities to the public and (2) the distribution of incomplete, false, or misleading information pertaining to security offerings. In discharging its responsibility, this Division

- Assists the Commission in the establishment of standards of economic and financial information to be included in documents filed with the SEC.
- Enforces adherence to such standards by issuers, underwriters, and others with respect to securities offered for sale to the public or listed for trading on securities exchanges or in over-the-counter markets by reviewing and processing registration statements and periodic reports under the applicable securities acts.

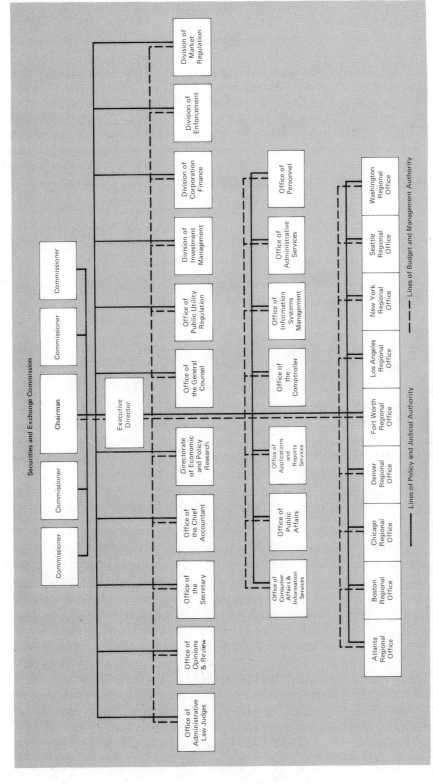

Figure 21-1. ORGANIZATION OF THE SECURITIES AND EXCHANGE COMMISSION. [Source: *The United States Government Manual 1984/85* (Washington, D.C.: U.S. Government Printing Office) p. 857.

- Prescribes and enforces the information to be included in proxy solicitations.
- Administers the disclosure requirements of the federal securities laws.
- Prepares Staff Accounting Bulletins (SABs) in conjunction with the Office of the Chief Accountant.

This Division also (1) drafts the rules, regulations, and forms to be used in filings with the SEC and (2) gives advice and answers inquiries pertaining to the application and interpretation of the statutes, and registration and reporting procedures.

Office of the Chief Accountant

The chief accountant is the SEC's principal expert adviser on all matters relating to accounting and auditing. The chief accountant

- Carries out SEC policy on accounting principles and the form and content of financial statements filed with it.
- Consults and rules on accounting questions from registrants and independent accountants.
- Directs administrative policy pertaining to accounting and auditing matters.
- Maintains liaison with accounting authorities, professional organizations, independent public accountants, and government officials.
- Participates in administrative and court proceedings involving accounting and auditing matters.
- Recommends to the Commission the taking of disciplinary action against accountants under the SEC's Rules of Practice.
- Considers cases on the independence and qualifications of independent accountants who practice before the SEC.
- Prepares Financial Reporting Releases (FRRs).
- Issues Accounting and Auditing Enforcement Releases (AAERs).
- Issues SABs in conjunction with the Division of Corporation Finance.

The chief accountant is in a position to exert substantial influence on the development of generally accepted accounting principles (GAAP) and generally accepted auditing standards (GAAS). There is no fixed term of office for the chief accountant.

REPORTING AND REGISTRATION REQUIREMENTS

The SEC has the authority to prescribe the accounting and reporting requirements for companies under its jurisdiction. Throughout its history, however, the SEC has cooperated with the private sector in the development of GAAP and it has indicated that it

> Intends to continue its policy of looking to the private sector for leadership in establishing and improving accounting principles and standards through the [Financial Accounting Standards Board] with the expectation that the body's conclusions will promote the interests of investors.[2]

The SEC's authority also generally extends to annual reports to shareholders that are issued by corporations, as well as to the periodic reports required under the 1934 Act and registration statements filed under the 1933 Act.

INTEGRATED DISCLOSURE SYSTEM

In 1980, the SEC adopted new requirements for reporting financial and other business information by publicly held companies. Known as the *integrated disclosure system,* the requirements provide for a standard package of information consisting of

- Audited consolidated financial statements consisting of balance sheets for the latest two years, and statements of income, retained earnings, and changes in financial position for the most recent three years.
- A five-year summary of selected financial data.
- A management discussion and analysis of the company's financial condition and results of operations.
- Market price and dividend information on the company's common stock and related security holder matters.

The requirements for this information are the same in all SEC forms. To avoid duplication, a company is permitted to *incorporate by reference* information required in one filing that is already contained in another filing. For example, information required in the SEC's annual report form, Form 10–K, can be incorporated by reference to the company's annual report to shareholders. The integrated disclosure system has significantly reduced the effort and cost of complying with the SEC's reporting requirements. The new system also requires *continuous reporting* through periodic and special reports that update the company's information included in its original registration statement. The integrative disclosure system is illustrated in Figure 21-2.

In addition to the standard information package, the SEC requires *supplementary financial information* in many filings. This information includes exhibits, schedules, and specialized financial and business data.

The SEC's reporting system is intended to serve both the average and the sophisticated investor. Certain of the disclosures required are intended to meet the needs of the average investor. In addition to being filed with the SEC, these disclosures must also be furnished to all present security holders or to any potential purchasers of the securities, as appropriate. Other disclosures

[2]SEC Financial Reporting Release No. 1, Section 101 (1982).

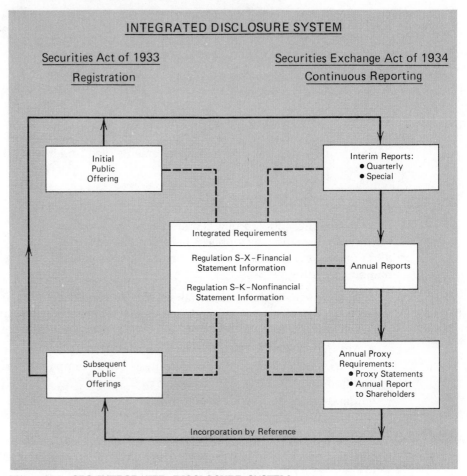

Figure 21-2. SEC INTEGRATED DISCLOSURE SYSTEM.

are intended primarily for institutional investors, security analysts, or the sophisticated individual investor. The information is contained in the filing made by a company with the SEC. Generally, all information in filings made with the SEC is considered public information. Copies of any reported data may be obtained from the SEC at nominal cost.

For companies required to report to the SEC, the first step is to select the proper form for filing. Although the instructions for each form contain the rule or eligibility requirements for its use, it often is necessary for legal counsel to be consulted in making this determination. Once the form has been selected, additional instructions on the form identify the number in the pronouncements of the SEC that specify the business disclosures and financial reporting requirements that are to accompany the filing.

TYPES OF ACCOUNTING PRONOUNCEMENTS

The SEC issues four major types of accounting-related pronouncements to be used by companies and their independent accountants in filings with the agency. These are Regulation S–X, Regulation S–K, FRRs, and SABs. In addition, administrative rulings may affect the filing of financial statements. Nearly all the disclosure requirements under the 1933 and 1934 Acts are contained in these pronouncements.

Regulation S–X

Regulation S–X is the principal accounting regulation of the SEC. It covers the requirements for financial statements to be filed with the SEC. The instructions specify the required time periods and the form and content of financial statements, including the classification, presentation, and disclosure of material financial statement items. Regulation S–X is subject to amendments in response to changing conditions and the need for additional or less information by investors. Amendments are made by issuing FRRs.

In accordance with the SEC's policy of cooperating with the private sector, Regulation S–X contains an explicit requirement that the financial statements are to be prepared in accordance with generally accepted accounting principles (GAAP). In a few instances, the financial statement disclosure requirements of the Regulation exceed the disclosure requirements under GAAP. These additional regulatory requirements are referred to as *compliance notes*.

Regulation S–K

Regulation S–K is referred to as the uniform disclosure regulation. It covers the disclosure requirements for nonfinancial statement or text information required under the Act in the same manner that Regulation S–X prescribes the requirements for financial statements.

The Regulation has nine major sections. Some of the sections include instructions regarding disclosures about the company's business, securities, management, and financial information other than the financial statements. Another section covers the information to be provided about the securities being sold. The final section lists the SEC-prepared industry guides to be used by companies operating in specialized areas, such as those with oil and gas operations, bank holding companies, and real estate limited partnerships.

The particular items that are to be included in filings under Regulation S–K are indicated by the instructions accompanying the form to be filed. Inclusion of an item of information as prescribed under Regulation S–K is required only to the extent that the form governing a particular document specifically directs the inclusion of such information.

Financial Reporting Releases (FRRs)

The Commission has the authority to amend existing rules and regulations of the securities acts and to issue new ones. Since 1982, notice of changes in accounting-related matters is made by publishing FRRs. These releases include

- New disclosure requirements or specified accounting treatment for certain types of transactions.
- Opinions of the Commission on major accounting issues.
- Amendments to the financial statement requirements.
- Clarification of existing rules and regulations, such as the rule on independence.

Prior to 1982, changes in accounting matters were issued as Accounting Series Releases (ASRs). FRR No. 1, issued as a Codification of Financial Reporting Policies, contains all ASRs that were still relevant for financial reporting. New amendments on accounting and auditing topics are issued in separate FRRs. Since the codification, 21 FRRs have been issued.

Releases on accounting and auditing matters are usually issued initially as proposals, and copies are distributed to various professional and other interested groups for their criticism and suggestions. Individuals and firms may also submit their views on proposals. Experience demonstrates that the SEC carefully considers comments on the proposals before adopting any changes.

Staff Accounting Bulletins (SABs)

The Division of Corporation Finance and the Office of the Chief Accountant have the authority to issue SABs.[3] They are issued to provide guidance for handling events and transactions with similar accounting implications.

SABs are not rules or interpretations of the Commission, and they are not published as bearing the Commission's official approval. However, they are generally regarded as "interpretations" of Regulation S–X and GAAP. When a registrant and its independent accountant believe that due to its peculiar circumstances, the appropriate accounting should be different than would result from following the practice expressed in an SAB, the registrant is encouraged to discuss the specifics with the staff.

Administrative Rulings

Some of the SEC's accounting requirements are informal and adopted administratively. Although such items may have general applicability to all registrants, they are not always publicized. In such case, the independent accountant may only learn of the Commission's position as a result of the SEC's review and related comments on a client's registration statement. There have been few administrative rulings since SABs were first issued.

---

[3]In 1981, the SEC codified all relevant SABs in *Staff Accounting Bulletin No. 40.*

QUALIFICATIONS OF INDEPENDENT ACCOUNTANTS

Regulation S–X prescribes the qualifications of accountants as follows:

(a) The Commission will not recognize any person as a certified public accountant who is not duly registered and in good standing as such under the laws of the place of his residence or principal office. The Commission will not recognize any person as a public accountant who is not in good standing and entitled to practice as such under the laws of the place of his residence or principal office.

(b) The Commission will not recognize any certified public accountant or public accountant as independent who is not in fact independent.

(c) In determining whether an accountant may in fact be not independent with respect to a particular person, the Commission will give appropriate consideration to all relevant circumstances, including evidence bearing on all relationships between the accountant and that person or any affiliate thereof, and will not confine itself to the relationships existing in connection with the filing of reports with the Commission.[4]

The SEC rules on independence closely parallel the AICPA's Rules of Conduct on independence (Rule 101), but there are exceptions. For example, the SEC will not consider the accountant independent if he provides any bookkeeping services to an audit client. The SEC believes that such services automatically impair the accountant's independence, whereas the American Institute of Certified Public Accountants (AICPA) permits the rendering of bookkeeping services to an audit client.

REQUIREMENTS FOR ACCOUNTANT'S REPORTS

Regulation S–X also sets forth the standards of reporting for accountant's reports. The requirements are as follows:

(a) **Technical requirements**. The accountant's report (1) shall be dated; (2) shall be signed manually; (3) shall indicate the city and state where issued; and (4) shall identify without detailed enumeration the financial statements covered by the report.

(b) **Representations as to the audit**. The accountant's report (1) shall state whether the audit was made in accordance with generally accepted auditing standards; and (2) shall designate any auditing procedures deemed necessary by the accountant under the circumstan-

[4]SEC Regulation S–X, Rule 2–01.

ces of the particular case, which have been omitted, and the reasons for their omission.

Nothing in this rule shall be construed to imply authority for the omission of any procedure which independent accountants would ordinarily employ in the course of an audit made for the purpose of expressing the opinions required by paragraph (c) of this rule.

(c) **Opinion to be expressed**. The accountant's report shall state clearly: (1) the opinion of the accountant in respect of the financial statements covered by the report and the accounting principles and practices reflected therein; and (2) the opinion of the accountant as to the consistency of the application of the accounting principles, or as to any changes in such principles which have a material effect on the financial statements.

(d) **Exceptions**. Any matters to which the accountant takes exception shall be clearly identified, the exception thereto specifically and clearly stated, and, to the extent practicable, the effect of each such exception on the related financial statements given. (See Section 101 of Codification of Financial Reporting Policies.)[5]

From the foregoing, it can be seen that the responsibility of the independent accountant resulting from the inclusion of his report on financial statements in a filing under the securities acts is, in substance, essentially the same as that involved in reporting on audited financial statements as explained in Chapter 17 of this text.

Pursuant to Rule 2–02, the SEC will not accept (1) an adverse opinion or (2) a qualified opinion on audited financial statements except when the qualification pertains to an inconsistency or an uncertainty. When the qualification pertains to the entity's ability to continue in existence, there should be full and fair disclosure of the registrant's financial difficulties and plans to overcome them. However, if the financial statements are prepared on a going concern basis but a liquidation basis would be more appropriate, the financials will be considered false and misleading.[6]

As in the case of financial statements used for other purposes, management has the responsibility for the assertions made in financial statements filed under the federal securities statutes.

REGISTRATION OF SECURITIES

Registration is a major part of all the acts administered by the SEC. The primary purpose of registration is to provide prospective investors with financial and other information concerning the company and its securities being offered for public sale. The reporting standard in a registration statement is disclosure of all material facts needed by investors to appraise the merits of the securities.

[5]SEC Regulation S–X, Rule 2–02.
[6]FRR No. 16, 1984.

Registration does not insure investors against loss in their purchase nor does it guarantee the accuracy of all the information presented. As stated earlier, the SEC does not pass on the merits of the securities. Moreover, it has no authority to disapprove a registration because securities lack merit. The Commission has the power to deny registration when disclosures are incomplete, inaccurate, or misleading. In addition, the federal securities acts prohibit false and misleading information under penalty of fine, or imprisonment, or both.

All data contained in a registration are kept by the SEC and are available to the general public. Securities cannot be sold until the registration is accepted by the SEC and the registration becomes effective.

Registration is a time-consuming, complex, and expensive undertaking. This is especially true the first time a privately owned company decides to "go public" with its equity securities. In a recent year, approximately 5,100 registration statements for securities valued at $220 billion were filed with the SEC.[7]

REVIEW OF REGISTRATION STATEMENTS

The SEC's review process is designed to ascertain compliance with the securities laws or, conversely, to detect materially untrue, incomplete, or misleading information in the filing of registration statements. Reviews are made by the Division of Corporation Finance.

A review may be complete or limited, based on an initial evaluation of the registration by the staff. The SEC's practice is to do a complete review of only certain filings, including

- Initial public offerings under the Securities Act of 1933.
- Initial registration statements under the Securities Exchange Act of 1934.

Other filings may be reviewed only on a sample basis. In some instances, registration statements of established companies may be allowed to become effective with no staff review.

In the case of a complete review, the examination of the registration statement is made by a team consisting of a financial analyst, an attorney, and an accountant. Memoranda are submitted by each reviewer, which culminate in a *letter of comments* (generally known as a *deficiency letter*) that is sent to the registrant for required amendments to the registration statement and other appropriate action.

If the prospective registrant is unwilling or unable to eliminate the deficiencies in its original filing, the SEC has three courses of action:

- *Allow the Deficient Financial Statements to Become Effective.* This is rarely done because it is contrary to the SEC's objective of protecting the investor, and it exposes the issuing company to possible lawsuits.
- *Issue a Refusal Order.* This action has been used sparingly because the

[7]Securities and Exchange Commission, *Annual Report 1984*, p. 114.

order must be issued within ten days of the filing and a hearing must be held during the next ten days to allow for correction.

- *Issue a Stop Order.* This action halts further consideration of the registration statement if issued before the effective date. Alternatively, it halts further trading of the security if it is issued after the effective date.

These actions ordinarily are not needed since most companies act promptly to correct any deficiencies in the filing.

REGISTRATION PROCESS

The registration process involves a number of participants including the board of directors, representatives of management (usually the president and/or vice president of finance), legal counsel, a lead underwriter (i.e., an investment brokerage firm that assumes responsibility for selling the securities), the independent accountant, and company accountants.

Once a decision to raise capital by issuing securities has been made, management has the responsibility of providing the necessary information to complete the registration statement. Management also is responsible for selecting the underwriter, outside legal counsel, and independent accountant. An illustrative timetable and specific steps in the registration process are presented in Figure 21-3. The example assumes an issue of common stock by a company that has a fiscal year ending December 31.

The foregoing are specifically applicable to the 1933 Act but also have general applicability to registrations under other acts.

SECURITIES ACT OF 1933

The 1933 Act pertains to the initial offer and distribution of securities to the public. Often referred to as the *truth in securities* law, the Act has two basic objectives:

- To provide investors with material financial and other information concerning securities offered for public sale.
- To prohibit misrepresentation, deceit, and other fraudulent acts and practices in the sale of securities generally (whether or not required to be registered).[8]

REGISTRATION UNDER THE 1933 ACT

Registration under the 1933 Act consists of preparing and filing a registration statement with the SEC. The registration statement consists of two parts: a prospectus and other detailed information.

A *prospectus* is a separate booklet or pamphlet, given to prospective purchasers of the security, that describes the company and the securities offered. The prospectus includes all information to be presented to prospective inves-

---

[8]Securities and Exchange Commission, *The Work of the Securities and Exchange Commission* (Washington, D.C.: U.S. Government Printing Office, 1974), p. 1.

June 1	Board of directors authorizes filing of registration statement and notifies independent auditors, lawyers, and underwriter(s) of the pending filing.
June 5	Management meets with underwriters and tentative agreement is reached concerning sale of securities.
June 15	Management, independent accountant, and legal counsel have prefiling conference with SEC staff in Washington, D.C.
June 20	Management and legal counsel select appropriate registration form.
June 25–July 25	Data for registration are collected by company accountants, reviewed by lawyers, and reviewed and/or audited by independent accountants.
July 28	Management prepares draft of registration statement and obtains board of directors' approval.
August 1	Management finalizes registration statement, which is filed with SEC by legal counsel.
August 25	Management receives letter of comment from SEC concerning deficiencies and necessary adjustments.
September 5	Management prepares amendments that are responsive to SEC's comments—these are filed with SEC by legal counsel.
September 7	Due diligence meeting is held to review registration statement and other matters affecting sale of issue—this meeting is primarily for the benefit of the underwriter(s) and is attended by management, legal counsel, the independent accountant, and underwriter(s).
September 10	SEC notifies management by phone of acceptance of registration statement.
September 11	Management approves offering price of securities and the agreement with underwriter(s) for sale of the stock is finalized.
September 12	Legal counsel files amendment to registration statement for offering price—registration statement becomes effective 5:00 P.M.
September 17	Underwriter transfers net proceeds of issue to issuer.

Figure 21-3. REGISTRATION PROCESS TIMETABLE.

tors. Part II of the registration statement contains ancillary information, including expenses of issuance and distribution, indemnification of directors and officers, and certain exhibits and financial statement schedules. Part II is required to be filed only with the SEC, although the information is available to interested investors on request.

There are four primary forms used by most companies in filings under the 1933 Act. The choice of form depends on the size of the company and the period of time it has been subject to the SEC's periodic reporting requirements.

- *Form S–4* is an abbreviated form that extends the integrated disclosure system to business combination transactions.
- *Form S–3* is an abbreviated filing that incorporates by reference information that is available in previous reports filed with the SEC. It is intended for use by large companies that are widely followed by financial analysts.

- *Form S–2* is designed for use by companies that have been subject to the periodic reporting requirements of the SEC for at least three years, but are not as widely followed by analysts. An S–2 filing may include only the information required for an S–3 filing, provided the company delivers its latest annual report to all potential investors. If the annual report is not included, then this information must be in the filing. Financial information for the most recent quarter also must be provided.
- *Form S–1* is used by companies that do not fit other categories.

Form S-1 is the most widely used under this Act, and it is the most comprehensive. The principal financial information requirements under this form are explained below.

Business Disclosures

Form S–1 requires disclosure of a considerable amount of information about the company and its business. These disclosures, which are described in Regulation S–K, include items such as the following:

- History and description of the business (including industry segments and foreign operations).
- Description of properties.
- Background information about directors and executive officers, including their security holdings, compensation, and material pending legal proceedings to which management is a party.
- Description of the securities being registered, including details of any underwriting arrangements, an estimate of the net proceeds, and the uses to which such proceeds will be put.

Financial Statements

Financial statements must be presented for the issuing company in one of the following forms:

- Financial statements for the company itself, if it has no subsidiaries that must be consolidated.
- Consolidated financial statements only, unless it is necessary to include "separate parent company" statements on a supplemental schedule.

In addition, under some circumstances, the issuer may have to present financial statements for (1) unconsolidated subsidiaries and 50% or less owned companies accounted for under the equity method, (2) affiliated companies whose securities are pledged as collateral for debt securities that are being registered, and (3) companies acquired or to be acquired.

Balance Sheets. Audited balance sheets must be filed as of the end of each of the two preceding fiscal years. In addition, the general rule is that the filing must include a balance sheet as of an interim date within 135 days of the date of the filing if the most recent audited balance sheet does not fall within this period. The interim balance sheet may be in condensed form and need not be audited.

Other Statements. An income statement must be filed for each of the three fiscal years preceding the date of the latest fiscal year-end balance sheet filed, and for the period, if any, between the close of the latest fiscal year and the date of the latest balance sheet filed. The statements of retained earnings, changes in financial position, and changes in stockholders' equity must be filed for the same periods as the income statement. All statements relating to the three fiscal years must be audited; comparative statements covering the period from the latest fiscal year to the date of the latest balance sheet may be in condensed form and need not be audited.

Selected Financial Data

Form S–1 requires a five-year summary of selected financial data. This requirement is intended to present significant trend data relating both to an enterprise's financial condition and its results of operations. The selected financial data are not required to be audited and are not encompassed within the auditor's report.

Elements from the company's balance sheet and income statement that must be presented include the following:

- Net sales or operating revenues.
- Income (loss) from continuing operations.
- Income (loss) from continuing operations per common share.
- Total assets.
- Long-term obligations (including capital leases) and redeemable preferred stock.
- Cash dividends declared per common share.

If the company is required by the Financial Accounting Standards Board to present a five-year summary of the effects of inflation and changing prices, this information may be presented under this caption. Alternatively, it may be presented as supplementary financial information. Figure 21-4 shows a five-year summary of selected financial data. A discussion of the factors that materially affect the comparability of the selected financial data also should be included.

Management's Discussion and Analysis

This selection is intended to provide a meaningful analysis of significant changes in financial condition and results of operations. The discussion must cover the three years presented in the audited financial statements and the statements for any interim period. When trends are discussed, reference has to be made to the five years of selected financial data, as appropriate. The discussion must include at least the following aspects of the business:

Integrated Software Systems Corporation
Five-Year Summary of Selected Financial Data

	Year Ended December 31				
	1980	1981	1982	1983	1984

INCOME STATEMENT DATA
(In thousands, except per share amounts)

	1980	1981	1982	1983	1984
Total revenues	$6,453	$10,705	$16,623	$24,177	$33,632
Total operating expenses	5,040	8,786	13,456	19,754	27,272
Operating income	1,413	1,919	3,167	4,423	6,360
Nonoperating income	8	67	162	1,128	1,808
Income before income taxes	1,421	1,986	3,329	5,551	8,168
Net income	787	1,051	1,749	3,001	4,228
Earnings per share	.21	.27	.43	.60	.80
Weighted average shares outstanding	3,743	3,944	4,084	5,023	5,293

	December 31				
	1980	1981	1982	1983	1984

BALANCE SHEET DATA
(In thousands)

	1980	1981	1982	1983	1984
Working capital	$1,665	$ 3,032	$ 4,040	$20,062	$21,917
Total assets	4,573	7,873	11,637	31,821	40,618
Long-term liabilities	746	723	362	432	636
Stockholders' equity	2,103	3,981	5,730	23,638	28,493

Figure 21-4. FIVE-YEAR SUMMARY OF SELECTED FINANCIAL DATA.

- The company's liquidity, capital resources, and results of operations.
- Favorable or unfavorable trends, significant uncertainties, and unusual or infrequent events and their possible effects.
- Causes of material changes in the financial statements.
- Narrative discussion of the effects of inflation and changing prices.

The discussion of liquidity and capital resources should deal with available sources of funds and the company's expected short- and long-term requirements. Trend information on cash flow from operations may be included, together with plans to deal with any insufficiency of funds from internal sources or changed circumstances.

At its option, the company also may include forward-looking information. This may be in the form of formal financial forecasts or simply information that may be useful to those who wish to work out a forecast of future operating results.

INDEPENDENT ACCOUNTANT'S INVOLVEMENT IN REGISTRATIONS

The independent accountant is an active participant in the registration process. His major responsibilities are to

- Make an examination of the financial statements in accordance with GAAS.
- Read any unaudited condensed financial statements included therein for matters that might require disclosure in the audited financial statements.
- Read the entire registration statement for data that may be materially inconsistent with the financial statements or be a material misstatement of fact.
- Perform a subsequent events review up to the effective date of the registration statement.
- Issue a comfort letter to underwriters.

The accountant advises the company on the SEC's reporting and disclosure requirements that are in addition to those required by generally accepted accounting principles; arranges for a prefiling conference with the SEC, if necessary, to resolve accounting or reporting problems; and advises the company's legal counsel on the financial portions of the registration statement. The accountant may also draft responses to deficiency letters, if any, received from the SEC staff.

Audited Financial Statements

The audit of the financial statements included in a registration is the same as the examination of any financial statements prepared in conformity with GAAP. Accordingly, the ten GAAS and the audit procedures described in previous chapters of this book are applicable.

Unaudited Financial Statements

When unaudited financial statements for an interim period are included with audited financial statements, the independent accountant who made the examination is associated with the unaudited statements. The independent accountant's responsibilities for the interim statements are basically the same as described in Chapter 18 for other unaudited financial statements. However, in an SEC registration, the accountant should consider withholding consent to the use of his report on audited financial statements if the client is unwilling to revise the unaudited statements to conform with GAAP.[9]

---

[9]Auditing Standards Board, *Codification of Statements on Auditing Standards* (New York: American Institute of Certified Public Accountants, 1985), Auditing Section 711.13 (hereinafter referred to and cited as AU §).

Other Data

The independent accountant is required to read the nonfinancial data in the prospectus and the other detailed information in the registration statement. The independent accountant is not expected to perform any auditing procedures on the data. The primary objective is to determine whether there are any material inconsistencies or statements in the text that contradict data relied on in preparing the financial statements included in the registration. When such instances are found, the independent accountant should see that appropriate revision is made.

Subsequent Events Review

The independent accountant's statutory liability under the 1933 Act extends to the circumstances existing as of the effective date of the registration statement. Specifically, the accountant is required to make a "reasonable investigation" and have "reasonable grounds" as to the fairness of the financial statements included in a registration up to the effective date of the filing.[10] To provide proof of a "reasonable investigation," the accountant should extend the subsequent events procedures described in Chapter 16 up to the effective date or as close thereto as possible.

In addition, the accountant should

- Read the entire prospectus and other pertinent parts of the registration statement.
- Inquire of and obtain written confirmation from officers and other executives having responsibility for financial and accounting matters (limited when appropriate to major locations) as to whether there have occurred any events other than those reflected or disclosed in the registration statement that, in the officers' or other executives' opinion, have a material effect on the audited financial statements included therein or that should be disclosed in order to keep those statements from being misleading.[11]

The performance of these procedures is facilitated when the client keeps the accountant informed during the progress of the registration proceedings. The subsequent events review described above is referred to as an S–1 review. This is not an accurate description, as the same review applies to other registration forms under the 1933 Act. This review was one of the key issues in the *BarChris* case discussed in Chapter 20. In the registration schedule shown in Figure 21-3, the S–1 review would extend from the date of the audit report through September 12, the effective date of the registration statement.

[10]Securities Act of 1933 § 11(b).
[11]Auditing Standards Board, *op. cit.*, AU § 711.10.

Letters for Underwriters

As indicated earlier in the chapter, an underwriting agreement is common in the issuance of securities under the securities acts. This agreement is a contract between the underwriter(s) and the issuer of the securities. Typically, the provisions of an underwriting agreement provide for a comfort letter from an independent accountant. The letter is so named because it is designed to give comfort (assurance) to underwriters that the financial and accounting data not covered by the independent accountant's opinion on the audited financial statements included in a prospectus are (1) in compliance with the Securities Act of 1933 and (2) in conformity with GAAP, consistently applied. Underwriters seek this comfort in the form of negative assurance as a due diligence (or reasonable investigation) defense against possible legal claims under the Act. Comfort letters are not required under the 1933 Act, and copies of such letters are not filed with the SEC. The rendering of this type of letter should be based on an agreement between the underwriter and the independent accountant. A comfort letter involves a limited review by the independent accountant of data requested by the underwriter rather than an audit. The review permits the expression of negative assurance, but not an opinion.

In a comfort letter engagement, the underwriter specifies the limited review procedures and takes responsibility for the adequacy of the procedures to be performed by the accountant. Normally, these procedures include

- Reading the minutes of stockholder and board of director meetings since the date of his report on the audited statements.
- Inquiring of company officials.
- Reading unaudited financial statements.

A comfort letter generally will refer to one or more of the following:

- The independence of the accountants.
- Compliance as to form in all material respects of the audited financial statements and schedules with the applicable accounting requirements of the Act and the published rules and regulations thereunder.
- Unaudited financial statements or condensed financial statements included in the registration statement.
- Changes in selected financial statement items during a period subsequent to the date and period of the latest financial statements in the registration statement.
- Tables, statistics, and other financial information in the registration statements.[12]

Based on his audit, the accountant should be able to express an opinion on compliance with SEC requirements. However, the CPA's comments on unaudited financial statements and other data should be in the form of negative assurance (i.e., nothing came to the accountant's attention that caused

[12]Auditing Standards Board, *op. cit.*, AU § 634.06.

him to believe the specified data does not meet a specified standard). The review procedures should be enumerated together with a statement that they do not constitute an examination made in accordance with GAAS and would not necessarily reveal matters of significance on items on which negative assurance has been given.

The comfort letter should conclude with the caveat that the letter is solely for the use of the underwriter in connection with the specified security issue under the Act, and that it is not to be used, circulated, quoted, or otherwise referred to, for any other purpose.[13]

ACCOUNTANT'S REPORTS

The Securities Act imposes a variety of reporting requirements on the independent accountant when he is associated with a registration statement. The major circumstances are explained below.

Report on Financial Statements

The accountant's report on the audited financial statements included in a registration statement is, for all practical purposes, identical with the auditor's standard report described in Chapter 17. The report must cover the two years of balance sheets and the three years of statements of income and changes in financial position that are included. In addition, the accountant reports on certain supporting schedules.

Accountant's Consent

The 1933 Act provides that "if any accountant is named as having prepared or certified any part of the registration . . . the written consent of such person shall be filed with the registration."[14] In addition, the Act requires consent to the use of the accountant's name as an expert.[15] These requirements are met by issuing a letter of consent, as illustrated in Figure 21-5. The letter of consent should be made only when a "reasonable investigation" has been made of the data to which the consent refers. The accountant's reasonable investigation must be premised on an audit; it cannot be accomplished short of an audit.[16] Thus, the expertizing declaration should be limited to the financial presentations covered by the accountant's certificate.

If the accountant has reported on unaudited financial information included in a registration statement, a second letter, known as a *letter of acknowledgement*, must be included. Although the accountant does not have a responsibility for a report on unaudited information within the meaning of Section 11 of the

---

[13]Illustrative comfort letters are presented in Auditing Standards Board, *op. cit.*, AU § 634.49–.60.

[14]Securities Act of 1933 § 7.

[15]Securities Act of 1933 § 11(b)(3)(B).

[16]Auditing Standards Board, *op. cit.*, AU § 634.02.

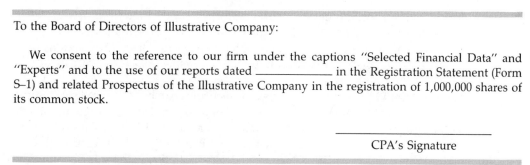

To the Board of Directors of Illustrative Company:

We consent to the reference to our firm under the captions "Selected Financial Data" and "Experts" and to the use of our reports dated _____ in the Registration Statement (Form S–1) and related Prospectus of the Illustrative Company in the registration of 1,000,000 shares of its common stock.

CPA's Signature

Figure 21-5. ACCOUNTANT'S CONSENT.

1933 Act, the SEC nevertheless requests that the accountant acknowledge awareness of the use of such a report in a separate letter included in the filing.[17]

Certain kinds of securities offerings are exempt from the requirement for registration under the 1933 Act. These include offerings of governmental units, offerings sold intrastate, and "private placements." An abbreviated registration statement, Regulation A, is available for certain offerings not exceeding $1,500,000. Further, certain other offerings are governed by special provisions.

SECURITIES EXCHANGE ACT OF 1934

The 1934 Act is known as the *continuous disclosure act*. It provides for both the registration of securities and the filing of annual and other periodic reports to keep current the data in the original filing. This Act originally applied to the public trading of securities on national securities exchanges. Through the enactment of a subsequent amendment to the securities acts, the provisions of the 1934 Act also apply to equity securities of companies traded over-the-counter when company assets exceed $3 million and shareholders number 500 or more. In general, transactions in securities that are consummated other than on a national exchange are said to be traded over the counter.

The scope of the Securities Exchange Act extends to (1) proxy solicitations, (2) tender offer solicitations, (3) insider trading, (4) margin trading, (5) market surveillance, and (6) registration of exchanges and broker dealers. These aspects of the 1934 Act are beyond the scope of this book.

REGISTRATION UNDER THE 1934 ACT

Before trading can occur on a national securities exchange, companies must file a registration application with both the exchange and the SEC. A similar registration form must be filed with the SEC for over-the-counter trading when the foregoing size test is met. The financial and other data prescribed under

[17]Auditing Standards Board, *op. cit.*, AU § 711.09.

a 1934 Act registration generally are identical with that required in a 1933 Act registration. However, there is no provision for the dissemination of the registration statement to investors through a prospectus or similar medium. Instead, the information is available for public inspection at the offices of the SEC and the exchanges.

Under the 1934 Act, an entire class of securities can be registered for trading at one time with no amount specified. Thus, the number of registrations is significantly fewer under this Act than under the 1933 Act. A variety of registration forms are prescribed under the Act. Form 10 (not to be confused with annual reporting Form 10–K, which is discussed later) is the most commonly used form. It is required when no other form applies.

Information to be filed in a listing application with an exchange may differ from SEC requirements. The New York Stock Exchange (NYSE), for example, requires a 10-year earnings summary. The requirements of an exchange are not a substitute for the SEC requirements or vice versa. The involvement of the independent accountant in the registration process under the 1934 Act is similar to the involvement in 1933 Act registrations.

ANNUAL REPORTING

The 1934 Act provides for continuous reporting by the registrant of "adequate and accurate disclosure of material facts" to investors because the securities may be actively traded for many years.[18] Such disclosure does not guarantee the worth or establish the value of any security. The foregoing disclosure requirement is met through annual, quarterly, and special reports.

Form 10–K is the general report form to be used by companies when no other report form is authorized or prescribed. The purpose of a Form 10-K filing is to provide an annual update of the data included in the registration statement. The information in Form 10-K is organized in four parts:

Part I. Description of the business, properties, legal proceedings, and matters voted on by security holders during the fourth quarter.

Part II. Financial statements and supplementary data, selected financial data, management's discussion and analysis, certain information about the market for the company's stock and related stockholder matters, and disagreements on accounting and financial disclosures.

Part III. Information about the directors and executive officers of the company, compensation, any transactions with the company, and security ownership of certain beneficial owners and management.

Part IV. Exhibits, financial statement schedules, and other data.

---

[18]Securities Exchange Act of 1934, Rule 12b–23.

The requirements for audited financial statements, selected financial data, and management's discussion and analysis are the same as those described under 1933 Act filings.

The SEC's regulations further prescribe that certain of the information in Form 10–K must be included in the annual report issued by the corporation to its shareholders. This requirement applies to a portion of the information about the business in Part I and all the information in Part II. The information in Part III may be provided separately to shareholders in a proxy or information statement. The remaining information in Part IV is required only in the filing with the SEC.

By requiring that only certain information on Form 10-K be provided directly to stockholders, the SEC is recognizing that not all financial statement users are interested in the detailed information that is provided. Some corporations voluntarily include all Form 10–K information in their annual reports. When this is not done, there must be a statement in the annual report that a copy of Form 10–K is available, without charge, to any shareholder on request. Conversely, all information in an annual report may not be included in a Form 10–K report. The president's letter, financial highlights, and graphic analysis of financial data are among the excluded items. The SEC regulations assure that owners of the company's securities receive at least basic financial information about the company.

The time constraints on the filing of Form 10–K often are demanding on both the company and the independent accountant. Parts I and II and a portion of Part IV of Form 10–K must be filed with the SEC within 90 days of the company's year-end. The remaining information may be filed separately and is due within 120 days. Few extensions of time are granted.

QUARTERLY REPORTING

A registrant under the 1934 Act is required to keep investors and other interested parties informed of interim changes in its operations and financial position by submitting quarterly reports to the SEC. Form 10–Q serves to update the most recent 10–K information for events during the current year. A company must file the 10–Q within 45 days after the end of each of the first three quarters of the fiscal year. Form 10–Q contains two major accounting requirements: (1) interim financial information (IFI) and (2) an accountant's letter on the preferability of changes in accounting principles.

Interim Financial Information

Form 10–Q requires condensed financial statements, management's analysis of financial condition and results of operations, and certain other information. The IFI is to be prepared in accordance with GAAP applied on a consistent basis.

The financial statement requirements for the Form 10–Q include (1) condensed balance sheets at the end of the most recent quarter and preceding fiscal year and (2) condensed statements of income and changes in financial position for the period from the beginning of the year and the corresponding period of the prior year. Disclosures for condensed interim statements must be adequate, within the context of the most recent audited financial statements, to prevent them from being misleading. Management's discussion and analysis should include material changes and give special attention to liquidity, capital resources, and operating results.

The SEC does not require that IFI be either audited or reviewed by an independent accountant. However, companies that meet certain trading and size tests must show quarterly revenues, gross profit, net income, and earnings per share data as supplemental information in the annual financial statements. The supplemental information must be reviewed by the independent accountant. For these companies, the question is whether to have quarterly reviews or to have only an annual review of interim financial information. Many companies elect the former to avoid year-end embarrassment or potentially more serious consequences if changes in quarterly data are needed. When a review has been made of IFI, the accountant's report should be included as an exhibit to the filing.

Changes in Accounting Principles

Registrants must report any change in accounting principles or practices or change in the method of applying them that will materially affect the financial statements filed or to be filed in the current year. This requirement must be met in the first Form 10–Q filed subsequent to the date of the accounting change.

Regardless of whether the independent accountant has reviewed interim financial information in a Form 10–Q filing, Regulation S–X requires

> [I]n the first Form 10–Q filed subsequent to the date of an accounting change, a letter from the registrant's independent accountants indicating whether any change . . . is to an alternative principle that in his judgment is preferable in the circumstances. Except that no letter from the accountant needs to be filed when the change is made in response to a standard adopted by the Financial Accounting Standards Board . . .

Thus, a preferability letter must be sent to the client to file as an exhibit to Form 10–Q. The wording of the accountant's letter should state

> In our opinion, the change in accounting principle described in Note X is preferable in your circumstances.

SAB 40 contains guidance to assist the independent accountant in meeting this requirement.

SPECIAL REPORTING

The SEC requires companies under the jurisdiction of this statute to file special reports when certain material corporate events have occurred. The reporting is done on Form 8–K and the report must be filed within 15 days after the occurrence of the event. The following are illustrative of events that should be considered for inclusion in a Form 8–K filing:

- Changes in control of the company.
- Major acquisitions and disposals of assets.
- Bankruptcy or receivership.
- Changes in the company's independent accountant.
- Resignation of the company directors.

A company is also expected to report any other significant events, such as losses from fire, flood, and so on, within a reasonable time after their occurrence. Form 8–K does not have a specific format but is a narrative report that gives the registrant considerable flexibility in reporting.

Form 8–K requires the registrant to submit written statements on any auditor changes. Auditor changes must be reported when the principal accountant resigns, declines to stand for reelection, or is dismissed, as well as when a new auditor is engaged. In addition, any changes in other auditors of significant subsidiaries or divisions relied on by the principal auditor must be reported. The report must state whether there were any disagreements with the former auditor during the audits of the last two fiscal years and subsequent interim period on any matter of (1) accounting principles, (2) financial statement disclosure, or (3) auditing scope or procedure, which would have caused the auditors to make reference in expressing their opinion to the subject matter of the disagreement regardless of whether the disagreement was resolved to the auditors' satisfaction.

The former auditor must also furnish the registrant with a letter, addressed to the SEC, stating whether he agrees with the statements made by the registrant, and if not, the reasons therefor. The general form of the auditor's letter is illustrated in Figure 21-6.

ENFORCEMENT OF THE SECURITIES ACTS

As indicated in Chapter 20, the SEC has the authority to initiate legal actions against independent accountants for violations of the securities acts. Through its Division of Enforcement, the SEC also has the authority to impose sanctions against independent accountants through administrative proceedings. Since 1982, actions taken by the SEC against accountants have been published in Accounting and Auditing Enforcement Releases (AAERs). To date, 68 AAERs have been published.

June 25, 19X1

Securities and Exchange Commission
Washington, D.C. 20549

To the Commissioners of the SEC:

We were previously principal accountants for Illustrative Company and, under date of March 15, 19X1, we reported on the consolidated financial statements of the Company and consolidated subsidiaries as of and for the two years ended December 31, 19X0. On June 10, 19X1, we resigned [or we declined to stand for reelection—or our appointment as principal accountants was terminated]. We have read Illustrative Company's statements included under Item 4 of its Form 8–K dated June 25, 19X1 and we agree with such statements.

Yours truly,

Reddy & Abel
_____
Reddy & Abel

Figure 21-6. LETTER OF AGREEMENT CONCERNING CHANGE OF AUDITORS.

INJUNCTIVE PROCEEDINGS

The SEC has the authority under both the 1933 and the 1934 Acts to initiate injunctive proceedings in the courts to restrain future violations of the provisions of these Acts. In addition to stopping the unacceptable practice, an injunction seeks assurances that future actions will be in compliance with the securities acts. The effect of an injunction may be damaging to a defendant in subsequent civil suits for damages, and it may expose the person(s) enjoined to criminal action.

The conditions under which the SEC will bring injunctive proceedings were generalized by an SEC chairman as follows:

> Put very simply, when the Commission discerns that the auditor has not been alert to his duty, that he has gone through an exercise by rote or that he has not been true to the duty of fair presentation, then in my estimation, the Commission should properly authorize an action to enjoin the accountant from a repetition of those faults.[19]

An injunction must be issued by a court of law. The SEC has consistently maintained that ordinary negligence is sufficient to support an injunctive action.

[19]A. A. Sommer, Jr., "Accountants: A Flexible Standard," *Litigation* (Winter 1975), pp. 35–39.

ADMINISTRATIVE PROCEEDINGS

Sanctions against auditors may be brought under the SEC's Administrative Rule 2(e), which states that

> *The Commission may disqualify and deny, temporarily or permanently, the privilege of appearing or practicing before it* to any accountant who is found by the Commission . . . (1) not to possess the requisite qualifications to represent others, (2) to be lacking in character or integrity, (3) to have engaged in unethical or improper professional conduct, (4) to have willfully violated, or willfully aided and abetted the violation of any provision of the federal securities laws.[20]

In addition, the Commission may suspend from appearing or practicing before it an auditor who has been (1) "convicted of a felony, or a misdemeanor involving moral turpitude," (2) the subject of a revocation or suspension of his license to practice, (3) "permanently enjoined . . . from violation . . . of any provision of the federal securities laws," or (4) "found by any court . . . or found by this Commission in any administrative proceeding . . . to have violated . . . any provision of the federal securities laws . . . (unless the violation was found not to have been willful)."

The SEC has imposed the following innovative sanctions against auditors under Rule 2(e):

- Peer reviews and inspections of accounting firms to determine the extent of compliance with professional and firm auditing standards and procedures.
- Restrictions for specified periods against mergers with other firms.
- Prohibitions for specified periods against undertaking new engagements likely to result in filings with the SEC.
- Requirements to develop and implement auditing procedures for certain types of transactions.
- Imposition of continuing education programs.

These sanctions are viewed by one commissioner as being neither punitive nor retributive but rather as providing assurance that the possibility of recurrence of specific problems caused by pervasive control deficiencies will be reduced.[21]

Rule 2(e) proceedings are public unless the SEC, on its own motion or at the request of a party, should direct otherwise. All known Rule 2(e) proceedings have involved consent decrees. Consent decrees are negotiated settle-

[20]*Ibid.*

[21]Sommer, *op. cit.,* p. 37.

ments in which the SEC publishes only the settlement and the CPA firm neither denies nor admits guilt.

CONCLUDING COMMENTS

The SEC has had a profound influence on the public accounting profession, accounting firms, and individual CPAs. In the exercise of its regulatory powers, the SEC has maintained direct interaction with such groups as the Financial Accounting Standards Board and the AICPA's Auditing Standards Board in the development of GAAP and GAAS. A number of the Statements on Auditing Standards, for example, were initiated by new disclosure requirements of the SEC.

The provisions of the federal securities acts administered by the SEC have significantly affected the day-to-day practice of accounting firms and independent public accountants. Moreover, these statutes establish the basis for both civil and criminal actions against independent accountants.

Based on its record to date and its ongoing responsibility to provide investors with reliable financial data, it appears likely that the SEC will continue to have a significant influence on the accounting profession and independent accountants.

REVIEW QUESTIONS

21-1 How extensive is the SEC's authority over the public sale of securities?

21-2 Describe the responsibilities and primary functions of the Division of Corporation Finance.

21-3 Enumerate the principal duties of the Chief Accountant.

21-4 a. Identify the components of the standard package of information required in the integrated disclosure system.
b. What is meant by (1) incorporation by reference and (2) continuous reporting?

21-5 Identify and briefly describe the types of authoritative pronouncements issued by the SEC and the specific types of information included in each.

21-6 Briefly describe the SEC's rules concerning (a) qualifications of independent accountants and (b) accountant's reports.

21-7 The registration of securities is designed to insure investors against loss. Do you agree or disagree? Why?

21-8 a. Describe the complete review that is made of a registration statement.
b. Indicate the courses of action the SEC may take when an original filing is deficient.

21-9 Identify the steps in the registration process that occur after the registration statement is filed with the Commission.

21-10 a. What are the two basic objectives of the Securities Act of 1933?
b. Distinguish between a registration statement and a prospectus.

21-11 Enumerate the basic information that is common to registrations under the 1933 Act.

21-12 Describe the basic types of financial data required under the 1933 Act, including the time period covered and whether the data must be audited.

21-13 Identify the major responsibilities of the accountant in a 1933 Act registration.

21-14 a. What is an S–1 Review?
b. List the specific steps required in making an S–1 Review?

21-15 a. What procedures are generally required in a comfort letter engagement?
b. Indicate the items included in a comfort letter.

21-16 Identify the four categories of data required in a Form 10–K filing and what data, if any, must be audited.

21-17 Briefly explain the two major accounting requirements in filing quarterly reports under the 1934 Act.

21-18 a. What data are required in a Form 8–K filing?
b. Indicate the information that must be submitted in regard to auditor changes?

21-19 Distinguish between injunctive and administrative proceedings in enforcement of the securities acts and indicate how the SEC publicizes its enforcement actions.

21-20 Identify the sanctions that may be imposed by the SEC under Rule 2E.

OBJECTIVE QUESTIONS FROM PROFESSIONAL EXAMINATIONS

Indicate the *best* answer choice for each of the following multiple choice questions.

21-21 These questions pertain to SEC accounting pronouncements.

1. Regulation S–X
   a. Specifies the information that can be incorporated by reference from the annual report into the registration statement filed with the SEC.
   b. Specifies the regulations and reporting requirements of proxy solicitations.
   c. Provides the basis for generally accepted accounting principles.
   d. Specifies the general form and content requirements of financial statements filed with the SEC.
   e. Provides explanations and clarifications of changes in accounting or auditing procedures used in reports filed with the SEC.
2. Financial Reporting Releases (FRR), called Accounting Series Releases (ASR) prior to 1982, issued by the SEC
   a. Provide the basis for generally accepted accounting principles.
   b. Specify the regulations and reporting requirements of proxy solicitations.
   c. Provide explanations, interpretations, and procedures used by the SEC in administering the federal securities laws.
   d. Specify the general form and content requirements of financial statements filed with the SEC.
   e. Provide explanations and clarifications of changes in accounting or auditing procedures used in reports filed with the SEC.
3. Staff Accounting Bulletins issued by the SEC.
   a. Specify the information that can be incorporated by reference from the annual report into the registration statement filed with the SEC.
   b. Specify the regulations and reporting requirements of proxy solicitations.

    c. Provide explanations, interpretations, and procedures used by the SEC in administering the federal securities laws.

    d. Specify the general form and content requirements of financial statements filed with the SEC.

    e. Provide explanations and clarifications of changes in accounting or auditing procedures used in reports filed with the SEC.

21-22 These questions relate to the SEC's integrated disclosure rules.

1. The primary intent for the integrated disclosure rules issued by the Securities and Exchange Commission (SEC) is
   a. To reduce the influence of SEC regulations in public financial reporting.
   b. To replace generally accepted accounting principles with Regulation S–X.
   c. To replace Regulation S–X with generally accepted accounting principles.
   d. To minimize the differences between published financial reports and financial reports filed on Form 10–K.
   e. To integrate the materiality criteria of Regulation S–X with generally accepted accounting principles.

2. The management discussion and analysis section of Form 10–K has been revised by the SEC's integrated disclosure system. The revised management and discussion section does *not* require a description of
   a. Factors affecting financial condition as well as the results of operations.
   b. Factors affecting international markets and currency exchange.
   c. Factors that are likely to increase or decrease liquidity materially.
   d. Material commitments for capital expenditures including the purpose of and source of financing for such commitments.
   e. The impact of inflation and changing prices on net sales and revenues and on income from continuing operations.

3. In its 19X2 shareholder report for fiscal year 19X2 (year end is October 31), James Co. presented audited financial statements that contained balance sheets, income statements, and statements of changes in financial position covering the fiscal years of 19X2 and 19X1. What changes must be made in fiscal 19X3 in order to comply with current SEC disclosure requirements?
   a. Expand balance sheet disclosure to three years: October 31, 19X3, 19X2, and 19X1.
   b. Expand income statement disclosure to three fiscal years: 19X3, 19X2, and 19X1.
   c. Expand statement of changes in financial position to three years: October 31, 19X3, 19X2, and 19X1.
   d. Expand all three statements to three fiscal years: 19X3, 19X2, and 19X1.
   e. Expand only the income statement and statement of changes in financial position to three fiscal years: 19X3, 19X2, and 19X1.

4. SEC regulations provide for a procedure known as *incorporation by reference*. Which of the following best illustrates the concept of *incorporation by reference?*
   a. A partnership is incorporated by reference to the U.S. Tax Code.
   b. The incorporation of a proprietorship or partnership.
   c. Inclusion of information on officers' remuneration in Form 10–K by reference to the same information in the proxy statement to shareholders.
   d. Footnote reference to market data per share since incorporation.
   e. Footnote disclosure that financial statements are incorporated into the annual report by reference from Form 10–K.

COMPREHENSIVE QUESTIONS

21-23 The U.S. Securities and Exchange Commission (SEC) was created in 1934 and consists of five commissioners and a staff of approximately 1,900. The SEC professional staff is organized into five divisions and several principal offices. The primary objectives of the SEC are to support fair securities markets and foster enlightened shareholder participation in major corporate decisions. The SEC has a significant presence in financial markets and corporation-shareholder relations and has the authority to exert significant influence on entities whose actions lie within the scope of its authority. The SEC chairman has identified enforcement cases and full disclosure filings as major activities of the SEC.

Required

a. The SEC must have some "license" to exercise power. Explain where the SEC receives its authority.

b. Discuss, in general terms, the major ways in which the SEC:
  1. Supports fair securities markets.
  2. Fosters enlightened shareholder participation in major corporate decisions.

c. The major responsibilities of the SEC's Division of Corporation Finance include full disclosure filings. Describe the means by which the SEC attempts to assure the material accuracy and completeness of registrants' financial disclosure filings.

d. The Division of Enforcement of the SEC is responsible for the review and direction of all enforcement activities.
  1. Give an example of a violation the SEC might identify.
  2. For the violation, indicate the sanction or penalty, other than fine or imprisonment, that the SEC could impose.

CMA

21-24 The Securities and Exchange Commission (SEC) has encouraged managements of public companies to disclose more information in the shareholders' annual report. As a consequence, a significant amount of the information required in the SEC's Form 10–K now appears in published annual reports.

At the same time, the SEC has attempted to make the annual financial reporting process simpler and more efficient. During 1980, the SEC approved a new integrated disclosure system.

Required

a. Identify the major classes of information that must be included in both the annual report to shareholders and Form 10–K filed with the SEC.

b. The integrated disclosure system is intended to simplify the annual reporting process with the SEC by expanding the ability to incorporate by reference.
  1. Define what is meant by *incorporating by reference* and identify the documents that are involved when incorporating by reference.
  2. Explain how the integrated disclosure system should reduce managements' efforts in filing annual reports with the SEC.
  3. Explain the SEC's principal reasons for making the changes in the annual reporting process.

    4. Identify and explain potential problems the integrated disclosure system could have on the annual reporting process from the aspect of users of financial information.

CMA

21-25 The accounting-related pronouncements issued by the SEC include: Regulation S–X, Regulation S–K, *Financial Reporting Releases* (FRRs), *Staff Accounting Bulletins* (SABs) and Accounting and Auditing Enforcement Releases (AAERs). Listed below are statements that relate to these five pronouncements:

    1. Contains accounting provisions that closely parallel GAAP.
    2. Includes opinions of the Commission on major accounting issues.
    3. Contains guidance for handling events and transactions with similar accounting interpretations.
    4. Pertains to disclosure of management remuneration.
    5. Contains disclosure requirements that may exceed GAAP.
    6. Sets forth the results of disciplinary proceedings against accountants.
    7. Requires disclosure of material pending legal proceedings to which management is a party.
    8. Provides clarification of existing rules and regulations.
    9. Requires disclosure of securities holdings of management.
    10. Includes amendments to financial statements requirements of various forms.

Required

a. Describe briefly the nature of the five pronouncements and identify who is authorized to issue each pronouncement.

b. List the number of the foregoing statements and indicate the pronouncement to which it pertains.

21-26 A number of steps are involved in the registration process under the 1933 Securities Act. Ten of these steps are listed below in random order:

    1. Data for registration are collected by company accountants, reviewed by lawyers, and reviewed and audited by independent accountants.
    2. Management and legal counsel select appropriate registration form.
    3. Management prepares amendments that are responsive to SEC's comments. These are filed with SEC by legal counsel.
    4. Management prepares draft of registration statement and obtains board of directors' approval.
    5. Management receives letter of comment from SEC concerning deficiencies and necessary adjustments.
    6. SEC notifies management by phone of acceptance of registration statement.
    7. Due diligence meeting is held to review registration statement and other matters affecting sale of issue.
    8. Management finalizes registration statement, which is filed with SEC by legal counsel.
    9. Legal counsel files amendment to registration statement for offering price. Registration statement becomes effective 5:00 PM.

10. Management, independent accountant, and legal counsel have prefiling conference with SEC staff in Washington, D.C.

Required

Arrange the steps in proper sequence.

21-27 Ensign Corporation is a manufacturing firm with ten domestic plants. Increased demand for the company's products and a near full capacity production have caused management to decide to build a new plant. The plant expansion is to be financed by a public issue of $10,000,000 of long-term bonds. Before the issue can be sold to the public, a registration statement will have to be filed with the Securities and Exchange Commission using a Form S–1. Ensign Corporation's financial statements have been certified by the corporation's independent accountants for many years.

Required

a. Several parties are involved in the preparation, filing, and approval of the registration statement. Briefly indicate the responsibility of (1) Ensign Corporation management, (2) Ensign's independent accountants, and (3) the Securities and Exchange Commission in this procedure.

b. Indicate the general types of financial information and statistical data that would be disclosed in the schedules and reports included in the registration statement and the time period(s) to which this information and data must refer.

CMA

21-28 Below are events pertaining to a public client subject to SEC jurisdiction:

1. There is a change in independent accountants not related to a disagreement over accounting principles.
2. There is a change in an accounting principle that the auditor believes is preferable.
3. Interim financial information is filed following review by the independent accountant.
4. A comfort letter is issued by the accountant to an underwriter.
5. Selected financial data for five years is filed.
6. There was a major acquisition during the year.
7. Unaudited financial statements for a "stub" period are included.

Required

a. Indicate the SEC reporting form(s), if any, on which each of the foregoing would appear.

b. Explain the independent accountant's responsibilities under 1 to 4 above.

21-29 The Jerford Company is a well-known manufacturing company with several wholly owned subsidiaries. The company's stock is traded on the New York Stock Exchange, and the company files all appropriate reports with the Securities and Exchange Commission. Jerford Company's financial statements are audited by a public accounting firm.

PART I: Jerford Company's Annual Report to Stockholders for the year ended December 31, 19X1, contained the following phrase in boldface type: The company's 10–K is available on written request.

Required

a. What is Form 10–K, who requires that the form be completed, and why is the phrase "The company's 10–K is available on written request" shown in the annual report?

b. What information not normally included in the company's annual report could be ascertained from the 10–K?

c. Indicate three items of financial information that are often included in annual reports that are not required for the 10–K.

PART II: Jerford Company changed independent auditors during 19X1. Consequently, the financial statements were certified by a different public accounting firm in 19X1 than in 19X0.

Required

What information is Jerford Company responsible for filing with the SEC with respect to this change in auditors? Explain your answer completely.

CMA

21-30 The most common annual report required by the SEC is Form 10–K. Form 10, another SEC report, is often used to register under the Securities Exchange Act of 1934. Both Form 10–K and Form 10 call for "Selected Financial Data." Form S–1, used in the registration of securities for public sale under the Securities Act of 1933, also requires this information. Thus, this summary is an important disclosure requirement in meeting annual reporting and initial filing requirements with the SEC.

Required

a. Identify the basic information that must be disclosed in the "Selected Financial Data," including the period covered and any explanatory notes needed.

b. Is the "Selected Financial Data" required to be audited?

CMA (adapted)

21-31 In order to aid in integrating quarterly reports to shareholders with Form 10–Q, the Securities and Exchange Commission issued *Accounting Series Release (ASR) 286* in February 1981. The ASR modifies and expands the financial information content of the previous Form 10–Q disclosures. Specific guidelines are set forth in the ASR as to what information must be included on Form 10–Q.

Required

a. Corporations are required by the SEC to file a Form 10–Q.
   1. What is Form 10–Q and how often is it filed with the SEC?
   2. Explain why the SEC requires corporations to file Form 10–Q.

b. Discuss the disclosure requirement now pertaining to Form 10–Q with specific regard to the
   1. Condensed balance sheet.
   2. Condensed income statement.
   3. Condensed changes in financial position.
   4. Management's discussion and analysis of the interim period(s).
   5. Footnote disclosures.

CMA

Appendix X

Content Specification Outline for the Auditing Section of the Uniform Certified Public Accountant Examination (Effective May 1986)*

The auditing section tests the candidates' knowledge of generally accepted auditing standards and procedures. The scope of the auditing section includes professional responsibilities, internal control, evidence and procedures, and reporting.

In preparing for this section, candidates should study publications such as:

- AICPA Code of Professional Ethics.
- Statements on Auditing Standards.
- Statements on Standards for Accounting and Review Services.
- Statements on Quality Control Standards.
- Statements on Management Advisory Services.
- Statements on Responsibilities in Tax Practice.
- AICPA Audit Guides.
- Auditing textbooks.
- Leading accounting journals.

*Board of Examiners, *Content Specification Outlines for the Uniform Certified Public Accountant Examination* (New York: American Institute of Certified Public Accountants, 1984), pp. 17–19.

AUDITING—CONTENT SPECIFICATION OUTLINE

I. Professional Responsibilities (15%).
   A. General Standards and Rules of Conduct
      1. Proficiency, Independence, and Due Care
      2. Rules of Conduct
   B. Control of the Audit
      1. Planning and Supervision
      2. Quality Control
   C. Other Responsibilities
      1. Client Errors, Management Fraud, and Defalcations
      2. Client Illegal Acts
      3. Responsibilities in Review and Compilation
      4. Responsibilities in Management Advisory Services
      5. Responsibilities in Tax Practice

II. Internal Control (30%).
   A. Definitions and Basic Concepts
      1. Purpose of Auditor's Study and Evaluation
      2. Definitions and Basic Concepts
   B. Study and Evaluation of the System
      1. Review of the System
      2. Tests of Compliance
      3. Evaluation of Weaknesses
   C. Cycles
      1. Sales, Receivables, and Cash Receipts
      2. Purchases, Payables, and Cash Disbursements
      3. Inventories and Production
      4. Personnel and Payroll
      5. Property, Plant, and Equipment
   D. Other Considerations
      1. Required Communication of Material Weaknesses
      2. Reports on Internal Control
      3. Sampling
      4. Flowcharting

III. Evidence and Procedures (30%).
   A. Audit Evidence
      1. Nature, Competence, and Sufficiency of Evidential Matter
      2. Analytical Review Procedures
      3. Evidential Matter for Receivables and Inventory
      4. Evidential Matter for Long-Term Investments
      5. Client Representations
      6. Using the Work of a Specialist
      7. Inquiry of a Client's Lawyer
   B. Specific Audit Objectives and Procedures
      1. Tests of Details of Transactions and Balances
      2. Documentation

C. Other Specific Audit Topics
1. Use of the Computer in Performing the Audit
2. Use of Statistical Sampling in Performing the Audit
3. Related Party Transactions
4. Subsequent Events
5. Operational Auditing
6. Omitted Procedures Discovered After the Report Date

D. Review and Compilation Procedures
1. Understanding of Accounting Principles and Practices of the Industry
2. Inquiry and Analytical Review
3. Unusual Matters
4. Other Procedures

IV. Reporting (25%).
A. Reporting Standards and Types of Reports
1. Scope of Examination
2. Generally Accepted Accounting Principles
3. Consistency
4. Disclosure
5. Reporting Responsibilities
6. Unqualified
7. Qualified
8. Adverse
9. Comparative
10. Disclaimer
11. Review and Compilation
12. Review of Interim Financial Information
13. Special Reports
14. Negative Assurance
15. Prospective Financial Statements

B. Other Reporting Considerations
1. Subsequent Discovery of Facts Existing at the Date of the Auditor's Report
2. Dating of the Auditor's Report
3. Part of Examination Made by Other Independent Auditors
4. Letters for Underwriters
5. Filing Under Federal Securities Statutes
6. Other Information in Documents Containing Audited Financial Statements
7. Supplementary Information Required by the FASB
8. Information Accompanying the Basic Financial Statements

Index